LAND DEED GENEALOGY
of
BEDFORD COUNTY
TENNESSEE
1861-1867
- VOLUME #2 -

Complied By:

Helen & Timothy Marsh

Southern Historical Press, Inc.
Greenville, South Carolina

This volume was reproduced
from a personal copy located in
the Publishers private library

Please direct all correspondence and book orders to:
SOUTHERN HISTORICAL PRESS, Inc.
1071 Park West Blvd.
Greenville, SC   29611

Copyright 2003 by: Southern Historical Press, Inc.
ISBN #0-89308-785-8
Printed in the United States of America

*** INTRODUCTION ***

This volume is the third in a series of Bedford County land deed publications, prepaired and edited by the authors, a detailed abstract of the land deeds and related genealogy of the county from its establishment.

The first volume, beginning with the formation of the county in 1807 was entitled, land Deed Genealogy Of Bedford County Tennessee, a unique title that has since been adopted by others.

The second volume was an index appropriately entitled, The burned Index, a volume that covered the years years 1852 to 1861 and listing the Grantor and Grantee index of the nine deed books that were destroyed when the Court House burned in March 1863.

DEED BOOKS DDD-EEE-FFF

This third volume 1861-1868 is a full abstract of all of the deeds recorded during that span of the Civil War years, when the courts and county offices met spasmodically, or often not at all, as the war raged on. This volume recorded the turbulent Restruction years, a time when many of the pre-war deeds were re-recorded to replace those that were destroyed by the Court House fire. Included in this practice were the many Processional Surveys and the registration of numerous soldiers discharges, an act that often produced valuable and vital information. This volume reflects a crucial time in the history of Bedford county and it's people. We believe it to be an interesting and informative volume.

Timothy R. & Helen C. Marsh

Page 1 - Robert C. Daniel Deed 50 acres to James R. Daniel and Solomon P. Daniel, made 27 March 1861.   Robert C. Daniel of Bedford County. Land in Bedford County on waters of Thompsons Creek a south branch of Duck River and on the road leading from R.C. Daniel's dwelling house to the Mulberry Road and bounded by John Dean's land and land sold to William Burnett.
Wit: Wm. W. Hunt   Signed: R.C. Daniel
     John A. Adams
Reg: August 7, 1861

Page 1 - John W. Tilford Deed 6 acres to Samuel B. Heard. Land in Bedford and District No. 3 near Wartrace Depot. Land adjoining A.H. Coffey 50 poles from the Depot in the center of the Nashville and Chattanooga Rail Road. This November 16, 1859.
Wit: G.G. Osborne, Jr.   Signed: J.W. Tilford
     Wm'son Haggard
Reg: August 7, 1861

Page 2 - Solomon G. Reaves Deed 84+ acres to John A. Landers. Land in Bedford County and District No. 11 and adjoining a 2000 acre tract granted to John Lock's heirs, and the school land tract. This 2 December 1860.
Wit: J.T. Williams   Signed: S.G. Reaves
     H.A. King
Reg: August 7, 1861

Page 3 - John Scott Deed of Gift to Mary S. Cannon. For the natural love and affection for my granddaughter Mary S. Cannon wife of Clement Cannon, I have given all my right title claim and interest in a tract of land lying in that part of the Town of Shelbyville known as Camp White adjoining Lot No. 6 Camp White Street, the same being Lot No. 5. Registered in Book AAA, page 586. This 12 June 1861.
Wit: B.M. Tillman   Signed: Jno. Scott
     J.S. Davis
Reg: August 16, 1861

Page 3 - John Scott Bill of Sale to John S. Davis. For seven slaves. This April 18, 1861.
Wit: M.T. Cooper   Signed: Jno. Scott
     A.A. Cooper
Reg: August 17, 1861

Page 4 - Eli Moss Mortgage to John G. Primrose. For all my right title claim and interest in a tract of land on which my mother still lives in District No. 25 of Bedford County, it being her dower. Containing 66 acres. This 16 August 1861.
Reg: August 17, 1861   Signed: Eli Moss

Page 4 - T.W. Jordan Deed to Robert Cannon. This 11 September 1860. Land in Bedford County beginning at the center of Duck River at Cannon's line.
Reg: August 19, 1861   Signed: T.W. Jordan

Page 5 - Samuel J. Moore Deed 65 acres to Sallie Sprouce. Land in Bedford County on the waters of Weakleys Creek adjoining lands of J.E. Batt. This 9 August 1861.
Wit: Jennings Moore   Signed: S.J. Moore
     J.R. Stem
Reg: August 19, 1861

Page 6 - Rich'd Nance Deed 155 acres to J.F. Elliott. Land in Bedford County and District No. 10, adjoining John W. M(illegible) and John Landrum. This November 27, 1860.
Wit: W.C. Cook   Signed: Richard Nance
     John Landrum
Reg: August 27, 1861

Page 7 - James T. Arnold Title Bond to John Reeves. I have sold to John Reeves a tract of land in District No. 24 adjoining lands of H.C. Ferguson, John Brinkley and Presley Prince. Containing 50 acres. This 19 August 1861.
Wit: Edm'd Cooper   Signed: J.T. Arnold
Reg: August 27, 1861

Page 7 - F.D. Haggard Bill of Sale to A.J. Greer. French D. Haggard sold to A.J. Greer a negro girl. This August 31, 1861.
Reg: September 3, 1861   Signed: F.D. Haggard

Page 8 - E.W. Stone Deed 37+ acres to T.F. Erwin. This 2 June 1858. E.W. Stone of Bedford County and T.F. Erwin of Lincoln County, Tennessee. Land in Bedford County and Civil District No. 23.
Wit: F.M. Morris   Signed: E.W. Stone
     J.F. Stone
Reg: September 3, 1861

Page 8 - John A. Moore Bill of Sale to F.N. Stokes. This September 4, 1861. For a black man.
Reg: September 6, 1861   Signed: John A. Moore

Page 9 - Richard H. Sims Deed 327 acres to Newcomb Thompson 2nd. This 11 September 1861. Land in Bedford County and Civil

District No. 21 adjoining Melchesidek Brame (now W.B.M. Brame), John Dougal, the Columbia Road, John Streater (now Fonville heir's), Thomas Greer, Gabriel Knight and Obediah Knight agreeable to the will of William Knight, deceased, and Samuel Anderson.
Reg: September 12, 1861   Signed: Richard H. Sims

Page 9 - Newcomb Thompson, 2nd Deed 174+ acres to Richard H. Sims. Land in Bedford County and District No. 21. Adjoining Mrs. Susan Burts. This 11 September 1861.
Reg: September 12, 1861   Signed: N. Thompson 2nd

Page 10 - A.M. Dean Power of Attorney to John Noblett. Appointed my attorney. For any portion of my interest in the estate of Henry Dean, deceased, late of Bedford County. This September 12, 1861.
Reg: September 12, 1861   Signed: A.M. Dean

Page 10 - Thomas B. Cannon Bill of Sale to Martha Wilhoite. September 13, 1861. For a negro man.
Reg: September 13, 1861   Signed: Thos. B. Cannon

Page 11 - Thos. B. and Charles L. Cannon Deed to James L. Scudder. Thos. B. and Charles L. Cannon, executors of the last will and testament of Clement Cannon, Sr., deceased, have conveyed unto James L. Scudder a tract of land in Bedford County, adjoining the middle of Duck River about 200 yards below the Scull Camp Ford, H.L. Davidson, Clement Cannon, and Scudder and W.J. Cochran. Registered in Book HH, page 532. This 16 September 1861.
Reg: 18 September 1861   Signed: Thos. B. Cannon, Exr.
                                   Charles L. Cannon, Exr.

Page 12 - M.E.W. Dunaway Mortgage to Wm. S. Jett and B.K. Coble. For guardians of my daughter Margaret F. Dunaway, I have conveyed unto Wm. S. Jett and B.K. Coble a lot of ground in the Town of Shelbyville on the road leading from Shelbyville to the Scull Camp Ford. Containing 105 poles. This September 16, 1861.
Reg: September 18, 1861   Signed: M.E.W. Dunaway

Page 12 - G.B. Sharp Trust Deed to John H. Rice. For all my interest in a house and lot in Rowesville, Bedford County, being the same lot conveyed to me by Wm. A. Loyd, also listed several items in original document. This September 16, 1861.
Reg: 18 September 1861   Signed: G.B. Sharp

Page 13 - John P. Steele Deed 3 ¼ acres to Hiram Hammond. Land adjoining a lot sold to me by C.G. Mitchell and now owned by W.H. Wisener, also Holland's or Cathorn's line. This 16 September 1861.

Reg: 18 September 1861   Signed: John P. Steele

Page 14 - Seymour Puryear Deed of Gift to Francis F. Holt and children. Seymour Puryear of Alamance County, North Carolina. For the love and affection I bear for my daughter Fanny F. Holt of Isaac B. Holt, have granted slaves. This 17 September 1860.
Reg: September 18, 1861   Signed: Seymour Puryear

Page 14 - Gilbert W. Wynn Deed 2 acres to Garrett Phillips. Land in Bedford County and District No. 7 adjoining C. McCuistion and the Warner Road. This 19 September 1861.
Wit: Thos. H. Coldwell   Signed: G.W. Wynn
Reg: September 20, 1861

Page 15 - Thos. H. Coldwell Deed 2 acres to Gilbert W. Wynn. Land in Bedford County and District No. 7 adjoining Claiborn McCuistion. This 6 September 1861.
Wit: J. Holt 4th   Signed: Thos. H. Coldwell
     Wm. S. Speer
Reg: September 20, 1861

Page 15 - James Dixon Deed of Gift to Cynthia Dixon. For the love and affection I bear towards my daughter Cynthia Dixon, I convey two negro slaves for life. This 4 April 1861.
Wit: Thos. C. Whiteside   Signed: J. Dixon
     Ro B. Davidson
Reg: September 21, 1861

Page 16 - James S. Boyd and wife Deed 187 acres to Robert B. McLean. Land in Bedford County and Civil District No. 7, adjoining Barnes' land, John L. Cooper, and Blankenship. This 27 September 1861.
Reg: September 27, 1861   Signed: James S. Boyd
                                   Martha L. Boyd

Page 16 - Wm. S. Speer and wife Title Bond to C.W. Cummings. William s. Speer and Susan Speer conveyed a tract of land in Bedford County and District No. 7. J.F. Cummings and Morris Barney, and Thomas Lipscomb, J.F. Thompson, named. This 14 September 1861.
Reg: September 30, 1861   Signed: Wm. S. Speer
                                   Susan Speer

Page 17 - Naomi Ward Deed to John C. Thompson. Naomi Ward late of Bedford County now of Izard County, Arkansas, sold to John C. Tompson of Izard County, Arkansas. Naomi is the widow of Burrell Ward, deceased, late of Bedford County. Burrell Ward about the month of November 1858 died intestate in Bedford County, leaving his widow Naomi and children. This 31 August 1861.
Wit: Wm. Arnold   Signed: Naomi Ward

B.F. Dixon
Reg: October 1, 1861

Page 19 - Edmund Cooper and Robt. Matthews, Executors, Deed Lot
No. 127 to Clement H. Wright. Robert Matthews and Edmund Cooper
are executors of the last will and testament of Erwin J.
Frierson, deceased, conveyed unto Clement H. Wright a Lot No.
127 in the Town of Shelbyville, adjoining the lot where Thomas
Turpin now lives. This 19 February 1850.
Reg: October 7, 1861   Signed: Edmund Cooper
                                    Robt. Matthews

Page 19 - Clement H. Wright Deed part of Lot No. 127 to Joseph
Anderson. Lot in Town of Shelbyville lying north west of the
Big Spring on the north side of the Unionville Turnpike Road and
adjoining the lot of Newcomb Thompson, Sr., and by Dr. Blakemore
and by E.J. Frierson in his lifetime. This 17 September 1861.
Wit: John L. Clardy   Signed: Clement H. Wright
     P.F. King
Reg: October 7, 1861

Page 20 - T.F. Barnes Bill of Sale to D.W. Barnes. A negro boy.
This 30 September 1861.
Wit: Edm'd Cooper   Signed: T.F. Barnes
Reg: October 9, 1861

Page 20 - J.C. Shapard Trust Deed to Robert Mathews. A tract of
land in Bedford County and Civil District No. __ in the Village
of Flat Creek, adjoining C.A. Crunk's lot and the church lot,
This October 2, 1861.
Reg: October 11, 1861   Signed: J.C. Shapard

Page 21 - William Hime Trust Deed to John Wallis. I owe Robert
Reed it being a debt I stayed for my son Henry Hime, a debt to
Dr. Ambrose Parks and also a debt to Robert Mathews, also a debt
to John Wallace, also to Mathew Cunningham, also to Dr. Evans,
also to William Gordon, and to Isaac Shook now in the hands of
the Wilhoites. This 5 October 1861.
Reg: October 11, 1861   Signed: William Hime

Page 22 - A.A. Cooper Bill of Sale to Elizabeth H. Stephens. On
19 November 1860 Joseph W. Stephens executed his Trust Deed to
A.A. Copoer upon contain properties. This 25 September 1861.
Wit: Wm. H. Wisener   Signed: A.A. Cooper
     S.B. Heard
Reg: October 11, 1861

Page 23 - James T. Moore and wife Power of Attorney to John C.
Thompson. James T. Moore and Naomi E. Moore, wife of James T.
Moore, residents of Izard County, Arkansas, have appointed John
C. Thompson of said place, our attorney in fact for us and in

our name &c to the estate of her grand father Burrell Ward late
of Bedford County. Naomi E. Moore was formerly Naomi E.
Thompson, daughter of James Thompson by his wife Ary, who was
Ary Ward, daughter of said Burrell Ward who died intestate in
Bedford County about November 1858. This 3 August 1861.
Wit: Jno. C. Claiborn   Signed: Jas. T. Moore
Reg: October 14, 1861   Naomi E. Moore

Page 23 - T.B. and L. Cannon Bill of Sale to R.S. Dwiggins,
October 7, 1861. Sold a negro boy to R.S. Dwiggins.
Reg: October 14, 1861   Signed: Thos. B. Cannon
                           Charles L. Cannon, exrs of
                           C. Cannon

Page 24 - Thomas Lipscomb Deed 3 or 4 acres to Phillip Haley.
Land in Bedford County on the south side of Duck River.
Beginning at the Warner Bridge, (illegible), to the Fishing Ford
to Shelbyville, adjoining Henry Earnhart. This 3 October 1861.
Wit: Terry D. Thompson   Signed: Thos. Lipscomb
     Wm. Gosling
Reg: October 12, 1861

Page 25 - Benjamin Farmer and James Young Power of Attorney to
Wm. B. Wheeler. Benjamin Farmer son and heir of Margaret
Farner, deceased, Jesse Young husband of Margaret Young, Cate
Hudgins daughter of Nancy Hudgins who was a daughter of Margaret
Farmer, appointed William B. Wheeler of Bedford County our
Attorney for us and in out name to ask and demand whatever may
be coming to us from the estate of said Margaret Farmer,
deceased, late of Bedford County. This 8 August 1861.
                 Signed: Benjamin Farmer
                        Jesse Young
Madisonville, Hopkins County, Kentucky. Wednesday 8 August
1861. Benjamin Farmer and Jesse Young appeared before the court
and acknowledged that they did sign and deliver the same. This
8 August 1861.
Reg: October 11, 1861

Page 25 - Clement Cannon, Jr. to James Searcy. October 11,
1861. Dr. James Searcy, Mississippi.
Dear Sir.
The farm in Bedford County which I bought of you on 15 August
1858 and executed to him my bond for title. I have paid you
your money. This October 11, 1861.
Reg: October 11, 1861   Signed: Clement Cannon

Page 25 - Chancery Court Decree to Wm. B. Wheeler for 150+
acres. David J. Wheeler. Exparte petition to sell land. Ordered
by the court at August Term 1857. I sold the tract of land at
the request of one of the heirs. I have sold 13 October 1857
said land containing 150 acres and 34 poles to William B.
Wheeler.
Reg: October 21, 1861.

Page 27 - William M. Williams and others Deed to M.J. Phillips.
We, William M. Williams and wife Martha A. Williams formerly
Martha A. Phillips, George Foreman and wife Margaret J. Former
formerly Margaret J. Phillips, have sold to M.J. Phillips land
which Mathew Phillips willed to the children and heirs of Jesse
Phillips, deceased, in Civil District No. 6. Land adjoining
Harrison Jennings and T.J. Brown, Garrett Phillips, Tabitha
Brown widow of Shadrack Brown, deceased, Elizabeth Robinson and
James Phillips. Land containing 85 acres our interest being two
sixths. (one sixth each in right of the said Martha A. Williams
and Margaret J. Foreman who are children and heirs of said
Martha A. Williams and Margaret J. Foreman who are children of
Jason Phillips, deceased). This 21 October 1861.
Reg: October 26, 1861   Signed: Wm. M. Williams
                                       Martha A. Williams
                                       George Foreman
                                       Margaret J. Foreman

Page 27 - James C. Powell Deed 213+ acres to C.W. Powell. I do
hereby convey to C.W. Powell a tract of land in Bedford County
and District No. 18, containing 213+ acres adjoining John Larue,
and the center of Rock Creek. This 14 October 1861.
Reg: October 26, 1861   Signed: James C. Powell

Page 28 - James A. Marr Deed 98+ acres to John A. McLain. Land
in Bedford County and Civil District No. 9, adjoining Tucker's
line, and Fisher's line. This 6 October 1861.
Wit: John McKey   Signed: James A. Marr
     Jas. Boyd
Reg: October 26, 1861

Page 29 - William P. Oneal Deed Lot to Daniel G. Stephenson.
Land in Bedford County and District No.7 and in the west part of
the Town of Shelbyville known as one half of Lot No. 7 and all
of Lot No. 8 as laid out by C.S. Dudley, surveyor for J.F.
Thompson and N. Thompson 3rd. Lot bounded by Buchanan Street,
by A.T. Eakin's land, and by Lots No. 14 and 15, and by half of
Lot No. 7. The other half of Lot No. 7 was sold to Wm.
Buchanan. This December 14, 1860.
Wit: Robert Williams   Signed: W.P. Oneal
     D.B. Smiley
Reg: October 26, 1861

Page 29 - William Morton Deed 51+ acres to Frederick Brown.
William Morton of Bedford County sold on 27 August 1851 unto
Frederick Brown of same place, land in Bedford County and
Lincoln County, Tennessee, adjoining Gilchrist, the Elk Ridge,
corner of Marshall and Lincoln County, A. Elzzy and Thomas Smith
and Robert Smith.
Wit: Joseph Trice   Signed: William Morton
     J.H. Curtiss, Jr.
Reg: October 26, 1861

7

Page 30 - William Nichols Deed 30 acres to Frederick Brown.
William Nichols of Lincoln County, Tennessee on 4 January 1855
sold unto Frederick Brown of Bedford County land in Bedford
County located on the top of Elk Ridge adjoining J. Morton and
Brown's line. This 4 January 1855.
Wit: James L. Adams   Signed: William Nichols
     William Morton
Reg: October 26, 1861

Page 31 - A.W.B. Patterson Deed to Susan Patterson. For the
natural love and affection for my sister Susan Patterson, I have
conveyed all my right title claim and interest to land in
Bedford County in Civil District No. 3, adjoining G. Blessing.
The same being the tract that was deeded to my mother Elizabeth
Patterson during her life and at her death to myself. Martha
H.J. Patterson and Isaac W. Patterson by William Gosling. This
October 26, 1861.
Wit: N.F. Thompson   Signed: Absalom W.B. Patterson
     James H. Neil
Reg: October 28, 1861

Page 31 - Albert Anderson Deed 50 acres to Andrew M. Anderson.
Land in Bedford County and District No. 19, adjoining where A.
Anderson lives on, also Dowdy's land, Joel Bradley and Thomas
Coffey. This 15 April 1861.
Wit: John Anderson   Signed: Albert Anderson
     James L. Hazlett
Reg: October 28, 1861

Page 32 - Andrew Vannoy, Sr. Deed 115 acres to Anna E. Temple
and others. Sold to Anna E. Temple, J.K.P. Temple and W.D.
Temple land in Bedford County and District No. 6, adjoining
Thomas B. Marks and James Clardy. This 26 October 1861.
Reg: October 28, 1861   Signed: Andrew Vannoy

Page 32 - M.M. Wilson and W.R. Hannaway Deed to Joseph trice.
We, Moses M. Wilson of Marshall County, Tennessee and William R.
Hannaway of Lincoln County, Tennessee sold unto Joseph Trice of
Bedford County land or lot in the Village of Richmond, Bedford
County, adjoining house of Jackson & Looney, and John Phillips.
Land containing 1 acre. This August 19, 1861.
Reg: October 28, 1861   Signed: M.M. Wilson
                                       W.R. Hannaway

Page 33 - Chancery Court to William Brown for lot. Garrett
Phillips, administrator &c VS Frances McQuistion and others.
Decree. Ordered that all claim and interest which said Frances
McQuistion and the heirs and children of Claiborne McQuistion,
deceased, have in said lot it being No. __ in the Town of
Shelbyville being divested out of them and vested in said
William Brown.
Reg: October 28, 1861

8

Page 34 - William W. Hastings Deed to Robert Hastings. All of my right title claim and interest in land in Bedford County on the waters of Big Flat Creek, partly in Burrow's District and partly in Hastings' District. Containing 46+ acres being the dower tract of Jane Hastings. This 28 October 1861.
Reg: October 29, 1861   Signed: William W. Hastings

Page 34 - Charles L. and Thos. B. Cannon Deed 1+ acres to James L. Scudder. Thomas B. Cannon and Charles L. Cannon, executors of the last will and testament of Clement Cannon, Sr. sold unto James L. Scudder 1+ acres adjoining Lot No. 15 in Moody's tract now or formerly owned by William J. Cochran. This 28 October 1861.
Reg: October 29, 1861   Signed: Charles L. Cannon
                               Thomas B. Cannon, Exrs.

Page 35 - William J. Cochran Deed or title Bond to James L. Scudder. W.J. Cochran conveyed to Jas. L. Scudder two tracts of land or lots. Lot No. 15, recorded in Bedford County in Book HH, page 532 which I bought of Clement Cannon, Sr., containing 1 acre and 92 poles lying south of Moody Street. Also Lot No. 16 containing 1 acre and 64 poles. This October 26, 1861.
Reg: October 29, 1861   Signed: W.J. Cochran

Page 35 - James L. Scudder Title Bond to W.J. Cochran. James L. Scudder is firmly bound to pay William J. Cochran. Conveyed Lots No. 104 and No. 111 in Town of Shelbyville which I once sold to Robert Denniston. This October 26, 1861.
Wit: R.F. Oneal   Signed: James L. Scudder
     Geo. W. Buchanan
Reg: 29 October 1861

Page 36 - Thomas Lipscomb Deed 2+ acres to Joseph Anderson. Land I first sold to Wm. C. Hay and in Bedford County, Civil District No. 7 a little north of Shelbyville, adjoining a lot by me sold to J. Tarpley. This 29 October 1861.
Reg: October 31, 1861   Signed: Thos. Lipscomb

Page 36 - E.M. Patterson and wife Deed to Wm. H. Wisener for 1/5 of 1/6 of 11 acres. Elijah M. Patterson and wife Lavina Jane sold to Wm. H. Wisener our undivided interest in remainder of the lands on which Thomas Holland, Sr. lived at the time of his death and on which his widow has a life estate and which life she has conveyed to said Thomas our interest being one fifth of one sixth of said tract of land with the right of possession at her death. This 4 April 1861.
Reg: October 31, 1861   Signed: Elijah M. Patterson
                               Lavina J. Patterson

Page 37 - Mrs. Susan Burt Deed 3 or 4 acres to B.C. Owen. Mrs. Susan Burt relinquished to Benj. Owen all right and interest to that portion of land containing 3 or 4 acres, adjoining the

Tract of land I now live on and on the west side of Big Sugar Creek. This 31 October 1861.
Wit: Nash H. Burt   Signed: Susan Burt
     Richard H, Sims
Reg: October 31, 1861

Page 38 - Grundy Fletcher Deed of Settlement to John W. Fletcher, a Trustee.
G. Fletcher sold to John W. Fletcher in trust a lot or parcel of land in the limits of the Town of Shelbyville, adjoining on Spring Street at the corner of Lot No. 82 and Lot No. 83 and a lot purchased by me of Rachel Hobbs. Registered in Book BBB, page 364. This October 20, 1861.
Reg: November 2, 1861   Signed: G. Fletcher

Page 39 - Winn Thomas and others Deed to John & William Thomas. This 29 January 1856. David Thomas late of Bedford County departed this life intestate seized of a tract of land in Bedford County on the waters of the Wartrace Fork of Duck River, is a part of a 5000 acre tract of land granted to John G. and Thomas Blount by patent No. 219. Registered in Book H, page 127. Whereas said David Thomas, deceased, left at the time of his death the following persons his children and heirs, to wit, William Thomas, Ava Thomas, Winn Thomas. R.S. Thomas and John Thomas, Martha Bird (formerly Martha Thomas who had intermarried with Bartlett Bird), Mary Fields (formerly Mary Thomas who had intermarried with L.P. Fields) and Huldah Mason (formerly Huldah Thomas) widow of Thomas Mason, deceased, his children. The widow Huldah Mason departed this life 8 October 1857 leaving children but leaving the aforesaid brothers and sisters surviving her as her only heir at law and leaving her brother Asa Thomas her executor of her last will and testament (which has been proven and registered in Coffee County where she resided as a citizen at the time of her death. This 4 October 1859.
Wit: R.D. Rankin   Signed: Asa Thomas
     Wm. J. Peacock   Winn Thomas
     Jo. P. Kelly   R.S. Thomas
     R.W. Pearson   B. Bird
Reg: November 13, 1861   Martha Bird
                                 L.P. Fields
                                 Mary Fields

41 - James H. Neil and wife Deed to James S. Newton. Land in Bedford County and District No. 20, adjoining Jordan Holt, L.W. Barrett, James S. Newton, Carlisle, Gabbert, William Forbes, and George W. Fogleman, Randolph Newsom, James G. Whitney, Joseph A. Whitney, James H. and Jane G. Neil, and Noah Scales. This 4 November 1861.
Reg: November 12, 1861   Signed: James H. Neil
                                        Jane Greer Neil

Page 42 - Mathew Dixon Deed 200 acres to Wm. S. Jett. Land in Bedford County and District No. 3, adjoining James G. Barksdale and J.F. Cummings. This November 9, 1861.
Reg: November 12, 1861   Signed: Mathew Dixon

Page 42 - R.H. Temple, Jr. R(illegible) of Title Bond to Bradley Gamble. Bradley Gamble has sold unto R.H. Temple, Jr. land in Bedford County and District No. 20, adjoining Gibson Gap Road, Powell Creek, Dougal, and Samuel Roan. Containing 20 acres and 60 poles. This 7 September 1859.
Reg: November 19, 1861   Signed: B. Gamble

Page 43 - Benton Gabbert Deed to W.P. Goodwin. Land sold to Washington P. Goodwin all the right title and interest in and to the dower interest of Mary Ann Hastings in the lands of William Gabbert, deceased, being part of said land owned by William Gabbert, deceased, to her during her natural life. This 11 November 1861.
Reg: November 19, 1861   Signed: Benton Gabbert

Page 44 - Philip R. Haley Bill of Sale to Thomas Thompson. For five negros. This November 20, 1861.
Wit: Daniel Earnhart   Signed: Philip R. Haley
     J.C. Haley
Reg: November 21, 1861

Page 44 - John A. Bramlett Deed 70+ acres to John R. Muse. Land to John R.C. Muse being in Bedford County and District No. 2, adjoining William Hall and William Cully. This __ February 1861.
Reg: November 25, 1861   Signed: John A. Bramlett

Page 45 - Garrett Phillips and J.H.C. Scales Deed to James S. Newton. 17 April 1860. There came to the hands of Garrett Phillips as Sheriff of Bedford County an execution in favor of J.H.C. Scales, administrator and against James H. Neill and others. Execution was levied on all rights title claim and interest which J.H. Neil and wife Jane G. Neil had in land in Bedford County and District No. 20, adjoining Jordan Holt, William Gabbert, Carlisle, William Forbes, George W. Fogleman, and Randolph Newsom. Others named were James S. Newton and George W. Greer. This November 1861.
Reg: November 25, 1861   Signed: G. Phillips
                                      Jas. H.C. Scales

Page 46 - Garrett Phillips, Sheriff, Deed to William T. Stamps for Lots No, 26 and 27. Lots in Bedford County, Civil District No. 7 in the Town of Shelbyville, adjoining by the street which divides said lot from the Presbyterian Church lot, on the street dividing said lot from the Frierson property, by lot of Thos. J. Nance, by Brittain street which divides said lots from property of Wm. P. Whitthorne being the lot on which A.L. Stamps resided

11

at the time of said levy and levied on as property of said
Stamps, being Lots No. 26 and 27, containing about 1 ½ acres.
This November 25, 1861.
Reg: November 25, 1861   Signed: G. Phillips

Page 47 - W.M. Tatum Deed 40+ acres to Wm. Murphree.   Land in
Bedford County and District No. 5, adjoining Horatio Coop and
Cooper and Ogilvie. This 18 November 1861.
Wit: Edm'd Coper   Signed: W.M. Tatum
     H.F. Holt
Reg: 26 November 1861

Page 48 - E.W. Jennings and wife Deed 160 acres to M.B.
Hamilton.   Edmund W. Jennings and wife Mary E. Jennings sold to
M(illegible) B. Hamilton land in Marshall and Bedford County,
Tennessee and Bedford County on the West Fork of the East Fork
of Rock Creek a branch of Duck River, containing 160 acres,
adjoins William Martin's Grant No. 678.   This 29 June 1860.
Reg: November 26, 1861   Signed: E.W. Jennings
                                    M.E. Jennings

Page 48 - Thomas Cook Deed to G.W. Cook.   Land in Bedford County
and District No. 18, adjoining Sam'l Crowell, James b. Jones,
and Mrs. Lawwell.   Containing 50 acres, being the place owned
and occupied by my father Wm. Cook at his death and my interest
being one ninth and my mother is entitled to a dower out of said
land.   This 26 November 1861.
Reg: November 27, 1861   Signed: Thomas Cook

Page 49 - County Court Decree to G.W. Cook for 50 acres.   G.T.
Neely, administrator of Wm. Cook, deceased, VS Nancy Cook
(widow), Thos. J. Cook, G.W. Cook, Mary E. Cook, Andrew J. Cook,
Sarah A. Cook, Emily M. Cook, Hugh L. Cook, Zachary T. Cook and
Mary Frances Cook, heirs at law of Wm. Cook, deceased.
Green T. Cook, administrator of Wm. Cook, deceased, VS Nancy
Cook heir at law of Wm. Cook, deceased.   Petition to sell land.
Land vested in George W. Cook.   Land in Bedford County on both
sides of Sinking Creek and adjoining Barrett and Newsom, Tyre
Harrison, W.B.M. Brame, and James B. Jones.
Reg: November 27, 1861

Page 50 - G.W.Cook Deed 50 acres to Thomas Cook.   Land in
Bedford County and District No. 18 on both sides of Sinking
Creek and adjoining Barrett and Newsom. Tyre Harrison, W.B.M.
Brame, and James B. Jones.   I covenant Thomas Cook that I am
lawfully seized of said land.   This November 26, 1861.
Reg: November 26, 1861   Signed: G.W. Cook

Page 50 - J.B. Dixon and others Bill of Sale to Wm. M. Reed.
For a negro woman Ary. This 26 November 1861.
Wit: Thos. C. Whiteside   Signed: J.B. Dixon
     Jo. Thompson   J.E. Dixon

11

Reg: November 27, 1861   J. Dixon

Page 51 - Frederick Batte Deed to 36 ½ acres to John W. and
Stacy Rucker. This 5 February 1861. Land in Bedford County it
being land lying west of the road from the Protestant Meeting
House and adjoining lands of J.W. and Stacy Rucker, A. Landers,
and F. Batte.
Wit: Abner Steed   Signed: Frederick Batte
     A.J. Chrisman
Reg: November 29, 1861

Page 51 - N.J.C. Keller and others Deed 332 acres to Reuben C.
Couch. We, J.W.C. Keller, James W. Keller and N.J.C. Keller,
calvin Ayres and his wife Sarah C. Ayres, William R. Roberts and
wife Eliza Roberts, Joel Parker and wife Sophia A. Parker,
Christopher Thomas and wife Mary W. Thomas, sold to Reuben C.
Couch land in Bedford County and District No. 2, adjoining
Joseph Couch, Sally Kelly, William Pepper, Asa Thomas, John
Douglas, and James Finch. This 20 January 1859.
Wit: James Bramlett   Signed: N.J.C. Keller
     G.A. Cortner   J.W.C. Keller
Reg: November 30, 1861   Calvin Ayres
                                      Sarah L. Ayres
                                      James M. Keller
                                      Joel H. Parker
                                      Sophia A. Parker
                                      C. Thomas
                                      Mary M. Thomas
                                      R.C.T. Keller
                                      Wm. R. Roberts
                                      Eliza J. Roberts

Page 53 - A. Freeman, Trustee Bill of Sale to Sarah B. Price.
N.C. Gambill by deed dated __ of __ 186_ conveyed to me in trust
property amongst other things a negro man. This 29 November
1861.
Reg: December 2, 1861   Signed: A. Freeman, Trustee

Page 53 - Enoch Williams Deed 40 acres to R.B. Freeman. Land in
Bedford County and District No. 8, adjoining M.F. Williams and
Hartwell Freeman. This 27 November 1861.
Reg: December 3, 1861   Signed: Enoch Williams

Page 54 - Lafayette Blackwell Power of Attorney to R.B.
Blackwell. Parker County, Texas. R.B. Blackwell of Bedford
County. Lafayette Blackwell of Parker County, Texas. Land in
Bedford County given to me by my grand father John Blackwell,
deceased, and in the possession of German Woodward legal
representative and Maria Coffee who are all citizens of Bedford
County. This 24 May 1861.
Wit: A.J. Batt   Signed: Lafayette Blackwell
     J.N. Roach
Reg: December 3, 1861

Page 55 - Josiah F. Blackwell and wife Power of Attorney to R.B.
Blackwell. Parker County, Texas. Josiah F. Blackwell and his
wife Elizabeth Blackwell, both of Parker County, Texas appointed
R.B. Blackwell of Bedford County their Attorney. Josiah F. and
Elizabeth Blackwell have a claim in a lot or parcel of land in
Bedford County and given to me the said Elizabeth Blackwell with
other heirs of S.B. Blackwell by my grand father John Blackwell
and now in possession of German Woodward and Maria Coffee all of
Bedford County. This 24 May 1861.
Wit: A.J. Batt   Signed: Josiah F. Blackwell
     J.N. Roach   Elizabeth Blackwell
Reg: December 3, 1861

Page 56 - Josiah F. Blackwell and others to German Woodward.
Josiah F. Blackwell and wife Elizabeth Blackwell and Lafayette
Blackwell sold to German Blackwell land in Bedford County and
adjoining J.L. Adams, James Price, Walter Coffey, and containing
50 acres. This 30 November 1861.
Reg: December 4, 1861   Signed: Josiah F. Blackwell
                                     Elizabeth Blackwell
                                     Lafayette Blackwell, by
                                     Atty R.B. Blackwell

Page 56 - H.A. Graves Bill of Sale to Jacob Greer. A negro man.
This 30 November 1861.
Reg: December 4, 1861   Signed: H.A. Graves

Page 57 - Samuel Morris Deed 65 + acres to David N. Wise. This
21 May 1861. Samuel Morris and David N. Wise, both of Bedford
County. Land in Bedford County on the head waters of Big Flat
Creek in District No. 22, adjoining Harris' line and Richard
Mullins.
Wit: T.S. Dean   Signed: Samuel Morris
Reg: December 5, 1861

Page 58 - E. Morris Trust Deed to John W. Greer. On 19 January
1860 I executed a Deed of Trust to Josephus Cunningham,
registered in Bedford County in Book CCC, pages 422, 423 and
424. I rented of Richard Phillips about 10 acres. Also about
250 acres I rented of F.F. Fonville. This 5 December 1861.
Reg: December 6, 1861   Signed: E. Morris

Page 58 - James F. Arnold Deed 2+ acres to A.L. Stamps. Land in
Bedford County and District No. 7, adjoining Lot No. 6 and the
road leading from Shelbyville to Skull Camp Ford. This December
3, 1861.
Reg: December 6, 1861   Signed: J.F. Arnold

Page 59 - John Williams Trust Deed to John S. Brown. A negro
man, one stallion horse, mare and colt, several other mares and
horses and three head of cattle. This 5 December 1861.
Reg: December 6, 1861   Signed: John Williams

Page 60 - Montgomery Little, Executor &c Bill of Sale to Rufus Smith. Montgomery Little as Commissioner for the sale of the slaves belonging to the estate of Benjamin Little, deceased, to Rufus Smith. This 5 November 1861.
Wit: Edm'd Cooper   Signed: M. Little, Extr.
Reg: December 9, 1861

Page 60 - G.W. McLain Deed to B.A. McLain. 1 July 1860. Bond for lot in Unionville, Bedford County, which is registered in Book CCC, pages 571 and 572. This December 6, 1861.
Reg: December 9, 1861   Signed: G.W. McLain

Page 61 - L.B. Morgan Trust Deed to Edmund Cooper. Len. B. Morgan sold to Edmund Cooper land in Bedford County and District No. 3, adjoining in the middle of a spring on south side of Duck River, Lot No. 5, and containing 62 acres and 96 poles. This 10 December 1861.
Reg: December 10, 1861   Signed: L.B. Morgan

Page 61 - Edmund Cooper and L.B. Knott Deed Lot to Warren & Co. Cooper and Knott conveyed to Charles A. Warren and Thomas J. Warren a lot in the Town of Shelbyville on the south side of Depot Street adjoining the south west corner of the original lot on the north edge of Depot Street. This 29 November 1861.
Reg: December 12, 1861   Signed: Edm'd Cooper
                                      L.B. Knott

Page 62 - Thomas J. Roane Deed part of Lot to B.M. Tillman. Thomas J. Roane sold to Barclay M. Tillman a lot in the Town of Shelbyville, adjoining Tillman and Roane, and west of the house now standing over the cistern. This 12 December 1861.
Reg: December 12, 1861   Signed: Thos. J. Roane

Page 63 - G. Phillips, Sheriff, Deed Lots to Wm. T. Stamps. 30 November 1857. Wilson & Hayden recovered a judgment against A.L. Stamps. Land in Civil District No. 7 as property of A.L. Stamps, adjoining by the street south of the Presbyterian Church and east of the street west of the Pierson property, south by Thos. J. Nance, and west by the street between Whitthorne and said lots, being the same lots on which A.L. Stamps at the time of levy resided. This December 12, 1861.
Reg: December 13, 1861   Signed: G. Phillips, Sheriff

Page 63 - David Chrisco Deed 61 acres and 84 poles to W.M. Daniel. Land lying on the head waters of Thompson Creek in District No. 24, adjoining George Orrick, Oneal's line, David Chrisco's fence, and Wm. H. Miles. This 23 September 1852.
Wit: H.J. Reed   Signed: Daniel Crisco
     John Tucker
Reg: December 13, 1861

Page 65 - John H. Oneal, Clk &c Deed 102 acres to James F. McCowan. Names in document: Elnathan Davis, Hugh H. Manly, and Land in Bedford County and District No. 4 adjoining the mouth of Spring Branch, school land, Pearson's line, and Hatchett's line. This December 13, 1861.
Reg: December 14, 1861   Signed: John H. Oneal

Page 65 - James F. McCowan Deed 43+ acres to Wm. J. Loyd. Land in Bedford County and District No. 4, adjoining the center of Wartrace Creek at the intersection of a cliff in said creek on the north side, David Frizzell, Chaffin's south boundary, and Pearson's line. This December 1861.
Reg: December 14, 1861   Signed: James F. McCowan

Page 66 - Wm. J. Loyd Deed 43+ acres to Henry H. Manly. Land in Bedford County and Civil District No. 4, adjoining in the center of the Wartrace Creek at the intersection of a cliff on the north side, J.F. McCowan, Frizzell, Chaffin and Pearson. This December 13, 1861.
Reg: December 14, 1861   Signed: W.J. Loyd

Page 67 - William E. Phillips Deed ½ of 85 acres to M.J. Phillips. Land which Mathew Phillips, deceased, willed to the children and heirs of Jesse Phillips, deceased, in Civil District No. 6 and adjoining lands of Harrison Jennings and T.J. Brown, by Garrett Phillips and Tabitha Brown widow of Shadrack Brown, deceased, and by Elizabeth Robinson, and James Phillips. Containing in all 85 acres. This December 14, 1861.
Wit: Thos. J. Brown   Signed: Wm. E. Phillips
     W.C. Gordon
Reg: December 14, 1861

Page 67 - Briant Landis Deed 1 ¼ acres to Wm. G. Cowan and others. Land sold to William G. Cowan, John F. Thompson, John T. Neil, Garrett Phillips, and Daniel Williams, Directors of the Southern Division of the Eagleville, Unionville and Shelbyville Turnpike, all citizens of Bedford County and Civil District No. 11, adjoining said Landis' tract, Widow Thompson, and Jackson Nichols. This 10 June 1859.
Reg: December 14, 1861   Signed: Briant Landis

Page 68 - L.B. Morgan & Edmund Cooper Deed to Joel Coggins. Land in District No. 3 of Bedford County, adjoining in the middle of a spring on the south bank of Duck River, Lot No. 3, and Lot No. 5. This 16 December 1861.
Reg: December 17, 1861   Signed: L.B. Morgan
                                        Edm'd Cooper

Page 68 - Sarah Damron Deed 56+ acres to Ann O. Damron. Both of Bedford County, adjoining Lot No. 1, to a field, and Jesse E. Williams, deceased. This 16 December 1861.
Wit: J.W. Damron   Signed: Sarah Damron

15

Reg: Dec 18, 1861

Page 69 - Rufus Smith Deed to Benjamin F. Wiggins. On 15 May 1854, sold land in Bedford County in 22 Civil District and on the waters of Flat Creek the same originally belonging to the school land, and adjoining Lot No. 4, Elijah Lacey, the stone lettered JWW, and a stone lettered JCH. It being part of the school land sold by John T. Neil on 27 October 1848. This February 14, 1861.
Reg: December 18, 1861   Signed: Rufus Smith

Page 70 - Benjamin F. Wiggins Deed to Rufus Smith. On 15 May 1854 sold land in Bedford County, Civil District No. 22, adjoining a stone marked HH, a stone marked DV. This 17 December 1861.
Reg: December 18, 1861   Signed: B.F.Wiggins

Page 70 - Lewis Tillman, Clk &c Deed 90 acres and 44 poles to C.L. Coffey. On 3 July 1858 sold land belonging to the heirs of Edmund Johnson, deceased. Land adjoining T.H. Allison and C. Coffey. This June 29, 1861.
Reg: December 20, 1861   Signed: Lewis Tillman

Page 71 - William Young, Trustee Deed to Mariah E. Phillips. Whereas James W. Dickerson by Deed of Trust dated 5 March 1860 and registered in Book BBB, pages 538 and 539 conveyed to William Young certain property and among other things. Said Wm. Young was authorized to sell any part of said property. Mariah E. Phillips paid for same. Land adjoining James W. Dickerson and Mrs. Phillips. Containing 56 acres and 92 poles. This 20 December 1861.
Reg: December 21, 1861   Signed: Wm. Young, Trustee

Page 72 - James F. Arnold Title Bond to G.W. Gardner. James F. Arnold sold to G.W. Gardner land in Bedford County and Civil District No. 25, adjoining S.B. Gordon and J.R. Burrow. This 20 December 1861.
Reg: December 21, 1861   Signed: J.T. Arnold

Page 73 - Briant Landis Deed 98+ acres to Howell Williams. Land in Bedford County and Civil District No. 11, adjoining Batte's corner, J.C. Wilson, Covington's heirs, Thompson's line, and lot sold to Unionville and Shelbyville Turnpike Company. This 29 December 1861.
Wit: R.H. Stem   Signed: Briant Landis
     W.J. Collins
Reg: December 21, 1861

Page 73 - Newsom & Thompson, Extr &c Deed 1+ acres to N. Thompson 2nd. Whereas Randolph Newsom and Terry D. Thompson, executors of the Last Will and Testament of Sterling Newsom,

deceased, did sell to John L. Burt a small tract of land belonging to the estate of said Sterling Newsom being near Shelbyville, adjoining the east side of a lane or street called Newsom Street, and by Samuel Doak now owned by John A. Blakemore. Land conveyed to Newcom Thompson 2nd. This 20 December 1861.
Reg: December 21, 1861   Signed: Randolph Newsom
                                      Terry D. Thompson

Page 74 - W.B.M. Brame Deed 308 acres to N. Thompson, 2nd. Land in Bedford County and District No. 21, adjoining school land, Dr. Christopher, center of the Shelbyville, Farmington and Lewisburg Turnpike Road at a bridge, William Collins, R.H. Sims, and M. Brame. This December 23, 1861.
Reg: December 23, 1861   Signed: Wm. B.M. Brame

Page 75 - N. Thompson 2nd Deed 183 acres to George V. Hebb. Land in Bedford County and District No. 7, adjoining the center of Flat Creek near a spring. This 20 December 1861.
Reg: December 23, 1861   Signed: N. Thompson, 2nd

75 - A.L. Adams Deed 110 acres to W.M. Tatum. Conveyed made 16 December 1861 between Adolphus Adams and William M. Tatum of Bedford County and Civil District No. 8, adjoining on the bank of Duck River, and John Fisher. This 16 December 1861.
Reg: December 23, 1861   Signed: A.L. Adams

Page 76 - Chas. L. & Thos. B. Cannon Deed 463 acres to Jo.D. & Thos. P. Wilhoite. Thomas B. Cannon and Charles L. Cannon as executors of the Last Will and Testament of Clement Cannon, Sr., deceased, have sold unto Joseph D. Wilhoite and Thomas P. Wilhoite all the right title claim &c in a tract of land in Bedford County, adjoining Thomas B. Cannon, Scudder, Duck River, R.T. Cannon, Reid & Gentry, and Robert Cannon. Play made by William Galbreath. This 23 December 1861.
Reg: December 24, 1861   Signed: C.L. Cannon
                                      Thos. B. Cannon

Page 77 - Nathaniel G. Norville Deed to John W. Norville. All my right title &c to 1/7 of 1/9 of a tract of land in Bedford County and Civil District No. 3, containing 270 acres being the place whereon John W. Norville now resided and formerly owned by David Norville now deceased, and adjoining lands of Elijah Bomar, Gilchrist or Whiteside, and Daniel Gilchrist. This 24 December 1861.
Reg: December 24, 1861   Signed: N.G. Norville

Page 77 - J.C. Shapard Trust Deed to R.T. Shapard. J.C. Shapard conveyed to R.T. Shapard land in Bedford County and Civil District No. 24, adjoining the Lynchburg Road, the Farrar lot, and a church lot. This December 26, 1861.

Reg: December 27, 1861   Signed: J.C. Shapard

Page 78 - D.F. Osteen Deed 128+ acres to Jesse Covington. David F. Osteen of Bedford County sold to Jesse Covington land in Bedford County and District No. 10, adjoining Osteen, a creek, and Cheatham's line. This 28 December 1861.
Wit: John T. Wilson   Signed: D.F. Osteen
     John Jordan
Reg: December 30, 1861

Page 79 - Archa. Prewett Deed ___ acres from James C. Lain. Land in Bedford County and Civil District No. 3, adjoining John Westley Brown, C.F. Sutton, H.C. Kinnard and W.B. Armstrong, Daniel Gilchrist, Abram Shriver, B.F. McElrath, and Mrs. Mullins. This 30 December 1861.
Wit: Thos. H. Coldwell   Signed: J.C. Lain
Reg: December 30, 1861

Page 79 - Mike Shofner and Ann E. Hix Title Bond to J.T. Arnold. Michael Shofner and Ann Eliza Hix are bound unto James T. Arnold and will convey land in Bedford County and Civil District No. 25?, adjoining S.B. Gordon and J.R. Burrow. Containing 100 acres. This 5 September 1861.
Wit: D.M. Shofner   Signed: Mike Shofner
     J.M. Phillips   Ann E. Hix
Reg: December 31, 1861

Page 80 - John Wallis, extr., Deed to Peter E. Clardy, admr. Whereas Geo. Pratt, late of Bedford County did on ___ May 1855 make his Last Will and Testament by which he appointed John Wallis and Andrew Pratt his executors. Said Geo. Pratt having died and said Wallis and Andrew Pratt having qualified will give bond and were directed to sell all his real estate and which they did on 25 September 1855 and sold to Andrew Pratt. Andrew Pratt having died and by his Last Will and Testament appointed James R. Reagor his executor and Peter E. Clardy was appointed administrator of Andrew Pratt. The land in Bedford County and Civil District No. 23, adjoining Flat Creek and Lot No. 2. Containing 142 acres. This 18 December 1861.
Wit: Thos. H. Coldwell   Signed: John Wallis
Reg: December 31, 1861

Page 81 - Asa L. Stamps Deed Lot to Joseph Cox. Deed in Book BBB, pages 437 and 438. Land in Bedford County and Civil District No. 7 and in the Town of Shelbyville, adjoining the Female Academy, and on west side of the Nashville Road. Containing about 1 acre. This 30 December 1861.
Reg: January 1, 1862   Signed: A.L. Stamps

Page 82 - Rufus Smith Deed 93 acres to James L. Hix. I have sold to J.L. Hicks a tract of land lying in the 22nd District of Bedford County, containing 93 acres. This 17 December 1861.

Reg: January 1, 1862   Signed: Rufus Smith

Page 82 - James L. Hix Deed 93 acres to John C. Hix.   Land in
22nd District of Bedford County.   Containing 93 acres.   This 21
December 1861.
Reg: January 1, 1862   Signed: Jas. L. Hix

Page 83 - John C. Hix Deed 93 acres to A.H. Evans.   Land in
Bedford County and Civil District No. 22.   Containing 93 acres.
This 21 December 1861.
Reg: January 1, 1862   Signed: J.C. Hix

Page 83 - R.S Dwiggins Deed in Trust to Jett & Cooper.   Robert
S. Dwiggins has sold to Wm. S. Jett and C.A. Warren 60 head of
mules now on my plantation near Shelbyville.   Some of the mules
I purchased of T.B. Marks, P.C. Steele, A. Webb, and George W.
Bell, Doak Murphy, Thomas Ogilvie, and C.T. Philpot.   This 31
December 1861.
Reg: January 1, 1862   Signed: R.S. Dwiggins

Page 84 - L.W. Barrett Bill of Sale to J.T. Patrick.   For four
negros.   This 18 November 1861.
Reg: January 1, 1862   Signed: L.W. Barrett

Page 84 - D.S. Evans Bill of Sale to S.D. Coble.   For a negro
woman.   This 31 December 1860.
Reg: January 1, 1862   Signed: D.S. Evans

Page 85 - R.T. Daniel and wife Bill of Sale to J.J. Shriver.
December 22, 1861 for a negro boy.
Wit: G.W. Cone   Signed: Emaline Daniel
     W.P. Cooper   R.T. Daniel
Reg: January 2, 1862

Page 85 - Robert Reed Deed 8 ½ acres to Wm. Hime.   Sale on ___
day of ___ 1861 to Wm. Hime.   In the case of Henry Hime and
others Nos. 5594 & 5595.   Land adjoining J.H. McGrew.   This
January 1, 1862.
Wit: Thos. H. Coldwell   Signed: Robert Reed
Reg: January 2, 1862

Page 85 - A.D. Fugitt and others Deed 218+ acres to R.D. Blair.
This ___ day of ___ 1859 James R. Clardy and Noble L. Clardy
conveyed all of their property in trust by two Trust Deeds
registered in Bedford County, on to James Wortham and Jesse F.
Vannoy and the other to Jesse F. Vannoy.   Alfred D. Fugitt was
appointed Trustee of said Trust.   Land being in Bedford County
near the Village of Bellbuckle, adjoining the Rail Road.   This
19 March 1861.
Wit: James Dunniston   Signed: J.R. Clardy

G.C. Fuggitt
Reg: January 3, 1862

N.L. Clardy
A.D. Fugitt, Trustees of
J.R. & N.L. Clardy

Page 86 - Thomas H. Hutson Deed 88+ acres to J.N. Blanton.
Thomas H. Hutson of Bedford County. Land in Bedford County and
District No. 24 being part of Lot No. 2 of the school land on
Flat Creek and purchased by William Heaslett, deceased,
adjoining Alfred Campbell, and a branch of Flat Creek. Being
two lots included in said boundaries hereto conveyed to the
school land and the church and burying ground. This 31 December
1861.
Wit: Edm'd Cooper   Signed: Thos. Hutson
Reg: January 1, 1862

Page 87 - J.N. Blanton Deed 88+ acres to J.C. Ray and E.A.
Reagor. Land in Bedford County and District No. 24, being part
of Lot No. 2 of the school land on Flat Creek and purchased by
William Heaslett, deceased, and adjoining the Big Road in Alfred
Campbell's line, and the top of a ridge. This 31 December 1861.
Reg: January 4, 1862   Signed: J.N. Blanton

Page 88 - John F. Thompson Deed 35+ acres to Martha Ann
Williams. This 7 November 1861. Martha Ann Williams wife of
W.M. Williams, all of Bedford County. Land in Bedford County
and in Civil District No. 18, adjoining Hiram Harris, Henry
Brown and L.E. Jones.
Wit: Wm. G. Cowan   Signed: John F. Thompson
     Robert Cowan
Reg: January 4, 1862

Page 88 - William Word Deed 42 acres to Garrett Phillips. Land
in Bedford County and Civil District No. 7, adjoining Thomas J.
Brown, W.S. Jett, J.A. Blakemore, Claiborne McCuistion, and Mrs.
Brown, being the place on which I now live and it being the land
I bought from Samuel McCuistion, Claiborne McCuistion and Geo.
Porter. This 2 January 1862.
Wit: Thos. H. Coldwell   Signed: William Word
Reg: January 4, 1862

Page 89 - Phillip R. Haley Title Bond to Young Wilhoite. I,
Philip R. Haily, have sold to Young Wilhoite land in Bedford
County. The home tract on which I am now residing. Adjoining
on the north bank of Duck River. Also one other small tract in
Bedford County and in District No. 18, adjoining on the east
side of Thompson Ford Road in the north boundary line of
Hartsfield tract. Also one other tract known as part of Henry
Earnhart tract and adjoining Ab. Parsons and wife, and the old
Warner tract. Also one other tract purchased by Thos. Lipscomb
3 October 1861 and adjoining the south west corner of Warner's
bridge, the north side of the road leading from the Fishing Ford
to Shelbyville, and land formerly owned by Henry Earnhart. This
19 October 1861.

20

Wit: Edm'd Cooper   Signed: Phillip R. Haley
Reg: January 4, 1862

Page 90 - William G. Cowan Deed 350+ acres to Wilson Turrentine.
Both of Bedford County and Civil District No. 8 and 6 and
adjoining in the center of the Shelbyville & Unionville Pike,
lands of said Cowan and Michael B. Thompson, and the old dirt
road, and Thomas Shearin, Lee Stewart, and Thomas Gregory. This
4 January 1862.
Reg: January 6, 1862   Signed: Wm. G. Cowan

Page 91 - Wilson Turrentine Trust Deed to Edmund Cooper. Land
in Bedford County on the waters of Hurricane Creek a branch of
Duck river, and adjoining in the center of the Shelbyville and
Unionville Turnpike, said Cowan and M.B. Thompspn, the Widow
Stewart, and Thomas Gregory. This January 4, 1862.
Reg: January 4, 1862   Signed: Wilson Turrentine

Page 92 - W.B. Grady Bill of Sale to Morris Burney. January 6,
1862. For a negro boy.
Wit: Euclid Waterhouse   Signed: W.B. Grady
Reg: January 7, 1862

Page 92 - Samuel L. Davidson Bill of Sale to S.S. Moody. For a
negro man. This January 7, 1862.
Reg: January 7m, 1862   Signed: Sam'l L. Davidson

Page 92 - Levi Turner Title Bond to A.J. Shofner. A tract of
land in Bedford County, and District No. 25 and containing 120 ½
acres. This 30 October 1856.
Wit: A.L. Landis   Signed: Levi Turner
     Martin Euliss
     G.W. Heard
     R.F. Setliff
     R.F. Arnold
Reg: January 8, 1862

Page 93 - Dabney Wade Deed in Trust to Samuel G. Thompson.
Dabney Wade of Bedford County has sold to Sam'l G. Thompson of
same place one yellow man and two horse wagon. I am indebted to
Thomas Mattox. This 8 January 1862.
Wit: James H. Neil   Signed: Dabney Wade
Reg: January 8, 1862

Page 94 - V.K. Stevenson Deed 281+ acres to Barton & Ramsey. 28
November 1855. Land. H.C. Hurst and J.L. Hurst sold much of
said land to William Barton and David Ramsey by deed on 1
September 1860 and registered in Book CCC, page 175. Whereas
said David Ramsey has since died leaving S.Mc. Ramsey his only
son and heir. Land in Bedford County and Civil District No. 4,
adjoining on the road from Shelbyville to McMinnville being

21

Charles Sutton's corner, Granville Frazier, R.D. Blair now Ransom's tract and the center of the Nashville and Chattanooga Rail Road. This __ December 1861.
Reg: January 15, 1862   Signed: V.K. Stevenson

Page 95 - William Barton and Sam'l Mc. Ramsey Deed 281+ acres to Edwin H. Ewing, Jr. On 1 September 1860, H.C. Hurst and J.L. Hurst conveyed to William Barton and David Ramsey a tract of land registered in Book CCC, page 175. Whereas David Ramsey has since died having first made his Last Will and Testament which was proven and recorded in Warren County, Tennessee of his residence by which will be vested to Sam Mc. Ramsey all the property and bequeath made to his wife Lucy Ramsey. Said Wm. Barton and Sam Mc. Ramsey has sold said land to Edwin H. Ewing, Jr. Land in Bedford County and Civil District No. 4 and adjoining the road leading from Shelbyville and McMinnville Road, Sutton's line, Charles Sutton, the Bradfords Creek, Granville Frazier, Whitthorne, and the Wartrace Creek, and to the mouth of Andersons Creek, R.D. Blair now Ransom's tract and the Nashville & Chattanooga Rail Road. This 19 December 1861.
Wit: Henry Cooper   Signed: Sam Mc. Ramsey
     Edm'd Coper   Wm. Barton
Reg: January 13, 1862

Page 96 - D.F. (David F.) Osteen Deed 100 acres to Alitha Collins. 3 January 1853. Alitha Collins the wife of Daniel Collins, all of Bedford County. All of Bedford County. Land in Bedford County adjoining Joshua White's field or land, and W. Daniel.
Reg: January 13, 1862   Signed: D.F. Osteen

Page 96 - P. Fay Deed Lot to Mary Haberlin. Land in the Town of Shelbyville, Bedford County and District No. 7, adjoining on the road to Jacob P. Thompson's mill, by Robert' Cannon, and William Little. This March 26, 1858.
Reg: January 13, 1862   Signed: P. Fay

Page 97 - G.W. Gardner Trust Deed to William McGill. A tract of land I purchased of James T. Arnold by deed 20 December 1861. This January 13, 1862.
Reg: January 14, 1862   Signed: G.W. Gardner

Page 97 - J.H. Roane Deed 14+ acres to Elijah Arnold. Land in Bedford County, Civil District No. 6, adjoining my tract of land, and the Turnpike. This 25 November 1861.
Wit: S.S. Arnold   Signed: J.H. Roane
     John S. Arnold
Reg: January 14, 1862

Page 98 - Louis Mankel Trust Deed to Morris Burney. All the material on hand belonging to the two cooper shops now in the Town of Shelbyville and under my control together with all the

cooper tools &c belonging to said shop, it being my intention to convey to Morris Burney all the finished and unfinished work &c on hand.
Reg: January 16, 1862   Signed: Louis Mankel

Page 98 - Thos. B. Laird and M.E.W. Dunaway Bill of Sale to John H. Wells. Mortgage registered in Bedford County in Book CCC, page 569. To sell negro man. This January 6, 1862.
Reg: January 17, 1862   Signed: T.B. Laird

Page 99 - J.C. Muse and Richard Anderson Deed 2 acres to Newcom Thompspon, 2nd. Richard Anderson and Jacob C. Muse with others as Trustees of the Baptist Church by John T. Muse which deed is registered in Bedford County in Book LL, page 159. We as trustees of the Friendship Baptist Church a tract of land lying on the waters of Sugar Creek, adjoining Asa Fonville, deceased, and said Thompson, also land formerly Streater's line. This May 21, 1861.
Reg: January 16, 1862   Signed: Richard Anderson

Page 100 - G.P. Baskett and others Deed 10+ acres to W.B.M. Brame. & October 1861. Land in Bedford County and District No. 7, adjoining old Manchester Road passing the old Thomas Holland place, and Mrs. Coats' line. This 11 January 1862.
Wit: R.N. Wallace   Signed: G.P. Baskett
     Thos. H. Coldwell   Leonard B. Fite
Reg: January 18, 1862   G. Phillips, Sheriff

Page 100 - D.G. Deason Deed Lot to P. Fay. Lot in the Town of Shelbyville, Bedford County, adjoining streets where Lane Street crosses Pike Street north of the Public Square, William Brown of my fence. This January 20, 1862.
Wit: Geo. W. Buchanan   Signed: D.G. Deason
     J.T. Taylor
     Daniel B. Shriver
Reg: January 21, 1862

Page 101 - Jeddediah A. McLain Deed 41+ acres to John A. McLain. Land in Bedford County and Civil District No. 9. This February 5, 1861.
Wit: J.R. Puckett   · Signed: J.A. McLain
     G.W. Holden
Reg: January 22, 1862

Page 102 - Thomas A. Sikes Deed 30+ acres to Edwin Batte. Land in Bedford County and District No. 11. This January 11, 1862.
Wit: T(F?). B. Jeffress   Signed: Thos. A. Sikes
Reg: January 23, 1862

Page 102 - Jos. Mc Williamson and others Deed to John and T.P. Williams. R.S. Williamson, Jos. Mc Williamson, F.B. Tuck and wife Caroline Tuck formerly Caroline Williamson sold to John Williams and Thomas J. Williams of Bedford County and Joseph Mc Williamson land in Bedford County, adjoining Widow Greer. Containing 240 acres. This 5 June 1858.

Wit: R.M. Speed   Signed: Joseph Mc Willliamson
     P.G. Huckabey   P.F. Tuck
Reg: January 23, 1862   Caroline T. Tuck
                                     R.S. Williamson

Page 103 - John and Thos. J. Williams Deed to George W. Greer. John Williams, Jr. and Thomas J. Williams sold to George W. Greer land in Bedford County, adjoining the Widow Greer. Containing 240 acres, it being the undivided two thirds of said tract being the shares of Joseph Mc. Williams and P.T. Tuck and wife Caroline T. Tuck in and to said land subject to the life estate of R.S. Williamson and which belong to during his life to Moses Neely and Samuel Neely and W.P. Goodwin. This 5 September 1861.

Reg: January 24, 1862   Signed: J.T. Williams
                                John Williams

Page 104 - Wm. D. Arnold and wife Deed to G.W. Story. Land in Bedford County and District No. 18. Adjoining a tract of land known as the Burkean tract, and containing 49 acres. Registered in Book BBB, pages 86 and 87. This January 2, 1860.

Reg: January 24, 1862   Signed: W.D. Arnold

Page 105 - E.W. Haile Trust Deed to C.T. Haley and W.W. Arnold. Property which was now in my possession at my residence in Bedford County. Also all my interest in a tract of land on which I live in District No. 6. Containing 80 acres. This January 25, 1862.

Wit: P.E. Clardy   Signed: E.W. Haile
     N.W. Haley
Reg: January 27, 1862

Page 106 - M.F. Thompson Deed to A.S. Stem for 102+ acres. Land in Bedford County and District No. 11. Adjoining W.C. Morris, A.M. Cooper, Joshua White, and the heirs of John Thompson, deceased. This 21 August 1861.

Wit: Wm. Collins   Signed: M.F. Thompson
     S.J. Terry
Reg: January 27, 1862

Page 107 - John A. Moore Deed of Gift to Nancy Y. Dickerson. For the natural love and affectiom for my daughter Nancy Y. Dickerson, wife of Lytle Dickerson. I have given unto her free from debts &c liabilities of her husband or any future husband and at her death to go to her children that may be living, a negro woman. This 7 January 1862.

Reg: January 27, 1862   Signed: John A. Moore

Page 107 - James M. and J.E. Stephens Deed to J.E. Couch. An undivided one half of the tract in Bedford County and District No. 24 which was deeded to James M. and Joseph E. Stevens by Thomas B. Rogers on 10 November 1856 and registered in Book YY, pages 190 and 191. This 6 January 1862.
Reg: January 30, 1862   Signed: J.M. Stephens
                                        J.E. Stevens

Page 108 - N.G. Dial and wife Power of Attorney to James H. Graham. N.G. Dial and Mary M. Dial wife of N.G. Dial, both citizens of Hopkins County, Texas, have appointed James H. Graham of Bedford County our attorney to receive our full share of the proceeds of two houses and lots in the Town of Shelbyville which was sold upon the petition of the devises and heirs of Rev. George Newton by decree of the County Court. Also the proceeds of the sale of all other property real and personal belonging to said estate of Rev. George Newton to which we are heirs. Also to forward our interest in said estate when collected to George A. Newton of Cherokee County, Texas. This 6 October 1860.
Reg: January 31, 1862   Signed: N.G. Dial
                                        M.M. Dial

Page 109 - John B. Murray and wife Power of Attorney to James H. Graham. Rush County, Texas. John B. Murray and his wife Julia J. Murray of Rush County, Texas has appointed James H. Graham of Bedford County our attorney to receive from the Clerk of County Court of Bedford County our full share of the proceeds of the houses and lots, rents &c in the Town of Shelbyville which was sold upon the petition of the devices and heirs of Rev. George Newton. Also to forward our said share and interest when received to George A. Newton of Charles County, Texas. This 2 October 1860.
Reg: January 30, 1862   Signed: John B. Murray
                                        Julia J. Murray

Page 109 - Sarah Newton and others Power of Attorney to James H. Graham. Penola County, Texas. Sarah Newton wife of Ebenezer Newton, deceased, James E. Newton, Sam M. Newton, Sarah M. Newton, and Nancy P. Mills are children and heirs of said Sarah and Ebenezer Newton, deceased, and James H. Mills husband of said Nancy P. Mills, all citizens of Penola County, Texas, have appointed James H. Graham of Bedford County our attorney to receive from the County Clerk of Bedford County in full our share and interest in the proceeds of the houses and lots, rents &c in the Town of Shelbyville. Heirs of Rev. George Newton. This 28 September 1860.
Reg: January 31, 1862   Signed: Sarah Newton
                                        James E. Newton
                                        Sam M. Newton
                                        S.E.M. Newton
                                        James H. Mills
                                        Nancy P. Mills
                                        Thos. G. Allison, Atty.

Page 110 - James H. Graham Deed Lot to J. Wesley Brown. John Wesley Brown bought a lot in the limits of Shelbyville from James H. Graham adjoining Ross D. Deery, Gideon P. Baskett (now Henry Cooper), and Robert Mathew. Containing 1 ¼ acre. This 30 January 1862.
Reg: January 31, 1862   Signed: J.H. Graham

Page 111 - C.P. Houston Deed 296 Acres to A.M. Webb. Land in Bedford County and District No. 5, adjoining west margin of the turnpike road, A.L. Adams, Hutton, Price C. Steele, and George W. Bills. This December 5, 1861.
Reg: January 31, 1862   Signed: C.P. Houston

Page 111 - R.J. Williams and wife Bill of Sale to John W. Tilford. For a negro girl. This 1 October 1860.
Wit: A.C. Wood   Signed: Rich'd J. Williams
                                       Mary Williams

Page 112 - John W. Tilford Bill of Sale to B.K. Coble. For negro boys and negro girls. This 20 November 1861.
Wit: J.M. Elliott   Signed: J.W. Tilford
Reg: February 1, 1862

Page 112 - T.M. Chapman and wife Bill of Sale to Thomas Davidson. For a negro girl. This March 19, 1861.
Wit: T.H. Bell   Signed: E.M. Chapman
     Thos. W. Coffey   T.M. Chapman
     A.P. Coffey
     J.M. Dysart
Reg: February 1, 1862

Page 113 - Mary Reaves Deed 79 Acres to H.H. Nease. Land in District No. 22 on the waters of Big Flat Creek and adjoining Wilhoite's field, and the school land. This 13 September 1851.
Wit: Thos. C. Whiteside   Signed: Mary Reaves
     John P. Steele
Reg: February 1, 1862

Page 114 - James B. Dixon and Jno. E. Dixon, Trustees, Bill of Sale to A.S. Riggs. For a slave for life to Adam S. Riggs. This January 1862.
Wit: Thos. C. Whiteside   Signed: J.E. Dixon
     N. Thompson, 2nd.
Reg: February 3, 1862

Page 114 - J.S. Nowlin Bill of Sale to Morgan H. Conway. Sold a negro woman and her child.
Wit: F.M. Chapman   Signed: J.S. Nowlin
     G.W. Stephens
Reg: February 14, 1862

Page 115 - James Clardy to James Vannatti, Bill of Sale. Sale
of negro boy. This February 5, 1862.
Wit: G.W. Buchanan   Signed: James Clardy
     R.F. Evans
Reg: February 20, 1862

Page 115 - N.C. Harris and Minos Wilks Deed to James M.
Smalling. This 2 July 1847. Newton C. Harris and Minos Wilks
of Bedford County sold to James M. Smalling of same place land
in Bedford County on the waters of Bell Buckle a branch of the
Wartrace Fork of Duck River, adjoining S. Marsh, William Knott,
Tillman Dixon, Stephen Murphy, the mouth of the Sugar Camp
Branch, the Bell Buckle (Creek), and John Rice. Containing 100
acres.
Wit: John Sutton   Signed: Newton C. Harris
     B.F. Smalling   Minos Wilks
Reg: February 20, 1862

Page 116 - W.F. Sutton Deed 89+ acres to William Brown. Land in
Bedford County and Civil District No. 4, adjoining Lot No. 5 of
John Sutton, and Dawson Skeins. This February 6, 1862.
Reg: February 20, 1862   Signed: W.F. Sutton

Page 117 - John W. Thompson Deed to G.W. Thompson. All the
right claim and interest which is one fourth of a tract of land
in Bedford County and Civil District No. 8, adjoining Robt.
Cannon, J.A. Blakemore, T.W. Jordan, and Steele & H(illegible).
Containing 6 acres, the same being Lot No. 7 in T.W. Jordan's
plan of Town Lots laid off on the Newsom tract and deeded by
said Jordan to J.F. Calhoon and by Calhoon to G.W. and J.W.
Thompson on 1st October 1860 and registered in Book CCC, page
205. This 6 February 1862.
Reg: February 20, 1862   Signed: Jno. W. Thompson

Page 117 - N.C. Harris Deed 104+ Acres to W.J. Whitthorne.
Newton C. Harris sold to Wm. J. Whitthorne two tracts of land in
BEdford County and Civil District No. 3 and the first being a
part of the John Taylor tract, adjoining Granville H. Frazier,
to the Wartrace and Bell Buckle Road. Containing 52 acres and
157 pqles. The other tract on both sides of the railroad,
adjoining H.C. Hunt, and the Wartrace Creek. Containing 104
acres and 80 poles. This 6 February 1862.
Wit: Wm. H. Wisener   Signed: N.C. Harris
     T.B. Ivie
Reg: February 20, 1862

Page 118 - Iverson Knott and others Deed to R.S. Holland & Co.
Iverson Knott sold a tract of land to Isaac M. Hix. This legal
document named the following persons: John A. Ganaway, Joseph H.
Freeman, John M. Henson, as Trustees, S.P. Carrick, and P.S.
Holland, merchants. First tract of land in Civil District No. 4
and adjoining Salem Camp Ground. Containing 179 acres and 70

poles. Second tract made out by C.S. Dudley July 28, 1857.
This 6 February 1862.
Wit: Thos. H. Coldwell   Signed: Iverson Knott
     Jas. L. Scudder   J.M. Hicks
                                        Jno. A. Ganaway
                                        J.H. Freeman
                                        Jno. M. Henson

Page 120 - John A. McLean Deed to G.W. Holden. Land in Bedford
County and Civil District No. 9 adjoining J.E. Hoskins, and D.
Wheelhouse. Containing 89 acres and 19 poles. This 6 February
1862.
Wit: J.R. Pucket   Signed: John A. McLean
     R.N. McLain
Reg: February 21, 1862

Page 120 - N.B. Hart Deed to T.C. Allison. Land in Bedford
County and District No. 6, adjoining the center of the
Shelbyville and Nashville Road in A. Vannoy's line. Containing
2 acres and 85 poles. This February 21, 1862.
Reg: February 21, 1862   Signed: N.B. Hart

Page 121 - M.F. Thompson Trust Deed Bryant Landers. Minos F.
Thompson sold to Bryant Landers all my interest in the estate of
my father Jno. Thompson, my interest in a saw mill and the real
estate upon which it stands and all other articles with said
mill in Van Buren County, Arkansas owned in connection with my
brother W.P.F. Thompson, also all my horses, buggy and other
items listed in original document. Also land of about 107 acres
in Bedford County being a tract where I now live about one mile
west of Unionville and on the east side of the turnpike. NOTE:
A very long document. This 7 February 1862.
Reg: February 21, 1862   Signed: M.F. Thompson

Page 123 - A.S. Stem Deed to M.F. Thompson. Land in Bedford
County adjoining the pike, and William Floyd. Containing 111
acres and 90 poles. This 21 August 1861.
Wit: Wm. Collins   Signed: A.S. Stem
     S.J. Terry
Reg: February 21, 1862

Page 124 - W.R. Muse Deed to L.P. Fields. William P. Muse sold
to L.P. Fields all his interest in the estate of my deceased
father Orville Muse. Land in Bedford County and adjoining
Martin Hancock, Nancy Muse, Jas. L. Woods, Sarah Wood, and
Rev's. Ransom, being the same place where Orville Muse resided
at the time of his death. My interest being one undivided 6th
part of which I have sold to L.P. Fields. This February 7,
1862.
Reg: February 21, 1862   Signed: W.R. Muse

Page 124 - William Oliver Trust Deed to Geo. W. Greer. Conveyed unto George W. Greer one horse, carryall, and harness. This February 8, 1862.
Wit: Jos. H. Thompson   Signed: Wm. Oliver
Reg: February 21, 1862

Page 125 - Wm. S. Jett Bill of Sale to Letitia Cannon. January 21, 1862. For a negro boy.
Wit: G.W. Thompson   Signed: Wm. S. Jett
     Jno. W. Thompson
Reg: February 22, 1862

Page 125 - L.J. Marbury and Jno. H. Oneal Deed Martin Sims. Land in Bedford County and Civil District No. 18, adjoining at Martin Sims' corner, and R. Stephens. Containing 21 acres. This 10 May 1860.
Reg: February 22, 1862   Signed: Jno. H. Oneal
                                        L.J. Marbury

Page 126 - Mary A. Cunningham Deed to Joseph H. Cunningham. Land in Bedford County and Civil District No. 19 on the waters of Sinking Creek and adjoining M.P. Gentry, Sinking Creek, and Freeman's corner. Containing 110 acres. This November 16, 1859.
Wit: Thos. W. Buchanan   Signed: Mary A. Cunningham
     E. Morris
Reg: February 22, 1862

Page 126 - D.G. Stephenson Deed to A.J. Sharan. Land in Bedford County and District No. 18 on the waters of Bryans Creek. This 5 December 1861.
Reg: February 22, 1862   Signed: D.G. Stephenson

Page 127 - Jo. M. Hutton Deed to William Murphree. Joseph M. Hutton of Bedford County sold unto William Purphree land in Bedford County and Civil District No. 5 and adjoining Jas. Claxton, the school land, Knott's corner, and Sarah Gibb. Containing 157 acres and 29 poles. This 10 February 1862.
Reg: February 22, 1862   Signed: Jo. M. Hutton

Page 128 - Wm. & W.C. Little Bill of Sale to Jno. T. Mederas. Shelbyville, February 12, 1862. For a negro man.
Reg: February 22, 1862   Signed: Wm. & W.C. Little

Page 128 - Grandison Fletcher Trust Deed to J.W. Fletcher. One half of a lot and house in the Town of Shelbyville on which William Pickett now lives. Title Bond of Joshua Zachery. Other names listed were Mary Fletcher, Gen. Robt. Cannon, and Lucretia Eakin. This 17 February 1862.
Reg: February 22, 1862   Signed: G. Fletcher

Page 129 - S.A. Bivins Trust Deed to G. Fletcher. Silas A. Bivins sold unto Grandison property, to wit, one lot and house in the Town of Shelbyville, adjoining the Unionville Turnpike, Jno. H. Oneal being the one on which I formerly lives. I am indebted to Wilhoite & Brothers, also G. and J.W. Fletcher, Shapard & Mitchell, Wendal & Watson, J.E. & R.S. Wendal, and T.J. Reaves. This 17 February 1862.
Reg: February 24, 1862   Signed: S.A. Bivins

Page 130 - S.A. and J.H. Bivins Trust Deed to G. Fletcher. Land sold to Grandison Fletcher a lot and house in the Town of Shelbyville and adjoining by the street leading to the Depot, and by Brittain Street, also the tan yard in Manchester known as the Hickerson tan yard owned jointly with Daniel Dillon. Also convey all of our stock of leather material. Names listed in original document are G. Fletcher, Shapard & Mitchell, C.G. Mitchell, J.A. Blakemore, and J.H. Graham. NOTE: A long document. This 17 February 1862.
Reg: February 24, 1862   Signed: S.A. & J.H. Bivins

Page 131 - Elizabeth Hall & others Deed to S.K. Whitson. Elizabeth Hall, D.W. Donaldson and wife Sarah E., W.A. Hall, Mary A. Hall, A.J. Hall, heirs at law of Miles M. Hall, deceased, sold to Samuel K. Whitson land in Bedford County and Civil District No. 2, adjoining Widow Hall, L.W. Hall and Lot No. 1, also to Down tract. Containing 82 acres and 85 poles. This March 1859.
Rutherford County, Tennessee
Reg: February 24, 1862   Signed: Elizabeth Hall
                                        W.A. Hall
                                        A.J. Hall
                                        M.A. Hall
                                        D.W. Donaldson
                                        S.E. Donaldson
                                        T.R. Hall

Page 132 - S.K. Whitson Deed 82+ acres to Willis M. Rippy. Land in Bedford County and Civil District No. 2, adjoining L.W. Hall. (Excepting and reserving the Hall family grave yard. This February 14, 1862.
Wit: J,S. Maupin   Signed: S.K. Whitson
     F.M. Yates
Reg: February 25, 1862

Page 133 - A.J. Greer Bill of Sale to Eleanor Gammill. For a negro girl. This 17 February 1862.
Reg: February 25, 1862   Signed: A.J. Greer

Page 133 - John M. Trollinger Deed Lot to Andrew M. Trollinger. Land in the corporate limits of the Town of Shelbyville being the same lot or part of lot I purchased of R.T. Foster and is registered in Bedford County in Book CCC, page 273. This February 17, 1862.

Reg: February 25, 1862   Signed: J.M. Trollinger

Page 134 - Samuel Little and others Deed __ acres to Montgomery
Little. William Little, Elizabeth Taylor, Samuel Little and
wife Emily Little, Wiley P. Chick and wife Patsey Chick have
sold to Montgomery Little, for debt of Benjamin Little, land in
Bedford County, adjoining the turnpike road leading from
Shelbyville to Fayetteville, and containing 397 acres and 104
poles, it being the place formerly owned by Benjamin Little and
our interest being one eighth part each, except the shares of
Montgomery Little, John Little and Rebecca Davis.   This 4
October 1861.
Wit: Edm'd Cooper   Signed: Samuel Little
Reg: February 25, 1862   Elizabeth Taylor
                                       Alfred Little
                                       Emily Little
                                       W.T. Chick
                                       Patsey Chick
                                       Wm. Little

Page 135 - Hiram Harris and others Deed 85 acres to William
Little. Hiram Harris in his own right and Hiram Harris' wife
Lucy Ann as one of the heirs at law of George W. Tilford,
deceased, W.C. Blanton and wife Elizabeth, John H. Laurence and
wife Tabitha, W.T. Green and wife Margaret, Henry Brown and wife
Mary, John W. Tilford, James S. Tilford and Samuel Tilford have
sold to William Little land in Bedford County and District No.
18, adjoining land sold by Robert B. Davidson to Hiram Harris,
and by Russell Freeman. Containing 85 acres. This 10 February
1860.
Reg: February 25, 1861   Signed: Hiram Harris
                                       Lucy Ann Harris
                                       J.W. Tilford
                                       W.T. Green
                                       M.J. Green
                                       Samuel Tilford
                                       W.C. Blanton
                                       Elizabeth B. Blanton
                                       M.M. Brown

Page 136 - Garrett Phillips Deed to Wm. S. Jett.   Land in
Bedford County and District No. 7 and adjoining lands of Thomas
J. Brown, W.S. Jett, J.A. Blakemore, C. McCuistion, and Mrs.
Brown, being the same place I bought of Wm. Wood for which his
deed to me is registered in Book DDD, pages 88 and 89.   This
February 8, 1862.
Reg: February 25, 1862   Signed: Garrett Phillips

Page 136 - Samuel Little and others Power of Attorney to
Montgomery Little. We, William Little, Samuel Little, Elizabeth
Taylor, Alfred Little and wife Emily, W.P. Chick and wife Patsey
Chick, being heirs at law of Benjamin Little, deceased, have
appointed Montgomery Little who is also one of the heirs of said
estate, our attorney in fact for us to sell or dispose all the

real estate formerly owned by Benjamin Little and which on his
death descended to us. Land in the State of Arkansas,
Mississippi and the western part of Tennessee near Memphis, and
in the City of New Orleans in Louisiana. This 4 October 1861.
Wit: Edm'd Cooper   Signed: Alfred L. Little
Reg: February 26, 1862   Emily Little
                                   Samuel Little
                                   Elizabeth Taylor
                                   W.P. Chick
                                   Patsey Chick

Page 137 - Allen Wallis Deed to Joel A. Wallis. Allen Wallis of
Bedford County in a Deed of Trust executed to me by Alfred G.
Wallis of the one third part of land allotted to Mrs. Ditto as
her dower out of the lands of William Ditto, deceased, which
(illegible) to said Alfred F. Wallis in right of his wife
Cynthia Wallis, now at the death of her mother Mrs. Ditto, the
dower contains near 100 acres being in Bedford County and Civil
District No. 3. Joel A. Wallis being the purchaser. This 10
October 1861.
Wit: J.M. Wallis   Signed: Allen Wallis
     Allen Wallis, Jr.
Reg: February 26, 1862

Page 138 - John Q. Davidson, Trustee, Deed Lot to Samuel R.
Haley. By a Deed in Trust to me made by Robert Buchanan and
dated 30 June 1859 and recorded in Book BBB, pages 124, 125 and
126, paid by Samuel R. Haley, land in Bedford County and
District No. 3 near the junction of the Shelbyville Branch Rail
Road with the Nashville and Chattanooga Rail Road, adjoining the
line of Wartrace Depot ground. This 20 January 1862.
Reg: February 26, 1862   Signed: John Q. Davidson, Trustee

Page 138 - Henry Swarp Trust Deed to James Stallings. Sold to
James Stallings one sorrel horse and one horse wagon and
harness. This February 10, 1862.
Reg: March 6, 1862   Signed: Henry Swarp

Page 139 - A.J. Greer and Jacob Harrison Bill of Sale to William
Wiggins. William Wiggins as executor of William O. Forbes,
deceased, conveyed unto Nancy Jackson during her natural life
and at her death to Sarah Jane Forbes, Riley H. Forbes and Alice
Forbes and if any of them should die before their mother Nancy
Jackson leaving child or children as child or children to have
their deceased parents share, and one negro girl. This 20
February 1862.
Reg: March 6, 1862   Signed: A.J. Greer
                                    Jacob Harrison

Page 139 - J.E. Prosser Title Bond to John F. Jenkins. J.E.
Prosser is bound to pay John F. Jenkins $8100. John F. Jenkins
has purchased a tract of land in Bedford County and District No.

20 and adjoining Nathan Evans, Jesse Evans, Thompson Snell, John Twonsend, and containing 162 acres. This 15 August 1859.
Wit: L.W. Barrett   Signed: J.E. Prosser
     James Carlisle
Reg: March 6, 1862

Page 140 - Friar Trail Power of Attorney to Wm. G. Cowan. Shelbyville, December 3, 1861. Wm. G. Cowan to act as my legal authorized attorney in fact to act for me and to sell and convey my land in Bedford County.
Wit: O. Cowan   Signed: F. Trail
     A.E. Cooper
     Robert Cowan
Reg: 7 March 1862

Page 140 - S.W. and T.S. Clay Deed Lot to Wm. J. Whitthorne. T.J. Clay conveyed a deed dated 21 April 1856 a lot and house in the Town of Shelbyville, adjoining a lot and house of Young Wilhoite on the turnpike road leading from Martin Street north to Murfreesboro. For the benefit of his wife Jane E. Clay and his children by her. This 6 February 1862.
Wit: Wm. H. Wisener   Signed: S.W. Clay, Trustee
     T.B. Ivie   T.S. Clay
Reg: March 7, 1862

Page 141 - Zadock Motlow Deed 50 acres to James Martin, Sr., both of Lincoln County, Tennessee. Land in Bedford County on the head waters of Big Flat Creek being the southern half of a 100 acre tract granted to Hugh McCall and John Woodward agreeable to a dividing line which was run sometime since by Wm. Boone. Land adjoining John Woodward, Jesse Phillips, Elijah Smith, and George Woodward. This 11 October 1859.
Wit: R.B. Parks   Signed: Zadock Motlow
     Mathew Hiles
     James Martin
     J.R. Sharp
Reg: March 8, 1862

Page 142 - Thomas Shearin Deed 197+ acres to William Shearin. Land in Bedford County and Civil District No. 11, adjoining the heirs of John E. Smith it being John W. Mayfield's corner, a cross fence, west bank of Duck River, and Michael Capley. This __ day of __ 1853.
Reg: March 10, 1862   Signed: Thomas Shearin

Page 142 - A. Claxton Deed 100 acres to Friar Trial. 1 October 1859. Abram Claxton conveyed unto Friar Trial all the right title and claim in land in Bedford County and Civil District No. __, adjoining John M. Warner, and Duck River. This 24 February 1862.
Wit: Robert Cowan   Signed: A. Claxton
     W.S. McClelland
Reg: March 10, 1862

Page 143 - Gray Linch Deed 25 acres to Louisa Robinson. Land in Bedford County and District No. 5 and adjoining G.W. C(illegible), C.A. Freeman, Jenny Wammack, and Jacob's land. This year 1862.
Reg: March 10, 1862   Signed: Gray Linch

Page 144 - Wm. G. Cowan Attorney &c Deed 100 acres to Wm. S. Jett. Agreement between Friar Trail and Wm. S. Jett, citizens of Bedford County sold to said Friar Trail paid by said Jett and conveyed to Wm. S. Jett a tract of land in Bedford County and Civil District No. 7, adjoining John M. Wisener, and Duck River. This 26 February 1862.
Reg: March 10, 1862   Signed: Wm.S. Jett

Page 145 - John M. Henson Deed to John A. Gannaway. Land in Bedford County and Civil District No. 4, and adjoining east corner of Salem Campground lot, Burrel Featherston, Bell Buckle Creek, the Shelbyville and Bell Buckle Road, and land laid off to Mary S. Elkins. Containing 68 acres. This 1 March 1862.
Wit: W.B. Norville   Signed: Jno. M. Henson
     R.H. Elkins
Reg: March 11, 1862

Page 145 - John G. Wilson Bill of Sale to Levi Madison. For a negro girl. This 1 March 1862.
Reg: March 11, 1862   Signed: Jno. G. Wilson

Page 146 - A.A. Cooper, Trustee, Deed Lots to Mrs. Elizabeth H. Stephens. J.W. Stephens executed to A.A. Cooper a Deed of Trust on property on _- day of __ 1860, containing among other property to lots and houses in the Village of Wartrace, Bedford County and registered in Bedford County, lots adjoining the Depot ground belonging to the Nashville and Chattanooga Rail Road Co., and by Mrs. Pruitt, Henry B. Coffee, A.H. Coffee, and __ Coffee being the same said J.H. Stephens purchased of James M. Chilton. This 14 February 1862.
Wit: J.G. Webster   Signed: A.A. Cooper
     S.B. Heard
Reg: March 11, 1862

Page 146 - James L. Scudder Deed Lots to Wm. J. Cochran. Two Town Lots in Camp White on October 26, 1861. Lots in Town of Shelbyville, Bedford County which I purchased of R.N. Jones by deed September 18, 1852 and known by Lots No. 104 and 111. This March 8, 1862.
Reg: March 11, 1862   Signed: J.L. Scudder

Page 147 - M.T. Cooper Bill of Sale to Catharine R. Hill. Free from her husband James Hill, sold a negro boy. This 28 January 1862.
Wit: A.A. Cooper   Signed: M.T. Cooper
     L.P. Fields

Reg: March 11, 1862

Page 147 - Elnathan Stephens Deed to James Finch. Land on
waters of Strait Creek in Bedford County, adjoining Strait
Creek, Anderson's land, John Cawthon's line, J. Douglass, and
Finch's original tract, and Slaton's tract. Containing __
acres. This __ of __ 1860.
Reg: March 12, 1862   Signed: E. Stevens

Page 148 - Luke Ramsey Bill of Sale to Joseph Ramsey. March 12,
1862. For a negro boy. David McCulloch as my security.
Reg: March 13, 1862   Signed: L. Ramsey

Page 149 - John H. Oneal and C.T. Philpott Deed 395+ acres to
A.L. Adams. Land in Bedford County and District No. 6, and
adjoining the center of the Shelbyville and Murfreesboro
Turnpike Road, Peyton Coats' corner, center of the Middleton
Road, and the original south east corner of the school land.
This January 20, 1862.
Reg: March 14, 1862   Signed: John H. Neal
                                     C.T. Philpott

Page 149 - A.L. Adams Deed 162 acres to Edmund Cooper. Land
originally sold to me by John H. Oneal and Charles T. Philpott,
land, for securing the unpaid purchase money going to Turner S.
Foster and Edm'd Cooper and which was a line on the land
conveyed to me. Land in Bedford County on the waters of Fall
Creek and adjoining the Shelbyville-Murfreesboro Turnpike Road,
the heirs of John and Margaret Hutton, deceased, and by Hughes.
This 20 January 1862.
Reg: March 14, 1862   Signed: A.L. Adams

Page 150 - J.S. Nowlin Deed 38+ acres to Joel Stallings. Land
in Bedford County and District No. 18, and adjoining James
Davis' lane, and Rock Creek. This June 8, 1860.
Wit: C.S. Dudley   Signed: J.S. Nowlin
     James Hicks
Reg: March 15, 1862

Page 150 - Joel Stallings Deed 10+ acres to J.S. Nowlin. Land
in Bedford County and District No. 18 and adjoining the land I
purchased of John H. Oneal, and center of the Turnpike Road.
This June 8, 1860.
Wit: C.S. Dudley   Signed: Joel Stallings
     James Hicks
Reg: March 15, 1862

Page 151 - Reuben Curry Deed 23+ acres to William Hoover. Land
in Bedford County and District No. 4 and adjoining the center of
the Wartrace Creek in Nathan Chaffin's line, to near Spout
Spring, and Wm. F. Pearson's water gate. This 27 April 1859.

Wit: E.G. Davis   Signed: Reuben Curry
     R.B. Bigham
Reg: March 18, 1862

Page 151 - William Hoover Deed 23+ acres to R.B. Bigham. Land
in Bedford County and District No. 4, and adjoining the center
of the Wartrace Creek in Nathan Chaffin's line, to Spout Spring,
and to Wm. P. Pearson's water gate. This 14, 1862.
Reg: March 14, 1862   Signed: William Hoover

Page 152 - A.L. Adams Deed 68+ acres to G.W. Bell. Land in
Bedford County and District No. 5, and adjoining G.W. Bell's
corner. This 15 March 1862.
Reg: March 15, 1862   Signed: A.L. Adams

Page 152 - D.S. Parker and William Brown Deed to Thomas C.
Ryall. 2 November 1858, conveyed to D.S. Parker by deed
registered in Bedford County in Book AAA, page 411 being in
District No. 23. Said Parker did on 15 August 1860 convey among
other property to Wm. Brown. Said land containing the same
tract aforesaid to Thomas C. Ryall. This March 14, 1862.
Reg: March 18, 1862   Signed: D.S. Parker
                                     William Brown

Page 153 - John C. Wood Deed 15+ acres to John Claxton. Land in
Bedford County and District No. 8, adjoining the old Arthur
Donalson, and D. Pates. This August 16, 1861.
Wit: John S. Dwyer   Signed: John C. Wood
     Jonathan Holden
Reg: March 19, 1862

Page 154 - Thos. H. Oneal and S.S. Arnold Deed 22+ acres to J.Y.
West. Land in Bedford County and Civil District No. 3, it being
part of a tract of land that S.S. Arnold sold to Thos. H.
Coldwell in 1855 and has Arnold's bond and is registered in
Bedford County, it being that portion of the land lying on the
right of Rail Road running from Shelbyville to Wartrace, and
adjoining the Rail Road. This 15 March 1862.
Reg: March 19, 1862   Signed: Thos. H. Coldwell
                                     S.S. Arnold

Page 154 - J.S. Nowlin Deed 4+ acres to Thomas H. Bell. Land in
Bedford County and District No. 18 and adjoining the pike. This
November 23, 1861.
Reg: March 19, 1862   Signed: J.S. Nowlin

Page 155 - Joseph H. Cunningham Deed to Mary A. Cunningham. For
all the right title claim and interest to the land owned by
J.W.C. Cunningham at the time of his death and said land
adjoining lands of John Cortner, M.P. Gentry, and Wm. Wood.
Also all interest in a small tract of cedar land owned by J.W.C.

Cunningham at the time of his death in Civil District No. __, it being the same land bought by J.W.C. Cunningham of Alex. Wilson, and containing 16 acres. This October 20, 1861.
Reg: March 19, 1862   Signed: J.H. Cunningham

Page 155 - William S. Puckett Deed 12+ acres to George W. Holden. Land in Bedford County and Civil District No. 9, and adjoining Dennis Wheelhouse. This 27 April 1858.
Wit: Dennis Wheelhouse   Signed: W.S. Puckett
     S.J. Holden
Reg: March 31, 1862

Page 156 - James Martin, Sr. Deed 50 acres to Medearis & Dean. James Martin, Sr., of Lincoln County, Tennessee and John T. Medearis and P.S. Dean of the firm of Medearis & Dean of Bedford County. Land in Bedford County on the head waters of Big Flat Creek being the southern half of a 100 acre tract granted to Hugh McCall and John Woodard agreeable to the line which runs by William Boone, and adjoining John Woodard, Jesse Phillips, Elijah Smith, and George Woodard. This 24, 1862.
Wit: James C. Martin   Signed: James Martin
Reg: March 24, 1862

Page 157 - P. Fay Deed 40 acres to W.S. Jett. Land in District No. 3, and adjoining in the center of the Shelbyville Branch Rail Road, by B.A. Nelson, Moses Nelson, Roger H(illegible), and containing 40 acres. This March 26, 1862.
Reg: March 31, 1862   Signed: P. Fay

Page 157 - Albert and Melinda Smith Agreement to Separate. We, G.G. Osborne and A. McMahan being called by Albert Smith and Melinda Smith to make a division of property between them as they have separated from each other as man and wife. We give to Albert Smith several animals and a bedstead and furniture, also other named items. We give to his wife Melinda several animals and three bed steads and furniture, and several other items. This 28 December 1861.
Wit: G.G. Osborne   Signed: Albert Smith
     Abram McMahan   Melinda Smith
Reg: March 31, 1862

Page 158 - Wilson Turrentine Deed 209+ acres to M.F. Williams. Land in Bedford County and Civil District No. 8, and adjoining Stephen Sanders. This 29 March 1862.
Reg: March 31, 1862   Signed: Wilson Turrentine

Page 159 - P. Fay Deed 20 acres to Roger Hassett. Land in District No. 3, and adjoining Wm. H. Wisener, Thos. G. Holland, Moses Nelson, and the center of the Rail Road. This January 1, 1858.
Reg: April 8, 1858   Signed: P. Fay

Page 159 - William Culley Deed 108+ acres to J.A. Bramlett. Land in Bedford County and Civil District No. 2, and on Lazy Branch of Doddys Creek waters of the Barren Fork of Duck River, and adjoining Bramlett and F. Thompson, J. Muse, and Wilson Hall. This 7 April 1862.
Wit: Isaac B. Holt   Signed: William Culley
Reg: April 10, 1862

Page 160 - Joseph Harrison and wife Deed undivided interest to John D. Webb. We, Rebecca Harrison and Joseph Harrison sold to John D. Webb all the right title which we have in and unto the dowry part of the tract of land owned by the late James K. Clark, deceased, and adjoining J.P. Marbury, Preston Frazier, and said Webb. This 25 March 1862.
Reg: April 10, 1862   Signed: Rebecca Harrison
                                     Joseph Harrison

Page 161 - James F. Calhoon Deed Lot in Camp White to D.J. Christopher. Land in Bedford County and Civil District No. 7 near the Town of Shelbyville and it being part of Lot No. 3 of lots sold in Camp White by Clement Cannon, Sr. and registered in Bedford County. Lot adjoining the north edge of Camp White, White Street and the east side of Lot No. 3, and Line Street. Containing one acre. It being the lot sold to me by Amos Hays and registered in Book YY, pages 392 and 393. This 10 April 1862.
Wit: Thos. H. Coldwell   Signed: J.F. Calhoon
Reg: April 11, 1862

Page 162 - Jesse B. McAdams Deed 10+ acres from W.B.M. Brame. Jesse B. McAdams of Marshall County, Tennessee. Land in Bedford County and Civil District No. 7, being the lot I purchased of A.L. Stamps and part of the Coats tract sold to said Stamps. This September 25, 1860.
Reg: April 12, 1862.   Signed: W.B.M. Brame

Page 162 - William O. Dwyer Bill of Sale to George W. McQuiddy. A negro man. This 29, April 1862.
Reg: May 2, 1862   Signed: Wm. O. Dwyer

Page 162 - R.S. Thomas Deed 321 acres to Waterhouse & Burney. R.S. Thomas of Bedford County sold to Euclid Waterhouse and Morris Burney land in Bedford County and District No. 4 and land lately sold by J.A. Gannaway, Styers A. Mash, Burrel Featherston, the Nashville & Chattanooga Rail Road, J.D. Blair, J.W. Rainwater, and by land sold by James Thomas to A.L. Stamps. This 7 March 1862.
Wit: A.A. Cooper   Signed: R.S. Thomas
     J.P. Brown
     L.P. Fields
     Daniel L. Reaves
Reg: May 3, 1862

Page 163 - James Porter Deed 166 acres to Lilborn P. Fields.
Montgomery County, Alabama. Lilborn P. Fields of Bedford
County. Land in Bedford County in District No. 1 on the waters
of Puncheon Camp Creek known as a part of the Abb Wood's tract
and adjoining John Coldwell and Caughran, Abb Woods, George D.
Stephenson, and McMahan & Cufman. This 2 April 1862.
Wit: J.F. Thompson   Signed: James Porter
     J.A. Elmore
Reg: May 5, 1862

Page L.P. Fields Deed 166 acres to Daniel L. Reaves. Land in
Bedford County and District No. 1 on the waters of Puncheon Camp
Creek, adjoining Absalom Woods, John Coldwell and Caughran, Abb
Woods, George D. Stephenson, McMahan & Caufman. This 3 May
1862.
Reg: May 7, 1862   Signed: L.P. Fields

Page 165 - C.B. Sutton Power of Attorney to I.T. Mayfield and
E.W. Sutton. Colman B. Sutton late of Giles County, Tennessee,
have appointed I.T. Mayfield and E.W. Sutton of same place, my
lawful attorney to receive all sums of money, debts &c which are
due to me. To take possession of all real estate belonging to
me in Giles County, Tennessee and sell, grant and convey any
part thereof. This 1 May 1862.
Wit: W.G. Cox   Signed: C.B. Sutton
     James Eaton
Reg: MAY 5, 1862

Page 165 - Patrick Fay Deed part Lot No. 23 to Wm. S. Jett. Lot
in Town of Shelbyville, Bedford County and adjoining an alley on
the south side of ___ Street, J.M. Hobbs, and Cumberland
Presbyterian Church lot. This May 8, 1862.
Reg: May 9, 1862   Signed: P. Fay

Page 166 - C.T. Philpott Title Deed to Alexander Philpott for
71+ acres. Land on both sides of the Middleton Road known as
part of land lying north of the tract of land conveyed for A.L.
Adams' 71 acres, by lands of W.T. Tune, Peyton Coats, and
others. This January 29, 1862.
Wit: Edm'd Cooper   Signed: C.T. Philpott
     Martin Hancock
Reg: May 12, 1862

Page 166 - C.T. and Alexander Philpott Title Bond to A.L. Adams.
We bind ourselves to A.L. Adams. Conveyed a tract of land in
District No. 6 and adjoining the Middleton Road, land conveyed
by Crutcher & Foster to Oneal, and Tune's line. Containing 41
acres. Surveyed by C.S. Dudley. This 8 May 1862.
Reg: May 12, 1862   Signed: Alexr. Philpott
                                   C.T. Philpott

Page 167 - William Brown Deed Lot to Mary McKinney. Town Lot or part of Town Lot in the Town of Shelbyville and near the Big Spring. Adjoining where Patrick McKinney now lives. This 8 May 1862.
Reg: May 12, 1862   Signed: William Brown

Page 167 - Leroy W. Barrett Deed 37 acres to James Carlisle. Land in Bedford County and District No. 20 on the waters of Sugar Creek and adjoining Joseph Morton, L.H. Barrett & Carlisle. This April 25, 1862.
Reg: May 13, 1862   Signed: L.W. Barrett

Page 168 - John F. Jenkins Mortgage Deed to L.W. Barrett. Land in Bedford County and Civil District No. 20 and on the waters of Sugar Creek and adjoining Jesse Evans, Nathan Evans, and John O. Townsend. This 12 May 1862.
Wit: Thos. H. Coldwell   Signed: J.F. Jenkins
Reg: May 13, 1862

Page 169 - Adam Anthony Deed 43+ acres to Daniel Anthony. Both of Bedford County. Land in Bedford County and District No. 25 on waters of Thompsons Creek of Duck River and adjoining the edge of a ridge. This 22 March 1862.
Wit: John Blackwell   Signed: Adam Anthony
     William Johnson
Reg: May 16, 1862

Page 19 - James Johnson and A.L. Parks Deed 170 acres to L.P. Fields & Co. Land conveyed to L.P. Fields and Edmund Cooper, partners under the firm of L.P. Fields & Co., land on which James Johnson is now residing and being in District No. 1 of Bedford County, adjoining lands of D.L. Reaves, McMichael, William Johnson, and Edmund Cooper. Land not including land sold to D.L. Reaves being the land purchased by Matt Martin and the Norton tract. This 20 May 1862.
Reg: May 20, 1862   Signed: James Johnson
                                      A.L. Parks

Page 170 - Isabella W. Crowell Deed 12+ acres to Jane Crowell. For the love and affection I bear to my Aunt Jane Crowell the wife of William Crowell, have conveyed land in Bedford County and District No. 11 and being Lot No. 4 of a division of land that Jos. Anderson and David Anderson heirs made a division, being 1/10 of said land my said grant father died seized and possessed of at the time of his death. This 27 May 1862.
Wit: Jno. Anderson   Signed: Isabella W. Crowell
     J.S. Anderson
Reg: May 27, 1862

Page 170 - John A. Moore Deed to Samuel S. Moody. This 28 May 1862. John A. Moore of Bedford County and S.S. Moody of same place. Land in Bedford County also an undivided interest in a

small tract of land owned by said John A. Moore and Robert
Cannon, adjoining on the north side of Duck River at or near the
land of Mr. Holt and Mr. Gosling's mill, west of Sims and Cross'
old corner now Jas. H. Bomar, a spring, Cannon's corner, and
Uriah Cross. This May 28, 1862.
Reg: May 29, 1862   Signed: John A. Moore

Page 171 - John M. Kimbro Power of Attorney to James M. Grimes.
John M. Kimbro of the City of Holly Springs, Marshall County,
Mississippi appointed James M. Grimes of Maury County, Tennessee
my attorney to collect and receive property &c that may be in
the hands of any person in Bedford County, in the hands of
William Wisener and Riley Kimbro of Bedford County as the
executors or administrators of my father's estate the late Eli
Kimbro and my grand father John Kimbro's estate. This 14 March
1861.
Reg: June 2, 1862   Signed: J.M. Kimbro

Page 172 - William H. Clark Deed 112+ acres to Henry Clark.
Land in Bedford County and Civil District No. 11 and adjoining
Widow Wadley, center of Alexanders Creek, the center of the
North Fork of Duck River, and Abraham Reaves. This 12 December
1861.
Wit: A.N. Vincent   Signed: W.H. Clark
     Wm. F. Capley
Reg: June 16, 1862

Page 173 - A.S. Stem Deed 102+ acres to Milton Birdwell. Land
in Bedford County and District No. 11, adjoining W.G. Morris,
A.M. Cooper, Joshua White, and the heirs of John Thompson,
deceased. This 5 June 1862.
Wit: S.R. Birdwell   Signed: A.S. Stem
Reg: June 16, 1862

Page 173 - A.L. Adams Bill of sale to William D. Murphy. For a
negro boy. This 5 February 1862.
Wit: B.F. Whitworth   Signed: A.L. Adams
     M.D. Clark
     A.M. Webb
Reg: June 16, 1862

Page 174 - B.F. Whitworth Deed 54 acres to Edmund Cooper. By
the conveyance of my daughter Ann E. Sutton wife of Charles F.
Sutton, Jr., of 163 acres of land in the deed this day executed
to her and for the purpose of fully securing the unpaid purchase
maney going to Turner S. Foster and Edmund Cooper and which was
a line on the land conveyed to Ann E. Sutton, I have sold unto
Edmund Cooper all the right title &c which I have in a tract of
land in Bedford County and adjoining Joseph R. McKinley, Wm. K.
Ransom, the Public Road, and Boothe & MCKinley. This 20 June
1862.
Reg: June 23, 1862   Signed: B.F. Whitworth

Page 174 - Edmund Cooper Deed 162 acres to Mrs. Ann E. Sutton.
By notes of Charles F. Sutton, Jr. and Benjamin F. Whitworth
conveyance to me a tract of land conveyed unto Ann E. Sutton
wife of Charles F. Sutton all the right title &c I have in a
tract of land in Bedford County and adjoining the Shelbyville,
Myrfreesboro & Fosterville Turnpike, land on which Anderson Webb
now lives, land belonging to the heirs of John and Margaret
Hutton, deceased, and land conveyed to William T. Hughes by
Margaret Hutton, and Benjamin Whitworth. This 19 June 1862.
Wit: B.F. Whitworth   Signed: Edm'd Cooper
     C.T. Philpott
Reg: June 26, 1862

Page 175 - James F. Calhoon Deed Lot to T.W. Jordan. Land
registered in Book CCC, pages 188 and 189. Lot of land in the
corporate limits of the Town of Shelbyville. This June 26,
1862.
Reg: July 7, 1862   Signed: J.F. Calhoon

Page 176 - William and James P. Taylor Deed 57 acres to Edward
Tarpley. William Taylor and J.P. Taylor, trustees for said
William Taylor, sold to Edward Tarpley land in Bedford County
and District No. 9, and adjoining T.D. Tarpley, Edward Tarpley,
W.S. Taylor, and William Taylor, it being the land that
Elizabeth Lile lived on at the time of her death and afterwards
sold by Jos. H. Thompson and purchased by William Taylor. This
April 26, 1862.
Wit: T.D. Tarpley   Signed: William Taylor
     H.W. Jones   J.P. Taylor, Trustees
Reg: July 7, 1862

Page 175 - Jacob F. Thompson Deed 50 acres to Eliza Ann Parsons.
Edmund Cooper as Trustee of Eliza Ann Parsons. Notes executed
by Eliza Ann Parsons and A.B. Parsons. Eliza Ann Parsons
assigned all right title &c in a tract of land in Bedford
County, adjoining Samuel Thompson, and W.S. Jett. This 22
December 1860.
Reg: July 12, 1862   Signed: J.F. Thompson

Page 177 - A.N. Cunningham Deed of Gift to Margaretta
Cunningham. For the natural love and affection I bear for my
daughter Margaretta Cunningham a certain negro girl. This 11
July 1862.
Reg: July 12, 1862   Signed: A.N. Cunningham

Page 177 - A.N. Cunningham Deed of Gift to Julia A. Cunningham.
For the love and affection I bear for my daughter Julia A.
Cunningham a certain negro girl. This July 11, 1862.
Reg: July 12, 1862   Signed: A.N. Cunningham

Page 177 - A.L. Stamps Deed 3+ acres to Wm. H. Wisener. On 25
November 1856, I sold to William H. Wisener three small lots of

land. Said lots of land are a part of the John T. Neil tract of land near Shelbyville and adjoining Patrick Fay, A.H. Berry, and a road leading from Shelbyville to Sims Bridge on Duck River. This 12 July 1862.
Reg: July 21, 1862   Signed: A.L. Stamps

Page 178 - B.F. Duggan Deed 1 acre to G.B. Moone. B.F. Duggan sold to George B. Moon, both of Bedford County, land in the Village of Unionville, Civil District No. 11 of Bedford County, adjoining M. Blanton. This 25 February 1860.
Wit: R.H. Stem   Signed: B.F. Duggan
   J.W. Simpson
Reg: August 29, 1862

Page 179 - Richard Foreman, Sr. Deed Lot to E. Braden and children. I, Richard Foreman, have sold to my daughter Elizabeth Braden and her children, Virgil, Sandy and Anne, for the love and affection that I have for my daughter a piece of ground in the Town of Shelbyville, Bedford County and known by part of Lot No. 40 and fronting on Martin Street, an alley, Mrs. Letsy Cannon, which alley I convey to her all the right conveyed to me by William Brown by deed 17 August 1846 and registered in Book OO, page 416. This 23 July 1862.
Wit: Edm'd Cooper   Signed: Richard Foreman
   Wm. Galbreath
Reg: August 29, 1862

Page 179 - Abram. Claxton Deed 23 acres to Granville T. Tucker. Land in Bedford County, District No. 8, adjoining John Brown and E. Wilson. This May 29, 1862.
Reg: August 29, 1862   Signed: A. Claxton

Page 180 - John G. Primrose Deed 54 acres to Sophia Johnston. Land adjoining B.C. Dobson and wife, and Alexander Allen. Land I purchased of N. Thompson, 2nd. This 15 December 1859.
Wit: Albert T. Johnson Signed: J.G. Primrose
   G. Roberts
Reg: September 3, 1862

Page 180 - Wm. S. Jett Deed 100 acres to Wm. G. Cowan. Paid by Wm. G. Cowan, Shelbyville, Tennessee, September 3, 1862 for land in Bedford County and Civil District No. 7, adjoining John W. Warner, and the bank of Duck River.
Reg: September 5, 1862   Signed: Wm. S. Jett

Page 181 - Margaret & Thomas A. Bradshaw Deed 18 acres to H. Bledsoe. This 2 September 1862. All of Bedford County. Land in District No. 20 on the head waters of Sugar Creek, adjoining west of said Bledsoe's house, Aaron Bledsoe, and Hillsman Bledsoe.
Wit: Thomas A. White   Signed: Margaret Bradshaw
   T.M. White   Thomas A. Bradshaw

Reg: September 8, 1862

Page 182 - D.H. Williams Deed 75+ acres to D.H. Skeen. This 17
September 1857. David H. Williams of Bedford County and Duncan
H. Skeen of Rutherford County, Tennessee. Land in Bedford
County on the north west of Duck River and adjoining the
Gollathan land, and by C.F. Sutton.
Wit: A. Prewett   Signed: David H. Williams
     A.D. Fugitt
Reg: September 10, 1862

Page 182 - R.B. Blackwell, Sheriff, Deed 70 acres to Henry
Brown. James Wortham a former Sheriff of Bedford County against
D.B. Shriver, D.C. Shriver and John H. Oneal in favor of V.K.
Stevenson, dated 16 May 1859 (being No. 3847 Circuit Court Clerk
Dockett) and by him levied on a tract of land in Bedford County
and District No. 3 as the property of D.C. Shriver, and
adjoining the Poor House tract, Reding George, G.W. Harmon, and
John McGuire (now owned by Dixon, Bennett and others) being
place Henry Brown died on. This 8 September 1862.
Reg: September 15, 1862   Signed: R.B. Blackwell, Sheriff

Page 183 - Joseph T. Bigger Deed 106+ acres to F.M. Ray. Land
in Bedford County and District No. 11, and adjoining the center
of Wilson Creek. This 8 December 1858.
Wit: Wm. Collins   Signed: J.T. Bigger
     D.A. Ozment
     A.M. Cooper
Reg: September 15, 1862

Page 184 - Gray Linch Deed 95+ acres to G.A. Conn. Land in
Bedford County and Civil District No. 4, it being Lot No. 5 and
No. 6. The first is the plat of land formerly owned by William
P. Elkins, deceased, and now by Linch and adjoining R.W.
Pearson's Lot No. 4, the old Dennison tract of land, Robert
Dennison, H.H. Elkins' old line and Elizabeth Elkins' corner of
Lot No. 3. Containing 40 ½ acres with a deduction of 1 acre as
laid off adjoining the church lot. One other tracts adjoins
W.T. Elkins' old tract, and Iverson Knott's original tract.
Containing 56 acres including the school house, also G.A. Conn
and heirs &c is to have the legal right of way to the spring and
the use of the water or the dwelling south of the spring
formerly owned by me and now by said G.A. Conn. This 3 January
1862.
Wit: J.N. Smith   Signed: Gray Linch
     C.C. Mayhew
Reg: September 15, 1862

Page 185 - C.W. Powell Deed 65+ acres to J.S. Nowlin. Land in
Bedford County and District No. 18 and adjoining John Larue,
J.C. Powell, Rock Creek, and Joel Stallings. This 15 February
1862.
Wit: W.H. McConnell   Signed: C.W. Powell

J.C. Powell
Reg: September 16, 1862

Page 185 - Edmund Cooper Deed 271+ acres to W.A. Ransom. Land sold to William A. Ransom, and being in Bedford County and District No. 1, and adjoining the Martin place, and Maxwell tract. This 26, July 1860.
Reg: September 16, 1862   Signed: Edm'd Cooper

Page 186 - Richard Anderson Deed to Selina A. Griffith. All the right title, claim &c which I have to a tract of land in District No. 18, adjoining Wiley Usery, William Kimmons, James Stalling, and Thos. Gambill. Containing 89 acres. This 16 September 1862.
Wit: Edm'd Cooper   Signed: Richard Anderson
Reg: October 9, 1862

Page 187 - Wm. T. Tune and others Deed to John B. Tune. R.B. Tune and L.B. Knott purchased of John P. Steele land lying in Bedford County on the waters of the North Fork of Duck River and adjoining John L. Cooper, John Webb, the heirs of Thomas Rankins, deceased, Wm. Gillman, David R. Hooker, Jonathan Cooper, and Thos. B. Moseley and wife. Containing 314 acres. This August 2, 1858.
Wit: K.L. Tune   Signed: Wm. T. Tune, Trustee
     C.D. Steele   John Knott, Trustee
Reg: October 9, 1862   L.B. Knott
                               R.B. Tune
                               John P. Steele
                               W.F. Cooper

Page 188 - S.F. Southern and wife Power of Attorney &c to W.P. Green. Dade County, Georgia. Stephen F. Southern and his wife Mary A, Southern (the said Mary A. being the daughter of Blan Maupin, late of Bedford County, deceased). W.P. Green, Trustee of said Mary A. Southern has paid us which we received in the full distributive share of said Mary A.'s in her father's real estate. W.P. Green is authorized to receive all such money. This 19 August 1862.
Reg: October 9, 1862   Signed: Stephen F. Southern
                                    Mary A. Southern

Page 188 - W.J. Nowlin and others Deed 217+ acres to J.S. Nowlin. W.J. Nowlin, B.H. Nowlin and J.W. Nowlin children and heirs at law of Jabus and Mary F. Nowlin, deceased, has sold to J.S. Nowlin land in Bedford County and Civil District No. 18 about twelve miles west of the Town of Shelbyville, and adjoining the farms of John Larue and James Davis, crossing Rock Creek, a graveyard, and crossing the pike. This 2 December 1859.
Wit: H.M. Oneal   Signed: W.J. Nowlin
     James Davis   B.W. Nowlin
Reg: October 9, 1862   J.W. Nowlin

Page 189 - C.W. Powell Deed 147÷ acres to Robert Williams. Land in Bedford County and District No. 18, and adjoining John Larue, J.S. Nowlin, J.C. Powell, and Davidson's corner. This 29 September 1862.
Wit: James W. Bell   Signed: C.W. Powell
    Richard C. Stephenson
Reg: October 10, 1862

Page 190 - State of Tennessee Grant No. 25136 for 106 acres to H.G. Holt. Shelbyville dated February 23, 1861, there is granted by the State of Tennessee unto Herod G. Holt assignee of B.F. Wiggins, a tract of land containing 106 acres on the waters of Flat Creek in Range 4, Section or Township 4, and a part of Section 4 being Lot No. 6 and adjoining Lot No. 5, a stone lettered JWW in Lacey's field, an old spring near a bluff of rocks, the original school land in the south boundary line of McKinney's 2000 acre grant, and Lot No. 1 and 2, 45. This 11 June 1861.
R.E.R. Ray, Sec.   Signed by the Governor
Reg: October 10m 1862   Isham G. Harris

Page 191 - Edmund Cooper, Trustee, Deed 106 acres to W. Blanton and wife. By Trust Deed from H.G. Holt which is registered in Bedford County, sold unto Willis Blanton and Mrs. Mary A. Newsom now Mrs. Mary A. Blanton, land in Bedford County and District No. 22, and adjoining Lacey's field, a bluff of rocks, the original school land in the south boundary line of McKinney's 2000 acre grant, Lot No. 1 and 2, and Lot No. 5. This 2 October 1862.
Wit: Robert B. Maupin   Signed: Edm'd Cooper, Trustee
    J.W. Tilford
Reg: October 10, 1862

Page 191 - Willis Blanton and wife Deed 106 acres to Alfred Campbell. Willis Blanton and wife Mary A. Blanton sold to Alfred Campbell land in Bedford County and District No. 22 and adjoining Lot NO. 5, Lacey's field, the original school land, and McKinney's 2000 acre grant. This 7 October 1862.
Wit: Edm'd Cooper   Signed: Willis Blanton
    John F. Thompson   Mary A. Blanton
Reg: October 10, 1862

Page 192 - Samuel Bobo Deed 57 acres to Willis Blanton. This 20 November 1860. Samuel Bobo of Lincoln County, Tennessee and Willis Blanton of Coffee County, Tennessee. Land in Bedford County on the waters of Flat Creek, a south branch of Duck River and adjoining Jo Farrar now lives, Shelbyville Road, Philpott's corner, and F. Farrar.
Wit: J.K. Cobb   Signed: Samuel Bobo
    D.W. Parker
Reg: October 11, 1862

Page 193 - Willis Blanton Deed 57+ acres to Alfred Campbell.
Land in Bedford County on the waters of Flat Creek a south
branch of Duck River, adjoining an old road bed, Jo Farrar now
lives on, Shelbyville Road, Philpott's corner, and F. Farrar.
This 7 October 1862.
Wit: Edm'd Cooper   Signed: Willis Blanton
     John F. Thompson
Reg: October 11, 1862

Page 194 - Willis Blanton and others Deed 29+ acres to Alfred
Campbell. Willis Blanton, Mary A. Blanton, John E. Pearson,
Jane Pearson, James T. Newsom and Nancy C. Newsom (by her
guardian Willis Blanton) sold to Alfred Campbell land in Bedford
County on the waters of Flat Creek and adjoining Campbell's
spring, the public road, center of Flat Creek, and the old
school land tract. This 26 September 1860.
Wit: Chas. Pearson   Signed: Willis Blanton
     Wilburn Hiles   Mary A. Blanton
Reg: October 11, 1862   J.C. Pearson
                                      Jane Pearson
                                      James T. Newsom
                                      N.C. Newsom

Page 195 - Alfred Campbell and wife Ratification to T.J. Reaves.
This __ day of ___ 18__. Alfred Campbell did convey to my
brother Tarleton J. Reaves my share and interest in the lands of
and left by our father Archibald Reaves to his heirs at our
mother's death being one eighth of said land. I have legally
passed my title to said interest we Sarah Campbell (formerly
Sarah Reaves amd daughter of said Archibald) and Alfred Campbell
ratify the said transfer and sale by my husband. This 7 October
1862.
Wit: Edm'd Cooper   Signed: Alfred Campbell
     John F. Thompson   Sarah Campbell
Reg: October 11, 1862

Page 195 - E.D. Bomar Power of Attorney to J.H. Bomar. Elijah
D. Bomar has appointed James H. Bomar his attorney in fact to
receive any legacy that may be coming to me during my life from
my father's estate and that may be in the hands of Bibby B.
Bomar and William Bomar that may fall to me and my children.
This 5 December 1860.
Wit: B.B. Bomar   Signed: E.D. Bomar
     Edm'd Cooper
Reg: October 11, 1862

Page 196 - Harry M. Oneal Deed 13+ acres to William Wood. Land
in Bedford County and District No. 18 and adjoining Michael
Moore, E. Bryant, and Bedford Endsley. This 1 October 1862.
Wit: Wm. Woodard   Signed: Harry M. Oneal
     Samuel D. Wood
Reg: October 11, 1862

Page 196 - G.W. Parsons, Admr. Deed 71 acres to James Purvis. G.W. Parsons, administrator of J.T. McElwrath, deceased, conveyed land in Bedford County and District No. 8 and adjoining Jesse Clanton. This 6 October 1862.
Wit: Jesse C. Wheeler   Signed: G.W. Purvis, admr. Of
     John A. Wheeler   J.T. McElwrath, deceased
Reg: October 13, 1862

Page 197 - James Purvis Deed 71 acres to Wm. T. McElwrath. James Purvis sold to William T. Nash land in Bedford County and District No. 8 and adjoining Jesse Clanton. This 6 October 1862.
Reg: October 13, 1862   Signed: James Purvis

Page 197 - G.W. Cunningham Deed of Right to Redemption to H.L. Davidson. For all my equity of redemption in 30 acres of land sold as my property in Civil District No. 21 in Bedford County and adjoining Duck River and Flat Creek, James Gambill, Young's line, and N. Cannon. The second tract adjoining Flat Creek of Duck River, the first tract, Wm. D. Orr, and Doak's line. Containing 60 acres, making in all of the original tract of 275 acres conveyed by Sam'l Thompson to John Blackwell by deed 5 January 1835 except the mill tract of about 15 acres. Also one other tract as the A.G. Wood's tract lying on both sides of the Shelbyville and Farmington Turnpike and adjoining the last named tract, Duck River, Samuel Doak's tan yard, Moseley's line, G.W. Cunningham, Chamberlain & Galbraith, and center of the Bluff Spring. Containing 55 acres and 8 poles. This October 4, 1862.
Reg: October 13, 1862   Signed: G.W. Cunningham

Page 199 - Edmund Cooper Deed Lot in Normandy to Riley Wilson. A bond executed on __ day of ___ 18__ to Thomas Daniel and the bond of Thomas Daniel to John W. Huffman and transfer of land January 5, 1858 to Willis Blanton and by him to Riley Wilson. Land a town lot in the Town of Normandy and adjoining Thomas Daniel. Containing one quarter of one acre. This 7 October 1862.
Reg: October 13, 1862   Signed: Edm'd Cooper

Page 199 - D.R. Hooker and wife Deed 197 acres to Iverson Knott. D.R. Hooker and Eliza Hooker sold to Iverson Knott land in Bedford County and District No. 8. This October 8, 1862.
Wit: J.L. Cooper   Signed: D.R. Hooker
Reg: October 14, 1862   Eliza Hooker

Page 200 - Leroy W. Barrett Release of Mortgage to John F. Jenkins. Release dated 12 May 1862 and registered in Bedford County in Book DDD, page 168. This October 8, 1862.
Reg: October 14, 1862   Signed: L.W. Barrett

Page 200 - John F. Jenkins Title Bond for 162 acres to Henrietta M. Gabard. John F. Jenkins bind myself to pay Mrs. Henrietta M.

Gabard for a tract of land in Bedford County and Civil District No. 20 and adjoining Nathan Evans, Jesse Evans, and Thompson Snell, and John Townsend. This October 8, 1862.
Reg: October 14, 1862   Signed: J.F. Jenkins

Page 201 - William Brown Deed 89+ acres to William B. Sutton. Land in Bedford County and Civil District No. 4, and adjoining Lot No. 5 in the partition of the Sutton land, and Dawson Skein's' line. Land being the same tract I purchased of W.F. Sutton. This 7 October 1862.
Reg: October 14, 1862   Signed: William Brown

Page 202 - Mary Ray Deed of Gift to Frances Fisher and heirs. Mary Ray of Bedford County conveyed unto my daughter Frances Fisher land where she and her husband now live and adjoining George Beavers, the heirs of Thomas Ray, deceased, and by the heirs of R. Ray, deceased. This 4 August 1862.
Wit: T.H. Wortham   Signed: Mary Ray
     Robt. F. Ray
Reg: October 15, 1862

Page 202 - William Crowell Deed 12+ acres to Joseph Anderson. Lot No. 1 conveyed to me by Richard Anderson and drawn in the division of David Anderson's land being in Bedford County and District No. 11, and adjoining David Anderson, Wm. Wortham's heirs, Joseph Anderson's corner of his father's tract, and Lot No. 2. This 19 September 1862.
Wit: B.S. Parsons   Signed: William Crowell
     Isabella W. Crowell
Reg: October 15, 1862

Page 203 - James H. Neil, Extr. &c Deed 5 acres to Nancy Cummings. By the Last Will and Testament of John T. Neil, deceased, I have conveyed to Nancy Cummings land in Bedford County and adjoining Geo. W. Cunningham and formerly Joseph Thompson's corner, A.W. Johnson, and Jonathan Moseley. This 13 October 1862.
Reg: October 15, 1862   Signed: James H. Neil,. Ectr. &c.

Page 203 - John W. Brown Deed 4 acres to Granville T. Tucker. Land in Bedford County and Civil District No. 8. Beginning at the center of Fall Creek. This October 16, 1862.
Reg: October 15, 1862   Signed: J.W. Brown

Page 204 - D.W.C. Bennett and others Deed to R.L. Landers. This 15 March 1861. D.W.C. Bennett, James M. Bennett, Louisa M. Bennett, Emerine Bennett, Austin Brinkley and wife Jane Brinkley of Bedford County and R.L. Landers of same place, sold land in Bedford County and District No. 25 and on the waters of Thompsons Creek and adjoining R.L. Landers, Rowesville Road, and Peter Graves. Containing 55 poles.
Wit: P.L. Shofner   Signed: Emerine Bennett

Hosea Cheshire
Reg: October 17, 1862

Louisa M. Bennett
Austin Brinkley
Margaret Jane Brinkley
L.W.C. Brinkley

Page 204 - J.M. Floyd and wife Deed undivided interest to D.W.C. Bennett. J.M. Floyd and wife Mary Ann Floyd of the State of Arkansas have sold to D.W.C. Bennett land in Bedford County and District No. 25 and adjoining N. Anthony, Peter Graves, R.L. Landers, and Robt. Mathews. Containing 120 acres and 48 poles, it being the same tract that we conveyed to said D.W.C. Bennett dated November 1, 1857(9?) and registered in Bedford County. This 18 November 1861.
Franklin County, Arkansas.
Reg: October 17, 1862   Signed: J.M. Floyd
                                       M.A. Floyd

Page 205 - D.W.C. Bennett and others Deed 4 acres and 70 poles to R.L. Landers. This 15 March 1861. D.W.C. Bennett, James M. Bennett, Louisa M. Bennett, Emerine Bennett, Austin Brinkley and wife Jane Brinkley of Bedford County and R.L. Landers of same place, conveyed land in Bedford County on the waters of Thompsons Creelk and adjoining Robert Landers, and J.M. Bennett.
Wit: P. Shofner   Signed: Emerine Bennett
     Hosea Cheshire   Louisa M. Bennett
Reg: October 17, 1862   Austin Brinkley
                                  Margaret Jane Brinkley
                                  D.W.C. Bennett

Page 206 - D.W. C. Bennett and others Deed 94+ acres to William J. Shofner. This 15 March 1861. D.W.C. Bennett, James M. Bennett, Louisa M. Bennett, Emerine Bennett, and Austin Brinkley and his wife Jane Brinkley of Bedford County of one part conveyed to Wm. J. Shofner land in Bedford County and on the waters of Thompsons Creek and adjoining Nicholas Anthony, bank of Thompsons Creek, J.M. Bennett, R.L. Landers, and Robert Mathews. NOTE: The name Landers should be Landis.
Wit: P.L. Shofner   Signed: Austin Brinkley
     Hosea Cheshire   Margaret Jane Brinkley
Reg: October 18, 1862   Louisa M. Bennett
                                  D.W.C. Bennett
                                  Emerine M. Bennett

Page 208 - A.L. Stamps by C.P. Houston, Agt. Bill of Sale to T.L. Coldwell. For a negro girl. This 16 October 1862.
Reg: October 16, 1862   Signed: A.L. Stamps

Page 208 - Thomas Dale Deed to one third patent to Jacob C. Fite. Thomas Dale of Logan County, Kentucky (Russelville) and Jacob C. Fite of Bedford County (Shelbyville). Paid 14 March 1862 from the patent office at the City of Richmond No. 82 which patent is called H(illegible) for placing a car or automobile on a Rail Road tract which patent was issued to me and signed Rufus

R. Rhodes, Commissioner of Patents and Thomas Bragg, Attorney General. Now J.C. Fite paid 1 March 1862 is to have one third of said patent and all the sales. This 17 October 1862.
Reg: October 17, 1862   Signed: Thos. Dale

Page 208 - Edmund Cooper Deed 54 acres to Thomas J. Ogilvie. Land in Bedford County and adjoining Joseph R. McKinley, William K. Ransom, and lands of Boothe. This 18 October 1862.
Reg: October 18, 1862   Signed: Edm'd Cooper

Page 209 - Adalaide V. Hatchett Power of Attorney to Thomas McKnight. I have appointed Thomas McKnight my attorney in fact to demand and receive from Bennett G. Fields or any other person having possession of a negro girl Mary bequeathed to me by Harriet Chaffin now deceased late of Bedford County. This 18 October 1862.
Reg: October 21, 1862   Signed: Adalaide V. Hatchett

Page 209 - N. Thompson,Sr. Deed of Gift to Jane A. Woods. Newcomb Thompson, Sr. have sold to my daughter Jane A. Woods wife of Alexr. G. Woods, a negro girl Mariah and a negro boy named Emmett. This 20 October 1862.
Reg: November 3, 1862   Signed: N. Thompson, Sr.

Page 210 - D.S. Bates Deed undivided interest to B.K. Coble. Land levied upon as my property, I have sold unto B.K. Coble all my right title claim and interest to a tract of land of which my father Jno. B. Bates, deceased, died seized of the same, adjoining J.M. Johnson, K. Stokes, A. Murphy's heirs, R.B. Maupin, not including the widow's dower. This 29 October 1862.
Reg: November 3, 1862   Signed: D.S. Bates

Page 210 - James F. Cunnings Deed 15 acres to Mayor and Aldermen. A tract of land in Bedford County and District No. 7 and on old Warner Road a short distance from Shelbyville. This 1 November 1862.
Reg: November 3, 1862   Signed: J.F. Cunnings

Page 211 - W.B.M. Brame Deed of Gift to Sarah A. Davidson. For the love and affection for my daughter Sarah A. Davidson wife of Robert H. Davidson, I have given unto her a negro girl Sydney. Several years ago I made a conveyance to Edmund Cooper as Trustee for my wife and children by which I conveyed property at the death of my wife descend to her children. This 1 January 1861.
Reg: November 3, 1862   Signed" W.B.M. Brame

Page 212 - Hezekiah Ray Deed 50 acres to William J. Bomar. Both of Bedford County. Land in Bedford County on the waters of Thompsons Creek a south branch of Duck River and adjoining Wm. Martin's survey. This April 19, 1859.

Wit: Manuel Ray   Signed: H. Ray
     John Riddle
Reg: November 3, 1862

Page 212 - Melinda Dryden Bill of Sale to James W. Dryden and others. Purchased by James W. Dryden, Alexr. R. Dryden, Docia M. Dryden, and Mary J. Stephenson from me Melinda Dryden all the right title claim and interest which I have into four sevenths of slaves, but sale not to take place until my death. This November 3, 1862.
Reg: November 3, 1862   Signed: Melinda Dryden

Page R.B. Blackwell, Sheriff, Deed to John W. Thompson. There came to the hands of my predecessor Garret Phillips former Sheriff of Bedford County sundry order of sales. One in favor of Wm. G. Cowan against S.A. Thompson No. 5593, another being No. 5597 in favor of Wm. Brown against S.A. Thompson, another No. 5603 in favor of Gardner & Co. against S.A. Thompson, another No. 5605 in favor of W.G. Cowan & Co. against S.A. Thompson, another No. 5607 in favor of Baskett Jett & Co. against S.A. Thompson, another in favor of Oliver Cowan against S.A. Thompson being No. 5611, another being No. 5612 in favor of Oliver Cowan against S.A. Thompson, another No. 5618 in favor of William Brown against S.A. Thompson. Land to be sold is in Bedford County and District No. 8 and adjoining lands of William Smith, Michael Fisher and wife, Abram Claxton, and Newcum Thompson, Sr. Containing 90 acres. This 3 November 1862/
Reg: November 3, 1862   Signed: R.B. Blackwell

Page 214 - Alfred Campbell Deed 106 acres to W.W. Gill. Land in Bedford County and Civil District No. 22 and adjoining Lot No. 5, Lacey's field, over an old spring near a bluff of rocks, the original school land in the south boundary line of McKinney grant, and Lot No. 1. This November 5, 1862.
Reg: November 6, 1862   Signed: Alfred Campbell

Page 214 - Alfred Campbell Deed 197+ acres from W.W. Gill. On 9 September 1859, W.W. Gill sold land in Bedford County and Civil District No. 22 and known as the H.F. Holt tract and adjoining Mrs. Sarah Chandler's corner, Mrs. Holt's line, and A.J. Long's corner. This 5 November 1862.
Reg: November 6, 1862   Signed: W.W. Gill

Page 215 - Geo. W. Holden Deed 102+ acres to D.M. Holden. Land in Bedford County and Civil District No. 9 and adjoining J.E. Hoskins' corner, and D. Wheelhouse. This 5 November 1862.
Wit: J.R. Head   Signed: G.W. Holden
     John M. Holden
Reg: November 6, 1862

Page 216 - James Caruthers Deed 2+ acres to Wm. W. Payne. This 5 November 1862. Both of Bedford County. For land in Bedford

County and adjoining William W. Payne's 50 acre tract on which he now lives.
Reg: November 6, 1862   Signed: James Caruthers

Page 217 - N. Thompson, Sr. Deed of Gift to Wm. M. Thompson. Newcomb Thompson, Sr. sold to my son William M. Thompson (during his natural life and at his death to be the property of his children and if he dies without children the negro man to be the property of William M. Thompson's pregnant wife during her life or widowhood) a negro named Granville. This 6 November 1862.
Reg: November 6, 1862   Signed: N. Thompson, Sen.

Page 217 - William J. Bomar Deed 23+ acres from Jason Ray. Land on the waters of Thompsons Creek in District No. 2 and adjoining Manuel Ray. This March 17, 1862.
Wit: Samuel Dunaway   Signed: Jason Ray
     H.W. Evins
Reg: November 7, 1862

Page 218 - Roger Hassett and P. Fay Deed 20 acres to Wm. S. Jett. Land in Bedford County and District No. 3 adjoining Wm. H. Wisener, Ed. Green, Moses Nelson, and W.S. Jett. This November 7, 1862.
Reg: November 8, 1862   Signed: Roger Hassett
                                       P. Fay

Page 218 - Richard Foreman, Sr. Deed 149 acres to L.H. Staten. Land in Bedford County and Civil District No. 7 about half mile from the Court House in Shelbyville a north west corner, adjoining on the old Harpeth Road, and Amos Hays. This 29 December 1860.
Reg: November 10, 1862   Signed: Richard Foreman

Page 219 - L.H. Staten Deed 149 acres to William H. Staten. Land in Bedford County and Civil District No. 7 about half a mile from the Court House in the Town of Shelbyville a north west corner, and adjoining on the west side of the old Harpeth Road, and Amos Hays' lot. This 8 November 1862.
Reg: 10 November 1862   Signed: L.H. Staten

Page 219 - W.R. Murray Deed 13+ acres to Howell Williams. Land in Bedford County and Civil District No. 11 and adjoining the dower issued to Mrs. Louisa Covington in the lands of Jesse Covington, deceased, Lot No. 2, James Ogilvie, and to the Shelbyville Road it being Lot No. 3 in the division of Jesse Covington's land by his heirs. This November 5, 1862.
Reg: November 10, 1862   Signed: W.R. Murray

Page 220 - James Carlisle Deed 127+ acres to J.K.P. Carlisle. I have in my hands as guardian of my son J.K.P. Carlisle a large sum of money and some increase from Wm. J. Whitthorne arising

from the sales of lands of James A. Gant, deceased, and I wish to save my son harmless from all or damages of loss of said money. I convey unto my son James J.P. Carlisle all the right to a claim &c I have in said land being in Bedford County on the waters of Sugar Creek and District No. 20 and adjoining Nathan Evans, Carlisle's corner, Goodwin's and Martha and Amanda Gabbart to the creek, and Newton's corner. This 26 October 1862.
Wit: Edm'd Cooper   Signed: James Carlisle
Reg: November 11, 1862

Page 220 - Nancy Stephens, Extr. Deed 100+ acres to W.H. Shelton. R(Richard). M. Stevens did on 10 October 1857 executed his bond for title to W.H. Shelton to make a title to a tract of land in Bedford County and Civil District No. 1 and adjoining Jacob Coffman, T.B. Moseley, a corner of a ridge, and McMahan's corner. This November 10, 1862.
Wit: Robert H. Temple   Signed: Nancy Stephens
      John Jakes
Reg: November 11, 1862

Page 221 - Sarah Hoover Relinquishment to D.D. Hoover. Relinquish all claim interest in a tract of land on which D.D. Hoover now resides deeded to him by his father Martin Hoover. This November 8, 1862. I do reserve my house room to live in or whenever I see proper.
Wit: A.H. Hoover   Signed: Sarah Hoover
      J.M. Hoover
Reg: November 11, 1862

Page 222 - Edm'd Cooper, Trustee &c Deed 73 acres to Joel C. Russell &c. This 17 January 1861 and registered in Bedford County conveyed to me the tract of land for the purpose of paying debts and authorized to sell said land at public sale. Sale on 8 November 1862 when Joel C. Russell bid and was the highest bid became the purchaser. This 10 November 1862.
Reg: November 11, 1862   Signed: Edm'd Cooper, Trustee of
                                G.W. Cunningham

Page 223 - William H. Shelton Deed 126+ acres to John Jakes. Land in Bedford County and Civil District No. 1 on Scotts Branch, the waters of the Garrison Fork of Duck River, adjoining on top of a ridge, Drake's line, Esq. Lee's corner, and Mrs. Stevens' corner. This 11 November 1862.
Wit: R.H. Temple   Signed: W.H. Shelton
Reg: November 11, 1862

Page 224 - Thomas Cox and wife Deed undivided interest to German B. Morgan. Thomas Cox and wife Sarah R. Cox sold to said German B. Morgan land on the south side of Duck River about three miles above the Town of Shelbyville and adjoining Thomas C. Ryall, Wm. Gosling and being the land devised by Robt. Morgan, deceased, to his grandsons our interest being whatever (illegible) from

George Morgan' deceased. Also convey to G.B. Morgan land on the south side of Duck River in Bedford County and adjoining lands of Thomas C. Ryall, J.H. McGrew, and G.B. Morgan. This November 1862.
Reg: November 15, 1862   Signed: Thos. Cox
                                        S.R. Cox

Page 224 - W.F. Sutton Bill of Sale to Elizabeth Sutton. A negro boy. This November 10, 1862.
Reg: November 15, 1862   Signed: W.F. Sutton

Page 225 - Silas R. Pratt Deed to A.L. Parks for 51 acres. Land in Bedford County and District No. 23 on the waters of Big Flat Creek and adjoining Joseph Hasty, said Parks, A.L. Parks and John Kizer being part of the land belonging to John Himes at the time of his death and the land allotted to David and John A. Himes at the division. Containing 50 acres. This 19 August 1862.
Reg: November 1862   Signed: Silas R. Pratt

Page John Kizer Deed 51 acres to Silas R. Pratt. Land in Bedford County and District No. 23 on the waters of Big Flat Creek and adjoining Joseph Hasty, A.L. Parks, John Kizer, and being a part of the land belonging to John Himes at the time of death and said land allotted to David and John A. Himes. This 19 August 1862.
Reg: November 15, 1862   Signed: John Kimes

Page 226 - William Williams Deed 140 acres to Aaron Williams. Land in Bedford County and District No. ___ and adjoining H. Pearson, B.G. Fields, and John Powell. This 15 November 1862.
Wit: J.D. Gilmore   Signed: William Williams
      S.G. Miller
Reg: November 17, 1862

Page 227 - Note: William Campbell processional survey and plat. Bedford County, October 27, 1858. Said survey being land on which said Campbell now lives in District No. 22. Land adjoining J. and W. Wilhoite, Thomas Conwell, Jas. Parker, the creek and the north side of a road. Containing 310+ acres.
Recorded November 17, 1862   Signed: C.S. Dudley,
                                        Surveyor of Bedford Co.

Page 228 - J.C. Russell Deed 35 acres to John Nance. Both of Bedford County. Land in Bedford County and Civil District No. 20 and adjoining said Nance's north west corner on J.A. Cunningham's east boundary line, the Gibson Gap, the center of Little Sinking Creek, J.C. Russell, Benjamin Gambill, and Nance's north boundary line. This November 15, 1862.
Reg: November 17, 1862   Signed: J.C. Russell

Page 228 - J.C. Russell Deed 26 acres to J.A. Cunningham. Both of Bedford County. Land in Bedford County and Civil District No.20 and adjoining the center of the Gibson Gap, J.A. Cunningham, James Carlisle, and Alcy Campbell. Edmund Cooper as trustee of G.W. Cunningham. This November 15, 1862.
Reg: November 17, 1862   Signed: J.C. Russell

Page 229 - G.W. Jakes Deed 235 acres to John Jakes. All my interest in land in Bedford County and District No. 1, lying on the waters of the Garrison Fork of Duck River and adjoining George Jakes, Sr. and Eli Eaton, Wm. Keel, Sr., Wm. F. Robinson, and John Jakes, and by G.D. Stephenson. This February 10, 1859.
Wit: G.M. Crawford   Signed: G.W. Jakes
     B.L. Chadwick
     G.D. Stephenson
Reg: November 19, 1862

Page 229 - H.N. Hutton Power of Attorney to John P. Hutton. Appointed John P. Hutton of Bedford County my agent and attorney in fact to transact my business in my name and stand in my interest in the estate of J.M. Hutton, deceased. This November 21, 1862.
Reg: November 20, 1862   Signed: H.N. Hutton

Page 230 - John H. Oneal and others Deed to A.L. Adams. Received of A.L. Adams and secured by payment of purchase money going to Turner S. Foster, trustee of John K. Hume. Land in District No. 6 and adjoining in the Middleton Road, Crutcher & Foster, and Tune's line. Containing 41 acres by survey of C.S. Dudley. This ___ 24, 1862.
Reg: December 1, 1862   Signed: John H. Oneal
                                       C.T. Philpott
                                       Alexr. Philpott

Page 230 - A.H. Coffey Deed Lot in Wartrace to Michael Robinson. A certain town lot in the Town of Wartrace, Civil District No. 3 in Bedford County and adjoining the north side of Nob Creek, the turnpike, an alley, and a stake 20 feet from my south blundary line. This 27 February 1860.
Wit: J.W. Tilford   Signed: A.H. Coffey
     T.W. Tarpley
Reg: December 1, 1862

Page 231 - John H. Oneal and C.T. Philpott Deed 20 acres to Peyton Coats. Land appraised by Edmund Cooper, all the right title &c to land in Bedford County and District No. 6 and adjoining at the turnpike Coats' south boundary line, and the center of Middleton Road. This 24 November 1862.
Reg: December 1, 1862   Signed: John H. Oneal
                                       C.T. Philpott

Page 232 - John H. Oneal Deed to C.T. Philpott. Land in Bedford County and District No. 6 and adjoining lands of W.T. Tune, Peyton Coats, A.L. Adams, and by the Middleton Road. Containing __ acres. This 24 November 1862.
Reg: December 1, 1862   Signed: John H. Oneal

Page 232 - John R. Eakin Power of Attorney to Andrew Erwin. To sell to who may purchase the same two several tracts or any part of them being in Bedford County. One being my place commonly known as Willowbeck and containing my house, stables, vineyard &c, about two and one half miles east of Wartrace. The tract is composed of several parcels purchased at different times from Wm. J. Webster, trustee, Jno. Q. Davidson, J.T. Armstrong, and Archibald Murphy containing all together near 100 acres and all are recorded. The other tract in north of the former about a mile distant, commonly known as the Factory Place and being formerly occupied by Jno. Myers and myself as a rope and bagging factory. Reference to Deed of Conveyance from Henry C. Erwin to my self, which is taken out of trust and conveyed by me to Mrs. Myers. The conveyance include a small tract conveyed by Jonas Myers to Myers & Eakin near the end of the factory of about one mile. This March 9, 1860.
Hempstead County, Arkansas   Signed: Jno. R. Eakin
Reg: December 2, 1862

Page 233 - John R. Eakin and wife Power of Attorney to Andrew Erwin.   John R. Eakin of Hempstead County, Arkansas and Elizabeth J. Eakin his wife do appoint Andrew Erwin of Bedford County our attorney in fact to sell land in Bedford County belonging to E.J. Eakin for her sole use. Said land is between the residence of Andrew Erwin and the said Eakin's Willowbeck place consists of about 60 acres the same conveyed by Wm. J. Webster, trustee to said E.J. Eakin and is recorded in Bedford County. Said Erwin is authorized to sell for cash. This 9 March 1860.
Hempstead County, Arkansas   Signed: Jno. R. Eakin
Reg: December 2, 1862   Elizabeth J. Eakin

Page 235 - H.L. Davidson Deed 121+ acres to Jesse Rogers. Land in District No. 23 and adjoining J.H. McGrew, John B. Johnson, first branch below Gosling's mill, and to the Winchester Road. This 28 February 1859.
Reg: December 3, 1862   Signed: H.L. Davidson

Page 235 - M.F. Thompson Deed to William Collins. Land in Bedford County and District No. 11, two shares of an undivided tract of land which John Thompson, deceased, willed to his wife Mary Thompson during her natural life then to be sold. Containing in whole tract 100 acres and bounded by land of D.F. Osteen, Asa S. Stem, the heirs of Thos. Ray, deceased, and G.W. Beavers. This 22 November 1862.
Reg: December 4, 1862   Signed: M.F. Thompson

Page 236 - John C. Akin and wife Deed Lot in Camp White to John A. Moore. John C. Akin and wife America Akin (of Warren County, Tennessee) sold to John A. Moore of Bedford County a certain house and lot in the Town of Shelbyville, District No. 7, being the house and lot which we purchased from D.B. Hall and adjoining Cannon tract, a lot of James Elliott, James Wortham's vacant lot, and by Camp White. Containing about one acre. This November 22, 1862.
Reg: December 11, 1862   Signed: J.C. Akin
                                        A. Akin

Page 236 - M.F. Thompson, Trustee &c Deed undivided interest to Wm. Collins. M.F. Thompson as trustee of John R. Orr. Trust registered in Book CCC, pages 248 and 249. Ann C. Orr was a daughter of John Thompson, deceased, my share and interest of 100 acres owned by said Thompson at his death, sold unto Wm. Collins land in Bedford County and District No. 11 and bounded by Asa S. Stem, the heirs of Thos. Ray, G.W. Beavers, and D.F. Osteen. Containing 100 acres. This 3 December 1862.
Reg: December 13, 1862   Signed: M.F. Thompson

Page 237 - Samuel Morris Deed 20+ acres to F.M. Morris. Land in Bedford County and Civil District No. 22 on the head waters of Big Flat Creek a branch of Duck River, a part of the land formerly owned by Jesse Phillips and adjoining on top of a ridge, and Well's line. This __ September 1860.
Reg: December 16, 1862   Signed: Samuel Morris

Page 238 - Buford Burnett and wife Power of Attorney to J.M. Townsend. Dade County, Georgia. Buford Burnett and Elizabeth Burnett (formerly Elizabeth Maupin) of Dade County, Georgia, appointed J.M. Townsend of Bedford County our attorney in fact to ask for demand and receive all the remaining of our part of the money devised from the sale of land which belonged to the estate of Blan Maupin, deceased, who was the former husband of said Elizabeth Burnett. This November 9, 1862.
Wit: Gabriel Maupin   Signed: Buford Burnett
     H.L.W. Allison   Elizabeth Burnett
Reg: December 16, 1862

Page 238 - Jo. D. Wilhoite Deed Lot to George D. Hutton. This __ day of ___ 1861. A certain lot of ground in the Town of Shelbyville on the east side of the turnpike or street leading north from the Public Square adjoining the lot of T.M. Coldwell, J.C. Coldwell and others being the same on which said Hutton formerly lived supposed to contain one half acre being the same I bought of T.M. Coldwell and afterwards was conveyed on 6 August 1861 to G.W. Hutton. This 15 December 1862.
Reg: December 17, 1862   Signed: Jo D. Wilhoite

Page 239 - William Brown Deed 33 acres to B.F. Sikes. By cash and transfer of a note on Mrs. Elizabeth Kimbro due 25 December 1863. I, William Brown have sold to B.F. Sikes land in Bedford

County and District no. 1 and adjoining lands of A.C. Potts and Thompson, and P.H. Thompson and Stephens. It being the same tract I bought at Sheriff's sale as the property of P. Fay. This 16 December 1862.
Reg: December 17, 1862   Signed: William Brown

239 - J.C. Ray Deed 80 acres to J.N. Blanton. Land in Bedford County and District No. 24 on the head waters of an east branch of Thompsons Creek and adjoining John Powell, to a point of a hill, and Walsh's line. This August 8, 1862.
Wit: J.T. Snoddy   Signed: J.C. Ray
     Alfred Campbell
Reg: December 17, 1862

Page 240 - Moses B. Wadley Deed 43 acres to Newman W. Haley. Land in Bedford County and Civil District No. 18 and adjoining a tract of 200 acres known as the Blue Spring Tract granted to Malcum Gilchrist, and Hammell's corner. It being land deeded to me by Thos. C. Cheaves January 10, 1862. This December 18, 1862.
Reg: December 18, 1862   Signed: Moses B. Wadley

Page 241 - Joseph and Amy Green Deed of Gift to Susan Earnhart. For the love and affection we have towards our niece Susan Earnhart wife of Benjamin Earnhart. Joseph Green and Amy Green his wife give unto Susan Earnhart (Formerly Susan Fuller) five named slaves, This 17 December 1862.
Wit: B.F. Wiggins   Signed: Joseph Green
Reg: December 19, 1862   Amy Green

Page 241 - Joseph Green and Amy Green Deed of Gift. For the love and affection we bear to our niece Mary Green, we give four named slaves. This 17, December 1862.
Wit: B.F. Wiggins   Signed: Joseph Green
Reg: 19 December 1862   Amy Green

Page 242 - Joseph and Amy Green Deed of Gift to Michael Green. For the love and affection we have for our nephew Michael Green, we have given three named slaves. This 17 December 1862.
Wit: B.F. Wiggins   Signed: Joseph Green
Reg: December 19, 1862   Amy Green

Page 242 - Bank of Tennessee Deed 100 acres to Wm. S. Jett. Land conveyed unto William S. Jett being in Bedford County and District No. 3 and adjoining land granted to the heirs of George Doherty on which Thomas McFarland once lived, by the meridian, and a 2500 acre tract. This November 18, 1862.
Hamilton County, Tennessee.
Wit: John W. Norville   Signed: Moses Nelson
     T.J. Purdie   G.C. Torbitt
Reg: December 20, 1862   B.A. Nelson

Page 243 - William S. Jett Deed 45 acres to Moses A. Nelson. Land sold to Moses A. Nelson, John T. Nelson, Sarah D. Nelson, Robert N. Nelson, and Levina Jane Nelson, children of Benjamin Nelson, for a tract of land in Bedford County and District No. 3 and adjoining Moses Nelson's tract which I purchased from the bank. This 18 December 1862.
Reg: December 20, 1862   Signed: Wm. S. Jett

Page 244 - James M. Gant Deed 1/3 of 80 acres to Mathew Shearin. Land in Bedford County and District No. 20 and being Lot No. 3 in the division of lands of James Gant, deceased, and adjoining Lot No. 2. Containing 80 acres and 7 poles. This 10 December 1862.
Reg: December 20, 1862   Signed: James M. Gant

Page 244 - Amanda F. Little Deed 18+ acres to A.F. Knott. Land in Bedford County and District No. 10, sold unto Albert F. Knott. Land being my share of the tract conveyed by William Little outside of the dower now occupied by Delila Litle and adjoining A.F. Knott and a lane. This December 19, 1862.
Wit: William Floyd   Signed: Amandy F. Litle
     A. Ransom
Reg: December 20, 1862

Page 245 - Wm. S. Jett Deed 42 acres to Garrett Phillips. Land in Bedford County and District No. 7 and adjoining lands of Thomas J. Brown, Wm. S. Jett and J.A. Blakemore, and McCuistion heirs, and Mrs. Brown. Registered in Book DDD, page 136. This December 22, 1862.
Reg: December 22, 1862   Signed: Wm. S. Jett

Page 246 - Thompson Lipscomb Deed 2 ½ acres to R.F. Evans. Land in Bedford County and District No. 7 and adjoining in the north part of corporate limits of the Town of Shelbyville, the Shelbyville and Murfreesboro Turnpike on the west side of the street, the Shelbyville Female Academy, and Thomas Lipscomb's spring. This November 15, 1862.
Reg: December 26, 1862   Signed: Thos. Lipscomb

Page 246 - James Jakes Deed undivided interest to George Jakes. 27 August 1850 by descent from the heirs of James Morrow, deceased, George Jakes and myself have devised title a tract of land in Bedford County and District No. 1 and adjoining John Jakes, Eli Eaton and others. Containing 185 acres. This 3 December 1855.
Wit: M.T. Cooper   Signed: James Jakes
     B.L. Chadwick
Reg: December 27, 1862

Page 247 - R.B. Blackwell, Sheriff, Deed 3 ½ acres to B.F. Sikes. On 30 March 1859 B.F. Sikes recovered a judgment against Andrew Smith and came by him levied on a lot which levy is in

property. I therefore levy this execution upon all right title claim and interest that Andrew Smith had in a house and lot in Bedford County and in Civil District No. 2 and adjoining lands of Jacob Thompson and M. Buckner. This 29, 1862.
Reg: December 30, 1862   Signed: R.B. Blackwell, Sheriff

Page 248 - R.B. Blackwell, Sheriff, Deed 50 acres to Enoch Williams. Several executions issued during the year 18__ in favor of Robert Mathews and others against C.S. Dudley and which executions in favor of Robert Mathews came into hands of R.B. Blackwell a constable for Bedford County and which was levied on a tract of land belonging to said Dudley. Sheriff was ordered to sell said land to highest bidder for cash. Sale to be 24 November 1860 and sold to Enoch Williams. Land in Bedford County and District No. 8 adjoining Hartwell Freeman, M.L. Williams, Robt. Terry and others, and J.W. Brown. This 27 December 1862.
Reg: December 31, 1862   Signed: R.B. Blackwell, Sheriff

Page 249 - Wm. S. Jett Deed 3+ acres to Garrett Phillips. Land in Bedford County and Civil District No. 7 and adjoining land that Wm. Word purchased of S.B. McCuistion, Alexander Eakin, Eakin & Jett, and the Porter tract. This December 27, 1862.
Reg: January 3, 1863   Signed: Wm. S. Jett

Page 249 - Randolph Newsom Deed 517+ acres to R.S. Dwiggins. Land in Bedford County and Civil District No. 20 on the waters of Sugar Creek. First tract adjoining Jordan C. Holt's old line, Ellis' old line, and Scales' old line. Containing 201 acres being the Thos. Greer tract. The second tract adjoining one of my lines and containing 116 acres, being the Benj. Moseley and wife tract. The third tract adjoins Jordan C. Holt's old corner, and a tract Holt purchased of J.R. White. Containing 100 acres being the John Moseley tract. The fourth tract joins Noah Scales' old corner and containing 60 acres and 20 poles being Jordan C. Holt's tract. The fifth tract joins my line, Hiram Holt's old line and containing 40 acres being the Benjamin Moseley tract. All of said tracts are adjoining each other. This January 5, 1863.
Wit: Wm. S. Jett   Signed: Randolph Newsom
     H.H. Neace
Reg: January 6, 1863

Page 251 - Robt. S. Dwiggins Trust Deed to Wm. S. Jett, cash &c. I, Robert S. Dwiggins of Bedford County sold unto Wm.S. Jett, cashier of the Shelbyville Bank of Tennessee land I purchased of Randolph Newsom being in Bedford County and District No. 20 on the waters of Sugar Creek adjoining lands of H.H. Neace, L.W. Barrett, J.S. Newton, James F. Arnold, and containing 517 acres and 20 poles, it being the place whereon Randolph Newsom now lives. This 5 January 1863
Reg: January 6, 1863   Signed: R.S. Dwiggins

Page 252 - Eli H. Stephens and wife Deed undivided interest in Dower to Edm'd Cooper. We, Eli H. Stephens and wife Sarah E. Stephens sold unto Edmund Cooper land on which Sarah Shearin now resides being the dower tract of Sarah Shearin in and to the lands of which her husband Thomas Shearin, deceased, the owner being in Bedford County on both sides of Duck River and partly in District No. 1 and 18. Sarah E. Stephens who was a grand daughter of Thomas Shearin and entitled to one half of one thirteenth interest in the same. This 18 October 1859.
Wit: Henry Cooper   Signed: E.H. Stephens
     Wilson Turrentine   Sarah E. Stephens
Reg: January 7, 1863

Page 252 - N. Thompson, Sr. Deed Lots 60 and 68 to Wm. S. Jett. Two town lots in the Town of Shelbyville conveyed to me by R.N. Jones on November 7, 1850, being Lots No. 60 and 78 with the exception of that portion which said Jones sold to Graham & Brown off of said lots. This 7 January 1863.
Reg: January 7, 1863   Signed: N. Thompson, Sr.

Page 253 - Wm. S. Jett Deed part Lot No. 54 to Jo D. Wilhoite. Lot in Bedford County and in the Town of Shelbyville on the south side of the Public Square being part of Lot No. 54 and adjoining the north west corner of the three story brick building on said lot lately occupied by Cochran & Stephens as a store house, to opposite the center of the dividing wall between said store house and the store house lately occupied by Coldwell & Co., and wife boundary line of Lot No. 54. This December 25, 1862.
Reg: January 8, 1863   Signed: Wm. S. Jett

Page 254 - Wm. S. Jett Deed 3 tracts to Silas A. Bivins. Land in Bedford County and Civil District No. 7, The first tract adjoins the Columbia Road and Thomas Lipscomb, and containing 111 acres and 32 poles. One other tract adjoins in the middle of the old Nashville Road by way of R.C. Jennings, the same being Alexander Eakin's corner, Thomas Lipscomb's corner, and the first tract, and containing 15 acres. Also one other tract adjoining land formerly owned by John A. Marr, Edm'd Green, McCuistion place, and containing 3 acres conveyed by L.B. Knott to William Martin by Deed of Gift and also about 1 ½ acres conveyed by L.B. Knott to C.D. Tarpley. There is also retained our of the above land 3 acres and 8 poles which I sold to Garrett Phillips by deed December 27, 1862. This December 29, 1862.
Reg: January 8, 1863   Signed: Wm. S. Jett

Page 255 - A.J. Maddox and wife Deed one sixth of 85 acres to Garrett Phillips. We, Malinda J. Maddox and A.J. Maddox in right of his wife Malinda J. Maddox sold to Garrett Phillips land which Mathew Phillips, deceased, willed to the children and heirs of Jesse Phillips, deceased, in Civil District No 6 and adjoins lands of Harrison Jennings and T.J. Brown, Garrett Phillips, Tabitha Brown widow of Shadrack Brown, deceased, and

Elizabeth Robinson, Jas. Phillips, and Harrison Jennings, in all containing 85 acres. This 8 October 1861.
Wit: Thos. H. Coldwell   Signed: A.J. Maddox
Reg: January 9, 1863   Malinda J. Maddox

Page 255 - C.T. and Alexr. Philpott Deed 27+ acres to A.L. Adams. Land in Bedford County and District No. 6, being part of the tract purchased of John H. Oneal by Charles T. Philpott and for which Alexander Philpott held title bond. Bounded by lands of Peyton Coats, W.T. Tune, and A.L. Adams. This 9 January 1863.
Wit: Edm'd Cooper   Signed: C.T. Philpott
Reg: January 9, 1863   Alex. Philpott

Page 256 - Randolph Newsom Deed 89+ acres to Edward Newsom. Land in Bedford County and District No. 20 and adjoining the original tract belonging to John Harrison, deceased, and a road. Containing 44 acres and 122 poles, being the dower tract allotted to Hannah Harrison widow of John Harrison, Deceased. Second tract on said road and containing 44 acres and 120 poles it being a part of said Harrison tract and deeded to me by Elisha Reed June 18, 1858. This January 10, 1863.
Reg: January 10, 1863   Signed: Randolph Newsom

Page 257 - Mrs. E.J. Dalton Quit Claim to G.C. Neely. A certain parcel of lot in West End near to and adjoining Shelbyville. Said lot being the lot bargain to e by said G.C. Neely for the title which was dated August 25, 1860 and registered in Book CCC, pages 183 and 184. This 12 January 1863.
Reg: January 13, 1863   Signed: E.J. Dalton

Page 257 - G.B. Harris Deed 15 acres to John T. Cannon. Both of Bedford County. Land in Bedford County and Civil District No. 4 adjoining lands of Sutton's heirs, by lands of Robt. Denniston, by Charles F. Sutton, it being a portion of land sold to James K. Norton by Robert Denniston and by him to T.B. Ivie and afterwards to me and registered in Book XX, pages 94 and 95. This 11 June 1862.
Wit: W.T. Myers   Signed: G.B. Harris
     A.A. Cooper
Reg: January 13, 1863

Page 258 - Wm. P. Oneal Bill of Sale to Lewis Tillman. Shelbyville, January 12, 1863. For a negro boy.
Reg: January 13, 1863.   Signed: W.P. Oneal

Page 258 - Wm. S. Jett and R.S. Dwiggins Deed 20+ acres to Hiram H. Nease. Land in Bedford County and District No. 20 and bounded by said Nease and containing 20 acres and 109 poles, being a part of the land sold by Randolph Newsom to said Dwiggins and by Dwiggins mortgaged to Wm. S. Jett in Trust. This January 13, 1863.

Reg: January 1863   Signed: R.S. Dwiggins
                                            Wm. S. Jett, Trustees

Page 259 - Matilda Shofner Bill of Sale to Allen Thedford. Flat
Creek. For a negro slave named Mecha. This 10 January 1863.
Wit: Martin Euless   Signed: Matilda Shoffner
     L. Shoffner
Reg: January 20, 1863

Page 259 - G.B. Harris Mortgage to James S. Maupin. J.S. Maupin
is my security on three notes due September 1, 1861 executed to
J.R. Ferrill notes now held by Edmund Cooper and held by the
estate of William Pepper and I am (illegible) securing to make
payment. I now transfer and convey to James S. Maupin all claim
&c which I have in land located in the Village of Wartrace,
Bedford County and bounded by the line of the Depot ground at
Willis Prewett's corner, and to John W. Chilton. This 9 June
1862.
Wit: Wm. T. Myers   Signed: G.B. Harris
     A.A. Cooper
Reg: January 26, 1863

Page 260 - Volney H. Steele and wife Bill of Sale to Charles H.
Cummings. Volney H. Steele and Sarah L. Steele his wife sold to
Charles H. Cummings a negro woman named Melinda. This January
26, 1863.
Reg: January 26, 1863   Signed: V.H. Steele
                                     S.L. Steele

Page 261 - Wm. S. Jett Deed part Lot No. 5 to Jo. D. Wilhoite.
Lot in Bedford County in the corporate limits of the Town of
Shelbyville on the south side of the Public Square being part of
Lot No. 5 and adjoining the house and lot I sold, and adjoining
this lot to said Wilhoite December 26, 1862 and lately occupied
by Cochran & Stephens as a store house, on this lot lately
occupied by Coldwell & Co. as a store house, to the east side of
the brick wall which divides the Coldwell & Co. store house and
G.W. Thompson & Co. family grocery house, and it being the house
and lot recently occupied by Coldwell & Co. as a store house. I
reserve out of the above lot an alley on the south end of said
lot. This 31 December 1862.
Reg: January 27, 1863   Signed: Wm. S. Jett

Page 261 - R.P. Setliff Deed Lots in Rowesville to Peter R.
Vanhouton. Land in Bedford County and District No. 25 being in
the Village of Rowesville and known by Lots No. 4, 5, 6, 7, 8,
9, 10 and 11 and adjoining Isaac Barnett's old corner, and land
owned by Miss Wardlow. This 9 February 1863.
Wit: M. Green   Signed: R.P. Setliff
     M.E.W. Dunaway
Reg: February 11, 1863

Page 262 - N. Burns Deed 269+ acres to .W. Gill. I, Nicholas Burns sold to said Gill land in Bedford County and District No. 20 and bounded by the Shelbyville Road, and to a ridge, it being the tract I now live on. This 9, February 1863.
Reg: February 9, 1863   Signed: N. Burns

Page 263 - W.W. Gill Deed 71+ acres &c to Mrs. Elizabeth Kingree. Land in Bedford County and District No. 22 and adjoining the Widow Burgess's dower tract and by a line of my tracts of land, and by Widow Bennett's line. This February 10, 1863.
Reg: February 10, 1863   Signed: W.W. Gill

Page 264 - Alexander Forbes Deed 164 acres to Thomas Lipscomb. Described as The South West Quarter of Section 18, Township 16, Range 6 west and being in the County of Green, Arkansas. This 10 February 1863.
Wit: Jennie C. Lipscomb   Signed: A. Forbes
     R.H. Lipscomb
Reg: February 14, 1863

Page 264 - G.B. Harris & S.B. Heard Deed or Title Bond to Jesse W. Chockley. Land being the same purchased from J.R. Ferrell and wife and registered in Book CCC, pages 161 and 162 in Bedford County. Reference to the same and said conveyance of Sue R. Ferrell and J.R. Ferrell dated July 19, 1860. This 16 February 1863.
Reg: February 17, 1863   Signed: G.B. Harris
                                        S.B. Heard

Page 265 - Edm'd Cooper Trustee of M.J. Erwin Deed 114 acres to S.B. Heard. Edmund Cooper, Trustee of Mary J. Erwin sold unto Sam'l B. Heard paid to Mrs. Mary J. Erwin land in Bedford County and District No. 2 and bounded by the bank of the Garrison Fork of Duck River at the upper or north east corner of a tract of land conveyed by James Erwin to Kinchen Stokes and now occupied by John M. Stokes and which is also the lower corner on the river of the old brick house tract, the Shelbyville Road, and by land conveyed by Andrew Erwin to Archibald Murphy, and to the center of the Rail Road. This 10 December 1862.
Wit: L. Shofner   Signed: Edm'd Cooper, Trustee of
     Jesse Chockley   M.J. Erwin
Reg: February 18, 1863

Page 266 - Samuel B. Heard Deed 114 acres to Joseph W. Tilford. Land in Bedford County and District No. 2 and adjoining the east bank of the Garrison Fork of Duck River the upper or north west corner of a tract of land conveyed by James Erwin to Kinchen Stokes and now occupied by John M. Stokes and which is also the lower corner on the river of the old brick house tract, thence south of gate on the road to Shelbyville now standing in said line, and which is land conveyed by Andrew Erwin to Archibald

Murphy, thence to the center of the Rail Road. This 6 February 1863.
Wit: Newton Harris   Signed: S.B. Heard
     L.P. Fields
Reg: February 20, 1863

Page 266 - W.H. & S.G. Dyer Deed 147+ acres to W.W. Gill. Land in Bedford County and Civil District No. 22 and adjoining Jarrel Smith, and the center of the pike. This 19 February 1863.
Reg: February 20, 1863   Signed: W.H. & S.G. Dyer

Page 267 - W.W. Gill Deed 269+ acres to W.H. & S.G. Dyer. Land in Bedford County and Civil District No. 20 and bounded by the Shelbyville Road. Land being the tract I purchased of N. Burns. This February 19, 1863.
Reg: February 20, 1863   Signed: W.W. Gill

Page 268 - Joseph H. Smith Deed 75 acres to Rich'd H. Sims. Land in Bedford County and district No. 21 and bounded by lands of said Richard H. Sims, J.M.H. Coleman, and M(illegible) Smith, it being a part of her dower. This 19 February 1863.
Reg: February 20, 1863   Signed: J.H. Smith

Page 268 - Wm. S. Jett Deed Lot to G.W. Thompson. All of Bedford County. A certain Town Lot in the Town of Shelbyville and bounded by a lot conveyed to A.H. Dashiell by Thos. Lipscomb at the junction of a street leading to Female Academy on the Nashville, Murfreesboro and Shelbyville Turnpike Road, to an alley, and to Spring Street. This 28 December 1862.
Reg: February 20, 1863   Signed: W.S. Jett

Page 269 - John Oneal Deed of Gift to Syntha E. Taylor and others. For the natural love and affection I bear towards my daughter Synthia E. Taylor wife of Joseph Taylor, have given unto her a negro woman named Edney and her three children, all free from any future husband and at her death to the heirs of such living. This February 20, 1863.
Wit: J.C. Russell   Signed: John Oneal
     John H. Oneal
Reg: February 25, 1863

Page 269 - M.P. Gentry Bill of Sale to Nancy J. Cummings. Received Hill side (illegible) of Nancy J. Cummings payment in full for a negro woman Florida and her four children. This January 22, 1863.
Wit: D.J. Low   Signed: M.P. Gentry
     Joseph Price
Reg: February 25, 1863

Page 270 - M.P. Gentry Bill of Sale to Mary A. Cunningham. Paid in full for one negro man Samuel. This 20 January 1863.

Reg: February 24, 1863   Signed: M.P. Gentry

Page 270 - Geo. W. Thompson Deed Lot to Charles A. Warren.   A
Town Lot being in the Village of Shelbyville and adjoining the
south and east side of the street leading to the University, and
the south side of the Skull Camp Road. This 24 February 1863.
Reg: March 3, 1863   Signed: G.W. Thompson

Page 271 - P. Fay Deed 5 acres to Moses A. Nelson and others.
Land in Bedford County and District No. 3 and adjoining A.
Nelson, and the center of the Rail Road. I transferred to Moses
A. Nelson, John T. Nelson, Sarah D. Nelson, Robert M. Nelson,
Lavina J. Nelson, and Mary J. Nelson, said land. This March 2,
1863.
Reg: March 4, 1863   Signed: P. Fay

Page 271 - Thomas Kimmons Trustee Deed to Wm. A. Allen, Trustee.
By a Trust Deed executed to me by Wm. Kimmons 29 January 1861
and registered in Bedford County in Book CCC, pages 446 and 447.
I have sold to Wm. A. Allen, trustee of Martha E. Kimmons wife
of Wm. Kimmons a negro boy Arch and a tract of land in Bedford
County and District No. 1 and bounded by lands of L(illegible)
Anderson, and by lands of B.F. Green and Richard Anderson, and
containing 85 acres, it being the place on which land William
Kimmons now live. This 2 March 1863.
Wit: Thos. H. Coldwell   Signed: Thomas Kimmons, Trustee of
     H.L. Davidson   Wm. Kimmons

Page 272 - J. Word and wife Deed Lot to Charles L. Powell. I,
Mary Ann Word, have this day sold to Charles L. Powell land in
the Town of Shelbyville and a portion of Lot No. 5 laid off by
C.S. Dudley for N. Thompson 3rd and deeded to me by W.F. Cooper
and Johnson Know and adjoining Lot No. 5, Buchanan's fence, to
an alley between said lot and a lot heretofore sold to Anderson
Sharp, and by him conveyed to his daughter Mrs. Goldathan(?).
This 10 February 1863.
Reg: March 11, 1863   Signed: John I(?). Word
                                     Mary A. Word

Page 273 - Phereba Elkins Deed of Gift to Elizabeth Pruitt. For
the love and affection which I have for Elizabeth Pruitt one
negro girl named Matt to use free from her husband. This
February 17, 1863.
Wit: J.B. Stevenson   Signed: Phereba Elkins
     D.H. Skeen
Reg: March 12, 1863

Page 273 - Wm. S. Jett Deed Lot to Geo. W. Thompson. Town Lot
No. 42 in the Town of Shelbyville and on the east side of Martin
Street and bounded by James Story and Martin Street. This 29
December 1862.
Reg: March 13, 1863   Signed: Wm. S. Jett

Page 274 - Winston W. Gill Deed of Gift to Mary R. Gill, For the love and affection for my daughter Mary R. Gill of Bedford County, have conveyed to her, separate and free from debts &c of any future husband in five named slaves, which said slaves are now been for some time at my brother A.G. Gill in Lincoln County, Tennessee. This 6 March 1863.
Wit: Thos. H. Coldwell   Signed: W.W. Gill
     Jesse W. Brown
Reg: March 13, 1863

Page 275 - Winston W. Gill Deed of Gift to John J. Gill. For the love and affection I have for my son John J. Gill, I have conveyed unto him five named slaves. This 6 March 1863.
Wit: Thos. H. Coldwell   Signed: W.W. Gill
     Jesse W. Brown
Reg: March 13, 1863

Page 275 - Winston W. Gill Deed of Gift to Winston W. Gill, Jr. Both of Bedford County. For the love and affection I have for my son Winston W. gill, Jr., have conveyed unto him two named slaves. This 6 March 1863.
Wit: Thos. H. Coldwell   Signed: W.W. Gill
     Jesse W. Brown
Reg: March 13, 1863

Page 276 - Wm. A. Allen Deed 91 acres to A.S. Riggs and John E. Davis. For $1800 (Confederate money) paid by Adam S. Riggs and John E. Davis for land in Bedford County and District No. 18 and adjoining Fugitt's old line, and being the place formerly known as the Hughes' place. This March 13, 1863.
Reg: March 16, 1863   Signed: Wm. A. Allen

Page 277 - Wm. S. Jett Deed 397 acres to Wm. J. Whitthorne. First tract of land in Bedford County and Civil District No. 3 and adjoining J.G. Barksdale and containing 200 acres and is the same tract I purchased of Mathew Dixon. The other adjoins the above tract on the east, and lands of Wm. H. Wisener & Mrs. Ed Green, lands of D.C. Shriver and Hammond's heirs, and lands of Moses Nelson, and containing 197 acres, being the same I purchased of James F. Cummings. This December 31, 1862.
Wit: Wm. B.M. Brame   Signed: Wm. S. Jett
     Thos. H. Coldwell
Reg: March 23, 1863

Page 278 - Wm. S. Whitthorne Deed Lot to Wm. S. Jett. One Town Lot in the Town of Shelbyville, Bedford County on which there is a two story brick house, said house and lot is on the Murfreesboro Pike and adjoins a lot and house belonging to Young Wilhoite on the turnpike leading from martin Street to Murfreesboro. This 13, March 1863.
Wit: Thos. H. Coldwell   Signed: W.J. Whitthorne
     Wm. B.M. Brame
Reg: March 24, 1863

Page 278 - Hugh Jones Transfer of Title Bond to James Stallings. We, Edmund Cooper and Robert Mathews bind ourselves to pay Hugh Jones $500. Whereas said Hugh Jones has this day purchased of us several listed notes and has executed his note, a tract of land in Bedford County and adjoins the old corporation of the Town of Shelbyville, and a two acre tract formerly owned by George W. Hively, and containing about 1 acre. This 2 January 1852.
Reg: March 24, 1863   Signed: Edmund Cooper
                                     Robt. Mathews, Exrs of
                                     E.J. Frierson, deceased

Page 279 - John A. Crockett Bill of Sale to Wm. J. Whitthorne. For five named slaves. This 16 March 1863.
Wit: Isaac Green   Signed: John A. Crockett
     G.W. Brown
     V.H. Steele
Reg: March 25, 1863

Page 280 - Garrett Phillips Deed 3+ acres to Silas A. Bivins. Land in Bedford County that I purchased of Wm. S. Jett which recorded in Book DDD, page 249. This March 26, 1863.
Reg: March 26, 1863   Signed: G. Phillips

Page 280 - Silas A. Bivins Deed 1 acre to Garrett Phillips. Land in Bedford County and District No. 7 and adjoins Wm. Word bought of S.B. McCuistion. This March 26, 1863.
Reg: April 1, 1863   Signed: S.A. Bivins

Page 280 - March 29, 1863 at about 11 o'clock P.M. the Court House in Shelbyville was destroyed by fire and most of the books and papers in the offices were lost from the 7 September 1852 to the 29 July 1861 were in office of Register (being nine books).
                             Test: M.E.W. Dunaway, R of BC

Page 281 - M.L.D. Dismukes Deed 120 acres to Jacob Kizer. Land in Bedford County and Civil District No. 21 and adjoining Kizer's line, to the center of Flat Creek, and Galbreath's 1000 acre grant. This January 6, 1863.
Reg: April 2, 1863   Signed: M.L. Dismukes

Page 281 - John and Lucy Noblett Deed of Gift to Henry D. Lipscomb et als. This 23 March 1863 between Lucy M. Noblett & John Noblett and Henry D. Lipscomb and Henry D. Lipscomb and Tappenas(?) Lipscomb for the love and affection which said Lucy M. Noblett as the mother of John Noblett as the step father of said Henry D. Lipscomb and Tappenas Lipscomb who are the children of said Lucy M. by a former husband have conveyed all the right title &c which said Lucy M. Noblett as the child and heir of Henry Dean, deceased, after first deducting and settling whatever may be due from said Lucy M. Noblett and John Noblett. This 23 March 1863.

Reg: April 3, 1863   Signed: John Noblett
                                    Lucy M. Noblett

Page 282 - J.S. Nowlin Deed 65+ acres to C.W. Powell. Land in
Bedford County and District No. 18 and joins John Larue, J.C.
Powell, to center of Rock Creek, and Joel Stallings' line. This
February 25, 1863.
Wit: R.M. Walton   Signed: J.S. Nowlin
     J.N. Dryden
Reg: April 6, 1863

Page 283 - Robert Mathews Deed 950 acres to C.L. Pyrom. Both of
Bedford County and for Confederate money have sold unto C.L.
Pyrom land in Bedford County and Franklin County, Tennessee and
joins Samuel Mitchell, crossing the Winchester Road, Crossing
the Thompsons Creek Road, Wm. Elliot, Jeremiah Holt, Adam
Anthony and an entry of 50 acres made in the name of Robert
Brinkley, Henry L(illegible), R.L. Landis, John Short, and
Benjamin Cross. Also a portion of 100 acre entry laying east of
the last line. Land lying on the waters of Shipman Creek. This
1 April 1863.
Reg: April 6, 1863   Signed: Robt. Mathews

Page 284 - Wm. G. High, C.B.C. Bill of Sale to A.L. Adams. For
a negro woman and child, Mary Jane and child. This March 25,
1862.
Wit: W.N. Gwinn   Signed: G.W. High, C.B.C.
     W. Perry
Reg: April 13, 1863

Page 285 - A.S. Riggs & John E. Davis Division Deed of 91 acres.
William H. Allen sold to Adam S. Riggs and John E. Davis a tract
of land jointly on 13 March 1863 and registered in Bedford
County in Book DDD, pages 276 and 277. John E. Davis taking the
east end and one half of the land and said Adam S. Riggs taking
the west end of said tract and one half of said land. Division
April 10, 1863.
Wit: R.F. Evans   Signed: Adam S. Riggs
     Geo. W. Buchanan   J.E. Davis
Reg: April 14, 1863

Page 285 - G.W. Buchanan Deed Lot to S.A. Bivins. Land being in
the Town of Shelbyville and being part of the enclosure of said
Bivins' same place and joining my flood gate on a branch, and
Oneal's & Bivins' corner. This 10 April 1863.
Reg: April 14, 1863   Signed: G.W. Buchanan

Page 285 - Silas A. Bivins Deed Lots to Wm. S. Jett. Lot in the
west end of the Town of Shelbyville, Bedford County, being
composed of first I purchased of John H. Oneal, the second of
G.W> Buchahah. The first joins the center of the Shelbyville &
Unionville Pike. The second joins the corner of my stable on

The above lot, the flood gate on a branch, G.W. Buchanan's lot, and Oneal's corner. This April 11, 1863.
Reg: April 14, 1863   Signed: S.A. Bivins

Page 286 - Wm. S. Jett Deed 3 tracts to Silas A. Bivins. Land in Bedford County and District No. 3. The first contains 20 acres and is the same that Roger Haslett conveyed to me dated November 7, 1862 and is recorded in Book DDD, page 218. The second contains 40 acres and is the same conveyed to me by P. Fay dated March 26, 1862 and recorded in Book DDD, page 157. The third tract contains 55 acres and is the west end of the 1000 acre tract that I purchased of the Bank of Tennessee and adjoins the 100 acre tract, a 2500 acre tract grant in the name of George Doherty's heirs, and a 45 acre tract that I sold to Moses A. Nelson and others. This January 1, 1863.
Reg: April 14, 1863   Signed: Wm. S. Jett

Page 287 - Dennis Hemby Deed 330+ acres to Robert Mathews. Plat of land on page 287. Land in Bedford County on Shipman Creek a south branch of Duck River. Land adjoining Solomon L(illegible), crossing Shipman Creek, Turner's corner, John Landers, Henry Landers, Dennis Hemby, William Shofner, and Nutt's line, and on the west side of the Manchester Road, Adam Anthony's corner, Brinkley's corner, and J.B. Burrow's line. This January 25, 1854. George Cortner.
Reg: April 15, 1863   Signed: Dennis Hemby

Page 289 - Wm. J. Whitthorne Deed 55 acres to Robert Mathews. Land in District No. 18 of Bedford County and joins Wm. B. Jones and Mathews' heirs. This January 27, 1853.
Reg: April 17, 1863   Signed: William J. Whitthorne

Page 290 - Wm. S. Jett Deed Lot to D.J. Christopher. For Confederate money. House and lot in the Town of Shelbyville and bounded by Young Wilhoite on the Murfreesboro Turnpike. This April 15, 1863.
Reg: April 17, 1863   Signed: Wm. S. Jett

Page 290 - D.J. Christopher Deed Lot to Wm. S. Jett (in Camp White) house and lot in the Town of Shelbyville being part of Lot No. 3 in the plat of lots laid off by Clement Cannon, Sr. and bounded by White Street, at the corner of Camp White Street, Lot No. 3, and containing 1 acre, it being the lot I purchased of James F. Calhoon. This April 15, 1863.
Reg: April 20, 1863   Signed: D.J. Christopher

Page 291 - William S. Taylor Deed 156+ acres to Frederic Batt, Jr. Land in Bedford County and District No. 9 and adjoining Jackson Lile, deceased, corner, John Jackson, and the bank of Weakley Creek. This November 3, 1862.
Wit: Wm. Taylor   Signed: William S. Taylor
     T.D. Tarpley

Reg: April 20, 1863

Page 291 - J.A. McLain Deed Lot to J.A.S. Shannon. Jeddiah A.
McLain sold to John A.S. Shannon a certain lot of ground and
wool carding factory in the Village of Unionville, District No.
11, Bedford County and adjoining a corner of a lot on which
Duggan and Moon's lot, and the edge of the turnpike. This 29,
December 1862.
Wit: John A. McLain   Signed: J.A. McLain
     Robert H. Barnes
Reg: April 20, 1863

Page 292 - George W. Thompson Deed Lot to T.B. Ivie. Land in
the Town of Shelbyville, on the north east side of the street or
road leading from the Depot of the N & C Rail Road to the Skull
Camp Ford and joins a lot owned by Joseph Edwards of Nashville
formerly occupied by Mrs. Fuqua, and the north east side of
Skull Camp Road. This April 20, 1863.
Reg: April 20, 1863   Signed: G.W. Thompson

Page 293 - George W. Thompson Deed Lot to T.B. Ivie. A certain
lot in the Town of Shelbyville and bounded by the street leading
from Skull Camp Ford Road to the street leading from the
graveyard to the Male University lot known as Thompson Street,
on the south west by street running from the graveyard to the
Male University, then a picket fence between Wm. Gosling and
this lot, and on the north east by Mrs. Rebecca Mathews' lot and
said T.B. Ivie's lot whereon he now lives. This April 20, 1863.
Reg: April 21, 1863   Signed: G.W, Thompson

Page 293 - John C. Coldwell, Jr. Deed Lot to Wm. S. Jett. Land
in Bedford County and District No. 7 and containing 2 acres and
bounded by L.B. Knott's corner on Turnpike Street and Wm. G.
Cowan. This 23 April 1863
Reg: April 25, 1863   Signed: JohnC. Coldwell

Page 294 - C.P. Cunningham Bill of Sale to Mrs. Sarah
Cunningham. For a negro girl Sarah. This 23 April 1863.
Wit: J.P. Baldridge   Signed: C.P. Cunningham
     George W. Johnson
Reg: April 27, 1863

Page 294 - George Smith Trustee and D.G. Deason Deed Lot to Wm.
Brown. A certain lot in the corporate limits of the Town of
Shelbyville and bounded by an alley, and the south east corner
of the Methodist Church lot. It being the same that D.G. Deason
purchased from Wm. Taylor, and containing 1 acre. This 23 April
1863.
Wit: C.C. Covington   Signed: George Smith
Reg: April 30, 1863   D.G. Deason

Page 295 - Wm. Brown Deed Lot to R.D. Porter. A certain lot or parcel of ground in Bedford County and District No. 7 in the corporate limits of the Town of Shelbyville adjoining an alley and opposite the south east corner of the Methodist Church lot, it being the lot bought by D.G. Deason from Wm. Taylor and containing 1 acre. This 28 April 1863.
Wit: Thos. H. Coldwell   Signed: William Brown
     W.J. Whitthorne
Reg: April 30, 1863

Page 295 - A.P. Eakin and D.H.C. Spence Title Bond to R.D. Porter. Condition is such that said A.P. Eakin has sold unto R.D. Porter his note under seal a store house and lot in the Town of Shelbyville on the east side of the Public Square in Bedford County and District No. 7, fronting said square running back to an alley on which lot there is a three story brick house known as the Escue house, it being the house which said Porter now occupies and adjoining the Drug Store of R.D. Deery. This 15 April 1863.
Wit: Thos. H. Coldwell   Signed: A.P. Eakin
     R.D. Deery   D.H.C. Spence
Reg: May 6, 1863

Page 296 - Thomas Lipscomb Deed House and Lot to Sarah E. Stephens. Sarah E. Stephens wife of John T. Stephens. Land in Bedford County and Civil District No. 7 in the Town of Shelbyville on the west side of the Murfreesboro and Shelbyville Turnpike and bounded by my lot on which I live, and T.C. Whiteside's lot. This May 4, 1863.
Reg: May 6, 1863   Signed: Thos. Lipscomb

Page 297 - M.P. Gentry Title Bond to Irby Morgan. M.P. Gentry of Bedford County and Irby Morgan of Davidson County, Tennessee now residing in Marietta, Georgia. Condition is such that said W.P. Gentry has sold unto Irby Morgan three tracts of land. The first being the tract on which I now live adjoining the lands of John Helton and Mary Cunningham, by J.H. Cunningham, by Stephen Freeman's estate and John Cortner, and by Benjamin Hazelett, Peter Cortner, James Helton and Miles Phillips, and containing 850 acres. The second tract being the tract purchased of Michael Moore on the waters of Sinking Creek and adjoining the lands of said Moore and Sarah Price, deceased, and containing 24 acres. The third tract lying on the waters of Rock Creek purchased of James Davis and adjoining the lands of Albert Anderson and others, and containing 12 acres. This May 11, 1863.
Wit: Sam'l Cowan   Signed: M.P. Gentry
     R.L. Caruthers, Jr.
Reg: May 12, 1863

Page 297 - H.L. Davidson 2 (illegible) Bond to John H. Wells. 25 September 1862. John H. Wells executed to me his notes &c. This May 16, 1863.
Reg: May 18, 1863   Signed: H.L. Davidson

73

Page 298 - R.S. Dwiggins Trust Deed to Charles A. Warren. Land on which I now reside adjoining the lands of Montgomery Little, Lewis Hix, W.W. Gill, A.H. Evans, H.H. Nease, and the estate of Evans' containing 860 acres. This 18 May 1863.
Reg: May 20, 1863   Signed: R.S.Dwiggins

Page 299 - C.W. Powell Deed to Robert Williams. Land in Bedford County and District No. 18 and bounded by John Larue, and with the center of the fence, the center of Rock Creek to an island, and by Joel Stallings. This 22 April 1863.
Wit: George Sewell   Signed: C.W. Powell
     R.M. Sikes
Reg: June 10, 1863

Page 299 - Patrick Fay Deed Lot to Mary Haberlin. Lot in the Town of Shelbyville, Bedford County and bounded by land conveyed to me by said Mary Haberlin on the street leading from Shelbyville to J.F. Thompson's mills, by J.F. Cummings, and William Brown. This June 9, 1863.
Reg: June 10, 1863   Signed: P. Fay

Page 300 - John Hastings Deed 50+ acres to John S. Cates. Land in Bedford County and Civil District No. 23 and bounded by Sprncer Brown, and John Woosley. This 13 June 1857.
Reg: June 10, 1863   Signed: Jno. Hastings

Page 300 - John Hastings Deed 5+ acres to John S. Cates. Land in Bedford County and District No. 23 and bounded by Spencer Brown, by 50 acre tract sold to me, and J.C. Woosley. This June 10, 1858.
Reg: June 10, 1863   Signed: Jno. Hastings

Page 301 - John W. Brown Deed 9+ acres to John S. Cates. Land in Bedford County and Civil District No. 23 and bounded by Cates and John Hastings' corner in the west margin of the road from New Hope Camp Ground to the Winchester Road, and containing 9 ¼ acres. This May 6, 1859.
Reg: June 10, 1863   Signed: J.W. Brown

Page 302 - H.L. Davidson Deed of Gift to Sallie B. Davidson. For love and affection I have for my son Robert H. Davidson and conveyed to his wife Sallie B. Davidson during the minority of their little son William B. Davidson my negro girl named a slave for life. This 9 June 1863.
Reg: June 10, 1863   Signed: H.L. Davidson

Page 302 - James F. Cummings Deed 250+ acres to Wm. Little. Land in Bedford County and District No. 24 and adjoining the center of the Shelbyville, Farmington and Lewisburg Turnpike Road opposite the center of the public road leading south by the

Place owned by Richard Phillips, J. Davis' corner, and Owens'
corner. This 4 February 1860.
Reg: June 10, 1863   Signed: J.F. Cummings

Page 303 - E.D. Winsett Deed 107+ acres to William Little. Land
in Bedford County and Civil District No. 10, and bounded by land
of the said Little of Maxwell, Stephen Woods' line, Widow Lamb's
corner, and Clay's line. This 25, March 1853.
Wit: Richard Nance   Signed: E.D. Winsett
     A. Wilson
Reg: June 11, 1863

Page 304 - Robert Mathews Deed to A.L. Landis. Both of Bedford
County one half of two tracts of land for Confederate money.
One tract to contain by deed executed by R.L. Landis and A.L.
Landis to said Mathews on 18 May 1853, 688 acres and 140 poles
and recorded on 3 September 1854. The other tract to contain by
deed executed by said R.L. Landis and A.L. Landis and A.M. Holt
to said Ro. Mathews on 10 December 1852, 636 acres and
registered 10 January 1853 and recorded in Winchester, Franklin
County, Tennessee in Book W, page 151, on 22 September 1854.
This 13 June 1863.
Wit: Wm. V. Mathews   Signed: Robt. Mathews
Reg: June 13, 1863

Page 304 - Henry Hill Title Bond to G.M. Ray. Bedford County
May 23, 1863. Land known as part of the school tract. Two lots
bounded by B. Philpott, Thomas Boyers, T.P. Wells, and G.M. Ray.
The second tract joins G.M. Ray, T.P. Wells, M.W. Watson, Mrs.
M.A. Bobo, J.W. Crunk supposed to contain about 122 acres. Also
one lot of farming tools, a mare and hogs.
Wit: Philegming(?) Putman   Signed: Henry Hill
     Benjamin Pollock
     Philegming(?) Putman
Reg: June 23, 1863

Page 305 - Wm.S. Jett Deed Lot in Camp White to Mrs. C. Burditt.
I have sold to Mrs. Charlotte Burditt wife of Joel H. Burditt
during her natural life and at her death to her children then
living, a tract of land known as Camp White near the Town of
Shelbyville and is the same house and lot deeded to me by D.J.
Christopher 15 April 1863 and recorded in Book DDD, page 290.
This June 18, 1863.
Reg: June 23, 1863   Signed: Wm. S. Jett

Page 306 - James Kincaid Trust Deed to C.P. Cunningham. Land in
the corporation of the Town of Shelbyville upon which there is a
brick cottage one story high laying between the Cumberland
Presbyterian and Catholic Churches being the lot conveyed from
Wm. S. Jett to me originally owned by P. Fay. This May 12,
1863.
Wit: E. Morris   Signed: James Kincaid
     W.J. Fletcher

Reg: June 23, 1863

Page 306 - C.P. Cunningham Trust Deed to Mrs. Sally Cunningham.
Whereas on 12 May 1863 James Kincaid executed a Deed of Trust to
me to secure payment by which he transferred a house and lot
being the lot conveyed by Title Bond from Wm. S. Jett originally
owned by P. Fay.   I have this day transferred to E. Morris as
trustee all the right title &c I have in said house and lot.
This 15 May 1863.
Reg: June 25, 1863   Signed: C.P. Cunningham

Page 307 - E. Morris Bill of Sale for girl Sarah to Mrs. Sally
Cunningham. This April 8, 1863.
Wit: P.L. Perry   Signed: E. Morris
     J.J. Kincaid
Reg: June 25, 1863

Page 307 - E. Morris Bill of Sale for girl Easter to Mrs. S.
Cunningham. This March 29, 1863.
Wit: S.M. A(illegible)   Signed: E. Morris
     Mrs. J.J. Kincaid
Reg: June 25, 1863

Page 307 - Marmaduke & Spence Co-partnership Agreement &c.   We
are now the purchaser of several parcels of real estate sold by
the Chancery Court and D.H.C. Spence has signed V. Marmaduke's
name. Murfreesboro, January 17, 1860.
Reg: June 25, 1863   Signed: V. Marmaduke
                                        D.H.C. Spence

Page 308 - George V. Hebb Deed 183 acres to Charles A. Warren.
Land in Bedford County and Civil District No. 7 and bounded at
the center of Flat Creek near a spring and through the spring
including house and lot. This 14, February 1863.
Wit: Thos. H. Coldwell   Signed: Geo. V. Hebb
     Joseph Ramsey
Reg: June 30, 1863

Page 309 - C.A. Warren Deed 198+ acres to Geo. W. Thompson,
clerk.   Land in Bedford County and Civil District No. 18 and
bounded by Seaton's line. This 1 May 1863.
Wit: Thos. H. Coldwell   Signed: C.A. Warren
     W.B.M. Brame
     Thos. C. Whitside
Reg: July 2, 1863

Page 310 - John T. Weaver Deed of Gift to Fannie Riggin. This
10 April 1863. Both of Bedford County. For and consideration
which he bears toward his said sister Fannie Riggin hath
conveyed unto her all the clothing and · stead that belongs
hereto, Several items listed.

Wit: A.L.S. Huffman   Signed: John T. Weaver
     George Huffman
Reg: June 25, 1863

Page 310 - John T. Weaver Deed 26 acres to David G. Weaver.
This 12 April 1863. John T. Weaver of Bedford County and David
G. Weaver of Coffee County, Tennessee. For the natural love and
affection he bears toward his brother the said David G. Weaver
hath given unto him a tract of land and adjoining a 60 acre
tract in the name of Jacob Hyles, south of the road leading from
Shelbyville to the Pond Spring, by Mathew Moss, and a line
between Weaver and John Turman.
Wit: A.L.S. Huffman   Signed: John T. Weaver
     George Huffman
Reg: June 25, 1863

Page 311 - John T. Weaver Deed of Gift to David G. Weaver. This
10 April 1863. John T. Weaver of Bedford County and David G.
Weaver of Coffee County, Tennessee and in consideration which he
bears towards his said brother said David G. Weaver hath given
unto him one bay mare, five head of shoats, and several listed
items.
Wit: A.L.S. Huffman   Signed: John T. Weaver
     George Huffman
Reg: June 25, 1863

Page 312 - Marmaduke & Spence Deed Lot to A.P. Eakin. A three
story brick house and lot situated on the east side of the
Public Square in the Town of Shelbyville, Bedford County and
bounded by the house now occupied by R.D. Deery as a Drug Store,
and the property of Robt. Cannon. Said lot fronts about 20 feet
on the Public Square and back to an alley and is generally known
as the Escue House. This 15 April 1863.
Reg: July 2, 1863   Signed: V. Marmaduke, by
                                     D.H.C. Spence, partner

Page 312 - A.P. Eakin Quit Claim Deed to Mrs. Charlotte
Chockley. On 3 July 1860 Jesse Chockley and wife Charlotte
Chockley executed to me a mortgage in Trust Deed in the Town of
Shelbyville, Bedford County the house being a brick house not
far from the Big Spring. Said mortgage is registered in Bedford
County. This June 22, 1863.
Reg: July 2, 1863   Signed: A.P. Eakin

Page 312 - Samuel Bowman Deed 250 acres to Bell & Webb. Land in
Bedford County and District No. 8 and adjoining Eben Nelson, A.
Goodwin, Mike Williams, and Robert Freeman. Sold to G.W. Bell
and A.M. Webb. This June 27, 1863.
Wit: J.P. Hutton   Signed: Sam'l Bowman
     R.B. Freeman
Reg: July 13, 1863

Page 313 - Edm'd Cooper, extr and others Deed 396+ acres to Wm.
G. Cowan. Wiley F. Daniel by his Last Will and Testament
appointed Edmund Cooper his executor and for him to sell all of
my real estate of land, money and stock &c and to pay over the
remainder if any to Henry B. Coffey and William R. Edmondson,
and whereas by agreement made between Henry B. Coffey and
William T. Edmondson the (illegible) legatees of one part and
William G. Cowan of other part. Land in Bedford County and
District No. 23 and adjoins Wiley F. Daniel, to the center of
Beech Creek, to the center of Duck River, to the center of
Little Flat Creek at the north of Singletons Branch, to the
mouth of Couchs Creek. This 19 June 1863.
Wit: W.W. Wilhoite   Signed: Edmund Cooper, Extr. Of
     Robert Cannon   Wiley F. Daniel
Reg: August 5, 1863   H.B. Coffey
                                    Wm. T. Edmondson

Page 315 - Spence & Marmaduke Deed &c to Wm. G. Cowan. Sale of
land on 25 June 1859 to highest bidder a town lot in Bedford
County and in the Village of Shelbyville fronting on the east
side of the Public Square and bounded by the Drug Store of Thos.
J. Roane, by the store house in the same block owned by Robert
Cannon including one half of the division wall between said
Robert Cannon's store house and the store house, and it being
the store house and lot now occupied by Wm. G. Cowan. Property
sold by Sheriff to David H.C. Spence and Vincent Marmaduke.
This 20 February 1863.
Wit: A.P. Eakin   Signed: D.H.C. Spence
     Robert Cannon   Spence & Marmaduke
Reg: August 5, 1863

Page 316 - D.H.C. Spence Receipt to Wm. G. Cowan. Received the
last payment for the store house and lot now occupied by him in
the Town of Shelbyville. This 20 February 1863.
Wit: A.P. Eakin   Signed: D.H.C. Spence
     Robert Cannon
Reg: 5 August 1863

Page 317 - Lodwick Holt Deed 106 acres to Presley Prince. Land
in Bedford County on Thompson Creek in 24th District and
containing 106 acres after deducting a small lot, say one
quarter of an acre for a school house and joins the creek and
the meeting house lot, and on the west side of the Shelbyville
Road. This 23, February 1863.
Wit: G.H. Castleman   Signed: Lodwick Holt
     Hezekiah Bennet
Reg: August 6, 1863

Page 318 - Wm. C. Atkisson and Mary Atkisson Deed to J.W. Clary.
Land in Bedford County and District No. 11 and adjoining William
Wilson, Stammer's line, Cooper's line, and containing 48 acres.
This 5 October 1858.
Wit: Jennings Moore   Signed: Wm. Atkisson
     James T. Williams   Mary Atkisson

Reg: August 13, 1863

Page 318 - Peter Berron Deed to John W. Clary. Lot of land in the Village of Unionville, Bedford County and adjoining the road running frim Unionville to Enoch Church and east of the Eagleville, Unionville and Shelbyville Turnpike Road, and containing about one third of a acre. This 17, December 1862.
Wit: J.T. Williams   Signed: Peter Berron
     Jennings Moore
Reg: August 13, 1863

Page 319 - R.S. Thomas Deed 68 acres to J.M. Henson. Land in Bedford County and Civil District No. 4. Land bounded by the Salem Camp Ground Lot, the Bell Buckle Creek, in the center of the Shelbyville and Bell Buckle Road, and the dower laid off to Mary S. Elkins. This 30 June 1859.
Wit: R.D. Rankin   Signed: R.S. Thomas
     Wm. J. Peacock
Reg: August 17, 1863

Page 320 - Chesley Williams Deed to William Collins. Chesley Williams of Williamson County, Tennessee, at Sheriff's sale as the land of James H. Lock in District No. 11 and containing 50 acres and bounded by Felix Turrentine, J.J. Long, James H. Lock and others. This 30, 1862.
Wit: A. Hatcher   Signed: Chesley Williams
     Thos. A. Knott
Reg: September 1, 1863

Page 321 - G.W. Cone and others Deed to A.M. Webb. Payment money going from G.W. Cone to Iverson Knott and other persons are G.W. Cone in his own right and Smith Bowlin as surviving trustees under trust and executed by G.W. Cone to W.F. Cooper and Smith Bowlin and Raleigh Miller as purchasers of the land at sale. Land in Bedford County and District No. 5 and by T.F. Smalling and containing 80 acres and 54 poles. This 24 November 1862.
Wit: C.F. Sutton, Sr.   Signed: G.W. Cone
     J.H. Ogilvie   Smith Bowlin, Trustee
Reg: September 1, 1863   J.R. Miller

Page 322 - William Houston Deed to W.W. Arnold. This __ January 186_. E.W. Hale conveyed by Deed in Trust to W.W. Arnold and E.T. Haley land in Bedford County and adjoining lands of E. Williams and others, being the same bought by E.W. Hale from said Arnold and by him bought of said Haley and containing 80 acres. This 7 September 1863.
Reg: October 28, 1863   Signed: Wm. Houston

Page 322 - Thos. W. Davis Deed to H.W. Jones. Land in Bedford County and Civil District No. 10 and containing 40 acres and 53 poles, This 18 December 1862.

Wit: G.W. Holden   Signed: Thos. W. Davis
     James W. Head
Reg: October 27, 1863

Page 323 - Francis Hale Deed to W.W. Arnold. Land which I now
live in Bedford County and adjoining E. Williams and others, has
been sold under a Trust Deed executed by her husband E.W. Hale
in his life time and was bought by Wm. Houston and has now been
redeemed by W.W. Arnold. This 7 September 1863.
Wit: S.S. Arnold   Signed: Francis Hale
     A.J. McAdams
Reg: October 29, 1863

Page 324 - D.M. Orr Deed to Johnathan Claxton. Land willed to
me by my grandfather David Orr, deceased, containing 106 acres
in Bedford County and Civil District No 11 and the land that Wm.
N. Orr is now living. This 22 September 1863.
Wit: Jos. Anderson   Signed: D.M. Orr
     M.J. Anderson
Reg: October 29, 1863

Page 324 - Young and Martha Wilhoite Deed Thos. C. Wilhoite.
Young Wilhoite and Martha Wilhoite his wife has sold to Thos. C.
Whitside a tract of land in Bedford County within the corporate
limits of the Town of Shelbyville and bounded by a junction of
Union Street with the Nashville, Murfreesboro and Shelbyville
Turnpike Road, by a lot sold by L.B. Knott to T.S. Clay and now
occupied by Geo. F. Blakemore, and by the side of Brittain
Street. This October 2, 1863.
Reg: October 29, 1863   Signed: Young Wilhoite
                                  Martha Wilhoite

Page 325 - Thos. Baxter Deed to Martha S. Russell. This 19
October 1863. Indenture made between Thos. B. Baxter and Martha
S. Russell wife of Wm. W. Russell, all of Bedford County in
Civil District No. 18 on Big Sinking Creek and bounded by
William H. Stephens, James H. Baxter, and the middle of Sinking
Creek, and containing 85 acres and 11 poles, and being the place
on which said Thos. M. Baxter now reside.
Reg: October 29, 1863   Signed: Thos. Baxter

Page 326 - R.P.S. Kimbro Deed to J.M. Elliott. R.P.S. Kimbro
sold to James M. Elliott land in Bedford County in what is known
as "Camp White" sold by Clement Cannon and bounded by said Camp
White or Lucust Street, Rev. S.S. Moody and lots, B.M. Tillman
to C.L. McKnight, Clem Cannon, J.A. Blakemore, (said alley being
a vacant space between the two lots) (not conveyed), and
containing three fourths of an acre. This August 18, 1859.
Wit: B.H. Coble   Signed: R.P.S. Kimbro
     J. Wortham
Reg: October 29, 1863

Page 326 - William S. Jett Deed to William Gosling. Lot in the west end of the Town of Shelbyville, Bedford County composed of two parcels. The first purchased by Silas Bivins of John H. Oneal and second by said Bivins of G.W. Buchanan. The first bounded by and at the center of the Shelbyville & Unionville Road. The second joins the corner of my stable on the above lot, to the corner of a flood gate to said branch to mine said Oneal's corner. The place purchased by me of Silas A. Bivins on 4 April 1863. This 23 September 1863.
Reg: November 3, 1863   Signed: Wm. S. Jett

Page 327 - Ezekiel M. Lacy Deed 3 acres to J.H. McGrew. Land in Bedford County and Civil District No. 3 on the road leading from Shelbyville to Rowesville and bounded by William Reaves, the Rowesville Road, Robert Reaves, and to the north bank of Duck River. This 13 October 1863.
Reg: November 3, 1863   Signed: E.M. Lacy

Page 328 - G.G. Osborne and Elizabeth Sutton, Marriage Contract. Both of Bedford County, have agreed to make a marriage contract. That at the death of said Elizabeth he will not claim any of her real estate or slaves should slaves still be property unless she should will or give said slaves to him. That at the death of said Osborne the will and claim of any portion &c should be willed or given to her. This 3 November 1863.
  Wit: W.W. Payne   Signed: G.G. Osborne
       W.B. Payne   Elizabeth Sutton

Page 328 - Jane Garrett Deed 133 acres to John Hailey. Jane Garrett of Rutherford County, Tennessee and relict of James Garrett, deceased, late of Bedford County, having become in possession of dower in the landed estate of said Garrett, I have sold to John Hailey of Williamson County, Tennessee all the dower allotted and laid off by the Commissioners Wm. Collins, Wm. Little, J.T. Street, and A. Wilson and surveyed by A. Nelson on 23 September 1863 and joining Stephen Wood, John Woods, Wm. Little, and Stephen Woods. This 28 September 1863.
  Wit: J.R. Stem   Signed: Jane Garrett
       James G. Williams
  Reg: November 1863

Page 329 - Martha A. Couch Deed for dower to Mary C. Couch et als. Martha A. Couch against the administrator and heirs of Joseph E. Couch it is provided that the administrator might pay out of the shares of the children of said Joseph E. Couch in his estate who are all minors, for the right of said Martha A. Couch to dower in his real estate upon her executor, a deed to them relinquishing to them her right to dower. Conveyed to Mary C. Couch, Sarah E. Couch, Joseph A. Couch, John E. Couch, Elijah P. Couch, Eliza A.R. Couch, and Jane B. Couch, the children and heirs of said Joseph E. Couch all her right to dower. This 13 November 1863.
  Wit: Wm. H. Wiseman   Signed: M.A. Couch
       Wm. Word

Reg: November 14, 1863

Page 330 - Hiram H. Holt and Mary J. Smith, Marriage Contract.
Both of Bedford County, have entered into an agreement and
contract to each other on 11 November 1863 in Bedford County for
the purpose of securing to said Mary J. Smith all the property
of which she is now owner both real and personal. Said Mary J.
Smith is to retain the title to all her property now in her
possession. Should Mary J. Smith die without leaving any child
of children or the issue of any child or children, it is to
belong to the said Hiram H. Holt. This 10 November 1863.
Wit: John R. Smith   Signed: H.H. Holt
     W.T. Lewellen   Mary J. Smith
Reg: November 21, 1863

Page 331 - Wm. J. Whitthorne Title Bond to Mathew Johnston. Wm.
J. Whitthorne of Bedford County am held and firmly bound unto
Mathew Johnson of Davidson County, Tennessee, have conveyed
title &c to a brick house and lot on Martin Street in the Town
of Shelbyville, Bedford County known as Mrs. Newton's house and
lot. Now if I should make warrant and deed to Mrs. Margaret
Whitthorne for the sole use of said Margaret Whitthorne and her
children free from debts and her husband Samuel H. Whitthorne.
Wit: W.M. Winbourn   Signed: William J. Whitthorne
     Jos. R. Winvourn
Reg: January 2, 1864

Page 332 - Lucretia and A.P. Eakin Mortgage to Cowan & Eakin.
John W. Cowan and Alexander Eakin paid cost of an execution now
in the hands of Thomas B. Laird, coroner of Bedford County,
being in favor of J.R. Kimbro has been levied on the real estate
with exception of Lot No. 1. Lucretia Eakin and Argyle P. Eakin
have this day sold to Alexander Eakin and John W. Cowan town
lots parts of town lots in the Town of Shelbyville and tracts of
land in District No. 7 of Bedford County. First, the dwelling
house in which Mrs. Lucretia Eakin now resides adjoining on the
street, by the lot on which is built the yellow house formerly
occupied as a residence by G.P. Baskett, by Alexander Eakin now
occupied by G.P. Baskett. Second, the house and lot joins the
street, by the north boundary Dixon Academy and lately occupied
as a residence by E. Morris. Third, the store house and lot
known as "Roane's Drug Store" located on the east side of the
Public Square at Shelbyville and bounded by the store house and
lot of W.G. Cowan, by the store house and lot of Eakin & Cowan,
by the corner store being now occupied by Thos. J. Roane.
Fourth, one lot of ground &c attached at present occupied by one
Guest, a shoemaker, and by the road leading to Murfreesboro and
east of the dirt road leading to Murfreesboro and bounded by
lands of Alexander Eakin, and containing 10 acres. Fifth, one
lot of ground lying between the Turnpike Road leading to
Murfreesboro and the dirt road leading to lands of Alexander
Eakin, and containing 8 acres. Note: a long document. This 28
November 1863.
Wit: Thos. M. Coldwell   Signed: Lucretia Eakin
     R.F. Evans

Reg: January 4, 1864

Page 333 - H.C. Kinnard Trust Deed to Arch Prewitt. All the
right title claim &c to a tract of land bounded by the lands of
Anderson Sharp and Jasper Smith, and W. Chambers, and Jackson
George. Tract in Civil District No.3 containing about 67 acres.
Also conveyed horses, stock and hogs. This December 10, 1863.
Reg: January 5, 1864   Signed: H.C. Kinnard

Page 334 - Wm. B. Wheeler Deed 75 acres to Nathaniel M. Wheeler.
Land in Bedford County and District No. 8 and adjoining the
center of the pike it being the north west corner of the
original tract of Thomas Wheeler, deceased, it being half of the
original tract. This October 26, 1863.
Reg: January 4, 1864   Signed: W.B. Wheeler

Page 334 - Benjamin and Margaret Crowell Deed 12+ acres to Wm.
Crowell. We, Margaret Crowell and Benj. Crowell her husband,
sold to Wm. Crowell paid to us by Jno. Anderson, a lot of land
by us drawn in the lands of David Anderson, deceased, being Lot
No. 3, being in Bedford County and being a part of David
Anderson's land and bounded by Jno. Anderson's line of his
brother's land and Lot No. 2, and Wortham's line. This 19
September 1862.
Wit: Jos. Anderson   Signed: Margaret Crowell
     B. ?. Parsons   Benj. Crowell
Reg: January 4, 1864

Page 335 - Lucretia Eakin Deed Lot to Argyle P. Eakin. Land in
the Town of Shelbyville, Bedford County and bounded by the
garden and stable lot of John W. Cowan, Brittain Street, Dixon
Academy lot, the street leading in front of Mrs. L. Eakin's
brick residence, said lot contains two framed dwelling houses.
This 12 September 1863.
Wit: Thos. M. Cowan, Dec 3, 1863
     R.F. Evans   Signed: Lucretia Eakin
Reg: January 4, 1864

Page 336 - Alexander H. Evans Deed Lot to Gwynn & Stewart.
Alexander H. Evans sold to W.M. Gwinn and Daniel Stewart lot of
land in the Town of Shelbyville and known as Lot No. 101, said
lot on the second block from the Public Square, said lot being
north of the street leading from the Public Square to the town
bridge over Duck River. This December 24, 1863.
Reg: January 5, 1864   Signed: A.H. Evans

Page 336 - Edmund Cooper, Trustee of Mary J. Erwin Deed to Berry
& Demoville. Whereas by marriage contract entered into between
Andrew Erwin and Mrs. Mary J. Erwin before their marriage. The
property then owned by Mrs. Mary J. Erwin was and remain her own
and separate property and power on her part at any time to sell.
Said land was vested in the Trustee under said marriage

contract. Edmund Cooper being trustee of Mrs. Mary J. Erwin. Also September 5, 1863 sold to Berry & Demoville of Davidson County, Tennessee land in District No. 2 of Bedford County and known as Beachwood now in the possession of Coleman F. Hord and formerly occupied by Mary J. Erwin. Land adjoining lands of John R. Erwin, by the heirs of Archibald Murphy, the heirs of Wm. Pepper, and by the Garrison Cork of Duck River, and by the Rail Road. Known as Beachwood, and containing 250 acres. This 5 November 1863.
Reg: January 21, 1864   Signed: Edmund Cooper, Trustee of
                                        Mary J. Erwin

Page 337 - Wm. Gosling Deed &c to William J. Whitthorne. In consideration of one half interest in the store house and lot on Depot Street in Shelbyville and adjoining the Shelbyville Bank of Tennessee and recently occupied by John Wells. I have sold unto William J. Whitthorne a half share of the stock in the cotton factory known as the Sylvan Mills and all machinery therein, grist mills and lands and dwellings &c. This 1 January 1864.
Wit: Robt. B. Davidson   Signed: Wm. Gosling
     Thos. Lipscomb
Reg: January 2, 1864

Page 338 - Robt. B. Ruth Deed Gift to Gartha A. Gillman. For the affection I have for my sister Gartha Ann Gillman the west part of Lot No. __ in the Town of Shelbyville on the south side of the street leading past the Jail, past Geo. W. Ruth's it being the west part of the lot on which David Ruth now lives and adjoining a lot belonging to John W. Thompson on which said G.A. Gillman now lives. This May 10, 1858.
Reg: January 21, 1864   Signed: Robt. B. Ruth

Page 338 - Martha A. Gillman Deed Lot to W.N. Gwynn. I, Gartha A. Gillman, have sold to said Gwynn a town lot in corporate limits of the Town of Shelbyville the same part of Lot No. __ adjoining David Ruth formerly resided, a street, and by the lot of Jno. W. Thompson. This 14 January 1864.
Reg: January 21, 1864   Signed: Gartha A. Gillman

Page 339 - James M. Neely Deed to Tira Harrison. Indenture made 23 November 1863 between Jas. M. Neely of Bedford County and the heirs of Tyra Harrison. F.M. Harrison and E.P. Harrison, William Harrison, Joshua Harrison, and Mary Harrison and Hulda Harrison of Bedford County sold to the heirs of Tyra Harrison land in Bedford County on Sinking Creek being a part of Grant No. 16516 granted to Moses Aron and containing 5 acres and 21 poles.
Reg: January 22, 1864   Signed: James H. Neely

Page 340 - A.F. Knott Deed 18+ acres to Amanda F. Little. Albert F. Knott sold to Amanda F. Little land in Bedford County and District No. 19, being my share of the tract of land owned

by William Little outside the dower now occupied by Delia Little and adjoining A.F. Knott, and a lane. This November 24, 1863.
Wit: William Floyd   Signed: A.F. Knott
     J.F. Marshall
Reg: January 22, 1864

Page 340 - G.C. Neely Deed Town Lot to Bartley Posey. Lot in the west end of the Town of Shelbyville, it being the same I purchased of Joshua Zachery adjoining Camey's(?) corner. This December 26, 1863.
Reg: January 22, 1864   Signed: G.C. Neely

Page 341 - John G. Bledsoe Deed 79+ acres to Martha Shaddie. Land sold unto Mrs. Martha Shaddie being in Bedford County and District No. 20 and on the head waters of Sugar Creek and bounded by Nathan Evans, Leadbetter's tract, and William Bledsoe's original tract. This 26 June 1858.
Wit: Benjamin Delf   Signed: John G. Bledsoe
     Martin Capley
Reg: January 22, 1864

Page 342 - J.A. Cunningham Deed of Settlement to E.G.M. Cunningham. For the love and affection I bear towards my beloved wife E.M.G. Cunningham all the further consideration of my having used her money in payment of purchase money of the land for the purpose of securing in their time of trouble a home for my wife and children. I, Joseph A. Cunningham of Bedford County do convey unto E.M.G. Cunningham during her natural live and at her death to be equally divided amongst our children then living, land on which I now reside being in Bedford County and District No. 20 and adjoining the Section Line, being G.W. Cunningham's corner and John Nance's line, Thomas Gambrell, and Richard Anderson, and William Porter. This 23 December 1863.
Reg: January 22, 1864   Signed: J.A. Cunningham

Page 343 - Geo. W. Greer Deed 57+ acres to Wash. P. Goodwin. Land adjoining lands of Samuel Neely, and Washington P. Goodwin purchase of the Gabbert's heirs. This 7 December 1863.
Reg: January 25, 1864   Signed: G.W. Greer

Page 343 - W.P. Goodwin Deed 212 acres to W.H. and S.G. Dyer. Land in Bedford County and District No. 20 and bounded by lands of Martha Dobson, Amanda Gabbert, James Carlisle, and by Mrs. Nathan Evans, Wm. H. and S.J. Dyer, and lands of Samuel Neely. This 7 December 1863.
Reg: January 26, 1864   Signed: W.P. Goodwin

Page 344 - William Little Deed 151+ acres to Joseph T. Dozier. Land in Bedford County and District No. 9 and adjoining E. Wallace, and Z. Moore. This 24 August 1858.
Wit: J.E. Frost   Signed: Wm. Little
     Wm. Dozier

Reg: (no date)

Page 345 - John A. Moore Deed Town Lot to A.G. Moore. Both of
Bedford County. A certain house and lot in the Town of
Shelbyville known as Camp White in Bedford County and District
No. 7, it being the house and lot which I purchased of John C.
Akin and A. Akin and bounded by Cannon Street, by James Elliott,
James Wortham's vacant lot, and Camp Street, containing about 1
acre. This January 29, 1864.
Reg: January 29, 1864   Signed: Jos. H. Thompson, Clerk

Page 345 - Thos. Lipscomb Deed 145+ acres to Wm. S. Jett. Land
in Bedford County and bounded by Newcum Thompson's land, James
H. Lock's land, and Theophilus Thompson. This 30 December 1863.
Reg: January 30, 1864   Signed: Thos. Lipscomb

Page 346 - Wm. S. Jett Deed 4 shares in Factory to Thos.
Lipscomb. Four shares of the capital stock in the manufacturing
company of Wm. Gosling & Co. engaged in manufacturing thread and
cloth in their two factories on Duck River, one at Shelbyville
and the other about two miles below including grist mill
together with all lands attached, and now by said company in the
Town of Shelbyville and with all machinery, water, power &c.
This 31 December 1863.
Reg: January 30, 1864   Signed: Wm. S. Jett

Page 347 - Robt. Galbraith Deed Town Lot to C.T. Martin. Land
in Bedford County and in the Town of Shelbyville and adjoining
Richard Foreman, a street, and Thomas Burnett. This 28 January
1864. Nashville, Tennessee.
Wit: C.A. Warren   Signed: Robt. Galbraith
     Wm. B.M. Brame
Reg: February 2, 1864

Page 347 - R.C. Cannon Deed Town Lot to Lewis Mankle. Lot of
ground in Camp White on which Lewis Mankle is now residing and
bounded by lands of John G. Johnson now John C. Coldwell, the
lot of Mary A. Thompson, and by ___ Street, and by John F. Neil.
Wit: Edmund Cooper   Signed: R.C. Cannon, Trustee for
     Thos. C. Whiteside   James Wortham
Reg: February 2, 1864

Page 348 - M.E.W. Dunnaway Deed Lot to Mrs. Rhoda Ann McKinney.
Lot in Bedford County in the Town of Shelbyville and known as
Camp White and bounded by a lot known in the place of lots laid
off and by C. Cannon, Sr. as Lot No. 8 in the edge of White
Street and Camp Street, by Lot No. 8 and by Locust Street. This
February 1, 1864.
Reg: February 2, 1864   Signed: M.E.W. Dunnaway

Page 348 - G.W. Bullock and wife Power of Attorney to Thos. Bullock. G.W. Bullock and Mary P. Bullock of Christian County, Kentucky and grand children of Jackson Liles and Betsey E. Liles his wife who living in Bedford County, do appoint Thomas Bullock of Christian County, Kentucky our attorney in fact to receive for us any money or property which may be coming to us from the estate of said Jackson Liles and Betsey E. Liles. We being two children of Betsey E. Bullock who is now dead and who was a daughter of said Jackson Liles and we are now over twenty one years of age. This 11 December 1863.
Reg: February 3, 1864   Signed: G.W. Bullock
                                       Mary P. Bullock

Page 349 - Robert Cannon Deed of Gift to Elizabeth M. Nellson. Robert Cannon of Bedford County and living in the Town of Shelbyville do give to my daughter Elizabeth M. Nellson land, house and lot &c. and the lands. The house brick house and some 5 ½ or 6 acres around the house. It being the former residence of the late Wm. Gilchrist formerly called the Gilchrist place but now called and named by me (Pleasant View), located on the north side of Lane Street and adjoining land of Ross Deery, a 5 acre tract conveyed to my daughter Nancy J. Fay and her husband Patrick Fay, by said Robt. Cannon, lands where Mrs. Wallace now lives on belonging to the heirs of J.W. Wallace, and also two lots (one Lot No. 4 containing 11 acres and 8 poles and the other Lot No. 5 containing 9 acres and 120 poles) which two lots I have purchased at the sale of the lands of the late Sterling Newsom and heris on the north side of Rowesville Road east of Shelbyville and adjoining land belonging to Charles Warren and his brother Albert Warren, and land of Volney H. Steele, and land said Cannon now lives on. Also I give to my daughter Eliza or Elizabeth M. Nellson the store house in Town of Shelbyville on the south side of Water Street now called Depot Street the store room No. 3 now at present occupied by ___ Wallace (it being on Lot No, 36). House listed as a brick house, This 14 April 1863.
Wit: Mary L. Dromgoole   Signed: Robert Cannon
     M.C. Fay
     Alex. Eakin
     P. Fay
     John W. Cowan, Sr.
     G.P. Baskett
     W,W. Wilhoite
Reg: February 3, 1864

Page 351 - N. Thompson Deed of Town Lot to Gwynn & Stewart. I have sold to W.N. Gwynn and Daniel Stewart a lot in the Town of Shelbyville, being part of Lot No. 94 and bounded by the street leading from the Public Square to the river, and by Lot No. 94. This January 114, 1864.
Reg: February 4, 1864   Signed: Newcum Thompson, Sr.

Page 351 - C.L. Powell Deed Town Lot to Gotha A. Gillman. I have conveyed unto Gotha Ann Gillman a lot in the Town of Shelbyville and District No. 7 and adjoining lands of G.W.

Buchanan being south east corner of Lot No. 3, to an alley, and a lot belonging to Anderson Sharp, by Mrs. Gollithan, and not including 10 feet between Mrs. Gollithan and the lot. This February __ 1864.
Reg: February 4, 1864   Signed: C.P. Powell

Page 352 - W.J. and B.W. Blessing Deed to J.H.C. Scales. Land and slaves belonging to the estate of James Coats, deceased, which said land and slaves were sold 5 February 1864 by said Scales under decree of Bedford County Court. This February 8, 1864.
Reg: February 9, 1864   Signed: W.J. Blessing
                                       Baley W. Blessing

Page 352 - Thos. C. Whiteside Trustee Deed 306+ acres to Nathan Evans. Whereas William A. Campbell on __ July 1859 conveyed in trust to Anderson Maxwell tracts of land and other property for the purpose of paying of debts &c of said Campbell. Sale to Nathan Evans portion of the lands. Land in Bedford County and Civil District No. 3 on the Wartrace Fork of Duck River and on both sides of the Nashville and Chattanooga Rail Road and adjoining Jeremiah Cleveland's corner, on the east side of the road leading from Wartrace Depot to Fairfield and in or near Mrs. Robt. Waite's line, and a corner of a 100 acre tract sold to Henry B. Coffey and Robt. Buchanan and by said Buchanan to said Wm. A. Campbell, thence to the mouth of said Coffeys Spring Branch in the center of the Wartrace Fork of Duck River, and a tract of 163 acres sold by trustees of said Campbell to Robt. S. Clark, and by Clark by A. Maxwell. This 26 December 1861.
Reg: February 9, 1864   Signed: Thos. C. Whiteside,
                                       Trustee

Page 354 - Wm. L. Thomas Deed 63 acres to Thos. Kimmons. Land in Bedford County and Civil District No. 20, it being the place known as the "Whitesell Place" and on which Milly Whitesell now resides and bounded by lands of James Coats estate, by lands of John W. Greer, by lands of Jno. w. Greer, and by lands of Thos. J. Robinson. My interest being one third of one eighth of said 63 acres. This February 8, 1864.
Reg: February 9, 1864   Signed: Wm. L. Thomas

Page 354 - James M. Hobbs Deed Town Lot to Thos. S. Sharp. Land in 7th Civil District of Bedford County within the corporate limits of the Town of Shelbyille and known as Lot No. 23 being the lot on which I now reside and being the lot conveyed to me by Wm. Brown and is registered in Book YY, pages 272 and 273. This March 1, 1861.
Reg: February 10, 1864   Signed: Jas. M. Hobbs

Page 356 - Joel Stallings Deed 100 acres to B.A. Haskins. Land in Bedford County and Civil District No. 18 and bounded by Eda Forbes' line, Thos. Coffey's line it being Eda Forbes' corner,

Page 356 - P.P. Ward Power of Attorney to Buchanan & Davidson. Prudence P. Ward of Livingston County, Kentucky appointed G.W. Buchanan and J.L. Davidson of Bedford County or either of them my trustee and lawful attorney to collect from Burrell Ward, Jr. administrator of Burrell Ward, Sr. my distributive share as one of the heirs at law of said Burrell, Sr. Also to collect from Wm. J. Whitthorne my distributive share as said heir at law of the fund arising from the sale of the real estate of said Burrell, Sr. Also slaves belonging to said Burrell, Sr. This February 17, 1864.
Reg: February 17, 1864   Signed: P.P. Ward

Page 357 - John and William Stephens Deed to E.H. & J.M.L. Stephens. This 14 April 1852. John H. and William Stephens of Bedford County sold to E.H. and J.M.L. Stephens of Bedford County land being our undivided interest in the land of which John Stephens, Sr. died seized and possessed in Bedford County on the west side of Duck River and containing 348 ¾ acres, adjoining R.H. Sims, H(illegible), Smith and W.E. Coleman, L.T. Williams, Mrs. E. Warner, John Streater, and R.H. and L.A. Temple.
Wit: R.H. Temple   Signed: John H. Stephens
     L.A. Temple   William S. Stephens
Reg: February 29, 1864

Page 358 - Thomas Thompson and wife Deed to E.H. & J.M.L. Stephens. We, Thomas Thompson and wife Tranquilla Thompson formerly Tranquilla Stephens, have sold to E.H. Stephens and J.M.L. Stephens land in Bedford County on the waters of Powell Creek and bounded by R.H. Sims, Temple's line, land of Warner's heirs, Leroy T. Williams' line, W.E. Coleman's corner, and containing 370 acres. This 9 July 1853.
Reg: February 29, 1864   Signed: Thos. Thompson
                                        T.A. Thompson

Page 359 - E.H. Stephens Deed to J.M.L. Stephens. Land in Bedford County on the waters of Powell Creek and bounded by R.H. Sims, Temple's line, lands of Warner heirs, Leroy T. Williams' line, W.E. Coleman's corner, and containing 370 acres. This 26 January 1858.
Reg: March 2, 1864   Signed: E.G. Stephens

Page 360 - Briant Landis Deed ___ acres to Rowland Landis. Whereas on 26 August 1858 Elijah Landis of Webster County, Missouri, executed to me as trustee a deed for land in Bedford County, said deed conveying to me his interest as one of the heirs of George Landis, deceased, and for payment of debts against him said Elijah Landis. Rowland Landis is not gained majority, then I as trustee to sell same for cash to highest bidder. Land adjoining lands of Francis Landis, Frederick Batte, Anderson Landis and Ziza Moore, lands formerly owned by Gabriel Lowe, and by lands formerly owned by Rowland Landis, Edward Whitworth and Jacob Morton, deceased, in Civil District No. 9 of Bedford County. This February 27, 1864.

Reg: March 2, 1864   Signed: Briant Landis, Trustee

Page 360 - James Rippey Deed 7+ acres to Hugh Morgan. This 30
January 1864. Both of Bedford County. Land in Bedford County
on the waters of Little Flat Creek being of Rippey's tract and
bounded by James Rippey.
Wit: W.W. Stanfield   Signed: James Rippey
     A.C. Wood
Reg: March 2, 1864

Page 361 - B.A. McLain Deed to Jedediah A. McLain, Land
containing a wool factory &c in the Village of Unionville, Civil
District No. 11 of Bedford County and adjoining a lot on which
Duggan & Moon's Store House now stands, land between Garrett's
lot and the factory lot, and the edge of the turnpike. This 5
December 1861.
Wit: John A. McLain   Signed: B.A. McLain
     J.M. McLain
Reg: March 4, 1864

Page 362 - D.J. Christopher Deed of Gift to Mary J. Christopher.
For the natural love and affection which I have towards my wife
Mary Jane Christopher and our children have granted unto said
wife a certain house and lot and all fixtures &c therein, being
in the Town of Shelbyville on the east side of Shelbyville and
Murfreesboro Turnpike and bounded by Thos. C. Whiteside formerly
belonging to Young Wilhoite and wife, and to a street back of
the said lot. I also convey to her personal property. Several
items listed in original document. This 5 March 1864.
Reg: March 12, 1864   Signed: D.J. Christopher

Page 363 - James S. Maupin Deed 37+ acres to Samuel Yates. This
19, December 1862. Both of Bedford County. Land in Bedford
County adjoining said Yates and the spring path.
Wit: David Throneberry   Signed: James S. Maupin
     Robert B. Maupin
Reg: March 12, 1864

Page 364 - G.W.C. Morton Deed 250 acres to Elijah A. Morton. My
interest in the lands of my deceased father Jacob Morton in
Bedford County and Civil District No. 9 and bounded by
Wheelhouse and Webb, by Frazier, by Primrose and Whitworth, by
Mrs. Fannie Landers. My interest being one thirteenth part.
This March 8, 1864.
Wit: Thos. B. Laird   Signed: G.W.C. Morton
     A.J. Greer
Reg: March 15, 1864

Page 364 - James H. Graham Deed 1 acre to J.W. Brown. Both of
Bedford County. Land being part of a town lot being in the
corporation of the Town of Shelbyville and Civil District No. 7
and bounded by Town Lot belonging to said J.W. Brown and

formerly owned by said Graham and sold to said Brown, by Robt.
Graham, by Wardlaw's line, and a lot formerly owned by Jas.
Deery, deceased. This 10 March 1864.
Reg: March 15, 1864   Signed: J.H. Graham

Page 365 - Thomas H. Coldwell Trustee Deed 263 acres to Robt. T.
Hall. Thomas H. Coldwell, trustee of John G. Hall. Sale of
land in the Village of Rover, Bedford County to highest bidder
on 14 June 1861. Land being part of land conveyed to me by said
Hall in his Trust Deed and is bounded by lands of Alfred Little
and wife and John Simpson, by lands of W.A. Knott, by
G(illegible) and Thomas Chambers, and by lands of Mrs. Thompson
and the heirs of D. Garrett. This 22 March 1864.
Reg: April 1, 1864   Signed: Thos. H. Coldwell, Trustee
                                   Of Robt. T. Hall.

Page 466 - A. Wilson Trustee Deed 100 acres to R. Warner & M.
Morris, administrators. This 9 April 1861. W.G.   Morris
executed to me as trustee a deed to a tract of land bought by
heirs of M.F. Thompson in Civil District No. 11 of Bedford
County bounded by Wm. Wilson's line. Land is registered in Book
CCC, pages 530 and 531. Richard Warner and Margaret Morris,
administrators of Allen Morris, deceased, by their agent. This
16 March 1864.
Reg: April 1, 1864   Signed: A. Wilson, Trustee

Page 367 - Terry D. Thompson Deed __ acres to Alex. Hodge. I
have sold to Alexander Hodge and Joseph Ramsey land in Civil
District No. 3 of Bedford County adjoining near the mouth of the
East Fork of Butlers Creek, Overton & Whiteside tract, and
Mullins' corner lettered M, except two acres and 18 poles
conveyed by Wm. Young to Jas. Mullins near said Mullins Mill.
Also except 3 ½ acres conveyed by said Young to his father James
Young on which the residence of Henry Davis is situated. Said
tract contains 168 ¾ acres. This 14 March 1864.
Wit: Jos. H. Thompson   Signed: Terry D. Thompson
     R.A. Coldwell
Reg: April 13, 1864

Page 368 - Martha Jane Harsett Decree VS Roger Harsett. This 8
April 1864. Roger Harsett is a non-resident of Tennessee and
that complainant and defendant intermarried in Bedford County in
the year 1853 and that have one child John Dennis Harsett aged
six years by said marriage. That said defendant was such
addicted to the use of liquors and that some eighteen months
since that the defendant treated the complainant with great
cruelty by driving her from her home and pursuing her and
beating her with his fist and with sticks and kicking her with
his feet &c. The defendant had and possessed and was seized of
a tract of land that he had a deed to the same from P. Fay dated
January 1, 1858 and registered in Book DDD, page 159 and is in
Bedford County, Civil District No. 8 and adjoining W.H. Wisener,
Thomas G. Holland, Moses Nelson, and the center of the Rail
Road, and containing about 20 acres. He devised unto her during

her natural life to her and her separate use and interest and at
her death the remainder be vested to John Dennis Harsett and the
defendant shall have custody of John Dennis Harsett.   Her
security P.M. Snelling. This 12 April 1864.
Reg: April 14, 1864

Page 369 - Thomas J. Gant and wife Deed 80 acres to Thomas
Baxter. Land in Bedford County and Civil District No. 18 and
bounded by Jonathan Ligett, John White's line, Thomas Coffee's
line, Haskins' tract, and to the road. This April 5, 1864.
Reg: April 14, 1864   Signed: Thomas J. Gant
                                     William J. Gant

Page 370 - B.F. White Deed 75 acres to R.F. Wallis. B.F. White
of Marshall County, Tennessee, hath on 2 April 1863 sold unto
R.F. Wallis of same place a tract of land in Bedford County and
Civil District No. 11 and bounded by land sold by A. Mathews to
J.S. Hart, land sold by C. Batts executor to Hopkins and said
White, G.W. Beavers' corner, and a line between Batts and White.
This April 3, 1863.
Wit: G. Bacon Moon   Signed: B.F. White
     W.H. Landis
Reg: April 18, 1864

Page 371 - T.W. Jordan Deed House and Lot to Thos. J. Warren.
Thomas J. Warren now resides in the City of Concinnatti, Ohio.
Ths house and lot being in the corporate limits of the Town of
Shelbyville and adjoins a corner post of the fence and the east
edge of Brittain Street, line of J.H. McGrew's lot, running west
by the Baptist Church lot and of the Grave Yard, and by B.M.
Tillman's lot and used as a garden, and containing one half
acre. This 18 April 1864.
Reg: May 25, 1864   Signed: T.W. Warren
                                  Ack'd April 18, 1864

Page 372 - Edmund Cooper Attorney Deed 170+ acres to Frederick
Jones. Edmund Cooper as attorney in fact of Sarah Cooper, L.B.
Knott, M.B. Knott, Samuel P. Phillips, Adeline J. Phillips, A.J.
Goodwin, Matilda Goodwin, W.F. Cooper, W.C. Holt and Mary E.
Holt and paid over to them and which money was paid by Samuel P.
Phillips executed to him dated October 2, 1855. Acknowledged by
them all and has sold to Frederick Jones land in Bedford County
and bounded by a 5000 acre tract granted to Martin Phifer, on
the bank of Flat Creek in Bedford County, by Grant No. 487 in
the name of James Patton and Andrew Erwin, and including 170+
acres, being the same tract sold to Charles Cooper on 3 February
1816. This 8 September 1860.
Ack'd August 22, 1863   Signed: L.B. Knott
Reg: May 25, 1864   M.B. Knott
                                   A.J. Goodwin
                                   Matilda Goodwin
                                   Samuel P. Phillips
                                   A.J. Phillips
                                   Mary E. Holt

Wm. C. Holt, by his Atty
Edmund Cooper

Page 373 - Richard P. Stephenson Deed 207+ acres to Thos.
Pickel. This 7 May 1864. Richard P. Stephenson of Marshall
County, Tennessee and Thomas Pickel (Pickle) of Bedford County.
Land in Bedford County on the East Fork of Rock Creek being part
of a tract granted to Capt. John Maderis by Grant No. __ and
bounded by the north west corner of the original tract.
Reg: May 25, 1864   Signed: Richard P. Stephenson

Page 374 - A.S. Adams Deed 27+ acres to Wm. T. Tune. Land in
Bedford County and District No. 6, lands deeded to me by C.T.
and Alexander Philpot January 9, 1863, and bounded by lands of
Peyton Coats, lands of Wm. T. Tune, by my own tract, and lands
of said Coats. This 10 May 1864.
Reg: May 25, 1864   Signed: A.S. Adams

Page 375 - Thos. Hastings Deed 1/8 of 46+ acres to Robt.
Hastings. Land in Bedford County on the waters of Big Flat
Creek, partly in Burrow's District and partly in Hasting's
District, and containing 46 ¾ acres, being tract assigned to
Jane Hastings on which she now resides, in which she has an
estate for life, it being understood that my interest in said
land is one eighth in right of my father Robt. Hastings,
deceased. I conveyed to Robert Hastings. This 14 May 1864.
Reg: May 26, 1864   Signed: Thos. Hastings

Page 376 - Robt. Cannon Deed 5+ acres to Joshua Reed. A small
tract of land in Bedford County about one mile or a little
upward nearly and east corner from the Town of Shelbyville it
being Lot No. 9 in the division of the lots of the late Wilson
Coats and sold by Joseph H. Thompson, Clerk of Bedford County
and sold on 10 June 1857. This 25 June 1863.
Wit: Thos. J. Brown   Signed: Robert Cannon
     E.B. McLain
     G.P. Dobson
Reg: May 26, 1864

Page 377 - B.A. Haskins Deed 30+ acres to H.D. Glasscock. Both
of Bedford County. Land in Bedford County and Civil District
No. 18 being a part of a tract of land conveyed by the heirs of
L.C. Temple to Forbes & Wiggins & Co., and by them to John H.
Oneal, and joining a corner of B.A. Haskins, and Temple's tract.
This 18 December 1863.
Wit: Charnel Glasscock   Signed: B.A. Haskins
     J.F. Haskins
Reg: May 26, 1864

Page 377 - Wm. S. Jett Deed Town Lot to Robert Cannon. Both of
Bedford County. Parcel of ground in the Town of Shelbyville and
adjoins a corner of the brick building owned by the Odd Fellows

and known as the Odd Fellow's Hall, and by Robt. Cannon's tavern. This 1 July 1860.
Wit: B. Martin, Jr.   Signed: Wm. S. Jett
    G.P. Basket
Reg: May 26, 1864

Page 378 - Calvin Ayers Deed 65 acres to N.J.C. Keller. Land in Bedford County and District No. 2 and adjoining John V. Biddle, and by Samuel Vance. This 27 November 1860.
Reg: May 26, 1864   Signed: Calvin Ayers

Page 379 - N.J.C. Keller Deed 65 acres to Michael Robinson. Land in Bedford County and District No. 2 and adjoining John V. Biddle, and Samuel Vance. This 18 May 1864.
Reg: May 26, 1864   Signed: N.J.C. Keller

Page 380 - James M. Stephens Deed 92+ acres to Nathan J.C. Keller. Both of Bedford County. Land in Bedford County and on the ridge between the waters of the Garrison and the Barren Fork of Duck River and bounded by a spring in the Bear Wallow which is a corner of land belonging to the heirs of Edmund Hord, deceased, Mrs. Eliza Davidson, and Furgus Hall's line. This May 18, 1864.
Reg: May 26, 1864   Signed: J.M. Stephens

Page 381 - James Hastings Deed 46+ acres to Robt. Hastings. Land in Bedford County and partly in Civil District No. 22 and partly in No. 23 which tract of land was owned by Robert Hastings, Sr., deceased, being the dower tract of Mrs. Jane Hastings. Bounded by lands of Thos. S. Wood, by Joshua M. Hix and Joseph Hasty, and lands belonging to me as one of the heirs of said Robert Hastings, Sr., deceased, and the other eight belongs to me of the share of Jonah Hastings' tract, deceased. I warrant the title of 2/8 or fourth to said Robert Hastings, Jr. Subject to the life estate of Mrs. Jane Hastings or a dowership. This 24 May 1864.
Reg: May 27, 1864   Signed: James Hastings

Page 382 - F.T. Burrow Deed 1+ acres to Willis Blanton and D.D. Holt. Both of Bedford County. Land in the Village of Normandy in Bedford County and bounded by the Nashville and Chattanooga Rail Road in Village of Normandy, James Phillips, and John W. Huffman. This 24 October 1857.
Wit: W.B. Phillips   Signed: F.T. Burrow
    Middleton Holland
Reg: May 27, 1864

Page 383 - Peter E. Clardy, admr. Deed 142+ acres to Harriett Berry. Peter E. Clardy, administrator of the will of Andrew Pratt, deceased, conveyed to Harriett Berry late widow of Larkin Johnson but now the side of Benj. H. Berry, a tract of land in Bedford County and Civil District No. 23, and adjoining the

center of Flat Creek and the north side of Flat Creek and corner of Lot No. 2. This April 30, 1864.
Reg: May 27, 1864   Signed: Peter E. Clardy, Admr.

Page 384 - Dabney Wade Trust Deed to Sam'l Thompson. For a yellow made and colt now in my possession, one two horse wagon and harness, and ten heads of sheep. This May 25, 1864.
Wit: M.E.W. Dunaway   Signed: Dabney Wade
     Williamson Gordon
Reg: May 27, 1864

Page 385 - R.S. Dwiggins Trust Deed to W.S. Jett. Both of Bedford County. Land known as the Newsom tract in District No. 20 of Bedford County on the waters of Sugar Creek, adjoining the lands of B.F. Greer and Edward Newsom, by lands of Montgomery Little and H.H. Neace, the lands of L.W. Barnett and J.S. Newsom, lands of Mrs. James F. Arnold, and containing about 500 acres. This 24 May 1864.
Reg: May 27, 1864   Signed: R.S. Dwiggins

Page 386 - James S. Maupin Deed 37+ acres to Robt. B. Maupin. Land in Bedford County and District No. 2 and adjoining Mary Franklin, deceased, line, the center of the Nashville and Chattanooga Rail Road, and by Elias Holt's line. This April 28, 1864.
Wit: W.M. Eason   Signed: J.S. Maupin
     M.A. Black
Reg: June 6, 1864

Page 386 - James S. Maupin Deed 8+ acres to Robt. B. Maupin. Land in Bedford County and District No. 2 and adjoining in the center of the Nashville and Chattanooga Rail Road, and Robert B. Maupin's corner of the Payne tract. This 29 April 1864.
Wit: W.M. Eason   Signed: James S. Maupin
     M.A. Black
Reg: June 7, 1864

Page 387 - James S. Maupin Deed ¼ acre to Nancy A. Eason. For the love and affection I entertain for Nancy A. Eason, I do hereby give her a lot of land in Bedford County and District No. 2, adjoining James S. Maupin, to center of the Nashville and Chattanooga Rail Raod, James Chilton's line, and Nancy A. Eason's corner. This May 11, 1864.
Wit: W.M. Eason   Signed: J.S. Maupin
     Robert B. Maupin
Reg: June 8, 1864

Page 388 - Robt. B. Maupin Deed 154 acres to Nancy A. Eason. For the love and affection I entertain for Nancy A. Eason, have conveyed unto her land in Bedford County and District No. 2 and

adjoining the Nashville and Chattanooga Rail Road in James Chilton's line. This March 30, 1864.
Wit: J.S. Maupin   Signed: Robert B. Maupin
    W.M. Eason
Reg: June 8, 1864

Page 388 - Robt. B. Maupin Deed 13+ acres to James S. Maupin. Land in Bedford County and District No. 2 and adjoining James S. Maupin where S.T. Southern lived, and to the center of the Nashville and Chattanooga Rail Road. This 29 April 1864.
Wit: W.M. Eason   Signed: Robert B. Maupin
    M.A. Black
Reg: June 9, 1864

Page 389 - James S. Maupin Deed 90+ acres to David Thronberry. Land in Bedford County and District No. 2, and adjoining J.S. Maupin's line. Samuel Yates' corner, Mary Franklin's corner, and James Chilton's corner. This 6 May 1864.
Reg: June 10, 1864   Signed: J.S. Maupin

Page 390 - Joseph Thompson, Sheriff, Deed Lot to James H. Graham. This 24 September 1858 James H. Graham recovered a judgment in Bedford County against W.W. Gavin and John Gavin. There being no personal property he levied upon all the right title &c of John Gavin and W.W. Gavin to a lot in that part of Shelbyville known as Camp White, and bounded by Locust Street, Lot No. 12, on the west by Cannon Street, it being Lot No. 12 in Camp White, to satisfy judgment. This 6 June 1864.
Reg: June 10, 1864   Signed: Jo. Thompson, Sheriff

Page 391 - Hiram Hammond Deed 3+ acres to James A. Moore. Lot of land on the north side of the Rail Road near Shelbyville and adjoining a 6 acre tract by John P. Steele to C.G. Mitchell and now owned by W.H. Wisener, to Holland's in Calhoon's line, and a 3 acre lot now owned by William C. Wisener, it being the place formerly owned by John P. Steele and Where I now live. This December 12, 1864.
Reg: June 14, 1864   Signed: Hiram Hammond

Page 391 - Walter F. Sutton Deed for 240 acres in fund to D.H. Skein. All my right title and claim &c to the fund raising from sale of land sold Jos. H. Thompson a Commissioner under decree of County Court of Bedford County and belonging to the estate of Overton Sutton estate and bought of said sale by Edmund Mullins now deceased and whose note for the purchase money. This June 18, 1864.
Wit: Jo. H. Thompson   Signed: W.F. Sutton
    B.F. Smalling
Reg: June 28, 1864

Page 392 - Martin S. Dean Procession Deed for 59+ acres. Tract
of land on which said Martin S. Dean now lives in District No.
24 on the waters of Thompson Creek and adjoining Wm. Daniel.
W.M. Daniel and William Anderton, C.C.
                              Signed: C.S. Dudley, Surveyor
Note: Plat of land on page 393.
Reg: July 4, 1864

Page 393 - R.C. Daniel Deed 55+ acres to James H. Lokey. Land
in Bedford County and District No. 24 on the head waters of
Thompson Creek and bounded by Hezekiah Bennett road, and by the
road from R.C. Daniel to Tullahoma, and by James Lokey. This 7
May 1857.
Wit: D.W.C. Bennett   Signed: R.C. Daniel
     R.K. Daniel
Reg: June 24, 1864

Page 394 - W.M. Tatum Deed 110 deed to Granville T. Tucker.
Both of Bedford County. Land in Bedford County the place on
which he now lives known as the place of Jacob Fisher, deceased,
and in the District No. 8, adjoining bank of Duck River,
formerly John Fisher's line. This 5 July 1864.
Reg: July 16, 1864   Signed: W.M. Tatum

Page 394 - Walter F. Sutton Deed 350+ acres to John T. Cannon.
I, Walter F. Sutton, bind myself to pay John T. Cannon. I have
an undivided interest in remainder to take effect and be united
with the possession after the death of my mother Mrs. Elizabeth
Osborne formerly Elizabeth Sutton who has a life estate in the
same in a tract of land in Bedford County and District No. 4,
known as my mother's dower tract and bounded by lands of John
Thomas, Joseph Freeman and N.C. Harris, and by lands of William
B. Sutton, by Gilchrist lands and Mrs. Louisa Terry's dower
tract, and by the Mullins' land and W.B. Sutton. This 12 July
1864.
Wit: W.W. Payne   Signed: W.F. Sutton
     J.C. Mash
Reg: August 29, 1864

Page 395 - W.C. Blanton Deed Lot to S.F. Smith. Land in Bedford
County and Village of Unionville, and containing 1 ½ acres and
bounded by J.R. Brown's lot. This October 24, 1859.
Wit: Wm. R. Burch   Signed: W.C. Blanton
     T.A. Knott
Reg: July 15, 1864

Page 396 - This Deed sold to George Woods. Lot of land on the
north side of the Rail Road near Shelbyville, adjoining a lot
sold by John P. Steele to J.G. Mitchell, and by a line Holland's
or Calhoun's line, and by lot claimed by Mrs. Wisener. Said
land containing 3 ¼ acres being the place formerly owned by John
P. Steele and where S. Hickerson now lives. This July 19, 1864.
Wit: Thos. H. Coldwell   Signed: James A. Moore

Wm. B. Brame
Reg: August 29, 1864

Page 396 - William Gosling Deed 2 acres to G.W. Thompson. Land being in the Town of Shelbyville and bounded by the street leading from Skull Camp Ford Road to street leading from the grave yard to the lot on which is located the Male High School Building known as Thompson Street in the south west by the above named street running from the grave yard to the Male High School lot, by lot owned by myself, and by Mrs. Rebecca Mathews and Thompson B. Ivy. This 29 December 1862.
Reg: 29 August 1864   Signed: Wm. Gosling

Page 397 - Joseph H. Thompson Deed to Jas. Russ. On 25 February 1860 J.P. Frazer, administrator of W.P. Temple, deceased, recovered a judgment against Samuel Woodfin and Samuel H. Thomas, and Moses Woodfin security. There being no personal property to be found in Bedford County levied on a tract of land adjoining the lands of P. Frazer and lands of __ Haile, John Gilmore, and lands of G. Miller being the place on which Sam'l Woodfin then lived. This 24 May 1864.
Reg: 29 August 1864   Signed: Jo. Thompson, Sheriff

Page 398 - Jo. Thompson Deed to Jas. Russ. On 17 March 1860 Wilson Wood Co. &C recovered a judgment against W.M. Boyce. No personal property to be found, he levied on the 16 January 1861 on all the right title and that W.M. Boyce had in a tract of land that he then lived upon, bounded by A. Boyce, John King, and by William Jackson. This 24 May 1864.
Reg: 29 August 1864   Signed: Jo. Thompson, Sheriff

Page 399 - Jo. Thompson Deed to Jas. Russ. On 17 March 1860 Wilson Wood &c recovered a judgment against W.M. Boyce, principal, and J. Boyce. No personal property to be found, levied on all right title and that W.M. Boyce had in a tract of land that said Boyce then lived upon being in District No. 10 of Bedford County as the property of said Boyce and bounded by A. Boyce, John King and by William Jackson, January 5, 1861. This 24 May 1864.
Reg: 29 July 1864   Signed: Jo. Thompson, Sheriff

Page 400 - Jo. Thompson, Sheriff, Deed to James Russ, Jr. on 5 January 1861 James A. Puckett recovered a judgment against J.T. McBride and W.C. Blythe before a Justice of the Peace of Rutherford County, Tennessee and filed in Bedford County on 24 January 1861. There being no personal property to be found on John T. McBride's undivided interest in a tract of land in District No. 9 Bedford County and bounded by lands of John Landrum. This 24 May 1864.
Reg: September 2, 1864   Signed: Jo. Thompson, Sheriff

Page 401 - Wm. T. Tune Deed to Peyton Coats and Thos. Nance. I have interest in 27 ¾ acres of land in Bedford County deeded to me by A.S. Adams 16 May 1864 and bounded by lands of Coat's line, and by lands of T.L. Tune. This 30 July 1864. Registered in Book DDD, page 401.
Reg: September 2, 1864   Signed: Wm. T. Tune

Page 401 - Blanton B. Burrow Deed to John Wilhoite. B.B. Blanton of Bedford County have sold unto John Wilhoite a tract of land in Bedford County and Civil District No. 22 on Goose Creek and containing about 90 acres, it being the land owned by Mary Wilhoite (my grand mother) at her death and said land sold to Isaiah Parker by Joseph H. Thompson and said Parker has executed his note with good securities. This 1 August 1864.
Reg: September 2, 1864   Signed: B.B. Blanton

Page 402 - N.J.C. Keller and wife Deed to Jas. M. Stevens. Nathan J.C. Keller and his wife Lovica Jane Keller of one part and James M. Stevens of other part. Lovica Jane Keller wife of Nathan J.C. Keller as the daughter of the late Francis H. Keller inherits and is the owner of an undivided interest of one eighth in the tract of land of which her father the late Francis H. Keller died seized and possessed and on which he resided at the time of his death and bounded by the lands of the late Joseph Couch, lands of Reuben and John Archa Couch, lands of the late William Pepper, and lands of Mrs. Barbbara Cortner and Myers' land, and containing 250 acres. This __ day of October 1863.
Reg: September 2, 1864   Signed: Lovica Jane Keller
                                    N.J.C. Keller

Page 404 - William T. Nash Deed to N.B. Parsons. Wm. T. Nash sold unto Newton B. Parsons land in Bedford County and District No. 8, containing 13 acres and bounded by Jane Nash and G.W> Parsons. This 5 January 1861.
Wit: Thomas T. Parsons   Signed: Wm. T. Nash
     G.W. Parsons
Reg: August 15, 1864

Page 404 - Elizabeth and Hannah Deed to John W. Parsons. We, Elizabeth and Hannah Dollarson have sold to J.W. Parsons land in Bedford County and District No. 8 and containing 40 acres and adjoining James Gregory, Anderson J. Goodrum, and the Fairfield Road. (no date)
Wit: G.W. Parsons   Signed: Elizabeth Dollarson
   N.B. Parsons   Hannah Dollarson

Page 405 - John C. Hicks Deed to Mary E. Stanfield and others. 7 April 186_. I as executor of Mary Norman, deceased, executed a bond for title to a tract of land to Alfred Campbell at public sale. Said Hix and said Campbell the later became the purchaser and whereas said Campbell paid me the purchase money for said land previous to his death, he being now dead. I as executor of said Mary Norman do hereby convey to Mary E. Stanfield wife of

W.W. Stanfield, Susan E. Sanders wife of H.H. Sanders, Caldonia Baker wife of James Baker, Martha J. Reager wife of M.H. Reager, and Sarah C. Campbell being the only children of said Alfred Campbell and his wife Sarah Campbell subject to the dower right of said land. Land in Bedford County and District No. 22 and bounded by L.S. Woods, T. Dean's corner, and by the old Butler tract. This August 2, 1864.
Reg: September 3, 1864   Signed: J.C. Hix

Page 406 - Jas. S. Turner Deed to W.P. Wood. Land in Bedford County and District No. 9 and bounded by the heirs of Elizabeth Williams, and by G.W. Bounds. This 14 November 1862.
Wit: W.J. Winsett   Signed: James S. Turner
     T.N.B. Turner
Reg: September 3, 1864

Page 407 - W.B.M. Brame Deed to Elzira McFarlin. This day have given a tract of land in Bedford County and District No. 7 and bounded by the lands of Moses Marshall and others, W.H. Wisener, by lands of said W.H. Wiseman and R.N. Jones, by lands of J.M. Brown and the Coats & Reed place, and by the lands of Thomas Holland, and containing 36 acres. Conveyed to Elzira McFarlin and her heirs. This 15 August 1864.
Reg: September 3, 1864   Signed: Wm. B.M. Brame

Page 407 - William Brown Deed to Louis Mankel. All that tract No. 108 lying south of the street running from the Square to the bridge on Duck River in the Town of Shelbyville, being the lot deeded to me by Chesly Williams and Wm. P. Cannon, executors of Gen. Robert Cannon, deceased, dated July 7, 1864. This 15 August 1864.
Reg: September 3, 1864   Signed: William Brown

Page 408 - Thomas J. Warren Deed to C.A. Warren. All my right title claim and interest (being the undivided one half thereof) in a house and lot in the Town of Shelbyville, on the north side of Depot Street and adjoining the original lot on the north edge of Depot Street. It being the house in which Warren & Co. formerly done business, now occupied by Elliott & Co. This 1 August 1864.
Reg: September 3, 1864   Signed: Thomas J. Warren

Page 409 - Thos. J. Warren Deed to Charles A. Warren. A house and lot in corporation of the Town of Shelbyville, Bedford County, and bounded by the east side of Brittain Street the intersection of the fence running with said street and the fence, by the line of J.H. McGrew lot, and the lot herein conveyed, about 250 feet to the street running west of the Baptist Church lot and of the grave yard, and by B.M. Tillman's garden lot. Containing one half acre. This 1 August 1864.
Reg: September 3, 1864   Signed: Thos. J. Warren

Page 409 - William Gosling Desd to Sallie Peacock.   I have sold
to Mrs. Sallie Peacock land in the west end of the Town of
Shelbyville, Bedford County, being composes of two parcels.   The
first purchased by Silas Bivins of John H. Oneal.   The second
purchased by said Bivins of G.W. Buchanan.   The first bounded by
the Shelbyville and Unionville Pike.   The second joins the above
lot and G.W. Buchanan lot, and by Oneal's corner.   Said land
being the place purchased by me of Wm.S. Jett on 23 September
1863.   This 25 July 1864.
Wit: Robt. C. White   Signed: Wm. Gosling
     D.S. Logan
Reg: September 3, 1864

Page 410 - Wm. B. Sutton Deed to W.W. Payne.   Conveyed land in
Bedford County and District No. 3 and containing 50 acres and
bounded by other lands of said Sutton, by lands of Anderson
Sharp and the McGuire tract, by the lands of A. Pruett, and
lands of the heirs of Daniel Gilchrist, deceased.
Wit: Thos. C. Whiteside   Signed: Wm. B. Sutton
     W.B. Armstrong
Reg: September 3, 1864

Page 411 - J.E. Gleaves Deed to Eakin & Cowan.   This 16 August
1864.   John E. Gleaves of Nashville, Davidson County, Tennessee.
Alexander Eakin and John W. Cowan of Bedford County.   By a
decree of court rendered at November Term 1859 in the cause of
David H.C. Spence and wife and other exparte.   John E. Gleaves,
Clerk & Master, did on 29 March 1860 sell at public auction the
real estate to Alexander Eakin and John W. Cowan.   Land in
Bedford County and in the Town of Shelbyville and being the
store house and lot at the corner of the Public Square and Depot
Street which formerly belonged to John Eakin, deceased, and
known in the plan of division by which the Shelbyville property
was sold in the case of Spence and wife and others exparte as
Lot No. 1.   Recorded in Minute Book H, page 262 Chancery Court
at Nashville.   The lot fronts on the Square and back to an
alley.
Recorded in Book DDD, pages 411 and 412.
Reg: September 3, 1864   Signed: J.E. Gleaves, C&M

Page 412 - Wm. J. Whitthorne Deed to Cummings & Coldwell.
Whereas Minos Cannon departed this life sometime in the month of
__ 185_ having first made and published his Last Will and
Testament by which he appointed Augustus Cannon his executor who
resigned and the undersigned was appointed by the Court of
Bedford County at the November Term 1855 the administrator of
said Minos Cannon, deceased.   By said land will his executor was
authorized to sell the real estate belonging to said Cannon,
lying in Bedford County in Bedford County.   Land to be sold to
highest bidder in Town of Shelbyville on 23 December 1855 where
James F. Cummings and Thomas M. Coldwell became the highest
bidder for a lot of ground in the Town of Shelbyville fronting
on Depot Street, and to the lot owned by S.D. Pannell at his
death.   Said lot being situated on the corner of Depot Street
and an alley running from the Dixon Academy lot, past lot and

West of the grave yard ground. On said lot there is a two story brick house which lot was sold off to said Coldwell and Cummings. This February 14, 1859.

Signed: William J. Whitthorne

Page 413 - James F. Cummings Deed to J.C. Coldwell, Jr. Land sold to Thomas M. Coldwell land in Bedford County and Civil District No. 7 and within the corporate limits of the Town of Shelbyville and bounded by Lot No. 3 the same being the corner of Water Street and the alley, and by Pannell lot. It being the lot and house occupied by Coldwell & Cummings. This 20 April 1858.
Reg: August 24, 1864   Signed: J.T. Cummings
                              J.C. Whitthorne

Page 414 - James F. Cummings Deed to Thos. M. Coldwell, Lot in Town of Shelbyville, Bedford County, situated on Depot Street, it being the same purchased by Coldwell & Cummings of Joseph F. Thompson. Deed recorded in Book TT, page 88. This 26 May 1860.
Reg: August 24, 1864   Signed: James F. Cummings

Page 414 - Jacob F. Thompson Deed to T.M. Coldwell & Cummings. Land in the said town, part of Lot No. ___ and bounded by Martin (alias Depot Street) at the junction of said street and the street which runs north and south by the Baptist Church. This 25 November 1856.
Reg: September 5, 1864   Signed: J.F. Thompson

Page 415 - William McGill Deed to Nancy C. Dean. Nancy C. Dean as guardian of the minor children Christopher C. Hix and Sarah E. Hix (by a former husband). Land in Bedford County and Civil District No. 23 on the waters of Little Flat Creek and bounded by lands of Wm. McGill, by lands belonging to the heirs of James McGill, deceased, and Robt. H. Terry, by lands of Barnett Stephens, and by land belonging to the heirs of Elijah Couch, deceased, the same being the lands heretofore purchased of Stephen Williams and Barnett Stephens for which I hold their deed, and containing 170 acres. This 11 July 1864.
Wit: Thos. H. Coldwell   Signed: Wm. McGill
     R.L. Landers
Reg: August 24, 1864

Page 416 - Thomas A. Sykes Deed to Wm. F. Capley. Land in Bedford County and District No. 11, it being the place whereon Rebecca Kener now lives and bounded by E. Batt's line, and containing about 12 acres and 15/160. This July 26, 1864.
Reg: September 5, 1864   Signed: Thomas A. Sikes

Page 416 - Newton A. Cummings Deed to Nancy J. Cummings. Contract made between Newton J. Cummings and Nancy J. Cummings, and James M. Buckaloo that a marriage contract executed by and between the parties of the first part and second part dated June

22, 1843 and registered in Bedford County. All the property of Nancy J. Cummings was then the owner vested for her own separate use &c and at her own disposal. And the Bill of Sale dated August 7, 1846Nancy J. Cummings the owner of a negro girl named Martha and bill registered in Bedford County. And that by deed from Moses Marshall dated 23 January 1855 Nancy J. Cummings became the owner of 20 acres adjoining the home place. Note: a very long document. This 24 August 1864.
Reg: September 8, 1864   Signed: N.A. Cummings
                                    N.J. Cummings
                                    Jas. M. Buckaloo

Page 418 - M.P. Gentry Trust Deed to J.N. Jones. September 23, 1863. Property, viz, one negro man named Dick and his wife Eliza, and farming tools &c, one farm wagon, yoke of oxen &c, all the horses now on my farm, one fine stallion named Bedford Chief now in the possession of J.M. Wisener of Franklin County, Tennessee, also several other items listed in original document.
Reg: September 5, 1864   Signed: M.P. Gentry

Page 420 - Wm. S. Jett Deed to Mrs. M.B. Knott. Land in Bedford County and District No. 7, containing 2 acres and adjoining Mrs. Martha Gentry's corner, on the turnpike road leading to Murfreesboro, and by Wm. G. Cowan's line. Mariah B. Knott and her heirs &c. This 31 December 1863.
Wit: Wm. J. Whitthorne   Signed: Wm, S. Jett
     Wm. Gosling
Reg: September 6, 1864

Page 421 - John W. Thompson Mortgage to John P. Steele. Land in Bedford County and District No. 8 and bounded by Thos. H. Coldwell, by A. Claxton, by Wm. Smith, and by N. Thompson, Sr., and known by the name of Sam'l A. Thompson's land, and containing about 93 acres. This September 14, 1864.
Reg: September 14, 1864   Signed: Jno. H. Thompson

Page 421 - Thos. J. Ladd Deed of Gift $600 to Barbara A. Ladd. For love and affection I have for my wife Barbara A. Ladd, both of Bedford County. I have conveyed unto her the sum of $600 out of my interest in the estate of my deceased father Wm. H. Ladd now in the hands of his administrator Wm. H. Ladd, Jr. and the Clerk of the Chancery Court at Franklin or my former guardian James M. Patterson of Marshall County any one of who is authorized to pay to her. This 6 August 1864.
Wit: R.A. Coldwell   Signed: Thomas J. Ladd
     W.W. Gunter
Reg: September 20, 1864

Page 422 - Robt. S. Dwiggins Trust Deed to Wm. Campbell. Personal property, to wit, cows, oxens, heifers and other items listed in original document. This 20 September 1864.
Reg: September 23, 1864   Signed: R.S. Dwiggins

Page 423 - Arch G. Moore Deed Lot in C.W. (Camp White) to James A. Moore. House and lot in that part of the Town of Shelbyville known as Camp White, Bedford County and District No. 7 being the house and lot that John A. Moore purchased of John C. Akin and wife America Akin and that I purchased of said John A. Moore and bounded by Cannon Street, by a lot owned by James M. Elliott, by James Wortham's vacant lot, and by Camp Street. Containing about one acre. This 4 October 1864.
Reg: October 6, 1864   Signed: Arch. G. Moore

Page 423 - James A. Moore Deed Lot in C.W. (Camp White) to Louis Mankel. House and lot in the Town of Shelbyville known as Camp White, Bedford County and District No. 7, being the house and lot that John A. Moore purchased of John C. Akin and wife America Akin and that A.G. Moore purchased of said John A. Moore and that I purchased of said A.G. Moore and bounded by Cannon Street, by a lot owned by James M. Elliott, and by James Wortham's vacant lot. This 4 October 1864.
Reg: October 4, 1864   Signed: James A. Moore

Page 424 - R.S. Brown and wife Deed 82 acres to Sargent H. Price. R.S. Brown and wife Martha Brown have sold unto Sargent H. Price land in Bedford County and Civil District No. 18 on the waters of Little Sinking Creek and bounded by Lot No. 6 formerly Thomas Moore's corner, and by lands formerly owned by Andrew Nail. This 11 October 1864.
Wit: Thos. H. Coldwell   Signed: Martha J. Brown
Reg: October 19, 1864   R.S. Brown

Page 425 - Sargent H. Price Deed 82 acres to Lee Martin. Land in Bedford County and Civil District No. 18 on the waters of Little Sinking Creek and bounded by Lot No. 6 formerly Thomas Moore's corner, and by lands formerly owned by Andrew Nail, it being part of the land granted to James Johnson and conveyed to Logan Henderson, by him to John Ray and he to Stephen Freeman, and by his children to S.H. Price. This 11 October 1864.
Wit: Thos. H. Coldwell   Signed: S.H. Price
     James A. Moore
Reg: October 19, 1864

Page 425 - Thomas J. Ogilvie Deed 27 acres to James H. Ogilvie. Land in Bedford County and District No. 5 and bounded by Lot No. __, by the line of the survey, and by Lot No. 1. This 28 November 1864.
Reg: November 5, 1864   Signed: Thos. J. Ogilvie

Page 426 - Thomas J. Ogilvie Deed 54 acres to Thomas B. Marks. Land in Bedford County and Civil District No. __ and bounded by lands of Joseph R. McKinley, by lands of Wm. K. Ransom, by a public road, and the lands of J.B. Booth, and lands of said Booth and J.R. McKinley. This 28 October 1864.
Reg: November 7, 1864   Signed: Thos. J. Ogilvie

Page 426 - J.R. Brown and J.M. Moore Deed to Mary A. Klien. Land in Bedford County and Civil District No. 11 and near the Village of Unionville and bounded by the rock in Blanton's south boundary line, by the road in Wilson's west boundary line, and by Doctor Moore's line. Containing 1 acre and 152 poles. This April 20, 1863.
Wit: E.C. Moore   Signed: J.R. Brown
     E. Blanton   J.M. Moore
Reg: November 17, 1864(4?)

Page 427 - Robert Williams Deed 130 acres to C.W. Powell. Land in Bedford County and bounded by Rock Creek, This 12 November 1864.
Wit: D.J. Low   Signed: Robert Williams
Reg: November 17, 1864

Page 428 - Francis V. Story Trust Deed to R.H. Lewis. Said Story old to Robert H. Lewis personal property, one wagon and harness, two sofas, one table, hat rack, and several other items listed in original document. This 14 November 1864.
Reg: November 17, 1864   Signed: F.V. Story

Page 429 - James D. Burrow Deed 6 acres to B.A. Burrow, Land in the waters of Flat Creek and bounded by lands of B.A. Burrow, Harris Austin, Catharine Raney, and lands of Mary Burrow. This November 8, 1864.
Wit: John Wilhoite   Signed: James D. Burrow
     J.J. Burrow
Reg: November 17, 1864

Page 429 - G.W. Gardner and Mike Shofner Title Bond 100 acres to Roane & Coble. Said Gardner and Shofner is firmly bound to Thomas J. Roane and N.B. Coble. Said George W. Gardner sold to Roane & Coble land in Bedford County and District No. 25 and bounded by S.B. Gordon and by J.R. Burrow. This 11 November 1864.
Reg: November 18, 1864   Signed: G.W. Gardner
                                      Mike Shofner

Page 430 - J.W. Greer Deed to R.S. Brown. Land in Bedford County and Civil District No. 20 and bounded by lands of John W. Greer, John Cotner, John Williams, John S. Brown, and M.P. Gentry, and containing about 85 acres. It being the same place on which Stephen Freeman resided at his death, two undivided interest is said land being one half or two undivided interest is said land or so much as is not conveyed to the widow dower and in the part conveyed by widow's dower, the two undivided interest or half of said dower at her death. This 3 April 1864.
Reg: November 18, 1864   Signed: J.W. Greer

Page 430 - B.F. Sikes Deed 33 acres to W.H. Locke. Land in Bedford County and Civil District No.11 and bounded by A.C.

Potts, by Potts & Thompson, and T(P).H. Thompson & Stephens, being the same as sold at Sheriff sale as property of T(P). F. King and bought by William Brown. This April 18, 1863.
Wit: R.W. Locke   Signed: B.F. Sikes
     Henry Stevens
Reg: November 18, 1864

Page 431 - N.B. Hart Deed 136+ acres to John H. Rice. Land in Bedford County and District No. 6 and adjoining A. Vannoy, Phifer's old corner, Clardy's corner, J. Tune's corner, and to the center of Hurricane Creek. This 17 November 1864.
Reg: November 18, 1864   Signed: N.B. Hart

Page 432 - Moses B. Wadley Deed 93 acres to W.C. Alexander. Land in Bedford County and District No. 6 and bounded by lands of John Barber, lands of Wm. Orr, lands of William J. Chunn and Mrs. Mallard, and by lands of Mrs. Sarah Mallard. Land being land from Thomas Knott and S.B. Knott dated May 28, 1859, except about 26 acres of said tract heretofore sold and conveyed by deed to Mrs. Sally Mallard. This 19 November 1864.
Reg: November 19, 1864   Signed: Moses B. Wadley

Page 432 - Chancery Court Decree 114+ acres to Sallie Phillips. B.B. Bomar and Wm. Bomar VS James H. Bomar and others - Decree. 9 March 1861. Report of the Commissioners as to the division of the land of Elijah Bomar, deceased, and it appearing that Lot No. 8 in said division was allotted to Sally Phillips. It is further ordered that all the right title claim and which B.B. Bomar and other legatees of Elijah Bomar, deceased, have in and to Lot No. 8 be divested of them and vested in Sallie Phillips. Lot No. 8 bounded by the original tract, by Lot No. 7, and by Lot No. 6. Containing 114 acres and 120 poles.
Reg: November 24, 1864   Signed: Wm. J. Whitthorne, C&M

Page 433 - R.P. Ransom Deed __ acres to David A. Vaughn. Land in Bedford County and Civil District No. 4 and adjoining and being on the public road running from Shelbyville to Fairfield, to the center of Wartrace, and by Anderson Creek, and a line between myself and Martin Hancock to the Rail Road including a small purchase of some 7 or 8 acres made by T.B. Ivie of said Hancock, and by E. Ewing. Containing 161 acres. This 25 July 1863.
Wit: Thos. H. Fletcher   Signed: Richard P. Ransom
     B.D. Fletcher
Reg: November 26, 1864

Page 434 - J.A. McLain & G.W. McLain Co-partnership Agreement. J.A. McLain and G.W. McLain are partners in a wool carding machine which is on J.A. McLain's land, the work in building the house and putting up the machinery was done by us jointly. Now for safety of G.W. McLain it is agreed that said G.W. McLain is to have the privilege of running the same on my land at the place where it is now located for fifteen years and to remove

his half of the same whenever he desires to do so. He nor the firm is to pay rent as long as he runs the wool factory &c. This 25 November 1864.
Reg: Nov 25, 1864   Signed: J.A. McLain
                                    G.W. McLain

Page 435 - John P. Bullock Power of Attorney to Thomas Bullock. John P. Bullock of Christian County, Kentucky and grandson of Jackson Liles and Betty E. Liles his wife who lived in Bedford County, did appoint Thomas Bullock of Christian County, Kentucky my true and lawful attorney in fact to receive for me any money or property which is or may be due or coming to me from the estate of said Jackson Liles or Betsey E. Liles. This 3 November 1864.
Wit: H.R. Littell   Signed: John P. Bullock
     A.H. Clark
Reg: December 23, 1864

Page 436 - A.L. Adams Deed 336+ acres to B.K. Coble. Land in Bedford County and Civil District No. 6 and adjoining in the center of the Shelbyville and Murfreesboro Turnpike Road, Peyton Coat's corner, to the center of the Middleton road, and a corner of the school land tract. Containing 295 acres and 78 poles being the same tract deeded to me by Jno. H. Oneal and C.T. Philpott. The second tract bounded by the Middleton Road, and by said Oneal. Containing 41 acres surveyed by C.S. Dudley. The whole containing 336 acres and 78 poles. The 41 acre tract I purchased of Jno. H. Oneal, C.T. Philpott and Alex. Philpott. This 3 January 1865.
Reg: January 5, 1865   Signed: A.L. Adams

Page 436 - Robert Dennis Deed to George W. Thompson. Land near the Town of shelbyville containing __ acres it being a part of the land known as the Wilson Coats' tract and the same purchased by me at a sale made by Joseph H. Thompson a special commissioner and upon which Thomas Dalton and others now reside. Survey of land made by Wm. Galbreath and by me purchased. This 13 November 1864.
Reg: January 5, 1865   Signed: Robert Dennis

Page 437 - Rich'd Warner and Margaret Morris Deed 100 acres to W.W. Hopkins. We, Richard Warner and Margaret Morris, administrators of Allen Morris, deceased, and of Marshall County, Tennessee, have sold to William W. Hopkins of Bedford County a tract of land in Bedford County and Civil District No. 11 and adjoining William Wilson's tract, which tract of land we, Richard Warner and Margaret Morris, did on 6 June 1863 by our agent buy at public sale of A. Wilson, Trustee of W.G. Morris and Wilson made us a deed to same on 16 March 1864. This 24 November 1864.
Wit: G.W. Brown   Signed: Richard Warner
    M.B. Fisher   Margaret Morris, admrs. Of
                            Allen Morris

Page 438 - James H. Graham Deed Lot in Camp White to E.M. Lacey. Land near the Town of Shelbyville and what is known as Camp White and bounded by Cannon Street on the west, and containing about three fourth of an acre, it being known as the Gaven lot purchased by me at Sheriff's sale. This 7 January 1865.
Reg: January 9, 1865   Signed: James H. Graham

Page 438 - Nancy J. Cummings Deed to Lucy Ann Edde. Land in Bedford County and District No. 7 and bounded by J.W. Cowan, and center of the McMinnville Road, and containing 108 acres. This 16 January 1865.
Reg: January 28, 1865   Signed: Nancy Jane Cummings

Page 439 - Jos. H. Thomas and wife Power of Attorney to Bailey W. Blessing. We, Joseph H. Thomas and Minerva Jane Thompson appointed our friend and relation Bailey W. Blessing as our attorney in fact to sell and convey all out interest in the proceeds of the sale of the slaves belonging to the estate of James Coats, and also our interest in the proceeds of a tract of land belonging to said estate known as the home place. This 26 November 1864.
Wit: Thomas Thomas   Signed: Joseph H. Thomas
     Sam D. Nichols   Minerva J. Thomas
Reg: February 6, 1865

Page 440 - Joseph H. Thomas and wife Deed to J.B. McAdams. Joseph H. Thomas and Minerva J. Thomas sold unto J.B. McAdams all out interest to the fund arising from the sale of the land of James Coats, deceased, which said land was sold by J.H.C. Scales and purchased by said McAdams. It being the same place on which said Coats resided at the time of his death and on which said McAdams now reside. This 16 January 1865.
Reg: February 6, 1865   Signed: J.H. Thomas
                                       Minerva J. Thomas

Page 440 - Thos. W. Jordan Deed Lot to J.J. Mankin. This 18 January 1865. Both of Bedford County. T.W. Jordan sold unto J.J. Mankin on a claim against W.G. Osborne now in the hands of William H. Wisener. Said Jordan has sold unto J.J. Mankin one house and lot being in the Town of Shelbyville, Bedford County, and bounded by the north edge of Scull Camp Road. Containing 1 ½ acres. This 18 January 1865.
Reg: February 7, 1865   Signed: T.W. Jordan

Page 441 - J.G. Barksdale Deed 267+ acres to Geo. W. Thompson. Both of Bedford County and Civil District No. 7, adjoining the lands of the late John Eakin, Moses Marshall and Wm.H. Wisener. Beginning at the south side of Air Creek where it run in 1841 and now between the old bed of said creek and where the main current now runs being the south east corner of the M(illegible) Nelson tract which was sold to me by Robert Moffett on 15 October 1841, by the McMinnville Road, near the mouth of the lane being a corner of the Eakin tract, and in Henry Brown's

line, and by Matthews' tract now owned by William J. Whitthorne, and by Daugherty tract, by McCuistion's tract, Nathan Ivy &c. Note: A long document. This 20 June 1865.
Wit: W.H. Wisener, Sr.   Signed: J.G. Barksdale
    W.H. Wisener, Jr.   J.G. Barksdale

Page 443 - John M. Miller, admr. Deed 384+ acres to W.G. Miller. J.M. Miller, administrator &c of Isaac J. Miller, deceased, conveyed a tract of land to William G. Miller a tract of land in Bedford County and District No. 4, and bounded by a lane of Martin Hancock, by John Thomas, by the east bank of Wartrace Creek, and by Burrel Featherston's corner. This 29 September 1863.
Reg: February 23, 1865   Signed: John M. Miller, admr. With
                       Will annexed of
                       Isaac J. Miller, dec'd.

Page 443 - Robbert Patton Title Bond 131+ acres to Phillip Cartright. This ___ February 1865. For a tract of land bounded by the center of Clems Creek, Thos. B. Allison's corner, to center of a well, by Widow King's corner, and by A. Wilson.
Reg: February 23, 1865   Signed: R.J. Patton

Page 444 - John M. Barber Deed 1 acre to William C. Alexander. This 3 February 1865. Both of Bedford County and Civil District No. 6 and adjoining east of the spring, and the creek, and to the mouth of Spring Creek.
Reg: February 25, 1865   Signed: J.M. Barber

Page 445 - Jno. P. Hutton and Jo. D. Wilhoite, Extrs. Deed 550 acres to Wm. S. Jett. Said executors of the Last Will and Testament of Robert Clark, deceased, we have sold unto William S. Jett a tract of land being in District No. 5 of Bedford County and adjoining in the center of the creek, and to a spring. This 1 July 1864.
Reg: February 25, 1865   Signed: John P. Hutton
                       Jo. D. Wilhoite, Extrs of
                       Robert Clark, deceased

Page 445 - William Gosling Lease for 15 years to Milroy, Miller & Co. This 25 February 1865. William Gosling of Bedford County and J.W. Milroy, W.H. Miller, partners under the name of Milroy, Miller & Co. for sale and only purpose of mining and excavating petroleum, coal, rock or carbon oil or other valuable minerals &c. all that tract of land in Bedford County and bounded to wit, to Civil District No. 3 and three miles north of the Town of Shelbyville, adjoining lands of Dan. C. Shriver, lands of George W. Thompson formerly owned by James G. Barksdale, by lands of William H. Wisener, and lands of George W. Thompson and Henry Brown. Containing 397 acres and land is known as the Horse Mountain Tract.
Wit: Thos. H. Coldwell   Signed: Wm. Gosling
Reg: February 28, 1865   J.W. Milroy

Page 447 - Samuel M. Logan and Robert Logan, Agreement. S.M. Logan conveyed to said Robert Logan two billiard tables, balls, stick and other articles belonging to said tables and also a lot of bar furniture being the same used by said S.M. Logan in this Tippling Saloon in Shelbyville such as bottles, glasses &c. This February 7, 1865.
Reg: February 28, 1865   Signed: S.M. Logan
                                  Robert Logan

Page 447 - Elisha W. & Evander Hendrix Deed 64+ acres to Joseph Haynes. This 25 October 1864 between Elisha W. Hendrix and Evander W. Hendrix of Christian County, Kentucky and Joseph Haynes of Bedford County and bounded by John Marices(?), Thomas Lamb, Pope & Haynes, and Elliott's line.
Reg: March 1, 1865   Signed: Elisha W. Hendrix
                                  Evander W. Hendrix

Page 448 - John P. Steele and others Deed 10 acres to Thos. and Henry Troop. James Deery departed this life this __ day of __ 185_. Will proven in Bedford County and directing a sale of land in Bedford County and District No. 7 on the north bank of Duck River and adjoining a corner of Alexander old tract and the factory tract. John P. Steele, administrator as aforesaid and Alexander Eakin and wife Margaret, W.B.M. Brame and wife Mary Ann, and G.P. Baskett and wife Eliza J., and R.D. Deery the only children of said James Deery, deceased.
Reg: March 1, 1865   Signed: John P. Steele
                                  Alex. Eakin
                                  G.P. Baskett
                                  Wm. B.M. Brame
                                  R.D. Deery
                                  Margaret Eakin
                                  Mary A. Brame
                                  Eliza J. Baskett

Page 449 - John W. Thompson Deed 23 acres to Wm. S. Jett. Land in Bedford County and District No. 7 and bounded by lands of J.T. Cannon, lands of Newcom Thompson, Sr., by the grave yard, and by Warner's Mill. This 16 February 1865.
Reg: March 1, 1865   Signed: Jno. W. Thompson

Page 449 - N. Thompson, Sr. Deed 5 acres to Wm. S. Jett. Land in Bedford County and District No. 7 and bounded by lands conveyed by John W. Thompson to W.S. Jett, land formerly owned by Jno. Dalton, by a street leading west, and by the lands of J.T. Cannon. It being the three half of an acre tract conveyed to Newcomb Thompson, Sr. by John W. Thompson on 25 March 1857. This 17 February 1865.
Reg: March 2, 1865   Signed: N. Thompson, Sr.

Page 450 - William Brown Deed Lot to J.T. Johnson. Land on
Martin Street in Shelbyville, Bedford County, and bounded by the
west side of the street, a framed house on it, it being the
house that the cannon ball passed through. The place or lot I
deeded to J.T. Johnson in 1863 but agent Wm. T. Zollicofer
having the deed entrusted in his hands to have it recorded
failed on his part to do so were recorded and lost. I give
another in the place of it. This 30 May 1863.
This 30 May 1863.
Reg: March 2, 1865   Signed: William Brown

Page 450 - Robert Galbraith Deed Lot to Lewis & English. Land
sold to Robert H. Lewis and P.S. English a lot in Town of
Shelbyville and District No. 7 of Bedford County and bounded by
Richard Foreman, an alley leading from the little spring to ___
street in front or east of the property of m. Galbraith, Sr., a
street leading west from the Big Spring, and by Thomas Bennett's
corner and Foreman's corner. Lot known as Lot No. 112. This 27
February 1865.
Wit: H.H. Holt   Signed: Robt. Galbraith
     Wm. E. Galbraith
Reg: March 3, 1865

Page 451 - Robert Galbraith Deed Lot to Lewis & English. Robert
Galbraith sold to Robt. H. Lewis and P.S. English a lot in the
Town of Shelbyville and District No. 7, Bedford County and
adjoins Lot No. __, and by Martin Street. This 27 February
1865.
Wit: H.H. Holt   Signed: Robt. Galbraith
     Wm. E. Galbraith
Reg: March 3, 1865

Page 451 - J.J. Shriver Deed 225 acres to John Thomas. Land in
Bedford County and District No. 4 and bounded by J.H. Freeman,
by A. Webb, and Wm. Murphree, and by J.W. Cone, J. Dwyer and
others, and by E. Sutton. This 28 November 1862.
Wit: E.A. Blanton   Signed: J.J. Shriver
     J.A. Erwin
Reg: March 3, 1865

Page 452 - J.J. Shriver Title Bond to Joseph H. Freeman. J.J.
Shriver is bound to J.H. Freeman and executed to me a tract of
land in Bedford County and District No. 4 and bounded by John
Hutton, J.H. Freeman, and Henry Cone's corner. This 1 December
1860.
Wit: Jno. T. Cannon   Signed: J.J. Shriver
     John C. Mash
Reg: March 4, 1865

Page 452 - J.J. Shriver Deed 100 acres to Joseph H. Freeman.
Land in Bedford County and District No. 4 and bounded by John
Sutton, Freeman's corner, and George Cone's corner. This March
1, 1865. Note: Plat of land on page 453.

Wit: John T. Cannon   Signed: J.J. Shriver
     John C. Mash
Reg: March 4, 1865

Page 453 - Robert B. Ruth Deed Lot to W.N. Gwinn. Robert B.
Ruth of Nashville, Tennessee sold to W.N. Gwinn of Shelbyville a
tract of land in Bedford County and Civil District No. 7 and in
the corporate limits of the Town of Shelbyville and bounded by
George W. Ruth's lot on Church Street. This 25 February 1865.
Reg: March 4, 1865   Signed: R.B. Ruth

Page 454 - George W. Greer Deed 86+ acres to Thomas Kimmons.
Land in Bedford County and District No. 18 and bounded by
William Kimmons. This 27 February 1865.
Reg: March 4, 1865   Signed: G.W. Greer

Page 455 - Geo. W. Story Deed 49 acres to James Story. Land in
Bedford County and District No. 18 and bounded by the Burkeen
tract. Said tract the same conveyed to me by deed from Minerva
Angeline Arnold and is registered in Book DDD, page 104. This
February 25, 1865.
Reg: March 6, 1865   Signed: G.W. Story

Page 455 - C.P. Houston and others Deed 131 acres to Joseph R.
McKinley. Land in Bedford County on the waters of the North
Fork and bounded by lands of John L. Cooper, by lands of the
heirs of L. Thompson, by W.R. Ransom, and by Joseph R. McKinley.
This 19 July 1864.
Reg: March 7, 1865   Signed: Jane M. Houston
                                    C.P. Houston

Page 456 - A.H. Coffey Deed Lot in Wartrace to John W. Tilford.
Lot in the Town of Wartrace, Civil District No. 3 and bounded by
the north side of Nob Creek Turnpike, and an alley, and by
Tilford's livery stable. This 28 November 1859.
Wit: Wm'son Haggard   Signed: A.H. Coffey
     J.M. Townsend
Reg: March 9, 1865

Page 457 - John W. Tilford Deed 2 Lots in Wartrace to W.R.
Tinsley. Lots in Village of Wartrace and bounded by the north
side of Knob Creek Turnpike, by a street, and by the livery
stable lot. Also the lot known as the livery stable lot. This
27 August 1864.
Reg: March 17, 1865   Signed: J.W. Tilford

Page 457 - A.M. Trollinger Deed Lot in Shelbyville to W.R.
Jewill. Said Trollinger has sold to said Jewill a tract of land
in the Town of Shelbyville and bounded by the lot on which James
H. Neill resides, and by lot of R.P. ___. This 2 January 1865.
Reg: March 27, 1865   Signed: A.M. Trollinger

Page 458 - Chesley Williams and Wm. P. Cannon, Executors of Gen. Robert Cannon. Deed 19 acres to G.W. Thompson. Gen. Robert Cannon, late of Bedford County made his Last Will and Testament and afterwards departed this life which will was after his death at the April Term 1865 duly proven &c. Robert Cannon appointed various persons therein named executors, among them was Chesley Williams and William P. Cannon. The executors was authorized to sell certain real estate (three lots) purchased at the sale of landed estate of Sterling Newsom. Executors conveyed two lots bounded in the Rowesville Road, by Newsom's tract, and to the Mill Road, and to corner between Doak and Cannon. This 7 July 1864.

Reg: March 27, 1865   Signed: Chesley Williams
                                      Wm. P. Cannon, Exrs.

Page 459 - Chesley Williams and Wm. P. Cannon, Executors of Robt. Cannon, deceased, Deed to G.W. Thompson for 25 acres. Land near James Bomar's on the Rowesville Road east of Shelbyville in Bedford County and being in four tracts, Nos. 1, 2, 3, & 4, containing 12 ½ acres. Lot No. 1 contains 12 ½ acres and 15 poles. Lots No. 3 & 4 is bounded on the Rowesville Road south east corner of Lot No. 2 conveyed to Mrs. L.S. Moody, by Woods' lot tract, west with said road 50 poles to include Lots 3 & 4 and containing 25 acres. This 7 July 18??.

Reg: March 27, 1865   Signed: Chesley Williams
                                      Wm. P. Cannon, Exrs.

Page 461 - William Brown Deed George W. Thompson. Land in the Town of Shelbyville and on the west side of Martin Street and bounded by a corner of the Odd Fellows Hall, and by a small brick house and owned by said G.W. Thompson. This 20 January 1865.

Reg: March 28, 1865   Signed: William Brown

Page 461 - Francis J. Thompson wife of Newcomb Thompson, 3rd, being a part of the proceeds of her interest in the real estate of her late father James Dixon. I, George W. Thompson have this day sold unto Francis J. Thompson a tract of land in Bedford County and District No. 7 and bounded by the division corner between S. Doak, Gen. R. Cannon, by the Rowesville Road, and a road leading to the mill. Containing 15 acres and 40 poles. The second tract bounded by the Rowesville Road and east of Lot No. 2, land conveyed to Mrs. T.L. Moody, and by Wood's lot tract. Containing 25 acres. This 7 March 1865.

Reg: March 28, 1865   Signed: G.W. Thompson

Page 462 - W.J. Whitthorne to Deed or Decree to Jas. H. Bomar. W.B. Bomar and W. Bomar, executors &c, Decree, and James H. Bomar. 9 March 1861. Reports of the division of the lands of Elijah Bomar, deceased. Lands allotted to James H. Bomar Lot No. 1 and adjoining the original tract, line of Lot No. 7, and by Peggy Ault's line. Containing 95 acres and 7 poles. This 20 January 1865.

Reg: March 28, 1865   Signed: William J. Whitthorne, C&M

Page 463 - R.W. Couch Deed to N.J.C. Keller. 2 February 1865. Reuben W. Couch sold unto Nathan J.C. Keller, both of Bedford County, land in Bedford County and bounded by land of William Cully and L.W. Hall, and on Cully Branch, and 100 ½ poles to a water pen. Containing 131 acres and 99/160 poles.
Wit: John Q. Davidson   Signed: R.W. Couch
Reg: March 28, 1865

Page 464 - N.J.C. Keller Deed to R.W. Couch. Nathan J.C. Keller sold to Reuben W. Couch, both of Bedford County, land containing 92 ¾ acres and 26 poles, being in Bedford County and on the ridge between the waters of the Garrison and the Barren Fork of Duck River, and beginning near a running spring in the head of Bear Hollow which is a corner of a tract belonging to the heirs of Edwin Hord, deceased, and corner of Mrs. Eliza Davidson tract of land, and by Fergus Hall's line. This February 2, 1865.
Wit: John Q. Davidson   Signed: N.J.C. Keller
Reg: March 28, 1865

Page 465 - William J. Whitthorne Deed to B.B. Bomar Lot No. 5. W.B. Bomar and William Bomar, executors &c. VS James H. Bomar - Decree. The division of the lands of Elijah Bomar, deceased, allotted to B.B. Bomar Lot No. 5 and adjoining J.W. Norville, Lot No. 4, and the original tract. This 21 February 1865.
Reg: March 28, 1865   Signed: William J. Whitthorne, C&M

Page 465 - W.B. Bomar and Wm. Bomar, Exrs. VS James H. Bomar and others - Decree. The division of the lands of Elijah Bomar, deceased. Land allotted to Elisha D. Bomar Lot No. 6 and adjoining Lot No. 5. This 30 January 1865.
Reg: March 29, 1865   Signed: William J. Whitthorne, C&M

Page 466 - George Smith of Bedford County sold unto Jesse W. Batton, William M. Ray, and William M. Robinson (under the firm of Batton & CO.) J.W. Batton of Bedford County being one half purchaser and W.M. Ray of Haywood County, W.M. Robinson being each one fourth purchaser of a tract of land in Bedford County and District No. 11 on east bank of Duck River and known as Pardee & White's Mills, and adjoining Duck River. Containing 3 acres and 78 poles. This 22 February 1862.
Wit: A.F. Smith   Signed: George Smith
     J.H. Freeman
Reg: March 29, 1865

Page 467 - William S. Jett Deed to J.W. Cowan. I have sold to John W. Cowan one share of the capital stock in the manufacturing company of Wm. Gosling and is engaged in manufacturing thread and cloth in their two factories on Duck River, one at Shelbyville, the other about two miles below, including grist mills, together with all lands, with all machinery, water power &c. This December 29, 1863.
Wit: Edm'd Cooper   Signed: Wm. S. Jett
     N. Thompson, 2nd

Reg: March 29, 1865

Page 467 - Wm. S. Jett Deed to Alex. Eakin and J.W. Cowan. For 5 ½ shares of the capital stock in the manufacturing company of William Gosling & Co. engaged in manufacturing thread and cloth in their two factories on Duck River, one at Shelbyville, the other about two miles below including grist mill, together with all lands, houses, and water power &c. Said company in the Town of Shelbyville. This 30 December 1863.
Wit: Edm'd Cooper   Signed: Wm. S. Jett
Reg: March 29, 1865

Page 468 - A.M. Webb and N.J. Webb Deed to James H. Ogilvie. Anderson M. Webb and wife Nancy J. Webb sold unto James H. Ogilvie land in Bedford County and District No. 5 and bounded by Lot No. 3, by B.F. Whitworth, and by the widow's dower. It being Lot No. 4 of the lands belonging to the estate of James Ogilvie, deceased. This 10 March 1864.
Reg: March 29, 1865   Signed: A.M. Webb
                                       N.J. Webb

Page 469 - James Finch Deed to Robt. S. Clark. Land in Bedford County and District No. 2 and bounded by John S. Davis, lands of Osborne & Anderson, lands of John A. Couch and Douglass, and by lands of Singleton's heirs. This 16 November 1864.
Reg: March 29, 1865   Signed: James Finch

Page 470 - N. Thompson 3rd and wife Frances J. Deed to Jas. B. Driver. Newcomb Thompson,3rd sold to James B. Dixon real estate in Bedford County and District No. 21 and bounded by the lands of Andrew Reid and the mill place formerly owned by Holt, by lands of M.L. Dismukes, and the heirs of Robert Dixon, and by lands of J.N. Dunaway and Jas. C. Martin. Containing about 400 acres. This 14 March 1865.
Reg: March 30, 1865   Signed: N. Thompson
                                Frances J. Thompson

471 - William J. Whitthorne Deed to William Gosling. Two tracts of land in Bedford County and Civil District No. 3. The first tract adjoining J.G. Barksdale and the top of another tract sold to him, and containing 200 acres, it being the same I purchased of William S. Jett. The other tract adjoining the above tract on the east and bounded by lands of Wm. H. Wisener and Mrs. Ed Green, by lands of D.C. Shriver and Harmon's heirs, and by lands of Moses Nelson and others. Containing 197 acres and is the same tract I purchased of Wm. S. Jett. This 11 January 1865.
Reg: March 30, 1865   Signed: William J. Whitthorne

Page 471 - G.W. Thompson Deed Chasen Lodge No. 11 (I.O.F.). I habe this day sold unto Chasen Friends Lodge No. 11. Independent Order of Odd Fellows located in the Town of Shelbyville working under a charter issued to them from the

Right Worthy Grand Lodge of the State of Tennessee Independent Order of Odd Fellows a tract of land in Bedford County and Civil District No. 7 and in the Town of Shelbyville and bounded by a building now owned by said Lodge as a Lodge Room on the west side of Martin Street, by west edge of Market Street, by a brick office owned by me, and by an alley between said Lodge and J.D. Wilhoite's property. This 16 March 1865.
Wit: Thos. H. Coldwell   Signed: George W. Thompson
     Absalom Mosley
Reg: March 30, 1865

Page 472 - A.M. Webb Deed to James R. Miller. Land in Bedford County and District No. 5 and bounded by B.F. Smalling, and containing 80 acres and 54 poles. This 21 November 1864.
Wit: A.M. McElroy   Signed: A.M. Webb
     L.S. Nichols
Reg: March 30, 1865

Page 473 - Thos. Holland, Sr. Deed to Henry Sipsy. Land in Bedford County and in the Town of Shelbyville and bounded by Lot No. 6 in the Town of Shelbyville, and by Main Street. This September 15, 1864.
Reg: March 30, 1865   Signed: Thomas Holland, Sr.

Page 474 - Anderson M. Webb Deed to John P. Hutton. Land in Bedford County and District No. 5 and bounded by the turnpike road, Charles F. Sutton's corner formerly A.L. Adams' corner, and by Price C. Steele's line, and by George W. Bell's corner, and by the Nashville and Murfreesboro and Shelbyville Turnpike. Containing 207 acres. This 7 November 1864.
Reg: March 31, 1865   Signed: A.M. Webb

Page 474 - Samuel Yates Deed to John F. Hall. Land in Bedford County and Civil District No. 3 adjoining the lands of said Hall, David Thornsbury and others and bounded by lands formerly Jeremiah Kimbro and Fergus Hall. Containing 50 acres. This 9 January 1865.
Wit: F.M. Yates   Signed: Samuel Yates
     J.V. Biddle
Reg: (no date)

Page 475 - M.P. Gentry Deed to Wm. S. Jett. Meredith P. Gentry of Bedford County sold to William S. Jett a tract of land in Bedford County and District No. 7. Bounded by the center of Flat Creek, and by the south boundary line of the Smith grant. Containing 231 acres and 82 poles. This 13 March 1865.
Reg: March 31, 1865   Signed: M.P. Gentry

Page 475 - G.G. Osborne and A.D. Fugett Deed to John Thomas. G.G. Osborne and Alfred D. Fugett sold to John Thomas a tract of land in Bedford County and District No. 3 and bounded by J.

Shriver, and a tract of which this is a part formerly owned by John Sutton. This 28 August 1863.
Wit: D.A. McCullock   Signed: G.G. Osborne
     W.B. Norvill   A.D. Fugett
Reg: March 31, 1865

Page 476 - Chesley Williams and Wm. P. Cannon Deed to G.W. Thompson. Whereas Gen. Robert Cannon, late of Bedford County, published his Last Will and Testament and afterwards departed this life which will was after his death at April Term 1864 duly proven &c. Chesley Williams and Wm. P. Cannon named executors to sell the small brick building occupied by Mr. Pitts and the lot of ground divided into three small lots. One lot corner of Martin and ___ Street, one lot fronting Martin Street on which is a small building Mr. Pitts occupies, and the other lot adjoining the same west of the Odd Fellows Hall a lot on Martin Street on which a small building occupied by Mr. Pitts. Adjoining Wm. Brown on Martin Street, by a lot sold to Robert Galbreath. Land sold to G.W. Thompson. This 7 July 1864.
Reg: March 31, 1865   Signed: Chesley Williams
                                      Wm. P. Cannon

Page 477 - Presley Holland and others Deed to James F. Calhoon. William Holland, Presley Holland, Sarah Lam formerly Sarah Holland, Elijah Patterson and Viney Patterson his wife formerly Viney Holland, William C. Spence and wife Elizabeth Spence formerly Elizabeth Holland have this day sold to James F. Calhoon landed estate of Thomas Holland, Sr., deceased, under a Deed of Gift made by Thomas Holland, Sr. to his wife Sarah Holland and at her death to be divided among his children and is registered. This October 2, 1860.
Wit: Daniel Hooser   Signed: Presley Holland
Reg: March 31, 1865   W. Holland
                                     W.C. Spence
                                     Elizabeth Spence

Page 478 - William H. Whitthorne, C&M, Deed to William Bomar. Bedford County. W.B. Bomar VS James H. Bomar and others - Decree. Report as to the division of the lands of Elisha(Elijah?) Bomar, deceased. Land allotted to Wm. Bomar Lot No. 7. Adjoining Lot No. 6, by Peggy Ault, Lot No. 8, and Lot No. 5. Containing 88 acres and 48 poles. This 21 February 1865.
Reg: April 1, 1865   Signed: William J. Whitthorne, C&M

Page 479 - W.B. Bomar and William Bomar, exrs. &c James H. Bomar and others - Decree. Report of the division of lands allotted to Reuben Bomar Lot No.2 and adjoining Lot No. 1, Butlers Creek, corner of the Poor House tract, and by the Shelbyville and Fairfield Road. Containing 93 acres and 40 poles. Lands of Elijah Bomar, deceased. This 27 February 1865.
Reg: April 1, 1865   Signed: William J. Whitthorne, C&M

Page 479 - J.W. Yancy Deed to Wm. L. Yancy. I have sold unto my brother Wm. L. Yancy all of my interest &c in a tract of land in ___ District of Bedford County and adjoining the lands of George W. Thompson and others. Containing about ___ acres, it being the place known as the Widow Marshall place on which she now resides. The interest herein conveyed being the interest inherited by me in right of my deceased mother who was a daughter of said Widow Marshall. This 9 March 1865.
Reg: April 1, 1865   Signed: J.W. Yancy

Page 480 - Thomas R. Gowen Deed to B.E. Bedford. Land in Bedford County and District No. 24. Containing 75 acres and adjoining James Stone, and Samuel Bobo. This February 10, 1865.
Reg: April 1, 1865   Signed: Thomas R. Gowen

Page 481 - Chesley Williams and W.P. Cannon Deed to Robt. Galbraith. Whereas Gen. Robert Cannon, late of Bedford County, made his Last Will and Testament and afterwards departed this life which will after his death was duly proven at April Term 1864. Executors appointed by said Cannon was Chesley Williams and Wm. P. Cannon. They were ordered to sell certain real estate, land mostly in the Town of Shelbyville called Green Hill to be divided into tracts of 5 or 6 acres commencing on a Lane Street to the center of the river, and by Primrose's boundary. Containing 5 ¾ acres. This July 7, 1864.
Reg: April 1865   Signed: Chesley Williams
                                 Wm. P. Cannon, Exrs.

Page 482 - Chesley Williams and Wm. P. Cannon Deed to Robert Galbraith. Lands of Gen. Robert Cannon, deceased. Sold was land about the small brick house occupied by Mr. Pitts which said lot is divided into three lots. One lot at the corner of Martin Street bounded by Lot o. 54. This 7 July 1864.
Reg: April 3, 1865   Signed: Chesley Williams
                                 Wm. P. Cannon, Exrs.

Page 483 - Chesley Williams and Wm. P. Cannon Deed to Wm. Brown. Whereas Gen. Robert Cannon, late of Bedford County, made his Last Will and Testament and afterwards departed this life which will was proven at April Term 1864. Chesley Williams and Wm. P. Cannon was appointed executors. Land sold to Wm. Brown granted near the bridge that was purchased by Clement Cannon's estate in the Town of Shelbyville and bounded by Lot No. 108 lying south of the street running from the Square to the bridge on Duck River. This 7 July 1864.
Reg: April 3, 1864   Signed: Chesley Williams
                                 William P. Cannon, Exrs.

Page 484 - Chesley Williams and Wm. P. Cannon Deed to David S. Evans. By the will of Gen. Robert Cannon, deceased, sold land in Bedford County on Martin Street in the Town of Shelbyville it being the lot formerly belonging to the Robinson heirs situated on MARtin Street north of Marr's corner and said Evan's line.

Reg: April 3, 1865   Signed: Chesley Williams
                                        Wm. P. Cannon, Exrs.

Page 485 - Chesley Williams and Wm. P. Cannon Deed to Louisa
Mankel. By the will of Gen. Robert Cannon, deceased. Sold land
in Bedford County a certain store house and lot occupied by R.D.
Deery as a drug store on the east side of the Public Square in
the Town of Shelbyville and bounded by lands known as the Deery
Drug Store, and by an alley. This 7 July 1865.
Reg: April 4, 1865   Signed: Chesley Williams
                                        Wm. P. Cannon, Exrs.

Page 486 - Chesley Williams and Wm. P. Cannon Deed to Jas. S.
Newton. By will of Gen. Robert Cannon, deceased, land sold to
James S. Newton land or part of lot purchased at the sale of the
late Lewis Shapard that lies near the Spinning Factory, and
bounded on Spring Street, to the river below the factory lot and
Rouzee in Town of Shelbyville. This 7 July 1864.
Reg: April 4, 1865   Signed: Chesley Williams
                                        Wm. P. Cannon, Exrs.

Page 487 - Chesley Williams and Wm. P. Cannon Deed to Mrs. S.T.
Moody. By will of Gen. Robert Cannon, deceased. Land sold
about 40 or 50 acres of land of said Robert Cannon on Rowesville
Road near James Bomar's east of Shelbyville. Lands divided into
four lots, three lots 12 ½ acres and one lot 12 ½ acres and 16
poles. Numberon the plat 1, 2, 3, and 4. Lot No. 1 on the
north side of the Rowesville Road and containing 12 ½ acres and
15 poles. Lot No. 2 adjoining Lot No. 1 and Lot No. 3
containing 12 ½ acres. This 7 July 1864.
Reg: April 5, 1865   Signed: Chesley Williams
                                        Wm. P. Cannon, Exrs.

Page 488 - Chesley Williams and William P. Cannon Deed to Robt.
Dennis. By will of Gen. Robert Cannon, deceased. Land sold a
tract of land that lies near Charles Warner's east of
Shelbyville in Bedford County and bounded by C.A. Warren's line,
and containing 24 acres and 40 poles. This 7 July 1864.
Reg: April 5, 1865   Signed: Chesley Williams
                                        Wm. P. Cannon, Exrs.

Page 489 - Chesley Williams and Wm. P. Cannon, Exrs. Deed to
W.W. Gunter. By will of Gen. Robert Cannon, deceased. Land
sold known as the tract of land purchased of Wilson Arnold and
his wife whereon Wm. Spencer formerly lived in Bedford County
and east of Shelbyville on the Rowesville Road and bounded on
the south by Duck River, by lands belonging to Robert Cannon
where he purchased said tract of land of Wilson Arnold and wife,
by lands belonging to the heirs of Wilson Coats, and by lands
purchased of said Cannon of Wilson Arnold and wife Margaret J.,
dated 6 October 1845. Containing 50 acres. This 7 July 1864.
Reg: April 5, 1864   Signed: Chesley Williams
                                        Wm. P. Cannon, Exrs.

Page 490 - James Story Deed to W.N. Gwin. Land in Shelbyville being part of Lot No. 83 and adjoining Mrs. Rachel Hobbs, by a spring branch. It being the same lot on which Thomas F. Nash now resides. This 4 April 1865.
Reg: April 5, 1865   Signed: James Story

Page 491 - Chesley Williams and Wm. P. Cannon, exrs., Deed to Henry Yancy. By the will of Gen. Robert Cannon, deceased. Land sold known as the Landis Store House at present occupied by S. Gumbert & Co. on the Public Square in the Town of Shelbyville and fronting on the Square and joining an alley, which house was formerly owned by John Eakin's heirs. This 7 July 1864.
RegL April 5, 1865   Signed: Chesley Williams
                                        Wm. P. Cannon, Exrs.

Page 492 - N.W. Haley Deed to Wm. T. Nance. Newman W. Haley sold to William T. Nance land in Bedford County and District No. 18, containing 43 acres and bounded by a 200 acres known as the Blue Spring tract granted to Malcomb Gilchrist, and by Hammell's corner. It being the same tract deeded to me by Moses B. Wadley 18 December 1862. This April 3, 1865.
Reg: (no date)   Signed: Newman W. Haley

Page 493 - James M. Stephens Deed to Reuben W. Couch. 6 December 1860. Both of Bedford County. Land in Bedford County and bounded by lands of William Culley, and L.W. Hall, and by Culleys Branch. Containing 131 92/160 acres.
Wit: G.A. Cortner   Signed: J.M. Stephens
Jno. R. Muse
Reg: (no date)

Page 493 - D.D. Martin Deed to Longsher Lamb. D.D. Martin as executor and guardian of W.M. Martin under the Will and Testament of Martha Martin, deceased, has conveyed and sold unto Longsher Lamb land in Bedford County on the head waters of Big Harpeth and bounded by Black's land, and the county line. Containing 51 acres conveyed to me. There is however 14 acres of the same land which belongs to me individually which I do sell and convey in my own name.
Reg: (no date)

Page 494 - Rufus Smith Deed to George H. Casselman. Land in Bedford County and District No. 22 and bounded by old school land tract. Containing 164 47/160 acres. This 16 January 1864.
Wit: J.C. Hix   Signed: Rufus Smith
     R.W. Castleman
Reg: April 6, 1865

Page 494 - W.W. Gill Deed to George Castleman. Land in Bedford County and Civil District No. 22 and bounded by Lot No. 5, Lacey's dield now Castleman, passing over an old spring near a bluff of rocks, by the original school land, and by McKiney's

2000 acre grant, and by Lot No. 1. Containing 106 acres. This
November 25, 1864.
Reg: April 6, 1865   Signed: W.W. Gill

Page 495 - D.D. Martin Deed to Longsher Lamb.   D.D. Martin as
executor and guardian of W.H. Martin under the Last Will and
testament of Martha Martin, deceased, sold unto Longsher Lamb
land in Bedford County on the head waters of Big Harpeth and
bounded by Black's line, and the county line. There is however
14 acres of the above land which belonged to me individually and
which I do hereby sell. This October 30, 1860.
Wit: G.W. Buchanan   Signed: D.D. Martin, Exr. &
     A. Wilson   Guardian
Reg: (no date)

Page 496 - James N. Hargrove and wife Deed to A.F. Knott. James
N. Hargrove and wife formerly Mary Emmons of Bedford County,
sold unto A.F. Knott land in Bedford County and Civil District
No. 7 and bounded by L.B. Knott. Containing one half of an
acre. This 24, January 1860.
Wit: Henry Cooper   Signed: James Hargrove
Reg: April 7, 1865   Nancy Hargrove

Page 496 - F.S. Brown Deed of Trust to J.W. Clary. F.S. Brown
sold to John W. Clary the following property, to wit, one tract
of land in Bedford County and District No. 10, containing 151
acres and bounded by Jordan Rucker, A. Poplin, A.F. Knott,
(illegible) Thompson and Lemuel Call, and by Keziah Steed, also
four head of mules, three horses and several other items listed
in original document. I am indebted to William Brown. Also to
Robert Reed. This April 24, 1865.
Reg: (no date)   Signed: S.F. Brown

Page 498 - A.S. Laurance Deed of Trust 330 acres to Thos. H.
Coldwell. Land in Bedford County and Civil District No. 25 on
the waters of Duck river and bounded by Duck River, lands of Z.
Culley, Isaac Troxler, George Cortner, Mrs. Hight and Sam
Stephens, by lands of Dr. J.H. Scott, J.L. Rowesborough and Mrs.
Wm. Troxler, and by Gabriel Maupin, and Josiah Maupin and Robert
Smith. It being the place on which I now live. This 27, April
1865.
Wit: D.A. Ramsey   Signed: A.S. Laurance
     Lewis Tilman
Reg: April 27, 1865

Page 499 - W.P. Wood Deed to F.G. Harris. William P. Wood sold
to F.G. Harris land in Bedford County and District No. 9.   It
being a part of the tract of Rolen Landers and bounded by the
heirs of Elizabeth Williams, and G.W. Burn's line, and by
Bounds' line. Containing 45 acres. This April 12, 1865.
Wit: G.W. Bounds   Signed: W.P. Wood
     E. Harris
Reg: May 2, 1865

Page 499 - Rich'd Warner, Admr., Deed to Thos. J. Brown. Shadrick S. Brown by his last Will and Testament authorized his executor to dispose of his land after the death of his widow Tabitha Brown. John T. Neil was appointed the executor of said will had departed this life and Richard Warner was appointed administrator with the will annexed. Thomas J. Brown became the purchaser and by an arrangement a part of said land was sold to George W. Brown leaving a remainder of said land to be conveyed to Thomas J. Brown. This 27 March 1865.
Reg: May 2, 1865   Signed: Richard Warner

Page 500 - William H. Wisener VS Patrick Fay. Chancery Court Decree. It appeared to the satisfaction of the court that the complainant had purchased of the defendant on 26 March 1856 a tract of land in Bedford County and Civil District No. 3 being a part of what was known as the Gilchrist tract lying on the north side of the Rail Road and adjoining at the center of the Rail Road at Gilchrist's tract being the corner of Wisener's tract as purchased of Nathan Ivy, by Blessing's tract, and near a house formerly owned by Benj. A. Nelson now owned by the family of Edmund Green. Containing 90 acres and 142 poles. This 11 March 1865.
Reg: May 8, 1865

Page 502 - William Phillips Deed 14+ acres to John H. Philpott. This 20 April 1865. Both of Bedford County. Land in Bedford County and District No. 8, bounded by Fall Creek, and C.T. Philpott.
Wit: John W. Cowan, Sr.   Signed: William Phillips
Reg: May 11, 1865

Page 503 - John H. McGee Deed of Trust to Thomas H. Coldwell. Land in Bedford County and Civil District No. 7 and adjoining the lands of John W. Cowan, by Union Street, and by lands of Mrs. Blackwell and Robert Mathews. Containing 6 acres and __ poles. This 2 May 1865.
Reg: May 11, 1865   Signed: John H. McGee

Page 503 - Joshua Reed Deed of Trust to J.H. McGrew. All my right title &c as one of the legatees &c of Robert Reed, deceased, and of the estate of Robert Reed my father which should consist of land monies notes &c in the hands of the executor of said Robert Reed. Several notes listed in original document. This 5 May 1865.
Reg: May 11, 1865   Signed: Joshua Reed

Page 504 - James Clardy Deed 214 acres to Peter E. Clardy. For the natural love and affection I bear to my son Peter E. Clardy I have given unto him land in Bedford County on the waters of Hurricane Creek being part of a tract of land allotted to Ann Phifer, deceased, or him as devises of Caleb Phifer and is bounded by the line of the original lots. This 22 April 1865.
Wit: H.L. Davidson   Signed: James Clardy

Geo. W. Buchanan
Reg: May 12, 1865

Page 505 - James Clardy to Mary L.P. Vannoy Deed 138 acres. For the love and affection I bear towards my daughter Mary L.P. Vannoy, widow of Jesse F. Vannoy, deceased, have granted unto her land. One tract conveyed to me by James Turrentine and being in Bedford County and District No. 2, 6th Section and 4th Range and on Falling Creek on the north side of Duck River and adjoining a claim in the name of Ephraim Peyton for 600 acres on the north side of Fall Creek. Also another tract conveyed by Dan'l Burton and which is being in Bedford County on the waters of Fall Creek of Duck River and adjoining James McAdams' corner, Phifer's corner, by John Burns, and by Alexander Turrentine, and Reuben Nance. Containing 138 acres. Also one other tract conveyed by Andrew Vannoy and is in Bedford County and district No. 6 called the Boiles Road that leads from Shelbyville to Nashville in line of said Clardy. Containing 4 acres. This April 22, 1865.
Wit: H.L. Davidson   Signed: James Clardy
     Geo. W. Buchanan
Reg: May 18, 1865

Page 506 - Chesley Williams and Wm. P. Cannon Deed ¾ acres to John W. Thompson. By will of Gen. Robert Cannon, deceased. Land adjoining John Thompson in the Town of Shelbyville on the north side of Lane Street, and Mrs. Cunningham. This 7 July 1864.
Reg: May 8, 1865   Signed: Chesley Williams
                                  Wm. P. Cannon, Exrs of
                                  Gen. Robert Cannon.

Page 57 - William Brown Deed Lot to Henry Beck, Jr. Land in the Town of Shelbyville and it being a part of the lot known as Lot No. 40, and bounded by the street leading out east from the north east corner of the Public Square at the intersection of said street and Brittain Street at the south east corner of the brick house on said lot, to the center of the cross wall, and to Mrs. Cannon's line, including all the buildings on the lot. This 8 May 1865.
Reg: May 8, 1865   Signed: William Brown

Page 508 - R.S. Dwiggins Mortgage to John H. Wells. May 9, 1865. I have this day sold to John H. Wells two bay mare mules and four horse wagons.
Reg: May 18, 1865   Signed: R.S. Dwiggins

Page 508 - Baskett & Stamps to Title Bond to A.P. Eakin. Bound to A.P. Eakin land near the Town of Shelbyville containing 13 acres which said Stamps since sold to John Dalton and afterwards sold and on which said Dalton resided at the time of his death to be paid in brick or brick work in the year 1860 and 1861. This December 12, 1859.

Reg: May 18, 1865   Signed: Baskett & Stamps

Page 509 - Henry Beck Deed Lot to William Brown. Land in the
Town of Shelbyville, it being part of the late known Lot No. 40
and adjoining north side of the street leading out east from the
north east corner of the Public Square at the intersection of
said street, with Brittain Street at the south east corner of
the brick house on said lot, by the cross wall, and by Mrs. L.
Cannon. It including all said lot and is the same house and lot
deeded to me by said Town on 8 of this month. This May 16,
1865.
Wit: S.T. Farrar   Signed: Henry Beck
Reg: May 18, 1865

Page 509 - E.M. Ousley Deed 65 acres to P.P. Petty. Land in
Bedford County and Civil District No. 22 and on the head waters
of Flat Creek and bounded by lands of James R. R____, by lands
of John W. White, by lands of John W. White, P. Bryant and said
Petty, and by lands of P.P. Petty. This 28 October 1863.
Reg: May 22, 1865   Signed: E.M. Ousley

Page 510 - Black & Jernigan Deed to Wm. N. Gwynn. George W.
Jernigan and W.A. Black sold to Wm. N. Gwynn a house and lot in
the corporate limits of the Town of Shelbyville known as the
"Mars Corner" and formerly belonging to Gen. Robt. Cannon and on
the north east corner of the Public Square, and bounded by the
square and Martin Street, and by D.S. Evans. This 10 May 1865.
Reg; May 25, 1865   Signed: George W. Jernigan

Page 511 - David M. Orr and others undivided interest to
Johnathan Claxton. We, David M. Orr, Anneybet and Sarah C. Orr
have sold unto Johnathan Claxton all the undivided interest in a
tract of land of 100 acres that was willed by our grandfather
Jno. Thompson, deceased, to our grandmother Mary Thompson, now
deceased, during her life time and we are entitled to our part
of our mother's share of said land. Said land in Bedford County
and District No. 11. This 5 November 1863.
Wit: J.H. Vincent   Signed: D.M. Orr
     M.J. Vincent   A.E. Orr
Reg: May 30, 1865   S.C. Orr

Page 511 - Barney Patterson Oil Lease to J.W. Milroy. This 21
March 1865 lease made between Barney Patterson of Bedford County
and James W. Milroy. For sole and only purpose of mining and
excavating for petroleum, coal, rock or carbon oil &c., all the
land in Bedford County and bounded by east bank of Normans
Creek. Supposed to be 83 acres. And also that tract adjoining
Normans Creek, the top of a hill, by John McQuiddy, Moses Ayres'
75 acre entry, A.L. Huffman, the Rail Road, and Zepheniah
Weavers' corner. This 1 March 1865.
Wit: E.C. Casion   Signed: Barney Patterson
Reg: June 13, 1865   J.W. Milroy

Page 512 - James Calhoon Deed to Wm. H. Wisener, Sr. Three fifths of one fifth that is three fifths of the share of James Holland in remainder in a small tract of land containing about 11 acres on which Thomas Holland, Sr. lived at the time of his death and in which Sarah T. Holland his widow had a life estate which she sold to said Wisener. The three fifths I convey are shares of Wm. A. Holland, ____ Holland and William Spencer and wife Elizabeth as heirs of said James Holland. This 28 March 1865.
Wit: S. Greenbaum   Signed: James F. Calhoon
     J.J. Mankin
Reg: June 14, 1865

Page 513 - F.P. McElwrath, wife and others Deed 120 acres to John S. Cooper. F.P. McElwrath and wife Mary E. McElwrath formerly Mary E. Thompson and John R. Thompson, have sold unto J.S. Cooper land in Bedford County and District No. 9 and containing 320 acres and bounded by the Murfreesboro Road, corner of Lot No. 2 in the division among the heirs of S.C. Thompson, deceased, by Lot No. 7 laid off to J.C. Bates and wife, by W.C. Brame, by S.V. Batts, and by Lot No. 3. This February 22, 1862.
Wit: Judith Thompson   Signed: John R. Thompson
     Louvice Thompson   F.P. McElwrath
Reg: June 14, 1865   M.E. McElwrath

Page 514 - C. Williams & W.P. Cannon Deed Marr's Corner to G.W. Jernigan. By will of Gen. Robert Cannon, deceased. A certain house and lot known and called the Marr's Corner within the Town of Shelbyville on the south east corner of the Public Square and adjoining at the corner of the Square and Martin Street, by Evans corner. This 7 July 1864.
Reg: June 14, 1865   Signed: Chesley Williams
                                    William P. Cannon, Exrs.

Page 515 - Dulcina Hemby Entry 60 acres on Shipmans Creek. Dulcina Hemby enters 60 acres of land in Bedford County and District No. 25 on the waters of Shipmans Creek and bounded by an entry in the name of Robert P. Harrison, by Burrow's land now Crawley's, by an entry in the name of Rachel Hemby, and by Daniel Hamby and Zachariah Dobbins' land. This June 8, 1865.
Reg: June 15, 1865   Signed: Dulcina Hemby

Page 515 - America A. Carrick Deed to James Y. West. Land in Bedford County and Civil District No. 3. This September 11, 1860.
Wit: William Bomar   Signed: James Carrick
     William McGee   America A. Carrick
Reg: June 15, 1865

Page 516 - Walter F. Sutton Deed Remainder Interest in land to John T. Cannon. Land in Bedford County and District No. 4, containing 350 acres known as my mother's dower tract and

bounded by the lands of John Thomas, Joseph Foreman and N.C. Harris, by lands of William B. Sutton, by gilchrist lands and Mrs. Louisa Terry's dower tract, and by the Mullins' land and Wm. B. Sutton's cedar tract, in which lands my mother Mrs. Elizabeth Osborne has a life estate and I transferred and an heir of John Sutton, Sr., deceased, and an heir of my deceased brother John Sutton, Jr. and James Overton Sutton and my deceased sister Slatira(?) Sutton. This 8 June 1865.
Wit: B.F. Smalling   Signed: W.F. Sutton
     J.C. Mash
Reg: June 15, 1865

Page 516 - W.F. Sutton Deed 15 acres to Henry R. Green. Land in Bedford County and Civil District No.4 and bounded by lands of M.W. Newsom and wife, by land formerly owned by Robert Demster, and by lands of Charles H. Sutton. It being a portion of land sold by Robert Demster to James R. Sutton. This June 12, 1865.
Reg: June 15, 1865   Signed: W.F. Sutton

Page 517 - W.P. Green Deed Lot in Wartrace to Sam'l R. Hailey. Lot in the Town of Wartrace and bounded by an alley, A.H. Coffey's line, by Knob Creek Turnpike, and by Green and Tarpley. This 7 February 1863.
Wit: J.W. Tilford   Signed: W.P. Green
     B.D. Holt
Reg: June 21, 1865

Page 517 - S.B. Heard Deed 6 acres to S.R. Hailey. Land in Bedford County and District No. 23 near Wartrace Depot. Adjoining A.H. Coffey 35 poles from the Depot, by the Rail Road, by Cleveland's line. This January 8, 1863.
Wit: J.W. Tilford   Signed: S.B. Heard
     James Carothers
Reg: June 21, 1865

Page 518 - Michael Robinson Deed Lot to W.P. Green. Michael Robinson sold to William P. Green a certain house and lot in the Town of Wartrace in Civil District No 3 of Bedford County and bounded by A.H. Coffey, north side of Knob Creek Turnpike, by Tarpley and Henry Green, and by an alley. This 11 March 1862.
Reg: June 21, 1865   Signed: Michael Robinson

Page 519 - S.R. Hgailey Deed Lot to John Murray. House and lot in the Town of Wartrace, Bedford County, and District No. 3 and bounded by A.H. Coffey, by north side of Knob Creek, by a lot now occupied by Tarpley and Henry Green, and by the Knob Creek Turnpike. This 14 June 1865.
Reg: June 21, 1865   Signed: S.R. Hailey

Page 519 - John W. Thompson Deed Interest in House and Lot to Geo. W. Thompson. House and lot situated on the Public Square in the Town of Shelbyville and sold by decree of the Chancery

Court of Bedford County in the case of Mathew Shearin and wife against J.K.P. Carlisle and others as the property of James A. Gaunt, deceased, and was purchased by G.W. and J.W. Thompson. Said house and lot situated on the south side of the Public Square in said town and adjoining the property of William C. Fletcher and others, it being the same house and lot that James A. Gaunt, deceased, formerly purchased of Robert Cannon. This 20 June 1865.
Reg: July 1, 1865   Signed: John W. Thompson

Page 520 - Rebecca Pannell Deed Town Lot to John W. Thompson. For the natural love and affection which I have for my daughter Mary J. Thompson wife of Jno. W. Thompson, I do convey to said Mary Jane Thompson a certain house and lot in the Town of Shelbyville known as the Pannell Lot and on which S.H. Pannell resided at the time of his death my said interest being a life estate for her own sole and separate use and free from her present or any future husband. This 15 May 1865.
Wit: M.E.W. Dunaway   Signed: Rebecca Pannell
Reg: July 3, 1865

Page 521 - A.W. Evins Deed 120 acres to W.J. Bomar. Land in Bedford County and District No. 24 on the waters of Flat Creek and bounded by Thomas Martin, and to the ridge at the corner of James Williams' fence. This October 5, 1863.
Wit: John Riddle   Signed: A.W. Evins
   M.G. Pearson
Reg: July 3, 1865

Page 521 - James T. Arnold Deed 70 acres to Thomas A. Hime. Land in Bedford County and Civil District No. 23 and bounded by H.L. Davidson now John H. Wells' corner, and by Bush Creek. Containing 70 acres. This June 24, 1865.
Reg: July 6, 1865   Signed: J.T. Arnold

Page 522 - John T. Cannon Deed to W.F. Sutton. Land in Bedford County and District No. 4 and bounded by lands of M.M. Newsom and wife, by lands formerly owned by Robert Dennison and afterwards Andy Mathews' heirs, by the lands of Charles F. Sutton, it being a portion of land sold to James K. Norton by Robt. Dennison and afterwards to T.B. Ivie and afterwards to G.B. Harris and afterwards to myself. This 8 June 1865.
Wit: B.F.Sutton   Signed: J.T. Cannon
   John C. Marsh
Reg: July 10, 1865

Page 523 - David F. Jackson Trust Deed to T.W. Buchanan. Interest in stock and other personal property, to wit, one black mare, one roan mare, one sorrel mare, one mule, one bay horse colt, ten head of cattle, fifty head of hogs, fifteen head of sheep, one corn sheller, one wheat fan, and one old buggy. (no date).
Reg: July 10, 1865   Signed: D.F. Jackson

Page 524 - John F. Wells Deed to Amasa(?) W. Morrice. This June 30, 1865. Land in Bedford County and Civil District No. 9 and bounded by James Foster, by Hastings' line, by John Landers' line, and by John Foster's corner. Containing 88 acres.
Reg: July 10, 1865   Signed: John F. Wells.

Page 524 - G.W. Bounds Deed to F.J. & M.H. Harris. Land in Bedford County and District No. 9, being a part of the tract of land granted to George Alexander and bounded by Rebecca Landers, and by F.J. Harris. Containing 95 acres. This July 3, 1865.
Wit: J. Ray   Signed: G.W. Bounds
     E.G. Harris
Reg: July 10, 1865

Page 525 - F.G. Harris & M.H. Harris Deed to G.W. Barns. Land in Bedford County and Civil District No. 8, it being a tract purchased of James Jarett. Containing 128 acres. This July 3, 1865.
Wit: E.G. Harris   Signed: F.G. Harris
     J. Ray   Mary H. Harris
Reg: July 10, 1865

Page 526 - Martin E. Sims Trust Deed to Martin Sims. For all my undivided interest in the distillery of Sims, Coffee & Clay in Bedford County and Civil District No. 18, consisting of one copper still tubs, worm and fixtures and all belonging to said distillery sold to Martin Sims. This July 4, 1865.
Reg: July 10, 1865   Signed: Martin E. Sims

Page 527 - J.M. Moor(e) Trust Deed to J.R. Brown. House and Lot in Unionville, Bedford County and bounded by L.F. Smith's lot, by lands of D.C. Moor(e), by Mary Ann Kliner lot, and by lands of M. Blanton. This July 3, 1865.
Wit: John A. Moore   Signed: J.M. Moore
     M.B. Blanton
Reg: July 11, 1865

Page 527 - David T. Chambers Trust Deed to Robt. Allison. Real and personal property, to wit, a tract of land in Bedford County and District No. 10 and bounded by lands of the heirs of Ebenezer Winn, and the lands of Esq. Street, and by R.T. Hall's land, and by lands of Widow Gaunt and said Hall, and by lands of Wiley Perry and Letitia Perry. Containing about 100 acres being the same place which I now reside. Also a lot in the Village of Unionville and bounded by the Turnpike Road, by lands formerly belonging to Wm. Foster being the same lot I purchased of Moses West and was occupied by me as a grocery house which house has since burned, the lot is now a vacant lot. I also convey personal property, to wit, one sorrel mare, one cow and calf, one carriage and harness. I am indebted to Robert S. and Eliza Brown as their guardian. D.A. Osment and Henry R. Stem are my securities. (no date).
Reg: July 6, 1865   Signed: D.T. Chambers

Page 529 - G.M. Ray, M.W. Watson, Daniel Parker to C. Pearson. All of Bedford County. We sold to Charles Pearson a tract of land in Bedford County and Civil District No. 24 and on the head waters of Thompsons Creek and bounded by John Dean, Wm. Bomar, to the center of a branch, and by McDavers' corner. Containing 152 acres including all the buildings and improvements and a steam mill and other machinery that we have built on the premises. This 26 April 1863.
Reg: July 11, 1865   Signed: G.M. Ray
                                  M.W. Watson
                                  Daniel Parker

Page 531 - John W. Key Trust Deed to J.M. Minter. John M. Minter of Rutherford County, Tennessee and John W. Key of Bedford County. Lands both adjoining each other and in Civil District No. 9 and bounded by lands of Preston Frazier and R.B. McLean, by lands of Samuel G. Thompson and Columbus Brown, by lands of Mrs. Vaughan, and by the lands of Robert Barns. Containing 242 acres conveyed by deed of George W. Jones and Robert Barns. Also one bay mare and colt, six stock hogs and several other items listed in original document. I am indebted to G.W. Holden and Martha A. Ray. This July 7, 1865.
Reg: July 12, 1865   Signed: John W. Key

Page 532 - Amasa V. Manier Deed to Henry V. Taylor. Land in Bedford County and District No. 10 and containing 48+ acres. This June 28, 1865.
Wit: C.P. Taylor   Signed: Amasa V. Manier
     W.F. Vinson
Reg: July 12, 1865

Page 533 - T.W. Jordan Deed to Robert Cannon. A small tract of land bounded by the Scull Camp Ford Roads by the way of Jordan's corner, and the north bank of Duck River. This 3 March 1857.
Wit: Thos. J. Roane   Signed: T.W. Jordan
     Thos. Walsh
Reg: July 12, 1865

Page 534 - Mary Forman Deed to John H. Deeryberry. This 3 July 1865. Mary Forman of Bedford County, executrix of the Last Will and Testament of Richard Forman, deceased, late of Bedford County, conveyed to John H. Deeryberry land in the Town of Shelbyville which is known as being a fraction of lot in said Yown of Shelbyville, conveyed from Wm. Brown dated 11 January 1848 and registered in Book DD, page 345.
Wit: John Bell   Signed: Mary Forman
     Wm. Galbreath
     J.H. Castleman
Reg: July 25, 1865

Page 536 - James Finch & P.H. Manier to M.T. Cooper. We bind ourselves to pay M.T. Cooper. We have sold to said Cooper a tract of land in Bedford County on Straight Creek and bounded by

said creek and James Finch, by Stephen Gallaghy and Hugh Montgomery's line, to Jesse Shelton, John S. Davis, and the tract known as the James A. Word tract lying and being north of the center of Straight Creek and contains 210 acres. (no date).
Wit: James Brown   Signed: James Finch
     Martin N. Uless
Reg: July 12, 1865

Page 537 - M.T. Cooper Title Bond to W.J. Osborn.   I bind myself to pay Wm. J. Osborn.   I have sold unto Wm. J. Osborn a tract of land in Bedford County on Straight Creek east and bounded by the creek, by Galleghy and Hugh T. Montgomery, by John S. Davis, and by James Finch.   Tract known as the old Word tract lying north of the center of Straight Creek and supposed to contain 210 acres,   This 10, November 1862.
Wit: B.M. Tilman   Signed: M.T. Cooper
     T.V. Parrish
Reg: July 10, 1865

Page 538 - James F. Cummings Deed of Gift to Margret F. Cummings.   For the love and affection I have for my wife Margret F. Cummings I have conveyed unto her a tract of land in District No. 7 of Bedford County and bounded by a lot owned by Wm. Galbreath at the stable, the old corporation line of the Town of Shelbyville, to a street that divides said land from the Fair Grounds, and by G.W. Buchanan's dwelling house, and to Atkins Street.   Containing 3 Town Lots and about 19 acres of land. This same being the place which I now live and purchased from Wm. Litle, and deed registered in Book BBB, pages 480 and 481. This 19 April 1860.
Reg: April 21, 1860 in Book BBB, pages 617 and 618.
                              Signed: J.F. Cummings

Page 539 - R.S. Dwiggins Trust Deed to John H. Wells.   I have sold unto John H. Wells one sorrel horse being the same I purchased of Wm. Raby and also other items listed in original document.   This July 11, 1865.
Reg: July 15, 1865   Signed: R.S. Dwiggins

Page 540 - R.S. Dwiggins Trust Deed to T.C. Whiteside.   I have sold unto Thomas C. Whiteside property, to wit, all the oats or my share of all the oats growing upon my plantation the present year being about four hundred dry bundles, also 100 shoats, one log wagon, a lot of wheat in the sheaf now in my barn or stable and other items listed in the original document.   Also a lot of land in the Town of Shelbyville on the north side of the river at the west end of the street leading out from the south west corner of the Public Square and adjoining the steam mill, also a lot on the Town of Shelbyville in which is called Camp White and containing about ¾ acres.   This 20 July 1865.   Note: A long document.
Reg: July 24, 1865   Signed: R.S. Dwiggins

Page 542 - Martha Burton Deed to William H. Steele. Land conveyed to Wm. H. Steele a lot of land in Bedford County and Civil District No. 7 and in the Town of Shelbyville and bounded by the lands belonging to the heirs of Gen. Robert Cannon, deceased, by the street north of Wm. G. Cowan's tanyard, by the lot owned by G.W. Ruth at the time of his death, and by a lot formerly owned by Robt. Ruth now owned by Dr. Garin. This 21 July 1861.
Reg: July 31, 1865   Signed: Martha Burton

Page 543 - C.W. Powell Deed to Sarah L. Williams. Land in Bedford County and bounded by Cokes' line formerly John Landers, and to the Rock Creek. This 10 July 1865.
Reg: July 31, 1865   Signed: C.W. Powell

Page 543 - W.H. Steele Deed to W.N. Gwin. A Town Lot or part of a Town Lot in the Town of Shelbyville, Bedford County and bounded by lands belonging to the heirs of Gen. Robert Cannon, by a lot owned by G.W. Ruth at the time of his death, and by a lot formerly owned by Robert Ruth now owned by W.N. Gwin.
Reg: July 31, 1865   Signed: W.H. Steele

Page 544 - Thomas Hill Deed to William Hill. A lot and house in the Village of Normandy, Bedford County, and bounded by a street leading eastward to the spring, and by Thomas Daniel now John Dwyer's corner near the Rail Road. Containing ½ acre. This 24 July 1865.
Reg: July 31, 1865   Signed: Thomas Hill

Page 544 - George T. Dobson and Martha Dobson Deed to J.S. Newton. Sold unto James S. Newton land in Bedford County and Civil District No. 20 and bounded by the lands of said James S. Newton, by lands of Sam'l and H. Dyer and foster Jackson, and by lands of said Dyer and Amanda Gabbet(?). Containing 97 acres and 10 poles. Said land being the tract that Martha Dobson formerly Martha Gabbet inherited in the division of the estate of her father William Gabbet. This 28 July 1865.
Reg: July 31, 1865   Signed: G.T. Dobson
                                     Martha Dobson

Page 546 - James M. Jones enters 150 acres of land in Bedford County and Civil District No. 22 and bounded by land whereon Thomas Martin now lives running south to the Bedford and Lincoln County line, by a tract of land Wash Bobo now claims, and to Wm. K. Stevens' corner, and with Casteel's line to Eliza Stevens' corner, by Dean and Medaris' line, and by Thomas Martin's corner. Entered July 31, 1865.
Reg: July 31, 1865   Signed: James M. Jones

Page 547 - James G. Barksdale Deed to Moses Marshall. Land in the Town of Shelbyville upon which recently stood the African Church and bounded by J.M. Elliott's lot, to Marshall's line to

the street running from or by Elliotts to the college. Containing about 50 acres. This July 27, 1865.
Reg: July 31, 1865   Signed: J.G. Barksdale

Page 548 - Joseph Etheridge, wife and others Deed to J.C. Paschal. Joseph Etheridge and wife Harriett A. Etheridge and Elizabeth Burlin(?) sold unto James C. Paschal land in Bedford County and District No. 18 and lying on the south bank of Duck River and bounded by Duck River, and by lands of L. Jones, by lands of James paschal, and by lands of Samuel Crowell. Containing 96 acres. This 22 July 1865.
Reg: August 2, 1865   Signed: Joseph Etheridge
                                     Harriett Etheridge
                                     Elizabeth Burlin

Page 549 - James F. McCowan Deed to D.W. Frizzell. This 10 March 1864. Both of Bedford County. Sold unto David W. Frizzell land in Bedford County on the Wartrace Fork of Duck River and bounded by Milton Giles' line where said line crosses the spring branch, to Wartrace Creek, to Wm. Loyd's corner, by A.J. Bingham's line, and by Thomas Hatchett and Giles' line. Containing 58 acres.
Reg: August 4, 1865   Signed: James F. McCowan

Page 550 - Abner Steed Deed to Wm. Floyd. Land in Bedford County and District No. 1 on the waters of the North Fork of Duck River it being the part of D.A. Osment's 268 acres of land and was conveyed to me by deed dated June 24, 1857 by Henry A. King, Preston F. King and John A. King. Containing 140 acres. Land bounded by the center of the old road leading from Shelbyville to Unionville. This 20 November 1862.
Wit: W.C. Blanton   Signed: Abner Steed
     F.S. Brown
Reg: August 11, 1865

Page 551 - George Jakes Trust Deed to John Jakes and G.G. Osborne. All of Bedford County. Property conveyed, to wit, two sorrel mares, one brown bay horse, one black filly, one mule, and one yoke oxens and a wagon, cows and calves, and several other items listed in original document. Also tract being described as west with John Jakes' line, and by George W. Jakes. Containing 185 acres. Note: A long document. This 7 August 1865.
Reg: August 11, 1865   Signed: George Jakes

Page 553 - B.D. Holt and James Mullins Trustee to O.P. Arnold. This ___ June 1858. One W.C. Holt executed his Trust Deed to B.D. Holt and James Mullins. Being William C. Holt's residence. Land in Bedford County and District No. 3 and on the Rail Road leading from Wartrace to Shelbyville and bounded by Mrs. Caruthers. Containing 201 acres and 37 poles. This 24 March 1865.
Reg: August 12, 1865   Signed: B.D. Holt, Trustee

Page 554 - Wm. T. Hughs Deed to John T. Stephens. Land in
Bedford County and District No. 5 and bounded by the lands of
G.W.T. Erwin and B.F. Whitworth, by lands of B.F. Whitworth and
Charles F. Sutton, by lands of Melton's heirs, and by Huston &
Huston's heirs, and by G.W.T. Erwin. Containing 300 acres.
This 9 August 1865.
Reg; August 22, 1865   Signed: W.T. Hughes

Page 555 - John W. Dameron Trust Deed to J.M.H. Coleman. Sold
two horses and one gray horse to say said Joseph Stallings and
James Dryden, admrs., have recovered a judgment against myself,
my mother and J.M.H. Coleman. J.M.H. Coleman and my mother are
my securities. I desire my debt to be paid. This 8 August
1865.
Reg: August 9, 1865   Signed: John W. Dameron

Page 556 - Wm. G. Wood Deed to Sarah B. Hensley and Ann Wood.
Sold my undivided interest to a tract of land in Bedford County
and Civil District No. 3 it being the tract originally owned by
Sarah Wood, deceased, my interest being one third of a tract of
land the whole containing 150 acres and bounded by lands of the
heirs of Orvill Muse, by lands of Mrs. Nancy B. Muse, James L.
Wood and Mrs. Mary B. Jones, and by lands of Mrs. Mary B. Jones
and James Mullins, and by the lands of Ed Ewing, Dr. Vaughn and
the heirs of Orvill Muse. This 11 August 1865.
Reg: August 12, 1865   Signed: W.G. Wood

Page 557 - Chancery Court Decree to Nancy H. Harris. Thomas E.
Davis VS Sally Spruse and Jennings - Decree. Nancy H. Harris
who has since intermarried with said Thomas S. Davis, a tract of
land in Bedford County that Jennings Moore was appointed by the
executor of her will that at February Term 1861, he proved said
will gave bond &c and that its personal estate of said Mickey F.
Atkinson was sufficient to pay her debts. Mickey F. Atkinson
publish my Last Will and Testament. I direct my executor to pay
all my just debts I will and bequeath to Nancy H. Marshall the
tract of land on which I lived on Clems Creek in Civil District
No. 11 and bounded by James Finney, and Silas Spruce.
Containing 63 acres. I appoint Jennings Moore executor of the
Last Will and Testament. This 8 April 1865.
Reg: August 14, 1865   Signed: Lewis Tilman, C&M by
                                       Lewis Tilman, Jr., Dpt.

Page 558 - James Dillard Deed to T.W. Brents. Land in Bedford
County and Civil District No. 19 and bounded by the Richmond and
Lewisburg Road, by Brents' former corner, and by John Trice's
corner. Containing 380 acres 134 poles. This 11 August 1865.
Reg: August 15, 1865   Signed: James Dillard

Page 559 - Joseph Thompson, Sheriff Deed to Robert L. Landis. The Bank of Tennessee recovered a judgment on 6 April 185? Against Thomas Hume, Jacob Harrison, John Harrison, Denis Henby. An execution issued to the Sheriff and placed in the hands of David R. Vance then Deputy Sheriff and thence being no property in Bedford County, he levied on a tract of land in Bedford County and Civil District No. 25 and containing 103 acres and adjoining a tract of 387 acre tract entered by said Henley. This 4 August 1865. Note: A very long document.
Reg: August 15, 1865   Signed: Jo. Thompson, Sheriff

Page 560 - Robert Terry Deed to Martha A.G. Smith. Land in Bedford County and District No. 8 and bounded by lands of William Orr, by lands of N. Thompson, by lands of S.A. Thompson, and by lands of G.W. Thompson and others. Containing about 56 acres. Conveyed to me by George W. Thompson by deed dated December 1857. This August 14, 1865.
Reg: August 15, 1865   Signed: Robert Terry

Page 562 - R.D. Deery Deed to N.P. Evans. Ross D. Deery sold unto Nathan P. Evans land in Bedford County and Civil District No. 7 and in the Town of Shelbyville and bounded by property known as the James Deery property, and by Union Street, by the Deery lot. Containing 9 acres and 28 poles. The same being a portion of the lands conveyed by James Deery in his lifetime to R.D. Deery and J.H. Deery and upon which said James Deery resided at the time of his death and on which I now reside with my family. All the improvements, houses, out houses &c. For the natural love and affection entertained by me for my wife Margret D. Deery and my children by her. This 10 August 1865.
Reg: August 15, 1865   Signed: R.D. Deery

Page 564 - James Merritt Trust Deed to R.S. McConnell. One filly, black spotted cow and calf, and a brown mare. This August 15, 1865.
Reg: August 15, 1865   Signed: James Merritt

Page 564 - H.L. Marbury, J.P. Marbury Deed to J.D. Web(Webb). Land in Bedford County and District No. 9 on the North Fork of Duck River and bounded by lands of the late J.K. Clark. Containing 30 acres. This 20 September 1865.
Reg: August 17, 1865   Signed: H.L. Marbury
                              J.P. Marbury

Page 565 - William Campbell, admr. Deed to William Hastings 10 acres. On 10 October 1859 Alfred Campbell now deceased, and of whose estate I am administrator, sold to R.W. Long a tract of land and whereas said R.D. Long sold to William Hastings. This August 15, 1865.
Reg: August 17, 1865   Signed: William Campbell, Admr.

Page 566 - John Woodward Deed to William Woodward. Land owned by the late German Woodward at the time of his death being on the waters of Sinking Creek in Bedford County and District No.19 and bounded by a 5000 acre survey in the name of George Dougherty, by the east bank of Sinking Creek and known as Stephen Porter's old corner (No. 6), to Alexander Dysart's line on Benj. Haslett's corner, and by lands of the heirs of J.W.C. Cunningham. Deceased. Containing 260 acres and 3 poles. This 10 August 1865.
Reg: August 17, 1865   Signed: John Woodward

Page 567 - N. Thompson, Sr. Deed to W.S. Jett. Land in Bedford County and District No. 8 and bounded by the Shelbyville and Unionville Turnpike Road in the east boundary line of the old original Lenoir Grant. Containing 58 acres and 62 poles.
Reg: August 17, 1865   Signed: N. Thompson, Sr.

Page 568 - James A. Puckett and others Deed to James T. Cothran. I, James B. Puckett, Lee A. Winn and Martha A. Wynn sold to James T. Cothran land in Bedford County and District No. 10 and adjoining the lands of Judith Lawrance, by lands of Joseph Harris, by lands of Cothran's heirs, and by lands of Parsons. Containing 72 acres. It being the place formerly owned by Henry Arnold and on which Lee A. Wynn and wife are at present residing and being the place purchased by James A. Puckett at Chancery Sale. This 18 August 1865.
Wit: Edm'd Cooper   Signed: James A. Puckett
Reg: August 18, 1865   Lee A. Wynn
                                      Martha J. Wynn

Page 569 - William Gunn, admr. Deed to Isaac M. West. I, William Gunn, administrator of John Gunn, deceased, sold to I.M. West land in Bedford County and District No. 25 and containing 34 acres and 21 poles, and bounded by a corner of W.R.H. Stem, and by Weavers' line. It being said land conveyed to Edmund Green by Thomas B. Karr dated 31 January 1850. This 10 December 1855.
Reg: August 22, 1865   Signed: Wm. Gunn, Admr.

Page 570 - R.D. Blair Deed to Wm.S. Jett. Land in Bedford County and Civil District No. 4 and bounded by E.G. Lewis, and by the center of Bellbuckle Creek. Containing 4 acres. This August 21, 1865.
Reg: August 22, 1865   Signed: R.D. Blair

Page 571 - Windsor Green Deed 259 acres to William M. Green. This 12 January 1861. Conveyed the interest being one eleventh of two tracts of land in Bedford County and District No. 2. One lot containing 140 acres on the west side of Doddys Creek and bounded by the lands of Edwin Hart's heirs east of David R. Vance, and by lands of James M. Isom. And another tract containing 119 acres on the east side of Doddys Creek and bounded by lands of James Green, deceased, by lands of Robert H.

Green and Thos. Holland, by lands of Elijah Green, and by lands of James M. Isom and William M. Green. This 24 August 1865.
Reg: August 24, 1865   Signed: Windsor Green

Page 572 - A.P. Eakin Deed to Sarah E. Porter. Argile P. Eakin in 1863 given my bond to convey title to certain property in the Town of Shelbyville to R.D. Porter. One lot in the Town of Shelbyville on the east side of the Public Square and fronting said Public Square, a three story brick house known as the Evans House and adjoining the house or Deery Drug Store and now owned by Lewis Mankle, and by a brick store house now owned by Henry Yancy and Moses Marshall. This 23 August 1865.
Reg: August 29, 1865   Signed: A.P. Eakin

Page 572 - Jo. D. Wilhoite, Young Wilhoite and T.P. Wilhoite Deed to Horatio Coop. The members of the family Wilhoite and brothers have sold to Hortatio Coop a tract of land in Bedford County and District No. 5 and bounded by lands of John L. Jacobs, by lands of G.W. Cone, by James Robinson and Mrs. Womack's dower, by James Cortner and perhaps Mrs. Coop. Containing 38 acres. This 19 August 1865.
Reg: August 29, 1865   Signed: Jo. D. Wilhoite
                                    Young Wilhoite
                                    Thos. P. Wilhoite

Page 573 - Thomas Burnett Deed to Samuel Morton. A certain town lot in the corporation limits of Shelbyville near the big spring on which A. McRoy now lives and is bounded by a street running west by the Big Spring, by a vacant lot lying between this lot and the Big Spring, by the lot of Richard Foreman, Jr., by the lot of C.T. Martin it being the same house and lot I purchased of Geo. Davidson and others. This 29 August 1865.
Reg: August 29, 1865   Signed: Thomas Burnett

Page 573 - J.P. Hutton and Robert Clark Deed from Wm. M. Statum. Land sold to John P. Hutton and Robert Clark of Bedford County a tract of land on the waters of Fall Creek, Civil District No. 5 and adjoining the road H. Coop's corner. Containing 66 acres and 35 poles. This 16 October 1862.
Reg: August 30, 1865   Signed: W.M. Tatum

Page 574 - W.W. Hastings Deed to C.J. Burrow. William W. Hastings have sold unto Calvin J. Burrow a tract of land in Bedford County and Civil District No. 23 adjoining lands of Jacob Kiser, John Koonce, Woodward and Smiley. Containing 10 acres, being the same tract that Wm. Campbell, admr. Of Alfred Campbell, deceased, deeded to me August 15, 1865. This August 30, 1865.
Reg: August 30, 1865   Signed: W.W. Hastings

Page 575 - Robert M. Smith and wife - Decree - Exparte. This 20 August 1865. After examination of Mary Jane Smith taken in

court separate from her husband and it appearing to the court that Mary Jane Smith is the owner in her own right and apart from her husband, the slaves and land mentioned in the petition and no trustee named. A trustee to be appointed by court and that she desires to have a trustee appointed for her. She desires that her husband Robert M. Smith be appointed.
Reg: August 30, 1865   Signed: R.K. Kercheval, C&M

576 - Middleton Holland Trust Deed to A.S. Colyar. Land in Bedford County and what is known as the Rowesville District and bounded by John Jamison, by Jack Bates, by Jack Hight south of the Rowesville Road, by M.C. Johnson, and by Wiley Riggins near a spring. Containing 167 acres. I am the senior partner indebted to the firm of Gardner & Co. of Nashville, Tennessee. This 29 August 1865.
Reg: August 31, 1865   Signed: M. Holland

Page 577 - Samuel S. Morton Deed to G.C. Neely. A lot in Bedford County and in the Town of Shelbyville known as a part of Lot No. 71 and bounded by spring Street. This 31 August 1865.
Reg: September 1, 1865   Signed: S.S. Morton

Page 578 - James Groomes to P.L. Wade. Deed of Trust. I am indebted to P.L. Wade. I do hereby convey my sorrel mare and colt. This 2 September 1865.
Wit: R.B. Davidson   Signed: James Groomes
     L. Evans
     Philamon Hillliard(?)
Reg: September 4, 1865

Page 578 - Robert Mathews Deed to Thomas H. Coldwell, Trustee of J.H. McGrew. Sold 6 acres and 3 poles of land near the Town of Shelbyville. This 5 September 1865.
Reg: September 6, 1865   Signed: Robert Mathews

Page 579 - Thomas H. Coldwell, Trustee of J.H. McGee(McGrew) Deed to Wm. J. Cochran. Whereas John H. McGee(McGrew) by deed dated 2 May 1865 to me interest in land in Bedford County and District No. 7 and containing 6 acres and __ poles and bounded by lands of John W. Cowan, on Union Street, by lands of Robert Mathews and the balance was made for the purpose of securing to Robert Mathews the balance of the purchase money still due on said lot and Thomas S. Sharp. This 5 May 1865.
Reg: September 6, 1865   Signed: Thomas H. Coldwell,
                                      Trustee of
                                      John B. McGee(McGrew?)

Page 579 - James H. Neil Title Bond to Elizabeth J. Knott. James H. Neil, executor of the Last Will and Testament of John T.Neil, deceased, am indebted to Elizabeth J. Knott wife of A.b. Knott. Sold unto Elizabeth J. Knott a Town Lot in the Town of Shelbyville, Bedford County and contains one half acre adjoining

T.D. Ledbetter and Edmund Cooper, by W.H. Wisener, by a street running North and south which is the first street west of the Big Spring, and by G.W. Buchanan. This March 29, 1865.
Reg: September 6, 1865   Signed: Jas. H. Neil, Exr. Of
                                        John T. Neil, deceased

Page 580 - John H. Rice Deed to George W. Gardner. Land in Bedford County and District No. 23 and bounded by John W. Gardner'' land, by Huffman's line, by John Martin's line, by W.W. Hyles, and by John W. Gardner. Containing 100 acres and being the tract I bought at Chancery sale except 3 acres I conveyed to John T. Martin. This 11 November 1864.
Reg: September 7, 1865   Signed: J.H. Rice

Page 581 - John T. Yancy Deed to William L. Yancy. Land in Bedford County and Civil Districts No. 3 and 7 on the old Wartrace Road known as the Widow Marshall place and containing about 25 acres. This 8 September 1865.
Reg: September 8, 1865   Signed: John T. Yancy

Page 582 - William T. Myers and others Deed to Andrew Myers. Whereas Wm. T. Myers, Martha Myers, L.S. Myers under the firm and style of W.T. Myers & Co. and indebted to W.T. Myers former guardian of Thomas R. Myers and Andrew E. Myers. Conveyed unto Andrew E. Myers land in Bedford County and District No. 3 and bounded by lands of Jonas Myers, by lands of known as the church property. Containing 18 acres and known as the Erwin & Myers hemp factory place. This 31 August 1865.
Wit: Thomas J. Myers   Signed: L.S. Myers
     H.A. Davidson   Martha Myers
Reg: September 8, 1865   Thomas R. Myers
                                        A.E. Myers

Page 583 - G.T. Tucker Deed to W.M. Tatum. Land in Bedford County and District No. 8 and containing 23 acres and bounded by James Sanders, and by John Brown, and by E. Wilson. This September 8, 1865.
Reg: September 8, 1865   Signed: G.T. Tucker

Page 583 - G.T. Tucker Deed to W.M. Tatum. Land in Bedford County and District No. 8 and bounded by said center of Fall Creek. Containing 4 acres. This September 8, 1865.
Reg: September 8, 1865   Signed: G.T. Tucker

End Book DDD

DEED BOOK EEE

1865 - 1866

THE RECONSTRUCTION YEARS

Page 1-47 - Index

Page 48 - A.P. Sherrill and wife to W.L. Riggins. This 19
August 1865. Andrew Sherrill and Elizabeth A. Sherrill his wife
sold to W.L. Riggin all the right title claim and interest to
which said Elizabeth A. Sherrill is entitled as sister and heir
at law of John T. Weaver in the following tracts of land in
Bedford County and Civil District No. 25 on the waters of
Normans Creek and bounded by Z. Weaver, by a log lying on
Normans Creek, by G. Hufman, by Holland's west boundary line and
Calahan's line. Containing 70 acres.
Reg: September 18, 1865   Signed: Andrew P. Sherill
                                     Elizabeth A. Sherrill

Page 49 - D.G. Weaver Deed to W.L. Riggins. This 9 September
1865. All the right title claim and interest to which D.G.
Weaver is entitled as brother and heir at law of John T. Weaver
in land in Bedford County and Civil District No. 25 on the
waters of Normans Creek and adjoining Z. Weaver, a log lying in
Normans creek, and by G.H. Hufman and by Holland's line.
Containing 70 acres.
Reg: September 18, 1865   Signed: D.G. Weaver

Page 50 - Thomas W. Warner Deed of Gift to Mary E. Rutledge.
For the love and affection which I have towards my Aunt Mary E,
Rutledge, I have this day do hereby give her one large black
horse free from debts or contracts of her present husband. This
January 7, 1864.
Wit: Edm'd Cooper   Signed: Thomas W. Warner
Reg: September 18, 1865

Page 51 - G.W. Thompson Deed to J.D. Wilhoite. Agreeing to
transfer to me a bill of exchange on A.J. Greer (illegible)
endorsed by G.W. Greer, C.A. Warren and W.S. Jett for
transferring to me a note on D.G. Wheeler and B.G. Field and
W.S. Jett. Said Wilhoite agreeing to pay me when collected
enough out of a note on Jno. H. Wells and Thomas L. Wells. I,
G.W. Thompson have this day sold unto J.D. Wilhoite a Town Lot
in the Town of Shelbyville and house thereon which house and lot
is on the south side of the Public Square and is known as the
Elliott Stand. This September 21, 1865.
Reg: September 18, 1865   Signed: George W. Thompson
                                     Jo. D. Wilhoite

Page 52 - R.B. McLean Deed to J.A. Oden. Land in Rutherford
County, Tennessee and District No. 14, it being the tract on
which I now reside and which was conveyed to me by Wm. T.
Baskett dated 1 January 1858 and in registered in said county in
Book No. 9, pages 389 and 390. Containing 331 acres and 5
poles. Also one other tract of land in Bedford County and Civil
District No. 9 and containing about 198 acres and joins the
lands of John L. Cooper, Robert Blankenship, deceased, Preston
Frazier, John W. Key, and R.H. Barnes, it being the same tract
conveyed to me by James S. Boyed and which is recorded in
Bedford County. I am indebted to Wm. T. Baskett. This 1
September 1865.
Wit: Richard Nance   Signed: R.B. McLean
     J.E. Dromgoole
Reg: September 18, 1865 .

Page 54 - P.H. Manier Deed to Henry J. Taylor. A certain lot in
the Town of Fairfield known as the Cooper lot and bounded by the
Manchester and Shelbyville Road, by John S. Davis, and by Lands
belonging to the estate of Jno. Scott, deceased. Containing
about 2 acres. This 14 September 1865.
Reg: September 19, 1865   Signed: P.H. Manier

Page 54 - James Finch Trust Deed to John E. Scruggs. James
Finch of Bedford County sold to John E. Scruggs all the right
title claim and interest in a tract of land in District No. 2
and bounded by lands of John S. Davis, by lands of Osborne and
Anderson, and by lands of John A. Couch and Douglas, and by
lands of Singleton's heirs. Containing about 460 acres. I am
indebted to David Jarrett. This 14 September 1865.
Reg: September 19, 1865   Signed: James Finch

Page 56 - Martha Sparrow Deed to Wm. A. Mann. Land in Bedford
County and Civil District No. 11 in Township or Section No. 6
and part of Section 6 on the waters of the North Fork of Duck
River and bounded by the original survey, and by Lot No. 7, and
Lot No. 3, and Lot No. 2, and by the widow Jones heirs' corner,
it being the same corner that R.W. (illegible) bought of Thos.
A. Sikes. This September 9, 1865.
Wit: E.S. Wortham   Signed: Martha Sparrow
     S.G. Reaves
Reg: September 14, 1865

Page 57 - Simon Greenbaum Deed to Janetta Greenbaum. Simon
Greenbaum of the City of Louisville, TN (KY). In the Circuit
Court of the State of Kentucky for the purpose of selling of
real estate in the Town of Owensboro the separate property of my
wife Janetta Greenbaum. This September 7, 1865.
Reg: September 19, 1865   Signed: Simon Greenbaum

Page 58 - William Brown Deed to John T. Stephens. Both of
Bedford County. A house and lot in North Shelbyville and
bounded by a corner of Silas W. Clay's lot on the west side of

140

Martin Street, and by a new street opened by Thomas Lipscomb. This 13 August 1857.
Reg: September 19, 1865   Signed: Wm. Brown

Page 58 - William Brown Deed to John T. Stephens.   Both of Bedford County.   A house and lot in North Shelbyville and bounded by a corner of Silas W. Clay's lot on the west side of Martin Street, and by a new street opened by Thomas Lipscomb. This 13 August 1857.
Reg: September 19, 1865   Signed: Wm. Brown

Page 59 - John T. Stephens Deed to R.P. Shapard.   A certain house and lot in the Town of Shelbyville, Bedford County and bounded by Silas W. Clay's lot, by Martin Street, by Thomas Lipscomb.   The same house and lot I purchased from Wm. Brown in the year 1857.   This 15 September 1865.
Reg: September 19, 1865   Signed: John T. Stephens

Page 60 - R.W. and W.F. Pearson Deed to B.F. Pearson.   This 12 April 1865.   Land in Bedford County on the waters of Bellbuckle Creek in Civil District No. 4 and bounded by S. Elkins' line, by corner of Lot No. 2 Elizabeth Elkins' lot, by Robert Davidson's line, by corner of Mary Elkins' dower, and by the Shelbyville Road.   It being the same land described in the decree rendered on 10 March 1865.   This September 17, 1865.
Reg: September 19, 1865   Signed: R.P. Parsons
                               W.F. Parsons

Page 61 - H.W. Holt Deed to Samuel R. Hailey.   H.W. Holt sold unto Samuel R. Hailey my entire interest in the W.T. Green lot, a certain lot of land in the Town of Wartrace known as the W.T. Green lot in Bedford County and District No. 3 and bounded by the Buchanan lot, and by Coffee & Mullins' lot.   This September 18, 1865.
Reg: September 19, 1865   Signed: H.W. Holt

Page 61 - C.L. Pyron Deed of Trust to Thomas H. Coldwell.   All the right title claim and interest which I have in and unto a certain tract in Bedford County and Civil District No. 2 and bounded by lands of James M. Johnson, by lands of Robert Moffatt, by lands of Elisha Reed, and by lands of John M. Johnson.   Containing 46 acres and known as the Three Forks Mill tract and on which three mills situated.   This 19 September 1865.
Reg: September 20, 1865   Signed: C.L. Pyron

Page 62 - James M. Johnson Deed to C.L. Pyron.   Land in District known as the Trigg tract which he purchased from Hay & Trigg, and containing about 3 acres, exchange for land sold and conveyed to said Johnson from the mill tract by said Pyron known as the Three Fork Mill in Bedford County.   Land beginning at the

center of the spring near the house of James M. Johnson, and by the Three Fork Mill tract. This 19 September 1865.
Reg: September 20, 1865   Signed: J.M. Johnson
                                         C.L. Pyron

Page 63 - W.M. Tatum Deed to Joseph Neil. Land in Bedford County and District No. 8 and containing 23 acres and bounded by James Sanders, by John Brown, and by E. Willson's heirs. This September 8, 1865.
Reg: September 20, 1865   Signed: W.M. Tatum

Page 64 - W.M. Tatum Deed to Joseph Neil. Land in Bedford County and District No. 8 and bounded by Fall Creek. This September 8, 1865.
Reg: September 20, 1865   Signed: W.M. Tatum

Page 65 - James M. Neely Deed to Edmund Cooper. Land containing 7 acres which I many years ago verbly sold to Green T. Neely, lying in the south west corner of his tract sold by said Cooper to Theophilus Thompson and bounded by a corner of one of Gilchrist's grants, by the beginning, and corner of the tract sold by Theophilus Thompson to G.W. Thompson. This 5 August 1865.
Reg: September 20, 1865   Signed: James M. Neely

Page 66 - Edmund Cooper Deed to Theophilus Thompson. Both of Bedford County and District No. 18. Containing 112 acres. This 7 August 1865.
Reg: September 20, 1865   Signed: Edmund Cooper

Page 66 - Theophilus Thompson Deed to G.W. Thompson. Theophilus Thompson of Bedford County sold unto George W. Thompson all the right claim and interest which I have in a tract of land in Bedford County and District No. 18. Containing 112 acres and 9 poles. This 7 August 1865.
Reg: September 20, 1865   Signed: Theo. Thompson

Page 67 - G.W. Thompson Deed to W.N. Gwynn. House and lot on the north east corner of the Public Square by transferring to me, I have sold unto W.N. Gwynn a tract of land in District No. 18 of Bedford County. Containing 112 acres it being the place known as the green T. Neely place and recently purchased by me from Theophilus Thompson. This 18 September 1865.
Reg: September 20, 1865   Signed: G.w. Thompson

Page 68 - W.N. Gwynn Deed to G.W. Thompson. Land in the 18th District of Bedford County known as the Green T. Neely place. I have sold unto G.W. Thompson a tract of land on the north east corner of the Public Square in the Town of Shelbyville known as the (illegible) corner and formerly owned by General Robt.

Cannon and bounded by the corner of the Public Square and Martin Street, and by D.S. Evans' corner. This 18 September 1865.
Reg: September 20, 1865   Signed: W.N. Thompson

Page 69 - James M. Johnson Deed to Rufus Smith. Land in Bedford County and Civil District No. 2 and bounded by Ann Batt's corner, by the Garrison Fork of Duck River in Cannon's line, by the corner of the mill tract, by Maupin's corner, and by Mrs. Batt's corner. Containing 253 acres. This land is made out from a survey (illegible) of said tract of land by W.M. Wallace December 1, 1852 and as my deed is not now before me I have made this deed. This September 19, 1865.
Wit: (illegible)   Signed: J.M. Johnson
     (illegible)
Reg: September 20, 1865

Page 70 - T.S. Word Deed to Ellen Farrar. Land containing 27 acres and 98 poles. This 19 September 1865.
Wit: John E. Frost   Signed: T.S. Word
     Robt. Hastings
Reg: September 21, 1865

Page 71 - Ellen Farrar Deed to T.S. Word. Land in District No. 22 south of the Columbia Road. Containing 9 acres and 58 poles, A second piece lying north of the Columbia Road. Containing 10 acres and 147 poles. This __ day of __ 1862.
Wit: John E. Frost   Signed: E.J. Farrar
     Robt. Hastings   I.J. Farrar
Reg: September 21, 1865

Page 72 - M.E.W. Dunaway Deed to Margret T. Wortham. Sold unto my daughter Margret T. Wortham wife of John Wortham, free from her husband a certain house and lot in the corporate limits of Shelbyville and bounded on the north edge of the Scull Camp Ford Road. Containing 104 poles. This 26 September 1865.
Reg: September 29, 1865   Signed: M.E.W. Dunaway

Page 73 - R.M. Smith Deed of Trust to William Gosling. For securing William Gosling, my security, I am complainant and Alexander Cotner is defendant. I hereby convey to said William Gosling in trust a tract of land in Civil District No. 25 of Bedford County and bounded by J.H. Scott in the Village of Roseville, by the Hillsboro Road, by west of the ridge on the mill race, and the cave spring, and a creek, and by W.S. Troxler's corner. This 28 September 1865.
Reg: September 29, 1865   Signed: R.M. Smith

Page 71 - John F. Neil and James H. Neil, Executors, Lease to Jo. H. Thompson. In September 1858 John F Neil and James H. Neil leased to John F. Neil a lot in the Town of Shelbyville then owned by them on which was an office and on the south west corner of the Square which office is now owned and occupied by

Thomas Lipscomb the said part leased being the west part of the said lot and is the same now occupied by John F. Neil as a smith shop and on which is a small brick house and bounded by a brick house belonging to R.S. Dwiggins, by Water Street, by Dr. Lipscomb's lot, and by a lot belonging to Paskiel Rousee. This 28 September 1865.
Reg: September 28, 1865   Signed: John F. Neil
                                        James H. Neil

Page 75 - Magdaline H. Sanders Power of attorney to G.W. Sanders. Magdaline H. Sanders do appoint G.W. Sanders my attorney in fact to demand and receive from all persons indebted and by note &c in State of Tennessee. This 15 August 1865.
Wit: G.W. Boyed   Signed: Magdaline H. Sanders
     Jacob M(illegible)
Reg: September 29, 1865

Page 76 - Elizia L. Cates and Willis H. Cates Deed to W.H. McFarling. Sold unto William H. McFarling a tract of land in Bedford County and District No. 23 and bounded by lands of Henry Hines, by the lands of Andy Hines, by lands of B. McFarling, and by lands of the heirs of Robert Reed, deceased. Containing 1 ½ acres. This September 29, 1865.
Reg: September 29, 1865   Signed: Elizia L. Cates
                                        Willis H. Cates

Page 76 - Sallie Sprouse Deed of Gift to Jennings Moor. In consideration of the Deed of Gift to me and granted by Sallie Sprouse, I bind myself to take proper care of and said Sallie Sprouse or cause the same to be done for the remainder of her life and cause her to be buried in good style after her death.
Wit: B.F. Duggan   Signed: Jennings Moor
     Wm. Collins
Reg: October 3, 1865

Page 77 - Horatio Coop Deed to Wm. J. Coop. I have this day sold unto W.J. Coop a tract of land in Bedford County and Civil District No. 5 and bounded by lands of John L. Jacobs, by the lands of G.W. Cone, by James Robinson and Mrs. Warmack, and by James Claxton. Containing 38 acres. This 2 October 1865.
Reg: October 4, 1865   Signed: Horatio Coop

Page 78 - C.P. Houston Deed to William Houston. For the love and affection for my son William Houston, I give unto him a tract of land. Containing 100 acres. This January 2, 1861.
Reg: October 4, 1865   Signed: C.P. Houston

Page 79 - Middleton Holland Deed to Willis Blanton. A tract of land in Bedford County and in the village of Normandy, bounded by the Nashville and Chattanooga Rail Road, by Blanton's line, by William Hyles, and by Chesley Arnold's line. This 14 January 1861.

Wit: G.E. Borden   Signed: Middleton Holland
     S.V. Blanton
Reg: October 4, 1865

Page 79 - M.P. Gentry Deed to Irby Morgan & Co. On 11 May 1863,
I gave a title bond to Irby Morgan of the firm Irby Morgan & Co.
of the City of Nashville, to make his a deed to a tract of land
in Bedford County and is registered in Book DDD, page 297. I,
Meredith P. Gentry, sold to Irby Morgan, Jno. P. White, Charles
A. Warren and Bolivar H. Cook of said firm of Irby Morgan & Co.
in Bedford County adjoining a corner of A. Ray, deceased, to
Freeman's corner, and west bank of Sinking Creek, and to the
center of the Hannah Gap Road. Containing 898 acres and 140
poles. Also one other tract of land in said county upon the
waters of Sinking Creek purchased by me of James Jeans and is
registered and it contains 12 acres of cedar land and adjoining
the above tract. Containing 28 acres and deeded to me by one
register by Michael Moore. This 11 September 1865.
Reg: October 5, 1865   Signed: M.P. Gentry

Page 81 - James Russ Mortgage to J.H. McGrew. The town lot on
which I now live in the Town of Shelbyville, Bedford County and
bounded by the old corporation opposite the center of Martin
Street, to a rock fence, and by a corner of a poultry house.
Containing 2 acres. This September 26, 1865.
Reg: October 5, 1865   Signed: James Russ

Page 82 - William G. Cowan Deed to James Russ. April 1, 1863.
Both citizens of the Town of Shelbyville. A tract of land known
as the Moffat Place being the same the said Russ now lives and
bounded by the old corporation opposite the center of Martin
Street, and by a rock fence, and by a poultry house. Containing
2 acres.
Reg: October 5, 1865   Signed: Wm. G. Cowan

Page 83 - E.G. Hamilton Mortgage to S.A. Harper and M.B.
Hamilton. I, Edward G. Hamilton of Bedford County sold unto
Sarah A. Harper and M.B. Hamilton land in Civil District No. 19
of Bedford County, containing about 160 acres and bounded by
Robert Montgomery, R.M. Sikes, by Elizabeth Chapman, and heirs
of H.M. Oneal, and by Robert Hardin, and by Jacob Birkin. I am
indebted to James L. Scudder, Charles (illegible), Davidson
McAdams, James Dillard, (illegible) Jones, and R.J. Orr. This 5
October 1865.
Reg: October 5, 1865   Signed: E.G. Hamilton

Page 84 - Robert Mathews Judgment against A.P. Eakin, Lucretia
Eakin and R.S. Kimbro. District No. 28. Plaintiff recover of
the defendant the balance of the debt interest and damages.
This 9 October 1865.
Reg: October 9, 1865   Signed: James H. Neil, Clerk

Page 85 - J.F. Elliott Deed of Trust to John Landrum. A tract of land bounded by Richard Nance, by A. Brice, by John Landrum, and John McGuire. Containing 155 acres lying in District No. 10 of Bedford County. This 11 October 1865.
Reg: October 20, 1865   Signed: J.F. Elliott

Page 86 - William L. Yancy Deed to John T. Yancy. Whereas my deceased mother Levina Yancy, whose maiden name Levina Marshall, was the owner of one share in the division, said share being an undivided one fourth of a certain tract of land near the Town of Shelbyville, containing 25 acres, being which said land is in the 3rd and 7th District of Bedford County and adjoining the lands of G.W. Thompson, Lucretia Eakin and Moses Marshall, known as the widow Marshall place and where at the death of my said mother her said share descended to her three children, to wit, James W. Yancy, John T. Yancy now the owner of my own share of my two brothers James W. and John T. being the entire share of my said mother which I now sell to my said brother John T. Yancy. This 13 October 1865.
Reg: October 16, 1865   Signed: Wm. L. Yancy

Page 87 - D.B. Huffman and wife Deed to W.L. Riggins. This 20 September 1865. D.B. Huffman and Sarah Huffman his wife sold unto W.L. Riggins a tract of land in Bedford County and Civil District No. 25 on the waters of Normans Creek and bounded by Z. Weaver, by said creek, by G. Hyman, by G.H. Huffman, and by Holland's south boundary line. Containing 70+ acres, being one eighth.
Wit: A. McLeroy   Signed: D.B. Huffman
Reg: October 16, 1865   Sarah Huffman

Page 88 - Amasa W. Manier Deed to George W. Reed. I have sold unto George W. Reed a tract of land in Bedford County and Civil District No. 9 and bounded by James Forbes, by Foster's line, by Hastings' line, by John Landrum's line, and by James Foster's corner. Containing 88 acres.
Wit: W.G. Ozburn   Signed: Amasa W. Manier
     Elisha C. Reed
Reg: October 16, 1865

Page 89 - Nance & McCord Deed to Amasa W. Manier. Whereas William G. Hight by deed dated 18 December 1860 conveyed to us in trust amongst many other things, a certain tract of land in Bedford County and District No. 10, containing 129 acres and 101 poles and bounded at the center of the pike, by Johnson's south boundary line, by Simmons' line, and by the corner of the church lot. This 13 September 1865.
Wit: Allen N. McCord   Signed: Richard Nance
     Benjamin F. Jarrell   Thomas N. McCord, Trustees
Reg: October 16, 1865   of William G. Hight

Page 90 - Nance & McCord Trustees Deed to Allen N. McCord. William G. Hight by deed dated 18 December 1860 convey to us in

trust amongst other things a certain tract of land in Bedford
County and District No. 10, containing 182 acres and 14 poles
and bounded by the center of Eagleville, Unionville and
Shelbyville Turnpike, and by Clems Creek and also a judgment in
favor of John Jordon for part of purchase money. This 30
September 1865.
Wit: Benj. F. Jarrell   Signed: Richard Nance
    C.S. Dudley   Thos. N. McCord
Reg: October 30, 1865

Page 91 - Alonzo Murphy Deed in Trust to A.A. Cooper. Land in
Bedford County and District No. 2, said interest being one sixth
of the entire tract except dower containing 525 acres including
dower of 150 acres and bounded by lands of Andrew Ewing and
Kinchen Stokes, by lands of R.B. Maupin and James Maupin, by
lands of B.B. Buchanan, deceased, and by Andrew Ewing it being
the original tract of Archibald Murphy, deceased, and my
interest being one sixth of the same as one of the legatees of
said Archibald Murphy. NOTE: Long document. This 17 October
1865.
Reg: October 18, 1865   Signed: Alonzo Murphy

Page 93 - Allen N. McCord Receipt and advance bid on land of
W.G. Hight. Whereas W.G. Hight executed his Trust Deed to
Richard Nance and T.N. McCord and on 30 September 1865 a part of
said land conveyed was sold to A.N. McCord by said trustees, he
being the highest bidder and whereas A.N. McCord has judgments
against W.G. Hight. Land sold as property of W.G. Hight by his
trustees and said Allen McCord makes bid for same. This October
17, 1865.
Reg: October 18, 1865   Signed: Allen N. McCord

Page 94 - Transcribe of Proceedings had in the Probate Court of
the Will of Daniel Gilchrist. This being 20th August 1865 and
probating the instrument dated 21 January 1851. Perporting to
the last Will and Testament of Daniel Gilchrist, late of
Lawrence County, deceased, said instrument in writing was
produced to the court by Malcolm Gilchrist and Philip P.
Gilchrist, executors in said instrument with a written agreement
waving all future notices signed by the parties at interest
which is in the words and figurers following, to wit, we, the
widow and heirs at law agree that the will of Daniel Gilchrist
and may be propounded for probate in Probate Court on Monday 20
August 1855. This 18 August 1855.
                Signed: John A. Gilchrist
                    Geo. M. Gilchrist
                    C.M. Gilchrist
Whereupon said cause came in for hearing and said instrument was
produced by Malcom Gilchrist and Philip P. Gilchrist, executors,
and record as the will and testament of Daniel Gilchrist,
deceased. A.W. Buntley, Witness.
In the name of God Amen. I, Daniel Gilchrist being of a sound
mind and disposing memory knowing the uncertainty of life and
the certainty of death and it is appointed for all men once to
die hath made this my Last Will, to wit, First, I give my sole

To God who gave it and my body to the grave until the judgment day. Item Second, that all my household debts shall be paid which are few. Item Third, I will to my beloved wife Nancy A. Gilchrist the following, to wit, Polly a negro woman and her children, Elmira and her children, Caroline and her children, and Becca and her children, and the Carney and Hays notes given for two tracts of land sold them, which (illegible) by her, also my dwelling house and out houses where I now live with the north east quarter of Section 6 and forty acres in the south east corner of the north west (illegible) of said land. Township 5 of Range 7 west with timber sufficiently for fuel and fencing in only given during her life and at her death goes to John A. Gilchrist our youngest son. Item Fourth, I give and bequeath to my beloved sons Malcum J. Gilchrist and Philip P. Gilchrist divisions three and four of lands in Alabama as in the described together with divisions three and four of negros to themselves and children after them and all the lands described in divisions three and four in any part of the state of Tennessee and Madison County, Alabama to themselves. Item Fifth, I will and bequeath to my beloved daughter Catharine M.E. Gilchrist and her body heirs all that land in division first of land first of land in Alabama and all negros described in division first and the land described in division first in Tennessee and Mississippi to herself. Item Sixth, I will and bequeath to my beloved and youngest son John A. Gilchrist and his children all the lands that are described in division Second in Alabama and all the negros in division Second reserving to his mother a lifetime in part of the Alabama division as heretofore specified the land described in Middle Tennessee and Western District to himself. Lots of Alabama First Division.
All the lands lying west of the west boundary line of Range 7 west south of the Tennessee River in Lawrence and Franklin Counties with about eighty six acres that lies adjoining east (illegible) in (illegible) on the south in Mississippi. Second Division all the lands east of the west boundary line of Range 7 south of the Tennessee River to the Huntsville meredian except the lands including fractional Township Three of Range 7 and Section 3 in north west quarter of Section 4 in Township 4, Range 7 west. Third and Fourth division all the lands in Limestone and Lauderdale Counties and in fractional Township 3 of Range 7 west and Section 3 and north west quarter of Section 4 in Township 4 of Range 7 west south of the Tennessee River lots of land in Middle Tennessee and Western District, first lot or division about 400 acres joining William Murphy, Bedford County in two tracts of about 200 acres where deceased Gilchrist now lives in Decatur County and 125 acres in Harden County near Hausbury(?), and other tract of 150 acres in Henderson County. Second lot in division about 730 acres in Bedford County my old place and 110 acres in McNairy County, Tennessee. Third and Fourth division, all the remaining lands in Bedford County, Tennessee including the connection of land joining John Moor east of Shelbyville, lots of negros.
First lot or division (illegible) Jerry and family division and Maria his wife, George Brown and Patsy his wife and his children and old Isaac and wife and two youngest. Second lot and division, Preston and family except Cary, Robert and his family, young Isaac, Jordan and old Jim.

Third lot or division, Peter and family, Lotie and two children and grandchildren, Jesse, Gilbert and Willa his wife and Rachel and child.

Fourth lot or division, George and family, Jerry, Silas, daughter, Daniel, Pheba and children Nancy Jane and child Prince and Caroline his sister.   It is my will also that all the balance of my property un-disposed of at my death shall be divided equally between my four beloved children or sold and the proceeds equally divided as my two executors may think best reserving to myself the privilege of altering or changing this will at pleasure and it is my wish that my two sons Malcum J. Gilchrist and Philip P. Gilchrist be my executors and that they be compelled not to give security as I have full confidence in them.   This the 21st day of January 1851.

Signed: D. Gilchrist

N.B. - It is my will that my son John A. Gilchrist have an equal interest in the Island at Bambridge of about 90 acres as well as the same interest in the water power that joins it on the north.

Wit: A.M. Keller   Signed: D. Gilchrist
    Jos. C. Baker
    A.W. Bently
State of Alabama
Lawrence County
Reg: October 19, 1865

Page 97 - D.A. McCullough Deed in Trust to J.C. Claxton.   Sold to John C. Claxton a horse and a colt.   Executed 2 October 1865. This October 19, 1865.
Reg: Ocyober 19, 1865   Signed: D.A. McCullough

Page 97 - A.M. Trollinger Deed from W.R. Jewell, Town Lot.   Said lot being in the corporate limits of the Town of Shelbyville, Bedford County.   Registered in Bedford County in Book DDD, page 458.   This 18 October 1865.
Reg: October 20, 1865   Signed: W.R. Jewell

Page 98 - Peggy Ault Prossession Deed (Registered).   On 2 July 1856, said land on which said Peggy Ault now lives in District No. 3.   Land containing 84 acres and 76 poles.
Wit: D.S. Shriver   Signed: C.S. Dudley, S.B.C.
    Elisha Harmon
NOTE: Plat on page 98.
Reg: October 21, 1865

Page 99 - Jo. Thompson, Sheriff, Deed to William Word.   This 4 April 1860.   James Story recovered a ·judgment against Wm. B. Phillips, James B. Phillips, Wm. Word and C.B. Word for a tract of land in Normandy, Bedford County and District No. 25 as the property of Wm. B. Phillips and is bounded by the edge of the Rail Road bank in John Jernigan's line.   This 20 October 1865.
Reg: October 21, 1865   Signed: Jo. Thompson, Sheriff

Page 100 - W.T. Adams Deed of Gift to Caroline May. Caroline May of Bedford County. The following property, to wit, horses, cows, hogs, sheep and other items listed in original document. This October 21, 1865.
Reg: October 21, 1865   Signed: W.T. Adams

Page 100 - Sallie Cunningham and G.W. Cunningham Receipt to C.P. Cunningham. Received from Cecero P. Cunningham cash for Deed in Trust made to him by James D. Kincaid on a house and lot in Shelbyville and registered in Book DDD in Bedford County October 18, 1865.
Wit: C.P. Cunningham   Signed: Sallie Cunningham
G.W. Cunningham   G.W. Cunningham
Reg: October 24, 1865

Page 101 - George A. Anderson Note and Levied on bay horse to Thos, Lipscomb. This 19 October 1865.
Wit: T.M. Johnson   Signed: George A. Anderson
     J.F. Johnson
Reg: October 25, 1865

Page 101 - James S. Newton Deed to William H. and Samuel G. Dyer. On 21 July 1863 George Dobson and wife Martha Dobson or Mattie Dobson transferred by deed to me all the right title claim and interest which the said Martha Dobson had in and to the dower tract of land which was allotted to Mary Ann Gabbot as the widow of William Gabbot, deceased, and whereas I have this day sold unto William H. Dyer and Samuel G. Dyer the land. Also I have sold to said W.H. and S.G. Dyer a small tract of land a fraction of that claimed by Martha Dobson in her own right, containing 15 acres and 34 poles. This 28 July 1865.
Reg: October 26, 1865   Signed: Jas. S. Newton

Page 102 - A.M. Trolinger Deed of Gift to Julia Ann and Ida Isibell Trolinger, I have this day given to them a certain house and lot in the corporate limits of Shelbyville, Bedford County and bounded by a street, running west to the Fair Grounds and by the residence of G.W. Buchanan, by the lot of Henry Trolinger formerly owned by R.P. Tatum, by the lot of G.W. Buchanan, and by the lot of Jos. H. Neil. This October 25, 1865
Reg: October 26, 1865   Signed: A.M. Trolinger

Page 103 - Martha A.G. Smith Deed to Edmund Cooper. On 1 January 1864, I have sold unto Edmund Cooper a tract of land on which I am now residing in District No. 8 and bounded by lands of Jo. Williams, by the lands of Newcom Thompson, by lands of S.A. Thompson, and by the lands of G.W. Thompson and others, containing 56 acres, being the place conveyed to me this day by Robert Terry. This 14 August 1865.
Reg: October 27, 1865   Signed: Martha A.G. Smith

Page 103 - John Lents Deed to Benjamin Earnheart, 48 acres.
Land in Bedford County and District No. 18 and bounded by the
bank of Duck River it being the corner of Lot No. 2 by the
division of the land belonging to the estate of George Busey,
deceased. Containing 48 acres. This 28 October 1865.
Wit: Wm. H. Wisener, Sr.   Signed: John Lents
Reg: October 31, 1865

Page 104 - Burrell Ward order to Lewis Tilman, Clerk and Master.
September 8, 1865.   W.J. Whitthorne or Lewis Tilman, Clk &
Master, give Richard Parson credit on his note in your court in
the case of R(illegible) Ward and others heirs of Burrell Ward,
deceased, petition to sell land against me in favor of Alfred
Ransom before Luthern Spear, J.P. of Coffee County.
Reg: October 31, 1865   Signed: Burrell Ward

Page 105 - W.F. Ogilvie Deed to R.C. and Jasper Ogilvie, 39
acres, District No. 5. Land in Bedford County it being the lot
originally willed to me by decree of the Chancery Court of
Bedford County in the division of the estate of James ogilvie,
deceased, and bounded by W.F. Cooper's original tract of land,
by the lot decreed to R.C. Ogilvie, by G.W. Bell and William
Murphy, by B.F. Whitworth, and by John Parker, Sr. Containing
39 acres. This October 28, 1865.
Reg: October 28, 1865   Signed: W.F. Ogilvie

Page 106 - Thomas J. Roane Deed to Lucretia Eakin, ½ lot. Lot
being in Bedford County and in the Town of Shelbyville on the
east side of the Public Square and adjoining a lot owned by A.L.
Stamps and on which he is erecting a brick store house, by the
store house lot of W.G. Cowan, by the store house of Alex. Eakin
and John W. Cowan formerly the property of John Eakin and
others, by the Public Square, and by a lot of A.L Stamps on
which said lot is situated the Drug Store formerly owned by
Roane, White & Jordan being same lot with the house thereon
purchased by Thomas J. Roane and C.A. Robinson, partners under
the style of Robinson & Roane from Wm. J. Whitthorne, admrs.,
with the will annexed of Minos Cannon, deceased.   This 15
October 1865.
Wit: Thomas C. Whiteside   Signed: Thomas J. Roane
     Robt. B. Davidson
Reg: November 1, 1865

Page 107 - Alex. Eakin, J.W. Cowan and Lucretia Eakin Deed to
Roane & Coble. Whereas Lucretia Eakin and Argyle P. Eakin by
conveyance dated 28 November 1863 and registered in Bedford
County in Book DDD, pages 332 and 333 conveyed to John W. Cowan
and Alex. Eakin the Town Lot sold to Thomas J. Roane and N.B.
Coble. Said lot known as Roane's Drug Store located on the east
side of the Public Square in Shelbyville and bounded by the
store house and lot of Wm. G. Cowan, by the store house of Eakin
& Cowan known as the Corner Store which said house was there and
now occupied as a drug store by Thomas J. Roane and known as Lot
No. 3. This 28 October 1865.

Reg: November 1, 1865   Signed: Alex. Eakin
                                       J.W. Cowan
                                       Lucretia Eakin

Page 108 - W.P. Proby and others Deed to Sarah Proby, 50 acres.
Payrom Proby and Joseph Ousley and wife Leatha conveyed to Sarah
Proby all the right title interest and claim that we have as two
of the heirs of J.W. Proby, deceased, real estate of J.W. Proby,
deceased, it being the place on which Sarah Proby now resides
under the will of said J.W. Proby during her life time being the
intention of this deed to relinquish and transfer all our
interest in said real estate to said Sarah Proby, land bounded
by Cowan's place, Gordon Hight, and Kimbro Stanfield place.
This October __ 1865.
Wit: W.W. Stanfield   Signed: W.P. Proby
     James Edmonson   Leatha B. Woosley, for
Reg: November 2, 1865   M. Woosley

Page 109 - L.H. Staton Deed to W.J. Staton. District No. 7.
Land in Bedford County and Civil District No. 7 about a half
mile to the Court House in the Town of Shelbyville and a north
west corner, adjoining the west side of the Old Harpeth Road, by
a corner of Amos Hays' lot, and containing 149 acres. This 12
June 1861.
Reg: November 2, 1865   Signed: L.H. Staton

Page 109 - Samuel R. Haily Deed to Catherine Jenkins, Lot in
Wartrace. Land known as the Buchanan lot being in Bedford
County and District No. 3. This May 6, 1865.
Wit: R.S. Clark   Signed: S.R. Haily
     L.P. Fields
Reg: November 2, 1865

Page 110 - William S. Jett Deed to Thomas B. Cannon.   34 ¾
acres. Both of Bedford County. Land in Bedford County and
Civil District No. 7 and bounded by Duck River at Thomas B.
Cannon's corner, and by Cannon Street. This 15 October 1865.
Reg: November 2, 1865   Signed: Wm. S. Jett

Page 111 - A. Wilson Deed in Trust to John C. Wilson. Augustus
Wilson of Bedford County sold to John C. Wilson a tract of land
in District No. 11, adjoining the lands of Thomas Allison and
Philip Cartright, by lands of Bryant Landers, by lands of Joseph
Anderson and Bryant Landers, and by lands of Kimbro Allison.
Containing about 500 acres and at which I am at present
residing. Also sold other items listed in original document.
NOTE: Long document. This 2 November 1865.
Reg: October 2, 1865   Signed: A. Wilson

Page 113 - W.J. Straton Deed Lot to R.L. Brown. William J.
Straton sold unto R.L. Brown a tract of land in Bedford County
and Civil District No. 7 about half mile from the Court House in

the Town of Shelbyville adjoining A(illegible) Hays' lot.
Containing 149 poles. This November 2, 1865.
Reg: November 3, 1865   Signed: W.J. Straton

Page 114 - Jerriah Dean Deed to F.T.D. Davis.   Jeremiah Dean
sold unto F.T.D. Davis land in Bedford County containing 125
acres adjoining lands of Wm. H. Miles, by lands conveyed is
situated on the head waters of Thompson Creek of Duck River in
Civil District No. 24.   This 19 August 1851.
Wit: Willis Blanton   Signed: Jeremiah Dean
     C.A. Dean
Reg: November 6, 1865

Page 115 - James P. McCuistion Deed to Thomas Thompson. Land in
District No. 7 of Bedford County and bounded by lands of James
Story, and by Claiborn McCuistion tract.   Containing 111 acres
and 7 poles. This 3 November 1865.
Reg: November 7, 1865   Signed: J.P. McCuistion

Page 116 - Lucretia Eakin Title Bond to Ishiel Ward. For a lot
of ground being in the Town of Shelbyville and bounded by
Lucretia Eakin, by Alexander Eakin, and by a street. This July
1, 1865.
Wit: J.H. Eakin   Signed: Lucretia Eakin
     George Eakin
Reg: October 7, 1865

Page 117 - G.W. Buchanan Deed to Sarah Peacock, Town Lot. Lot
in the west end of the Town of Shelbyville surveyed by C.S.
Dudley for N. Thompson, 3rd and conveyed to G.W. Buchanan. Said
lot sold conveying a (illegible) spring known as Spring Lot and
adjoining at a branch, by F(illegible) place, and by Gothain's
line. This November 2, 1865.
Reg: November 7, 1865   Signed: Geo. W. Buchanan

Page 117 - Cornelius Womble and wife Deed to W.W. Gill.
Cornelius Womble and Mary H. Womble, daughter of Isac and
Margaret Bennett sold unto Wilson W. Gill real estate in Bedford
County, This November 8, 1865
Reg: November 8, 1865   Signed: Cornelius Womble
                                       Mary Womble

Page 118 - William T. Thompson and wife Deed to 13 acres to Mary
E. Rutledge. We, Thomas W. Thompson and Hulda B. Thompson, have
sold to Mary E. Rutledge 13 ½ acres of land in Bedford County in
the north west corner of land belonging to Hulda B. Thompson and
adjoining lands of Alexander Sanders, and James Story. This 22
July 1865.
Reg: November 9, 1865   Signed: William T. Thompson
                                       Huldah B. Thompson

Page 119 - Robt Mathews Deed of Gift to Martha Mathews. Robt. Mathews of Bedford County give unto my daughter Martha Ann Mathews, for the love and affection unto her, a lot in the Town of Shelbyville, Bedford County on which there is a brick building for two store houses and now occupied as such, the lot is bounded by the street leading to the bridge across Duck River at Shelbyville, by the property of the Branch Bank of Tennessee, and to the Public Square. This 7 November 1865.
Reg: November 9, 1865   Signed: Robt. Mathews

Page 121 - Robert Mathews Deed of Gift to Virginia B. Armstrong. Robt. Mathews of Bedford County bequeathed unto my daughter Virginia Bell Armstrong of Bedford County a tract of land in Bedford County on the waters of Shipmans Creek and bounded by lands deeded to Dennis Hemby dated 26 January 1854 of which is a place now made by George Cortner, a surveyor, by all the land said Dennis Hemby owned on 14 June 1853 in District No. 25. NOTE: Long document. This 7 November 1865
Reg: November 9, 1865   Signed: Robt. Mathews

Page 123 - Robt. Mathews Deed of Gift to Margaret A. Mathews. I bequeathed unto my daughter (Margaret) Mathews of Bedford County for the love and affection I bear unto her, a tract of land near the Town of Shelbyville, containing about 11 acres it being the place on which I now reside and have resided for many years, and bounded by lands of Wm. G. Cowan where he now lives, by lands of James H. Graham, and by land sold by me to Mrs. Nancy Blackwell in 1863. I reserve the right to residing during my natural life. This 7 November 1865.
Reg: November 11, 1865   Signed: Robt. Mathews

Page 125 - G.B. Moon Deed to B.F. Duggan. George B. Moon of Bedford County sold unto B.F. Duggan, Sr. of the firm of Duggan & Moon of same place, a one half interest in a lot on which the store house of Duggan and Moon stood in the Village of Unionville and in Civil District No. 11 and bounded by D.A. Osment, and in the road leading from Unionville to Chapel Hill, and by J.A. Shannon's lot. Containing 16 acres. This October 23, 1865.
Wit: W.F. McLain   Signed: G.B. Moon
     J.R. Hendon
Reg: November 14, 1865

Page 126 - W.D Cates and James F. Cates Deed to John McAdams. Land in Bedford County and District No. 6 and bounded by lands of P.H. Coats, by lands of Thos. C. Whiteside, by John McAdams and James H. Roan, by Eakin & Cowan. Containing about 200 acres. Our interest being two fifth of one tenth of one ninth of said land. This November 10, 1865.
Reg: November 14, 1865   Signed: James F. Cates
                                        W.D. Cates

Page 126 - Victoria J. Bowers Deed to Henry C. Bowers. Land in 4th District of Bedford County known as the Widow Elkins dower and containing about 125 acres and adjoining the lands of Morris Burney, Harrison Elkins, and others. This 11 November 1865.
Reg: November 14, 1865   Signed: Victoria J. Bowers

Page 127 - Joseph Hastings Deed to Joshua Woosley. Land in Bedford County and District No. 23 and bounded by said Woosley, and John Hastings' line. Containing 11 acres. This November 10, 1865.
Wit: C.S. Dudley   Signed: Joseph Hastings
     James H. Wallace
Reg: November 14, 1865

Page 128 - J.J Kincaid and others to James Kirkpatrick. On 14 October 1862, W.S. Jett executed a deed or bond for a title for James Kincaid for the purpose by which he transferred to and sold to him a lot of ground in the Town of Shelbyville and known as the east part of Lot No. 23, adjoining at an alley, by J.M. Hobbs, and by the Cumberland Presbyterian Church lot. It being the same lot that P. Fay formerly owned and whereon 12 May 1863 said James Kincaid conveyed said lot in trust to secure said W.S. Jett for payment to C.P. Cunningham. Registered in Bedford County in Book DDD, page 306. This 27 October 1865.
Reg: November 14, 1865   Signed: J.J. Kincaid
                                     C.P. Cunningham
                                     W.S. Jett

Page 129 - J.M. Ledbetter Bond for Title to G.W. Cook & P.M. Pickle. I am indebted to G.W. Cook and P.M. Pickle. I conveyed unto them a tract of land in Bedford County and District No. 11 and bounded by Duck River, by lands I sold to Jack Crowell, by lands of Bailey Jones, and by lands of W.W. Hopkins. Containing 225 acres. This 5 November 1865.
Wit: Edm'd Cooper   Signed: J.P. Ledbetter
     William Foreman
Reg: November 14, 1865

Page 130 - T.C.H. Miller Deed to E.M. Cooper, 80 acres. This 20 September 1865 between Thomas C.H. Miller of Marshall County, Tennessee and E.M. Cooper of Bedford County. W.F. Cooper husband of E.M. Cooper. Land in Bedford County and District No. 5 and bounded by the Shelbyville Road, and by W.F. Cooper.
Wit: G.W. Cone   Signed: T.C.H. Miller
     G.W. Bell
Reg: November 15, 1865

Page 131 - Thomas Holland Deed to Martha E. Spencer. Lot of ground in Civil District No. 7 of Bedford County and bounded by a stake in the road leading from Shelbyville to Wartrace in John W. Cowan's line, and by an alley near Steele's line. Containing 2 acres. This 1 October 1865.
Reg: November 13, 1865   Signed: Thomas Holland

Page 132 - R.S. Dwiggins Deed in Trust to C.A. Warren. I have sold unto C.A. Warren all the corn standing in the field and the land transferred to W.W. L(illegible), trustee by me and one of said fields is opposite the school house on the left and side of the Fayetteville Road. Containing 40 acres the interest belonging to Lecil Bartlett is not hereby transferred the other field contain 30 acres on the west side of the road nearest of the house Lecil Bartlett in trust is not transferred in this field, also all the corn standing in the field cultivated by B(illegible) and McCane on the tract of land purchased by me of Randolph N(illegible). Containing 30 acres. Other illegible names in original document. I am indebted to Wiley Perry. This 14 November 1865.
Reg: November 15, 1865   Signed: R.S. Dwiggins

Page 133 - Edmond Cooper Deed to Elizia W. Cummings. I sold by title bond to J.F. Thompson the tract of land. Whereas Jacob F. Thompson has sold the same land by title bond to Salie Spear, wife of Wm. Spear. This 15 November 1865.
Reg: November 16, 1865   Signed: Edm'd Cooper

Page 134 - A. McRoy Mortgage to C.A. Warren. For goods, wares, merchandise and liquors which was sold in the house belonging to Evans & Co. of Nashville on the north east corner of the Public Square of Shelbyville, tables being in said house. This 16 November 1865.
Wit: J.L. Scudder   Signed: A. McRoy
Reg: November 16, 1865

Page 136 - Mary J. Proby Power of Attorney to W.W. Bobo. Mary J. Proby of Lawrance County, Missouri, appointed W.W. Bobo of Morgan County, Illinois my true and lawful attorney to collect and receive all moneys or property which may be and be due me on which Mary become due to me from the estate of Peter R. Proby, deceased, which I full hereto by the death of my father Thomas B. Proby. This 12 October 1865.
Wit: W.J. Furguson   Signed: Mary J. Proby
Reg: November 16, 1865

Page 136 - S.A. Mash Deed 86 acres to Marion A. Mash. This 17 November 1865. Both of Bedford County. Land in Bedford County bounded by William Murphy's land deeded to him by W.J. Davis, by Williams' line and others. Containing 86 acres. Recorded in Book LL, pages 160 and 166 on 27 December 1841.
Wit: Wm. Murphree   Signed: S.A. Mash
     E.A. Blanton
Reg: November 18, 1865

Page 138 - Joel Shofner Deed to William Hiles. Land in Bedford County adjoining Bartlet Philpot and James D. Snody. Containing 111 acres. This 21 November 1861.
Wit: Thompson Hiles   Signed: Joel Shofner
     Daniel P. Shofner

Reg: Nov 18, 1865

Page 139 - Robt. Mathews Trust Deed to James F. Farrer. Bedford
County.   I have sold to the highest bidder a house and lot
containing 1 acre and 140 poles as conveyed to me in trust by
J.C. Shapard and by Deed of Trust dated 2 October 1861 and
registered in Bedford County, page 18 and 19 (book not given).
Said land was struck off to me said Farrer by Wm. Brown,
auctioneer. This 18 November 1865.
Reg: November 20, 1865   Signed: Robt. Mathews, Trustee

Page 140 - Thomas Flynn Deed of Trust to Martin Glynn.   Land
which I purchased of the executors of Robt. Cannon, deceased,
containing about 2 acres situated in or near the N(ewsom ?)
grave yard and between that and the lands of B.B. Bivins. This
18 November 1865.
Reg: November 18, 1865   Signed: Thomas Flynn

Page 141 - A.P. Eakin and Lucretia Eakin Deed to Oliver Cowan.
Lot in the Town of Shelbyville on which is now situated a
cottage house, containing 3 rooms and out buildings &c and
bounded by corner of J.W. Cowan and on the street running in
front of Mrs. L. Eakins' residence, to Brittain Street, to J.W.
Cowan's corner. This November 14, 1865.
Wit: November 18, 1865   Signed: A.P. Eakin
                                      Lucretia Eakin

Page 142 - J.H. McGrew Deed to Louis Mankel Lot in Shelbyville,
adjoining Lot No. 8 on the north side of Main Street, and an
alley, being the south half of Lot No. 82.   This 16 October
1865.
Reg: November 20, 1865   Signed: J.H. McGrew

Page 143 - W.S. Brame Deed to Silas Williams.   Land in Civil
District No. 9 of Bedford County, containing 45 acres, my
interest being the one ninth part thereof and bounded by lands
of J.T. Wheelhouse, by lands of myself and William Primrose, by
lands of the Harris', and by lands of L.M. Rankin it being the
land belonging to the heirs of Elizabeth Williams, deceased.
This 20 November 1865.
Reg: November 20, 1865   Signed: W.S. Brame

Page 143 - State of Tennessee Deed to Richardson Clardy.   Paid
unto the Treasurer of State of Tennessee for use of the common
school, sold unto Richardson Clardy land containing 69 acres and
28 poles in Bedford County on the waters of North Fork in Range
3, District No. 6 and bounded by Lot No. 5.   Nashville, 17 April
1856.
Wit: L.M.W. Burton, Sec.   Signed: Andrew Jackson
Recorded in Book No. 9 in Nashville 17, 1856.
Reg: November 20, 1865

Page 144 - John Burcheen Deed to Thomas N. Ray. Land in District No. 18 and bounded by Lot No. 5 in the division of the lands belonging to the estate of Lewis Gant, deceased, and adjoining Earnhart's line. Containing 105 acres. This 5 September 1865.
Wit: Edm'd Cooper   Signed: John H. Burcheen
Reg: November 20, 1865

Page 145 - Thomas H. Coldwell Deed to James T. Cannon. Land executed to me by him some time in June 1857 a tract of land in Bedford County and Civil District No. 7, bounded by the center of the Shelbyville and Unionville Turnpike Road where the old Warner Dirt Road comes unto said turnpike road, and by where T.J. Williams now lives. Containing 1 ¾ acres. This 22 November 1865.
Reg: 22 November 1865   Signed: Thos. H. Coldwell, Trustee
                                             Of W.B. Parker

Page 146 - John S. Norvell and wife Deed to H.C. Kanard. John S. Norvell and Mary A. Norvell sold unto H.C. Kanard land in 3rd District of Bedford County and bounded by lands of Jack George, by lands of M.C. George, by lands of R.J. King, and lands of H.C. Kanard. Containing 100 acres. This 22 November 1865.
Reg: November 23, 1865   Signed: John S. Norvell
                                             Mollie A. Norvell

Page 147 - A.C. Wood Deed to Edm'd Cooper, Executor of W.F. Daniel, deceased. Wiley F. Daniel, deceased. All the land on which I am living in District No. 23 of Bedford County adjoining lands of John Wells, W.G. Cowan, and on the south side of Duck River. Containing 100 acres. This 22 November 1865.
Wit: William Frierson   Signed: A.C. Wood
     William Drummons
Reg: November 22, 1865

Page 148 - Thomas Nance Deed to E.A. Reagor. Land in Bedford County on the waters of Big Flat Creek in District No. 24 and bounded a (illegible) spring of Flat Creek, and Reagor's spring. Containing 15 ½ acres. This 18 November 1865.
Reg: November 23, 1865   Signed: Thos. Nance

Page 149 - John W. Cowan Deed from William Frierson. Shelbyville, July 23, 1865. Sold unto John W. Cowan, Sr. to one fifth share (illegible) stock as one of the legatees of Ervin J. Frierson, deceased, in two tracts of land, one being at Shelbyville and other a half mile below on Duck River, also one grist mill with houses and land on both sides of said river, and attached to the cotton factory and grist mill.
Wit: Minos Cannon   Signed: William Frierson
     Thos. M. Coldwell
Reg: November 23, 1865

158

Page 150 - Joseph D. Wilhoite Deed to W.S. Jett, 463 acres. Land in Bedford County near the Town of Shelbyville and bounded by a store, corner of Thomas B. Cannon lived, by the Duck River, and to the corner of Robt. T. Cannon's land, and by Gentry's line. Containing 463 acres. This 3 May 1865.
Reg: November 24, 1865   Signed: J.D. Wilhoite

Page 151 - George Hufman Deed to D.P(T?). Hufman and others. This 1 November 1865. George Hufman of Bedford County sold unto Daniel P(T?). Hufman, Moses T. Hufman and Michael D. Hufman of Bedford County a tract or plantation in Bedford County and containing 367 acres on the waters of Gage Mill Creek a south branch of the Barren Fork of Duck River, bounded by a tract known Ake's tract, by John Blanton's tract, and by Blanton's spring, and by Lemuel Blanton's line and by others.
Reg: November 24, 1865   Signed: George Huffman

Page 153 - Jo. Thompson and others Deed to Chasen Friends Lodge No. 11, IOOF. On 22 December 1847 John Eakin, William Eakin and Thomas Eakin conveyed to us and James R. Terry by deed a house and lot in the Town of Shelbyville known as the Odd Fellows Lodge, part by the lodge known as Chasen Friends Lodge No. 11 in Town of Shelbyville, bounded by the west side of Martin Street, and by a brick building. The house and lot used and occupied by the Lodge as a Lodge Room. This 26 September 1865.
Wit: Thomas H. Coldwell   Signed: Jo. Thompson
Reg: November 27, 1865   William Brown
                                         B.F. Whitworth

Page 154 - Joel Shofner and John H. O'Neal Deed to Joshua Woosley. This 7 April 1856. John H. O'Neal as trustee of said Joel Shofner by virtue of a Deed of Trust made of said deed of Joel Shofner and registered in Book __, page __. I have this day conveyed to Joshua Woosley a tract of land in Bedford County and Civil District No. 23 and bounded by T. Roberts' line, and by J. Hastings' line. Containing 20 acres and 22 poles.
Reg: November 27, 1865   Signed: Joel Shofner
                                        John H. O'Neal, Trustee of
                                        Joel Shofner

Page 155 - W.A. Coffey Conveyance of land and personal property to R.A. Coffey. This 2 September 1865 Weighstill Avery Coffee and Rice A. Coffee, both of Jackson County, Alabama, sold unto R.A. Coffey all the right title &c which he has now as one of the legatees of Alexander H. Coffey, father, deceased, including all the personal and landed estate of land in Bedford County and District No. __ on the waters of Big Wartrace Depot on the Nashville and Chattanooga Rail Road and containing 100 acres.
Reg: November 27, 1865   Signed: W.A. Coffey

Page 156 - T. Williams and others Deed to J.W. Molder. November 27, 1865 this indenture made by Theophilus Williams and Sarah E. Williams and Christina A. Molder and Joseph Molder paid by

Jasper W. Molder, land in Bedford County and District No. 11 and bounded by Jacob B. Delk, John F. Swan, and heirs of Benjamin Crowell and others. Containing 50 acres and 105 poles.
Reg: November 27, 1865   Signed: Thos. Williams
                                        Sarah E. Williams
                                        Christina A. Molder

Page 157 - James M. Ledbetter Title Bond to Eathan Lowell and others. I am indebted to Eathan Lowell, William Lowell and James M. Lents. I have sold unto Eathan Lowell, William Lowell and James M. Lents land in Bedford County and District No. 11 and bounded by Duck River, F.V. Jones, Richard Warner, G.W. Cook, and P.M. Pickle. Containing 290 acres and 44 poles. This 27 November 1865.
Reg: November 27, 1865   Signed: J.M. Ledbetter

Page 158 - Robt. Rich and Violet Deed to J.C. Green, Robt. Rich and Violet Rich, his wife, sold to J.C. Green land in Bedford County and District No. 11 and containing 100 acres and bounded by J.C. Green, by the bank of Weakley Creek, and by Ruben Thompson. This 2 February 1863.
Wit: Eden Wortham   Signed: Robt. Rich
     E.D. Winset   Violet Rich
Reg: November 28, 1865

Page 159 - Morgan & Co. Assignment of Equity to Town Lot to C.P. Houston, Jr. C.P. Houston, Jr. of Bedford County and Morgan & Co. of Nashville, do release unto C.P. Houston, Jr. a Town Lot in the Village of Shelbyville it being the property of A.L. Stamps. Lot bounded by the street running by the Presbyterian Church and by the street running by the Baptist Church and graveyard, from the Dixon Academy lot, and by the spring, and by the Cumberland Presbyterian Church. It being known as the Stamps lot. This 24 November 1865.
Reg: November 28, 1865   Signed: Morgan & Co.

Page 160 - Jo. Thompson, Sheriff, Deed to M.B. Moorman. Land in the corporation limits of Shelbyville and bounded by T. Gosling, by the street running in front of the Presbyterian Church, by M.B. Moorman, and by the Pike Street. Containing 1 acre. Said land was sold to me as the property of W.F. Davidson to satisfy an execution in favor of Lewis Tilman and R.B. Davidson was security. This November 25, 1865.
Reg: November 28, 1865   Signed: Jo. Thompson, Sheriff of
                                        Bedford County

Page 160 - Wm.S. Jett Mortgage to Thomas M. Coldwell. Land in Bedford County and Civil District No. __ and on the waters of Flat Creek and the south bank of Duck River near the Town of Shelbyville and bounded by the lands of Minos T. Cannon and Duck River, by lands of Robt. T. Cannon, by the lands of Andrew Reed and Flat Creek, and by the Shelbyville and Fayetteville Road. Containing 375 acres. It being all the land I own on the south

bank of Duck River and the land includes the old J.B. Cummings place the lands M.P. Gentry purchased of E.J. Frierson heirs and the land I purchased of J.D. Wilhoite about 18 acres conveyed by me to M.T. Cannon. Sold land free forever any right my wife may have to dower &c. This 27 November 1865. NOTE: Long document.
Wit: Thomas H. Coldwell   Signed: Wm. S. Jett
     Jas. D. Tilman
Reg: Nov 29, 1865

Page 162 - Louis Mankel Deed to Jo. D. Wilhoite. I have sold to Joseph D. Wilhoite a certain house and lot in the Town of Shelbyville formerly occupied by R.D. Deery as a Drug Store on the east side of the said block, and bounded by the house known as the Deery Drug Store running with the Square to the north west corner, by an alley. It being the same house and lot transferred and sold unto said Louis Mankel by Chesley Williams and W.P. Cannon, executors of the Last Will and Testament of Robt. Cannon, deceased, and dated 7 July 1864 and registered in Book DDD, page 485. This 29 November 1865.
Reg: November 29, 1865   Signed: Louis Mankel

Page 163 - T.F. Cartright Title Bond to Daniel Allerson (colored). Land being the southern half of a tract of land in Bedford County and Civil District No. 11 and bounded by a spring of Clem Creek, it being the place I bought from Robert J. Patton. Containing 133 acres. This 29 November 1865.
Reg: November 29, 1865   Signed: T.F. Cartright

Page 163 - John P. Hoover Title Bond to Lucinda Burks. This 25 September 1865. John P. Hoover of Bedford County sold to Lucinda Burks of same place land in Bedford County and bounded by D.D. Hoover's land, by a public road, by A.M(illegible), and by Henry Prewett. NOTE: Long document.
Wit: D.D. Hoover   Signed: John P. Hoover
     K.L. Burks   Lucinda Burks
Reg: November 29, 1865

Page 165 - Richard Anderson Deed to W.H. Anderson. Several years prior to 1860, I am indebted as the owner of a tract of land in 18th Civil District of Bedford County and bounded by lands of C.A. Warren, by lands of Wiley J. Usery, by the lands of William K(illegible), by lands of James Carlisle. Containing 89 ½ acres. Whereas I agree to vest will (to) my two sons G.B. Anderson and W.H. Anderson land. Said son G.W. Anderson has departed this life. NOTE: Long document. This 1 December 1865.
Reg: December 1, 1865   Signed: Richard Anderson

Page 166 - Jane R. Murphy Trust Deed to A.A. Cooper. District No. 2. Land in 2nd District of Bedford County and bounded by the lands of Ervin & Eakin, by lands of Ervin, and by lands belonging to the heirs of Arch Murphy. Containing 145 acres, it being my dower in the estate of my deceased husband Arch Murphy. I am owning the following persons, to wit, Wm. Meadows,

Elizabeth Franklin, Gosling & Co., Heart & Hogg, C.F. Herd, Jonas Myers, L.P. Fields, Thomas Heart, W.H. Sims, Dr. Hickerson, Jo. B. Muse, William Cully, Greenfield & Paterson, James Mullins, T.C. Thompson, and Jno. R. Jones. This 2 December 1865. NOTE: Long document.
Reg: December 2, 1865   Signed: Jane R. Murphy

Page 168 - John A.S. Shannon Deed to B.F. Duggan. John A.S. Shannon of Bedford County sold to B.F. Duggan of same place, land in Unionville, Bedford County and Civil District No. 11 and bounded by a lot owned by said Duggan, by the middle land between S.A. Garrett's line and this lot. This 23 November 1865.
Wit: J.W. Clarry(Clary)   Signed: J.A.S. Shannon
     J.R. Hendon
Reg: December 2, 1865

Page 168 - George W. Thompson Deed to Henry Cooper. Land in Bedford County and District No. 3 and bounded by the Rosewville Road, by the corner of Lot No. 18, and by Moody's corner. Containing 27 acres and 93 poles. This 15 September 1865.
Reg: December 2, 1865   Signed: G.W. Thompson

Page 169 - John W. Nelson Deed to Jack Smith, colr'd. Lot of ground lying and being in the Town of Shelbyville the north east corner of Lot No. 74 and bounded by a street. It being the lot of ground descended to me by Littlebery Green. This 9 March 1857.
Reg: December 5, 1865   Signed: John W. Nelson

Page 170 - F.C. Carter Power of Attorney to J.C. Carter. F.C. Carter, late F.C. McGowan, daughter and heir of Samuel McGowan, deceased, late of Bedford County, appointed J.C. Carter my agent and attorney in fact to receive from Thomas Tarpley guardian of said F.C. Carter such money or sums of money coming to her from her said guardian. He also to be authorized to institute any proceedings of any connection whatever there may be necessary to secure and collect any money. This 25 November 1865.
State of Kentucky   Signed: F.C. Carter
Graves County, Town of Mayfield. F.C. Carter examined separate from her husband. This 25 November 1865.
Reg: December 5, 1865

Page 171 - Thomas Hart Deed to W.R. Tinsley, 20 acres. Land in Bedford County and Civil District No. 3, containing about 20 acres and bounded at the old bridge where the McMinnville Road crosses the Wartrace Creek, and to where the road leaves the creek to the brink of the hill to Coble's line, to the line of Henry Coffey, by a line of Nathan Evans. This 4 July 1865.
Wit: W.B. Armstrong   Signed: Thos. Hart
     J.W. Tilford
Reg: December 5, 1865

Page 171 - James T. Wheeler and Nancy Wheeler Deed to Francis P. Arnold. All our interest in the real and personal estate of Joseph A. Arnold, deceased. This 10 October 1860.
Wit: J.P. Taylor   Signed: Nancy Wheeler
     Isaac Vickery   James T. Wheeler
Reg: December 5, 1865

Page 172 - Jennings Moore Deed to J.C. Wilson and others, Trustee. For the desire I have to the Worship of Almighty God, the love which I have for the M.E. Church, South, I have given and transferred unto John C. Wilson, J.R. Brown, Dr. W.F. Clary, Wm. J. Osteen, Wm. Knott, A.F. Knott, and Thomas D. Tarpley, Trustees for the use of the members of the M.E. Church, South, a lot in Bedford County and Civil District No. 11 on the south side of the road running west from Unionville opposite the Male Academy and bounded by Dr. J.W. Clary's lot. Containing about one half acre. This 12 June 1862.
Reg: December 6, 1865   Signed: Jennings Moore

Page 173 - Ruth Hutton Deed to W.M. Hutton. All the lands of which John Hutton, deceased, died seized. Also all the lands of which Margret M. Hutton, deceased, died seized. Said lands being in Bedford County and Civil District No. 5 and on the waters of Fall Creek. This November 25, 1865.
Wit: J.P. Hutton   Signed: Ruth Hutton
     James M. Smith
Reg: December 6, 1865

Page 174 - Andrew Vanoy, Sr. Deed to Jeremiah B. Booth. Land in Bedford County and District No. 6 and containing 118 ½ acres. Also another tract adjoining James Clardy's corner in James C. Bennett's line, by the center of the old Nashville Road. Containing 135 acres. Both tracts containing 253 ½ acres. I reserve for my use during my life time or the life time of my wife my dwelling house and my other outbuildings, my garden and orchard together with timber. I also reserve about 10 acres to include the house where my son Andrew now lives. This December 5, 1865.
Reg: December 5, 1865   Signed: Andrew Vanoy

Page 175 - Morgan Smith Deed to C.P. Huston, Jr. Land in Bedford County and District No. 6, bounded by John Overcast and by C.P. Huston, by John P. Steele. Containing 52 acres. This 5 December 1865.
Reg: December 6, 1865   Signed: Morgan Smith

Page 175 - John W. Cowan, Sr. Deed to Title Bond to John A. Moore. I have sold unto John A. Moore land this 20 November 1865. Land beginning in the center of the McMinnville Road. Containing 18 acres and 6 poles. This ___ December 1865.
Reg: December 6, 1865   Signed: J.W. Cowan, Sr.

Page 176 - J.W. Crunk Deed of Trust to Jordan Hale and C.A. Crunk. For the purpose of securing my father William Crunk who are my security in a Guardian Bond for the heirs of another Crunk named Letitia Crunk, Faney Crunk, Martha Crunk, Morgan Crunk and J.P. Crunk, minor children of J.J.B. Crunk and said Martha Crunk for a tract of land. Also to secure E. Cooper, executor of Wiley F. Daniel a note. NOTE: Other notes listed in original document. I now convey unto Jordan Hale and C.A. Crunk in trust property a tract of land on which I now reside in Bedford County and District No. 24. Containing 200 acres which I purchased of James Check(?). NOTE: Long document naming Dewitt C. Orr, Wiley Stone, Dick Stone and A. Hughs. Names of my children Martha and J.J.B. Crunk. Other named, A.G. Gill. This 7 December 1865.
Reg: December 8, 1865   Signed: J.W. Crunk

Page 178 - Marian A. Mash Deed of Gift to Harriett Mash. Both of Bedford County. Land in Bedford County and District No. 4 adjoining William Murphy, by land deeded to him by W.J. Davis, by Halling's line, by Morris Burney's line, and by John W. Mash. Containing 86 acres it being the same premises which S(illegible) A. Mash by indenture dated 17 November 1865 did grant to said Marian A. Mash. Recorded in Book EEE, pages 137 and 138 in Bedford County. NOTE: Long document.
Wit: D.C. Shriver   Signed: Marian A. Mash
     C.S. Dudley
Reg: December 9, 1865

Page 180 - P.R. Reynolds Transfer of Judgment to F.M. Prewett. Whatever amount may be coming to me by reason of decree that may be (illegible) in the Chancery Court of Bedford County in a bill filed against James Mullins, J.M. Stokes, Holt, Williams and Powell. December 3, 1865.
Reg: December 9, 1865   Signed: P.R. Reynolds

Page 180 - J.F. Elliott Deed to John Landrum. Land in Bedford and District No. 10 and containing 300 acres and 10 poles and bounded by Landrum's original tract. This November 13, 1865.
Wit: G.P. Hastings   Signed: J.F. Elliott
     G.M. Lamb
Reg: December 9, 1865

Page 181 - J.F. Elliott and John Landrum Deed to W.C. Taylor. Land in Bedford County and District No. 10 and containing 125 acres and 70 poles and adjoining J.W. Manier's corner. This November 13, 1865.
Wit: G.P. Hastings   Signed: J.F. Elliott
     G.M. Lamb   John Landrum, as
Reg: December 9, 1865   Trustees

Page 181 - C.A. Crunk Deed to George H. Castleman. Land on which Samuel L. Rogers now lives in Bedford County and District No. 24 and containing about 2 acres and 140 poles, adjoining the

lands of Thomas H. Hutson and John Farrar, and lands of Sam'k
Bobo, by lands of James Farrar, the heirs of Abrm. Reager and
E.A. Reager, and by lands of E.A. Reager and James Baker. This
December 9, 1865.
Reg: December 9, 1865   Signed: C.A. Crunk

Page 182 - James Deery Title Bond to J.H. McGrew, 10 acres.
Both of Bedford County. Land bounded by Robt. Reed and said
McGrew, all on south side of Duck River now McGrew. I bind
myself to make him a general warrant deed. This 12 November
1856.
Wit: Minos Cannon   Signed: James Deery
     Thos. S. Burt
Reg: December 11, 1865

Page 183 - John P. Steele Deed to J.H. McGrew, 10 acres. This
13 November 1856 James Deery, now deceased, sold to J.H. McGrew
10 acres of land in Bedford County and bounded by lands of Robt.
Reed and said McGrew and on the north side of Duck River. This
9 December 1865.
Reg: December 11, 1865   Signed: John P. Steele, Admr. Of
                                        James Derry, deceased

Page 183 - Louis Mankel Bond to R.H. Lewis. This 13 November
1865. Louis Mankel sold to Robt. H. Lewis a house and lot in
the Town of Shelbyville on the north west corner of the Public
Square known as the Strickler property and was being used by
said Lewis in the brewery business. I have also sold to said
Lewis another lot of land in said town and in the south of said
Strickler property and was originally a part where is known as
the Kincaid property and by me purchased of Doc. J.H. McGrew.
NOTE: Long document. This 13 November 1865.
Reg: December 11, 1865   Signed: Louis Mankel

Page 185 - John R. Eakin Mortgage to Wm. S. Eakin. I have sold
unto Wm. S. Eakin of Davidson County, Tennessee a tract of land
upon which I reside in Bedford County on the waters of Garrison
Fork of Duck River composing my residence buildings vineage &c
and known as Willowbeck. One tract of about 70 acres purchased
by me and conveyed to me by Wm. J. Webster, trustee for Mrs. A.
Erwin and her husband A. Erwin and registered in Book TT, pages
229 and 230 about the year 1851 or 1852. Another small tract
conveyed unto me by Whiteside, Lipscomb and Armstrong of about 8
acres dated 13 September 1853 and registered in Book OO, pages
689 and 590. Another small tract conveyed to me by Archabald
Murphy and registered in Book YY, pages 463 and 464. Another
small tract conveyed to me by John Q. Davidson containing about
3 acres and registered in Book YY, pages 491 and 492 off of
which said Willowbeck place I have sold to John Q. Davidson a
small tract of about 2 ½ acres. NOTE: Long document. Other
names in document are Wm. S. Eakin, and estate of Thos. L.
Eakin. I am indebted to Wm. S. Eakin. This November 7, 1857.
Reg: December 11, 1865   Signed: Jno. R. Eakin

Page 187 - W.W. Koonce Deed to Julia B. Morton, 100 acres. Sold unto Mrs. Julia Morton wife of G.W.C. Morton a tract of land in 3rd District of Bedford County and adjoining a corner of a tract owned by John Reaves, and to the west bank of Duck River. Containing 38 acres and 15 poles. Also one other tract beginning in the center of a spring on the bank of Duck River, and to John Reaves' corner. Containing 32 acres and 100 poles. Also one other tract beginning at the east corner of John Reaves. Containing 29 acres and being the tract conveyed to me by Benjamin Reaves. This 7 September 1865.
Reg: December 11, 1865   Signed: W.W. Koonce

Page 188 - Nicholas Troxler and H.C. Troxler Agreement with Troxler & Lowe. I, Nicholas Troxler of Bedford County and Civil District No. 25, have conveyed (illegible) Step-son Albert Lowe and my son Henry C. Troxler for the term of seven years commencing 1 January 1866 and ending 1 January 1873 including the house place, the purchase (illegible) from John Hufman, also to use any timber on the land known as the B(illegible) tract or Riggins purchases (illegible). NOTE: Document difficult to read. This 14 November 1865.
Wit: L.J. Anthony   Signed: Nicholas Troxler
     L.J. Marbury   H.C. Troxler
Reg: December 13, 1865   Albert Lowe
                                    R.L. Landis

Page 189 - J.W. Cully Deed to J.A. Jordan, Lot in Rowesville. Land together with the buildings being in Bedford County and Civil District No. 25 in the Village of Roseville and known as Lot No. 15 and adjoining on Main and Fourth Streets, to South Street, and by Setliff's line. This 10 October 1865.
Reg: December 15, 1865   Signed: James W. Cully

Page 190 - Bryant Landers and others Deed to John Jordan. N.G. Unionville Lodge IOOF No. 80. We, Bryant Landers, Joseph R. Brown and A. Wilson of Bedford County, Trustees in behalf of the board of stock holders of the Male Academy of Unionville, Tennessee, have sold unto John Jordan, Noble Grand of Unionville Lodge No. 80 of the Independent Order of Odd Fellows of Tennessee and his successors the said Male Academy and lot bounded by the center of a road running from the Village of Unionville. Containing 1 acre. This __ day of __ 1857.
Wit: December 15, 1865   Signed: Briant Landis
Wit: F.M. Atkinson   Augustus Wilson
     W.H. Moon   Joseph R. Brown
Reg: December 16, 1865

Page 191 - John T. Fisher Deed of Trust to Jordan Smith. I have conveyed unto Jordan Smith one four house wagon, one bay horse, about forty five head of stock hogs jointly owned by me and said Jordan Smith, one clock and one sugar chest. I am indebted to N. Thompson 1st and to Richard Sims, to G. Fletcher, to John Thompson, to Samuel Crowell, to Thomas Gregory, and to

166

Kirkpatrick by note transferred by A.J. Maddox.   This 18
November 1865.
Reg: December 18, 1865   Signed: John T. Fisher

Page 192 - J.T. Johnson Deed to J.P. Brown, Lot in Shelbyville.
Lot on Martin Street in the Town of Shelbyville, Bedford County,
a frame house and it being the house that the Cannon Ball passed
through commencing at the south east corner.   This October 9,
1865.
Reg: December 18, 1865   Signed: J.T. Johnson

Page 192 - Willis Blanton and Mary A. Blanton Deed to R.H.
Reaves and James P. Newsom. Land in Bedford County and District
No. 22 and bounded by lands of Wm. Cambell, by the lands of John
Hix and George Castleman, by lands of Jarrel Burrow, by lands of
John Wilhoite and said Campbell and known as the old Archie
Reaves' tract upon which ___ Reaves now resides and which is
eight fully ___ Martha Elizabeth Reaves during her life time
containing in all 159 acres.   We sell 7/8 of the above land.
This 11 September 1865.
Wit: Lewis Tilman   Signed: Willis Blanton
     W.J. Whitthorne   Mary A. Blanton
Reg: (no date)

Page 193 - John A. McGuyre Deed to W.W. Payne. This 9 December
1865.   John A. McGuyre of Hopkins County, Kentucky sold unto
W.W. Payne of Bedford County the dower interest for Phoeby
Elkins of whom the grantor is a grandson, said grantor interest
being one eighth of one third of said dower which said dower was
allotted to her out of the estate of William Ditto, deceased,
and is in Bedford County and District No. 3 being a portion of
the lands upon which W. Ditto resided at the time of his death.
State of Kentucky, County of Hopkins.
Madisonville, Kentucky.
Reg: December 18, 1865   Signed: John A. McGuyer

Page 194 - W.D. McGuyre Deed to W.W. Payne. This 2 December
1865.   W.D. McGuyre of Hopkins County, Kentucky sold to W.W.
Payne of Bedford County his undivided interest in and to the
dower interest of Phoeby Elkins of whom the grantor is the
grandson, said grantor's interest being one sixth of one third
of said dower which dower was allotted to her out of the estate
of William Ditto, deceased, and which interest is in Bedford
County and District No. 3 and being a portion of the land upon
which William Ditto resided at the time of his death.
State of Kentucky, County of Hopkins.
Madisonville, Kentucky.
Reg: December 18, 1865   Signed: W.D. McGuyer

Page 195 - John P. Steele Entry No. 1 - Since 1 October 1865.
Entry No. 1.   John P. Steele enters 100 acres of land in Bedford
County on the waters of Sinking Creek of Duck River and bounded
by a corner of William Stephenson's land, by Wm. Galbreath's

line, by Richard Sims' line, and by Moses Chamberline. The land conveyed by Entry No. 3112 made by said Steele 1 October 1849. But destroyed by fire. This 18 December 1865.
Reg: Dec 18, 1865   Signed: John P. Steele, Locator

Page 196 - R.D. Rankin Conveyance to Reliance Lodge No. 268. R.D. Rankin in his individual or private capacity conveyed unto R.D. Rankin, W.M. James, H. Woodfin, T.W., and William M. Robinson, J.W., of Reliance Lodge No. 268 the privilege of building their hall above the store house of said Rankin in the Town of Bellbuckle Depot in which B.D. Blair formerly did business, now occupied by W.B. Blunderfield, the lot on which said store house stands being bounded by the Depot grounds, by W.B. Norville, by William Howland. Said Lodge is authorized to have the free and occupation of the same for the purpose of a large room and any other purpose authorized by them by the rules &c of the Grand Lodge of Masons of Tennessee. This 1 November 1865.
Wit: Wm. J. Peacock   Signed: R.D. Rankin
     John Thomas   R.D. Rankin, W.M.
Reg: November 18, 1865   James H. Woodfin, S(T?).W.
                                     William F. Robinson, J.W.

Page 197 - Jesse Wood Power of Attorney to W.N. Gwynn. Registered in Bedford County. I have appointed one John L. Cooper of Bedford County my true and lawful attorney in fact for and in my name to manage and control my business &c to sell said estate which I was at the time the owner and to collect any money &c. This 23 September 1865.
Reg: December 19, 1865   Signed: Jesse Wood

Page 198 - W.W. Payne Deed to H.C. Kanard. Land in Bedford County and District No. 2 and bounded by H.C. Kanard, by Eliza George, by J.F. King, by the widow Isabel George and Widow A. Sharp. Containing 100 acres. My interest being the two shares belonging to John A. McGuyer and W.D. McGuyre as heirs at law of Pheoby Elkins, deceased, and transferred from them to me W.W. Payne and their interest being one sixth of one third each. This 18 December 1865.
Reg: December 19, 1865   Signed: W.W. Payne

Page 199 - Benjamin McFarlin Deed to Sarah M. Miller. Land in Bedford County and District No. 23 and bounded by lands of T.C. Ryal, by lands of Benjamin McFarlin, by lands of the heirs of John W. Brown, deceased. Containing 2 acres. This 21 December 1865.
Reg: December 21, 1865   Signed: Benjamin McFarlin

Page 199 - Robert Mathews Transfer of Deed to Wm. V. Mathews. State of Arkansas. Conveyed lands approved 28 September 1850. Reclaiming of swamp and over flooded lands d(illegible) to the State by the Unites States approved 6 January 1851. Land in

Green County, in said State and containing 179+ acres.   This 11
June 1860.
S.M. Weaver, Sec.   Elias N. Conway
I hereby transfer unto my son William V. Mathews.   This 9
November 1865.
Reg: December 21, 1865   Signed: Robt. Mathews

Page 201 - Wm. V. Mathews Deed of Gift from Robt. Mathews. By
an Act of Congress of the United States of America an act to
unable the State of Arkansas and other States to reclaim the
swamps and within their limits approved 28 September 1850, it is
provided that to enable the State of Arkansas to construct the
many levies and drain to reclaim the swamps and over flooded
land therein the whole of the swamp and over flooded lands made
unfit thereby for cultivation which shall remain unsold at the
passage of this said, shall be hereby granted to said State and
whereas the General Assembly of the State of Arkansas passed an
act for the reclaiming of the swamp and over flooded lands
donated to the State by the United States approved 6 January
1851 and on act supplemental to said act approved 15 January
1851 and an act (illegible) of existing laws regulating the land
in trust of the State approved 12 January 1856 and also an act
to enable the Governor to make deed to swamp and over flowed
lands after such lands shall have been p(illegible) by the
United States to the State of Arkansas approved 20 January 1855
and whereas the land agent for the office established by said
act of the 30 December 1856 at Batesville in State of Arkansas
did grant his certificate dated 14 November 1857 and No. 305
under said act of 12 January 1853 to and in favor of Robt.
Mathews as the original purchaser showing that the said Robt.
Mathews was entitled by law to a certificate of purchase upon
which to obtain from the State of Arkansas a deed vesting in him
the title in fee simple to the foregoing described and to will
the south west corner of Section 10, the north west quarter of
Section 15 the east half of the south east quarter of Section 27
and the west half of the south west quarter of Section 26 in
Township 20 north of the base line in Range 6 east of the 5th
principal meridian 480 acres.   NOTE: Long document. City of
Little Rock on 11 June 1860.
S.M. Weaver, Sec.   Elias N. Conway
I hereby convey to my son William V. Mathews for the affection I
have for my son. This 9 November 1865.
Reg: December 21, 1865   Signed: Robt. Mathews

Page 202 - John A. Moor Title Bond to R.A. Coldwell.   I have
sold unto R.A. Coldwell of Bedford County land being in District
No. 2 of Bedford County and adjoining the north bank of Duck
River. Containing 82 acres. This December 19, 1865.
Reg: December 22, 1865   Signed: John A. Moor

Page 203 - Phebe and Robt. Taylor Power of Attorney to B.B.
Taylor.   Phebe Taylor and her husband Robt. Taylor of Weakley
County, Tennessee appointed Benj. B. Taylor of Rutherford
County, Tennessee out true and lawful attorney in fact to attend
to our business in the undivided lands of our brother Thomas

Cheatham who died in Bedford County, either to sell or divide said land. This 5 October 1865.
Reg: December 23, 1865   Signed: Phebe Taylor
                                        Robt. Taylor

Page 204 - Sarah W. Gillaspie and James D. Gillaspie Power of Attorney to B.B. Taylor. Sarah W. Gillaspie and James D. Gillaspie of Benton County, Tennessee appointed Benjamin B. Taylor of Rutherford County, Tennessee our attorney in fact for us and in our names to attend to our business in the lands that our brother Thomas Cheatham died possessed in Bedford County. This 1 December 1865.
Wit: Wm. Johnson   Signed: Sarah W. Gillaspie
     Wm. S. (illegible)   James D. Gillaspie
Reg: December 25, 1865

Page 205 - J.R. Millor Deed to S.G. Millor (Miller). Land in Bedford County and District No. 5 bounded by B.F. Smalling. Containing 80 acres and 54 poles. This 25 December 1865.
Reg: December 25, 1865   Signed: J.R. Miller

Page 205 - James Kirkpatrick Deed to James M. Hobbs. A certain house and lot in the Town of Shelbyville, Bedford County and bounded by ___ Street, by J.M. Hobbs, by the Cumberland Presbyterian Church lot, and by an alley. Being Lot No. 23 being the lot conveyed by deed to me by J.J. Kincaid, C.P. Cunningham and Wm. S. Jett, and recorded in Book EEE, pages 128 and 129. This 25 December 1865.
Reg: December 25, 1865   Signed: James Kirkpatrick

Page 206 - William J. Coop Deed to Horatio Coop. Land in Bedford County and Civil District No. 5 and bounded by lands of John J. Jacobs, by lands of G.W. Cone, by James Robinson and Thomas Womack, by James Claxton. Containing 98 acres. This December 13, 1865.
Reg: December 25, 1865   Signed: Jo. H. Thompson, Clerk

Page 207 - Edmond Cooper Deed to W.B.M. Brame. In the case of Isaac Green against Orren Mobley, I was authorized to sell the property at public auction in Town of Shelbyville and known as the Mobley place and bounded by John Fletcher place, by Spafford (illegible) & Co. lands on the west side of the street or alley, by the Dickson Academy lot, by the Baptist Church and graveyard. Conveyed to W.B.M. Brame. This December 25, 1865.
Reg: December 25, 1865   Signed: J. Thompson, Reg. Of BC

Page 207 - M.T. Cooper and Lavina Minter, Agreement. M.T. Cooper and Lavina Minter to enter into the State of Matrimony and have agreed together in order to preserve and protect the estate of said Lavina separate and apart from the estate of M.T. Cooper and to have and keep the same free from debts contracts

or control of the said intended husband it is hereby constructed
by and between them. This December __ 1865.
Wit: J.H. G(illegible)   Signed: M.T. Cooper
     J.A. Eagleton   Lavina Minter
Reg: December 26, 1865

Page 208 - Thomas W. Muse Deed to John G. Bledsoe. Land in
Bedford County and District No. 18 on Little Sinking Creek and
bounded by a road leading from Shelbyville to Pulaski, by Z.
Roberts' corner, and by John Primrose' line. Containing about
60 acres. This 13 December 1860.
Wit: James A. Muse   Signed: Thomas W. Muse
     Richard Anderson
Reg: December 26, 1865

Page 209 - D.T. Mayfield and E.F. Mayfield Deed to W.C.
Mayfield. This 6 September 1862. D.T. Mayfield and his wife
Elizabeth F. Mayfield who was a daughter of the late John
Sutton, Sr., deceased, of Bedford County, sold unto William C.
Mayfield, all being of Giles County, Tennessee, land in Bedford
County on the head waters of Fall Creek and on both sides of the
Turnpike Road leading from Shelbyville to Fairfield and about
seven miles from the former place being and known as the dower
of Elizabeth Sutton, wife of the late John Sutton, Sr.,
adjoining lands of Newton Harris, by Louisa Sutton, by William
B. Sutton. Containing 375 acres.
Reg: December 26, 1865   Signed: D.T. Mayfield
                                        E.F. Mayfield

Page 210 - William C. Mayfield Deed to D.T. Mayfield. This 15
December 1862. W.C. Mayfield of Giles County, Tennessee sold
unto D.T. Mayfield of same place all of my undivided interest in
a certain tract of land in Bedford County on the head waters of
Fall Creek and lying on both sides of the turnpike road leading
from Shelbyville to Fairfield about seven miles from the former
place being known as the dower of Elizabeth Sutton wife of the
late John Sutton Sr., deceased, of Bedford County, and bounded
by the lands of Newton Harris, by the lands of Louisa Terry, and
by Wm. B. Sutton. Containing 375 acres.
Wit: Thos. D. Davenport   Signed: W.C. Mayfield
     John C. Rolland
Reg: December 26, 1865

Page 211 - E.B. Kelley Deed to R.S. Brown. I, Enoch B. Kelley
of Williamson County, Tennessee, have sold unto Robert S. Brown
of Bedford County, land in Bedford County and District No. 10
and containing 70 acres and 12 poles and bounded in the Vickery
south west corner of Jackson's line, by W.T. Vernon's land, and
by Bellefant's line. It being the tract of land sold by order
of the Chancery Court to E.B. Kelley in the course of W.A. Sims
and wife against Burrell Drumright and others. This 25 December
1865.
Wit: Chesly Williams   Signed: E.B. Kelley
Reg: December 26, 1865

Page 212 - Nathan W. Thompson Deed to J.C. Green.   Land in Bedford County and District No. 11, containing about 12 ½ acres, adjoining Ellen Thompson's corner, and Robt. And Vio;et Rich. This 2 February 1863.
Wit: E. Wortham   Signed: Nathan W. Thompson
     E.D. Winsett
Reg: December 27, 1865

Page 212 - Robert Mathews Deed to R.L. Landis.   All the lands that said R.L. Landis and A.L. Landis conveyed to me by deed in the year 1851 or 1852, it being the half of said land A.L. Landis having paid me for one half of the same, being all the land conveyed by the said R.L. Landis and A.L. Landis, A.M. Holt by the deed. This 27 December 1865.
Reg: December 27, 1865   Signed: Robt. Mathews

Page 213 - H.H. Nease Deed to Allice J. Morgan.   Isadore Allice Morgan wife of German B. Morgan paid to me and the receipt of which I acknowledged.   I, Hiram H. Nease, have sold to said Isadore Allice Morgan wife of G.B. Morgan land in 21st Civil District of Bedford County and bounded by land known as the Robt. Dixon land, by lands of John T. Neil's estate and Harbert Wiggins, and land of John E. Davis.   Containing 91 acres and known as the Parks place. This 28 December 1865.
Reg: December 28, 1865.   Signed: H.H. Nease

Page 215 - Wm. S. Jett and Jo. D. Wilhoite Deed to James L. Scudder.   Land in Bedford County and District No. 7 it being a portion of the Clement Cannon land which Wm. S. Jett purchased of Jo. D. Wilhoite by deed dated 3 May 1865 and bounded by J.L. Scudder, and by Duck River. This 28 December 1865.
Reg: December 28, 1865   Signed: Wm. S. Jett
                                        Jo. D. Wilhoite

Page 216 - H.L. Trescott and D.G. Christopher, Agreement. Article of Agreement between H.L. Trescott and D.G. Christopher have this day formed a partnership under the firm and style of Trescott & Christopher for the purpose of carrying on in Shelbyville the business of Saddles and Harness making and other articles connected in the said business of said partnership to continue at least twelve months. This December 29, 1865.
Reg: December 29, 1865   Signed: H.L. Trescott
                                        D.J. Christopher, of
                                        Trescott & Christopher

Page 216 - D.J.Christopher Mortgage to W.H. Christopher. Partnership for the purpose of carrying on the Saddle and Harness business in the Town of Shelbyville. This 20 December 1865.
Wit: Jno. C. Thompson   Signed: D.J. Christopher
Reg: December 29, 1865

Page 217 - H.L. Trescott Mortgage to Wm. Brown. For the purpose
of carrying on the Saddle and Harness business and other
articles connected with said business. This December __ 1865.
Reg: December 29, 1865   Signed: H.L. Prescott

Page 218 - Edmond Cooper Deed to Elizia Holt. This 20 January
1855. I conveyed unto Sarah Chandler a tract of land in Bedford
County and District No. 22 and containing 104 acres and 45 poles
and on 29 October 1864 Sarah Chandler transferred said land to
John Wilhoite and on 18 November 1865 John Wilhoite assigned
said title bond to Elizia Holt wife of Herod F. Holt and the
deed be made to B.F. Wiggins and wife Jane H. Wiggins. I hereby
transfer unto Elizia Holt all the interest and which I have in
42 acres adjoining a spring, and by R. Smith's line. This 20
November 1865.
Reg: December 29, 1865   Signed: Edm'd Cooper

Page 219 - Joseph Trice Deed to J.H.C. Scales. Both of Bedford
County. Lot of land in the Town or Village of Richmond, Bedford
County and bounded by a certain house known as the Jackson and
Loony house, and by John Phillips place to a cedar fence.
Containing 1 acre. This December 27, 1865.
Reg: December 30, 1865   Signed: Joseph Trice

Page 220 - T.M. Pickle Deed to A.J. Mount. Land in Bedford
County and Civil District No. 18 and bounded by lands of
Fielding Bell's heirs, by lands known as the Temple tract, by
William Stallings, and by the lands of Dysart & Burkeen.
Containing 67 acres and 132 poles. This January 1, 1866.
Reg: January 1, 1866   Signed: T.M. Pickle

Page 221 - M.L.D. Parks Deed to John Wortham. Land in Bedford
County and Civil District No. 11 and bounded and known as part
of tract of land formerly owned by Samuel G. McGowan, now
deceased, at McGowanville, Tennessee, called Poplins Cross Roads
and adjoining the edge of the Thompson Ford Road, and by Jonas
Sikes' line. Containing 2 acres. This October 4, 1865.
Reg: January 2, 1866   Signed: M.L.D. Parks

Page 221 - James Kirkpatrick Mortgage to J.H. Rook. A certain
cotton gin, wheel and press and inclined plain and g(illegible),
sixty gin saw made at Bridge Water, Massachusetts, now the gin
house of John Hart 4 ¾ miles from the Town of Shelbyville on the
Murfreesboro Turnpike. This 1 January 1866.
Reg: January 2,   Signed: James Kirkpatrick

Page 222 - John P. Steele Deed to James Mullins. John Hart
purchased ay Sheriff's sale a lot and house in the Village of
Wartrace as the property of A.E. Mullins on __ day of March
1860. John P. Steele redeemed said lot from said Hart on __ day
of __ 1861. Said lot was sold by W.J. Whitthorne, Commissioner.

Said lot is bounded by Green & Tilford lot. January 2, 1866.
Reg: January 2, 1866   Signed: John P. Steele

Page 223 - William Brown Deed to William Key. Land in Bedford
County and District No. 7 and bounded on the west side of the
Shelbyville and Murfreesboro Turnpike Road, by land of Thomas
Lipscomb sold to Willey Chockley, by a street laid off by Thomas
Lipscomb, and by land Thomas Lipscomb sold to A.P. Eakin.
Containing 2 ½ acres. This September 22, 1865.
Reg: January 3, 1866   Signed: William Brown

Page 224 - W.H. Moon and others. Division Deed. We are the
heirs of Alexander B. Moon, deceased, viz, W.H. Moon, G. Bacon
Moon, John A. Moon, Susan E. Wallis and R.F. Wallis her husband,
Mary Ann R. Landis and J.A. Landis her husband, and N.C. Moon
the widow guardian for Sarah L. Moon and Elizabeth J. Moon,
minors, all of Bedford County entertain the following agreement,
whereas A.B. Moon died leaving a will and recorded in
Shelbyville, Bedford County. We agree to distribution of the
estate of A.B. Moon, deceased, to W.A. Moon and Susan C. Wallis
married to R.F. Wallis by A.B. Moon before his death a piece of
land each and other articles. Land to each named heir. Also
one tract of land of 84 ¾ acres in Marshall County, Tennessee
and bounded by the lands of J.A. Landis, by lands of E.J. Moon,
and by Duck River. NOTE: Long document. This 20 December
1865.
Reg: January 3, 1866   Signed: W.H. Moon
                                      G. Bacon Moon
                                      Susan C. Wallis &
                                      R.F. Wallis
                                      John A. Moon
                                      Ripley A. Landis &
                                      J.A. Landis
                                      N.C. Moon, guardian for
                                      J.L. and E.J. Moon

Page 226 - W.H. Moon and others Deed to W.M. Shaw. This
indenture made ___ ___ by and between the heirs of Alex. B.
Moon, deceased, and W.M. Shaw, all of Bedford County witnessed
that the heirs of said Alex. B. Moon, deceased, hath given unto
W.M. Shaw land in Bedford County and on the bank of the North
Fork of Duck River and adjoining the bank of said (illegible)
(illegible) the remains of an old still house, to the mill road,
by George Smith's old line, and to north corner Moon's line.
Containing 32 ¾ acres.
Wit: W.H. Landis   Signed: W.H. Moon
Reg: January 4, 1866   G.B. Moon
                                        J.A. Moon
                                        Susan C. Wallis &
                                        R.F. Wallis
                                        Ripley A. Landis &
                                        J.A. Landis
                                        N.C. Moon, guardian for
                                        T.L. & E.J. Moon

Page 227 - Joseph Trice and J.H.C. Scales Deed to Jno. Trice. I, Joseph trice of Bedford County, conveyed unto John Trice of same place, land in Bedford County and District No. 19 on the head waters of Sinking Creek and bounded by a bluff it being the south east corner of said tract of land, by original school tract, and by Lot No. 2 the beginning corner. Containing 45 acres and 126 poles. This January 1, 1866.
Reg: January 4, 1866   Signed: Joseph Trice
                                      J.H.C. Scales, Trustee

Page 229 - Joseph Thompson, Sheriff, Deed to James Mullins. Recovered on 8 August 1860 against James Deniston, Smith Ballin(?) as makers of a note or bid and James Mullins as first endorser and L.P. Fields as second endorser. Sheriff did levied on a tract of land in Bedford County and District No. 4 and bounded by the lands of Thomas Hatchett, by lands of James Frizell, by lands of John McCrory and Smith Bollin or the Ruben Manley land, by lands of Thomas Hatchett, and being the same purchased by Smith Bollin of William Manley. Containing 75 acres. This 5 August 1865.
Reg: January 4, 1866   Signed: Jo. Thompson, Sheriff

Page 230 - William Word Deed to Hardy Prince. This 30 December 1865. Land in Bedford County and which is known as follows, to wit, beginning on the edge of the Rail Road bank in John Jamison's line. Containing 2 acres.
Wit: Wm. T.Tune   Signed: William Word
     Wm. Gabreath
Reg: January 8, 1866

Page 231 - Robt. B. Mopin Deed to Robt. C. Maupin, 290 acres. Land in Bedford County and District No. 25, the same being a portion of 5000 acre tract containing 290 acres. This 2 January 1866.
Wit: W.H. Eason   Signed: Robert B. Maupin
     James Bramblett
Reg: January 9, 1866

Page 232 - Eathan Lawell and William L. Lawell Deed to N.F. Neil. Conveyed to Newton F. Neil one lot, adjoining John K. Lawell's tract, and on the bank of Weakley Creek. Containing 44 acres and 132 poles. One other tract adjoining the above tract and containing 19 acres and 3 poles. Other tract containing 20 acres and 20 poles. This January 9, 1866.
Reg: January 10, 1866   Signed: Eathan Lawell
                                       William Lawell

Page 233 - R.C. Daniel Entry 1000 acres. R.C. Daniel enters a tract of land containing 1000 acres being in Bedford County and adjoining a 200 acre entry in the name of said Daniel near the county line, by Solomon Bennett's line, by Daniel's 400 acre tract at the head of Rock Creek. Recorded November 24, 1856.
Reg: January 13, 1866   Signed: M.E.W. Dunaway, R & Entry

Page 233 - C.C. Grizzard Deed Lot to A.C. Grizzard. Christopher C. Grizzard of Bedford County sold unto my brother A.C. Grizzard of Davidson County, Tennessee one undivided half of the house and lot that I purchased of Wm. Word in the Town of Shelbyville being part of Lots 67 and 59 in said Town of Shelbyville and upon which there is a large brick dwelling house &c. This 3 May 1859.

Wit: Young Wilhoite   Signed: C.C. Grizzard
     S.J. Wilhoite
Reg: January 13, 1866

Page 234 - A.P. Eakin Deed to Oliver Cowan. A strip of land in the Town of Shelbyville, Bedford County and bounded by the lot which I convey to said Cowan November last and being on the west side of the street leading in front of Mrs. Lucretia Eakin's residence, and by a stake on Brittain Street. This 13 December 1865.

Reg: January 16, 1866   Signed: A.P. Eakin

Page 234 - William Conwell and Mahala Bowner(?), Contract. William G. Conwell sold unto Mahala Bowner a tract of land in Bedford County and District No. 22, adjoining the lands of John and Wm. Wilhoite, by lands of William Cambell, by lands of Thomas Conwell, and by the lands of John Wilson. Containing 35 acres. Mahala Bowner to pay off debt on said land which is going to Robert Mathews, A.G. Gill, J.L. Bryant, Blanton and Newsom and others. This 23 December 1859.

Wit: Edm. Cooper   Signed: William Conwell
Reg: January 16, 1866   Mahala Bowner

Page 235 - Isham Stamers Deed to Simon Patterson. This 31 October 1865. Both of Bedford County. Land in Bedford County on the waters of Wilson Creek in the 11th District. Bounded by the bank of Wilson Creek. Containing 169 acres.

Wit: W.M. Shaw   Signed: Isham Stammer
     J,R. Haskins
Reg: January 17, 1866

Page 236 - Thomas Rushing Deed to Mary E. Lynn and Jos. M. Sikes. This 15 January 1865. All of Bedford County. Land in Bedford County on the waters of Wartrace Fork of Duck River and adjoining David Frizzell on the north side of the Widow Giles, by Thos. Rushing, and by the heirs of Thomas Hatchett. Containing 8 acres.

Wit: J.P. Majors   Signed: Thomas Rushing
     T.B. Majors
Reg: (no date)

Page 237 - Thomas Thompson and wife Deed to James Carlisle, 140 acres. We, Thomas Thompson and Elizabeth T. Thompson formerly Elizabeth T. Evans, have this day sold to James Carlisle land in Bedford County and District No. 20 and adjoining Jesse Evans' corner, Snell's line, and the center of Sugar Creek, and to Williams' corner. Containing 125 acres and 39 poles. This January 15, 1866.
Reg: January 17, 1866   Signed: Thomas Thompson
                                        Lizzie T. Thompson

Page 239 - John W. Thompson Deed to W.N. Gwinn. Land in Bedford County and Civil District No. 8 and bounded by lands of Wm. Smith, by lands of Michael Fisher and wife, by lands of A. Claxton, and by lands of N. Thompson. Containing 93 acres and 140 poles. This January 19, 1866.
Reg: January 19, 1866   Signed: John W. Thompson

Page 239 - Joseph Anderson Deed to David M. Orr, 12 ½ acres. Land that was willed and descended to Wm. N. Orr's children by their grand father David Orr, deceased, said land in Bedford County and Civil District No. 11 and the same tract that Wm. N. Orr and family now lives on. Land being the same that I purchased of John R. Orr, and his trustee E.D. Winsett who sold the same on 29 December 1860 and I bought the same. This 10 October 1865.
Wit: Mahala J. Anderson   Signed: Jos. Anderson
     Richard Anderson
     James C. Wortham
Reg: January 22, 1866

Page 240 - J.R. Russell Deed to E.W. Adams. James R. Russell of Coles County, Illinois, have sold to Edwin W. Adams of Bedford County undivided interest (it being the one fourth of one eighth) in a tract of land in Bedford County on the waters of Lawell Creek the same owned by Edwin Adams, deceased, by deed dated _ day of October 1822. Containing 150 acres which is now described in the original deed from Joseph B. Porter to the heirs of Edwin Adams, deceased. This 20 January 1866.
Reg: January 22, 1866   Signed: J.R. Russell

Page 241 - W.B.M. Brame Deed to Daniel Ray (col). A Town Lot in the Town of Shelbyville being a portion of the lot sold to me by Edmond Cooper on 23 December 1865 and bounded by the center of a branch at a little bridge on the street running from the Dixon Academy which is west of the Baptist Church, to the line of S(illegible) T(illegible) & Co., and by the lot formerly owned by John Fletcher. It being the said land sold to me by Edmond Cooper. This 6 January 1866.
Wit: J.L. Scudder   Signed: Wm. B.M. Brame
     J.W. Thompson
Reg: January 24, 1866

Page 241 - J.M. Elliott, Thos. C. Whiteside and G.W. Thompson Deed to T.B. Cannon. We, J.M. Elliott, George W. Thompson and Thomas C. Whiteside, of Bedford County, have sold unto Thos. B. Cannon a tract of land in Bedford County and in the corporate limits of Shelbyville. Beginning on Martin Street, to the north east corner of a lot now occupied by and belonging to James Russ, and by a lot formerly owned by Letitia Newsom, deceased. This 1 January 1866.
Reg: January 25, 1866   Signed: J.M. Elliott
                                  Thos. C. Whiteside
                                  G.W. Thompson

Page 242 - Margret Craig Deed to Wm. F. Barnett. Land in Bedford County and Civil District No. 18 on the waters of Sinking Creek, and adjoining my lands. Containing 30 acres and 45 poles. This November 24, 1862.
Wit: G.W. Story   Signed: Margret Craig
     J.G. Bledsoe
Reg: January 26, 1866

Page 243 - Willey B. Snell Deed to Acton Y. Snell. Land in Bedford County and Civil District No. 23 and containing 8 acres and 64 poles. This 25 January 1866.
Wit: Wm. T. Tune   Signed: Willie B. Snell
     W.P. Bridges
Reg: January 26, 1866

Page 244 - A.J. Mount Deed to Elizabeth Helton. Land in Bedford County and Civil District No. 18 and bounded by lands of Fielding Bell, by the land known as the Temple land, by William Stallings, and by lands of Dysart and Burkeen. Containing 67 acres and 132 poles, it being the same land purchased by me of P.M. Pickle and is registered in Book EEE, page 220. This February 1, 1866.
Reg: February 1, 1866   Signed: A.J. Mount

Page 244 - D.C. Bennett Entry No. 2   Since October 1, 1865. D.C. Bennett entered 500 acres of land in Bedford, County and bounded by land granted to Washington Walch now owned by Isaac Troxler, by C,L. Lynn's line, by Entry No. 3235 in the name of R.C. Daniel, and by Solomon Bennett's corner.
Reg: February 2, 1866   Signed: D.C. Bennett, locator

Page 245 - Frank M. Stamps Deed to C(illegible). J. Thompson. One cow and her calf, one sow and six pigs and one shoat. This January 30, 1866.
Reg: February 7, 1866   Signed: F.M. Stamps

Page 246 - We, James H. Neil, A.E. Kincaid, W.H. Kincaid and Sarah M.J. Kincaid, the last two being children of Dr. Joseph Kincaid. Whereas several years ago Mrs. Ary E. Kincaid became

The guardian of her two minor children, to wit, William H. and
Sarah M.J. Kincaid, gave bond. The said A.E. Kincaid, as
guardian received from sundry sales or real estate in the State
of Tennessee, Kentucky and Missouri the sum of $3997.87
belonging to said William H. and Sarah M.J. Kincaid. Also house
and lot in the Town of Shelbyville near the Female Institute on
which said A.E. Kincaid now resides and which she purchased from
John M. Trollinger. This January 30, 1866.
Reg: February 7, 1866   Signed: James H. Neil
                                        A.E. Kincaid
                                        W.H. Kincaid
                                        Sarah M.J. Kincaid

Page 247 - Jesse Evans to Joseph Reager. Two tracts of land
both of which are in the 20th Civil District of Bedford County
being bounded by land known as the Bell tract of Nathan Evans'
land. Containing 70 acres and 6 poles. Be the same and is
known as Lot No. 6 in the division of lands of Nathan Evans,
deceased. Also one other tract known as Lot No. 14 in division
of lands of Nathan Evans, deceased, and bounded by the Bell
tract. Containing 33 acres and 32 poles. This February 3,
1866.
Reg: February 7, 1866   Signed: Jesse Evans

Page 249 - Thomas Stephens Deed to R.L. Landis. I convey to
R.L. Landis whatever may be coming to me in the case of John
Huffman against me and others in the Chancery Court at
Shelbyville from the sales of the mills in said case after
paying the debts. This 30 January 1866.
Reg: January 31, 1866   Signed: Thomas Stevens

Page 249 - W.G. Knight Deed to W. Waite & Co. I, William G.
Knight of Bedford County, sold unto Warren Waite, F.M. Yell and
G.W. Richardson, partners, trading under the firm of W. Waite &
Co. in Tullahoma, Tennessee, have sold unto W. Waite & CO. a
tract of land in Bedford County on the Barren Fork of Duck River
on which said Knight at present resides and bounded by the
Barren Fork, by lands of the heirs of John McQuiddy, by lands of
Thomas C. Cribbs, by Duck River and lands of George Huffman.
Another small tract adjoining the tract above conveyed to me by
C.C. Brown by deed dated 7 June 1852 and bounded by the bank of
the Barren Fork of Duck River being my south boundary. Said two
tracts containing 162 acres. This 30 January 1866.
Wit: Ro. B. Davidson   Signed: W.G. Knight
     Geo. W. Buchanan
Reg: February 7, 1866

Page 251 - State of New York, County of New York. I, James F.
Cummings of said County and State, have appointed Robert F.
Evans of Bedford County my true and lawful attorney in fact for
me and in my name to collect and receive all sums of money which
may be due me in Bedford County. I am the owner of sundry small
lots of real estate in or near the Town of Shelbyville. This 24
January 1866.

Reg: February 7, 1866   Signed: James F. Cummings

Page 252 - William Collins Deed to Peter Brown. Both of Bedford
County. Land bounded on the west side of the turnpike. This 28
December 1865.
Wit: J. Hatchett   Signed: Wm. Collins
     John C. Blanton
Reg: February 8, 1866

Page 253 - P.F. King Deed to N. Thompson 2nd. One yellow filly.
This December 4, 1865.
Reg: February 8, 1866   Signed: P.F. King

Page 253 - P. Berron(?) Deed to J.T. Williams and W.H. Moon.
All of Bedford County.   House and lot in the Village of
Unionville, District No. 11 of Bedford County.   Land on the
north side of the turnpike. This 29 January 1866.
Wit: W.C. Blanton   Signed: P. Berron
     P.F. King
Reg: February 8, 1866

Page 254 - John L. Burt Deed to N. Thompson, 2nd.   I, John L.
Burt, have sold to N. Thompson, 2nd one horse hereto purchased
of Henry Brown and which is now on the farm of my mother Mrs.
Susan Burt near the Town of Shelbyville. I am indebted to Henry
Brown upon which the said N. Thompson, 2nd is one of my
securities. This February 3, 1866.
Reg: February 9, 1866   Signed: J.L. Burt

Page 255 - Hutton & Clark Deed to William Murphree. We, Robert
Clark and John Hutton, have sold unto William Murphree a tract
of land in Bedford County and Civil District No. 5 on the waters
of Fall Creek and bounded by Horatio Coop's corner. Containing
66 acres and 35 poles. This 6 November 1862.
Wit: G.D. Hutton   Signed: J.P. Hutton
     J.B. Booth   Robt. Clark
Reg: February 9, 1866

Page 256 - R. Terry Deed to A.W. Terry. For the love for my son
Alexander W. Terry, I do hereby give to him a tract of land in
Bedford County and District No. 8 and bounded by my south west
corner, to the center of the old Harpeth Road, by the line of
the land known as the Head tract, and to Bell & Hall's corner.
Containing 44 acres and 126 poles. This May 31, 1865.
Wit: A.J. Goodwin   Signed: Robert Terry
     C.S. Dudley
Reg: February 9, 1866

Page 256 - W.H. Moon Deed to J. Haynes. I, William H. Moon,
have sold unto John Hands(Haynes) a tract of land in Bedford
County and District No. 11, containing 159 acres and 5 poles,

Adjoining in the Shelbyville and Unionville Turnpike Road in J.R. Brown's east boundary line, and by A. Reaves' line, to the center of North Fork. This 25 January 1866.
Wit: G.W. Parsons   Signed: Wm. H. Moon
     M.E. Thompson
Reg: February 9, 1866

Page 257 - J.A. Blakemore Trust Deed to John P. Steele. I have sold to John P. Steele the following property, to wit, two tracts of land in Bedford County of 100 acres each. One in the 6th Civil District adjoining the lands of Robert Jennings and others and known as the Enoch place. The other near the Shelbyville, Farmington and Lewisburg Pike on the south side of the road about eight miles from Shelbyville, adjoining the lands of Geo. Stevenson and others and known in the neighborhood as my cedar tract, also a lot of 13 acres near Holt's Mill a part of the old Sterling Newsom tract lying east of Shelbyville near the town. 2 ½ acre lot near or in the Town of Shelbyville, in what is known as Camp White. Two other lots in the Town of Shelbyville 1 ½ acre lot near W. Powel's, the other the lot on which I live on Depot Street. Also an interest in the lot of ground on which Rose Porter the widow of George Porter, deceased, lives on or near Shelbyville, Unionville and Eagleville Pike about one mile from Shelbyville, and one small lot back of the aforesaid church. Also property, to wit, four head of horses, one four horse wagon and harness and other items listed in original document. This 6 February 1866.
Reg: February 9, 1866   Signed: J.A. Blakemore

Page 259 - Wm. H. Christopher Deed to Newcom Thompson, 2nd. Land in Bedford County and District No. 21, six miles from the Town of Shelbyville on the Shelbyville - Farmington Turnpike Road and adjoining the Section line and being the school land. Containing 80 acres. This 6 February 1866.
Reg: February 9, 1866   Signed: W.H. Christopher

Page 260 - L.B. and T.D. Fite Deed to Wm. H. Christopher. We, L.B. Fite and Thomas D. Fite sold on 7 October 1857 to Wm. H. Christopher interest we have and to a tract of land in Bedford County and Civil District No. 21, six miles from the Town of Shelbyville on the Shelbyville and Farmington Turnpike Road and bounded by the Section line the same being south west corner of the school land. Containing 80 acres. This 21 December 1865.
Reg: February 9, 1866   Signed: L.B. Fite
                                       Thos. D. Fite

Page 261 - R.D. Porter Deed to William Brown. A house and lot in the corporate limits of the Town of Shelbyville, Bedford County and adjoining the south side of an alley and opposite the south east corner of the Methodist Church lot. It being the lot that D.G. Deason bought from William Taylor and the same lot I purchased from William Brown. Containing 1 acre. This February 9, 1866.
Reg: February 10, 1866   Signed: R.D. Porter

Page 261 - Jas. F. Allen Deed to Jas. C. Paschall. This 2 December 1865. James F. Allen and his wife Susannah Allen of Sumner County, Tennessee, sold to James C. Paschal of Bedford County a tract of land containing 96 acres in Bedford County lying on the south side of Duck River in 18t[h] Civil District and bounded by the river, by James Paschal, and James Jones, deceased, by D.E. Jones. Said land belong to Susannah Parker, deceased, which she willed to heirs of my mother Elizabeth Paschall. James C.J. Paschal and one eighth of another share which belong to my father James Paschal, deceased.
Wit: S.A. Paschal   Signed: James F. Allen
    M.E. Allen   Susannah Allen
Reg: February 10, 1866

Page 262 - James F. Allen Deed to John W. Paschal. This 2 December 1865. James F. Allen and Susannah Allen his wife of Sumner County, Tennessee sold unto John W. Paschal of Bedford County land containing about 75 acres in Bedford County on the south side of Duck River in the 18th Civil District of Bedford County and bounded by Samuel Crowell, by James Jones, deceased, by Parker tract of land it being an undivided tract of land which belong to my father James Paschal, deceased. I, James F. Allen and wife Susannah Allen do bind ourselves to defend the title to the one eighth of said land to John W. Paschal.
Wit: S.A. Paschal   Signed: James F. Allen
    M.E. Allen   Susannah Allen
Reg: February 10, 1866

Page 263 - Entra, No. 3 Since 1 October 1865. I, James G. Gunn, enters 32 acres of land being on the head waters of Shipman Creek, District No. 25 of Bedford County and bounded by J.G. Gunn, Mrs. Burk Tyron and others. This February 10, 1866.
Reg: February 14, 1866   Signed: James G. Gunn

Page 264 - I, Hugh C. Hurst, am bound unto Samuel Cowan, Robert Cannon and J.W. Cowan a tract of land in Bedford County and District No. 21 adjoining the lands of James F. Cummings, Berry C. Owens and Geo. W. Cunningham and Duck River and being the place where I formerly resided and contains 242 acres. This 25 December 1858.
Wit: Edm'd Cooper   Signed: H.C. Hurst, by his
    P.E. Clardy   Atty in fact
Reg: February 14, 1866   I.L. Hurst

Page 265 - H.C. Hurst Deed to Robert Cowan. On 25 October 1858 executed my bond for title. I so convey unto Robert Cowan a tract of land in Bedford County and Civil District No. 21. Beginning in the pike, and bounded by the Toll Gate, to the bank of Duck River, and by Woods' line. Containing 223 acres and 72 poles. This 5 February 1866.
Wit: William Frierson   Signed: H.C. Hurst
    Byars Logan
Reg: February 14, 1866

Page 266 - Coldwell & Holland Deed to Henry Sipsey. On 15 September 1864, Thomas Holland sold unto Henry Sipsey a town lot in the corporate limits of the Town of Shelbyville and on 23 day of __ 1860 I, Thomas M. Coldwell causes an execution to issue on a judgment in my favor rendered on 3 November 1859 which was levied on a portion of said town lot on the 23 August 1860, on the property of Thomas G. Holland, said judgment being against him. Lot bounded by Main Street. I, Thomas M. Coldwell became the purchaser. This 30 January 1866.
Reg: February 14, 1866   Signed: Thos. M. Coldwell
                                        Thomas Holland

Page 267 - Solomon Claxton Deed to C.A. Freeman. Land in Bedford County and Civil District No. 5 and containing 29 acres and 52 poles and bounded by S. Lisenby's corner, by Jane Warmack's dower, by James Robinson's land, and by E.W. Jones' line. This January 27, 1860.
Wit: G.B. Price   Signed: Solomon Claxton
     James C. Claxton
Reg: February 14, 1866

Page 268 - Alex. Smith Power of Attorney to Joseph McFadden. I appoint Joseph McFadden of Shelbyville, agent and attorney in fact for me and in my name to manage and control or rent or lease a certain house and lot in the Town of Shelbyville near the Big Spring and belonging to the estate of Jack Smith, deceased. This 15 February 1866.
Reg: February 15, 1866   Signed: Alex. Smith, Admr. Of
                                        Jack Smith, deceased

Page 269 - Watson M. Gentry and wife Deed to Asa L. Stampson. Watson M. Gentry and his wife Martha A. Gentry of Bedford County sold unto Asa L. Stampson land in Bedford County and Civil District No. 7 on the east side of Shelbyville, Murfreesboro and Nashville Turnpike Road and bounded by said turnpike road being the south west corner of the land of Edmond Cooper, to the dividing line between the lands of Wm. G. Cowan and the tract hereby conveyed, and by a lot of land purchased by L.B. Knott from John C. Coldwell, Jr. Containing 4 acres and 35 poles. This 2 January 1866.
Reg: February 21, 1866   Signed: W.M. Gentry
                                        Martha A. Gentry

Page 270 - W.M. Gentry and M.A. Gentry Bond. W.M. Gentry and M.A. Gentry his wife. I have bargained and not yet conveyed unto A.L. S(illegible) a certain house in the Town of Shelbyville lying on the east side of the Murfreesboro Turnpike Road in Civil District No. 7 of Bedford County. Hereby made to the deed of John R. Jones to the said Martha A. Gentry deeded February 5, 1858, vested in Martha A. Gentry a life estate. This January 2, 1866.
Reg: February 21, 1866   Signed: W.M. Gentry
                                        Martha A. Gentry
                                        Thos. L. Gentry

Page 271 - P. Berron Deed to W.H. Moon. A lot of ground in Bedford County and District No. 11 and Village of Unionville. Containing about one half acre and bounded by J.T. Williams & Co. on the east side of the turnpike, and to W. Collins' line. (no date)
Wit: J.T. Williams   Signed: P. Berron
     D.P. Wheeler
Reg: February 21, 1866

Page 272 - F.T. McAlrath Deed to R.D. Rankins. I, Franklin T. McAlrath, have sold unto Robert D. Rankin land in Bedford County and Civil District No. 3 and bounded by the turnpike road leading from Shelbyville to Fairfield Archa Pruitt's corner, and to Joseph Ramsey's corner. Containing 14 acres. This 14 February 1866.
Wit: Archabald Pruitt   Signed: F.T. McAlrath
     David G. Rankin
Reg: February 22, 1866

Page 273 - W.W. Gill Deed to Mary H. Womble. Both of Bedford County. Land being in Lincoln County, Tennessee on the head waters of West Mulberry Creek. Bounded by the County Line, and by Raby's corner. It being 50 acres. This 1 December 1865.
Reg: February 23, 1866   Signed: W.W. Gill

Page 274 - R.D. Porter and wife Deed to R.C. White. I, R.D. Porter and Sarah E. Porter of Trigg County, Kentucky sold unto R.C. White a town lot in the Town of Shelbyville on the east side of the Public Square being the same conveyed by A.P. Eakin to Mrs. Sarah E. Porter wife of Mr. R.D. Porter on 23 August 1865 and registered in Book DDD, page 572. This 16 February 1866.
Reg: February 23, 1866   Signed: R.D. Porter
                           S.E. Porter

Page 275 - Louis Mankel Deed to R.H. Lewis. House and lot in the corporation of Shelbyville, Bedford County and bounded by John G. Johnson now John C. Coldwell, by Mary E. Thompson, by ___ Street the place now occupied by me and the same lot purchased from R.T. Cannon, trustee. This 25 February 1866.
Reg: February 23, 1866   Signed: Louis Mankel

Page 276 - C.T. Philpot Deed to W. Brown, 57 acres. I, Charles T. Philpot sold unto W. Brown land in Bedford County and Civil District No. ___ and bounded by the lands of Mrs. Terry, by the lands of Fredrick Jones, and by a lane. Containing 57 acres. It being the same land sold under decree of the Circuit Court in the case of Sutton's heirs and purchased by Wm. A. Philpot. This 24 February 1866.
Wit: R.B. Davidson   Signed: C.T. Philpot

William Frierson
Reg: February 28, 1866

Page 277 - Wm. S. Jett and Jo. D. Wilhoite Deed to J.L. Scudder.
Land in Bedford County and a portion of the land bounded by
Scudder's line, by Samuel E. Gilliland's corner, to the center
of Cannon Street, and by Charles Cannon's lot. Containing 17 ¾
acres. This 6 March 1866.
Reg: March 7, 1866   Signed: W.S. Jett
                                    Jo. D. Wilhoite

Page 278 - D.D. Hoover Deed to J.M. Hoover. This 14 February
1866. Both of Bedford County. Land in Bedford County and
District No. 4 adjoining Grizzard's corner, by the public road,
and by a branch. Containing 10 acres.
Reg: March 8, 1866   Signed: D.D. Hoover

Page 279 - James F. Arnold and wife Deed to Jno. W. Wiggins.
James F. Arnold and wife Mary V. Arnold have sold unto John W.
Wiggins land in the 20th District of Bedford County and bounded
by corner of H(illegible) Green's survey. Containing 34 acres
and 119 poles. Land being a part of the original Thomas Green
tract and by which the will of said Green was bequeathed to said
Mary V. Arnold who was his daughter. This 19 February 1866.
Reg: February 20, 1866   Signed: James F. Arnold
                                    Mary V. Arnold

Page 280 - John H. Oneal Deed of Trust to Charles T. Philpot. I
am indebted to Charles Philpot and I hereby sell, mortgage and
convey unto said Charles T. Philpot a certain house and lot in
the Town of Shelbyville and bounded by Unionville Turnpike, by
lands of James H. Neil, by lands of George W. Buchanan, and by
lands of the heirs of Silas A. Bivins. This 24 February 1866.
Wit: Ro. B. Davidson   Signed: John H. Oneal
     William Frierson
Reg: 8 March 1866

Page 282 - Cornelius Wamble Deed to Mrs. E.P. Kingree. Land in
Bedford County and District No. 20 and bounded by Gill's corner,
Evans' line, and to the Fayetteville Pike. Containing 50 acres.
This 12 February 1866.
Reg: March 8, 1866   Signed: Cornelius Wamble

Page 283 - George W. Greer Deed to Jesse Phillips. Land in
Bedford County and Civil District No. 20 and bounded by the
lands formerly owned by George W. Cunningham, by Joseph
Cunningham's land, by the lands of Richard Anderson, and by
lands of C.A. Warren and Ashly Cambell. Containing 106 acres.
This 26 February 1866.
Reg: March 8, 1866   Signed: G.W. Greer

Page 284 - William Henderson Deed to Green Murphy. One gray horse, one sorrel horse, one two horse wagon, and one buggy. This 20 December 1865.
Wit: S.H. Williams   Signed: William Henderson
Reg: 8 March 1866

Page 284 - Dabney Wade Trust Deed to S.G. Thompson. One two horse wagon and harness, one yellow mare, twenty head of sheep, ten head of hogs, one bed and stead, one bureau, two (illegible) saddles now in my possession. This 5 February 1866.
Reg: March 9, 1866   Signed: Dabney Wade

Page 285 - T.B. Allerson to E. Tarpley. I, Thomas B. Allerson sold unto Edward Tarpley two tracts of land in Bedford County and Civil District No. 11. First tract whereon the said T.B. Allison now lives. Adjoining lands belonging to D.A. Osment and a corner of Benjamin Blanton's land, by the old Franklin Road, Samuel J. (illegible)'s corner, to the center of Clems Creek, by lands of K.L. Allerson, and by the estate of George Harrison. Containing 83 acres and 21 poles. Second tract bounded by the Franklin Road. Containing 15 acres and 118 poles. This 28 February 1866. NOTE: Name could be T.B. Allison, ed.
Reg: March 9, 1866   Signed: T.B. Allerson

Page 287 - William Henderson Deed of Trust to S.H. Whitthorne. I have sold unto Samuel H. Whitthorne one spring wagon and harness, one buggy and harness, one feather bed and one longe. This 6 March 1862.
Wit: T.L. Marshall   Signed: William Henderson
Reg: March 9, 1866

Page 287 - Mike Shofner and others to James T. Arnold. We, Michael Shofner and Ana Eliza Hix on 5 September 1861 executed a title bond for a tract of land in District No. 25 and bounded by S.B. Gardner, and J.R. Burrow. Containing 100 acres. This 17 February 1866.
Reg: March 9, 1866   Signed: Mike Shofner
                                   Jordan C. Holt
                                   Ann E. Holt

Page 289 - G.W. Gardner Deed to Roane & Coble. Conveyed unto Thomas J. Roane and N.B. Coble a tract of land in Bedford County and District No. 25, adjoining S.B. Gardner's and J.R. Burrow's corner. Containing about 100 acres. This 17 February 1866.
Reg: February (March) 9, 1866.
                              Signed: G.W. Gardner

Page 290 - James T. Arnold Deed to G.W. Gardner. This 20 December 1861. Sold unto G.W. Gardner land and conveyed a title bond and registered in Bedford County in Book DDD, page 72 on 21 December 1861. Land in Bedford County and Civil District No. 25

and bounded by lands of S.B. Gordon and J.R. Burrow's corner. Containing 100 acres. This 19 February 1866.
Reg: March 10, 1866   Signed: J.T. Arnold

Page 291 - W.G. Osborn Deed of Trust to Chesley Williams. Land in Bedford County and 10th Civil District and containing 305 acres and bounded by the lands of John M. Hicks. This 2 March 1866.
Wit: Ro. B. Davidson   Signed: G.W. Osborn
     Geo. W. Buchanan
Reg: 10 March 1866

Page 292 - W.T. Thompson and wife Deed to <u>Mary R.Rutledge</u> (marked out). We, William T. Thompson and Hulda B. Thompson, have sold unto Narcisa Wilhoite a tract of land in Bedford County and District No. 7 and includes the south part or end of the tract of land belonging to me Hulda B. Thompson and being south of the land sold to Mary E. Rutledge and bounded by the lands of Hall & Warner, the old Swift tract, by the lands of said Narcisa Wilhoite, by the lands of Jacob T. Thompson, and beginning at the south west corner of Lot No. 2. Containing 35 acres. This 8 February 1866.
Reg: March 10, 1866   Signed: W.T. Thompson
                        H.B. Thompson

Page 294 - W.T. Thompson and wife Deed to Mary E. Rutledge. We, William T. Thompson and Hulda B. Thompson, have sold unto Mary E.Rutledge land in Bedford County on the north side of the tract of land belonging to Hulda B. Thompson and south of the land containing 13 ½ acres sold unto Mary E. Rutledge dated 22 July 1865, adjoining lands of Jacob F. Thompson, by John E. Hall and the W(illegible) the Swift, and by the lands. I have this day transferred to Narcisa Wilhoite. Beginning at the south west corner of Lot No. 1, and by the heirs of the Swift tract. Containing 20 acres. This 8 February 1866.
Reg: March 10, 1866   Signed: W.T. Thompson
                        H.B. Thompson

Page 295 - Narcissa Wilhoite Deed to Mary E. Rutledge. I, Narcisa Wilhoite for the love and affection I have for my aunt Mary E. Rutledge who is the sister of my deceased mother, have granted unto her land purchased by W.T. Thompson and wife H.B. Thompson lying in Bedford County and District No. 7 and including the south part or end of the tract of land owned formerly by said H.B. Thompson and bounded by lands of Mary E. Rutledge, by Hall & Warner, Old Swift tract, and by lands of Jacob F. Thompson. Land containing 35 acres. This 8 February 1866.
Reg: March 10, 1866   Signed: N. Wilhoite

Page 296 - Asa W. Elkins Deed to Scintha A. Holt. I have sold unto Syntha A. Hall a lot of land in Bedford County and District No. 25 and adjoining the old mill tract, and by Hufman's mill

tract. Containing 133 acres, it being the same lot of land I purchased of John Keck by deed dated 2 November 1849. This __ March 1866.
Reg: March 10, 1866   Signed: A.W. Elkins

Page 297 - Fred Batte Deed to L.J. Winsett. This 31 January 1866. Frederick Batte of Bedford County sold unto L.J. Winsett and her heirs a tract of land containing 108 acres in Bedford County and on the waters of Alexander Creek a branch of the North Fork of Duck River and adjoining a tract of land belonging to James Harris formerly now owned by John Tarpley, and by Anderson Landers' corner. Except a cotton house. This 25 December 1864.
Wit: A.M. Winsett   Signed: Fred Batte
     T.E. Batte
Reg: March 10, 1866

Page 298 - Michael B. Thompson Deed from Thomas Gregory. I have this day sold unto Michael B. Thompson land in Bedford County and District No. 8 and bounded by my original tract. Containing 8 acres. This January 18, 1866.
Wit: A.S. Turrentine   Signed: Thomas Gregory
     W.M. Tatum
Reg: March 12 1866

Page 299 - Michael B. Thompson Deed to W.M. Tatum (Granville Tucker). I do hereby transfer unto Granville Tucker land in Bedford County and District No. 8 and bounded by a corner of Thomas Gregory's original tract. Containing 8 acres. This December 6, 1866(3).
Reg: March 12, 1866   Signed: M.A. Thompson

Page 299 - James Carlisle Deed to G.W. Greer. I, James Carlisle, have sold unto George W. Greer a tract of land in Bedford County and Civil District No. 20 and bounded by the lands of George W. Cunningham, by lands of Joseph Cunningham, by lands of Richard Anderson, and by lands of C.A. Warren and Aily Campbell. Containing 126 acres. This March 2, 1866.
Reg: March 10, 1866   Signed: James Carlisle

Page 300 - William Phillips Deed of Rebecca R. Philpot. Land in Bedford County and District No. 8 and bounded by the center of Fall Creek. Containing 57 acres and 90 poles. This 10 February 1866.
Reg: March 13, 1866   Signed: William Phillips

Page 301 - Minos T. Cannon Deed to William G. Cowan. This 22 February 1866. Land in Bedford County and Civil District No. __ and bounded by Duck River, by west of Shelbyville and Lewisburg Turnpike Road, by a 2 acre tract willed by General Robt. Cannon to his son Minos T. Cannon, and to the middle of Duck River, making ¾ acres of 10 acres and 37 poles.

Wit: John T. Stephens   Signed: Minos T. Cannon
     Robt. Cowan
Reg: March 13, 1866

Page 302 - Joseph Trice Deed to Sallie Trice and others.   I,
Joseph Trice of Bedford County, sold unto Sally Trice, Nancy
Trice and Maria Antonettie Trice land in Bedford County and
District No. 20 and bounded by lands of John Nance, by the lands
of Joel C. Russell, deceased, by the lands of Sarah B. Trice and
John Cortner, and by lands of John C. Cortner.   Containing 80
acres, it being the same land upon which my mother Elizabeth
Trice now lives.   My undivided interest being one tenth of said
land I further convey my interest estate of said Elizabeth Trice
unto the said Sally Trice, Nancy Trice and Maria Anthonette
Trice that being one tenth of said personal property.   I was
appointed the administrator of the estate of my father John
Trice about the year 1849 and not being able to make the
payment, do convey to secure their right in the estate of John
Trice, deceased.   This March 7, 1866.
Reg: March 13, 1866   Signed: Joseph Trice

Page 303 - Jesse Nutt Lease to T.A. Atchison and others.   This
24 February 1866.   Jesse Nutt of Bedford County to T.A.
Atchison, J.M. Burrough, J.C. Shappard and James W. Bussey land
in Bedford County on the waters of Shipman Creek and Civil
District No. 25.   Containing 156 acres and bounded by lands of
Robert Mathews, by lands of Robt. Mathews and Wm. Shofner for
the term of 40 years.
Wit: H.H. Landis   Signed: Jesse Nutt
     A.J. Shofner
Reg: March 13, 1866

Page 304 - Albert J. Shofner Deed to T.A. Atchison and others.
This 24 February 1866.   Albert J. Shofner of Bedford County
lease to T.A. Atchison, J.M. Burrough, J.C. Shappard and Jas. W.
Bussey a tract of land in Bedford County on the waters of
Shipman Creek and in District No. 25.   Containing 120 acres and
bounded by lands of Harmon Landis, by lands of Robert Mathews,
by the lands of B. Blackman and Gabe Mopin, by lands of Robert
Mathws and R.L. Landis for the time of 40 years.
Wit: H.H. Landis   Signed: Albert J. Shofner
     Jesse Nutt
Reg: March 14, 1866

Page 305 - John W. Thompson Deed to Thomas Scott and others.   I
have sold unto Thomas Scott, Henry Holden and Frank Stump as
trustees of the Baptist Church by the name and style of Mont
Pisga Church located at Shelbyville the following lot or parcel
of land lying and being in the Town of Shelbyville and being on
the north side of Lane Street.   Adjoining a lot formerly owned
by Pat Neligan(?), to an old Ford Bridge, and to Mrs. J.F.
Cummings.   This March 14, 1866.
Reg: March 14, 1866   Signed: John W. Thompson

Page 306 - Henderson Shofner Deed to Calvin E. Jenkins. I, Henderson Shofner of Bedford County (being one of the lawful heirs of Austin Shofner, deceased, and as suck known in the late willand testament of said Austin Shofner) paid to me by Calvin E. Jenkins. I do sell unto said Calvin E. Jenkins a tract of land in Bedford County upon the waters of Thompson Creek being the same tract upon which said Austin Shofner was living at the time of his death. This 5 October 1865.
Wit: William Jenkins   Signed: Henderson Shofner
Reg: March 14, 1866

Page 307 - R.D. Deery Deed to John W. Thompson. A certain lot or parcel of land lying in the corporate limits of Shelbyville, Bedford County, and bounded by the street running north from the old grave yard by and in front of the residence of E.J. Frierson, deceased, by the lot owned by Price C. Steele, Edmond Cooper and C.A. Warren, by the lot of Thomas Holland, by the lot of Thomas G. Trollinger, and by the street running east and west by and on the south side of the Cumberland Presbyterian Church. This 31 October 1865.
Reg: March 15, 1866   Signed: R.D. Deery

Page 307 - Jo. Thompson, Sheriff, Deed to A.L. Stamps. On 1 February 1860 R.G. Green recovered a judgment against B. Neligan and P. Neligan. Which came into the hands of J.F. Vanoy, a constable of Bedford County, a tract of land in Civil District No. 7 in the corporate limits of Shelbyville and bounded by J. Neligan, by P. Fay, by Wm. Ditto, and by the street leading from the Big Spring to the old Fair Ground. Containing 160 acres levied on by said property of B. Neligan &c. This 7 March 1866.
Reg: March 15, 1866   Signed: Jo. Thompson, Sheriff

Page 309 - C.L. Pyron Deed from Robert Mathews. Land in Bedford County and containing 950 acres and known as the Short Mill place and which said Mathews purchased from Jacob Short several years past. This 15 March 1866.
Reg: March 15, 1866   Signed: Robt. Mathews

Page 309 - Richard B. Wilhoite Deed to William B. Offitt. W.B. Offitt, executed his note to me. I, Richard B. Wilhoite, have sold unto W.B. Offitt land in 7th District of Bedford County and adjoining John Frazier, by Alexander Sanders, and by Streeter's line. Containing 107 acres and 84 poles. This March 15, 1866.
Reg: March 16, 1866   Signed: R.B. Wilhoite

Page 310 - T.B. Ivie Deed to W.W. Gill, a Town Lot in the Town of Shelbyville on the Scull Camp Ford and being on the said road, by a street between said lot and C.A. Warren's lot, where he now resided, to a partition fence between said lot and the lot whereon Mrs. Andrew Mathews now reside, by William Gosling's line, and by the street leading from the grave yard to the Male University. Containing 3 ¾ acres is intended to convey by the

lot whereon I now live which includes the two lots which I bought from R.P. Ransom and G.W. Thompson. This March 17, 1866.
Reg: March 17, 1866   Signed: T.B. Ivie

Page 311 - Edmond Cooper Deed to Benjamin F. Wiggins and wife. On 20 January 1865, I conveyed to Sarah Chandler a tract of land in Bedford County and District No. 23 and containing 104 acres and 45 poles and on 29 October 1864 Sarah Chandler transferred a bond to John Wilhoite and on 18 November 1865 John Wilhoite assigned said title bond for 42 acres to be made to Eliza Holt wife of Herod H. Holt and deed he made to B.F. Wiggins and wife Jane H. Wiggins. Conveyed unto Benjamin F. Wiggins and his wife Jane H. Wiggins 62 acres and 45 poles, bounded by H.F. Holt, by a spring, and by Rufus Smith. This 20 November 1865.
Reg: March 19, 1866   Signed: Edm'd Cooper

Page 312 - W.W. Gill Deed of Gift to Mary R. Evans. For the love and affection I entertain for my daughter Mary R. Evans, I do give to her my town lot in the Town of Shelbyville and containing 3 ¾ acres and bounded by the south side of Scull Camp Ford Road, by a street opened between said lot and the lot whereon C.A. Warren now resides, to a partition fence between said lot and the lot whereon Mrs. Andrew Mathews now resides, by William Gosling's line, and to the street leading from the Male Academy. It being the lot I purchased of T.B. Ivie and whereon said Ivie now resides. This 18 March 1866.
Reg: March 19, 1866   Signed: W.W. Gill

Page 314 - J.B. McAdams Deed to Worley White. James B. McAdams sold unto Worley White land near the Town of Shelbyville Branch Rail Road and bounded by lands of Thomas Holland, by lands of J.B. McAdams, by lands belonging to the heirs of John Reed, and by lands of Mrs. Elizabeth Jones. Containing 3 acres and __ poles, the same being the part of the Wilson Coats' land. This March 19, 1866.
Reg: March 19, 1866   Signed: J.B. McAdams

Page 314 - Dabney Wade Deed of Trust to S.G. Thompson. Dabney Wade conveyed unto S.G. Thompson one two horse wagon and harness, one yellow mare, twenty head of sheep, ten head of hogs, one bed and stead, one bureau, two mans saddle and also several other items listed in original document. I am indebted to Bartlet Tyler. This 17 March 1866.
Reg: March 20, 1866   Signed: Dabney Wade

Page 315 - Wm. Gosling Deed to Nathan Cowan. Wm. Gosling sold unto Nathan Cowan (col.) a tract of land in Bedford County and Civil District No. __ about one mile from the Town of Shelbyville on the wide of the Murfreesboro...(Road), adjoining Jessy Cowan's land. Containing 1 acre. This 8 January 1866.
Reg: March 20, 1866   Signed: Wm. Gosling

Page 316 - Suan & Allerson Mortgage to Henry Clark. We agree to pay Henry Clark $723.72 bond money which said Suan (illegible) lecied his tract of land, containing 106 acres, adjoining E.S. Wortham, M. Crowell, by Molder and others, and by J. Crowell and Delk. This March 10, 1866.
Reg: March 21, 1866   Signed: Suan & Allerson

Page 317 - Wm. S. Jett and Jo. D. Wilhoite Deed to J.L. Scudder. I, Wm. S. Jett sold unto James L. Scudder for which he has executed his two notes for a tract of land in Bedford County and formerly owned by Clement Cannon and bounded by James L. Scudder, by center of Cannon Street, and to the top of the bluff on the west side of Duck River. Containing 18 acres and 12 poles which land was surveyed by William Galbreath March 21, 1866. This 22 March 1866.
Reg: March 22, 1866   Signed: Wm. S. Jett
                                      Jo. D. Wilhoite

Page 318 - A.B. Dryden and L.P. Dryden Deed to Thomas J. Gant. We, Alexander B. Dryden and wife Lydia P. Dryden, have sold unto Thomas J. Gant land partitioned to the heirs of law of Harriet Murgrave, deceased, in the division of the land of her mother Edith Forbes, deceased, and bounded by the land allotted to the heirs of William Forbes, deceased, by lands allotted to Thomas M. Forbes, and by lands of Coffey. Containing 60 acres and in District No. 18 of Bedford County. This 22 March 1866.
Reg: March 22, 1866   Signed: Alexander B. Dryden
                                      Lydia P. Dryden

Page 319 - N. Thompson, 2nd Deed to Thomas Thompson, Trustee. I, N. Thompson, 2nd, have sold unto Thomas Thompson, my son, a tract of land in Bedford County and Civil District No. 21 and bounded by Bradley Gambill's corner, and by lands known as Ransom's or school land. Containing 139 acres and 152 poles, being the same being the whole of the lands recently known as the Dr. Christopher place and being a part of the lands known as the Brame place and a part of the lands known as the Sims or Knight lands and all of which are near the Shelbyville and Lewisburg Pike. But this conveyance is made for no other purpose whatever that is to say that in consideration of the affection for my daughter Elizabeth Thompson, wife of my said son Thomas Thompson I am determined to secure to her and her children by him a comfortable house which will not be subject to the debts &c. NOTE: Long document. This March 21, 1866.
Reg: March 22, 1866   Signed: N. Thompson, 2nd.

Page 321 - James Grooms Deed of Trust to Ezekiel Lacy. I have sold unto Ezekiel Lacy one sorrel horse colt, one bay mare, and ten head of stock hogs.
Wit: N.F. Thompson   Signed: James Grooms
Reg: March 23, 1866

Page 321 - James M. Miller Deed to James W. Keel. I, J.W.
Miller with the will annexed of J.J. Miller, deceased, have
conveyed unto James Woodfin and transferred to Jas. W. Keel land
in the Town of Fairfield in Bedford County and District No. 1
and bounded by the Mosely lot and Mrs. Singleton, by a lot
supposed to belong to Paterson, and by the old road. This 30
November 1865.
Wit: Henry J. Taylor   Signed: J.M. Miller, Admr.
     T.H. Manier
Reg: March 23, 1866

Page 322 - R.S. Dwiggins and T.B. Ivie, Agreement. It is agreed
that said Ivie take all the cedar rails now on the land
purchased by said Ivie of Minos T. Cannon furnished by said
Dwiggins. This March 26, 1866.
Wit: J.A. Blakemore   Signed: R.S. Dwiggins
     W.H. Wisner   T.B. Ivie
Reg: March 26, 1866

Page 323 - James Russ Mortgage to Wm. G. Cowan. I, James Russ,
have sold unto Wm. G. Cowan a house and lot on Martin Street in
the Town of Shelbyville adjoining the lands of Thos. B. Cannon,
being the place where I now live and have conveyed to J.H.
McGrew in Trust Deed and registered in Book EEE, pages 81 and
82. Containing 2 Acres. This 26 March 1866.
Reg: March 26, 1866   Signed: James Russ

Page 324 - A.L. Adams Deed from Wm. S. Jett and Jo. D. Wilhoite.
Wm. S. Jett and Jo. D. Wilhoite sold unto Adolphus L. Adams land
in Bedford County and District No. 7 and bounded by T.B.
Cannon's corner, by Cannon Street, and to the middle of Duck
River. Containing 43 acres and 53 poles, surveyed by Wm.
Galbreath, surveyor. This 27 March 1866.
Reg: March 27, 1866   Signed: Wm. S. Jett
                                      Jo. D. Wilhoite

Page 325 - E.A. Reagar Deed to John C. Ray. Land in Bedford
County and Civil District No. 24 and bounded by a stone in the
Big Road in Alfred Cambell's line, to the top of the ridge, and
to the center of Flat Creek. Containing 91 acres and 158 poles,
surveyed by C.S. Dudley. This 1 October 1865.
Reg: March 27, 1866   Signed: E.A. Reagar

Page 326 - James Russ Deed to E.C. Russell and A.G. Russell. I
have sold unto Mrs. E.C. Russell a house and lot in the Town of
Shelbyville and bounded by the line of the old corporation
opposite the center of Martin Street, by a poultry house, and by
the north boundary fence on said property. Containing 2 acres
to have to the said Mrs. E.C. Russell and A.G. Russell. This 29
March 1866.
Reg: March 29, 1866   Signed: James Russ

Page 327 - James Carlisle Deed to Jesse Evans. I, James Carlisle, have sold unto Jesse Evans two tracts of land in Bedford County and Civil District No. 20 and bounded by the center of Sugar Creek, and by Snell's line. Containing 4 acres and 28 poles. Also another tract bounded by Lot No. 20, Lot No. 5 of the plat of Nathan Evans' land, and by Lot No. 19. Containing 16 Acres. This March 24, 1866.
Reg: March 29, 1866   Signed: James Carlisle

Page 328 - W.W. Evans Deed to Jesse Evans. I, William W. Evans, have sold unto Jesse Evans land in Bedford County and Civil District No. 20 and bounded by McCommons' tract, and by Lot No. 20 of the Nathan Evans plat. Containing 29 acres. This March 24, 1866.
Reg: March 29, 1866   Signed: W.W. Evans

Page 329 - Jesse Evans Deed to W.W. Evans. I, Jesse Evans, have sold unto William W. Evans land in Bedford County and Civil District No. 20 and bounded by Lot No. 20 of the Nathan Evans' plat, by Lot No. 5 of said plat, and by line of Lot No. 19. Containing 16 acres. This March 24, 1866.
Reg: March 29, 1866   Signed: Jesse Evans

Page 330 - John R. Eakin Deed of Trust to Albert Eakin. I have sold and conveyed unto Albert Eakin a tract of land in Bedford County upon which the hemp factory of Eakin & Myers is located. Bounded by the original factory tract being which corner is to extended 20 poles, to line between myself and Wm. T. Myers' tract, and by Pepper's line. Containing 140 acres.
Wit: At Washington County, Arkansas 3 January 1866.
Reg: March 30, 1866   Signed: Jno. R. Eakin

Page 332 - W.W. Gunter Deed to Henry Cooper. Both of Bedford County. Land in Bedford County and bounded by a road a short distance above the Jordan Holt mill, with an old fence, to the middle of the Roseville Road, to or near a dry branch, and to the north bank of Duck River. Containing 22 ¾ acres surveyed by Wm. Galbreath. This 30 March 1866.
Reg: March 30, 1866   Signed: W.W.Gunter

Page 333 - Daniel Dillon Deed to Asa L. Stamps. Davidson County, Tennessee. I, Daniel Dillon of Coffee County, Tennessee, have sold unto Asa L. Stamps of Bedford County in the Town of Shelbyville in Civil District No. 7 in Bedford County, bounded by the center of a street east and west which connects Lot No. 17, 15 and 18, and by a street that runs north and south to the corner of Wades' lot. Being about 1 acre and it being the same purchased by me by Asa L. Stamps about 1861. This March 21, 1866.
Reg: March 30, 1866   Signed: Daniel Dillon

Page 334 - James Russ Deed of Trust to Wm. S. Jett. I have conveyed unto William S. Jett the printing press and materials and fixtures of Shelbyville Expositor. This 30 March 1866.
Reg: March 30, 1866   Signed: James Russ

Page 335 - Henry Cooper Deed to Zebuland Evans. Land in Bedford County and Civil District No. 3 and bounded by the Roseville Road, by corner of Lot No. 18 of the Robt. Cannon tract, and by Mrs. Moody's corner. Containing 27 acres and 93 poles. This 31 March 1866.
Reg: March 31, 1866   Signed: Henry Cooper

Page 335 - John W. Thompson Deed to N. Thompson, Sr. Land in the Town of Shelbyville, Bedford County and bounded by the street running north and south from the old grave yard, by the lot of P.C. Steele, Ed. Cooper and Thomas Holland, by Thomas C. Trollinger, by the south side of the C.P. Church. This March 17, 1866.
Reg: March 31, 1866   Signed: Jno. W. Thompson

Page 336 - Title Bond to Elizabeth W. Chapman. Elizabeth W. Chapman wife of Thomas Chapman. NOTE: Instrument very hard to read. Land in Bedford County and Civil District No. 19. This November 19, 1861.
Wit: Thos. W. Coffey   Signed: Thos. Davidson
     A.T. Coffey
     J. ?. Dysart
Reg: April 2, 1866

Page 337 - J.W. Coffey, Extr. Of E.W. Chapman to Thos. Davidson. On 19 November 1861, I, Thomas Davidson executed my bond to Elizabeth W. Chapman a deed to the following tract of land in Bedford County and bounded by lands bought of Hugh A. Hall, to John Larue's corner, and to the homestead line. Registered in Bedford County in Book EEE, pages 335 and 336. This April 2, 1866.
Reg: April 2, 1866   Signed: J.W. Coffey, Extr. Of
                                    T. Davidson

Page 337 - James Snoddy Deed to Thomas Hutson and Sarah E. Haislett. This 9 June 1865. Between James T. Snoddy and Thomas Hutson and Sarah E. Haislett, all of Bedford County. Land in Bedford County and Civil District No. 24 bounded near Shook Branch, near Shofner's saw mill, and to the Winchester Road. Containing 51 acres and 39 poles.
Wit: James Bryant   Signed: James T. Snoddy
     J.F. Smith
Reg: April 5, 1866

Page 338 - William A. Mann Deed to Emily A. Neal, Deed to land. Land in Bedford County and Civil District No. 11 in Township or Section 6 and part of Section 6 on the waters of the North Fork

of Duck River and bounded by Lot No. 3 and a corner of Lot No. 7, by Lot No. 2, to the Big Road, by the Widow Jones' corner, by corner of P.W. Lock bought of Thos. A. Sikes, and by Turrentine's line. Containing 107 acres. This March 24, 1866.
Reg: April 2, 1866   Signed: William A. Mann

Page 339 - L.C. White Deed to Tennessee Davidson and others. For the love and affection I have for my sisters in law Tennessee Davidson, Martha Davidson, Margret A. Davidson wife of William Patton and for the consideration that the land came by my wife who is their sister and at her death it descended to our son who has since died leaving the right to me. I do hereby convey unto them all the right title &c which I have in and to said land which being in Bedford County and Civil District No. 20 and bounded by Jas. C. Snell, by the lands of Thos. Snell, by the lands of Thomas and Mrs. Nathaniel White, and by the lands of H. & S. Dyer, Mathew Shearin and Mrs. White. Containing 120 acres. This 13 September 1865.
Wit: T.M. Snell   Signed: L.C. White
     T.W. Brents
Reg: April 5, 1866

Page 340 - Argile P. Eakin Deed to Town Lot to John W. Thompson. Land in Town of Shelbyville, Bedford County by the old Pannell lot being on the south side of the same, and by the line of Thos. C. Whiteside Lot. This April 3, 1866.
Reg: April 6, 1866   Signed: A.P. Eakin

Page 340 - Alford Campbell Title Bond to C.A. Crunk. Land on the waters of Big Flat Creek and bounded by Elijah Reagor, by Joseph Farrar, by Abraham Reagor, and by J.C. Shephard and Thomas Nance. Containing 57 acres. This October 21, 1862.
Wit: William Campbell   Signed: Alford Campbell
     J.W. Crunk
Reg: April 6, 1866

Page 341 - William S. Jett Deed to A.P. and Lucretia Eakin. House and lot in the Town of Shelbyville in Civil District No. 7 and bounded by the lands of Jason T. Cannon, by a street running to the Fair Grounds by the residence of G.W. Buchanan, by the new graveyard, and by the Warner's mill road. Containing 28 acres, it being the land purchased by me of John W. Thompson and N. Thompson, Sr.
Reg: April 6, 1866   Signed: William S. Jett

Page 341 - A.P. and Lucretia Ekin Deed to William S. Jett. House and lot in Shelbyville, Bedford County and bounded by the street running in front of Mrs. Lucretia Eakin's residence, by the south side of the Dixon Academy lot, on the west of Brittain Street, and by Oliver Cowan's lot. This 5 April 1866.
Reg: April 9, 1866   Signed: A.P. Eakin
                                   Lucretia Eakin

196

Page 342 - Deed from Charles N. Harris and others to John L. Cooper. We, Charles N. Harris, Jane Harris, William C. Wood and wife M. Elizabeth and James P. Marbery and wife Harriet L., have sold unto J.L. Cooper, land in Bedford County and District No. 9 on the waters of the North Fork of Duck River and containing 100 acres and 36 poles and bounded by Haywood Oakley. Except one half acre including the grave yard which has been laid off. This 26 October 1864.

Wit: C.A. Dudley   Signed: C.N. Harris
      R.W. Couch   Jane Harris
      W.T. Landers   J.P. Marbery
      L.A. Puckett   H.L. Marbery
Reg: April 9, 1866   W.P. Wood
                               M.E. Wood

Page 343 - Transfer of Title Bond from J.W. Crunk, C.A. Crunk and Jordan Hale to J.C. Ray and E.A. Reagor. Sold bond to Alfred Campbell October 21, 1862 and a part of the instrument to J.C. Ray. According to a division of land in a plat of C.S. Dudley dated March 6, 1866, 14 acres and 104 poles, and 13 acres and __ poles. This April 3, 1866.

Wit: J.L. Scudder   Signed: C.A. Crunk
      W.P. Bridges   J.W. Crunk
Reg: April 9, 1866   Jordan Hale

Page 343 - Deed from William H. Moore to R.H. Stemm. Both of Bedford County. Land in Bedford County and Civil District No. 11 and containing 118 ½ acres bounded by the lands of the late E.D. Winsett, by lands of J.C. Green and wife, by J.R. Brown, and by the lands of Mrs. L. Winsett lately purchased from J.W. Stemm, by the road leading from Unionville to the North Fork Meeting House, by the heirs of said J.C. Green and wife, by lands of William Floyd, by Floyd's and Mrs. L. Winsett's line, and by the old Farrar tract. This April 3, 1866.

Wit: B.F. Duggins, Sr.   Signed: Wm. H. Moore
      W.C. Blanton
Reg: April 10, 1866

Page 344 - Edmond Cooper Deed to Sarah J. Moss. Eli Moss and wife Sarah J. Moss by deed dated 16 March 1859 conveyed to me a tract of land which belonged to Sarah J. Moss. I did sell and convey a part of said land to James H. Harrison say 17 acres and 85 poles. I do hereby convey all the remainder of said tract of land to James H. Harrison to the said Sarah J. Moss during her natural life free from debts &C and at her death to her children. Land consists of about 40 acres adjoining the lands of Edmund Jenkins, by the lands of Alexander Dysart, by lands of James H. Harrison, by lands of Joseph H. Smith and Matilda Harper in District No. 19 of Bedford County. This 6 April 1866.

Reg: April 11, 1866   Signed: Edm'd Cooper

Page 345 - Wm. B.M. Brame (illegible) to John H. Wells. W.B.M. Brame, Moses Marshall, a Justice of the Peace of Bedford County

that he has lost, mislaid a note on John A(H). Wells due 12 September 1862. This July 25, 1865.
Wit: Moses Marshall, J.P.   Signed: Wm. M.B. Brame
Reg: April 11, 1866

Page 345 - Joseph Hastings Deed to James H. Wallace and others. Joseph Hastings sold unto James H. Wallace, Joseph E. Wallace and Cyntha E. Wallace a tract of land in Bedford County and Civil District No. 23 and bounded by Kizer's corner. Containing 66 acres and 46 poles. This 10 April 1866.
Wit: Wm. T. Tune   Signed: Joseph Hastings
     S.S. Wallace
Reg: April 11, 1866

Page 346 - F.K. Daniel and wife Deed to William M. Green. We, F.K. Daniel and Malissa Daniel his wife conveyed unto William M. Green all the right title and interest and claim which said Malissa M. Daniel formerly Malissa Green had as one of his children and heirs of James Green, deceased, there being at the time of his death eleven heirs, have in a tract of land in Bedford County and Civil District No. 2. First tract bounded on the west side of Doddys Creek, by David R. Vance and Edward Hoard, by James Isom and John McQuiddy. Second tract bounded on the east side of Doddys Creek, by James Green, deceased, land, by Thomas and James Holland, by lands of Eliza Green and James Isham. First tract containing 140 acres and second tract 126 acres. This April 3, 1866.
Reg: April 11, 1866   Signed: F.K. Daniel
                                     Malissa Daniel

Page 346 - Wm. M. Green Deed to Emily Green. Interest in land. Land in Bedford County and Civil District No. 2 and on the waters of Doddys Creek, waters of the Barren Fork of Duck River and bounded by the head of an old walled spring which has now changes its channel, by a crop fence, to top of a ridge in E. Hall's line, and by J.M. Isom's corner. Containing 29 acres and 35 poles. This 17 March 1866.
Reg: April 11, 1866   Signed: W.M. Green

Page 347 - H.L. Davidson Title Deed to John H. Wells. I bind myself to John H. Wells for three adjoining tracts of land on the north side of Duck River in District No. 22 in Bedford County, containing after deducting about 5 acres when purchase money is paid being secured to me in his three notes. This September 25, 1862.
Reg: April 12, 1866   Signed: H.L. Davidson

Page 348 - George W. Thompson Deed to C.E. Peacock. Lot of land with the house on the north east corner of the Public Square in the Town of Shelbyville and known as the Marr's corner formerly belonging to Robert Cannon, deceased, and bounded by the Public Square and Martin Street, and by D.S. Evans' line. This 12 April 1866.

Reg: April 12, 1866   Signed: G.W. Thompson

Page 348 - James A. Puckett Deed to L.P. Vaughn, 20 acres.   Land
in Bedford County and Civil District No. 9 and adjoining the
lands of John A. Webb, by John W. Key, by L.P. Vaughn, by Mary
J. Puckett.   Containing 20 acres.   This 12 April 1866.
Wit: Wm. T. Tune   Signed: James A. Puckett
Reg: April 12, 1866

Page 343 - (Second page numbered 343) - James L. Scudder to
George W. Buchanan, Deed.   I, James L. Scudder, have sold unto
George W. Buchanan and Robert C. White a lot of ground the same
being one half situated in the Town of Shelbyville and bounded
by lot that D.S. Evans purchased of R.D. and James H. Deery, by
the north side of the Public Square, by Lot No. 2, by Lots No. 1
and 2, and by D.S. Evans' corner.   The lot is the interest of
J.L. Scudder in the lot formerly purchased of Wm. And M.E.
Churchwell now owned by Buchanan and Scudder.   This 12 April
1866.
Reg: April 16, 1866   Signed: James L. Scudder

Page 344 - (Second page numbered 344) - Louisville, Kentucky,
April 2, 1864. R.P. Shapard to Jane P. Black.   Deed.   I, Robert
P. Shapard, have conveyed unto Mrs. Jane P. Black a tract of
land in Bedford County and District No. 7 and in the corporate
limits of the Town of Shelbyville and known as Lot No. 97 and
bounded on the north by Lane Street, by an alley, by the little
spring, and by Lot No. 104.
Reg: April 16, 1866   Signed: R.P. Shapard

Page 344 (and 353) (As read on microfilm)   (Second No. 344) -
Samuel G. Hays to Rob. P. Shapard, Deed.   Land in Bedford County
and District No. 7 and in the corporate limits of the Town of
Shelbyville and known as Lot No. 77 and bounded on the north
Lane Street, by an alley, by the little spring, and by Lot No.
104 now owned by James L. Scudder.   This 26 April 1856.
Wit: C.G. Mitchell   Signed: Sam'l G. Hays
     J.W. Jordan
Reg: April 16, 1866

Page 353 (and 352, as read on microfilm) - N. Thompson, Sr. to
John M. Trollinger, Deed.   I, Newsom Thompson, Sr., have sold
unto John M. Trollinger a lot of land in corporate limits of the
Town of Shelbyville and bounded on the Shelbyville and
Unionville Turnpike road opposite the south west corner of Lot
No. 133, by Sarah Trollinger's line, and by an alley.   It being
part of Lot No. 133 and purchased by me of James L. Turpin in
1852.   This 18 February 1860.
Reg: April 17, 1866   Signed: N. Thompson, 2nd.

Page 352 - (As read from microfilm) - James A. Jarrett Deed to
F.J. and Mary H. Harris, 128 acres.   Land in Bedford County and

District No. 8 it being a tract of land purchased of W.M. Gilmore. Containing 128 acres. This December 30, 1865.
Wit: James Turpin   Signed: James A. Jarrett
     J.A. Elam
Reg: April 18, 1866

Page 352 - N.J.C. Keller Deed to G.A. and Daniel Cotner, 131+ acres. All of Bedford County. Land in Bedford County and bounded by lands of William Cully and L.W. Hall, and by Cully Branch. Containing 131+ acres.
Reg: April 18, 1866 .   Signed: N.J.C. Keller

Page 353 - Sarah A. Huffman Deed to G.A. Cotner, 4 acres. Land in Bedford County being the one third of one eighth of 114 acres of land and bounded by lands of the heirs of F.H. Keller, by lands of the heirs of Joseph Couch and G.G. Osborne, by lands of J.W. Welch, by lands of Myers, it being the original tract of land that Mathias Cotner owned at his death, the said Sarah A. Huffman being an heir and grand daughter of Mathias Cotner, deceased. This 7 March 1866.
Wit: F.M. Keller   Signed: Sarah A. Huffman
     N.J.C. Keller
Reg: April 18, 1866

Page 353 - Joseph and Cenar B. Holcomb Deed to M.N. Moore. This 16 April 1866, of Hempstead County, Arkansas and said Moore of Bedford County. Interest which said Cenar B. Holcomb and Joseph Holcomb the former being one of the heirs to the land, it being in two separate tracts, which are laid off after the death of William Boone out of the lands of which Boone died seized and possessed for his widow Margaret Boone's dower. Said lands lying in Bedford County and District No. 22 on the waters of Big Flat Creek and adjoining the lands of John Stone, Jordan Hale, Joseph Parker, P.S. Dean, Richard Mullins, and W.G. Harris. Containing in all 321 acres.
Reg: April 19, 1866   Signed: Joseph Holcomb
                                 Cenar B. Holcomb

Page 354 - Erwin C. Russell and others to Winston W. Gill, House and lot. House and lot in the Town of Shelbyville and bounded by near the south west boundary line of the old corporation opposite the center of Martin Street. Containing 10 acres. This April 23, 1866.
Reg: April 23, 1866   Signed: Erwin C. Russell
                                 A.G. Russell
                                 B.L. Russell

Page 355 - W.B. Sutton Deed to W.W. Payne. William B. Sutton sold to William W. Payne a tract of land in Bedford County and Civil District No. 3 and bounded by lands of Anderson Sharp and the Mcguire tract, by lands of A. Pruitt now by the lands of James Caruthers, by lands of the heirs of Daniel Gilchrist, deceased. Containing 50 acres. This 20 April 1866.

Reg: April 23, 1866   Signed: W.B. Sutton

Page 356 - A. Pruitt Deed to W.W. Payne, 10 acres.   Land in
Bedford County and Civil District No. 3 and bounded by Wm. B.
Sutton's line, by W.W. Payne's line, and by James Caruthers'
line. Containing 10 acres. This April 23, 1866.
Reg: April 23, 1866   Signed: A. Pruitt

Page 356 - Minos T. Cannon Deed to T.B. Ivie, 94 acres.   I have
sold unto Thomas B. Ivie land in Bedford County on the south
west side of Duck River near the Town of Shelbyville and bounded
by follows, Beginning in the forks of the Fayetteville and
Farmington Turnpike roads about three quarters of a mile from
the Town of Shelbyville, by Erwin J. Frierson line a little
south of the toll gate on the Fayetteville Turnpike, and by the
Farmington Road. Containing 94 acres. This April 1, 1866.
Reg: April 24, 1866   Signed: Minos T. Cannon

Page 357 - D.F. Jackson Deed & Tract to T.W. Buchanan.   This 1
June 1865. I executed to Thos. W. Buchanan as Trustee which is
registered in Book DDD, a certain property to pay and save
debts. The first deed (Which is destroyed) is one note due John
W. Wiggins. Also a note due Herbert Wiggins on three notes due
John W. Cowan. Three notes are to be paid by 1 June 1866 and
the note due the Jackson Wallace. This 24 April 1866.
Wit: Samuel Neely   Signed: D.F. Jackson
     Thos. P. Richardson
Reg: (illegible)

Page 358 - R.H. Lewis Deed to S.G. Reeves, Bond.   I, Robt. H.
Lewis, am bound unto S.G. Reeves. I have sold to said Reeves a
tract of land in 7th District of Bedford County near the Town of
Shelbyville and bounded by a lot of W.G. Cowan, by the
Shelbyville and Fayetteville Turnpike, on the west by Duck
River. Containing 12 acres and 120 poles. (no date)
Reg: April 25, 1866   Signed: R.H. Lewis

Page 358 - W.W. Payne Deed to James Caruthers, 10 acres.   Land
in Bedford County and Civil District No. 3 and bounded by
Gilchrist's corner, by James Caruthers' line, and by W.W.
Payne's line. Containing 10 acres. This 24 April 1866.
Reg: April 26, 1866   Signed: W.W. Payne

Page 359 - Lucy Ann Edde to Margaret Ann Whitthorne and others,
lot.   I have conveyed unto Lewis Tillman, Commissioner and
Trustee for the use of Margaret Ann Whitthorne and her children,
a tract of land in Civil District No. 7 Bedford County and
bounded by J.W. Cowan's line, and to the center of the
McMinnville Road. Containing 108 poles. This 25 April 1866.
Wit: Walter S. Bearden   Signed: Lucy Ann Edde
     W.J. Whitthorne
Reg: April 25, 1866

Page 360 - Kindred and K.J. Pearson, Agreement. Both of Bedford County. For one half of all his stock, corn, oats, hay and other articles made by M.W. Watson and G.M. Ray. Kindred Pearson is to pay the taxes on the same. K.J. Pearson is to pay to Kindred Pearson for one half of the rent of the place. This 6 February 1866.
Wit: Charles Pearson   Signed: Kindred Pearson
     John Norton   K.P. Pearson
Reg: April 26, 1866

Page 360 - Jennings Moore Deed to Benjamin Blanton, 124 acres and 106 poles. Land in Bedford County and Civil District No. 11 in and near the Town of Unionville and bounded by the lands of the N.A. Ozment (3)'s old tract, the corner of the Methodist Church Lot, by the Pike Road, by the Camp Ground Lot, by J.C. Wilson's line, and to the Chapel Hill Road. Containing 124 acres and 106 poles. This 20 March 1866.
Wit: W.C. Blanton   Signed: Jennings Moore
     John A. Moore
Reg: April 27, 1866

Page 361 - George W. Thompson Deed to Wm. H. Christopher, 174 acres and 136 poles. Land in Bedford County and Civil District No. 18 and bounded by James Stallings' line, and by the old Section line. Containing 197 acres and 136 poles. This 27 April 1866.
Reg: April 27, 1866   Signed: G.W. Thompson
                                      C.A. Warren

Page 362 - Polina C. Wilson Deed to Martha J. Haynie, Lot. I, Polina C. Wilson of Evansville, Indiana, sold land in Bedford County and within the corporate limits of the Town of Shelbyville on the east side of said town between Rowesville and Skull Camp Ford Road fronting on Rowesville Road and bounded by said road containing 1 acre being the lot of land sold years ago by Gen. Robt. Cannon to Zebulon Evans and including the house and enclosure occupied by said Evans for several years and until lately being also part of a 10 acre tract formerly owned by Peter Chilcut, Sr. This 13 April 1866. Vanderburgh, Indiana.
Reg: April 28, 1866   Signed: Polina C. Wilson

Page 363 - Minos T. Cannon Deed to William S. Jett, 22 acres and 107 poles. Land in Bedford County and containing 220 acres and 109 poles being the south west corner of the 200 willed by my father Robert Cannon, adjoining Gen. Robert Cannon's line, and to the middle of the Shelbyville and Fayetteville Turnpike Road. This 24 March 1866.
Reg: April 30, 1866   Signed: Minos T. Cannon

Page 364 - Robert L. Landers Deed to James C. Leming, 103 acres. Land in Bedford County on the waters of Normande (Normandy) Creek in Civil District No. 25. Containing 103 acres and adjoining Dennis Hively. This August 9, 1865.

Wit: William H. Wisner   Signed: R.L. Landers
Reg: April 30, 1866

Page 364 - William Frierson Deed to Jo. D. Wilhoite, House and
lot. One Town lot, to wit, one store house on the south side of
the Public Square of Shelbyville and for the last twenty five or
thirty years owned by Erwin J. Frierson, deceased, and for many
years occupied by Wilhoite & Bros., merchants, and for a year or
two by C.P. Houston, Jr., and at present by J.C. Coldwell & Co.,
said lot with the store house thereon fronts on the south side
of said square and adjoining the store house of C.A. Warren, and
by Robert Cannon's Hotel, and by a small house occupied by
Steele & Sharp as a grocery. This 28 April 1866.
Reg: April 30, 1866   Signed: William Frierson

Page 365 - John P. Phillips Deed to James Moore.   Lot in
Normandy.   Land in Bedford County and District No. 25 and
bounded by the edge of the Rail Road near the stock gap.
Containing 2 acres and 20 poles. This 30 October 1865.
Reg: April 30, 1866   Signed: John P. Phillips

Page 366 - William S. Jett Deed to Minos T. Cannon, 16 ½ acres.
Land in Bedford County on the west side of Duck River above the
Town of Shelbyville, beginning at a Hotel Gamble about 4 poles
from the river bank being the (illegible) in a line from Clem
Cannon to Newton Cannon, and to M.T. Cannon's stable.
Containing 16 ½ acres. This 31 May 1865.
Wit: J.M. Elliott   Signed: William S. Jett
     L.D. Akin
Reg: April 30, 1866

Page 366 - C.A. Warren Title Bond and William Frierson.   I,
Charles A. Warren bind myself to pay William Frierson and have
purchased of me the estate of Robert Cannon, deceased, a lot in
the Town of Shelbyville and bounded by the store house owned by
the estate of Erwin J. Frierson, deceased, on the south side of
the Public Square and formerly occupied by Wilhoite & Co., by
the first street running parallel with the south side of the
square. This 27 April 1866.
Wit: E.R. Bearden   Signed: C.A. Warren
     F.E. Dunaway
Reg: May 1, 1866

Page 367 - Harriet L. Hall Deed to W.M. Ripley, 15 acres and
house. I have sold unto Willis M. Ripley a tract of land in
Bedford County and Civil District No. 2. Deed registered in
Book DDD, pages 132 and 133 on 25 February 1863. This 2 May
1866.
Reg: May 2, 1866   Signed: Harriet L. Hall

Page 368 - W.W. Gill Deed to Elizabeth P. Kingrey, 100 acres.
This 13 February 1866. Both of Bedford County. Land in Bedford

County on the waters of Sugar Creek in Civil District No. 22, adjoining the lands of said Elizabeth P. Kingrey and others. Beginning at the east side of the pike near Wm. Gammel's near a branch Mr. Gammel's corner, and by Mrs. Kingrey. Containing 100 acres.
Reg: May 7, 1866   Signed: W.W. Gill

Page 368 - B.F. Whitworth Deed to E.M. Whitworth, 150 acres. I, Benjamin F. Whitworth for the love and affection I have for my son Edward M. Whitworth, have given and bequeathed the following tract of land containing 102 acres of the 150 acres and embraces the following remaining 50 acres. Land bounded by Price C. Steele, and by J.B. Booth's corner. This 1 May 1865.
Wit: Kittie Whitworth   Signed: Benjamin F. Whitworth
     Bell Whitworth
Reg: May 7, 1866

Page 369 - Isaac B. Webb Deed to Morgan Smith, 52 acres. Land in Bedford County and District No. 6 and bounded by John Overcast, by John Knott, and by John James. This 24 May 1855.
Wit: H.R. Green   Signed: I.B. Webb
     D.J. Dearing
Reg: May 7, 1866

Page 370 - Jo. Thompson, Sheriff, Deed to W.D. Jenkins. 25 October 1865, W.D. Jenkins recovered a judgment against Mary R. Easly, Rachel Easly, principal and E.A. Easly. On 28 October 1865 levied on the property of defendants on a tract of land in Bedford County and Civil District No. 3 as the property of Mary R. Easly and Rachel Easly which is bounded by g. Frazier, by C.F. Sutton, by J.M. Smith and Chambers, and by Erwin where Roberts now lives. Containing 80 acres. This 7 May 1866.
Reg: May 8, 1866   Signed: Jo. Thompson, Sheriff

Page 371 - John Murray Deed & Trust to J.J. Phillips. This 7 May 1866. Both of Bedford County. Land in the Town of Wartrace in Civil District No. 3 and bounded by an alley near A.H. Coffey's line, by side of Nob Creek Turnpike, by a lot now occupied by Tarpley J. Green.
Reg: May 8, 1866   Signed: John Murray

Page 372 - William A. Earnhart, Discharge. William A. Earnhart a Sergeant of Captain Hartwell N.T. Shipp's Company © 5th Regiment of Tennessee Cavalry Volunteers who was enrolled on the 7th day of August 1863 to serve three years or during the war is hereby discharged from the service of the United States this 14th day of August 1865 at Pulaski, Tennessee, by reason of Special Order No. 18 C.S. Mil Div Tenn. No objection to him re-enlisted is known to exist. Said William A. Earnhart was born in Bedford County, Tennessee is twenty six years of age, five feet ten inches high, dark complexion, dark eyes, dark hair and by occupation when enrolled a farmer. Given at Pulaski, Tenn. This 14th day of August 1865.

Francis Jackson, Captain   H.N.T. Shipp, Captain

Oath of Indentity.
William A. Earnhart of the Town of Shelbyville, County of
Bedford and State of Tennessee on the 28th day of April in the
year 1866 personally appeared before me the undersigned a
Justice of the Peace for the county and state above mentioned
William A. Earnhart who being duly sworn according to law
declares that he is the identical William A. Earnhart who was a
Sergeant in the Company commanded by Capt. H.N.T. Shipp in the
Regiment 5th T.C. Commanded by W.J. Clift that he enlisted on
the 7th day of August 1863 for the term of three years and was
discharged at Pulaski, Tennessee on the 14th day of August 1865
by reason of Special Order No. 18, C.S. Mil Div Tenn.
Reg: May 11, 1866   Signed: William A. Earnhart
                            Moses Marshall, J.P.

Page 372 - L.B. Fite and others Deed to Ann M. Wallace. We,
L.B. Fite and T.D. Fite and G.P. Baskett, have sold unto Miss
Ann M. Wallace a tract of land in Bedford County and Civil
District No. 7 and bounded by the Nashville & Chattanooga Rail
Road branch that runs from Wartrace to Shelbyville, by the lands
of G.W. Jarnigan purchased in his lifetime from the executors of
Gen. Robert Cannon, by lands belonging to the estate of said
Cannon, and by lands belonging to Mrs. Eliza J. Wallace mother
of said Ann. Containing about 4 acres.
Reg: May 11, 1866   Signed: Leonard B. Fite
                            Thos. D. Fite
                            G.P. Baskett

Page 373 - William Collins and wife Decree to Sally Russel.
Petition to sell land. Land belonging to the heirs of James
Garret in Bedford County, Marshall and Williamson Counties
containing by survey of C.S. Dudley 443 acres and 21 poles and
on 13 January 1866 sold to highest bidder to John C. Haley and
William C. Haley.
                    Signed: Chesly Williams, Spl.
                        Comm.
Land in District No. 10, of Bedford County and bounded by land
of William Little and Stephen Wood, by lands of Presley Jones,
by lands of McClure and others, by lands of Hemphill and others.
Containing 443 acres and 21 poles being the land known as the
James Garret tract.
Reg: May 12, 1866

Page 374 - John H. Derrybury's Discharge. John H. Derrybury,
Principal Musician, 10th Regiment of Tennessee Infantry
Volunteers who was enrolled on the 10th day of April 1862 to
serve three years of during the war is hereby discharged from
the service of the United States this 9th day of June 1865 at
Nashville, Tennessee by reason of expiration of Term of Service,
no obligation to his re-enlisted is known to exist. Said John
H. Derrybury was born in Warren County in the State if Tennessee
is twenty two years of age, five feet three inches high, light
complexion, gray eyes, light hair and by occupation when

enrolled a shoe maker. Given at Nashville, Tennessee the 9th June 1865.

> Signed: W.P. Hargram, Capt.
> U.S.V. A.C.K. 4 Dev.
> D(illegible) Gamble

Oath of Identity - John H. Derrybury of the Town of Shelbyville, County of Bedford in State of Tennessee on this 12 day May 1866 personally appeared before me the undersigned a Justice of the Peace for the county and state above mentioned. John H. Derrybury who being duly sworn according to law declares that he is the identical John H. Derrybury who was a principal musician in the company commanded by Tenth Tenn. In the Regiment commanded by J.W. Sully that he enlisted on the 10th day of April 1862 for the term of three years and was discharged at Knoxville, Tennessee on 9th June 1865 by reason of expiration of term of service.

Reg: May 12, 1866   Signed: John H. Derrybury

Page 375 - Joel Whirly Deed and Trust to John F. Brown. Personal property, to wit, one brown horse mule, one gray horse, about twenty five head of sheep, one yoke of small oxen. This May 18, 1866.

Reg: May 18, 1866   Signed: Joel Whirly

Page 376 - Joseph Thompson, Sheriff, Deed to Mary E. Stanfield and others. W.B.M. Brame recovered three judgments against Thomas J. Stanfield and W.W. Stanfield as principals Thomas Boyers first endorser and Wm. S. Jett second endorser and stayed by B.P. Stanfield before William Galbreath a Justice of the Peace for Bedford County on 25 January 1860. All the interest of the said Wm. W. Stanfield had in a tract of land and in Civil District No. 23, containing about 250 acres adjoining the lands of Taylor Hayley, by Mrs. Proby and Kimbro, by W.F. Daniel. This 18 May 1866.

Reg: May 19, 1866   Signed: Jos. Thompson, Sheriff

Page 377 - A.G. Thornsbury and others Deed to James Y. West. 333 acres. The undersigned distributees of Sarah D. West, deceased, have this day sold unto James Y. West a tract of land in Bedford County and District No. 3 and bounded by lands of John Bower, by lands of John Snelling, by lands of Robert Cannon, and by lands of Joseph Bomar, said land being the dower tract of said Sarah D. West, deceased, in the lands of her deceased husband Isaac West being the distribution share of Elender Thornsbury the daughter of said Sarah D. West, we being the heirs at law of Elender Thornsbury. This 4 December 1865.

Reg: May 21, 1866   Signed: A.G. Thornsbury
                                    B.L. Thornsbury
                                    J.K.P. Thornsbury
                                    A.J. Thornsbury
                                    I.S. Roberts
                                    S.E. Roberts

Page 378 - James F. Calhoun Deed to Thos. W. Jordan. Lot. This
11 September 1860. J.F. Calhoun of Bedford County sold unto
T.W. Jordan of same place one house and lot being in the Town of
Shelbyville, Bedford County and being at the north edge of the
Scull Camp Road. Containing 1 ½ acres.
Reg: MAY 21, 1866   Signed: J.F. Calhoun

Page 378 - B.M. Tillman and wife Deed to Thos. W. Jordan. We,
Barclay M. Tillman and wife Elizabeth F. Tillman sold unto T.W.
Jordan on 8 December 1856 and registered in Book YY, pages 141
and 142. Land in Bedford County in the Town of Shelbyville on
Brittain Street on the east side of the said street and bounded
at the edge of said street that the intersection of the fence,
by the south boundary line of J.H. McGrew's lot, being the south
west corner, and with the street running west of the Baptist
Church lot, and by the graveyard, by the cedar fence, and by the
lot owned by B.M. Tillman. Containing ½ acre. This 20 May
1857.
Reg: May 21, 1866   Signed: B.M. Tillman
                                       E.F. Tillman

Page 379 - B.M. Tillman Deed to T.W. Jordan, lot. T.W. Jordan,
Barclay M. Tillman have this day sold unto Thos. W. Jordan
tracts of land in Bedford County and near the Town of
Shelbyville and bounded by the lands of Gen. Robt. Cannon, by
the lands formerly owned by Hon. H.L. Davidson now owned ot in
possession of Robert B. Davidson, by the lands of Haskel &
Rucker or the lands formerly known as the Haskel & Rucker lands,
and by lands of Robert Cannon. Containing 4 acres. This 18 May
1858.
Reg: May 21, 1866   Signed: B.M. Tillman

Page 380 - R.L. Singleton Deed to T.W. Jordan, 47 acres and 147
poles. Land in Bedford County and District No. 7 containing 47
acres and 147 poles and bounded by the north side of the road
leading to the Skull Camp Ford from Shelbyville,by the road
leading from Cowan's mills, and by the grave yard. It being
reserved by the executors of Sterling Newsom, deceased, in their
deed to me on 4 August 1852. This 13 January 1855.
Wit: A. Hughes   Signed: R.L. Singleton
     J,F. Thompson
Reg: May 21, 1866

Page 381 - William S. Jett Deed to W.N. Guinn, 58 acres. Both
of Bedford County. Land in Bedford County and Civil District
No. 8 and bounded by the Shelbyville and Unionville Road, and by
the old Lenoir Grant. This 21 May 1866.
Reg: May 21, 1866   Signed: Wm. S. Jett

Page 382 - L.S. Nichols and wife Deed to Green B. Damron,
Interest in Dower. We, Laban S. Nichols and Martha Ann Nichols
formerly Martha Ann Mullins, have this day sold unto Green B.
Damron all our right title claim and interest in a tract of land

in 5th Civil District of Bedford County and bounded by the lands known as the dower of the widow of John Sutton, Jr., by lands of G.W. Erwin and Nehemiah Parker, by lands of Louisa Terry and others, and by the lands of M.M. Newsom. About 127 acres, it being the same land on which Jane Mullins the widow of said Edward Mullins now resides and out of which has been assigned to her one interest in said land conveyed being an undivided one eighth in the part not covered by dower. This 14 March 1865.
Reg: May 23, 1866   Signed: L.S. Nichols
                                     Martha Ann Nichols

Page 383 - Robert S. Dwiggins Trust Deed to J.H.C. Scales. I, Robert S. Dwiggins, have sold unto J.H.C. Scales one note on Peyton G. King. I do convey the following property, to wit, one sorrel horse, one bay horse, one sorrel mare and her suckling horse colt and several other items listed in original document. All of said property is upon the farm known as the Dwiggins' farm some five or six miles from Shelbyville. This 22 May 1866.
Reg: May 23, 1866   Signed: R.S. Dwiggins

Page 384 - Robert Galbreath - Marriage Contract to Sarah F. Myers. This 13 February 1860. Whereas a marriage is intended shortly to be solemnized between Robert Galbreath and Sarah F. Myers, made the following agreement and marriage contract. Robert Galbreath on his part to secure unto said Sarah F. Myers all of her property of every description so that the same cannot be taken for any of his debts &C. If the said Sarah F. Myers should die leaving no children and the said Robert Galbreath surviving her then the said property shall descend to and belong to him. This 13 February 1860.
Wit: Wm. T. Myers   Signed: Sarah F. Myers
     S. Woodbury   Robt. Galbreath
Reg: May 23, 1866

Page 385 - William S. Jett and J.D. Wilhoite Deed to A.L. Adams, 100 acres. I, William S. Jett, have sold unto Adolphus L. Adams land in Bedford County near the Town of Shelbyville and bounded as follows, said land being a part of the Clement Cannon tract, beginning at T.B. Cannon's corner, to Charles Cannon's corner, to the middle of Duck River a portion of said above said land has already been sold on 27 March 1866 said land conveyed being 43 acres and 53 poles. This 25 May 1866.
Reg: May 25, 1866   Signed: William S. Jett
                                     Jo. D. Wilhoite

Page 386 - Claiborn A. Fowler, Discharge. Claiborn A. Fowler, Sergeant of Captain Reuben C. Couch Company F, 5th Regiment of Tennessee Cavalry Volunteers who was enrolled on the 7 day of September 1862 to serve three years or during the war is hereby discharged from the service of the United States this 25 dau June 1865 at Fayetteville, Tennessee by reason of General Order No. 83 dated War Dept. May 8, 1865. No objection to his re-enlisted known to exist. Said Claiborn A. Fowler was born in Rutherford County, Tennessee is 32 years of age, five feet nine

inches high, fair complexion, blue eyes, black hair and by
occupation when enrolled a farmer. Given at Fayetteville,
Tennessee this 28 June 1865.
Francis Jackson, Captain   Signed: Reuben C. Couch, Captain
6th Div Cav Corps Mil Div
Oath of Identity - Claiborn A. Fowler of the Town of
Shelbyville, Bedford County, Tennessee on the 27 May 1866
appeared before a Justice of the Peace. Claiborn A. Fowler duly
sworn according to law declares that he is the identical
Claiborn A. Fowler who was a Sergeant in the company commanded
by Captain R.C. Couch in the Regiment 5 Tenn Cavalry commanded
by Col. Clift that he enlisted on the 7 September 1862 for the
term of three years and was discharged at Fayetteville,
Tennessee on 25 June 1865 by reason of General Order No. 83
dated War Dept. 1865.
Moses Marshall, J.P.   Signed: Claiborn A. Fowler
Reg: May 30, 1866

Page 387 - Mathew Mullins, Discharge. Mathew Mullins, Private
of Captain Hartwell N.T. Shipp Company © 5th Regiment of Tenn
Cavalry Volunteers who was enrolled on the 18th day of May 1863
to serve three years or during the war is hereby discharged from
the service of the United States this 14 day of August 1865 at
Pulaski, Tennessee by reason of Special Order No. 18 C.S. Mil
Div Tenn. No objection to his being re-enlisted is known to
exist, said Mathew Mullins was born in Bedford County, is
eighteen years of age, five feet four inches high, fair
complexion, blue eyes, dark hair and by occupation when enrolled
a miller. Given at Pulaski this 14 August 1865.
Francis Jackson, Captain   Signed: H.N.T. Shipp, Captain
Oath of Identity - Mathew Mullins of the Town of Shelbyville,
Bedford County on the 28 April 1866 personally appeared before
me the undersigned a Justice of the Peace for Bedford County.
Mathew Mullins who being duly sworn according to law declares
that he is the identical Mathew Mullins who was a private in the
Company commanded by Capt. Hartwell N.T. Shipp in the Regiment
5th Commanded by ___ Clift that he enlisted on the 18th day of
May 1863 for the term of three years and was discharged at
Pulaski, Tennessee on 14th day of August 1865 by reason of an
Order No. 18 C.S. Mil Div Tenn.
Moses Marshall, J.P.   Signed: Mathew Mullins
Reg: May 31, 1866

Page 387 - Jane Hutton Deed to W.M. Hutton, 60 acres. I, Jane
Hutton of Bedford County, sold unto W.M. Hutton all the land of
which John Hutton, deceased, died seized. I also sold unto him
all the land of which Margaret M. Hutton, deceased, died seized.
I also sold unto W.M. Hutton all the land in Bedford County and
Civil District No. 5 and on which the waters of Fall Creek.
This November 25, 1865.
Wit: J.P. Hutton   Signed: Jane Hutton
     James M. Smith
Reg: May 31, 1866

Page 388 - Thomas B. Marks and wife Deed to Thomas J. Ogilvie and wife. 112 acres. I, T.B. Marks and wife T.F. Marks of Civil District No. 6 of Bedford County, have sold unto T.J. Ogilvie and wife M.A. Ogilvie land in Bedford County and same district being a part of our tract is Mrs. E.M. Bells' dower and bounded by the division line of said dower east of the grave yard. Containing 68 8/10 acres and also another tract separate from the one first described by a narrow lane and lying east, adjoining the dower line, by T.J. Ogilvie's line, and by the Capal lane. Containing 102 acres and 127 poles. This 16 February 1866.

Wit: N.W. Haley   Signed: Thos. B. Marks
     J.W. Hill   Tennessee F. Marks
Reg: June 4, 1866

Page 389 - Thos F. Ogilvie and wife Deed to Thos. B. Marks and wife, 72 acres. This 15 February 1866. I, T.F. Ogilvie and wife M.A. Ogilvie of the 6th Civil District of Bedford County, have sold unto Thos. B. Marks and wife T.F. Marks of same place, Land in same place and bounded by the Middleton Road north west corner of E.M. Bell's dower near T.B. Marks' house. Containing 72 acres. This 15 February 1866.

Wit: N.W. Haley   Signed: Thos. J. Ogilvie
     J.W. Hill   Mary A. Ogilvie
Reg: June 4, 1866

Page 390 - R.W. and W.F. Parsons Bond to A.F. Bingham. We, R.W. and Wm. F. Parsons, have sold unto A.F. Bingham land in Bedford County and District No. 4, containing 130 acres and bounded by the lands once owned by John Nelson, by lands of E.G. Davis, by lands once owned by Rubin Curry, and by lands of Nathan Chafin, William Logue and David Frizsell, and by lands of Thomas Hatchell and R.D. Rankin. This September 27, 1859.

Wit: James Denniston   Signed: Wm. F. Parsons
     E.G. Davis   R.W. Parsons
Reg: June 5, 1866

Page 391 - William S. Jackson, Discharge. William S. Jackson of the Town of Shelbyville of Bedford County on this 27 day of April in the year 1866 personally appeared before me the undersigned a Justice of the Peace for the county and state above mentioned. William S. Jackson who being duly sworn according to law declares that he is the identical William S. Jackson who was a Sergeant in the Company commanded by Captain Philips in the Regiment Co. F 1st Regiment Ind. Vidette Cavalry Vols. Commanded by P.M. Radford that he enlisted on the 27th day of August 1863 for the term of one year and was discharged at Stevenson, Alabama on the 16th day of June 1864 by reason of an order from Secretary of War. Sworn to and subscribed to before me the day and year above written.

Signed: W.S. Jackson

William Galbreath, J.P.
Copy. To all whom it may concern know ye that William S. Jackson, a Sergeant of Capt. Philips' Company F 1st Regiment of Independent Vidette Cavalry Volunteers who was enrolled on the

27th August 1863 to serve one year or during the war, is hereby discharged from the service of the United States this 15th day of June 1864 at Stevenson, Alabama by reason of an order of the Secretary of War. No objection to his being re-enlisted is known to exist. Said William S. Jackson was born in Franklin County in the State of North Carolina, is thirty five years of age, five feet ten inches high, fair complexion, gray eyes and sandy hair and by occupation when enrolled a farmer at Stevenson, Alabama. This 16th day of June 1864.
Sworn this 24 November 1865 Signed: Wm. T. Wid(illegible)
William Galbreath, J.P.   1st (illegible) In Cav Vol
                                           Commands the Regiment
                                           A.C. & C.D.C.

Page 392 - William S. Jenkins, Discharge. Know ye that William S. Jenkins, Sergeant of Captain George W. Gray's Company (A) 4th Regiment of Mounted Infantry Tennessee Volunteers who was enrolled on the 18 day of August 1864 to serve one year or during the war is hereby discharged from the service of the United States this 25th day of August 1865 at Nashville, Tennessee, by order of G.O. No. 18 Mil Div Tenn July 11th 1865. No objection to his being re-enlisted is known to exist. William S. Jenkins was born in Franklin County in the State of North Carolina is thirty five years of age, five feet eight inches high, fair complexion, blue eyes, light hair and by occupation when enrolled a farmer. Given at Nashville, Tennessee this 25th day of August 1865.
George W. Gray, Captain   Cyrus N. Gray
Co. A. 4th Regt Tenn Inf   Capt. 15th U.S.C.I.
                               Muster Office
NOTE: Another Oath of Identity made 27 April 1866.
Reg: June 5, 1866

392 - Hiram J. Edde, Discharge. Hiram J. Edde, a private of Captain H.N.T. Shipp's Company © 5th Regiment of Tennessee Cavalry Volunteers who was enrolled on the 4th day of September 1862 to serve three years or during the war, is hereby discharged from the service of the United States the 25th day of June 1865 at Fayetteville, Tennessee by reason of General Order No. 83 War Dept May 8th 1865. No objection to his being re-enlisted is known to exist. Said Hiram J. Edde was born in Bedford County, Tennessee is twenty six years of age, six feet one inch high, fair complexion, blue eyes, dark hair and by occupation when enrolled a farmer. Given at Fayetteville, Tennessee this 25 day of June 1865.
Francis Jackson, Captain   Hartwell N.T. Shipp, Capt.
Oath of Identity - Hiram J. Edde of the Town of Shelbyville, Bedford County, Tennessee on this 7 day June 1866 appeared before me the undersigned a Justice of the Peace for the county and state above mentioned who being duly sworn according to law declares that he is the identical Hiram J. Edde who was a private in the Company commanded by Capt. H.N.T. Shipp in the Regiment of Cavalry commanded by _____ that he enlisted on the 4th day of September 1862 for the term of three years and was discharged at Fayetteville, Tennessee on the 25th June 1865 by reason of General Order No. 83 War Dept May 6, 1865.

Reg: June 7, 1866   Hiram J. Edde

Page 393 - L.P. Fields Deed to G.D. Stephenson, 29 acres. Both
of Bedford County. Land in Bedford County on the north waters
of Puncheon Camp Creek and in Civil District No. 1 and bounded
by top of the ridge, by Abram McMahan's line, and by said
Stephenson's corner. Containing 29 acres. This 1 November
1865.
Wit: J.P. Miller   Signed: L.P. Fields
     Anthony Thomas
Reg: June 8, 1866

Page L.P. Fields Deed to Abram McMahan, 30 acres. Both of
Bedford County. Land in Bedford County on the north waters of
Puncheon Camp Creek in Civil District No. 1 and bounded by lands
of said McMahan and G.D. Stevenson. Containing one quarter of
an acre for school house and 30 acres and 15 poles. This 1
December 1865.
Wit: J.P. Miller   Signed: L.P. Fields
     Anthony Thomas
Reg: June 8, 1866

Page 395 - Talton F. Williams, Discharge. Talton F. Williams,
private of Capt. H.N.T. Shipp's Company @ 5th Regiment of
Tennessee Cavalry Volunteers who was enrolled on the 30th day of
July 1862 to serve ___ years or during the war is hereby
discharged from the service of the United States. This 25th day
of June 1865 at Fayetteville, Tennessee by reason of General
Order No. 83 War Dept. May 8, 1865. No objection to his being
re-enlisted is known to exist. Said Talton F. Williams was born
in Bedford County, Tennessee is twenty six years of age, five
feet eleven inches high, fair complexion, blue eyes, auburn hair
and by occupation when enrolled a farmer.   Given at
Fayetteville, Tennessee. This 25 day of June 186_.
Francis Jackson, Captain   Hartwell N.T. Shipp, Captain
Oath of Identity - Talton F. Williams of the Town of
Shelbyville, Bedford County, Tennessee on the 12th day of June
1866 appeared before me the undersigned a Justice of the Peace
of Bedford County. Talton F. Williams who being duly sworn
according to law declared that he is the identical Talton F.
Williams who was a private in the Company commanded by Captain
H.N.T. Shipp in the Regiment 5th Regiment Cavalry commanded by
.F. Clift that he enlisted on the 20th day of July 1862 for the
term of three years and was discharged at Fayetteville,
Tennessee on 25 day of June 1865 by reason of General Order No.
83 War Dept. May 8, 1865.
Moses Marshall, J.P.   Signed: Talton F. Williams
Reg: June 15, 1866

Page 395 - William S. Jett Deed to A.L. Adams, 144 acres. Sold
two houses and a livery stable and lot on which they are
situated being in the Town of Shelbyville being a portion of the
old Cannon tract on which Clement Cannon resided at the time of
his death and bounded by Cannon Street, by Scudder's corner, to

212

the bluff of Duck River, to Robert T. Cannon's corner, and by Cannon's spring. This June 15, 1866.
Reg: June 15, 1866   Signed: Wm. S. Jett

Page 396 - A.L. Adams Deed to Town Lot to Wm. S. Jett. Tract of land described in the deed of said William S. Jett being in the Town of Shelbyville and bounded by a corner of Holland and Jones' lot which they now have a livery stable, and by a ___ Street. Also a portion of lot and bounded by corner of lot owned by A.L. Adams and formerly owned by R.K. Jones, the above said lots, to the margin of Brittain Street, it being the lot upon which the livery stable stands and the above lot is taken from the deed to Thos. Holland dated June 16, 1860 and both of said lots is only one Town Lot. This 13 June 1866.
Reg: June 15, 1866   Signed: A.L. Adams

Page 397 - William S. Jett Deed to W.P. Goodwin. Lot of land in the Town of Shelbyville and is fully described in a deed of A.L. Adams to said Jett dated 13 June 1866 and bounded by corner of Holland's and Jones' lot on which the livery stable is situated. Also another lot bounded on the east by Brittain Street, it being the lot which the livery stable is situated. This 13 June 1866.
Reg: June 15, 1866   Signed: Wm. S. Jett

Page 398 - W.P. Goodwin Mortgage to J.H.C. Scales and others. On 6th November 1866, J.H.C. Scales and Joseph H. Thompson became the securities of said W.P. Goodwin in Bedford County and by which the undersigned was appointed the guardian of his child Mary C. Goodwin. I have in and to the undivided half of two lots of land in the Town of Shelbyville and bounded by a corner of Holland and Jones and on which the livery stable is situated, then to ___ Street. Also another lot adjoining the corner of the above said lot. It being the lots on which the livery stable is built. It being the undivided half that I purchased of W.S. Jett by deed dated 13 June 1866. This 14 June 1866.
Reg: June 15, 1866   Signed: W.P. Goodwin

Page 399 - P.S. English Deed to T.B. Cannon, ¾ of an acre. I, P.S. English of Bedford County, have this day sold unto Thos. B. Cannon of same place, a tract of land in Bedford County and Civil District No. 7, being part of a 300 acre tract owned by the late Gen. Robert Cannon 100 acres of which off the north side of said tract and has been sold by his executors. The land now being a part off the north end of Lot No. 8, adjoining the original tract at the north west corner of the pork house lot and a corner of T.B. Cannon's mill lot, and by the pike. Containing 98 poles. This 15 June 1866.
Reg: June 15, 1866   Signed: P.S. English

Page 400 - Henry Cannon and others Deed to mills to Thos. B. Cannon. We, the heirs &c of Clement Cannon, Sr., deceased, have sold unto Thos. B. Cannon a tract of land bounded on the north

east by the corporation line of the Town of Shelbyville and the
lands of Gosling &C to Duck River, and by the lands of James F.
Cummings on which the port house is situated, by the lands of
Robert Cannon subject to the right of way along the west
boundary heretofore granted to the Pork House Company, and by
Gosling & CO. about the mill dam and water power and on which
land is situated a grist mill. Containing about 4 acres. This
November 3, 1860.
Wit: G.P. Baskett   Signed: Henry Cannon
     John P. Steele   C. Cannon
Reg: June 18, 1866   Clem Cannon
                                   L.T. Mosely

Page 401 - J.A. McLain Deed to Willie Perry, 65 acres. Land in
Bedford County and District No. 9 and bounded by E. McMahan, by
B. Harris, by a creek, and by C.G. M(illegible). Beginning at
A.P. Mc(illegible) boundary. This 30 March 1861.
Wit: J.B. Stem   Signed: J.A. McLain
     J.L. T(illegible)
Reg: June 18, 1866

Page 402 - R.S. Dwiggins Mortgage to C.A. Warren. On 7 August
1865, W.W. Gill as Trustee of R.S. Dwiggins by deed dated and
sold unto C.A. Warren a tract of land in the Town of Shelbyville
on which the Steam Mill is situated. Whereas William E.
Galbreath had a lot of ground sold under and by virtue of an
other warrant in the Town of Shelbyville and bounded by the mill
lot and the lot of Mr. Rowzer, by the Spring Street, and by the
factory property and by said Duck River it being that was
purchased by said R.S. Dwiggins of one James Newton. This 18
June 1866.
Reg: June 19, 1866   Signed: R.S. Dwiggins

Page 403 - William Grissom and wife Power of Attorney to M.E.W.
Dunaway. We, William Grissom and Jemima Grissom, have appointed
Mictchell E.W. Dunaway out true and lawful attorney for us and
in our name to collect and receive all money due or owning to us
from the estate of William, deceased, late a resident of Bedford
County. Jemima Grissom being heir to the estate by virtue of
being the daughter of Ellis Williams and said Ellis Williams was
the son of said William Williams, deceased, the said Ellis
Williams being also dead. This 9 June 1866.
Williamson County, Ill.   Signed: Jemima Grissom
Reg: June 20, 1866   William Grissom

Page 404 - M.B. Howell, C&M, Deed to D.H.C. Spence, Lot. This 3
May 1866. M.B. Howell, Clerk & Master of Davidson County,
Tennessee sold unto D.H.C. Spencer and Vincent Marmaduke of ___
County, State of _____ a tract of land in Bedford County and
bounded on Depot Street, near a corner of Brittain Street being
the corner common to Lot No. 5 and 6, by an alley, and being Lot
No. 5 in the Town of Shelbyville and recorded in Minute Book H
of this book, page 262.
Reg: June 22, 1866   Signed: Morton B. Howell, C&M

Page 404 - Vincent Marmaduke Power of Attorney to D.H.C. Spence.
I appoint D.H.C. Spence my Attorney in fact for me and in my
name to convey to A.L. Stamps a deed to the Town Lot in
Shelbyville sold by Marmaduke & Spence to said Stamps some years
ago and being a part of the lot sold at the sale for division of
the estate of Julia Marmaduke and Sarah J. Spence upon which
said Stamps has built a house. He may also being and presented
in my name any suit that may be necessary for the money due by
Stamps. This 19 May 1866.
Reg: June 22, 1866   Signed: V. Marmaduke

Page 405 - D.H.C. Spence VS John Coltart(?) and Argyle P. Eakin,
Transcript. Judgments September 14, 1864. Names: Clerk (David
C.) of Bedford County, Love, Sheriff Hawkins and Phillips and
Raney.
Reg: June 22, 1866

Page 405 - A.M. Welch VS J.R. Miller and G.W. Cone, Transcript
of Judgment. Rutherford County, Tennessee March Term 1866. To
defend the suit brought against them, came not but made default.
It was considered by the court that said plaintiff recover of
said defendant the sum of $1200 debt. Judgment made March 25,
1866. Named: Stamp and W.A. Johnson, Sheriff, and W. Jackson.
Reg: June 22, 1866

Page 406 - C.A. Warren Deed to D.S. Logan, House and lot. A
house and lot in the corporation of the Town of Shelbyville
adjoining a fence in the east edge of Brittain Street the
intersection of the fence, by line of J.H. McGrew's lot being
the south west corner of the lot conveyed, by the west of the
Baptist Church lot and of the grave yard, by the lot, and B.M.
Tillman's garden lot. Containing one half acre, it being the
same house and lot purchased by me from Thos. J. Warren. This
23 June 1866.
Reg: June 25, 1866   Signed: C.A. Warren

Page 407 - John H. Derrybury Bond to George W. Frankford, house
and lot. This 23 January 1866. House and lot in the Town of
Shelbyville and Civil District No. 7, Bedford County being a
fraction of Lot No. 40 conveyed by deed from William Brown dated
11 January 1849 and registered in Book II, page 345 and fronting
on Pike Street near the Public Square.
Reg: June 25, 1866   Signed: John H. Derrybury

Page 407 - M.M. Wilson Deed to J.H.C. Scales, 10 acres of land.
Land in Civil District No. 19 and bounded by John Trice, by J.S.
Davidson, by the lands known as the William Trice land, being
the same by me purchased of the Clerk & Master in the case of
myself against Benjamin Mosely and Joseph Trice. This 23 June
1866.
Reg: June 25, 1866   Signed: M.M. Wilson

Page 408 - Contract between D. Morris and T.H. Colvin, Merchants. Contract made 22 June 1866. T.H. Colvin has this day purchased of D. Morris in the firm of D. Morris & Co. in the Mercantile business carried on at the Town of Wartrace, Bedford County. Said firm having erected from and after the date of March 9, 1866.
Wit: J.A. Tuck   Signed: D. Morris
     M.N. McKeny   T.H. Colvin
Reg: June 25, 1866

Page 409 - Thos. B. Ivie Deed to T.F. Nash, Town lot. A lot in the Town of Shelbyville on the north side of the street on road leading from the Depot on the Nashville and Chattanooga Rail Road to Skull Camp Ford on Duck River and bounded by a lot by Joseph Edwards of Nashville and mine. Containing 1 acre. This June 9, 1866.
Reg: June 25, 1866   Signed: T.B. Ivie

Page 410 - William E. Sutton Deed to W.J. Brown. Land in Bedford County and District No. 19 and containing near one half acre in the Town of Richmond and adjoining the old salt house, and the line between Jno. R. Smith and J.H. Curtiss, Jr. and a line between Jno. R. Smith and W.J. Thorp's heirs. This 30 June 1866.
Wit: John H. Oneal   Signed: W.E. Sutton
     James H. Oneal
Reg: July 2, 1866

Page 410 - W.F. Brown Title Bond to W.E. Sutton. This 30 June 1866. I have this day sold unto Wm. W. Sutton land in Richmond, Bedford County and bounded by the road or street that runs north and south through railroad passing the residence of J.H. Curtiss, Jr., on the south by the grave yard and the lands of J.R. Smith. Containing about 2 acres the same being the land sold by Mrs. R. Smith to ___ H(illegible), by H(illegible) to Dr. Landers and by Landers to S.G. Reeves and by him to me.
Wit: John H. Oneal   Signed: W.F. Brown
     James H. Neil
Reg: July 2, 1866

Page 411 - Mary Foreman Deed to W. Rowzee, Town lot. I, Mary Foreman, executrix of Richard Foreman, deceased, have sold to Winston Rowzee land in Bedford County and Civil District No. 7 near the Town of Shelbyville containing one fourth of an acre, lying between the Unionville Turnpike Road and the mouth of the Female Academy Pike in front of Elizabeth Daniel, by J.H. Oneal's lot known as the Bucket Factory lot. This 17 May 1866.
Wit: D.J. Low   Signed: Mary Foreman
     D.S. Logan
Reg: July 2, 1866

Page 412 - Eliza Daniel Deed to W. Rowzee, Town lot. Land in Bedford County and Civil District No. 7 near the Town of

Shelbyville on the north side of the Female Academy near the entrance with the Unionville Turnpike Road and bounded by the north side of the Academy Pike, and by E. Daniel's corner. Containing 1 acre and 26 poles. This 17 May 1866.
Wit: D.J. Low   Signed: Eliza Daniel
     D.S. Logan
Reg: July 2, 1866

Page 412 - John H. Oneal Deed to C.T. Philpot, Town Lot. I have sold unto Charles T. Philpot a certain house and lot in the Town of Shelbyville, Bedford County and on which Leonard Marbury at present lives and is bounded by the street or road called the Unionville Pike, by M.E. (illegible)'s lot, by G.W. Buchanan's lot, and by James H. Neil's lot. Containing 2 ½ acres. This 2 July 1866.
Reg: July 3, 1866   Signed: John H. Oneal

Page 413 - John A. McGuire Deed to W.B. Armstrong, 83 acres. This 22 June 1860. John A. McGuire sold unto Wm. B. Armstrong, all of Bedford County, land in Bedford County known as Lot No. 3 in John Sutton's land and bounded by Lot No. 2. Containing 83 acres.
Wit: W.N. Guinnn   Signed: John A. McGuire
     H.C. Kinard
Reg: July 3, 1866

Page 414 - T.W. Jordan Deed to R.B. Davidson, Town Lot. House and lot on which I now reside situated on the east of Shelbyville and containing 4 acres, being the place purchased by me from B.M. Tillman. This 6 July 1866.
Wit: Arch H. (illegible)   Signed: T.W. Jordan
     B.M. Tillman
Reg: July 5, 1866

Page 414 - B.F. White Deed to Eliza J. Sanders, 32 acres. B.F. White sold unto Eliza Jane Sanders, Joshua P. Sanders, Garrett S. Sanders, and Thadeus C. Sanders land in Bedford County and Civil District No. 11 and bounded by the lands of Abe Cooper, by lands of Eliza Sanders, by Fletcher Osteen, by lands of Mrs. Charlotte Phillips, the same being the part of the land assigned to me as one of the heirs of Joshua White and known as Lot No. 2. Containing 32 acres. This 7 July 1866.
Reg: July 7, 1866   Signed: B.F. White

Page 415 - Williams & Cannon against W.P. Goodwin, Copy of Judgment. Williams & Cannon VS Minos T. Cannon, Ame S. Fay and Eliza M. Nelson. On motion of Lewis Tillman, on 29 May 1866, said that W.P. Goodwin purchased about 15 September 1865 at a sale a part of a town lot in the Town of Shelbyville and that he did not pay any cash. This 12 July 1866.
Reg: July 12, 1866   Signed: Lewis Tillman, C&M

Page 416 - F.J. Harris Title Bond to James E. Wadley. F.J. Harris sold unto James E. Wadley a tract of land in Bedford County and District No. 9 on the waters of Alexanders Creek and bounded by a corner of the C.F. Haskins' tract, and by a corner of Mary Dozier's dower. Containing 96 acres and 69 poles. This July 12, 1866.
Wit: C.S. Dudley   Signed: F.J. Harris
     Q.E. Morton
Reg: July 13, 1866

Page 416 - F.J. Harris Deed to Q.E. Morton, 53 acres. Land in Bedford County and District No. 9 on the waters of Alexanders Creek and bounded by the west side of Alexanders Creek, by the old Gabe Lowe tract, and by Mary Dozier's dower. Containing 53 acres. This July 12, 1866.
Wit: C.S. Dudley   Signed: F.J. Harris
     James E. Wadley
Reg: July 14, 1866

Page 417 - Robert Galbraith, Mortgage to William and William E. Galbraith.   On 14 September 1865 Chesley Williams and W.P. Cooper, executors of Gen. Robert Cannon, deceased, made a sale of estate belonging to the testator at the time of his death known as the Green Hill property and which I became the purchaser of said property being near the Town of Shelbyville. My father William Galbraith and my brother W.E. Galbraith are the securities for me. This 14 July 1866.
Reg: July 16, 1866   Signed: Robt. Galbraith

Page 418 - Dennis Hemby Deed to James C. Lemons, 103 acres. Land in Bedford County and District No. 25, containing 103 acres and bounded by a line of a 380 acre tract entered in the name of Dennis Hemby. This September 9, 1865.
Wit: R.L. Sanders   Signed: Dennis Hemby
     Thos. B. Kaar
Reg: July 16, 1866

Page 419 - John S. Davis Deed to Thos. H. Clay and others. I have transferred to Mrs. Ann Finch the following property, to wit, four beds and steads and furniture and bureau, two (illegible), one book case, two tables, forty head of hogs, twenty head of sheep, six head of cattle, five head of horses, one thrasher and mill, four plows and gears, two yoke of oxen and one wagon. December 5, 1865.
Wit: Thos. H. Clay   Signed: Jno. S. Davis
     R. Morgan
Reg: July 16, 1866

Page 419 - Thos. Allen Duncan Deed to Samuel D. Morgan, House and Lot. South Carolina, B.D.(?)   I have sold unto Samuel D. Morgan of the City of Nashville, Tennessee, my one tenth interest in property, to wit, two lots and improvements thereto belonging, bounded on the north by the street running by the

Presbyterian Church, on the east by the street dividing it from the Frierson property, on the south by the land of Thomas Nance, on the west by Brittain Street which divides it from the property of William J. Whitthorne being the lot on which C.T. Houston, Jr. now resides No. 26 and 27 and containing about 1 ½ acres. Recorded in Book CCC, page 299. This 20 March 1866.
Reg: July 17, 1866   Signed: Jas. A. Duncan

Page 420 - S.D. Morgan and Charles J. Chany Deed to C.P. Houston and others. House and Lot. Land sold to C.P. Houston, Jr., C.P. Houston, Sr., and William Houston, to wit, two lots of ground and improvements thereto belonging, bounded on the north by the street running by the Presbyterian Church, on the east by the street dividing it from the Frierson property, on the south by the lot of Thomas Nance, on the west by Brittain Street which divides it from the property of William J. Whitthorne, lying in the Town of Shelbyville, Bedford County and known as Lot No. 26 and 27 and containing 1 ½ acres. This 12 July 1866.
Reg: July 17, 1866   Signed: S.D. Morgan
                                     Charles J. Ch(illegible)

Page 421 -- B.F. Dugan Deed to D.A. Ozment, House and Lot. Both of Bedford County. Land in Bedford County and Civil District No. 11 and bounded in the big road, the south west corner of the Male Academy lot in Unionville, Tennessee, by Thos. Allison's corner, by D.A. Ozment's line, and by J.W. Clary's line. Containing 7 ¼ acres. This September 17, 1859.
Wit: T.D. Tarpley   Signed: B.F. Duggan
     J.R. Brown
Reg: July 19, 1866

Page 421 - Jo. Thompson, Sheriff, Deed to Lewis Tillman, 410 acres. This deed made by and between Joseph Thompson, Sheriff of Bedford County, and Lewis Tillman. When said Lewis Tillman, a Clerk & Master, recovered a judgment at the December Term 1860 against Smith Bowlin, Gray Lynch, William Wood and others. Said Thompson on 10 May 1866 on a tract of land and containing 98 acres and 110 poles and bounded by the Townsend Fugit place and by R.D. Rankins, by the Widow Hatchett, by the lands bought by William Mosely at the sale of the lands of Reuben Manly, deceased, and by lands of John McCrory, and by Mrs. Hatchett, and by A. Bingham in Bedford County. This 12 July 1866.
Reg: July 19, 1866   Signed: Joseph Thompson, Sheriff

Page 423 - John C. Hix VS Robert S. Dwiggins. It appears that W.W. Lacy who sues by his guardian John Wilhoite recovered a decree against said John C. Hix. Said R.S. Dwiggins, security.
Reg: July 20, 1866

Page 423 - R.S. Brown Deed to M.N. and S.C. Brown. My distributive share in the estate of my father George W. Brown both real and personal. This 21 July 1866.
Reg: July 23, 1866   Signed: R.S. Brown

424 - W.G. Davis Deed to Francis M. Prewit, House and Lot. I, William G. Davis of Bedford County, have sold unto Francis M. Prewit a house and lot in Bedford County in the Village of Bell Buckle and bounded by R.S. Thomas' line in Bell Buckle Creek, thence to the Rail Road so as to include the fence first built by Featherston's line, and by where William M. Robinson lived. Containing 2 acres and 90 poles. Also a black mare and colt. This 21 July 1866.
Reg: July 23, 1866   Signed: W.G. Davis

Page 424 - T.B. Fite and others Deed to J.H. Graham, Town Lot. We, T.B. Fite, Thos. D. Fite and G.P. Baskett have sold a tract of land in Bedford County and Civil District No. 7 and in the corporate limits of the Town of Shelbyville and bounded by lands of Jos. M. Brown, by the lands belonging to R.D. Deery's estate, by the Deery's and Henry Cooper, and by the lands of Margaret Wardlaw and Sarah Wardlaw. Containing 1 ½ acres. This 30 May 1866.
Reg: July 23, 1866   Signed: T.B. Fite
                                    Thos. D. Fite
                                    G.P. Baskett

425 - Robert S. Dwiggins Mortgage to Charles A. Warren. Conveyed land in 7t^h District of Bedford County near the Town of Shelbyville the same being a portion of the lands owned by Gen. Robt. Cannon at the time of his death and is bounded by Duck River, by corner of Lot No. 1 of 200 acres willed to Minos L. Cannon by said Gen. Robert Cannon, and by the center of the turnpike. This July 23, 1866.
Reg: July 24, 1866   Signed: R.S. Dwiggins

Page 426 - P.S. English Deed to William S. Jett. On 26 October 1861. I sold by title bond all my interest being one fourth of the port and beef slaughter and packing establishment near the Town of Shelbyville, Bedford County situate on the bank of Duck River, to William S. Jett. This July 18, 1866.
Reg: July 25, 1866   Signed: P.S. English

Page 427 - T.B. Marks Deed to T.J. Ogilvie, 45 acres. Land in District No. 5 of Bedford County and beginning in the lane the north boundary of T.J. and M.S. Ogilvie, and by F.P. McElrath's line. Containing 45 acres. This February 15, 1866.
Wit: _. W. Haley   Signed: Thos. B. Marks
     J.W. Hill
Reg: July 26, 1866

Page 427 - Thomas Overcast Deed to Green B. Damron. We, James Overcast and wife Susan A. Overcast formerly Susan A. Mullins, have this day sold unto Green B. Damron a tract of land known as the dower of the widow of John Sutton, by lands of G.W.P. Erwin and Nehemiah Parker, by lands of Louisa Terry and others, and by lands of Dr. M.M. Newsom. Containing about 127 acres. It being the same land bought by Edward Mullins at a sale made by Joseph

H. Thompson and known as a part of John Sutton land and part of which Jane Mullins the widow of said Edward Mullins now resides. This May 25, 1866   Signed: Susan A. Overcast
Reg: July 27, 1866   James M. Overcast

Page 428 - 428 - D.P. Huffman and others to George Huffman and wife, Obligation. This 1 November 1865. Daniel P. Huffman, Moses Huffman and Mitchel D. Huffman of Bedford County of one part and George Huffman and Lucinda Huffman of other part, all of Bedford County. We, Daniel P. Huffman, Moses Huffman and Mitchel Huffman for in and consideration that George Huffman has deeded said land to us and have put and placed said George Huffman and Lucinda Huffman and family in full possession of our tract of land or plantation of which we bind ourselves to keep said George Huffman and his wife and family in possession of the said plantation during their lives. And all that is attached to said plantation, of all the stock, all the house hold and kitchen furniture, the use of both shop and tools and the entire use of both mills.
Reg: July 28, 1866   Signed: Daniel P. Huffman
                                               M.P. Huffman
                                               M.D. Huffman

Page 429 - James L. Adams and wife Deed to William Woodward. Registered. We, James L. Adams and wife Catharine sold to William Woodward our undivided interest of one fourth in to a tract of land owned and resided on by the late German Woodward at the time of his death being on the waters of Sinking Creek in the 19th Civil District of Bedford County and bounded by the section line and a line of a 5000 acre survey in the name of George Daugherty, and by lands of Stephen Porter's old corner, by Alexander Dysart, by Ben Haslet's corner, and land owned by the heirs of J.W.C. Cunningham, deceased, and by John Cotner. This 23 July 1860.
Reg: July 30, 1866   Signed: James L. Adams
                                               Catharine Adams

Page 430 - W.W. Gunter Deed to Lewis Erwin, F.M.C., 10 acres. I, W.W. Gunter of Bedford County, have sold unto Lewis Erwin (a colored freeman) of same place, land in Bedford County and Civil District No. 3 and bounded by the Rowesville Road, and by Cates' old line now McAnnally's. Containing 9 acres and 120 poles. This 28 July 1866.
Reg: July 30, 1866   Signed: W.W. Gunter

Page 431 - Jo. Thompson, Sheriff, Deed to Kissam ? Kesler, 50 acres. On 2 August 1859 Edward Kissam(?) and John E. Kesler recovered a judgment against John P. Drumgoole, Rolly Drumgoole, Daniel B. Shriver and B.A. Nelson. And on 24 May 1860 an alias execution was issued on said judgment and placed in the hands of the undersigned Joseph Thompson, then a Deputy Sheriff, and listed on a tract of land as the property of said Benjamin A. Nelson situated in Bedford County and Civil District No. 3 and bounded by a corner on P. Fay's line, a corner of Redding

George's land, and by a line of Moses Nelson's land. Containing 50 acres. There being no personal property. This 30 July 1866.
Reg: July 31, 1866   Signed: Jo. Thompson, Sheriff

Page 432 - T.J. Ogilvie Deed to T.B. Marks, 45 acres. Both of Bedford County. Land in Civil District No. 3 of Bedford County and bounded by lands of G.D. Hutton, by land of T.B. Marks, and by land of T.J. Ogilvie and F.P. McElrath. Containing 45 acres. This 15 February 1866.
Wit: N.W. Kenly   Signed: T.J. Ogilvie
     J.W. Hill
Reg: July 31, 1866

Page 433 - Duncan L. Barrett Deed to A.S. Reaves. I have sold all right claim and interest I have in and to the estate of my deceased brother Lewis B. Barrett, deceased, of whose estate John E. Barrett is the administrator to the said interest consists of an interest in land, stocks, money in action. My interest in said land and being one seventh in said estate. This July 31, 1866.
Reg: August 1, 1866   Signed: D.L. Barrett

Page 433 - F.P. McElrath Deed to George D. Hutton, 125 acres. Land in 5th Civil District of Bedford County and bounded by lands of William Houston, by lands of Thos. B. Marks and wife and Thos. J. Ogilvie, by the Hutton's land. Containing 125 acres. This July 31, 1866.
Reg: August 1, 1866   Signed: F.P. McElrath

Page 434 - H.L. Davidson Deed to M.E.W. Dunaway. Registered. Land in the corporation of the Town of Shelbyville, Bedford County situate on the street leading from the Nashville and Chattanooga Rail Road Depot to the Skull Camp Ford. I have lost of mislaid the (illegible) notes of the survey. Land bounded by the Skull Camp Road the north east corner of the lot of G.W. Thompson purchased of J.H. illegible), and by land of J.H. Oneal sold to Johnson. Containing 1 ¼ acres. This June 27, 1857.
Reg: August 1, 1866   Signed: H.L. Davidson

Page 435 - M.E. W. Dunaway Deed to Henry Cooper, Trustee Relinquishment. Both of Bedford County. For the love and affection which I have for my wife Martha G. Dunaway and my children and for the purpose of securing them a house and maintenance, this day have sold unto Henry Cooper, as trustee, a lot of land in the Town of Shelbyville and in the place on which I now live. Deed Registered in Book YY, page 324 and 325, which said lot contains 1 ¼ acres. This 27 February 1860.
Reg: August 2, 1866   Signed: M.E.W. Dunaway

Page 436 - J.S. Roberts Deed to Z. Roberts, 812 acres. This 22 January 1860. James S. Roberts sold to Zacheus Roberts, both of Bedford County, land in Bedford County on the waters of Sinking

Creek adjoining the lands of Thomas Greer and others and bounded
by a tract of land containing 100 acres conveyed by the heirs of
William Neil to Thomas Greer, by lands of conveyed by Wright
Oliver and Thomas Greer, by land owned by William D. Davis
formerly, by James Neill's line and Andrew Neills formerly line,
by James M. Ray's tract, and through the middle of the spring.
It being a tract of land conveyed to me James M. Roberts and
Zacheus Roberts by Miles Philips.
Reg: August 2, 1866   Signed: J.S. Roberts

Page 437 - Miles Philips Deed to J.S. and Z. Roberts.
Registered. This 22 February 1854. Miles Philips sold unto
James Sims Roberts and Zacheus Roberts, all of Bedford County on
the waters of Sinking Creek adjoining the lands of Thomas Greer
and others. Bounded by a tract of 100 acres conveyed by the
heirs of William Neill and Thomas Greer, by land conveyed by
Wright Oliver to Thomas Greer, by land owned by Wm. D. Orr, by
James D. Neill and Andrew Neill's line, by corner of James M.
Ray, and through the spring. Containing 80 ¾ acres.
Reg: August 2, 1866   Signed: Miles Philips

Page 438 - James Bramlett and wife Deed to James M. Stephens.
James Bramlett and his wife Rachael C. Bramlett sold unto James
M. Stephens. Said Rachael C. Bramlett, wife of James Bramlett
is the daughter of the late Francis H. Keller and is the owner
of an undivided interest of one sixth in the tract of land of
which her father the late Francis H. Keller, deceased, seized
and possessed and on which he received at the time of his death.
Bounded by lands of the late Joseph Couch, by the lands of
Reuben and John Ortha Couch, by lands of the late William
Pepper, and by the lands of Mrs. Barbara Cortner and the Myers'
land. Containing 250 acres. This 13 April 1865.
Reg: (no date)   Signed: James Bramlett
                                Rachael Bramlett

Page 439 - State of Illinois, Perry County. I, David M. Hoge,
Clerk of the County Court of said County and State do hereby
certify that Henry F. Hambleman, Esquire, is now and was on the
13 April 1865 an Acting Justice of the Peace for said county and
state. This 17 May 1865.
Reg: August 3, 1866   Signed: David M. Hoge, Clerk

Page 439 - William Cully Deed to W.F. Thompson's heirs, 89 ½
acres. On __ day of February 1861 sold unto William F. Thompson
land in Bedford County and Civil District No. 2 and on the
waters of Lazy Branch of Doddys Creek and bounded by where said
Cully formerly lived and where the said Thompson ten lived, and
by a spring. This 1 August 1866.
Wit: R.B. Davidson   Signed: William Cully
Reg: August 3, 1866

Page 440 - James H. Neil, Exr., Deed to Elizabeth J. Knott, Town
Lot. By Virtue of the power vested in me by the last will and

testament of John T. Neil, deceased, have sold unto said
Elizabeth J. Knott wife of A.B. Knott a Town Lot or part of lot
in the Town of Shelbyville, Bedford County supposed to contain 1
acre and bounded by T.D. Ledbetter and Edmund Cooper, by an
alley which runs on the south of William H. Wisener, by the
street running north and south which is the first street west of
the Big Spring, and by the street which runs westward the Fair
Grounds passing G.W. Buchanan. This 30 July 1866.
Reg: August 3, 1866   Signed: James H. Neil

Page 441 - P.F. Young Trust Deed to Carithers. Property, to
wit, one gray horse, one suckling colt, one mule colt, and
several other items listed in original document. This Aug 3,
1866.
Wit: H.L. Davidson   Signed: P.F. Young
Reg: August 4, 1866

Page 442 - Mary A. and S.A. Cunningham Deed to John W. Woodward,
153 acres. Mary A. Cunningham and Samuel A. Cunningham have
sold unto John W. Woodward a tract of land owned by J.W.C.
Cunningham at the time of his death. Land bounded by lands of
John Cortner, by lands known as the M.P. Gentry tract, and by
lands of William Woodward and others. Containing 153 acres.
This August 3, 1866.
Reg: August 4, 1866   Signed: Mary A. Cunningham
                                       S.A. Cunningham

Page 443 - Mary F. Daniel Deed to Dennis Hemby. Land in Bedford
County and Civil District No. 25 on the waters of Gages Creek.
Containing 52 acres it being the same tract of land conveyed to
me by Robert Mathews by deed dated 21 December 1864. This 23
August 1865.
Wit: Daniel Hemby   Signed: Mary F. Daniel
     Rufus T. Daniel
Reg: August 6, 1866

Page 443 - Beverly Harris Deed to B.N. Davis and Elizabeth
Williams. Land in Bedford County and District No. 9.
Containing 9 acres, 3 rods and 24 poles and bounded by Elizabeth
Williams' corner, by A.H. McLean's line, and by James Alexander.
This July 25, 1866.
Wit: C.L. Cooper   Signed: Beverly Harris
     M.B. Damron
Reg: August 6, 1866

Page 444 - F.M. Keller Deed to M. Robertson. I, Francis M.
Keller, have sold unto Michael Robertson a tract of land in
Bedford County and District No. 2, consisting 1 acre and 134/160
poles and bounded by a short distance south west of the spring.
This 10 October 1865.
Wit: D.F. Tolly   Signed: F.M. Keller
     J.W. McGill
Reg: August 7, 1866

Page 445 - John Morrow Deed to John F. May. I, John Morrow, conveyed unto John F. May in trust for his wife Caroline E. May and their two sons George F. May and John H. May or any other children that may be born to then in marriage as husband and wife for the sole use of said Caroline E. May during her natural life and at her death to descend to said children George and John. Land in Bedford County and District No. 2, containing 1 ½ acres and bounded by the lands of the late Robert L. Singleton, deceased, and known as Lot No. 4 in the original plan of the Town of Fairfield. This 21 January 1859.
Reg: August 7, 1866   Signed: John Morrow

Page 446 - Thomas Hart Transfer of Deed to Mrs. John F. May, House and Lot. I, Thomas Hart of Bedford County, do covenant with said Mrs. John F. May said deed the same she gave me two cows and calves, one yearling, fifty bushels of wheat and one sorrel horse. This August 6, 1866.
Reg: August 7, 1866   Signed: Thos. Hart

Page 446 - F.J. Harris Deed to Mary Dozier. A lot of land known as "Mary Dozier's dower." This July 12, 1866.
Wit: C.S. Dudley   Signed: F.J. Harris
     James E. Wadley
Reg: August 7, 1866

Page 447 - R.L. Landers Deed to L.D. Hickerson, 412 acres. Robt. L. Landers of Bedford County sold unto Lytle D. Hickerson of Coffey County, Tennessee land. One tract purporting to contain by Grant No. 9675 and Entry No. 2860 made in Franklin County, Tennessee and entered 21 February 1846 and granted by the State of Tennessee to Wm. Turner on the waters of Rock Creek and bounded by a corner of Gunn's entry, on the south side of the Powell Road, and by Joab Short's line. Containing 825 acres. Also one half of 636 acres of land granted to William Turner by State of Tennessee Grant No. 9815 and Entry No. 3032 made in Franklin County, Tennessee 26 November 1848 dayed 24 February 1849, lying in Franklin County, Tennessee on the waters of Rock Creek and bounded by the south east corner of the above tract, and by James H. Carty and Miles Purdee, by a road and by a field, and by William Turner (now Josiah Gunn's) corner. Containing 1000 acres. This 27 July 1866.
Wit: Albert Lowe   Signed: R.L. Landers
     A. Brook
Reg: August 8, 1866

Page 448 - H.L. Davidson Trust Deed to R.B. Davidson. I have sold unto Robert B. Davidson a tract of land adjoining the Town of Shelbyville being the same tract on which I now reside, bounded on the north east by the Skull Camp Ford Road, by Duck River, and by the line between James L. Scudder and myself. Containing 40 acres. Also one bay horse and an old family carriage. Robert B. Davidson and George W. Buchanan are my securities on my guardian bond. This August 6, 1866.
Reg: August 8, 1866   Signed: H.L. Davidson

Page 449 - John F. Ray Lease to Harry Ray and wife, Lot. I, John F. Ray of Bedford County, have this day given to my old friend Harry Ray and his wife Milly Ray of same place, a lease of land whereon said Harry and his wife lives on my land embracing all the lot in which three houses is situated supposed to be 15 or 20 acres to have and to hold occupy and enjoy during the said Harry and Milly's natural life uninterrupted possession but I return the use of the lot for my own and benefit but for no other. They have the use of the lot timber, water and rock and full control of all the improvements on and attached to said lot for the consideration that he Harry Ray was a good and (illegible) land in raising me up to manhood from infancy and his wife Milly Rau has been like a mother to me. This 6 September 1865.
Wit: Jos. Anderson   Signed: John F. Ray
     T.B. Allison
     F.A. Ray
Reg: August 9, 1866

Page 450 - J.W. Allison Deed to Fredic Batte, 4 acres. I have sold unto Frederick Batte, both of Bedford County, and bounded Batte's and Chrismon's corner, to the bank of Weakleys Creek, and by Allison's line formerly Allison and Batte corner. This 11 May 1866.
Wit: J.B. Cooper   Signed: J.W. Allison
     J.W. Rucker
     S.W. Chrismon
Reg: August 9, 1866

Page 451 - E. Tarpley Deed to L.J. Winsett, 56 acres. I, Edward Tarpley, have this day sold unto L.J. Winsett a tract of land in Bedford County and District No. 11 on the waters of North Fork of Duck River and bounded by Floid's (Floyd's) corner, by A.E. Allison's corner, and by J.R. Stem's corner. This January 29, 1866.
Wit: F.D. Tarpley   Signed: Edward Tarpley
     Jno. A. Ganaway
Reg: August 9, 1866

Page 451 - Willliam S. Puckett Deed to Dennis Wheelhouse. Land in Bedford County and District No. 9, containing 20 acres and bounded by Dennis Wheelhouse's corner, and by Frazier's line. This 11 June 1866.
Wit: W.W. Puckett   Signed: Wm. S. Puckett
     G.S. Barnes
Reg: August 9, 1866

Page 452 - Jonathan Clanton Deed to W.N. Orr, undivided interest. I, Jonathan Clanton, have sold unto William N. Orr during his life time and unto Ann E, Orr, Sarah C. Orr, Susan A. Orr, Mary G. Orr, J.?. Orr heirs of William N. Orr, land whereon said William N. Orr now lives. Containing 106 acres. This 14 March 1865.
Wit: A. Wilson   Signed: Jonathan Clanton

A. Shaw
Reg: August 11, 1866

Page 453 - A.P. Eakin Mortgage to John P. Steele. I am indebted
to the estate of Samuel E. Gilliland, deceased. I have sold
unto said Steele a tract of land in Bedford County near the Town
of Shelbyville in District No. 7 and bounded by J.T. Cannon, by
a street, and George W. Buchanan, by new grave yard, by the
Warner Mill Road lately conveyed to me by William S. Jett.
Containing 28 acres. This August 10, 1866.
Reg: August 11, 1866   Signed: A.P. Eakin

Page 453 - Moses Marshall Deed to J.W. Brown, 3 acres and 28
poles. Land in Bedford County and District No. 3, containing 3
acres and 128 poles and bounded by J.G. Barksdale's corner, by
Thos. Holland, Sr.'s spring branch, by Air Creek, and by the
road leading from Shelbyville by the Thos. Holland's place.
This 11 August 1866.
Reg: August 14, 1866   Signed: Moses Marshall

Page 454 - H.L. Davidson Deed to Alford Reed, 24 acres, 3 rods,
15 poles. Land in Civil District No. 23 in Bedford County and
bounded by Robert Reed's tract, by Andrew Reed's tract, and by a
small tract purchased by John Reed from me. This March 1, 1864.
Reg: August 15, 1866   Signed: H.L. Davidson

Page 455 - J.E. Stem and others to Thos. P. Cooper and others,
Contract. We or either of us promise to pay Thomas P. Cooper
and J.W. Vincent $200 for an (illegible) and bind our crops of
cotton (say 14 acres) as security for payment. This August 7,
1866.
Wit: J.S. Cooper   Signed: J.E. Stem
     J.L. Cooper   C.W. Smotherman
Reg: August 16, 1866

Page 455 - W.J. Davis Deed to William Murphree, 100 acres. Land
in Bedford County and District No. 5 and containing 100 acres
bounded by Holling's land, by Wilson Skidmore tract, by S.
Marsh's corner by Wesley Rainwater's corner, by the Dugan tract,
and by Thos. Dugan. This 20 November 1862.
Wit: Burrel Featherston   Signed: W.J. Davis
     George W. Ivey, Jr.
Reg: August 16, 1866

Page 456 - Thos. C. Whitesides and others Trustees &c to R.C.
Russ. As Trustee of James M. Elliott under a deed of trust
executed to us by said Elliott in September 1857 we have sold to
Robt. C. Russ a lot situated in Bedford County in Camp White
near the Town of Shelbyville, beginning at corner of Cannon
Street and Line Street, and by Hob's lot being part of the lot
formerly purchased by Helbert and Burditt of said Elliott. This
24 December 1862.

Reg: August 20, 1866   Signed: Thos. C. Whiteside
                                        G.W. Thompson
                                        J.M. Elliott

Page 457 - Robert C. Russ Deed to John F. Yancy. House and lot
in Camp White. Lot of ground in Bedford County in Camp White
near the Town of Shelbyville and bounded by Cannon Street and
Line Street, by James Hobb's lot being part of the lot formerly
purchased by Helbert and Burditt of said Elliott. This 20
August 1866.
Reg: August 21, 1866   Signed: R.C. Russ

Page 457 - H.L. Davidson Trust Deed to R.B. Davidson. Whereas
previous to the death of Mrs. E.W. Harrison I executed to her by
note and by her last will and testament gave to her daughter in
law Mrs. Adeline Harrison and which is now in the hands of Judge
Cooper executor of E.W. Harrison and whereas to make said Addie
Harrison more secure in payment thereof. I hereby convey to him
in trust a small tract of unimproved land in the 21st District
of Bedford County adjoining Alford Reed, John Reed and ___
McFarland and R.T. Cannon, and by Cannon and Robert Reed's
heirs. Containing 32 or 33 acres. This August 23, 1866.
Reg: August 23, 1866   Signed: H.L. Davidson

Page 458 - Samuel Bobo Deed to Jason Ray and Thos. Dean and
others successors to Old Flat Creek Church. I, Samuel Bobo,
sold unto Jason Ray (pastor) and Thomas Dean Deacon of the
Baptist Church at Flat Creek and their successors in office a
small tract of land in Bedford County on waters of Flat Creek
south branch of Duck River and bounded by a corner of old Flat
Creek Baptist Meeting House, and by a road leading from
Winchester to Columbia. Including said church house and
graveyard, also use of a spring 4 rods from the north east
corner of said tract. This 7 May 1854.
Wit: P.H. (illegible)   Signed: Samuel Bobo
     Lacy L. Bobo
Reg: August 23, 1866

Page 459 - Wm. L. Yancy, Discharge. William L. Yancy, Private
of Captain H.N.T. Shipp Company © 5th Regiment of Tenn Cavalry
Volunteers who was enrolled on the 14 August 1862 to serve three
years or during the war, is hereby discharged from the service
of the United States this 25 June 1865 at Fayetteville,
Tennessee by reason of General Order No. 83 War Dept. May 8,
1865. No objection to his being re-enlisted is known to exist.
Said William L. Yancy was born in Bedford County, Tennessee is
fifteen years of age, (illegible) feet seven inches high, fair
complexion, blue eyes, dark hair and by occupation when enrolled
a farmer. Given at Fayetteville, Tennessee this 25 June 1865.
Francis Jackson, Captain   Signed: Hartwell N.T. Shipp, Capt.
Oath of Indentity. William L. Yancy of the Town of Shelbyville,
Bedford County, Tennessee on this 29 May 1866 personally
appeared before me the undersigned a Justice of the Peace for
the County and State above mentioned William L. Yancy who being

duly sworn according to law declared that he is the identical William L. Yancy who was a private in the Company commanded by Captain H.N.T. Shipp in the Regiment 5th Tenn Cav commanded by Col. W.J. Clift that he enlisted on 14 August 1862 for the term of three years and was discharged at Fayetteville, Tennessee on 23 June 1863 by reason of General Order No. 83 War Dept. May 8, 1865.
Reg: August 25, 1866   Signed: William L. Yancy

Page 460 - Michael Crowel and others to William Crowel, 12 ½ acres. We, Michael Crowel and his wife Sarah R. Crowel of Bedford County and Samuel G. Delk and his wife Isabella W. Delk both of Maury County, Tennessee, have this day sold unto William Crowel a small lot of land that we inherited from our grand father David Anderson now deceased, late of Bedford County the same is a part of Anderson's land in District No. 11 and known as Lot No. 2 of the land that was (illegible) by Joseph Anderson and said other heirs &c. Bounded by division line of said Joseph Anderson's Lot No. 1, by Lot No. 3, and by Wortham's line now the dower of Mary Wortham's line. This 30 August 1865.
Wit: B.S. Parsons   Signed: Michael Crowel
     Joseph B. Delk   Sarah R. Crowel
     Jos. Anderson   Samuel G. Delk
Reg: August 25, 1866   Isabella W. Delk
                                  Joshua Crowel

Page 460 - Andrew Johnson, Gov. Deed to R.H. Sims and J.S. Newton, 28 88/160 acres. For the use of school lands dated January 6, 1857. There is granted by the State of Tennessee unto Richard H. Sims and James S. Newton, assignees of Randolph Newsom a tract of land containing 78 acres and 88 poles in Bedford County on the waters of Powel Creek in Range 4 Township or Section 5 and part of Section 5 and bounded by the Range line, Lot No. 3 Daugherty's old corner now Allen's corner, and by said tracts of school land. This 10 January 1857.
F.M.W. Barton, Sec.   Signed: Andrew Johnson,
                                     By the Governor

Page 461 - William F. Dryden Deed to James N. Dryden. Land in Bedford County and Civil District No. 18 and bounded by Dr. J.A. Blakemore and J.M. Oneal, by lands of Z. Roberts and Thos. W. Muse, by lands of Sarah Neill, and by Mike Moore. Containing 148 1 ½cres which is encumbered by the dower of Mrs. Malinda Dryden which has been assigned to her. This 29 August 1866.
Wit: Thos. H. Coldwell   Signed: William F. Dryden
Reg: August 29, 1866

Page 462 - G.G. Osborne Deed to James L. Wood. Registered, 42 acres and 100 poles. Land in Bedford County and Civil District No. 2 and adjoining W.H. Finch's corner in my north line, by Wood's east line of his original tract and my north west corner of the Rich'd Muse purchase, and by the Furguson tract. This November 26, 1858.
Reg: August 30, 1866   Signed: G.G. Osborne

Page 463 - Mary McNutt Power of Attorney to C.S. McNutt. State of Texas, County of McLennan. I, Mary McNutt, do appoint C.S. McNutt of same place my attorney in fact for me and in my name to ask for and receive any and all money due me from the estate of James Gaunt, deceased, and Andrew Gant, deceased, both of Bedford County. Also to sell and convey any interest in the dower of Elizabeth Gant of Bedford County and all the other business for me. This 8 August 1866.
Reg: August 31, 1866   Signed: Mary McNutt

Page 463 - E.M. Lacy Deed to Jo. McFadden, Col., House and Lot in Camp White. I, E.M. Lacy, have sold unto Joseph McFadden (colored) a tract of land in the Town of Shelbyville and in what is known as Camp White and bounded on Cannon Street. Containing about ¾ of an acre. Said lot being known as the Gavin lot purchased by me of J.H. Graham. This September 3, 1866.
Wit: M.E.W. Dunaway   Signed: E.M. Lacy
     J.M. Elliott
Reg: September 4, 1866

Page 464 - G.W. Edmondson Deed to A.L. Adams, 1 acre and 110 poles. A partial lot of land in Civil District No. 7 it being a portion of the Wilson Coats' tract sold by Joseph H. Thompson, Commissioner and bounded by corner of Lot No. 18 of said Coats' tract, and by Lot No. 17. This 3 September 1866.
Reg: September 4, 1866   Signed: George W. Edmondson

Page 465 - G.W. Thompson Deed to G.W. Edmondson, 1 acre and 110 poles. Land near the Town of Shelbyville in District No. __ it being a portion of Wilson Coats' tract sold by Joseph H. Thompson, Commissioner, and the same that William Stewart now lives, and bounded by Lot No. 18 of said Coats' tract, and by Lot No. 17. This 14 November 1864.
Wit: Thos. J. Roane   Signed: G.W. Thompson
     N.B. Coble
Reg: September 4, 1866

Page 465 - W.S. Bates Deed to C.L. Pyron, undivided interest. Land it being a child's part as one of the children of John B. Bates, deceased, being in Bedford County and District No. 2. The said land being the dower of Ann B. Bates, containing about 75 acres, she having a life estate the remainder to the children and heirs at law of said Bates. This 3 September 1866.
Reg: September 4, 1866   Signed: D.S. Bates

Page 466 - J.H. Lawrence and wife Deed to R.H. Blankenship, undivided interest. Land being my undivided interest purchased from J.W. Blankenship, Benj. A. Blankenship and G.W. Blankenship, to a tract of land which Benj. Blankenship died seized in Bedford County and District No. 7 and containing 88 acres and bounded by Harrison's old entry, by S.V. Butts, by Preston Frazier, and by G.L. Poplin. Also, we, J.H. Lawrence and Tabitha Lawrence his wife formerly Tabitha Blankenship have

sold to R.H. Blankenship out undivided interest in the above said tract. This 22 December 1855.
Wit: J.V. Butts   Signed: J.H. Lawrence
     J.L. Cooper   Tabitha H. Lawrence
     M.B. Damron
Reg: September 5, 1866

Page 467 - M.W. Wood and Jesse Wood Bond to Jas. A. Jarrett. I, Moses W. Wood and Jesse Wood by our attorney J.L. Cooper, bind ourselves to Jas. A. Jarrett. We have sold to said James A. Jarrett money in notes. Notes to: Adam Comer, Robert b. Rucker, John Clanton, F.J. Harris, M.W. Wood and Jesse Wood, F.J. and Mary H. Harris, A.M. McElroy. Land in Bedford County and District No. 8 on the waters of Falling Creek and bounded by the bank of Falling Creek it being the beginning corner of a lot laid off to Minos W. Wood. Containing 155 acres and 112 poles. This December 19, 1861.
Wit: R.H. Blankenship   Signed: M.W. Wood
     John S. Cooper   Jesse Wood, by
Reg: September 5 1866   J.L. Cooper, Atty.

Page 468 - R.H. Lewis Deed to Louis Mankle, for Brewery. I, Robert H. Lewis, have sold unto Louis Mankel houses and lots in the Town of Shelbyville. One house and lot in said town on the north west corner of the Public Square known as the Strickler property used as a brewery together with the fixtures belonging to said property including engine and boiler M(illegible) mill kittle and in short everything belonging to the brewery on the 6 July 1866. This __ September 1866.
Wit: J.L. Scudder   Signed: R.H. Lewis
     W.J. Reagor
Reg: September 6, 1866

Page 469 - Louis Mankle Mortgage to Thos. H. Coldwell. A house and lot in the Town of Shelbyville and known as Lot No. __ and bounded by Main Street, by the Public Square, by the Bank of Tennessee lot on which the banking house is situated, by an alley, by Stewart's and Gwinn's livery stable on which my brewery is situated and all fixtures. This August 13, 1866.
Reg: September 6, 1866   Signed: Louis Mankle

Page 470 - William S. Jett Deed to James L. Turner, 145 acres and 95 poles. Land in Bedford County and Civil District No. 11 and bounded by a line of Newcomb Thompson's land, by a line of James H. Lock's land, and by Theophilus Thompson's north boundary line. This 5 September 1866.
Reg: September 7, 1866   Signed: Wm. S. Jett

Page 470 - J.J. Mankin Trust Deed to William H. Wisener. I have sold unto William H. Wisener a house and lot in the Town of Shelbyville on which I now reside and bounded by the street or road leading to the Skull Camp Ford, by Thomas B. Laird, by lands formerly belonging to J.L. Burt, and by Robt. B. Davidson.

Containing about 1 ½ acres. Also my interest in a tract of land of 107 acres purchased by W.O. Rickman at the sale of the lands of General Cannon and on which said Rickman now lives in Civil District No. 3 and on the north side of Duck River. This 6 September 1866.
Reg: September 7, 1866   Signed: John J. Mankin

Page 471 - William Collins Receipt to J.M. Moore. For one Town Lot in Unionville purchased at public sale on 1 September 1866 which credit is a note I hold on him.
Reg: September 8, 1866   Signed: Wm. Collins

Page 472 - George and John Frazier Power of Attorney to Daniel Earnhart. We authorize Daniel Earnhart to sell and transfer lands known by reference to a will made by our father John Frazier by record of Deed of Transfer. William Frazier one of the heirs of said John Frazier is not. This April 19, 1866.
Reg: September 8, 1866   Signed: George Frazier
                                        John Frazier

Page 472 - J.P. Hutton Deed to A.J. Cotton, 185 acres. Land in Bedford County and District No. 5, containing 185 acres and 20 poles and bounded by P.C. Steele's corner, E.M. Whitworth's corner, to the center of Fall Creek, by my original tract of land, and by P.C. Steele's house. This 5 September 1866.
Wit: Sue Clark   Signed: J.P. Hutton
     W.K. Ransom
Reg: September 12, 1866

Page 473 - Jo. P. Kelly Deed to Madison H. Webb, 113 ½ acres. This 7 August 1860. Both of Bedford County lying in the counties of Bedford and Rutherford on the west side of Nashville and Chattanooga Rail Road and bounded by the lane between Benjamin Webb and the aforesaid tract hereby conveyed being said Webb's south east corner and John M. Pearson's corner, by Daniel Gilchrist's line, by Robert Clark's line, and by John D. Bingham's corner. Containing 113 ½ acres.
Wit: B.F. Webb   Signed: Jo. P. Kelly
     Benjamin Webb
Reg: September 12, 1866

Page 474 - M.M. Moore Deed to W.J. Shofner, 70 acres. This 1 September 1866 between M.M. Moore and William J. Shofner, both of Bedford County. Deed for interest sold to said Shofner all his right title claim he has to two interests (each being one ninth) in Margaret Boone's dower. Said Moore having before purchased the above named interest, one from Benjamin Boone, the other from Joseph and Cenar Holcomb. Said dower being on the waters of Big Flat Creek of Bedford County and lying in two tracts joining the lands of Joseph Parker, Jordan Hale, John Stone, P.S. Dean, Rich'd Mullins, Warren Harris and others. The dower containing in all including both tracts that 321 acres.

The above claim to take effect at the death of said Margaret Boone.
Reg: September 13, 1866   Signed: M.M. Moore

Page 474 - John P. Steele and G.B. Sharp Deed to S.B. Gordon, 110 acres. All that part of the John Koonce old tract in Bedford County lying on the west side of the big road leading from Shelbyville to Flat Creek store and Lynchburg, adjoining the lands of the late Robert Reed, by Benjamin McFarland, by Benj. Berry. This 14 September 1866.
Reg: September 14, 1866   Signed: John P. Steele
                                         G.B. Sharp

Page 475 - James H. Roane Deed to Morgan Smith, 100 acres. By a conveyance of a tract of 50 acres of land to C.P. Houston on 5 December 1865 by my request. I hereby convey to said Smith land in Bedford County and District No. 6 and bounded by said Smith's land, to the center of the turnpike road leading from Shelbyville to Fairfield. This __ May 1866.
Reg: September 14, 1866   Signed: J.H. Roane

Page 476 - George W. Cook Deed to Hiram B. Crowel, 75 acres. Land in Bedford County and Civil District No. 18 and adjoining a corner of James N. and W.H. Clark's field, and by a 170 acre survey. Containing 75 acres. It being the same land conveyed by George W. Buchanan as administrator of J.W. Wallace and John H. Oneal to said George W. Cook on 18 February 1857. Also one other tract in Bedford County and same District containing 40 acres known as the William Cook tract. This 25 July 1865.
Wit: Jas. L. Scudder   Signed: G.W. Cook
     John Chapman
Reg: September 15, 1866

Page 477 - Hiram B. Crowel Deed to William B. Cowan, 75 acres. Land in Bedford County and Civil District No. 18 and bounded by corner of James N. and W.H. Clark's field, and by a 170 acre survey. Containing 75 acres it being the same land conveyed by G.W. Buchanan as administrator of J.H. Wallace and John H. Oneal to G.W. Cook on 18 July 1857 by said Cook to Hiram B. Crowel on 25 July 1865. Also one other tract in Bedford County and same District containing 40 acres and joining the above tract of land known as the William Cook tract of land. This 15 September 1866.
Reg: September 17, 1866   Signed: Hiram B. Crowel

Page 477 - Henry C. Bowers Deed to John S. Elkins. Land known as the Mary Elkins' dower it being part of the William Elkins' land and bounded by lands of Morris Barney, by the lands of H.D. Fugitt, by H.H. Elkins, and by the lands of R.Q. Hollins & Co. Containing 125 acres. This 13 August 1866.
Reg: September 17, 1866   Signed: H.C. Bowers

Page 478 - W.N. Gwynn and wife Deed to W.A. Black, House and Lot. House and lot in the corporate limits of the Town of Shelbyville and bounded by the lot of G.W. Buchanan, by an alley and lot belonging to Anderson Sharp by him conveyed to Wm. Gollathan, by a side wall in front on said street and not enclosed. Also retained the same having been retained by G.W. Buchanan. It being the same lot on which he now resides and purchased by us of C.L. Powell and when deed to Gartha Ann Gillman now Gartha Ann Gwynn. Registered in Book DDD.
Reg: September 17, 1866   Signed: W.N. Gwinn
                                       G.A. Gwinn

Page 479 - James M. Lentz and wife Deed to John W. and Jordan Rucker. This 8 December 1865. James M. Lentz and Elizabeth his wife sold unto John W. and Jordan Rucker, all of Bedford County, land in Bedford County it being a part of the land formerly owned by J.K. Lowell in District No. 10 on Weakley Creek. Containing 38 acres and 135 poles.
Wit: Newton F. Neil   Signed: James M. Lentz
     A. Poplin   Elizabeth Lentz
Reg: September 17, 1866

Page 479 - Joshua Reed Deed to J.P. Blessing and others.   I, Joshua Reed, have sold unto J.P. Blessing, Matt Brown, William Blessing, Thos. Dalton and Baily Blessing as Commissioners &c a tract of land containing one half acre being in Civil District No. 3 in Bedford County, being part of the tract known with Coat's land and bounded lands of William Grissom.   This 17 September 1866.
Reg: September 19, 1866   Signed: Joshua Reed

Page 480 - Margaret Smith Deed to B.F. Hazlett, 29 acres. Margaret Smith sold unto Benjamin F. Hazlett a tract of land in Bedford County and Civil District No. 19 and bounded by James H. Harrison's corner.   Containing 29 acres and 40 poles.   This September 6, 1866.
Wit: H.M. Hastings   Signed: Margaret Smith
     Eli Moss
Reg: September 19, 1866

Page 481 - W.A. Black Deed to Mary E. Miller, House and Lot. Land in the corporate limits of the Town of Shelbyville and bounded by the lot owned by G.W. Buchanan, to an alley and lot belonging to Anderson Sharp and by him conveyed to Mrs. Gollathan, by a retained __ __ for a side wall in front on said street and not enclosed, and by the street of 10 feet between Mrs. Gollathan and the said lot is also retained, the same having been retained by G.W. Buchanan in original sale of said lot it being the same lot on which Luther Ramsey now resides and purchased by me of W.N. Gwinn and Martha A. Gwinn.   This 17 September 1866.
Reg: September 19, 1866   Signed: W.A. Black

Page 481 - Richard Ransom Deed to John C. Jackson. Land all the west half of the tract bought by me at Shelbyville in the case of Theophilus R(illegible) and others VS Sarah Patterson and others and which tract if situated in Civil District No. 10 and bounded by the line of the original tract. Containing 127 acres. This 20 September 1866.
Reg: September 20, 1866   Signed: Richard Ransom

Page 482 - Richard Ransom Deed to Alfred Ransom. Land, all the east half of the tract of land bought by me in the case of Theophilus R(illegible) and others VS Sarah Patterson and others and which land is situated in Civil District No. 10 of Bedford County and bounded by the north east corner of the original tract. Containing 143 ½ acres. And I also convey the south half of the cedar tract of land purchased by me situated in District No. 10 of Rutherford County, Tennessee and containing 29 acres and 148 ½ poles. This September 20, 1866.
Reg: September 21, 1866   Signed: Richard Ransom

Page 483 - F.J. Harris Deed to W.D. Cates, 72 acres. Land in 9th Civil District of Bedford County and bounded by Rebecca Landers, and by N.B. Turner. Containing 72 acres. This 21 September 1866.
Wit: Wm. T. Lane   Signed: F.J. Harris
     Wm. Galbreath
Reg: September 22, 1866

Page 484 - Rebecca Mathews Deed to William H. Mathews. I, Rebecca Mathews widow of Andrew Mathews, deceased, late of Bedford County, convey unto William H. Mathews son of said Andrew Mathews all interest &c in said deceased estate as well as that of my now personal interest, ans all that which might or may be coming to me as inherited through my deceased children John and Mary Inze (?) Mathews both of whom were the children of my body by my husband. Both of said children departed this life after the death of their father at the same time, reserving my right of dower in the house and lot on which I now live and have lived since and at the time of my late husband's death. This 24 September 1866.
Reg: September 25, 1866   Signed: Rebecca Mathews

Page 485 - William J. Whitthorne Deed to N & C Rail Road Company. The Town Lot being in the Town of Shelbyville on the north west corner of the Public Square and bounded by the south east corner of said lot and the north west corner of the Public Square, by the west side of Spring Street, by the corner of a lot purchased by John H. Oneal from John G. Fulgham, by a street leading from the north west corner of the square west toward the river. This 25 August 1866.
Reg: September 25, 1866   Signed: William J. Whitthorne

Page 485 - J.L. Cooper Deed to C.L. Cooper, 185 acres. I, J.L. Cooper give and bequeath to C.L. Cooper 185 acres of land in

District No. 9 of Bedford County and bounded by R.A. McLean and T.F. Barnes, by the heirs of C.G. McLean, deceased, and the heirs of Edmund Damron, deceased, and by the heirs of Ephraim Turner. This December 28, 1865.
Reg: September 25, 1866   Signed: J.L. Cooper

Page 486 - Thos. H. Coldwell, Extr., Deed to Jacob Kizer, 104 acres and 45 poles. Whereas Robert Reed did on 29 March 1860 make and publish his last will and testament in which he appointed myself and one Isaac Reed his executors and in which he devised all his real and personal estate to his wife Elizabeth Reed during her life and at her death the property was directed to be sold. Robert Reed died seized and possessed and did sell them. Jacob Kizer being the highest bidder became the purchaser. Land in Bedford County and Civil District No 23 and bounded by Koonce's corner. This 26 September 1866.
Reg: September 26, 1866   Signed: Thos. H. Coldwell, Exr. Of
                                       Robert Reed

Page 487 - John Wortham, Discharge. John Wortham a Major of 5th Regiment of Tennessee Vol Cav Volunteers who was enrolled on the 30 day of June 1862 to serve three years or during the war is hereby discharged from the service of the United States this 14 August 1865 at Pulaski, Tennessee by reason of Special Order No. 18 C.S.Mil Div Tenn. No objection to his being re-enlisted is known to exist. Said Major John Wortham was born in Graves County, Kentucky is nineteen years of age, five feet eight inches high, fair complexion, blue eyes, dark hair and by occupation when enrolled a farmer. Given at Pulaski, Tennessee this 14 August 1865.
Francis Jackson, Captain   W.J. Clift, Lieut Col.
Oath of Identity - John Wortham of the Town of Shelbyville, County of Bedford County, Tennessee, on this 27 September 1865 personally appeared before me the undersigned a Justice of the Peace for said county and state above mentioned. John Wortham who being duly sworn according to law declared that he is the identical John Wortham who was a Major in the Company commanded by Captain Tenn Cav Vol in the Regiment 5th commanded by Lt. Col. Clift that he enlisted on the 31 day of July 1862 for the term of three years and was discharged at Pulaski on the 14 day of August 1865 by reason of Order No. 18 C.S. Mil Div Tennessee.
Reg: September 27, 1866   Signed: John Wortham

Page 488- C.C. Cummings and Margaret C. Foster, Marriage Contract. Whereas a marriage is about to be solemnized between C.C. Cummings and Margaret C. Foster and it is desired that a marriage settlement shall be made and entered into by which C.C. Cummings relinquish all right of property that Margaret C. Foster whereon said marriage ceremony is performed. It is mutually agreed that the said Margaret C. Foster and said C.C. Cummings that the said Margaret C. Foster retains full title and ownership belonging to her either by gift purchase or devise. This 8 October 1866.
Wit: C.W. Cummings   Signed: Margaret C. Foster
     B.M. B(illegible)   C.C. Cummings

Page 489 - James Whelan Deed to Patrick A. Fehan. Church and
Lot. James Whelan of Nashville, Tennessee, sold unto Patrick A.
Fehan a certain lot lying and being in Bedford County and Civil
District No. 7 and within the corporate limits of the Town of
Shelbyville and known as Lot No. 44 (sometimes referred to as
Lot No. 24) formerly occupied as a Presbyterian Church but
recently used by a Catholic Church, adjoining a corner of lot
owned by William McClure and purchased from A.L. Stamps on
Brittain Street, and by an alley. Land conveyed 6 January 1859
by Patick Fay to Richard T. Miles and registered in Book AA,
page 554 and by the last will and testament of said R.T. Miles
and registered in Book of Wills and Inventories Book No. 18,
pages 298 and 299.
Davidson County, Tennessee   Signed: James Whelan
Reg: October 15, 1866

Page 490 - William S. Jett to George E. Calhoun, Two Lots.   I
have sold unto George E. Calhoun two Town Lots in the Town of
Shelbyville conveyed to me by N. Thompson, Jr. by deed dated 7
January 1863 being Lots No. 60 and 68, which R.N. Jones sold to
Graham & Brown off said lots.
Reg: October 15, 1866   Signed: Wm. S. Jett

Page 490 - William J. Whitthorne Deed to Seaborn Jones, 157 ½
acres. Land in Bedford County and District No. 3 containing 157
½ acres on the waters of Wartrace Creek on both sides of the
Nashville and Chattanooga Rail Road about 1 ½ miles north of the
Village of Wartrace and adjoining the lands of E.H. Ewing, by
Granville Frazier, and the Chambers' land, by Miss Taylor, and
being the tract of land purchased by me from Newton C. Harris,
Esq. This 11 October 1866.
Wit: J. M. Jarrell   Signed: William J. Whitthorne
     J.W. Gollithan
Reg: October 18, 1866

Page 491 - Seaborn Jones Deed to Mortgage to William J.
Whitthorne. I have sold unto William J. Whitthorne my tract of
land in Bedford County and Civil District No. 3 on the waters of
Wartrace Creek on both sides of Nashville and Chattanooga Rail
Road about 1 ½ miles north of the Village of Wartrace and
adjoining the lands of E.H. Ewing, by Granville Frazier, and by
Chambers' land, and by Miss Taylor. Being the tract of land
purchased by me from William J. Whitthorne and containing 157 ½
acres. This 11 October 1866.
Wit: Jo. M. Jarrell   Signed: Seaborn Jones
     J.W. Gollithan
Reg: October 19, 1866

Page 492 - Robert Murphree Deed to William Cully, 62 acres.
This 5 June 1866. Robert Murphree sold unto William Cully, both
of Bedford County and District No. 3, between the waters of the
Garrison and Barren Fork of Duck River one or two miles from the
junction thereof and bounded by a tract of land owned by Kinchen
Stokes, deceased, and now occupied by John M. Stokes in the

north boundary line of a tract now owned by said William Cully, by Robert B. Maupin, by land belonging to the minor heirs of Arch'd Murphy, deceased, and by Alonzo Murphy.
Wit: Alonzo Murphy   Signed: Robert Murphy
     J.H. Alderman
Reg: October 20, 1866

Page 493 - W.N. Gwinn Deed to W.A. Neely, 10 acres. Land in Bedford County and bounded by the corner of the land I bought of W.S. Jett. This October 18, 1866.
Reg: October 22, 1866   Signed: W.N. Gwinn

Page 493 - A.M. Smith Deed to J.C. Snell, undivided lot in Richmond. I, A.M. Smith of Gibson County, Tennessee, have sold unto J.C. Snell of Bedford County the half of a certain lot of land in the Town of Richmond, Bedford County and bounded by a lot which Freeman's Store House is situated, by a street running north and south through said town, and by street running east and west through said town. Containing near 1 acre. This September 18, 1866.
Wit: J.S. Davidson   Signed: A.M. Smith
     J.R. Freeman
Reg: October 22, 1866

Page 494 - William Burns Power of Attorney to John H. Burns. Bell County, Texas. I, William Burns of Bell County, Texas, have appointed John H. Burns of Benton County, Arkansas as my only true and lawful general agent and attorney to make and execute a deed to John Barbour of Bedford County to 225 acres of land in Bedford County on Parch Corn Creek the same that formerly belonged to the heirs of McElrath, to sign my name to a deed. This 28 October 1865.
Reg: October 23, 1866   Signed: Wm. Burns

Page 495 - William Burns and others Deed to John Barbour, 226 acres. William Burns purchased a tract of land from F.P. McElrath in Bedford County on the north side of Parch Corn Creek and bounded by William Orr and the heirs of John Orr, deceased, on the south side of said creek and the lands of Wm. Alexander, by Sarah Mallard and Elizabeth Wood, and by F.P. McElrath and James Pervis. Containing 226 acres. This 19 October 1866.
Wit: John B. Steele   Signed: F.P. McElrath
     John P. Steele   William Burns, by
Reg: October 23, 1866   John H. Burns, Atty.

Page 496 - William Gosling Deed to George Davis, Lot. Land in Bedford County and bounded about 1 ½ miles east of the Town of Shelbyville bounded on the west by the Coat's tract, by the lands of Joshua Reed and Mrs. Patterson, by the lands of William Gosling and M. Brown, and by the lands of Widow Lane. Containing 10 acres. This 17 September _____.
Reg: October 23, 1866   Signed: Wm. Gosling

Page 496 - Wiliams and Cannon, Extrs &c Deed to Mary Ann Grissom. On 1 December 1858 Robert Cannon executed his title bond to Mary Ann Grissom for Lot No. 8 sold by Joseph H. Thompson, Clerk of the County Court of Bedford County on 10 June 1857 that formerly belonged to the estate of Wilson Coats, deceased, which lot contains 4 acres and 29 poles and which lies in Civil District No. 7, Bedford County near the Town of Shelbyville on the east. Robert Cannon departed this life in January 1864 having made and publish his Last Will and Testament and at the April Term 1864 the County Court two of the executors named therein proved said will, gave bond &C. This April 3, 1865.
Wit: H.L. Davidson   Signed: Chesley Williams
     G.W. Buchanan   Wm. P. Cannon
Reg: October 23, 1866

Page 497 - G.M. Ray Bond to Watson & Parker. I am indebted to M.W. Watson and Elijah Parker. I have this day sold to them my lands in Bedford County being in several tracts and adjoining each other in all 320 acres the three including the Shook tract in Civil District No. 24 and bounded by the lands of John W. Crunk and Mrs. Lyon, by the creek the Bobo land, and by T.P. Wells and Thomas Boyers, by Philpot and Mrs. Shofner. This 24 October 1866.
Reg: October 25, 1866   Signed: G.M. Ray

Page 498 - Minos T. Cannon Lease to Bedford County for Court House. Minos T. Cannon has leased to Jo. Thompson, Thomas C. Coldwell and Edmond Cooper, Commissioners on the part of Bedford County appointed by the County Court of said County at the January Term 1866 to lease a Court House and offices for and during the term of three years and five months said lease to terminate 1 January 1870. The following property, to wit, the house known as Cannon's Old Tavern House and the grounds in the rear of said building, said building is on the south side of the Public Square in the Town of Shelbyville and adjoining the frame house of Henry Yancy, on the east and the grocery house now occupied by Thomas S. Sharp, on the west and running back to an alley or street that runs east to the Baptist Church lot and running west to Spring Street near the cotton house of the factory. We are to have the possession of all the building except the two rooms now occupied by John W. Ruth as a Jeweler's Store. This 26 July 1866.
Reg: October 25, 1866   Signed: Minos T. Cannon

Page 499 - Directors of the Bank of Tennessee Trust Deed to Sam'l Watson. This 4 April 1866 between the President and directors of the Bank of Tennessee on one part and Sam'l Watson of Cheatham County of the other part. Conveyed unto Samuel Watson in the state of Tennessee described by a certain tract of land in the City of Nashville known in the plan or part of Lot No. 51 at the corner of Cherry and Union Streets on which is situated the Banking House of said Bank of Tennessee which was conveyed to said party of first part by the Union Bank of Tennessee by deed dated March 6, 1843 and registered March 20,

1843 in Book 5, page 58 in Davidson County. Also a tract of land in the City of Clarksville on which is situated the Banking House of the Branch of said Bank of Tennessee at Clarksville. Also a tract of land in the City of Memphis on which is situated the Banking House of Branch of said Bank of Tennessee. Also a tract of land in the Town of Somerville on which is situated the Banking House of the Branch of said Bank at Somerville. Also a tract of land in the Town of Trenton on which is situated the Banking House of the Branch of said Bank of Trenton. Also a tract of land in the Town of Columbia on which is situated the Banking House of the Branch of said Bank at Columbia. Also a tract of land in the Town of Shelbyville on which is situated the Banking House of the Branch of said Bank of Shelbyville. Also a tract of land in the Town of Sparta on which is situated the Banking House of the Branch of said Bank at Sparta. Also a tract of land in the Town of Athens on which is situated the Banking House of the Branch at Athens. Also a tract of land in the City of Knoxville on which is situated the Banking House of the Branch at Knoxville. Also a tract of land in the Town of Rogersville on which is situated the Banking House of the Branch at Rogersville. Also a tract of land in the Town of Brownsville on which is situated a brick house now occupied by one (illegible). Also (illegible) any lands or interests in lands or real estate owned by said first part in any of the Counties of said state of Tennessee and in any of the State of Mississippi, Arkansas, Louisiana, or Texas. Also several notes listed in original document. NOTE: Very long document. This 4 May 1866.

W.J. Cothran, Cashier   Signed: Samuel Watson, President
Wit: C. Robinson   of the Bank of Tennessee
     R.L. Cain
Reg: October 26, 1866

Page 503 - C.P. Houston Deed to W.Y. Elliott, Town Lot. I, C.P. Houston of Bedford County, have sold unto W.Y. Elliott property, to wit, two Lots No. 26 and 27 in the Town of Shelbyville, Bedford County containing 1 ½ acres being the property on which I now reside and bounded by Dawdy Street which divides it from the property of John W. Cowan and the Presbyterian Church, on the east by Jefferson Street which divided it from the Frierson property, on the south by an alley which divides it from the property formerly owned by Thomas Nance, on the west by Britain Street which divides it from the property of Wm. J. Whitthorne and the New Methodist Church. This October 22, 1866.
Reg: October 27, 1866   Signed: C.P. Houston

Page 504 - G.M. Ray Trust Deed to William J. Bomar. I have conveyed unto William J. Bomar the following articles of personal property, to wit, two horses, one horse mule, one suckling colt, one colored cow, one speckled cow, one red cow, one yoke of oxen &c, thirty head of stock hogs, twenty five head of sheep, my interest in a distillery establishment owned by M.W. Watson and myself and several other items listed in original document. I am indebted to Thomas Anderton, to Riddles' heirs, B.D. Fitzhugh, John Brinkley, Cunningham and McGill, J.N. Blanton, M.W. Watson, Asa Elkins, Joseph Horniday,

Martin Friddle, Elijah Pearson, Dawson Dean, Jordan Hale, James K. Floyd, and Balis Davis. This 25 October 1866.
Reg: October 29, 1866   Signed: G.M. Ray

Page 505 - Robt. J.J. Cates, Discharge. Robt. H.J. Cates a Private in Capt. JAmes Clift Company (M) 5th Regiment of Tennessee Cavalry Volunteers who was enrolled on the on the 28th day of August 1863 to serve three years or during the war is hereby discharged from the service of the United States this 14th day August 1865 at Pulaski, Tennessee, by reason of Special Order No. 18 C.S. Mil Div Tenn. No objection to his being re-enlisted is known to exist. Said Robert H.J. Cates was born in Bedford County, Tennessee is eighteen years of age, six feet two inches high, fair complexion, blue eyes, fair hair and by occupation when enrolled a farmer. Given at Pulaski, Tennessee this 14th August 1865.
Francis Jackson, Captain   James Clift, Captain, Copy
Oath of Identity - Robt. H.J. Cates of the Town of ___ of Bedford County, Tennessee on this 27 day of July 1866 personally appeared before me the undersigned a Justice of the Peace for said County and State above mentioned. Robert H.J. Cates who being duly sworn according to law declares that he is the identical Robert H.J. Cates who was a Private in the Company commanded by Captain James Clift in the Regiment 5th Regiment commanded by Jas. Clift that he enlisted on the 28th day of August 1863 for the term of three years and was discharged at Pulaski, Tennessee on the 14th day of August 1865 by reason of Special Order No. 18 C.S. Div Tenn.
Reg: October 29, 1866   Signed: Robert H.J. Cates

Page 506 - J.F. Price and others, Contract, To divide a tract of land known as the Nancy Durham tract as follows in four equal shares. I, J.F. Price will take his quarter off of the west end. Sarah J. Durham will take hers off. W.C. Durham will take his off next. Alexander M. Price will take his next. N.B., J.F. Price, W.E. Durham and Sarah J. Durham will pay A.M. Price the sum of money to make his share. This 23 October 1862.
Wit: T.H. Bell   Signed: W.C. Durham
     John Lacy   Nancy E. Price
Reg: (no date)   J.F. Price
                                    Sarah J. Durham
                                    Mary M. Price

Page 507 - Richard Anderson Deed to Wm. H. Anderson and James Story, 89 ½ acres. This 1 December 1865. Land in District No. 19 bounded by lands of C.A. Warren, Wiley J. Ussery and others and containing 89 ½ acres and registered in Book EEE, pages 165 and 166. This 14 September 1866.
Reg: October 30, 1866   Signed: Richard Anderson

Page 507 - Lewis Tillman, Clk & Com. Certified Copy to R.H. Lewis (Chancery Court). Chesley Williams and William P. Cannon, executors of Robert Cannon, deceased, VS Minos T. Cannon, Mrs. Eliza J. Nelson and Mrs. Ann S. Fay. To R.H. Lewis. Sold the

tract of land No. 3, 12 acres 120 poles. The tract of land No. 3 lying on the north side of Duck River to the west of the Fayetteville Road. Adjoining Lot No. 2 purchased by Wm. Cowan and Thomas C. Whiteside, the Fayetteville Road, and to the center of Duck River. Containing 12 acres and 120 poles.
Reg: October 30, 1866   Signed: Lewis Tillman, C&M

Page 508 - Robert H. Lewis Deed to S.G. Reaves, 12 acres and 120 poles. This ___ October 1866. Both of Bedford County. Land in 7th District of Bedford County and bounded by Duck River, by the Fayetteville Road, and by Lot No. 2 purchased by William Cowan and Thomas C. Whiteside of Lewis Tillman. This ___ October 1866.
Reg: October 30, 1866   Signed: R.H. Lewis

Page 509 - John A. King, Discharge. John A. King a Private of 2nd Lt. Gabriel T. Johnson's Company (I) 5th Regiment of Cavalry Tennessee Volunteers who was enrolled on the 18th day of January 1863 to serve three years or during the war is hereby discharged from the service of the United States this 14th day of August 1865 at Pulaski, Tennessee by reason of Special Order No. 18 C.S. Mil Div Tenn. No objection to his being re-enlisted is known to exist. Said John A. King was born in Bedford County, Tennessee is thirty two years of age, five feet ten inches high, fair complexion, blue eyes, light hair and by occupation when enrolled a farmer. Given at Pulaski, Tennessee. This 14th day of August 1865.
Francis Jackson, Captain   Gabriel Johnson, 2nd Lt.
Oath of Identity - John A. King of the Town of Shelbyville, Bedford County on 28 day of October 1866 personally appeared before me the undersigned a Justice of the Peace for said County and State. John A. King who being duly sworn according to law declares that he is the identical John A. King who was a Private in the Company commanded by Captain R.C. Couch in the Regiment 5th commanded by J. Clift, Lieut., that he enlisted on the 18 day of January 1863 for the term of three years and was discharged at Pulaski, Tennessee on the 14th day of August 1865 by reason of Special Order No. 18 C.S. Mil Div Tenn.
Reg: October 30, 1866   Signed: Jno. A. King

Page 510 - William R. Dixon, Discharge. William R. Dixon, a Sergeant of Capt. H.N.T. Shipp Company (C) 5th Regiment of Tennessee Cavalry Volunteers who was enrolled on the 4th day of September 1862 to serve three years or during the war, is hereby discharged from the service of the United States this 25th day of June 1865 at Fayetteville, Tennessee by reason of Special Order No. 83 War Dept. May 8th 1865. No objection to his being re-enlisted is known to exist. Said William R. Dixon was born in Bedford County, Tennessee is nineteen years of age, five feet eleven inches high, fair complexion, gray eyes, dark heir and by occupation when enrolled a farmer. Given at Fayetteville, Tennessee this 25th day of June 1865.
Francis Jackson, Captain   Heartwell N.T. Shipp, Capt.
Oath of Identity - William R. Dixon of the Town of Shelbyville, Bedford County, Tennessee, on this 27th day of October 1866 appeared before me the undersigned a Justice of the Peace for

the County and State aforesaid. William R. Dixon, who being
duly sworn according to law, declared that he is the identical
William R. Dixon who was a Sergeant in the Company commanded by
Captain H.N.T. Shipp in the Regiment commanded by Lt. Clift that
he enlisted on the 4th day of September 1862 for the Town of
three years and was discharged at Fayetteville, Tennessee on the
25th day of June 1865 by reason of General Order No. 83 War
Dept. May 8, 1865.
Reg: October 31, 1866   Signed: Wm. R. Dixon

Page 511 - James M. Reed, Discharge. James M. Reed, a Private
of Captain Reuben C. Couch Company (F) 5th Regiment of Tennessee
Cavalry Volunteers who was enrolled on the 6th day of September
1862 to serve three years or during the war, is hereby
discharged from the services of the United States this 25th day
of June 1865 at Fayetteville, Tennessee by reason of General
Order No. 83 dated War Dept. May 8, 1865. No objection to his
being re-enlisted is known to exist. Said John M. Reed was born
in Bedford County, Tennessee is twenty three years of age, five
feet five inches high, fair complexion, gray eyes, dark hair and
by occupation when enrolled a farmer. Given at Fayetteville,
Tennessee, this 25 day of June 1865.
Francis Jackson, Captain   Reuben C. Couch, Captain
Oath of Identity - James M. Reed of the Town of Shelbyville,
County of Bedford in the State of Tennessee on this 25th day of
June in the year 1865 personally appeared before me the
undersigned a Justice of the Peace for the County and State
above mentioned. James M. Reed who being duly sworn according
to law declared that he is the identical James M. Reed who was a
Private in the Company commanded by Captain R.C. Couch Co. (F)
in the Regiment 5th Tenn. Commanded by Col. R. Galbraith that he
enlisted on the 5th day of September 1862 for the term of three
years or during the war and was discharged at Fayetteville,
Tennessee on the 25th day of June 1865 by reason of General
Order No. 83 dated War Dept. May 8th 1865.
Reg: October 31, 1866   Signed: James M. Reed

Page 512 - Ziza Moore Deed to M.B. Dameron, 150 acres. I, Ziza
Moore, have this day sold unto Elizabeth Dameron, M.B. Dameron
and Nancy E. Dameron and their heirs a tract of land in Bedford
County and District No.9, containing 150 acres and bounded by
Anderson Landers' corner, by George S. Landers, deceased, old
tract of land, by E. Kimmons' old tract of land, and by William
Brown's line. Being 42 ½ acres of this land to descend to
Elizabeth Dameron and Nancy E. Dameron equally and remainder to
M.B. Dameron. This September 11, 1866.
Wit: E.C. Landers   Signed: Ziza Moore
     S.L. Landers
Reg: October 31, 1866

Page 513 - H.L.W. Bearden, Discharge. Hugh L.W. Bearden, a
Private of Captain Reuben C. Couch's Company (F) 5th Regiment of
Tennessee Cavalry Volunteers who was enrolled on the 6th day of
September 1863 to serve three years or during the war, is hereby
discharged from the service of the United States this 25th day

of June 1865 at Fayetteville, Tennessee by reason of General Order No. 83 dated May 8, 1865. No objection to his being re-enlisted is known to exist. Said Hugh L.W. Bearden was born in Bedford County, Tennessee, is eighteen years of age, five feet nine inches high, fair complexion, gray eyes, black hair and by occupation when enlisted a farmer. Given at Fayetteville, Tennessee this 25th day of June 1865.

Francis Jackson, Captain   Reuben C. Couch, Captain

Oath of Identity - Hugh L.W. Bearden of the Town of Shelbyville, Bedford County, Tennessee, on this 21st day of August 1866 personally appeared before me the undersigned a Justice of the Peace for the County and State above mentioned. Hugh L.W. Bearden who being duly sworn according to law declares that he is the identical Hugh L.W. Bearden who was a Private in the Company commanded by Captain Reuben C. Couch in the Regiment commanded by Joseph Clift. That he enlisted on the 6th day of September 1862 for the term of three years and was discharged at Fayetteville, Tennessee on the 25th day of June 1865 by reason of General Order No. 83, date War Dept. May 8th 1865.

Reg: November 8, 1866   Signed: Hugh L.W. Bearden

Page 514 - R.S. Dwiggins Trust Deed to P.D. Marony. I, Robert S. Dwiggins, have this day sold unto P.D. Marony ten thousand pounds of seed cotton, all of the corn and hay and oats on my premises either on the place known as the home or the Newsom place. Also one bay horse, also sixty heard of pork hogs now on my home place. I am indebted to R.H. Sims as executor of B.C. Owens. This October 31, 1866.

Reg: November 1, 1866   Signed: R.S. Dwiggins

Page 514 - William H. Mathews and others, Agreement, to Robert Mathews. Whereas Robert Mathews of Bedford County, a Commissioner, to sell the slaves belonging to the estate and the heirs at law of Andrew Mathews, deceased, late of Bedford County. Rebecca Mathews, administratrix on said estate. Said Commissioner was duly appointed guardian &c for all the minor heirs of said deceased by the County Court of Bedford County in the year 1859. All claims to the above for the benefit of said estate therefore we, William H. Mathews and Arthur P. Mathews promise and pledge aforesaid for the said Robert Mathews and Rebecca Mathews, the widow of said deceased, having sold all interest in the estate of the said deceased, except her dower in the home place. This 1 November 1866. NOTE: A very long document.

Wit: M.B. Moorman   Signed: Wm. H. Mathews
     N.F. Thompson   Arthur P. Mathews
Reg: November 2, 1866   Rebecca Mathews

Page 517 - Frank Hodgkins Trust Deed to R.C. White. I, Frank Hodgkins, have sold unto Robert C. White all my stock of Brood mares and merchandise, furniture and fixtures at my store house and bakery in the Town of Shelbyville including the bill of merchandise purchased from Messers Gardner & Co. on the 26th day of October 1866. I am indebted to said White by judgment rendered 31 October 1866 by Moses Marshall and to George W.

Buchanan and to Henry Berry, and to John Wortham.   This 1
November 1866.
Reg: November 2, 1866   Signed: Frank Hodgkins

Page 518 - G.W. Thompson Deed to J.M. Brown. Land in Bedford
County and District No. 3 and bounded by Lot No. 20 sold by
Lewis Tillman, Clerk & Master, as the property of Robert Cannon,
deceased, in September 1866 and purchased by me at the sale.
Containing 20 acres and 40 poles. This 6 April 1866.
Wit: Wm. S. Jett   Signed: G.W. Thompson
     Wm. T. Lane
Reg: November 2, 1866

Page 519 - James H. Ogilvie Deed to J.P. Hutton, 73 acres.   I,
James H. Ogilvie, have sold unto J.P. Hutton of Bedford County
land being in District No. 5 and it being the land allotted to
the heirs of James Ogilvie, deceased, in the division of his
estate in November 1864 and which I am the owner by right of
division of one share in said land and by purchase of two other
tracts the deeds of which have been acknowledged and registered.
Number first as Lot No. 1 adjoining the corner of the dower and
George Bell, and by the center of the Shelbyville and
Murfreesboro Turnpike.   Containing 18 acres.   Lot No. 2
containing 27 acres and bounded by Lot No. 1.   Lot No. 4
adjoining a corner of Lot No. 3, by B.F. Whitworth, and by the
dower.   Containing 28 acres making in all 73 acres.   This
November 2, 1866.
Reg: November 3, 1866   Signed: J.H. Ogilvie

Page 520 - Sarah H. Ogilvie Deed to J.P. Hutton, 37 acres.   I,
Sarah H. Ogilvie of Bedford County, have sold unto J.P. Hutton
land in said county and lying and being in Civil District No. 5,
the same being the portion of the land allotted to me in the
division of the estate of James Ogilvie, deceased. Said Lot No.
3 and bounded by Lot No. 2. Containing 37 acres. This November
5, 1866.
Reg: November 5, 1866   Signed: S.H. Ogilvie

Page 521 - Herod J.M. Holt, Discharge - Herod J.M. Holt, a
Private in Captain James Clift's Company (M) 5th Regiment of
Tennessee Cavalry Volunteers who was enrolled on the 18th day of
May 1863 to serve three years or during the war, is hereby
discharged from the service of the United States this 14th day
of August 1865 at Pulaski, Tennessee by reason of Special Order
No. 18 C.S. Mil Div Tenn. No objection to his being re-enlisted
known to exist.   Said Herod J.M. Holt was born in Bedford
County, Tennessee is thirty four years of age, six feet high,
dark complexion, black eyes, black heir and by occupation when
enrolled a farmer. Given at Pulaski, Tennessee. This 14th day
of August 1865.
Francis Jackson, Captain   James Clift, Captain
Oath of Identity - Herod J.M. Holt of the Town of ___ Bedford
County, Tennessee on this 3rd day of November 1866 personally
appeared before me the undersigned a Justice of the Peace for

the County and state above mentioned. Herod J.M. Holt who being duly sworn according to law declared that he is the identical Herod J.M. Holt who was a Private in the Company commanded by Captain James Clift in the Regiment commanded by Joseph Clidt, that he enlisted on the 18th day of May 1863 for the term of three years and was discharged at Pulaski, Tennessee on 14th August 1865 by reason of Special Order.
Reg: 3 November 1866   Signed: H.J.M. Holt

Page 521 - Charles B. King, Discharge - Charles B. King a Private of Captain Reuben C. Couch Company (C) 5th Regiment of Tennessee Cavalry Volunteers, who was enrolled on the 7th day of September 1862 to serve three years or during the war is hereby discharged from the service of the United States, this 25th day of June 1865 at Fayetteville, Tennessee by reason of General Order No. 83 dated War Dept. May 8th 1865. No. 83.
Reg: November 5, 1866   Signed: Charles B. King

Page 522 - A.P. Eakin and John P. Steele, Executors &c Deed to J.L. Scudder. This 9 June 1860 Sarah E. Gilliland sold to A,P. Eakin a lot of land then having a house upon it, two acres in the Camp White near the Town of Shelbyville, Bedford County and bounded by S.S. M(illegible)'s corner. Containing 2 acres being the lot purchased by said Gilliland from Lucretia Eakin 2 December 1859. This November 3, 1866.
Reg: November 6, 1866   Signed: A.P. Eakin
                                       John P. Steele, Exrs.

523 - James K.P. Harmon, Discharge - James K.P. Harmon, Bugler of Captain Reuben C. Couch Company (F) 5th Regiment of Tennessee Cavalry Volunteers who was enrolled on the 7th day of September 1862 to serve three years or during the wat, is hereby discharged from the service of the United States, this 25th day of June 1865 at Fayetteville, Tennessee by reason of General order No. 83 dates War Dept. May 8th 1865. No objection to his being re-enlisted is known to exist. Said J.K.P. Harmon was born in Bedford County, Tennessee is twenty three years of age, five feet seven inches high, dark complexion, black eyes, dark hair and by occupation a farmer. Given at Fayetteville, Tennessee. This 25th June 1865.
Francis Jackson, Captain   Reuben C. Couch, Captain
James K.P. Harmon of the Town of Shelbyville, Bedford County on the 25th day of July 1865 personally appeared before me the undersigned a Justice of the Peace for the County and State above mentioned. James K.P. Harmon who being duly sworn according to law declared that he is the identical James K.P. Harmon who was a Bugler in the Company commanded by Captain Reuben C. Couch in the Regiment of Cavalry commanded by Col. Robt. Galbraith, that he enlisted on the 7th day of September 1862 for the term of three years or during the war and was discharged at Fayetteville, Tennessee on the 25th day of June 1865 by reason of General Order No. 83 dated War Dept. May 8th 1865.
Reg: November 6, 1866   Signed: James K.P. Harmon

Page 524 - W.L. Riggins Trust Deed to Hardy Prince. Normandy, November 5th 1866. I promise to pay Hardy Prince and do hereby give to said Hardy Prince a lien of my interest in a tract of land being in Bedford County and known as the John F. Weaver tract of land, the Cole Tract of land containing 70 acres and being the place I now live on, my interest being about 33 acres.
Wit: R.L. Landers   Signed: W.L. Riggins
     D.C. Word
Reg: November 6, 1866

Page 525 - James N. Solomon, Discharge - James N. Solomon a Private of Captain James Clift Company (M) 5th Regiment of Tennessee Cavalry Volunteers who was enrolled on the 20th day of August 1863 to serve three years or during the war is hereby discharged from the service of the United States this 14th day of August 1865 at Pulaski, Tennessee by reason of Special Order No. 18 C.S. Mil Div Tenn. No objection to his being re-enlisted is known to exist. Said James N. Solomon was born in Bedford County, Tennessee is nineteen years of age, five feet ten inches high, fair complexion, gray eyes, light hair and by occupation when enrolled a farmer. Given at Pulaski, Tennessee this 14th day of August 1865.
Francis Jackson, Captain   James Clift, Captain
Oath of Identity - James N. Solomon of the Town of Shelbyville, Bedford County on this 9th day of October 1865 personally appeared before me the undersigned a Justice of the Peace for the County and State above mentioned. James Solomon who being duly sworn according to law declares that he is the identical man who was a Private in the Company commanded by Captain James F. Clift in the Regiment 5 Tenn. commanded by Joseph Clift that he enlisted on the 20th day of August 1863 for the term of three years and was discharged at Nashville on the 14th day of August 1865 by reason of proper authority.
Reg: November 12, 1866   Signed: James N. Solomon

Page 526 - William M. Marly Discharge.
Battles of the 89th Illinois Volunteers
Stone River   Pickett's Mill
Liberty Gap   Pine Top Mountain
Chickamauga   Kenesaw Mount.
Chattanooga   Chattahoochee
Orchard Knob   Peach Tree Creek
Missionary Ridge   Atlanta
Knoxville   Jonesboro, Ga.
Rocky Face Ridge   Lovejoy Station
Resaca, Ga.   Franklin
Dallas, Ga.   Nashville
William M. Marly, a Private of Captain James F. Clift Company (F) 89th Regiment of Illinois Infantry Volunteers who was enrolled on the 17th day of August 1862 to serve three years or during the war, is hereby discharged from the service of the United States this 4th day of June 1865 at Nashville, Tennessee in accordance with instructions from War Dept. No objection to his being re-enlisted is known to exist. Said Private Marly was born in Calvin in the State of Illinois is thirty one years of age, five feet seven five-eighth inches high, dark complexion,

black eyes, black hair and by occupation when enrolled a blacksmith. Given at Nashville, Tenn. This 10th day of June 1865.

> David A. Geiger, Captain of
> 15th Ohil V. A.C.M.
> 3rd Div 4th A Co. Mustering
> officer.

Oath of Identity - William M. Marly of the Town of Shelbyville, Bedford County, Tennessee, on this 12th day of November 1866 personally appeared before me the undersigned a Justice of the Peace for the County and State above mentioned. Wm. M. Marly who being duly sworn according to law declares that he is the identical Wm. M. Marly who was a Private in the Company commanded by Captain James F. Clift in the Regiment Infantry commanded by Col. Chas. Hodgkin, that he enlisted on the 15th day of August 1862 for the term of three years and was discharged at Nashville, Tennessee on the 10th day of June 1865 by reason of order from War Dept.

Reg: November 12, 1866   Signed: William M. Marly

Page 527 - Ezekiel M. Lacy Discharge - Ezekiel M. Lacy a Private of Captain R.C. Couch Company (F) 5th Regiment of Tennessee Cavalry Volunteers, who was enrolled on the 6th day of September 1862 to serve three years or during the war is hereby discharged from the service of the United States by reason of gun shot wound through his neck received at Shelbyville, Tennessee June 27th 1863. No objection to his being re-enlisted is known to exist. Said E.M. Lacy was born in Randolph City in the State of North Carolina is thirty seven years of age, six feet one inch high, dark complexion, blue eyes, light hair and by occupation when enrolled a farmer. Given at Nashville, Tenn. This 24th day of February 1864.

> Robt. Galbraith, Lt. Col.
> Commanding the Detachment

Oath of Identity - E.M. Lacy of the Town of Shelbyville, Bedford County, Tennessee, on this 13th day of November 1866 personally appeared before me the undersigned a Justice of the Peace for said County and State above mentioned who being duly sworn according to law declares that he is the identical E.M. Lacy who was a Private in the Company commanded by Captain R.C. Couch in the Regiment commanded by Lt. Col. R. Galbraith that he enlisted on the 6th day of September 1862 for the term of three years and was discharged at Nashville on the 24th day of February 1864 by reason of gunshot wound received while in service.

Reg: November 13, 1866   Signed: E.M. Lacy

Page John P. Phillips Discharge - John P. Phillips a Private of Captain Wm. A. Rickman Company (H) 5th Regiment of Tennessee Cavalry Volunteers who was enrolled on the 10th day of November 1862 to serve three years or during the war is hereby discharged from the service of the United States this 14th day of August 1865 at Pulaski, Tennessee by reason of Special Order No. 18 C.S. Mil Div Tenn. No objection to his being re-enlisted is known to exist. Said John P. Phillips was born in Rutherford County, Tennessee is thirty eight years of age, six feet two inches high, fair complexion, blue eyes, dark hair and by occupation when enrolled a farmer. Given at Pulaski, Tenn. This 14th day of August 1865.

Francis Jackson, Captain   W.O. Richman, Captain

Oath of Identity - John P. Phillips of the Town of Shelbyville, Bedford County, Tennessee on this 13th day of November 1866 personally appeared before me the undersigned a Justice of the Peace for the County and State above mentioned.   John P. Phillips who being duly sworn according to law declares that he is the identical John P. Phillips who was a Private in the Company commanded by Captain Wm. O. Rickman in the Regiment commanded by Col. Galbraith, that he enlisted on the 8th day of November 1862 for the term of three years and was discharged at Pulaski, Tenn. On 14th day of August 1865 by reason of Special Order No. 18.

Reg: November 13, 1866   Signed: John P. Phillips

Page 528 - Wm. C. Blanton Deed to B.F. Duggan, Sr., two lots. Both of Bedford County. Two lots or parcel of land lying in Bedford County and District No. 11 and in the Village of Unionville and bounded by Lot No. 1, near the turnpike, by J.W. Clary's store lot, by Duggan's lot on which he now lives, by a corner of the M.P. Church lot, and by a lane running from B. Blanton's to said church lot, and by a lot owned by P. Barron. Containing 3 ¾ acres. Lot No. 2, adjoining Duggan's lot, by E. Blanton's corner, and by M. Blanton's line.   Containing 1 ¼ acres. This August 31, 1866.

Wit: Robert Allison   Signed: W.C. Blanton
     J.T. Williams
Reg: November 13, 1866

Page 529 - M.W. Turner and wife Deed to J.D. Webb, undivided interest. We, Mary Ann Turner and M.W. Turner have sold unto J.D. Webb all the right title claim and interest which we have in and unto the dower part of the land owned by the late James H. Clark, deceased, and bounded by lands of J.D. Webb, and by lands of P. Frazier's land.   Containing 65 acres and our interest being the 1/11 part. This 6 November 1865.

Reg: November 14, 1866   Signed: M.W. Turner
                                     Mary Ann Turner

Page 530 - William E. Bearden Discharge - William E. Bearden a Sergeant of Captain Reuben C. Couch Company (A) 5th Regiment of Tennessee Cavalry Volunteers who was enrolled on the 6th day of September 1862 to serve three years or during the war is hereby discharged from the service of the United States this 25th day of June 1865 at Fayetteville, Tennessee by reason of General Order No. 83 dated War Dept. May 8th 1865. No objection to his being re-enlisted is known to exist. Said William E. Bearden was born in Bedford County, Tennessee is twenty years of age, five feet seven inches high, fair complexion, blue eyes, light hair and by occupation when enrolled a farmer.   Given at Fayetteville, Tenn. This 25th day of June 1865.

Francis Jackson, Captain   Reuben C. Couch, Captain

Oath of Identity - William E. Bearden of the Town of Shelbyville, Bedford County, Tennessee on this 15th day of

November 1866 personally appeared before me the undersigned a Justice of the Peace for said County and State above mentioned. William E. Bearden who being duly sworn according to law declares that he is the identical William E. Bearden who was a Sergeant in the Company commanded by Captain R.C. Couch in the Regiment commanded by Col. W.B. Stokes, that he enlisted on the 6th day of September 1862 for the term of three years and was discharged at Fayetteville, Tennessee on the 25th day of June 1865 by reason of General Order No. 83 dated War Dept. May 8th 1865.

Reg: November 15, 1866   Signed: William E. Bearden

Page 531 – Cohn & Strossman Trust Deed to Kuhn & Netter & Co. and others. We have sold unto Kuhn Netter & Co. of the City oc Cincinnatti, Ohio and to Joseph D. Wilhoite of the Town of Shelbyville, all of our stock of goods, wares, merchandise of every kind consisting of prints, shoes, boots, clothing, groceries &c in our store house of business situated in the Town of Shelbyville, Bedford County. H. Frankle and S. Rothchild, securities. NOTE: A very long document. This 16 November 1866.

Reg: November 16, 1866   Signed: Cohn & Strossman
                                       Gabriel Cohn
                                       Adolphus Strossman

Page 533 – B.M. Tillman Deed to Lavina . Pittman, Town Lot. I, Barclay M. Tillman, have sold unto John J. Pittman, she the said Lavina S. Pittman together with her husband the said John J. Pittman, a tract of land a house and lot and improvements in the Town of Shelbyville, Bedford County and being a part of Lot No. 43 and bounded by the street from Martin or Pike Streets, by the corner of the coal house. This 9 November 1866.

Wit: Lewis Tillman   Signed: Barclay M. Tillman
     J.A. Couch
Reg: November 16, 1866

Page 534 – John A. Couch, Discharge – John A. Couch a Saddler of Captain Reuben C. Couch Company (F) 5th Regiment of Tennessee Cavalry Volunteers who was enrolled on the 6th day of September 1862 to serve three years or during the war is hereby discharged from the service of the United States this 25th day of June 1865 at Fayetteville, Tennessee by reason of General Order No. 83 dated War Dept May 8th 1865. No objection to his being re-enlisted is known to exist. Said John A. Couch was born in Bedford County is thirty years of age, five feet eight inches high, fair complexion, blue eyes, light hair and by occupation when enrolled a farmer. Given at Fayetteville, Tenn. This 25th June 1865.

Francis Jackson, Captain   Reuben C. Couch, Captain

Oath of Identity – John A. Couch of the Town of ___, Bedford County, Tennessee on this 15th day of June 1866 personally appeared before me the undersigned a Justice of the Peace for the County and State above mentioned. John A. Couch who being duly sworn according to law declares that he is the identical John A. Couch who was a Saddler in the Company commanded by Captain Reuben C. Couch in the Regiment 5th Tenn. Commanded by

___ that he enlisted on the 6th day of September 1862 for the term of three years and was discharged at Fayetteville, Tennessee on 25th June 1865 by reason of General Order No. 83.
Reg: November 16, 1866   Signed: John A. Couch

Page 535 - Lewis Williams Mortgage to Edmund Cooper. A tract of land on which I am living and being the tract of land conveyed to me by my father John Williams, Sr., by Deed of Gift and which money was paid by said Cooper to Thomas J. Williams in payment of a debt which he had against my father John Williams, Sr. and which lands adjoins the land of S.A. Blakemore, by the lands of M. Shearin, by the lands of Green Newsom, and by the lands of Benj. Adams. Containing 100 acres. This 22 September 1866.
Reg: November 17, 1866   Signed: Lewis Williams

Page 536 -Wiley Farmer, Discharge - Wiley Farmer a Private of Captain Reuben C. Couch Company (F) 5th Regiment of Tennessee Cavalry Volunteers who was enrolled on the 11th September 1862 to serve three years or during the war is hereby discharged from the service of the United States this 25th day of June 1865 at Fayetteville, Tennessee by reason of General Order No. 83 dated War Dept. May 8th 1865. No objection to his being re-enlisted is known to exist. Said Wiley Farmer was born in Marion County, Tennessee is forty years of age, five feet seven inches high, fair complexion, blue eyes, dark hair and by occupation when enrolled a farmer. Given at Fayetteville, Tenn. this 25th day of June 1865.
Francis Jackson, Captain   Reuben C. Couch, Captain
Oath of Identity - Wiley Farmer of the Town of Shelbyville, Bedford County, Tennessee on the 17th day of November 1866 personally appeared before me the undersigned a Justice of the Peace for the County and State above mentioned. Wiley Farmer who being duly sworn according to law declares that he is the identical Wiley Farmer who was a Private in the Company commanded by Captain R.C. Couch in the Regiment Cavalry commanded by Col. R. Galbraith that he enlisted on the 11th day of September 1862 for the term of three years and was discharged at Fayetteville, Tenn. on the 25th June 1865 by reason of General Order No. 83 War Dept. May 8th 1865.
Reg: November 17, 1866   Signed: Wiley Farmer

Page 537 - James M. Lusk, Discharge - James M. Lusk a Corporal of Captain James Clift Company (H) 5th Regiment of Tennessee Cavalry Volunteers who was enrolled on the 14th day of September 1863 to serve three years or during the war is hereby discharged from the service of the United States. This 14th day of August 1865 at Pulaski, Tenn. by reason of Special Order No. 18 C.S. Mil Div Tenn. No objection to his being re-enlisted is known to exist. Said James M. Lusk was born in Hamilton County, Tennessee is twenty one years of age, five feet nine inches high, fair complexion, blue eyes, fair hair and by occupation when enrolled a farmer. Given at Pulaski, Tenn. This 4th day of August 1865.
Francis Jackson, Captain   James Clift, Captain

Oath of Identity - John M. Lusk of the Town of Shelbyville, Bedford County, Tennessee on this 17th day of November 1866 personally appeared before me the undersigned a Justice of the Peace for the County and State above mentioned. James M. Lusk who being duly sworn according to law declared that he is the identical James M. Lusk who was a Corporal in the Company commanded by Captain James Clift in the Regiment Cavalry commanded by Col. R. Galbraith that he enlisted on the 14th day of september 1863 for the term of three years and was discharged at Pulaski on the 14th day of August 1865 by reason of Special Order No. 18 Mil Div Tenn.
Reg: November 17, 1866   Signed: James M. Lusk

Page 537 - Robert C. Maupin, Discharge - Robert C. Maulin a Sergeant of Captain Reuben C. Couch Company (F) 5th Regiment of Tenn. Cavalry Volunteers who was enrolled on the 6th day of September 1862 to serve three years or during the war is hereby discharged from the service of the Unites States this 25th day of June 1865 at Fayetteville, Tenn. by reason of General Order No. 83 dated War Dept. May 8th, 1865. No objection to his being re-enlisted is known to exist. Said Robert C. Maupin was born in Bedford County, Tennessee is twenty eight years of age, six feet high, fair complexion, blue eyes, light hair and by occupation when enrolled a farmer. Given at Fayetteville, Tenn, 25th day of June 1865.
Francis Jackson, Captain   R.C. Couch, Captain
Oath of Identity - R.C. Maupin of the Town of Shelbyville, Bedford County, Tennessee on the 7th day of July 1865 personally appeared before me the undersigned a Justice of the Peace for the County and State above mentioned. Robert C. Maupin who being duly sworn according to law declares that he is the identical Robert C. Maupin who was a Corporal in the Company commanded by Captain Reuben C. Couch in the Regiment 5th Cavalry commanded by Lt. W.J. Clift that he enlisted on the 6th day of September 1862 for the term of three years and was discharged at Fayetteville, Tenn. on 25th June 1865 by reason of General Order No. 83 dated War Dept. May 8th 1865.
Reg: November 17, 1866   Signed: Robert C. Maupin

Page 538 - George W. Burrow, Discharge - George W. Burrow a Sergeant of Captain Reuben C. Couch Company (F) 5th Regiment of Tennessee Cavalry Volunteers who was enrolled on the 7th day of September 1862 to serve three years or during the war is hereby discharged from the service of the United States this 25th day of June 1865 at Fayetteville, Tennessee by reason of General Order No. 83 dated War Dept. May 8th 1865. No objection to his being re-enlisted is known to exist. Said George W. Burrow was born in Bedford County, Tennessee is twenty one years of age, five feet six inches high, fair complexion, blue eyes, light hair and by occupation when enrolled a farmer. Given at Fayetteville, Tenn. This 25th day of June 1865.
Francis Jackson, Captain   Reuben C. Couch, Captain
Oath of Identity - George W. Burrow of the Town of Shelbyville, Bedford County, Tennessee on this 17th day of November 1866 personally appeared before me the undersigned a Justice of the Peace for the County and State above mentioned. George W.

Burrow who being duly sworn according to law declares that he is the identical George W. Burrow who was a Sergeant in the Company commanded by Captain Reuben C. Couch in the Regiment commanded by ____ that he enlisted on the 7th day of September 1862 for the term of three years and was discharged at Fayetteville, Tennessee on the 25th day of June 1865 by reason of General Order No. 83 War Dept. May 8th 1865.
Reg: November 17, 1866   Signed: George W. Burrow

Page 539 - Daniel M. Jenkins, Discharge - Daniel M. Jenkins a Private of Captain Reuben C. Couch Company (F) 5th regiment of Tennessee Cavalry Volunteers who was enrolled on the 10th day of September 1862 to serve three years or during the war is hereby discharged from the service of the Unites States this 25th day of June 1865 at Fayetteville, Tenn. by reason of Order from War Dept. No objection to his being re-enlisted known to exist. Said Daniel M. Jenkins was born in Bedford County, Tennessee is twenty three years of age, six feet high, fair complexion, blue eyes, black hair and by occupation when enrolled a farmer. Given at Nashville, Tenn. this 20th July 1865 in accordance with c(illegible) of June29, 1865 near Depot also …
                    Cyrus H. Grass, Captain
Oath of Identity - Daniel M. Jenkins of the Town of Shelbyville, Bedford County, Tennessee on this 30th day of April 1866 personally appeared before me the undersigned a Justice of the Peace for the County and State above mentioned.   Daniel M. Jenkins who being duly sworn according to law declared that he is the identical Daniel M. Jenkins who was a Private in the Company commanded by Captain Reuben C. Couch in the Regiment commanded by Lt. Col. W.J. Clift that he enlisted on the 10th day of September 1862 for the term of three years and was discharged at Fayetteville, Tenn. on the 25th day of June 1865 by reason of Order from War Dept.
Reg: November 17, 1866   Signed: Daniel M. Jenkins

Page 540 - James R. Burrow, Discharge - James R. Burrow a 1st Sergeant of Captain Reuben C. Couch Company (F) 5th Regiment of Tennessee Cavalry Volunteers who was enrolled on the 6th day of September 1862 to serve three years or during the war is hereby discharged from the service of the United States this 25th day of June 1865 at Fayetteville, Tenn, by reason of General Order No. 83 dated War Dept. May 8th 1865. No objection to his being re-enlisted is known to exist. Said James R. Burrow was born in Bedford County, Tennessee is thirty two years of age, five feet seven and one half inches high, fair complexion, blue eyes, dark hair and by occupation when enrolled a farmer.   Given at Fayetteville, Tenn. this 25th day of June 1865.
Francis Jackson, Captain   R.C. Couch, Captain
Oath of Identity - James R. Burrow of the Town of Shelbyville, Bedford County, Tennessee on this 17th day of November 1866 personally appeared before me the undersigned a Justice of the Peace for the County and State above mentioned. James R. Burrow who being duly sworn according to law declared that he is the identical James R. Burrow who was a 1st Sergeant in the Company commanded by Captain R.C. Couch in the Regiment commanded by ____ that he enlisted on the 6th day of September 1862 for the term

of three years and was discharged at Fayetteville, Tennessee on the 25th day of June 1865 by reason of General Order No. 83 War Dept. May 8, 1866.
Reg: November 17, 1866   Signed: James R. Burrow

Page 541 - Nimrod C. Burrow, Discharge - Nimrod C. Burrow a Private of Captain Reuben C. Couch Company (F) 5th Regiment of Tennessee Cavalry Volunteers who was enrolled on the 6th day of September 1862 to serve three years or during the war is hereby discharged from the service of the United States this 25th day of June 1865 at Fayetteville, Tennessee by reason of General Order No. 83 dated War Dept. May 8, 1865. No objection to his being re-enlisted is known to exist. Said Nimrod C. Burrow was born in Bedford County, Tennessee is nineteen years of age, five feet eight inches high, fair complexion, blue eyes, light hair and by occupation when enrolled a farmer.   Given at Fayetteville, Tennessee this 25th day of June 1865.
Francis Jackson, Captain   Reuben C. Couch, Captain
Oath of Identity - Nimrod C. Burrow of the Town of Shelbyville, Bedford County, Tennessee on this 17th day of November 1866 personally appeared before me the undersigned a Justice of the Peace for the County and State above mentioned who being duly sworn according to law declared that he is the identical Nimrod C. Burrow. Nimrod C. Burrow was a Private in the Company commanded by Captain Reuben C. Burrow in the Regiment commanded by ___ that he enlisted on the 6th day of September 1862 for the term of three years and was discharged at Fayetteville, Tennessee on the 25th day of June 1865 by reason of General Order No. 83 War Dept. May 8th, 1865.
Reg: November 17, 1866   Signed: Nimrod C. Burrow

Page 542 - Franklin L. Chandler, Discharge - Franklin L. Chandler a Corporal of Captain Reuben C. Couch Company (F) 5th Regiment of Tennessee Cavalry Volunteers who was enrolled on the 6th day of September 1862 to serve three years or during the war is hereby discharged from the service of the United States this 25th day of June 1865 at Fayetteville, Tennessee by reason of General Order No. 83 dated War Dept. May 8th 1865. No objection to his being re-enlisted is known to exist. Said Franklin L. Chandler was born in Leak County in the State of Mississippi is twenty four years of age, five feet eleven inches high, fair complexion, blue eyes, light hair and by occupation when enrolled a farmer. Given at Fayetteville, Tennessee this 25th day of June 1865.
Francis Jackson, Captain   Reuben C. Couch, Captain
Oath of Identity - Franklin L. Chandler of the Town of Shelbyville, Bedford County, Tennessee on this 7th day of July 1865 personally appeared before me the undersigned a Justice of the Peace for the County and state above mentioned. Franklin L. Chandler who being duly sworn according to law declares that he is the identical Franklin L. Chandler who was a Corporal in the Company commanded by Captain Reuben C. Couch in the Regiment 5th Company commanded by Lt. Col. W.J. Clift that he enlisted on the 6th day of September 1862 for the term of three years and was discharged at Fayetteville, Tennessee on the 25th day of June

1865 by reason of General Order No. 83 dated War Dept. May 8th 1865.
Reg: November 17, 1866   Signed: Franklin L. Chandler

Page 542 - James Russ Agreement to Lewis Tillman. Whereas Lewis Tillman has paid me $150, I bind myself as Publisher of the Republican, a newspaper in the Town of Shelbyville to continue its publication weekly to the end of a half volume from its commencement and in order to secure him that I will perform my agreement to do so. This November 17, 1866.
Reg: November 19, 1866   Signed: James Russ

Page 543 - John W. F. Miller Trust Deed to John D. Allen. I have sold unto John M. Miller, as Trustee, land situated in the Village of Fairfield, Bedford County and bounded by the lands belonging to the estate of John Scott, deceased, and supposed to contain 2 acres, it being the same house and lot I purchased of Henry B(illegible) and McIntire a firm in Cincinnatti, Ohio. This 15 November 1866.
Wit: Phillip S. Scudder   Signed: John W. Miller
     James L. Scudder
Reg: November 19, 1866

Page 544 - George W. Pearson, Discharge - George W. Pearson a Private of Captain Reuben C. Couch Company (F) 5th Regiment of Tennessee Cavalry Volunteers who was enrolled on the 11th day of September 1862 to serve three years or during the war is hereby discharged from the service of the United States this 25th day of June 1865 at Fayetteville, Tennessee by reason of General Order No. 83 dated War Dept. May 8, 1865. No objection to his being re-enlisted known to exist. Said George W. Pearson was born in Walker County in the state of Georgia is eighteen years of age, five feet six inches high, fair complexion, gray eyes, dark hair and by occupation when enrolled a farmer. Given at Fayetteville, Tenn. this 25th day of June 1865.
Francis Jackson, Captain   Signed: Reuben C. Couch, Captain
Oath of Identity - George W. Pearson of the Town of Shelbyville, Bedford County, Tennessee on this 17th day of November 1866 personally appeared before me the undersigned a Justice of the Peace for the County and State above mentioned. G.W. Pearson who being duly sworn according to law declared that he is the George W. Pearson who was a Private in the company commanded by Captain R.C. Couch in the Regiment Cavalry commanded by Col. R. Galbraith that he enlisted on the 11th day of September 1862 for the term of three years and was discharged at Fayetteville, Tenn on the ___ day of _____ by reason ...
Reg: November 19, 1866   Signed: George W. Pearson

Page 545 - James H. Pearson, Discharge - James H. Pearson a Private of Captain Hartwell N.T. Shipp Company (C) Regiment of Tennessee Cavalry Volunteers who was enrolled on the 31st day of August 1863 to serve three years or during the war is hereby discharged from the service of the United States this 14th day of August 1865 at Pulaski, Tennessee by reason of Special Order

No. 18 C.S. Mil Div Tenn. No objection to his being re-enlisted is known to exist. Said James H. Pearson was born in Bedford County, Tennessee is thirty seven years of age, five feet nine inches high, fair complexion, gray eyes, sandy hair and by occupation when enrolled a farmer. Given at Pulaski, Tenn. this 14th day of August 1865.

Francis Jackson, Captain   H.N.T. Shipp, Captain

Oath of Identity - James H. Pearson of the Town of Shelbyville, Bedford County, Tennessee on this 10th day of November 1866 personally appeared before me the undersigned a Justice of the Peace for the County and State above mentioned. James H. Pearson who being duly sworn according to law declared that he is the identical James H. Pearson who was a Private in the Company commanded by Captain H.N.T. Shipp in the Regiment commanded by Lt. Col. Clift, that he enlisted on the 21st day of August for the term of three years and was discharged at Pulaski on the 14th day of August by reason of Special Order No. 18 C.S. Mil Tenn.

Reg: November 19, 1866   Signed: James H. Pearson

Page 546 · Thomas Pearson, Discharge - Thomas Pearson a Private of Captain Reuben C. Couch Company (F) 5th Regiment of Tenn. Cavalry Volunteers who was enrolled on the 11th day of September 1862 to serve three years or during the war is hereby discharged from the service of the United States this 25th day of June 1865 at Fayetteville, Tennessee by reason of General Order No. 83 dated War Dept. May 8, 1865. No objection to his being re-enlisted is known to exist. Said Thomas Pearson was born in Morgan County, Tennessee is forty four years of age, five feet ten inches high, fair complexion, blue eyes, dark hair and by occupation when enrolled a farmer. Given at Fayetteville, Tenn. this 25th day of June 1865.

Francis Jackson, Captain   Reuben C. Couch, Captain

Oath of Identity - Thomas Pearson of the Town of Shelbyville, Bedford County on this 17th day of November 1866 personally appeared before me the undersigned a Justice of the Peace for the County and state above mentioned. Thomas Pearson who being duly sworn according to law declared that he is the Thomas Pearson who was a Private in the Company commanded by Captain R.C. Couch in the Regiment Cavalry commanded by Col. R. Galbraith that he enlisted on the 11th day of September 1863 for the term of three years and was discharged at Fayetteville, Tennessee on 25th day of June 1865 by reason of General Order No. 83 War Dept. May 8th, 1865.

Reg: November 20, 1866   Signed: Thomas Pearson

Page 547 - Marion Stone, Discharge - Marion Stone a Private of Captain Reuben C. Couch Company (F) 5th Regiment of Tennessee Cavalry Volunteers who was enrolled on the 17th day of October 1863 to serve three years or during the war is hereby discharged from the service of the United States this 14th day of August 1865 at Pulaski, Tennessee by reason of Special Order No. 18 C.S. Mil Div Tenn. No objection to his being re-enlisted is known to exist. Said Marion Stone was born in Bedford County, Tennessee is nineteen years of age, five feet eight inches high, fair complexion, blue eyes, auburn hair and by occupation when

enrolled a farmer.   Given at Pulaski, Tennessee this 14th day of
August 1865.
Francis Jackson, Captain   R.C. Couch, Captain
Oath of Identity - Marion Stone of the Town of ___, Bedford
County, Tennessee on this 20th day of November 1866 personally
appeared before me the undersigned a Justice of the Peace for
the County and State above mentioned.   Marion Stone who being
duly sworn according to law that he is the identical Marion
Stone who was a Private in the Company commanded by Captain
Reuben C. Couth in the Regiment ___ commanded by ___ that he
enlisted on the 17th day of October 1863 for the term of three
years and was discharged at Pulaski, Tennessee on the 14th day
of August 1865 by reason of Special Order No. 18 Mil Div Tenn.
Reg: November 20, 1866   Signed: Marion Stone

Page 547 - Nathaniel Troup Trust Deed to Thomas W. Troup.   I,
Nathaniel Troup, have this day deeded in trust all my claim &c a
certain two horse wagon together with a certain mare mule.   This
20 November 1866.
Reg: November 20, 1866   Signed: Nathaniel Troup

Page 548 - Adam E. Gordon, Discharge - Adam E. Gordon a Corporal
of Captain Reuben C. Couch Company (F) 5th Regiment of Tennessee
Cavalry Volunteers who was enrolled on the 6th day of September
1862 to serve three years or during the war is hereby discharged
from the service of the United States this 25th day of June 1865
at Fayetteville, Tennessee by reason of General Order No. 83
dated War Dept. May 8th 1865.   No objection to his being re-
enlisted is known to exist.   Said Adam E. Gordon was born in
Bedford County, Tennessee is twenty years of age, six feet high,
fair complexion, blue eyes, light hair and by occupation when
enrolled a farmer.   Given at Fayetteville, Tenn. this 25th day
of June 1865.
Francis Jackson, Captain   Reuben C. Couch, Captain
Oath of Identity - Adam E. Gordon of the Town of Shelbyville,
Bedford County on this 21st day of August 1866 personally
appeared before me the undersigned a Justice of the Peace for
the County and State above mention.   Adam E. Gordon who being
duly sworn according to law declares that he is the identical
Adam E. Gordon who was a Corporal in the Company commanded by
Captain Reuben C. Couch in the Regiment commanded by Joseph
Clift that he enlisted on the 6th day of September 1862 for the
term of three years and was discharged at Fayetteville, Tenn. on
the 25th day of June 1865 by reason of General Order No. 83 War
Dept. date May 8, 1865.
Reg: November 21, 1866   Signed: Adam E. Gordon

Page 549 - Robert Allison Deed to Robert S. Brown, House and
Lot.   One lot in Unionville, Bedford County, Tennessee, District
No. 11.   Containing one fourth acre.   Bounded by the Unionville
Pike at the corner of Duggan's lot, and by Garrett's line.   This
October 31, 1866.
Reg: November 22, 1866   Signed: Robert Allison

Page 550 - David T. Chambers, Discharge - David T. Chambers a Private of Captain Reuben C. Couch Company (F) 5th Regiment of Tennessee Cavalry Volunteers who was enrolled on the 13th day of September 1860 to serve three years or during the war is hereby discharged from the service of the United States this 25th day of June 1865 at Fayetteville, Tennessee by reason of General Order No. 83 dated War Dept. May 8, 1865. No objection to his being re-enlisted in known to exist. Said David T. Chambers was born in Lincoln County, Tennessee is thirty two years of age, five feet six inches high, fair complexion, blue eyes, dark hair and by occupation when enrolled a ... Given at Fayetteville, Tenn. this 25th day of June 1865.

Francis Jackson, Captain   Reuben C. Couch, Captain

Oath of Identity - David T. Chambers of the Town of Unionville of Bedford County, Tennessee on the 22nd day of November 1866 personally appeared before me the undersigned a Justice of the Peace for the County and State above mentioned. D.T. Chambers who being duly sworn according to law declares that he is the identical David T. Chambers who was a Private in the Company commanded by Captain Reuben C. Couch in the Regiment commanded by Col. R. Galbraith, that he enlisted on the 13th day of September 1862 for the term of three years and was discharged at Fayetteville, Tenn. on the 25th day of June 1865 by reason of General Order No. 83 War Dept. May 8, 1865.

Reg: November 22, 1866   Signed: David T. Chambers

Page 551 - Daniel Boone Deed to Howard Boone, 287 acres. I, Daniel Boone of the County of Madison, State of Arkansas, have sold unto Howard Boone of same place a tract of land in Bedford County and lying in a south east direction from the Town of Shelbyville, ten miles from said town on the road leading from the same to Mulberry Village, and on Big Flat Creek, being the land and all the land bequeathed to me by my father William Boone, deceased. Containing 287 acres. This 17 February 1866.

Wit: John C. Garrett   Signed: Daniel Boone
     Elisha Dodson
Reg: November 23, 1866

Page 552 - Joseph Thompson, Sheriff, Deed to James C. Snell. This 21 November 1866. On the 12 April 1864, James C. Snell as the administrator of the estate of W.L. Brown, deceased, recovered a judgment against Meredith P. Gentry. There being no personal property of the defendant to be found in his county, its said Joseph Thompson on 8 June 1864 levied said execution on the following tract of land in Bedford County and bounded by the lands of John Helton, the Wash Cunningham place on which Mary Cunningham then lived, by the lands formerly belonging to Stephen Freeman's esstate, Joseph H. Cunningham's land, and the lands of John Cortner, and by Benj. F. Haslett, and by the lands of Peter Cortner, James Helton and Miles Philips, deceased. Containing 850 acres, on which M.P. Gentry then resided. This 22 November 1866.

Reg: November 23, 1866   Signed: Jo. Thompson, Sheriff

Page 553 - H.H. Elkins Deed to Elizabeth Elkins. Elizabeth Elkins VS Harrison H. Elkins was directed to convey all right title claim and interest which I have in and to the following tract of land in Bedford County. Land bounded by corner No. 2, to the widow's line, by a corner of Salem Camp Ground, and by Iverson Knott's line. Containing 45 acres and 60 poles to the said Elizabeth Elkins during her natural life and at her death to her children then living. This 22 November 1866.
Reg: November 24, 1866   Signed: H.H. Elkins

Page 554 - James E. Wadley Transfer Title Bond to L.A. Clark. I assign this title bond to L.A. Clark and authorize F.J. Harris to make said L.A. Clark a deed instead of me. The said Clark having taken up my note from said F.J. Harris and executed his own notes to said Harris. November 22, 1866.
Wit: W.T. Tune   Signed: James E. Wadley
Reg: November 24, 1866

Page 554 - A.E. Claxton and J.S. Jones Deed to James B. Jones, 50 acres. Bedford County and District No. 11, September 15, 1865. We, A.E. Claxton and J.S. Jones, sold unto James B. Jones land in Bedford County and District No. 11 and bounded by Mahulah H. Jones dower, by V. Len's boundary, and by Felix Turrentine's line. Containing 50 acres. This September 15, 1865.
Reg: November 24, 1866   Signed: A.E. Claxton
                                        J.S. Jones

Page 555 - James H. Galbreath, Discharge - James H. Galbreath a Sergeant of Captain H.N.T. Shipp Company (C) Regiment of Tennessee Cavalry Volunteers who was enrolled on the 31st July 1862 to serve three years or during the war is hereby discharged from the service of the United States this 25th day of June 1865 at Fayetteville, Tennessee by reason of General Order No. 83 War Dept. May 8th 1865. No Objection to his being re-enlisted is known to exist. Said James H. Galbreath was born in Bedford County, Tennessee is twenty one years of age, five feet eleven inches high, fair complexion, gray eyes, dark hair and by occupation when enrolled a saddler. Given at Fayetteville, Tenn. This 25th day of June 1865.
Francis Jackson, Captain   Hartewell N.T. Shipp, Captain
Oath of Identity - James H. Galbreath of the Town of Shelbyville, Bedford County, Tennessee on this 24th day of November 1866 personally appeared before me the undersigned a Justice of the Peace for the County and State above mentioned. James H. Galbreath who being duly sworn according to law declares that he is the identical James H. Galbreath who was a Sergeant in the Company commanded by Captain H.N.T. Shipp in the Regiment 5t^{h} Tenn Cavalry commanded by Robt. Galbreath that he enlisted on the 31st day of July 1862 for the term of three years and was discharged at Fayetteville, Tenn. on the 25th day of June 1865 by reason of General Order No. 83 War Dept. May 8th 1865.
Reg: November 24, 1866   Signed: James H. Galbreath

Page 556 - W.J. Sharp Trust Deed to G.P. Sharp. Land in Bedford
County and bounded by the lands of the heirs of Dill's and H.C.
Kenmore, Jasper N. Smith, by James Carothers, by lands of the
Gilchrist's, and by the heirs of Samuel Phillips in District No.
3. Containing 205 acres. Also all my undivided interest (the
former being an undivided interest) in a tract of land in said
county and District No. 3, known as the dower of the widow E.G.
Sharp now occupied by G.W. Chambers. Containing 97 acres
bounded by lands of J.N. Smith and others. Also all my interest
whatever which I have in the household and kitchen furniture and
every king of property included in an agreement made by myself
and brother and sisters for the benefit of my mother Nicy Sharp.
Also all my own household and kitchen furniture consisting of
beds, bedsteads and other property now in my possession in my
house. This 24 November 1866.
Reg: Nov 24, 1866   Signed: W.J. Sharp

Page 557 - William Campbell, admr. Deed to Robert F. Blankenship
and others. On 20 January 1859 Alfred Campbell, deceased, sold
to Wilson D. Blankenship, deceased, both then of Bedford County
a tract of land in Bedford County and bounded by a lane, to the
center of a cross lane on Barnet Stephens' line, and to the
center of a spring. Containing 42 acres and 27 poles. Alfred
Campbell departed this life intestate about the __ day of June
1863 and that his widow Sarah C. Campbell was appointed at the
April Term 1864 administrix of said estate. Wilson D.
Blankenship departed this life intestate in Bedford County in
the month of April 1863 leaving Mary Jane Blankenship his widow
and Robert F. Blankenship a son by a former marriage, Elizabeth
C. Blankenship, Marilda A. Blankenship, and James W. Blankenship
children by his last marriage, being the only children and heirs
at law. This 24 November 1866.
Reg: November 24, 1866   Signed: Wm. Campbell, admr.

Page 558 - Mary Jane Blankenship Deed to Robert Hastings. Land
in Bedford County on the waters of Big Flat Creek partly in the
22nd District and partly in the 23rd District. Containing 46 ¾
acres being the same tract assigned to Jane Hastings on which
she now resides and in which she had an interest for life. It
being my interest in said land is one half of an eighth in right
of my father Willis Hastings. This 3 November 1866.
Wit: G.W. Buchanan   Signed: Mary Jane Blankenship
     Wm. Campbell
Reg: November 24, 1866

Page 559 - James T. Snell, Discharge - James T. Snell a Private
of Capt. Reuben C. Couch Company (F) 5th Regiment of Tennessee
Cavalry Volunteers who was enrolled on the 10th day of September
1862 to serve three years or during the war is hereby discharged
from the service of the United States this 25th day of June 1865
at Fayetteville, Tennessee by reason of General Order No. 83 War
dept. May 8, 1865. No objection to his being re-enlisted is
known to exist. Said James T. Snell was born in Bedford County,
Tennessee is eighteen years of age, five feet six inches high,

fair complexion, blue eyes, and auburn hair and by occupation when enrolled a farmer. Given at Fayetteville, Tenn. this 25th day of June 1865.

Francis Jackson, Captain   Reuben C. Couch, Captain

Oath of Identity - James T. Snell of the Town of Shelbyville of Bedford County, Tennessee on the 24th day of November 1866 personally appeared before me the undersigned a Justice of the Peace for the County and State above mentioned. James T. Snell who being duly sworn according to law declares that he is the identical James T. Snell who was a Private in the Company commanded by Captain Reuben C. Couch in the Regiment commanded by ____ that he enlisted on the 10th day of September 1862 for the term of three years and was discharged at Fayetteville, Tennessee on the 5th day of June 1865 by reason of General Order No. 83 War Dept.

Reg; November 26, 1866   Signed: James T. Snell

Page 560 - Thomas J. Shoffner, Discharge - Thomas J. Shoffner a Private of Captain Reuben C. Couch Company (F) 5th Regiment of Tennessee Cavalry Volunteers who was enrolled on the 6th day of September 1862 to serve three years or during the war is hereby discharged from the service of the United States this 25th day of June 1865 at Fayetteville, Tennessee by reason of General Order No. 83 War Dept. May 8, 1865. No objection to his being re-enlisted is known to exist. Said Thomas J. Shoffner was born in Bedford County is eighteen years of age, five feet seven inches high, fair complexion, blue eyes, dark hair and by occupation when enrolled a farmer. Given at Fayetteville, Tenn. this 25th day of June 1865.

Francis Jackson, Captain   Reuben C. Couch, Captain

Oath of Identity - Thomas J. Shoffner of the Town of Shelbyville, Bedford County, Tennessee on this 24th day of November 1866 personally appeared before me the undersigned a Justice of the Peace for the County and State above mentioned. Thomas J. Shoffner who being duly sworn according to law declares that he is the identical Thomas J. Shoffner who was a Private in the Company commanded by Captain Reuben C. Couch in the Regiment 5th Tenn Cav commanded by Wm. T. Clift that he enlisted on the 6th day of September 1862 for the term of three years and was discharged at Fayetteville, Tenn. on 25th day of June 1865 by reason of General Order No. 83 War Dept. May 8, 1865.

Reg: November 26, 1866   Signed: Thomas J. Shoffner

Page 1 - A.M. Webb VS J.R. Miller, Judgment. A.M. Webb late in our Rutherford Circuit Court at Murfreesboro recovered against them on 23rd March 1866 for debt, interest and cost. This July 2, 1866.
Reg: November 26, 1866   Signed: M.L. Fletcher, Clerk

Page 1 - John R. Wright, Discharge - John R. Wright a Private of Captain James Clift Company (M) 5th Regiment of Tennessee Cavalry Volunteers who was enrolled on the 4th day of August 1863 to serve three years or during the war is hereby discharged from the service of the United States this 14th day of August 1865 at Pulaski, Tennessee by reason of Special Order No. 18 C.S. Mil Div Tenn. No objection to his being re-enlisted is known to exist. Said John R. Wright was born in Campbell County, Virginia is forty four years of age, five feet seven inches high, fair complexion, gray eyes, gray hair and by occupation when enrolled a blacksmith. Given at Pulaski, Tenn, this 14th day of August 1865.
Francis Jackson, Captain   James Clift, Captain
Oath of Identity - John R. Wright of the Town of Shelbyville, Bedford County, Tennessee on this 26th day of November 1866 personally appeared before me the undersigned a Justice of the Peace of the County and State above mentioned. John R. Wright who being duly sworn according to law declares that he is the John R. Wright who was a Private in the Company commanded by Captain Clift in the Regiment commanded by Col. W.B. Stokes, that he enlisted on the 7th day of August 1863 for the term of three years and was discharged at Pulaski, Tennessee on the 14th day of August 1865 by reason of Special Order No. 18 C.S. Mil Div Tenn.
Reg: November 26, 1866   Signed: John R. Wright

Page 2 - Jerry L. Burrow, Discharge - Jerry L. Burrow a Private of Captain James Clift Company (M) 5th Regiment of Tennessee Cavalry Volunteers who was enrolled on the 7th day of September 1863 to serve three years or during the war is hereby discharged from the service of the United States this 14th day of August 1865 at Pulaski, Tennessee by reason of Special Order No. 18 C.S. Mil Div Tenn. No objection to his being re-enlisted is known to exist. Said Jerry L. Burrow was born in Bedford County, Tennessee is forty one years of age, five feet four inches high, fair complexion, blue eyes, dark hair and by occupation when enrolled a farmer. Given at Pulaski, Tennessee this 14th day of August 1865.
Francis Jackson, Captain   James Clift, Captain
Oath of Identity - Bedford County, Tennessee on this 26th day of August 1865 personally appeared before me the undersigned a Justice of the Peace for the County and State above mentioned. Jerry L. Burrow who being duly sworn according to law declared

that he is the identical Jerry L. Burrow who was a Private in the Company commanded by Captain James Clift in the Regiment Tenn. line, commanded by W.B. Stokes, that he enlisted on the 7th day of September 1863 for the term of three years and was discharged at Pulaski, Tennessee on 14th day August (1865) by reason of Special Order No. 18.
Reg: November 26, 1866   Signed: J.L. Burrow

Page 3 - William W. Koonce, Discharge - William W. Koonce a Private of Captain Reuben C. Couch Company (F) 5th Regiment of Tennessee Cavalry Volunteers who was enrolled on the 8th day of September 1862 to serve three years or during the war is hereby discharged from the service of the United States this 25th day of June 1865 at Fayetteville, Tennessee by reason of General Order No. 83 dated War Dept. May 8th 1865. No objection to his being re-enlisted is known to exist. Said William W. Koonce was born in Bedford County, Tennessee is thirty four years of age, five feet ten inches high, fair complexion, gray eyes, dark hair and by occupation when enrolled a farmer.   Given at Fayetteville, Tennessee this 25th day of June 1865.
Francis Jackson, Captain   Reuben C. Couch, Captain
Oath of Identity - William W. Koonce of the Town of Shelbyville, Bedford County, Tennessee on this 26th day of November 1866 personally appeared before me the undersigned a Justice of the Peace for the County and State above mentioned. W.W. Koonce who being duly sworn according to law declares that he is the Wm. W. Koonce who was a Private in the Company commanded by Captain R.C. Couch in the Regiment Cavalry commanded by Col. R. Galbreath that he enlisted on the 8th day of September 1862 for the term of three years and was discharged at Fayetteville, Tennessee 25th day of June 1865 by reason of General Order No. 83 War Dept. May 8, 1865.
Reg: November 26, 1866   Signed: William W. Koonce

Page 3 - James W. Floyd, Discharge - James W. Floyd a 1st Sergeant of Captain Reuben C. Couch Company (F) 5th Regiment of Tennessee Cavalry Volunteers who was enrolled on the 14th day of October 1863 to serve three years or during the war, is hereby discharged from the service of the United States this 14th day of August 1865 at Pulaski, Tennessee by reason of Special Order No. 18 C.S. Mil Div Tenn. No objection to his being re-enlisted is known to exist.   Said James W. Floyd was born in Bedford County, Tennessee is twenty years of age, five feet (illegible) inches high, fair complexion, black eyes, red hair and by occupation when enrolled a farmer.   Given at Pulaski, Tennessee this 14th day of august 1865.
Francis Jackson, Captain   Reuben C. Couch, Captain
Oath of Identity - James W. Floyd of the Town of Shelbyville, Bedford County, Tennessee on this 26th day of November 1866 personally appeared before me the undersigned a Justice of the Peace for the County and State above mentioned.   James W. Floyd who being duly sworn according to law declares that he is the identical James W. Floyd who was a 1st Sergeant in the Company commanded by Captain R.C. Couch in the Regiment commanded by Lt. Col. C;ift, that he enlisted on the 14th day of October 1863 for the term of three years and was discharged at Pulaski, Tenn. on

14th day of August 1865 by reason of Special Order No. 18 C.S.
Mil Div Tenn.
Reg: November 26, 1866   Signed: James W. Floyd

Page 4 - W.W. Gill Deed to Edmund Cooper. Robert S. Dwiggins by
mortgage dated July 10, 1856 and registered in Bedford County
conveyed to me in trust the tract and which conveyed in trust
was by R.S. Dwiggins.   For the purpose of securing Edmund
Cooper, Henry Cooper and Winston W. Gill from liability.   I
proceeded on the Public Square in the Town of Shelbyville and
offered all the right title claim and interest which Richard S.
Dwiggins had in and to the tract of land known as R.S. Dwiggins'
home place. Containing 640 acres.   I, W.W. Gill convey unto
Edmund Cooper all the right title claim and interest which I
have in and to all the tract of land lying on both sides of the
Shelbyville and Fayetteville Turnpike Road adjoining the lands
of W.W. Gill, Leroy W. Barrett, Hiram Nease, Benjamin Little now
owned by A.M. Webb, and of the heirs of Jarrel Smith and Lewis
Hicks, being the home place of R.S. Dwiggins.   Containing 640
acres.   This 26 November 1866.
Reg: November 27, 1866   Signed: W.W. Gill

Page 5 - Samuel M. Cannon, Discharge - Samuel M. Cannon a
Corporal of Captain H.N.T. Shipp Company (C) 5th Regiment of
Tennessee Cavalry Volunteers who was enrolled on the 14th day of
August 1862 to serve three years or during the war is hereby
discharged from the service of the United States this 25th day
of June 1865 at Fayetteville, Tennessee by reason of General
Order No. 83 War Dept May 8th 1865. No objection to his being
re-enlisted is known to exist. Said Samuel M. Cannon was born
in Bedford County, Tennessee is sixteen years of age, five feet
six inches high, fair complexion, blue eyes, dark hair and by
occupation when enrolled a farmer.   Given at Fayetteville,
Tennessee this 25th June 1865.
Francis Jackson, Captain   Signed: Hartwell N.T. Shipp, Capt.
Oath of Identity - Samuel M. Cannon of the Town of Shelbyville,
Bedford County, Tennessee on this 24th day of November 1866
personally appeared before me the undersigned a Justice of the
Peace for the County and State above mentioned.   Samuel M.
Cannon who being duly sworn according to law declares that he is
the identical Samuel M. Cannon who was a Corporal in the Company
by Captain Hartwell N.T. Shipp in the Regiment Cavalry commanded
by Col. Clift that he enlisted on 14th day of August 1862 for
the term of three years and was discharged at Fayetteville,
Tenn. on 25th day of June 1865 by reason of General Order No. 83
War Dept. May 8th 1865.
Reg: November 27, 1866   Signed: Samuel M. Cannon

Page 6 - Wiley Riggins Deed to Hardy Prince, 26 acres. Land in
Bedford County and Civil District No. 25 on the waters of Gages
Creek adjoining Mathew Moss' corner of a 100 acre survey, and by
Callahan's corner.   Containing 26 acres.   This 28th day of
November 1866.
Reg: November 30, 1866   Signed: Wiley Riggins

Page 7 - William S. Jett Deed to English & Coble, House and Lot. I have sold unto P.S. English and S.D. Coble trading under the name and style of English & Coble, a house and lot in Shelbyville, Bedford County and bounded by the street running in front of Mrs. Lucretia Eakin's residence, by the street or alley running on the south side of the Dixon Academy lot, on the east by Brittain Street and on the south by Oliver Cowan's lot. This 1 July 1866.
Reg: November 30, 1866   Signed: William S. Jett

Page 7 - Joseph Thompson Deed to A.M. McElroy and others. Whereas Anderson Rucker recovered a judgment against R.B. Rucker as principal one A.M. McElroy and A.M. Webb as securities on the appeal on 12th Dacember 1865 and which came unto my hands as Sheriff on 10 May 1866 and there not being personal property of said Robert B. Rucker, I have levied on 10 May 1866 on a tract of land as the property of said R.B. Rucker, containing 462 acres lying in District No. 5 of Bedford County and bounded by lands of Benjamin F. Ransom and A.M. McElroy, by the lands of S.G. Miller, by the lands of John Claxton and Mrs. Wheeler, and by Horatio Coop and others. This 26 November 1866.
Reg: November 30, 1866   Signed: Jo. Thompson, Sheriff

Page 9 - Mike Shoffner Trust Deed to Wm. T. Tune.   Land in Bedford County and Civil District No. 3 and bounded on the south and west by Duck River, and by D.M. Shoffner, T.D. Thompson and John C. Shofner and John Booth.   Containing about 170 acres being on which I now reside. Also all my right title claim and interest the same being an undivided interest in a certain tract of land in Civil District No. 23 of Bedford County and bounded by the west by Duck River, by the south by the lands of Robert Cannon, on the east by Mrs. Johnson, and on the north by lands of Henry Cooper and Joseph Ramsey. Containing 104 acres being the same land that I and A.G. Marr purchased from the executors of Robert Cannon, deceased. Also six bales of cotton at the gin of John Norville and also a lot of cotton in the seed now at the gin of said John Norville and all the cotton in seed at my own dwelling house and included all cotton. Also named others in original document. Other names in said document were: James F. Arnold, F.F. Arnold, William J. Shofner, Loton Shofner, James E. Wadley, Newton McQuiddy, Thomasa S. Coldwell, Joel Hogg, Chesly Williams, Perkins Cannon, Moses Marshall, Lewis Tillman, William B.M. Brame, Wm. J. Whitthorne, John P. Steele, William H. Wisener, E. Cooper, John Stephens, and W.T. Tune. NOTE: A very long document. This 29 November 1866.
Reg: December 1, 1866   Signed: Mike Shofner

Page 11 - C.P. Houston Deed to R.W. Houston.   For the love and affection I have to my son R.W. Houston, I give and convey a tract of land in Bedford County adjoining my north east corner, then the north east corner of a 100 acre tract this day conveyed by me to William Houston. Containing 50 acres. This January 2, 1861.
Reg: December 1, 1866   Signed: C.P. Houston

Page 12 - J.J. Long Deed to F. Wilson. Land in Bedford County
and District No. 11 beginning in the Columbia Road. Containing
65 acres. This 26 November 1866.
Wit: J.A. Moore   Signed: J.J. Long
     A.N. Vincent
Reg: December 1, 1866

Page 12 - Daniel Bartlett, Discharge - Daniel Bartlett a Private
in Captain James Clift Company (M) 5th Regiment of Tennessee
Cavalry Volunteers who was enrolled on the 21st day of September
1863 to serve three years or during the war is hereby discharged
from the service of the United States this 14th August 1863 at
Pulaski, Tennessee by reason of Special Order No. 18 C.S. Mil
Div Tenn. No objection to his being re-enlisted is known to
exist. Said Daniel Bartlett was born in Bedford County is
twenty nine years of age, five feet five inches high, fair
complexion, gray eyes, dark hair and by occupation when enrolled
a carpenter. Given at Pulaski this 14th day August 1865.
Francis Jackson, Captain   James Clift, Captain
Oath of Identity - Daniel Bartlett of the Town of Shelbyville,
Bedford County, Tennessee on the 1st day of December 1866
personally appeared before me the undersigned a Justice of the
Peace for the County and state above mentioned. Daniel Bartlett
who being duly sworn according to law declares that he is the
identical Daniel Bartlett who was a Private in the Company
commanded by Captain James Clift in the Regiment Cavalry
commanded by Col. R. Galbreath that he enlisted on the 21st day
of September 1863 for the term of three years and discharged at
Pulaski, Tennessee 14th day of August 1855 by reason of Special
Order No. 18.
Reg: December 1, 1866   Signed: Daniel Bartlett

Page 13 - Wm. S. Smith Deed to Cornelius Womble. Land in
Bedford County and District No. 20 and bounded by the lands of
W.W. Gill, by lands (illegible), by John R. Wright, and by Isaac
Ortner. Containing about 78 acres. This 1st December 1866.
Reg: December 1, 1866   Signed: W.S. Smith

Page 13 - Fowler & Frankfort Trust Deed to R.A. Shapherd. We,
C.A> Fowler and George W. Frankfort trading under the firm and
style of C.A. Fowler & Co., have sold unto R.A. Shapherd a Town
Lot and house in the Town of Shelbyville, Bedford County known
as the Foreman House on Washington Street being the house
whereon we are now doing business and bounded by the lot of Mrs.
Wright, by the lot of Hodgkins & Shire, and by a lot.
Containing __ acres. We are indebted to the firm of Gardner &
Co. of Louisville, also John W. Derrybury. This 1st day of
December 1866.
Reg: December 1, 1866   Signed: C.A. Fowler & Co.

Page 15 - James M. Elliott Deed to Edmond Cooper. Land in
Bedford County and in the corporate limits of the Town of
Shelbyville on the east side of Martin Street and bounded by
Mrs. B.M. Tillman, by a lot owned by Thomas J. Roane, and by

Martin Street, the same being the house and lot formerly owned by Mrs. Letitia Morton, deceased, and on which she resided at the time of her death. This 28th November 1866.
Reg: December 1, 1866   Signed: J.M. Elliott

Page J.F. Thompson Deed to J.M. Elliott. I, Jacob F. Thompson, sold unto James M. Elliott a lot of land in Bedford County and in the corporate limits of the Town of Shelbyville on the east side of Martin Street, bounded by the lot owned by Mrs. Mary Dobson, by a lot of B.M. Tillman, by a lot owned by George Davidson, deceased, on which Thos. J. Roane now resides, and by Martin Street the same being the house and lot formerly owned by Mrs. Letitia Morton, deceased, and on which she resided at the time of her death. This 10 February 1866.
Wit: H.P. Cleveland   Signed: J.F. Thompson
     Thos. J. Roane
Reg: December 1, 1866

Page 16 - William S. Jett Deed to Edmund Cooper. Lot of ground in the Town of Shelbyville, to wit, the lot of ground on which my dwelling house is situated bounded by Union Street, by the Murfreesboro Turnpike, by the lot of Montgomery Coldwell, by the (illegible) lane running between W.G. Cowan and myself. Containing about 4 acres. The other one half interest in the livery stable lot which I purchased of A.L. Adams and bounded by Holland Street, by ___ Street, by the alley between the lots and the warehouse, and by Church Street. This 28 November 1866.
Reg: December 1, 1866   Signed: Wm. S. Jett

Page 17 - Barclay M. Tillman Mortgage to Lewis Tillman. I, Barclay M. Tillman, am indebted to Lewis Tillman. I have conveyed unto Lewis Tillman my tract of land in Bedford County and Civil District No. 1 and bounded by the lands of Thomas b. Mosely, and by the lands of B. & R. Beechboard, by lands of Dr. J.L. Armstrong, by lands of John E. Scruggs, and by lands of Scruggs & Winn. Containing 329 acres. This 9 November 1866.
Reg: December 1, 1866   Signed: Barclay M. Tillman

Page 18 - B.M. Tillman Trust Deed to Lewis Tillman and Blount G. Green. I have sold unto Lewis Tillman, Sr., and Blount G. Green a tract of land in Bedford County and Civil District No. 1 and bounded by T.B. Mosley and Benjamin Beechboard, by the lands of Dr. James L. Armstrong, by lands of John E. Scruggs, and by lands of Scruggs & Wynn and being the lands on which I now reside. Containing 330 acres. Also a small tract of timbered land in Coffee County, Tennessee containing about 33 acres and bounded by Stephen Galleghy and being the same land conveyed by J.G. Patton to Jas. C. Word and by said Word to me. Also the following town lots in the Town of Shelbyville, Bedford County, to wit, a lot of land adjoining a corner of Mrs. B.M. Tillman's lot, by Brittain Street, by a street running between said lot and the grave yard, and by Mrs. Tillman's line. One other town lot conveyed to me by P.S. Kimbro and adjoining Brittain Street and corner of the lot above described, by lands formerly

occupied by Drumgoole lot now by James M. Elliott. The said two
lots were conveyed to me by R.P.S. Kimbro. Also a lot on Main
Street and conveyed to me William Brown by deed dated 19th
December 1850. NOTE: A very long document. This 1 December
1866.
Reg: December 1, 1866   Signed: Barclay M. Tillman

Page 21 - Simon Greenbaum Deed to Jennette Greenbaum. September
7, 1865. This declaration of trust made by me Simon Greenbaum
of the City of Louisville, <u>Tennessee</u>(Kentucky?). Whereas a suit
was recently instituted in the Davis Circuit of the State of
Kentucky for the purpose of selling certain real estate in the
Town of Owensboro the separate property of my wife Jennette
Greenbaum. Said estate was sold and that the interest she said
about to acquire in a certain merchantile concern at Shelbyville
and Fayetteville, Tennessee is partnership with John J. Manken.
This September 7, 1865.
Reg: December 11, 1866   Signed: Simon Greenbaum

Page 21 - Joel Stallings Deed to Sam'l Carpenter. Land in Civil
District No. 18 Bedford County and containing 45 acres and
adjoining Helton's corner. This 7 November 1866.
Wit: R.S. Montgomery   Signed: Joel Stallings
Reg: December 3, 1866

Page 22 - T.C.H. Miller Deed to Susan G. Cooper and others. I,
T.C.H. Miller conveyed unto Susan G., John T., Margaret P., and
Virgil E. Cooper, minor heirs of W.F. Cooper, deceased. The
said land was bought by said Miller sold under a Deed of Trust
and he believing that there was property enough besides the
portion allotted to each heir belonging to Wm. F. Cooper the
father of said minors to pay debts of said Wm. F. Cooper. Land
in Bedford County and District No. __. Containing 43 acres and
128 poles. This 28 November 1866.
Wit: T.J. Moore   Signed: T.C.H. Miller
     J.B. Hunter
     A. Wilson
     B. Reg: December 4, 1866

Page 23 - G.W. Cone Deed to John H. Philpot, 62 acres. December
3, 1866. Both of Bedford County. Land bounded by Jacob's line,
W.N. Price's north east corner, and S. Claxton's east line.
Containing 62 acres in Bedford County and Civil District No. 5.
Wit: Wm. J. Peacock   Signed: G.W. Cone
     C.T. Philpot
Reg: December 4, 1866

Page 23 - M.R. Rushing Deed to W.F. Cooper, 245 acres and 144
poles. Milton R. Rushing sold unto William F. Cooper, both of
Bedford County, land in said county on the waters of Falling
Creek in Civil District No. 5. Containing 245 acres and 144
poles and bounded by A.S. Lawrance's line it being James

Ogilvie's corner, and by the Shelbyville Road. This 16 December 1859.
Wit: James Ogilvie   Signed: M.R. Rushing
     J.H. Ogilvie
Reg: December 4, 1866

Page Plummer W. Shoffner, Discharge - Plummer W. Shoffner a Private of Captain Reuben C. Couch Company (F) 5th Regiment of Tennessee Cavalry Volunteers who was enrolled on the 6th day of September 1862 to serve three years or during the war is hereby discharged from the service of the United States this 9th day of February 1865 at Tullahoma, Tennessee by means of _____. Said Plummer W. Shoffner was born in Bedford County is forty one years of age, five feet four inches high, fair complexion, brown eyes, dark hair and by occupation when enrolled a farmer. Given at Tullahoma this 9th day of February 1865.
                                   John F. Armstrong, Major
Oath of Identity - Plummer W. Shoffner of the Town of Shelbyville, Bedford County, Tennessee on 3rd day of November 1866 personally appeared before me the undersigned a Justice of the Peace for the County and State above mentioned. Plummer W. Shoffner who being duly sworn according to law declared that he is the identical Plummer W. Shoffner who was a Private in the Company commanded by Captain Reuben C. Couch in the Regiment Cavalry commanded by Col. Wm. B. S(illegible) that he enlisted on the 6th dy of September for the term of three years and was discharged at Tullahoma, Tenn. on 9th day of February 1865 by reason of ...
Reg: December 4, 1866   Signed: Plummer W. Shoffner

Page 25 - Louis Mankel Title Bond to James G. Grier. I am bound unto J.G. Greir. I make to said Greir a deed to a house and lot known as the John C. Akin house and lot which I purchased from James Moore situated near the Town of Shelbyville in Camp White part of the old Cannon tract about 2 acres and is bounded by lands of John Yancy, by James Wortham, and by __ Steele. This November 30, 1866.
Reg: December 6, 1866   Signed: Louis Mankel

Page 26 - A. Evans and others Deed to Martin Euliss. We, Abraham Evans and Mary Evans his wife and John Evans and Elizabeth Jane Evans his wife, Wilson C. Shofner, George Morrison and wife Nancy Catharine Morrison, have this day sold unto Martin Euliss a tract of land in District No. 25 of Bedford County and bounded by J.T. Ayers' corner. Containing 137 acres and 40 poles. This 25 September 1866.
Wit: Wm. H. Smith   Signed: A. Evans
     T.T. Harrison   Mary Evans
Reg: December 6, 1866   W.C. Shoffner
                                   John Evans
                                   Eliz. J. Evans
                                   G.D. Evans
                                   G.D. Morrison
                                   N.C. Morrison

Page 27 - Wm. G. Osburn Deed to James H. Elmore, 58 acres and 99 poles. Wm. J. Osburn of Bedford County. Land in Bedford County and Civil District No. 10. Containing 58 acres and 99 poles. Beginning at the center of the Eagleville and Unionville Turnpike. Bounded by Woods' line and Wm. Little's corner. It being the tract of land where James H. Elmore resides. This 21 August 1866.
Wit: Chesly Williams   Signed: W.G. Osburn
    B.F. Jarrell
Reg: December 6, 1866

Page 27 - Samuel W. Statum, Discharge - Samuel W. Statum a Private of Captain David Flurkin's Company (D) 10th Regiment of Tennessee Infantry Volunteers who was enrolled on the 4th day of April 1862 to serve three years or during the war is hereby discharged from the service of the United States this 10th day of June 1865 at Knoxville, Tennessee by means of expiration of term of service. No objection to his being re-enlisted is known to exist. Said Samuel W. Statum was born in Franklin County, Tennessee is nineteen years of age, five feet seven inches high, light complexion, blue eyes, light hair and by occupation when enrolled a laborer. Given at Knoxville, Tennessee 10th day of June 1865.
                W.P. Hargon, Captain
Oath of Identity - Samuel W. Statum of the Town of Shelbyville, Tennessee, Bedford County, on this 6th day of November 1866 personally appeared before me the undersigned a Justice of the Peace for the County and State above mentioned. Samuel W. Statum who being duly sworn according to law declares that he is the identical Samuel W. Statum who was a Private in the Company commanded by Captain David Flurkins in the Regiment commanded by Col. James W. Schelly that he enlisted on the 10th day of April 1862 for the term of three years and was discharged at Knoxville, Tenn. on 10th day of June by reason of expiration of term of service.
Reg: (no date)   Signed: Samuel W. Statum

Page 28 - G.W. Bell and A.M. Webb Deed to W.M. Tatum, 114 acres. Land in Bedford County and District No. 8 on the waters of Fall Creek and bounded by land known as the Smokey Wilson tract, and by A.J. Goodrum's corner, and by R.B. Freeman's corner. Containing 114 acres. This December 6, 1866.
Wit: C.S. Dudley   Signed: G.W. Bell
    Thos. Lamb   A.M. Webb
Reg: December 7, 1866

Page 29 - Benjamin F. Reed, Discharge - Benjamin F. Reed a Private of Lt. William G. Davis Company (A) 5th Regiment of Tennessee Cavalry Volunteers who was enrolled on the 7th day of September 1862 to serve three years or during the war is hereby discharged from the service of the United States this 25th day of June 1865 at Fayetteville, Tennessee by reason of General Order No. 83 War Dept. May 8, 1865. No objection to his being re-enlisted is known to exist. Said Benjamin F. Reed was born in Bedford County, Tennessee is nineteen years of age, five feet

ten inches high, fair complexion, gray eyes, light hair and by occupation when enrolled a farmer. Given at Fayetteville, Tenn. this 25th day of June 1865.
Francis Jackson, Captain   Signed: William G. Davis, 1st Lt.
Oath of Identity - Benjamin F. Reed of the Town of Shelbyville, Bedford County, Tennessee on this 25th day of June 1865 personally appeared before me the undersigned a Justice of the Peace for the County and State above mentioned. Benjamin F. Reed who being duly sworn according to law declared that he is the identical Benjamin F. Reed who was a member of the Company commanded by Lieut. William G. Davis in the Regiment 5th Tenn. commanded by ___ that he enlisted on the 7th day of September 1862 for the term of three years or during the war and was discharged at Fayetteville, Tennessee on 25th day of June 1865 by means of General Order No. 83 War Dept. May 8, 1865.
Reg: December 7, 1866   Signed: Benjamin F. Reed

Page 30 - Jasper N. Smith and others Title Bond to Wm. T. Sugg. Jasper N. Smith, James Carothers and wife Nancy Ann Carothers bind themselves to and sold unto W.T. Sugg all the right title claim and interest which we have to 93 acres of land in District No. 3 of Bedford County and adjoining lands of Johnson Townsend, and by lands of Harriet Arnold, by lands of Johnson Townsend and Edmund Cooper. This 5 November 1866.
Wit: Edm'd Cooper   Signed: J.N. Smith
     J.W. George   James Carothers
Reg: December 7, 1866   Nancy A. Carothers

Page 30 - Jos. Anderson Deed to Thomas Freeman, 2 acres and 23 poles. Land in Bedford County and Civil District No. 7 lying in the Town of Shelbyville on the road out of the Sulphur Spring and bounded by a lot sold by Dr. Lipscomb to J. Tarpley. Containing 2 acres and 23 poles. This 7 December 1866.
Reg: December 8, 1866   Signed: Jos. Anderson

Page 31 - John W. Thompson and Jo. D. Wilhoite Deed to Isaac McAdams. I have this day sold unto Isaac McAdams a lot of land lying and being in the corporation of the Town of Shelbyville and bounded by the road leading from Shelbyville by C.W. Cummings, and by the lot formerly owned by Pat Neligan and known as the Barclay Neligan place. This 4 December 1866.
Wit: Jo. Thompson   Signed: Jno. W. Thompson
     Wm. Wood   J.D. Wilhoite
Reg: December 8, 1866

Page 32 - Levi Mitchell, Discharge - Levi Mitchell a Private of Captain Benjamin F. Green Company (L) 9th Regiment of Tennessee Cavalry Volunteers who was enrolled the 30th day of September 1863 to serve three years or during the war is hereby discharged from the service of the United States this 11th day of September 1865 at Knoxville, Tennessee by means of (illegible) and Special Order No. 48 Dept. Tenn. August 22nd 1865. No objection to his being re-enlisted is known to exist. Said Levi Mitchell was born in Spartenburg District in South Carolina is twenty six years of age, six feet three and three eight inches high, dark complexion, blue eyes, dark hair and by occupation when enrolled a carpenter. Given at Knoxville, Tenn. this 11 September 1865.

Jno. A.B. Williams, Captain

Oath of Identity - Levi Mitchell of the Town of Shelbyville, Bedford County, Tennessee on this 10th day of November 1866 personally appeared before me the undersigned a Justice of the Peace of the County and State above mentioned. Levi Mitchell who was a Private in the company commanded by Captain Benj. G. Green in the Regiment commanded by Col. Jo. Parsons that he enlisted on the 30th day of September 1863 for the term of three years and discharged at Knoxville, Tenn. on the 11th day of September by reason of Special Order No. 48 Dept. Tenn.
Reg: December 10, 1866   Signed: Levi Mitchell

Page 33 - James B. Rodgers and wife Deed to S.B. Gordon. We, James B. Rodgers and his wife Alsey E. Rodgers, have sold unto S.B. Gordon a tract of land this day purchased from him by said Alsey E. Rodgers, all the interest which said Alsey has in and unto the one eleventh part of a fund in the lands of Thomas H. Coldwell, executor of Robt. Reed, deceased, arising from the sale of the land of which Robert Reed died seized and possessed and a small amount of personal property, said property been sold by said executor. Said Alsey being entitled to said one eleventh part of said land she being one of the children of said Robert Reed. Also convey the one eleventh part of the lands in the hands of T.D. Thompson, administrator of Elizabeth Reed, deceased, the mother of Alsey E. Rodgers. This 6 December 1866.
Wit: Thos. H. Coldwell   Signed: James B. Rodgers
Reg: December 10, 1866   Alsey E. Rodgers

Page 33 - James M. Reed Deed to S.B. Gordon. I have this day sold my interest in the estate of Robert Reed, deceased, in the hands of Thomas H. Coldwell his executor. This 6 December 1866.
Wit: Thos. H. Coldwell   Signed: James M. Reed
Reg: December 10, 1866

Page 34 - F.J. Harris Title Bond to T.N.B. Turner. Land in Bedford County and District No. 9 and bounded by the heirs of Elizabeth Williams, and by L.A. Clark. Containing 68 acres and 44 poles. This 13 August 1866.
Wit: Q.E. Morton   Signed: F.J. Harris
    L.A. Clark
Reg: December 10, 1866

Page 35 - Young Wilhoite Deed to James Wadly, 250 acres. Land in Williamson County, Tennessee, all the right title claim and interest which I have in and unto the one half of a tract of land in Bedford County and Civil District No. 7 and 18 and bounded by center of Duck River, a line between the woods between S.M. Wilhoite and this tract to S.M. Wilhoite's new ground fence, by fence to the Warner Road, and by Daniel Earnhart's corner, by the center of the Fishing Ford Road, and then along the center of said road to the Warner Bridge on Duck

River. Containing 250 acres. Also 10 acres of cedar land in the 18th District cornering on the land of Crecy Trollinger. This 11 December 1866.
Wit: Thomas H. Coldwell   Signed: Young Wilhoite
Reg: December 11, 1866

Page 35 - C.S. Dudley Surveyor's provision Deed to Horatio Coop. November 30, 1866. I, C.S. Dudley, surveyor for Bedford County do certify that I went on the premises of Horatio Coop this day after giving notice of the time and place. The land on which said Coop now lives. Bounded at the Unionville Road. Containing 270 acres and 15 poles. NOTE: Plat of land on page 36.
W.A. Mash and James T. Coop, CC   C.S. Dudley, Surveyor
Reg: December 11, 1866

Page 36 - G.E. Calhoon Trust Deed to P.S. English. I have this day conveyed unto Jos. H. Thompson, as trustee, the house and lot on which I now live being the same I purchased of W.S. Jett. Said house and lot is situated in the Town of Shelbyville opposite the factory of L.B. Knott. I am indebted to J.D. Wilhoite. I have procured P.S. English to become my stayor for stay of execution now to save him harmless and protect him. This 12 December 1866.
Reg: December 12, 1866   Signed: G.E. Calhoon

Page 37 - James F. Stephenson Deed to E.N. Stephenson. Land in District No. 18 of Bedford county the same being the land assigned to me by the Commissioners of John Stephenson land. This December 2, 1866.
Reg: December 15, 1866   Signed: James F. Stephenson

Page 38 - W.H. Stephenson Deed to E.N. Stephenson, 18 acres. Land in District No. 18 of Bedford County the same being the land assigned to me by the Commissioners of said county for that purpose of the division of the John Stephenson land. This 26 November 1866.
Reg: December 15, 1866   Signed: W.H. Stephenson

Page 38 - William H. Word, Discharge - William H. Word a Private of Lieut. William G. Davis Company (A) 5th Regiment of Tennessee Cavalry Volunteers who was enrolled on the 4th day of September 1862 to serve three years or during the war is hereby discharged from the service of the United States this 25th day of June 1865 at Fayetteville, Tennessee by reason of General Order No. 83 War Dept. May 8, 1865. No objection to his being re-enlisted is known to exist. Said William H. Word was born in Bedford County, Tennessee is twenty two years of age, five feet eight inches high, fair complexion, gray eyes, black hair and by occupation when enrolled a farmer. Given at Fayetteville, Tenn. this 25th day of June 1865.
Francis Jackson, Captain   William G. Davis, 1st Lt.

Oath of Identity - William H. Word of the Town of ___, Bedford County, Tennessee on this 14th December 1866 personally appeared before me the undersigned a Justice of the Peace for the County and State above mentioned. William H. Word who being duly sworn according to law declared that he is the identical William H. Word who was a Private in the Company commanded by Captain Lieut. Wm. G. Davis in the Regiment 5th Tenn. commanded by Wm. H. Stokes, that he enlisted on the 4th day of September 1862 for the term of three years and was discharged at Fayetteville, Tenn. on 25th day of June 1865 by reason of General Order No. 83 War Department. 1865.
Reg: December 15, 1866   Signed: W.H. Word

Page 39 - R.A. Lewis, Trustee, Transfer to Mollie Story. By virtue of the power vested in me as trustee of F.V. Story. I have this day sold to Miss Mollie Story a piano. This November 10, 1865.
Reg: December 15, 1866   Signed: R.H. Lewis, Trustee
                                        Of F.V. Story

Page 39 - Jo. Thompson, Sheriff, Deed to P.H. Thompson. On 7th May 1859 P.H. Thompson recovered a judgment against J.H. Locke. J.F. Smith levied on a tract of land on the undivided interest that J.H. Locke has or may have in a tract of land on Weakley Creek in District No. 11 of Bedford County adjoining the lands of T.B. Jeffries, E. Batts, H. Clark, J. Green, the Thompson's line &c. willed by Wm. Locke, deceased, to his widow her life time then to his children or heirs. This December 15, 1866.
Reg: December 15, 1866   Signed: Jo. Thompson

Page 41 - James Mullins Deed to M.E. Peacock, House and lot. House and lot in Bedford County and District No. 7 in the Town of Shelbyville and north of the square of said town on the west side of Martin or Pike Street and bounded by Martin or Pike Street, by an alley or Jail Street, by the lot where the western boundary line of said Martin or Pike Street crosses the southern boundary line of the alley or Jail Street, and by a small lot owned by ___ Brooks. Containing __ acres and ___ feet known as Town Lot No. __. This 15 July 1866.
Reg: December 16, 1866   Signed: James Mullins

Page 41 - Henry Mankle Trust Deed to S. Rothchild. I have sold unto Solomon Rothchild all my stock of goods, wares and merchandise in the house in which I am doing business in the Town of Shelbyville adjoining the house of John F. Brown and others, consisting of calicoes, boots, shoes, hats &c. Also all my stock of goods, wares and merchandise consisting of calicoes, clothing and all the wares in the house in which I am doing business as a merchant in the Town of Fayetteville, Tennessee, said house is situated I believe on the west side of the Public Square in which Jas. F. Calhoon sold goods formerly. Also one gray horse, bridle and saddle. NOTE: A long document. This December 18, 1866.
Reg: December 18, 1866   Signed: H. Frankle

Page 43 - Robert H. Barnes Deed to Josch Marshall, 97 acres.
Land in District No. 8 of Bedford County, containing 97 acres
and 4 poles, bounded by John W. Kay, John A. Webb, T.F. Barnes's
line, by J.L. Cooper's line and B.B. McLean, and by Bird Land.
Containing 97 acres and 4 poles. This 30 November 1865.
Wit: John A. McLain   Signed: Robt H. Barnes
     W.N. (illegible)
Reg: December 18, 1866

Page 44 - Josch Marshall Deed to T.F. Barnes, 97 acres. I,
Josiah Marshall, have this day sold unto T.F. Barnes land in
District No. 9 of Bedford County, containing 97 acres and 4
poles and bounded by John W. Key, John A. Webb, T.F. Barnes'
line, by C.L. Cooper and R.B. McLain, and by Bird lands. This
December 1, 1866.
Reg: December 18, 1866   Signed: Josiah Marshall

Page 44 - John Richardson and wife Deed to Thomas Kimmons,
undivided interest. All our right title claim and interest
being an undivided interest of one half of one eighth of a tract
of land in the 20th Civil District of Bedford County, containing
63 acres, it being the place known as the Whitesell place and
bounded by lands of James Coats' estate, by the lands of John W.
Greer, by the lands of Thomas J. Robinson. Our interest in land
being one half of one eighth of 63 acres. This 19 December
1866.
Reg: December 19, 1866   Signed: John Richardson
                                        Mary C. Richardson

Page 45 - William Word Deed to John W. Woosley, House and Lot.
House and lot in Camp White near the Town of Shelbyville,
Bedford County and bounded by the street running south from the
colege ground fronting on said street, by the lot formerly owned
by S.H. T(illegible) on the street by J.P. Calhoun, and by Thos.
J. Roane's lot. Containing 120 poles the same being the lot
deeded by James Wortham, Sheriff, to T.P. Cooper April 22, 1858
and by C.A. Robinson to Amos Hays in April 1858 and from Amos
Hays to me in December 1858. And also a redemption deed from
T.P. Coper to me. This December 20, 1866.
Reg: December 20, 1866   Signed: William Word

Page 46 - John S. Wiggins, Discharge - John S. Wiggins a
Sergeant of Captain James Clift Company (M) 5th Regiment of
Tennessee Cavalry Volunteers, who was enrolled on the 21st day
of August 1863 to serve three years or during the war is hereby
discharged from the service of the United States this 14th day
of August 1865 at Pulaski, Tennessee by reason of Special Order
No. 18 C.S. Mil Div Tenn. No objection to his being re-enlisted
is known to exist. Said John S. Wiggins was born in Bedford
County, Tennessee is eighteen years of age, five feet eleven
inches high, fair complexion, gray eyes, black hair and by
occupation when enrolled a farmer. Given at Pulaski, Tenn. this
14th day of August 1865.
Francis Jackson, Captain   James Clift, Captain

Oath of Identity - John S. Wiggins of the Town of ____ Bedford
County, Tennessee on this 20th day of December 1866 personally
appeared before me the undersigned a Justice of the Peace for
the County and State above mentioned. John S. Wiggins who being
duly sworn according to law declared that he is the identical
John S. Wiggins who was a Sergeant in the Company commanded by
Captain James Clift in the Regiment 5th Tenn Cav commanded by
Wm. B. Stokes, that he enlisted on the 21st day of August 1863
for the term of three years and was discharged at Pulaski, the
14th day of August 1865 by reason of General Order.
Reg: December 20, 1866   Signed: John S. Wiggins

Page 47 - John R. Thompson, Discharge - John R. Thompson a
Private of Captain Wm. O. Rickman Company (H) 5th Regiment of
Tennessee Cavalry Volunteers who was enrolled on the 1st day of
October 1862 to serve three years or during the war is hereby
discharged from the service of the United States this 14th day
of August 1865 at Pulaski, Tennessee by reason of Special Order
No. 18 C.S. Mil Div Tenn. No objection to his being re-enlisted
is known to exist. Said John R. Thompson was born in Franklin
County, Tennessee is twenty five years of age, five feet ten
inches high, fair complexion, blue eyes, dark hair and by
occupation when enrolled a blacksmith. Given at Pulaski this
1st day of August 1865.
Francis Jackson, Captain   Wm. O. Rickman, Captain
Oath of Identity - John R. Thompson of the Town of Shelbyville,
Bedford County, Tennessee on this 21st day of December 1866
personally appeared before me the undersigned a Justice of the
Peace for the County and State above mentioned. John R.
Thompson who being duly sworn according to law declares that he
is the identical John R. Thompson who was a Private in the
Company commanded by Captain W.O. Rickman in the Regiment __
commanded by __ that he enlisted on the __ day of __ for the
term of __ on the __ day of __ by reason…
Reg: December 22, 1866   Signed: John R. Thompson

Page 47 - Willlis Blanton Deed to Thomas Allison, Town Lot.
Land lying in Bedford County and in Civil District No. 25 and in
the Village of Normandy being the lot that William Hyles
conveyed to me and bounded near the Nashville and Chattanooga
Rail Road. This 25 September 1866.
Wit: W.T. Cully   Signed: Willis Blanton
     J.C. Word
Reg: December 22, 1866

Page 48 - William J. Loyd Deed to Henry Gibson, undivided
interest. This December 1st 1866. William J. Loyd and Rhoda
Ann Loyd his wife of Bedford County sold unto Henry Gibson of
Rutherford County, Tennessee all their interest in the following
tracts of lands, to wit, one tract lying in Bedford County and
Civil District No. 1 and bounded by the dower land of Nancy
Shelton widow of Jesse Shelton and A. Bird, by John S. Davis,
by Wm. Osburn and Hugh Montgomery, and by Ed. Scruggs.
Containing 99 acres. The other tract in Coffee County adjoining
the lands of C(illegible) Galleger and others called the Barren

Tract supposed to contain 22 acres. The same being descended to the said Rhoda Ann Loyd as daughter and heir at law of Jesse Shelton, deceased, not including any interest in the dower.
Reg: December 22, 1866   Signed: Wm. J. Loyd
                                   Rhoda Ann Loyd

Page 49 - Elizabeth Knight Deed of Gift to James L. Payne. Registered. I, Elizabeth Knight for the love and affection which I bear towards and for my son, J.L. Payne, give by Deed of Gift the following property of which I am the owner, viz, all my household and kitchen furniture, all of my stock of horses, cows, oxen, hogs, sheep now on the farm where I live devised to me during my life by Allen Knight, all my corn &c now on hand including the present growing crop on the place, also my life estate in the land whereon I now live divested to me by Allen Knight, also my life estate in the slaves (five named in original document). This 20 September 1854.
Wit: James G. Maupin   Signed: Elizabeth Knight
     Sam Yates
Reg: December 26, 1866

Page 50 - Ready Patterson, Discharge - Ready Patterson a Private of Captain James Clift Company (M) 5th Regiment of Tennessee Cavalry Volunteers who was enrolled on the 8th day of September 1863 to serve three years or during the war is hereby discharged from the service of the United States this 14th day of August 1865 at Pulaski, Tennessee by reason of Special Order No. 18 C.S> Mil Div Tenn. No objection to his being re-enlisted is known to exist. Said Ready Patterson was born in Bedford County, Tennessee is eighteen years of age, five feet six inches high, fair complexion, gray eyes, light hair and by occupation when enrolled a farmer. Given at Pulaski, Tenn. this 14th day of August 1865.
Francis Jackson, Captain   Signed: James Clift, Captain
Oath of Identity - I, Ready Patterson of the Town of Shelbyville, Bedford County, Tennessee on this 26th day of December 1866 personally appeared before me the undersigned a Justice of the Peace for the County and State above mentioned. Ready Patterson who being duly sworn according to law declares that he is the identical Ready Patterson who was a Private in the Company commanded by Captain James Clift in the Regiment Cavalry commanded by said Clift that he enlisted on the 18th day of September 1863 for the term of three years and was discharged ___ at ___ on the ___ day ___ of ___ by reason of ___...
Reg: December 26, 1866   Signed: Ready Patterson

Page 51 - G.E. Calhoon Trust Deed to William S. Jett, Agent. I, George C. Calhoon, have this day sold unto W.S. Jett and as attorney in fact for Edmund Cooper two town lots in the Town of Shelbyville being Lots No. 60 and 68 with the exception of the portion of said lots which R.N. Jones sold to Graham & Brown. I am the security on a note dated 26th December 1866 and due 1st day of January 1868 executed by W.P. Goodwin. This 26 December 1866.
Wit: T.S. Steele   Signed: G.E. Calhoon

Reg: December 27, 1866

Page 51 - Wm. P. Gowan Deed to Jno. D. Floyd. This October 15,
1866. Both of Bedford County. Land lying on the Elk Ridge and
cut into two parts by the Lynchburg and Shelbyville Road and
bounded by Kindred Pearson, Jr. and O.G. Stegall, by W. Bobo and
Samuel Morris, by James B. Gowan, and by Benj. Bedford and Jesse
Tucker.
Wit: H.D. Blythe   Signed: William P. Gowan
     Asa D. Blyhe
Reg: December 27, 1866

Page 52 - G.W. Thompson Deed to John Haberlin, Town Lot. Part
of Town Lot No. 43 in the Town of Shelbyville on the east side
of Martin Street and bounded by James Story's lot. This 28
December 1866.
Reg: December 28, 1866   Signed: G.W. Thompson

Page 53 - R.N. Wallace Deed to Joseph Ramsey, 6 acres. Land in
Bedford County and Civil district No. 7 and bounded by the road
leading from Holt's mill. Containing 6 acres, being the same
Lot No. 7 in T.W. Jordan's plan of Town Lots laid off by him on
the Newsom tract of land and which was deeded by said Jordan to
J.F. Calhoun and by him to G.W. and S.W. Thompson and by them to
me adjoining the Steele and Hammond Mill tract originally. This
3 April 1866.
Wit: John R. Wallace   Signed: R.N. Wallace
     Joseph Brown
Reg: December 28, 1866

Page 53 - Henry Sipsy Deed to C.A. Warren, Deed to House and
Lot. Land in the Town of Shelbyville and within the corporate
limits of said town and bounded by Lot No. 6, and by Main
Street, it being the lot conveyed to me first by deed from Thos.
Holland, Sr. dated September 15, 1864 and by another deed from
said Thomas Holland and T.M. Coldwell dated 30 January 1864.
This December 28, 1866.
Wit: J.L. Scudder   Signed: Henry Sipsy
     R.N. Jones
Reg: December 28, 1866

Page 54 - C.A. Warren Deed to Henry Sipsy, 115 acres. Land in
Bedford County and District No. 18 and adjoining in Trice's
line, Brad Gambill's corner, and by Stallings' corner.
Containing 115 acres and 127 poles. This December 28, 1866.
Wit: J.L. Scudder   Signed: C.A. Warren
     R.N. Jones
Reg: December 29, 1866

Page 55 - Henry Sipsy Deed to Arnold N.D. Delffs, 14 acres.
Land in Bedford County and Civil District No. 18 and bounded by
Bradley Gambill's corner. Containing 14 acres. Said land

surveyed by C.S. Dudley dated December 27, 1866.   This 28
December 1866.
Wit: J.L. Scudder   Signed: Henry Sipsy
     R.N. Jones
Reg: December 29, 1866

Page 56 - Andrew Reed Deed of Gift to W.M. Reed, 180 acres. For
the love and affection I have for my son W.M. Reed and by the
acts of kindness and affection rendered to me by him, I have
conveyed unto said W.M. Reed a tract of land in Bedford County
on the north and west side of Big Flat Creek, adjoining Kiziah
Galbreath's old tract, and to center of said creek, and to where
a line of 150 acre tract sold by L. Wood to me crosses said
creek going north, by formerly Cummings now Gentry's line.   It
being all the tract of 150 acres sold to me by said Levin Wood
by deed of April 1841 and about 30 acres of a tract sold to me
by Robt. Reed by deed October 1822. The whole about 180 acres.
This August 24, 1861.
Wit: John P. Steele   Signed: Andrew Reed
     James H. Neil
Reg: December 29, 1866

Page 56 - J.P. Casteele and others Trust Deed to James A. Moore.
I, James P. Steele of Bedford County, have sold unto James A.
Moore of same place a tract of land in Bedford County and Civil
District No. 2 and bounded by the lands of Charles Womack, by
the lands of James Morris, by the lands of Wm. Casteele and
Peyton Dean, and by the lands of Sarah Casteele et als.
Containing about 140 acres on which I now live. I am indebted
to Wisener & Ivie. This 29 December 1866.
Reg: December 31, 1866   Signed: J.P. Casteele
                                        R.C. Eaton
                                        Jas. Bruton

Page 57 - Thos. B. and C.L. Cannon, Extrs, Deed to W.T. Tune and
others. We, Thomas B. Cannon and Charles L. Cannon as executors
of the last will and testament of Clement Cannon, Sr., deceased,
have this day sold unto Wm. T. tune and Thos. C. Allison a tract
of land in Bedford County and bounded by a tract of land owned
and resided upon by the late John Woods at the time of his death
on the waters of Fall Creek in District No. 6, by Thos. C.
Allison's line, by Andrew Vannoy's line, and by John Woods'
tract. Contain 19 ½ acres and 20 poles.
Reg: December 31, 1866   Signed: Thos. B. Cannon
                                        C.L. Cannon, Extrs.

Page 58 - Philoman Gosling Deed to W.H. Shipperson, Town Lot.
Land in the corporate limits of the Town of Shelbyville, Bedford
County and bounded by the junction of Brittain Street and Union
Street, and by the lands of the Dixon Academy. This 31 December
1866.
Reg: December 31, 1866   Signed: P. Gosling

Page 59 ~ David Rozar Deed to M.S. Rozar, 100 acres. This 31 December 1866. David Rozar sold unto Milton S. Rozar, both of Bedford County, a certain tract of land the same on which I now live lying and being in Bedford County on the head waters of Flat Creek, said land was deeded to me in several parcels and by different persons all of which deeds are in my possession and in all about 100 acres. Said land bounded by Wm. Woodward and Ellen Gambill, and by James Burrow, by Catharine Leathers and W.W. Gill. This 31 December 1866.
Wit: William Bartlett   Signed: David Rozar
     J.M. White
Reg: January 2, 1867

Page 59 - N. Wilhoite Deed to Joseph Robertson and Wiley Thompson, 28 acres. I have sold unto Joseph Robertson and Willie Thompson a tract of land in Bedford County and District No. 6 and bounded at the center of Duck River my south west corner, by Swift's line, and to an island in Duck River. Containing 28 acres and 40 poles. This 29 November 1865.
Reg: January 3, 1867   Signed: N. Wilhoite

Page 60 - Howard Boone Deed to Wm. J. Shofner, undivided interest. I, Howard Boone of Bedford County, have sold to William J. Shofner of same place a tract of land known as the Widow Margaret Boone's dower or the old home place of William Boone, deceased, and one other tract known as the John Brown tract, all being in Bedford County. This 24 December 1866.
Wit: Thos. Hutson   Signed: Howard Boone
     Martin Fridel
Reg: January 3, 1867

Page 61 - A.J. Ray Deed to William H. Stephens, 43 acres. This 1 January 1867. Andrew J. Ray of Bedford County, have sold unto William H. Stephens of same place a tract of land in Bedford County on the north side of Duck River and bounded by J.F. Ray, by Mary Ray and J.W. Shearin, by Martha C. Stephens, and by Duck River. Containing 33 acres. This also includes 10 acres of cedar land lying on the north side of the North Fork of Duck River and bounded by the Bellefant land, and by Mary Ray, and by Martha C. Stephens, and by Louis A. Ray.
Wit: James F. Ray   Signed: Andrew J. Ray
     John C. Anderson
Reg: January 4, 1867

Page 61 - G.W. and James Gregory, extrs. Deed to Robert Cowan. We the executors of Thomas Gregory, deceased, having the will annexed, advertised the lands of said Gregory for sale which lands are in Bedford County and Civil District No. 8 being the same that said Thomas Gregory lived on at his death. Robert Cowan being the best and highest bidder for Lot No. 3 in the division of said land. Land bounded by corner of Lot No. 2 made by John W. Rutledge and Thomas Gregory, Sr., and by a corner of a 10 acre tract sold to Fisher.
Wit: Wm. G. Cowan   Signed: G.W. Gregory, Extr.

John T. Stephen   James Gregory, Extr.
Reg: January 4, 1867

Page 62 - R.H. Tucker Trust Deed to Peter Barren. I, Robert H.
Tucker for the security of Peter Barren, who is my security in
favor of John A. McLain and against myself principal and T.B.
Ivie, stayer. I have this day Deed in Trust, convey to said
Peter Barren a gray horse and a two horse wagon my own property.
This 3 January 1867.
Reg: January 5, 1867   Signed: R.H. Tucker

Page 63 - W.T. Tune and W.F. Cooper Trust Deed to Smith Bowlen.
I, W.F. Cooper, have this day sold unto W.T. Tune and Smith
Bowlen all the right title claim and interest which I have in a
tract of land in Bedford County and District No. 5 and bounded
by lands of Wm. Cooper and William Tatum, by lands of Joseph
Hutton, by lands of John Jacobs, Jr., James Clanton and John
Parker, and by lands of James Ogilvie. Containing 245 acres and
115 poles. One jack, one sorrel mare, one gray mare, one bay
horse, one black mare, one sorrel filly, one sorrel horse, and
others listed in original document. All which I own on the
shares with T.C.H. Miller about 20 or 23 head of stock hogs, one
book case, one b(illegible). I am indebted to Solomon Claxton.
I am guardian of my children, Sarah A., William C., and Mary C.
I owe Elisha Hunter, E.A. Wilson, T.C.H. Miller, R.P. Hunter,
Joseph Wilhoite, Richard Shidmore, A.D. Fugitt, R.D. Bowlin,
Bowlin & McElroy, A.M. McElroy, William Thomas, and Miss Mary
A(illegible). This 1 December 1866.
Reg: January 5, 1867   Signed: W.F. Cooper

Page 64 - W.C. Hill Deed to J.W. Hill. Land in Bedford County
and District No. 6 and bounded by J.M. Burnett, and by W.J.
Chunn. This January 5, 1867.
Reg: January 5, 1867   Signed: W.C. Hill

Page 65 - D. Wade Trust Deed to S.G. Thompson. Dabney Wade Deed
of Trust to S.G. Thompson. Conveyed unto said S.W. Thompson on
two horse wagon and harness, one yellow mare, twenty head of
sheep, ten head of hogs, one bed and stead, one bureau, two mans
saddles, also in trust one gray horse, ten head of sheep, one
clock, two chests, one cow and calf, one safe, one side saddle
now in my possession, and in addition to this trust one bay mule
now in my possession. I am indebted to Bartlett Tyler by note,
also F.B. Price. S.G. Thompson is my security. This 5 January
1867.
Wit: H.H. Holt   Signed: D. Wade
Reg: January 5, 1867

Page 66 - M.C. Thompson and others Deed to C.C. Covington.
Bedford County. We, Manerva C. Thompson, Rachel C. Reeves, C.C.
Covington and Jesse Covington, all being children and heirs at
law of Jesse Covington, deceased, are the dowers in common of a
tract of land known as the Lucy Covington dower lying in

District No. 11 Bedford County near the Village of Unionville, containing 70 acres and 99 poles. Lot No. 3 to C.C> Covington and bounded by the Crowel Mill Road, and by Lot No. 2. Containing 21 acres and 148 poles. We, Manerva C. Thompson, Rachel C. Reeves and Jesse Covington convey said land unto C.C. Covington. This January 7, 1867.

Reg: January 8, 1867   Signed: M.C. Thompson
                                                P.H. Thompson
                                                R.C. Reeves
                                                S.G. Reeves
                                                Jesse Covington

Page 67 - Thos. Thompson Deed to A.J. Shearin, 15 acres.   This __ of __ 1866.   Thomas J. Stephenson sold unto A.J. Shearin, both of Bedford County, land in Bedford County and in District No. 18 and bounded by James Thorn's corner about 10 poles and north of the old Fishing Ford Road.   Containing 15 acres.
Wit: J. Wortham   Signed: Thos. J. Stephenson
Reg: January 9, 1867

Page 67 - M.C. Thompson et als Deed to R.C. Reeves et als.   We, Manerva C. Thompson wife of P.H. Thompson, Rachel C. Reeves, C.C. Covington and Jesse Covington, all being children and heirs at law of Jesse Covington, deceased, assigns are the owner of a tract of land known as the Lucy Covington's dower lying in Civil District No. 11 of Bedford County near the Village of Unionville.   Lot No. 4 to Rachel C. Reeves containing 70 acres and 99 poles.   Land is near the Crowel Mill Road, by Lot No. 3, containing 12 acres and 92 poles.   This January 7, 1867.

Reg: January 9, 1867   Signed: C.C. Covington
                                        M.C. Covington
                                        Jesse Covington
                                        P.H. Thompson

Page 68 - M.C. Thompson and others Deed to Jesse Covington and others.   We, Manerva C. Thompson, Rachel C. Reeves, C.C. Covington, and Jesse Covington, all being children and heirs at law of Jesse Covington, deceased, and are the owners of a tract of land known as the Lucy Covington's dower lying in Civil District No. 11 of Bedford County near the Village of Unionville, containing 70 acres and 99 poles.   Lot No. 2 to Jesse Covington bounded in the middle of the Crowel Mill Road and Lot No. 1.   Containing 16 acres and 20 poles.   This January 7, 1867.

Reg: January 9, 1867   Signed: M.C. Thompson
                                        P.H. Thompson
                                        R.C. Reeves
                                        S.C. Reeves
                                        C.C. Covington

Page 69 - C.C. Covington and others Deed to M.C. Thompson and others.   We, Manervy C. Thompson, Rachel C. Reeves wife of S.G, Reeves, C.C. Covington, Jesse Covington all being children and heirs at law of Jesse Covington, deceased, and assigns are the

owner of a tract of land known as the Lucy Covington's dower lying in Civil District No.11 of Bedford County near the Village of Unionville. Containing 70 acres and 99 poles. Lot No. 1 to Manervy C. Thompson and bounded by the middle of the Thompson Ford. Containing 8 acres and 73 poles. This January 7, 1867.
Reg: January 9, 1867   Signed: C.C. Covington
                                      R.C. Reeves
                                      S.G. Reeves
                                      Jesse Covington

Page 70 - M.B. Dameron Deed to C.L. Cooper, 85 acres. We, Elizabeth Dameron, M.B. Dameron, Berthia F. Blankenship, and Nancy E. Dameron, have sold unto C.L. Cooper a tract of land in Bedford County and Rutherford County, Tennessee and lying partly in District No. 9 of Bedford County in District No. 14 of Rutherford County. Containing 85 acres. Land bounded by C.L. Cooper, by the dower of Lucy Moore, and by G.P. Cooper, and by lands of Louisa Turner and children. This September 11, 1866.
Wit: J.G. Thompson   Signed: Elizabeth Dameron
     J.W. Key   M.B. Dameron
Reg: January 10, 1867   B.F. Blankenship

Page 70 - J.A.S. Shannon Note to J.W. Clary. I promise to pay J.W. Clary. I give to J.W. Clary a lein upon my Carding Factory and fixtures belonging thereto. This Note is paid July 25, 1866.
Wit: S.J. Moore   Signed: J.A.S. Shannon
     J.M. Moore
Reg: January 10, 1867

Page 71 - G.G. Osborne Deed to Martha W. Welch. Undivided interest. I have sold unto Martha W. Welch a tract of land in Bedford County and District No. 2. One parcel lying in the bend of the Garrison Fork of Duck River and bounded by said river and adjoining my land, by Jeremiah Cleveland and Jonas Myers, by lands of Matthias Cortner, deceased, there being two fields the lower one called the Huffman's field and the other the bent field. The lower I purchased of Alford Huffman and the other of a part of the heirs of Solon Jones, deceased. Containing 23 or 24 acres. I convey 9/12 of the whole of the land of the heirs of Solon Jones, deceased, 3/12 of the same belonging to the estate of Mathias and Daniel Cortner, deceased. The whole of said Jones Heirs' land supposed to contain 36 or 37 acres. And 8/12 of another tract known as the dower of the wife of Solon Jones, deceased, and bounded by lands of Mathias Cortner, deceased, by Jonas Myers and John Eakin, and by the lands of Mathias Cortner estate until it runs through the spring and to the center of the Garrison Fork of Duck River. Containing 36 acres. The other 4/12 of this tract I convey during the life of the widow of Solon Jones, deceased. This 6 April 1866.
Wit: J.A. Couch   Signed: G.G. Osborne
     N.J.C. Keller
Reg: January 10, 1866(7)

Page 72 - William H. Wisener, Sr. Deed to Daniel Stewart, 14 acres. Land in Bedford County a part of the Cannon tract of land lying near Shelbyville on the south side of Duck River and being the Lot No. 5 in the division of the late Robert Cannon, and adjoining at Duck River, being the north west corner of Lot No. 4 purchased by William G. Cowan and Thomas C. Whiteside and now owned by them, and by the Turnpike Road. Containing 14 acres. This 8 January 1867.
Reg: January 10, 1867   Signed: Wm. A. Wisener

Page 72 - Thomas M. Ray Deed to H.L. Shearin, 30 acres. I have sold unto Hugh L. Shearin two lots of land that I drawn in the division of my father Robt. Ray's land. The land and lots is in Bedford County and Civil District No. 11 on Duck River at the mouth of the North Fork and known and bounded by Lot No. 5 in the field, a corner of Lot No. 4, to the mouth of the North Fork. Containing 20 acres and 10 poles. Also Lot No. 3 of the cedar land north of the North Fork. Containing 10 acres and 120 poles. This 15 September 1858.
Wit: William Shearin   Signed: Thomas M. Ray
     John W. Shearin
Reg: January 11, 1867

Page 73 - Joseph Welch, Discharge - Joseph Welch a Private of Captain Wm. O. Ruckman Company (H) 5th Regiment of Tennessee Cavalry Volunteers who was enrolled on the 11th day of October 1862 to serve three years or during the war is hereby discharged from the service of the United States this 14th day of August 1865 at Pulaski, Tennessee by reason of Special Order No. 18 C.S. Mil Div Tenn. No objection to his being re-enlisted is known to exist. Said Joseph Welch was born in Burke County in the State of North Carolina is thirty two years of age, five feet eight inches high, fair complexion, blue eyes, brown hair and by occupation when enrolled a carpenter. Given at Pulaski, Tennessee this 14th day of August 1865.
Francis Jackson, Captain   Wm. O. Rickman, Captain
Oath of Identity - Joseph Welch of the Town of ____, Bedford County on this 18th day of June 1866 personally appeared before me the undersigned a Justice of the Peace for the County and State above mentioned. Joseph Welch who being sworn according to law declared that he is the identical Joseph Welch who was a Private in the Company commanded by Captain W.O. Rickman in the Regiment 5 Tenn Cav Vol commanded by ____ that he enlisted on the 11th day of October 1862 for the term of three years and was discharged at Pulaski, Tennessee on the 30th day of August 1865 by reason of Special Order No. 18 C.S. Div Tenn.
Reg: January 11, 1867   Signed: Joseph Welch

Page 74 - Susan Davidson and others Deed to Wm. H. Dyer. We, Susan Davidson and William Patton and wife Anne Patton, Thomas A. Davidson and Martha Davidson and Tennessee Davidson and J.C. Davidson, have this day sold unto William H. Dyer all the tract of land lying on the waters of Sugar Creek and District No. 20. Bounded by William H. Dyer's corner on James C. Snell's line, by the corner of the school and church lot known as Moores Chapel,

and by Susan Davidson's dower line. Containing 248 poles. This
5 October 1865.
Reg: January 12, 1867   Signed: Susan Davidson
                                       T.A. Davidson
                                       William Patton
                                       Martha E. Davidson
                                       T.V. Davidson
                                       J.C. Davidson
                                       Margaret A. Patton

Page 75 - Robert C. Cock and wife Deed to Jordan Rucker. This
20 September 1866. Robert E. Cock and Virginia Cock his wife of
Marshall County sold unto Jordan Rucker of Bedford County, a
tract of land in Bedford County it being part of the land
formerly owned by J.K. Lawell in District No, 10 on Weakley
Creek and bounded by the bank of Weakley Creek. Containing 40
acres.
Wit: John W. Rucker   Signed: Robert E. Cock
     J.A. Patterson
Reg: January 12, 1867

Page 76 - Wilson & Hayden Deed to William Brown, House and Lot.
Pollock Wilson and Peter Hayden, partners under the name and
style of Wilson & Hayden of Cincinatti, Ohio have sold unto
William Brown of Shelbyville, Tennessee a certain tract of land
situate in the center part of the Town of Shelbyville, Bedford
County and bounded by Main Street, Wm. Brown, by land belonging
to Margaret Cummings formerly owned by John T. Neil, and by a
lot owned by A.L. Stamps. Containing 1 acre, being the lot
purchased by said Wilson and Hayden of Henry Hebbert and Joel H.
Burdett. This 21 December 1866.
Wit: Sam'l Carpenter   Signed: Pollock Wilson
     T.P. Carter   Peter Hayden
Reg: January 12, 1867

Page 77 - Smith Bowlin, as Trustee, Trust Deed to T.C.H. Miller.
Wm. F. Cooper by deed dated 1 December 1860 conveyed unto me in
trust a tract of land in Bedford County and District No. 5,
containing 245 acres and 144 poles and bounded by James
Ogilvie's corner, and by the Shelbyville Road. Said deed was
made secure by Solomon Claxton by note for his children. Other
names on notes: E.W. Hunter, E.A. Wilson, T.C.H. Miller, R.P.
Hunter, R.D. Rankin, J. Wilhoite, and Rich Shidmore. This 28
__ 1861.
Wit: Joseph Galleghy   Signed: Smith Bowlin, Trustee
     W.C. Cooper
     Jesse Boothe
Reg; January 12, 1867

Page 78 - William Gosling Deed to William Brown.   Land in
Bedford County and Civil District No. 7 and adjoining a corner
of William Brown's lot near the 1st mile post on the west side
of Shelbyville and Murfreesboro Road, and to the old Middleton
Road. Containing 2 acres and 4 poles. This 28 October 1866.

Reg: January 12, 1867   Signed: Wm. Gosling

Page 79 - Smith Bowlin Deed to James T. Coop. This 9 January 1867. Both of Bedford County. Land situated in Bellbuckle in Bedford County lying on the west side of the Nashville and Chattanooga Rail Road known as the lot of land Capt. Burrell Featherston sold to James Smalling and the same lot that James T. Coop, Jr. built a one story house on this lot and contains one half acre of land.
Wit: Horatio Coop   Signed: Smith Bowlin
     John M. Bowlin
Reg: January 12, 1867

Page 80 - Wm. S. Jett Deed to P. Gosling, House and Lot. I have sold unto Philomon Gosling. The town lot in Shelbyville on which is situated the brick house now occupied by the Shelbyville Bank of Tennessee and known as the Shelbyville Banking house fronting nineteen feet on the north side of Depot Street and running back to an alley in the rear of said Banking house. This 30 December 1863.
Wit: N. Thompson, Sr.   Signed: Wm. S. Gosling
     W.H. Martin
Reg: January 12, 1867

Page 80 - S.N. Elliott Transfer to W.Y. Elliott, Book. I have this day sold unto William Y. Elliott my law books. Several named books listed in original document. This 11 January 1867.
Reg: January 14, 1867   Signed: Sam'l N. Elliott

Page 81 - P. Gosling Deed to William Gosling, House and Lot. All the right title claim and interest in the Town Lot in Shelbyville, Tennessee on which is situated the brick house now occupied by the Shelbyville Bank of Tennessee and known as the Shelbyville Banking House fronting on the north side of Depot Street and to an alley in the rear of said Banking House together with all the fixtures and vault in said Banking House. This 30 December 1863.
Reg: January 14, 1867   Signed: P. Gosling

Page 82 - Wm. M. Tatum Deed to Madison M. Williams. Land in Bedford County and adjoining R.B. Freeman, by Hartwell Freeman, and by A.J. Goodrum's corner. Containing 135 acres and 39 poles. This 14 December 1866.
Reg: January 14, 1867   Signed: W.M. Tatum

Page 83 - Enoch Williams Deed to W.M. Tatum, 52 acres. Both of Bedford County. Enoch Williams sold unto William M. Tatum land in Bedford County and containing 52 acres and bounded by M.F. Williams, and by Hartwell Freeman. This December 14, 1866.
Reg: January 15, 1867   Signed: (Enoch Williams)

Page 83 - Joseph E. Stephens Deed to Hosea Cheshire, 27 acres
and 50 poles. All my right and interest being one half unto an
undivided tract of land the other half belonging to the heirs of
Elijah Couch, deceased, being in Bedford County upon the waters
of Thompson Creek in Civil District No. 24 and containing 54
acres and 100 poles and bounded by Jonathan Parker's old corner,
by Leighton Anthony's line, by Epps Parker's line being Hosea
Cheshire's corner and by Nathaniel Cheshire's corner, and by
Mrs. Anthony's line. This 18 October 1865.
Reg: January 15, 1867   Signed: J.E. Stevens

Page 84 - Thos. Dalton Deed to G.W. Thompson. G.W. Thompson and
James Wortham as my security and Robert Dennis in two notes
executed to Joseph H. Thompson. I have sold unto G.W. Thompson
land in Bedford County near the Town of Shelbyville, containing
about 7 acres and 78 poles, it being a part of the land known as
the Wilson Coats' tract and the same purchased by myself and
Robert Dennis and being the same upon which myself and others
now reside and bounded by Elizabeth Hampton formerly McAnnally
and others, by Robt. Cannon, by J.F. Cummings, and by Philip
Brooks. Surveyed by Wm. Galbreath, Esq. as Lot No. 17 of the
Wilson Coats' tract and was sold to said G.W. Thompson. This 5
January 1867.
Reg: January 15, 1867   Signed: Thomas Dalton

Page 85 - G.W. Thompson Deed to Thos. Dalton. Land or lot
situated in Bedford County and near the Town of Shelbyville and
near the Nashville and Chattanooga Rail Road and bounded by Lot
No. 17 sold by Joseph H. Thompson of the lands of Wilson Coats,
deceased, and purchased by said Dalton and Robert Dennis. This
25 January 1867.
Reg: January 16, 1867   Signed: G.W. Thompson

Page 85 - W. McKiney and wife Deed to Sutton Gosling, Col.
House and Lot. We, Wm. M. McKinney and his wife Rhoda Ann
McKiney conveyed to Sutton Gosling (col) a tract of land in
Bedford County and near the Town of Shelbyville in what is known
as Camp White and bounded by a lot known in the plan of lots
laid off and sold by Clement Cannon, Sr., as Lot No. 8 in the
edge of White Street and Camp Street, and by Locust Street.
This 14 January 1867.
Wit: Charlotta Burditt   Signed: W. McKinney
Reg: January 16, 1867   Rhoda Ann McKinney

Page 86 - W.T. Lewellen Deed to Thomas M. White, undivided
interest. Land in 20th Civil District of Bedford County known
as the Nat. White farm and on which said Nat. White resided at
the time of his death and bounded by lands of Susan Davidson, by
the lands of Susan Davidson and Mrs. Bradshaw, by the lands of
Hillsman Bledsoe, by the lands of W.W. Evans. Land being my
life estate in to an undivided one fifth in said land which life
estate I acquired through my deceased wife Jane A. Lewellen who
was a daughter of said Nat. White. This January 14, 1867.
Reg: January 16, 1867   Signed: W.T. Lewellen

Page 87 - H.H. Holt and wife Deed to Thomas M. White, undivided
interest. All our interest in the personal estate of Nathaniel
White, deceased, which consists of stock, money, notes &c. Also
a tract of land in 20th Civil District of Bedford County and
bounded by lands of Susan Davidson, by Susan Davidson and Mrs.
Bradshaw, by the lands of Hillsman Bledsoe and W.W. Evans, and
by the lands of Mrs. Bradshaw. Containing 130 acres. The same
being known as the Nat. White farm and on the said Nat. White
resided at the time of his death. This 14 January 1867.
Reg: January 16, 1867   Signed: H.H. Holt
                                       M.C. Holt

Page 88 - Joseph Thompson Deed to Howel Williams, 24 acres.
Land in Bedford County and District No. 11, it being Lot No. 7
of the division of the lands of D.W. Thompson and bounded by the
center of Weakley Creek a corner of Lot No. 1 of said division,
by Lot No. 8, by Howel Williams' corner, and by Lot No. 6.
Containing 24 acres and 40 poles. This 14 January 1867.
Wit: James G. Wheeler   Signed: Joseph Thompson
     Reuben Thompson
     W.T.B. Moore
Reg: January 17, 1867

Page 88 - J.B. Gambill Deed to Thomas Kimmons, undivided
interest. All my undivided interest of one half of one eighth
of a tract of land in the 20th District of Bedford County and
consisting 63 acres, it being the place known as the Whitesell
place bounded by the lands of James Coats' estate, by lands of
John W. Greer(Green?), and by lands of Thomas J. Robinson. The
17 January 1867.
Reg: January 17, 1867   Signed: J.B. Gambill

Page 89 - Abner C. Potts Deed to Thomas F. Simmons, 80 acres.
Land in Bedford County and District No. 11 on the North Fork of
Duck River and bounded by Joseph Williams, and by the old school
land line. Containing 30 acres. This January 18, 1867.
Wit: J.S. Jones   Signed: Abner C. Potts
     H.G. Culbertson
Reg: January 18, 1867

Page 90 - William B. Cowan Deed to Hiram B. Crowel. I having
bought of Hiram B. Crowel a tract of land in Bedford County,
District No. 18 the same that George Cook sold to said H.B.
Crowel and containing 115 acres. This December 29, 1866.
Wit: Wm. G. Cowan   Signed: Wm.B. Cowan
     John T. Stephen
Reg: January 19, 1867

Page 90 - James B. Puckett Deed to John L. Cooper, Trustee of
M.G. Puckett. On 12 April 1860 a decree was rendered in favor
of John L. Cooper as Trustee of Mary G. Puckett in which that
James A. Puckett should make a deed to said John L. Cooper as
Trustee for a tract of land in Bedford County and Civil District

288

No. 9, containing about 84 acres. Land bounded by John A. Webb, by G.W. Holden, by Moses Foster and others, and by a 20 acre tract owned by J.A. Puckett. This 21 January 1867.
Wit: N.F. Thompson   Signed: James A. Puckett
Reg: January 21, 1867

Page 91 - Thomas F. Coleman, Discharge - Thomas F. Coleman a Private of Captain Reuben C. Couch Company (F) 5th Regiment of Tennessee Cavalry Volunteers who was enrolled on the 18th day of August 1863 to serve three years or during the war is hereby discharged from the service of the United States this 14th day of August 1865 at Pulaski, Tennessee by reason of Special Order No. 18 C.S. Mil Div Tenn. No objection to his being re-enlisted is known to exist. Said Thomas F. Coleman was born in Lincoln County, Tennessee is twenty seven years of age, five feet five inches high, dark complexion, gray eyes, brown hair and by occupation when enrolled a farmer. Given at Pulaski, Tenn. this 14th day of August 1865.
Francis Jackson, Captain   R.C. Couch, Captain
Oath of Identity - Thomas F. Coleman of the Town of ____ Bedford County on the 4th day of September 1865 personally appeared before me the undersigned a Justice of the Peace for the County and State above mentioned. Thomas F. Coleman who being duly sworn according to law declared that he is the identical person who was a Private soldier in the Company commanded by Captain Reuben C. Couch in the Regiment 5th Cavalry commanded by Joseph Clift that he enlisted on 19th August 1863 for the term of three years and was discharged at Nashville on the 22 August 1865 by reason of special Order September 5, 1865.
Reg: January 22, 1867   Signed: Thomas F. Coleman

Page 92 - R.W. Houston Deed to W.B. Overcast. Land in District No. 6 of Bedford County and bounded by the lands of G.W.P. Ervin, by lands of C.P. Houston, Sr., by lands of Wm. Houston, and by lands of John R. Thompson and F.E. McElrath. Containing 50 acres. This 22 January 1867.
Reg: January 22, 1867   Signed: R.W. Houston

Page 92 - Jo. Thompson, Sheriff, Deed to James Woods and others. On 6 August 1861 in Bedford County James Woods, Henry C. Yeatman and John Bell recovered a judgment against Robert Galbreath and A.P. Eakin an execution was issued on 25 April 1866 and came to the hands of Joseph Thompson, Sheriff, and which levied upon 5 ¾ acres of land in the Town of Shelbyville and beginning on the south side of Lane street, by Primrose's boundary, and to the center of Duck River. Containing 44 acres levied on as the property of Robert Galbreath being the same lot conveyed to him by Williams & Cannon on 7 July 1864. This 22 January 1867.
Reg: January 22, 1867   Signed: Jo. Thompson

Page 93 - Jo. Thompson, Sheriff, Deed to James Woods and others. On 24 August 1860 James Woods and Henry C. Yeatman recovered a judgment against John L. Burt and James F. Cummings. An execution was issued on 8 October 1860 and delivered to Garret

Philips who levied the same on a house and lot belonging to said Cummings in the Town of Shelbyville near the Rail Road Depot, and containing __ acres being the same lot conveyed by William Gosling to said Cummings dated __ day of August 1859. On 1 December 1860 sold to highest bidder to said James Woods and Henry C. Yeatman. This __ January 1867.
Reg: January 22, 1867   Signed: Jo. Thompson

Page 94 - T.C.H. Miller Deed to E.M. Cooper. Land in Bedford County and District No. 5, containing 23 acres. This 28 November 1866.
Wit: L.S. Moore   Signed: T.C.H. Miller
     J.B. Hunter
     A. Wilson
     W.C. Cooper
Reg: January 24, 1867

Page 95 - T.C.H. Miller Deed to Benjamin Whitworth. T.C.H. Miller sold unto Benjamin F. Whitworth a tract of land in Bedford County and District No. 5, containing 92 acres and 136 poles. Said land adjoining land belonging to Jos. Ogilvie's heirs. This 28 November 1866.
Wit: S.J. Moore   Signed: T.C.H.Miller
     J.B. Hunter
     A. Wilson
Reg: January 24, 1867

Page 95 - George Smith and others Deed to Thomas Shearin and others. We, George Smith, John L. Rainy and Martha his wife, have this day sold unto Thomas Shearin a tract of land in Bedford County and District No. 11 and bounded by Samuel Crowel's' corner, by Michael Capley's line, and by Jacob Fisher's corner. Containing 179 acres and 40 poles. This 5 September 1855.
Wit: W.M. Robinson   Signed: G. Smith
     W.M. Ray   Jos. L. Rainy
Reg: January 25, 1867   Martha F. Rainy

Page 96 - J.L. Cooper, Extr. &c Deed to J.A. Jarrett, 92 ½ acres. J.L. Cooper, executor of J.C. Wood, have sold to J.A. Jarrett a tract of land in Bedford County and District No. 8 containing 92 acres and 80 poles and bounded by a tract of F.P. McElrath's line, by John Claxton to Harriet Pate's line, to Falling Creek, and by Wm. Phillips' line. This October 11, 1866.
Wit: J.F. Gray   Signed: J.L. Cooper, Extr.
     Tempie E. Cooper
Reg: January 25, 1867

Page 97 - Henry Yancy Deed to Moses Marshall. Henry Yancy sold unto Moses Marshall one half of a store house and lot in the Town of Shelbyville on the east side of the Public Square and purchased by me at a sale by executors of Gen. Robt. Cannon. It

is known as "The Lands Store House" fronting on the square. This January 24, 1867.
Reg: January 25, 1867   Signed: Henry Yancy

Page 98 - N. Sugg Deed to R.B. Bigham. Both of Bedford County and District No. 4 and adjoining a line of Sugg's, a Fugitt's tract, B.C. Johnson's corner, to center of Murfreesboro and Shelbyville Road, by R. Beechboard's corner, and to center of Wartrace Creek above the water gate. Containing 67 acres and 5 poles. This 18 December 1866.
Wit: B.G. Field   Signed: N. Sugg
     Wm. Hoover
Reg: January 28, 1867

Page 98 - Reuben Curry Deed to R.B. Bigham. I, Reuben Curry of Caldwell County, Kentucky sold unto Robert B. Bigham of Bedford County a tract of land on the waters of Duck River, Bedford County and adjoining the Wartrace Fork where Murfreesboro and Shelbyville Road crosses said creek, to Williams branch, and to west of the Fosterville Road. Containing 116 poles. This 30 November 1865.
Wit: J. McK. Clark   Signed: Reuben Curry
     B.G. Fields
Reg: January 28, 1867

Page 100 - R.B. Bigham Deed to William Hoover. Both of Bedford County. Land in Bedford County and Civil District No. 4 adjoining in the center of Wartrace Creek in the south boundary line of the Eoff land, to near the Spout Spring, and by A.J. Bigham's water gate. Containing 23 acres and 63 poles. This 18 December 1866.
Wit: B.G. Fields   Signed: R.B. Bigham
     N. Sugg
Reg: January 29, 1867

Page 100 - J.T. Hoover Deed to Alex. Mourland. This 31 October 1862. John T. Hoover of Bedford County sold to Eli Mourland of Rutherford County, Tennessee land in Bedford County and bounded by said Hoover's north boundary line side of a road running east. Containing 6 acres.
Wit: J.H. Woodfin   Signed: J.T. Hoover
     William Hoover
Reg: January 29, 1867

Page 101 - Joel S.S. Wallis and others to H.C. Kinard, undivided interest. We, Joel S.S. Wallis and Allen M. Wallis, have sold to H.C. Kinnard all our right title claim and interest in and to a tract of land in the 3rd District of Bedford County and bounded by lands of H.C. Kinnard and Eliza George, by lands of Eliza George, by lands of Mrs. R.J. King, and by lands of Isabella George. Containing 100 acres, it being the tract of land known as the Widow Ditto's dower the interest therein conveyed being two thirds of one third in said land which said interest descended to us in right of our mother Cynthia Wallis who was a daughter of Phereba Ditto or Phereba Elkins. This 11 January 1867.

Signed: Joel S.S. Wallis
Allen M. Wallis

Christian County, Kentucky - Allen M. Wallace a grantor, which is certified at Hopkinsville 21 January 1867.
Reg: January 27, 1867

Page 102 - A.L. Stamps Deed to Jos. D. Wilhoite. All of Bedford County. Land in the 7th Civil District of Bedford County in the corporate limits of the Town of Shelbyville and bounded by P. Nelligan, by P. Fay, by Wm. Little, by the street leading from the Big Spring branch to the old fair ground, it being the lot redeemed of James Russ and sold by Jos. Thompson, Sheriff, on 27 July 1861, the same having been levied on and sold as the property of B. Nelligan.
Reg: January 30, 1867   Signed: A.L. Stamps

Page 103 - Nimrod Burrow and others Deed to James S. Newton. This 10 January 1867. Nimrod Burrow, Wiley B. Snell, Herod F. Snell(Holt?) and Adam S. Riggs (Trustees and committee appointed by (illegible) Conf. Of Rich Valley Ct.) to James S. Newton, all of Bedford County and District No. 21 and bounded at a beech marked FRS on Richard Phillips' line, and by Phillips' line to a beech marked BT and except 10 poles which is reserved as a right of way to the grave yard. Containing 1 acre and 2 ½ poles. This 10 January 1867.
Reg: January 30, 1867   Signed: Nimrod Burrow
Willie B. Snell
H.F. Holt
Adam S. Riggs

Page 103 - J.B. McAdams Deed to Nancy Marshall. I, Jesse B. McAdams, have sold to Nancy Marshall a tract of land in the 7th District of Bedford County near the Town of Shelbyville and bounded by the lands of (illegible) Reed, by lands of Mrs. Robert ?. Jones, by the Shelbyville Branch Rail Road, and by my own land. Containing about 3 acres. This 28 January 1867.
Reg: January 30, 1867   Signed: J.B. McAdams
Nancy Marshall

Page 104 - Bartley Posey Deed to Jefferson White. I convey and sell unto Jefferson White (a colored man) a tract of land in the Town of Shelbyville, Bedford County and known as Lot No. __. Beginning at Carney's (old corner was Henry Brown), by Carney's (now Brown's) line. This October 2, 1866.
Wit: G.W. Buchanan   Signed: Bartley Posey
H.L. Davidson
Reg: January 30, 1867

105 - Henry Clark Deed to W.H. Clark, 112 acres. Land in Bedford County and Civil District No. 11, containing 112 acres

and 42 poles, bounded by John W. Maxwell, to the center of
Alexander Creek, to Widow Short's corner, to center of the North
Fork of Duck River, and to Absalom Reeves' corner.   This 27
September 1866.
Wit: Wm. N. Orr   Signed: Henry Clark
      H.C. Clark
Reg: January 30, 1867

Page 106 - R.H. Temple Trust Deed to James Story.   This 9
January 1867.   Robert H. Temple sold unto James Story, both of
Bedford County, the following property, to wit, one tract of
land in Civil District No. 21 of Bedford County and bounded by
lands of Nancy Stephens, by lands of Thos. Lipscomb, by lands of
Patsy Stephens, and by lands of R.H. Sims.   Containing 100 acres
being the land on which said Temple resides.   Also one gray and
one sorrel horse, fifteen head of sheep, also fifteen head of
large hogs, one bureau and one chins press.   The said Robert H.
Temple is indebted to said Story by note, also Wiley J.
(illegible), also to Miss Nancy Streeter, also indebted to G.W.
Brown, to Dr. Thos. Lipscomb for medical services, also to Dr.
Christopher for medical services.   This 9 January 1867.
Wit: Thos. C. Whiteside   Signed: Robert H. Temple
      William Frierson
Reg: January 30, 1867

Page 107 - Nancy E. Gooch and Roland Gooch Deed to Jeremiah
Culverhouse, 25 ½ acres.   This 18 September 1866.   Nancy E.
Gooch and Roland Gooch of Maury County, Tennessee sold to
Jeremiah Culverhouse of Bedford County Lot No. 1 being a part of
the lands owned by Henry W. Jones, deceased, of Bedford County,
given to Nancy E. Jones now present wife of Roland Gooch, lying
in 9th Civil District of Bedford County and bounded by Jeremiah
Culverhouse's corner.   Containing 8 acres.   Also Lot No. 2 being
a part of same tract and bounded by Thomas Culverhouse's tract,
and by Jeremiah Culverhouse's tract.   Containing 17 ¼ acres.
Reg: January 31, 1867   Signed: N.E. Gooch
                                      Roland Gooch

Page 108 - E.P. Kingree Deed to W.W. Gill, 47 acres.   This 18
December 1866.   Elizabeth P. Kingree sold unto W.W. Gill, both
of Bedford County, a tract of land in Bedford County on the head
waters of Sugar Creek and Civil District No. 22, it being the
west portion of said land sold to her by W.W. Gill and deed the
13 February 1866 and bounded in the center of the pike, south of
Sam Bird's corner, and W.W. Gill's line, and by Mrs. Gammel's
line.   Containing 47 acres.
Reg: January 31, 1867   Signed: E.P. Kingree

Page 109 - Lewis Sears Deed to Emma Morgan.   I, Lewis Sears,
have sold to Emma Morgan the south half to her heirs by James
Kerling and the north half of the heirs of Daniel Morgan the
present husband of E. Morgan a tract of 10 acres of land in
Bedford County and District No. 7 about ¾ of a mile north west
of the Town of Shelbyville on the west side of the old Nashville

Road and adjoining E. Green's line, and R. Foreman's corner.
This 2 May 1856   Signed: Lewis sears
Reg: January 31, 1867

Page 109 – Jason T. Cannon Deed to Alexr. Sanders. Land in 7th District of Bedford County near the Town of Shelbyville on the Unionville Turnpike and bounded by the center of the Shelbyville and Unionville Turnpike where the old Warner Dirt Road comes into said Turnpike Road, by a 2 ½ acre lot owned at one time and perhaps now owned by Thomas H. Coldwell, and by the south east corner of the place on which T.J. Williams formerly resided. Containing 1 ¾ acres. It being the lot originally owned by Thomas H. Coldwell and by him conveyed to Walter B. Perkins and was conveyed by said Perkins to Thomas H. Coldwell as Trustee and then conveyed to me. Registered in Book EEE, pages 145 and 146. This 30 January 1867.
Reg: February 1, 1867   Signed: J.T. Cannon

Page 110 – R.S. Montgomery Deed to Sam'l Carpenter, 105+ acres. Land in Civil District No. 19 of Bedford County, being a part of the lands of John Larue and known as Lot No. 3 and bounded by a corner of Lot No. 1. Containing 105+ acres. This 20 September 1866.
Wit: Thos. S. Montgomery   Signed: Robert S. Montgomery
     J.H. Brecheen
Reg: February 1, 1867

Page 111 – J.H. Brecheen Deed to Samuel Carpenter, 101 acres. Land known as Lot No. 2 of the John Larue land. Situated in District No. 19 of Bedford County and bounded by Thomas N. Bell's corner, and by a corner of Lot No. 1. Containing 101 acres. This 25 September 1866.
Wit: R.S. Montgomery   Signed: J.H. Brecheen
     H.C. Montgomery
Reg: February 1, 1867

Page 111 – D. Morris and others Deed to Oliver P. Arnold, House and Lot in Wartrace. This 29 January 1867. D. Morris and T.H. Calvin, both of Granger County, Tennessee, sold to Oliver P. Arnold of Bedford County a certain piece of land or Town Lot in the Village of Wartrace, Civil District No. 3 and bounded by Pike Street, by Robt. Chambers' lot sold by Lewis Tillman and afterwards sold by D. Morris to T.H. Calvin and recorded in Book EEE, pages 408 and 409. The said Tillman sold under decree in the case of Sarah A. Hicks and others against John E. Dromgoole and others.
Reg: February 1, 1867   Signed: D. Morris
                                       T.H. Calvin

Page 112 – Thomas H. Coldwell Deed to H.O. Huffman, House and Lot. I, Thomas H. Coldwell, have sold unto H.O. Huffman a horse and buggy and harness. He executed his note 1 July 1867 all the right title claim and interest which I have in and unto a house

and about 2 ½ acres of land near the Town of Shelbyville, Civil District No. 7 and bounded by the Shelbyville and Unionville Turnpike Road, and by a lot belonging to Jason T. Cannon, by the old Warner Dirt Road, and by the place on which I now live which land is all enclosed. This 5 January 1867.
Wit: L.D. Warder?   Signed: Thos. H. Coldwell
      Jesse ?. Gosling
Reg: February 2, 1867

Page 113 - W.J. Whitthorne Deed to Jo. D. Wilhoite.   On 9 November 1859.   I sold unto Joseph D. Wilhoite a parcel of ground in Bedford County and District No. 7, adjoining the lands of said Wilhoite on the Rail Road near the corporation of the Town of Shelbyville, by the McMinnville Road, and by Ramsey's smoke house. This 17 March 1866.
Reg: February 2, 1867   Signed: W.J. Whitthorne

Page - 113 - Wm. J. Whitthorne Title Bond to J. Wilhoite, Trustee.   Joseph D. Wilhoite has this day purchased of me his note this 1 January 1867.   One note dated 30 October 1866 a town lot in the Town of Shelbyville on the corner of Depot and Martin Streets being the corner house and lot of the Gen. Cannon block at present occupied by John F. Brown, also being the house and lot purchased by me at the sale of said Cannon's property sold by his executors. This 30 October 1866.
Reg: February 2, 1867   Signed: Wm. J. Whitthorne

Page 114 - Jason Ray Deed to Amos Ray, 46 acres and 24 poles. Jason Ray and Amos G. Ray, both of Bedford County and Civil District No. 24 and bounded near the school house, by W.J. Bomar's line, and by Manuel Ray's land. Containing 46 acres and 24 poles. This 20 June 1866.
Wit: K.J. Pearson   Signed: Jason Ray
      B. Stephens
Reg: February 2, 1867

Page 114 - Jordan Holden Deed to C.H. Lamb and Wm. Williams. Land in Bedford County and Civil District No. 7(9?) and bounded by James Foster's corner, by the Middleton Road, and to a rock buried in the ground James Foster's corner.   Containing 200 acres. This January 6, 1866.
Wit: D.M. Holden   Signed: Jourdon Holden
      Lafayette C. Lamb
Reg: February 4, 1867

Page 115 - John S. Arnold and wife Deed to H.C. Kinnard. We, John S. Arnold and Sarah Arnold sold unto H.C. Kinnard all the right title claim and interest is a tract of land in the 3rd Civil District of Bedford County and bounded by lands of Mrs. Jack George, by lands of Mrs. C. George, by lands of R.J. King, and by lands of H.C. Kinnard's land estimated at 100 acres and known as the Widow Ditto's dower. This 6 November 1865.
Reg: February 4, 1867   Signed: John S. Arnold

Page 116 - Wm. Gosling Bond to J.O. Soaps and George Parsons. I, William Gosling. Bind myself to J.O. Soaps and Geo. Parsons. I have this day sold unto J.O. Soaps and Geo. Parsons a tract of land in Bedford County and Civil District No. 11 and bounded by lands of David J. Osment, by Mrs. Wm. Smith's land, by lands of Abe Parsons and Wm. B.M. Brame, and by the lands of Dr. Jeff Long. Containing 100 acres. It being the same land I purchased from Wm. S. Jett some years since. This 2 February 1867.
Reg: February 4, 1867   Signed: William Gosling

Page 117 - S.W. Jones Deed to John A. McLain. I have sold unto John A. McLain a tract of land in Bedford County and Civil District No. 9 and bounded by land in K. Tucker's Dist., and by McLain's original corner. Containing 109 1/10 poles. This 8 May 1866.
Wit: J.?.?. Wallace   Signed: S.W. Jones
     L.A. Clark
Reg: February 4, 1867

Page 117 - J.W. Hill and wife Deed to Daniel F. Cocke. Brazoria County, Texas. We, James W. Hill and his wife Sarah J. Hill of Brazoria County, Texas, sold to Daniel F. Cocke of the Town of Gainesville, Alabama, a tract of land in Bedford County about ten miles from the Town of Murfreesboro and near the Town of Middleton being the same tract of land received by Sarah J. Hill one of the heirs of her father C.G. McLain in the partation of the estate of said McLain, which was made in 1861. Land contains 97 acres. This 29 January 1866.
Reg: February 5, 1867   Signed: Sallie Hill
                                       J.W. Hill

Page 118 - J.C. Claxton, Procession Deed. Bedford County November 1866. I went on the premises of James C. Claxton this day. I proceeded to survey and procession the tract of land on which said Claxton now lives, adjoining Erwin's line, and by the Shelbyville Road. Containing 149 acres and 56 poles.
Wit: Wm. J. Philpott   Signed: C.S. Dudley, Surveyor
     B.F. Smith
NOTE: Plat on page 119
Reg: February 5, 1867

Page 119 - D.C. Moore et als Power of Attorney to Samuel P. Moore. We, Don C. Moore in his own right and as guardian of Sarah J. Moore and Francis S. Moore, children and heirs of Don C. Moore and Sarah Y. Moore, deceased, and as guardian of Joseph A. Moore, sole surviving heirs of John F. Moore, deceased, said John F. Moore a son of the said Don C. Moore and Sarah Y. Moore, deceased, and Leonard C. Moore, Green M. Moore, James N. Moore and James R. McAnaly and Mary E. McAnaly his wife but formerly Mary E. Moore, all of Randolph County, Arkansas, have appointed Samuel P. Moore, of same place, our true and lawful attorney for

us and in our names to ask, demand, sue, receive for all such sums of money which is due and belonging to us as being or legatees in and to the estate of Samuel Phillips, deceased, said estate being in Bedford County. This 31 December 1866.
Reg: February 5, 1867   Signed: D.C. Moore
                              Francis C. Moore
                              Green M. Moore
                              James N. Moore
                              James M. McAnaly
                              Mary E. McAnaly

Page 121 - W.T. Nance Deed to W.H.H. Baxter. I, W.T. Nance, have sold to W.H.H. Baxter a tract of land in Bedford County and Civil District No. 18, containing 43 acres and bounded by the blue spring that granted by Malcomb Gilchrist, by Hammell's corner, by an entry made in the name of said Gilchrist, and by a 3 acre tract. It being the same tract of land deeded to me by N.W. Haly October 3, 1865. This February 4, 1867.
Reg: February 5, 1867   Signed: W.T. Nance

Page 121 - E.W. Adams, Procession Deed. Bedford County, January 31, 1867, I went on the premises of E.W. Adams. I proceeded to survey &c the tract of land that E.W. Adams now lives bounded by a branch C.R. Head's corner, and by old Township Corner. Containing 160 acres and 112 poles.
Wit: C.R. Head, C.C.   Signed: C.S. Dudley, Surveyor
     F. Capley, C.C.
NOTE: Plat on page 122
Reg: February 6, 1867

Page 122 - A. Prewitt and wife Deed to H.C. Kinnaird. We, Archibald Prewitt and wife Elizabeth Prewitt, have sold unto H.C. Kinnaird all the right title claim and interest that is coming to us from the estate of Polly McGuire, deceased, the same being an undivided interest in the tract of land known as the Widow Ditto tract being in the 3rd District of Bedford County and bounded by Ziza George and H.C. Kinnaird, by Mary King, by Mrs. Eliza George, and by Mrs. Isabella George. Containing 100 acres. It being the one eighth of one third in said land. This 26 January 1867.
Wit: N,C. Harris   Signed: A. Prewitt
keg: February 6, 1867   Elizabeth Prewitt

Page 123 - H.H. Renegar Deed to Nancy E. Renegar et als, 56 acres. I, H.H. Renegar, have sold to Mary E. Renegar, Sarah E. Renegar and Victoria E. Renegar a tract of land in Bedford County and District No. 25. Containing 56 acres. This January 15, 1867.
Wit: R.L. Renegar   Signed: H.H. Renegar
     Santford Renegar
Reg: February 6, 1867

Page 124 - George Hooser Deed to Mary Williams. On 15 September 1860 Daniel Hooser did bind himself unto Benjamin K. Coble. I, having this day sold to Benjamin K. Coble a tract of land in Bedford County and Civil District No. 25 and adjoining Duck River. Containing 70 acres and 27 poles, I, George M. Hooser, by virtue of the power vested in me as executor of Daniel Hooser, deceased, have this day sold unto the devises of said Benjamin K. Coble, deceased, to wit, Mrs. Mary Williams his mother during her natural life and at her death to S.D. Coble, A.B. Coble, N.B. Coble, Mrs. Fannie Carter, Mrs. Martha Ann Miller and Catherine Callaway his (illegible), another tract of land in Bedford County and Civil District No. 25 bounded by Duck River. Containing 70 acres and 29 poles. This 4 February 1867.
Reg: February 7, 1867   Signed: Geo. M. Hooser, Extr. Of
                                            Daniel Hooser, deceased

Page 125 - B.B. Morgan Trust Deed to E.T. Haley. I have sold unto E.T. Haley one two horse wagon and harness, one fine house and five head of cattle and one good rifle gun and a silver watch. I am indebted to E.T. Haley. This 2 February 1867.
Reg: February 7, 1867   Signed: B.B. Morgan

Page 126 - William Phillips, Procession Deed. Bedford County, January 31, 1867, I went on the premises of William Phillips to survey &c the tract of land on which Wm. Phillips now lives. Bounded by B.G. Gambill's north boundary line. Containing 87 acres and 157 poles.
Wit: C.R. Head, C.C.   Signed: C.S. Dudley, Surveyor
     Lewis Sutton, C.C.
NOTE: Plat on page 126.
Reg: February 7, 1867

Page 126 - N.F. Pickle and wife Deed to Thos. S. Gant. We, Newton F. Pickle and wife Margaret E. Pickle, have sold unto Thomas S. Gant a tract of land partitioned to the heirs at law of Harriet Musgrove, deceased, in the division of the land of her mother Edith Forbes, deceased, and bounded by lands allotted to the heirs of William Forbes, deceased, by lands of John C. Liggett, by lands allotted Thomas M. Forbes, and by lands of Coffey said lot of land they partitioned to the heirs of Harriet Murgrove, deceased. Containing 60 acres. This 2 January 1867.
                         Signed: N.F. Pickle
                                    Margaret E. Pickle
Johnson County, Illinois - N.F. Pickle and Margaret E. Pickle are personally known to me.
Reg: February 7, 1867

Page 127 - C.P. Houston, Sr. Deed to F.P. McElrath. I have on 28 July 1859 sold to F.P. McElrath a tract of land in Bedford County on Dry Fork of Fall Creek in District No. 5, adjoining the lands of William Houston, George D. Hutton, Thos. B. Marks and wife, Thos. Ogilvie and wife, and known as the Joana Nash dower tract. Containing 125 acres. This July 31, 1866.
Reg: February 8, 1867   Signed: C.P. Houston

Page 128 - F.P. McElrath Deed to C.P. Houston. I conveyed to
C.P. Houston land in Bedford County and District No. 6 and
bounded by lands of Wilie Ellis, C.P. Houston, Sr., and John
Overcast, by lands of George W. P. Erwin, by a tract conveyed to
C.P. Houston by John Smith, and by Thomas C. Whiteside.
Containing 250 acres. This January 29, 1867.
Reg: February 8, 1867   Signed: F.P. McElrath

Page 128 - Iverson Knott Deed to James Purvis. I, Iverson Knott
of Bedford County, have sold unto James Purvis of same place one
yellow mare, one iron gray horse colt, and one sorrel colt.
Said Purvis has become stayor of execution on a judgment in
favor of J.R. McKinley VS Iverson Knott dated 31 January 1867.
This 1 February 1867.
Wit: H.C. Turner   Signed: Iverson Knott
     J.E. Wallace
Reg: February 8, 1867

Page 129 - W.R. Tinsley Bond to M.T. Griswell.   December 1,
1866. I, W.R. Tinsley of Franklin County, Tennessee, sold unto
M.T. Griswell a certain Town Lot in the Village of Wartrace,
Bedford County as described in deed from S.W. Tilford to W.R.
Tinsley registered in Shelbyville August 27, 1864.
Wit: Dewitt Bennett   Signed: W.R. Tinsley
     R.R. Enochs
Reg: February 8, 1867

Page 129 - H.J.T. Moss and others Deed to Wiley Riggins and
Margaret Riggins.   This 23, January 1867 between Harry J.T.
Cook, J.T. Moss, Jasper Cook and Mary J. Cook by their attorney
in fact. Harry J.T. Cook of Franklin County, Illinois and Wiley
Riggins and Margaret Riggins of Bedford County and District No.
25.   Said Harry J.T. Moss, Jasper Cook and Mary J. Cook wife of
said Cook sold unto Wiley Riggins and Margaret Riggins all the
right title claim and interest to which said Harry J.T. Moss,
Jasper Cook, Mary J. Cook, heirs of Felix Moss, deceased, in a
tract of land in Bedford County and District No. 25 known as the
Mathew Moss tract of land of about 102 acres being one ninth.
Reg: February 8, 1867   Signed: Mary J. Cook
                                        Jasper Cook, by
                                        Harry J.T. Moss, Atty.

Page 130 - Nancy J. Cummings Deed to Peyton Steele (col).   I,
Nancy J. Cummings, have sold unto Peyton Steele (a free man of
color) a tract of land in the 21st Civil District of Bedford
County and bounded by the center of the Fayetteville Pike.
Containing in all according to survey made by C.S. Dudley 6
acres. This 7 February 1867.
Reg: February 8, 1867   Signed: Nancy J. Cummings

Page 131 - John Murry Deed to Charlotta Murry. I have had and
sold of my wife, Charlotta Murry, money which belonged to her
for the sale and separate use. I transfer to her the house and

lot whereon I now live being in the Town of Wartrace in Civil District No. 3 of Bedford County and bounded by an alley 20 feet from A.H. Coffey, by Nob Creek Turnpike, and by a lot now occupied by Thos. Hart with a store. Charlotta Murry (my wife). This February 7, 1867.
Reg: February 8, 1867   Signed: John Murry

Page 131 - J.J. Burrow and John Wilson to John Wilhoite. We, Jarrel J. Burrow and John Wilson, have sold unto John Wilhoite land in Civil District No. 22 of Bedford County and bounded by lands of John Wilhoite, by lands of William Campbell, and by lands of Mahala Bomar and Thomas Conwell. Containing 20 acres. This 10 February 1867.
Reg: February 9, 1867   Signed: J.J. Burrow
                                       John Wilson

Page 132 - J.J. Burrow Deed to John Wilhoite. J.J. Burrow did on 7 April 1866 in Bedford County sold to John Wilhoite a tract of land in Bedford County on the waters of Flat Creek a south branch of Duck River, and adjoining John Wilhoite and J.J. Burrow's old corner, and by Sally Chandler's line. Containing 11 acres and 22 ½ acres.
Reg: February 9, 1867   Signed: J.J. Burrow

Page 133 - Jo. Thompson, Sheriff, Deed to Sam'l D. Morgan. Whereas Sam D. Morgan, Chas. J. Cheny(?) and Joseph A. Duncan, partners under the name and style of Morgan & CO. recovered three several judgment against Willis Blanton, W.F. Davidson and W.M. Barton. Thereon were levied upon two lots with houses thereon in the Town of Normandy, Bedford County, there being no personal property of said Willis Blanton to be found in said county which executions were returned to its December Term 1860 upon which lives, the court ordered a (illegible) &c which came to the hands of Garrett Phillips, then Sheriff of Bedford County on 8 January 1861. Said lots lying in the Town of Normandy of Bedford County and bounded by the 1st by lands of Holland's heirs, and by lands of Bennett Cully. The 2nd by the Rail Road, the lands of John McQuiddy, by lands of Chasley Arnold, and by the lands of B.L. Hubbard. This 11 February 1867.
Reg: February 11, 1867   Signed: Jo. Thompson, Sheriff

Page 134 - Wiley Riggins and wife Deed to Middleton Holland. We, Wiley Riggins and Margaret Riggins formerly Margaret Moss, daughter of Mathew Moss, deceased, have sold to Middleton Holland a tract of land in Bedford County and District No. 25. Containing 11 1/3 acres it being the one part of land whereon Mathew Moss, deceased, known as the Moss tract of land. Containing 102 acres. This 18 February 1854.
Wit: A.?. Huffman   Signed: Wiley Riggins
     Wm. Holder   Margaret Riggins
     J.L. (illegible), Esq.
Reg: February 11, 1867

Page 134 - G.P. Baskett and A.L. Stamps Bond to Frank Stamps (col). G.P. Baskett and A.L. Stamps of Bedford County is firmly bound unto Frank Stamps, a free man of color, said Frank Stamps has purchased a tract of land in Bedford County and District No. 7 and bounded by a street, by G.W. Buchanan, by Dillon, and by a lot held by G.W. Buchanan supposed to contain 1 ½ acres, for the sum of $300 one half of which has been paid in work at the Carriage Factory of William Powel. The other half to be paid on the 25 December 1866. This 25 December 1865.
Reg: February 12, 1867   Signed: G.P. Baskett
                                         A.L. Stamps

Page 135 - James A. Jarrett Deed to W.C. Alexander. This 11 February 1867, District No. 8 of Bedford County. I, James Jarrett, have sold to said W.C. Alexander a tract of land and bounded by John Claxton's line, to the center of Fall Creek, and to F.P. McElrath's corner. Containing 35 acres and 7 poles.
Wit: J.M. Barber   Signed: James A. Jarrett
     J.W. Hill
Reg: February 12, 1867

Page 136 - W.J. Reager, admr. Deed to Wm. McGill. Whereas W.F. Gardner on 6 August 1858 executed to Wm. McGill his land to convey him a tract of land in Bedford County and Civil District No. 23 which amount has been settled and paid to the administrator of Jas. R. Reager, deceased, to which the note was transferred and since that time M.F. Gardner has died and I have been appointed his administrator at October Term of Bedford County 1865 which land is bounded by lands of Joseph Hiles, by lands of Elijah Couch, by lands of Jas. McGill and Wm. McGill, and by lands of James McGill. Containing 128 acres and 75 poles. This 6 August 1866.
Reg: February 13, 1867   Signed: Wm. J. Reager, admr. Of
                                         M.F. Gardner, deceased

Page 136 - James B. Reager Deed to John W. Reager, Re-registered. This 13 October 1856. James B. Reager sold unto J.W. Reager, both of Bedford County, a tract of land in Bedford County and Civil War No. 23 and bounded by D.D. Hix's land, to the middle of the road, to James Chessor's west boundary, and to Wm. S. Hix's south boundary line it being Dr. Gordon's corner. Containing 152 ½ acres.
Reg: February 15, 1867   Signed: J.B. Reager

Page 137 - H.C. Furguson Deed to A.D. Furguson. I, H.C. Furguson, have conveyed to the heirs of A.D. Furguson and father for the benefit of his wife during her life a tract of land in Bedford County and District No. 24, adjoining the school land. Containing 58 acres and 15 poles. T his September 1, 1866.
Reg: February 16, 1867   Signed: H.C. Furguson

Page 138 - John Claxton and D.A. Powers, Bill of Sale to R.S. Miller. R.S. Miller has bought of John Claxton one gelding, one

bay gelding, which horses were bought with the money of Mrs.
Ruth Miller wife of R.S. Miller. This February 14, 1867.
Reg: February 16, 1867   Signed: D.A. Powers
                                        John Claxton

Page 138 - Samuel Bobo Deed to J.H. Tucker. I, Samuel Bobo of
Lincoln County, Tennessee, have sold unto Jesse Tucker of
Bedford County, a tract of land in Bedford County and Civil
District No. 24 on the head waters of Flat Creek and bounded by
Jas. F. Farrar's line, by Benjamin Bedford's line, by William C.
Hix's corner. Containing 106 acres and 50 poles.
Wit: W. Motlow   Signed: Samuel Bobo
     E.P. Bobo
Reg: February 18, 1867

Page 139 - John W. Adams Deed to T.W. Coffey, 15 ½ acres. I
have conveyed with T.W. Coffey a tract of land in the 17th Civil
District of Bedford County and bounded by Thomas Coffey's
corner, to the Pulaski Road, and by S.J. Adams' corner.
Containing 15 ½ acres. This 25 December 1866.
Reg: February 18, 1867   Signed: John W. Adams

Page 140 - C.R. Head, Procession Deed. Bedford County January
31, 1867. I went on the premises of Craven R. Head this day and
proceeded to survey and procession the tract of land on which
said C.R. Head now lives according to his title papers, and
adjoining B. Gambrel's line. Containing 78 acres and 114 poles.
Wit: Wm. Phillips   Signed: C.S. Head
     S.S. Russel, C.C.
NOTE: Plat on page 140
Reg: February 18, 1867

Page 140 - W.P. Goodwin, G.E. Calhoun, Articles of Agreement.
W.P. Goodwin and George E. Calhoun for the purpose of carrying
on a general livery stable business in the Town of Shelbyville,
have this day entered into a co-partnership, and they are to
share equally in the profits. Calhoun puts in the stock he now
has on hand such horses, buggies &c. Said Goodwin puts in stock
such as horses, wagon, hack &c. which he purchased of W.S. Jett,
agent &c. This 28 December 1866.
Reg: February 19, 1867   Signed: G.P. Goodwin
                                        G.E. Calhoun

Page 141 - Wm. Galbreath Deed to J.B. McAdams. I, William
Galbreath, have this day sold unto Jesse B. McAdams a tract of
land in Bedford County and District No. 18, containing 27 acres
and bounded by a 40 acre tract sold by me to Berry Owens, by
land claimed by Wm. Stephenson, and by Richard H. Sims' line.
This February 18, 1867.
Reg: February 19, 1867   Signed: Wm. Galbreath

Page 142 - G.A. Conn, Power of Attorney to M.T. Griswell and H. Whitfield. Bedford County. I, George A. Conn, have this day appointed Harrison Whitfield and Griswell my true and lawful attorneys for me and in my name to wind up my business that is now to do or not I may have heretofore to transact and I give them full power. This __ day of February 1867.
Wit: Gilbert W. Land   Signed: G.A. Conn
     James Whitfield
Reg: February 20, 1867

Page 142 - Samuel L. Colville and David Ramsey, Admrs. Of William Ramsey, deceased, VS Joseph Ramsey, A. Hodge and G.W. Ramsey. This day came the plaintiff and filed the following Power of Attorney, to wit, we, Joseph A. Ramsey, A. Hodge and G.W> Ramsey hereby authorize C.J. Spurlock to I9llegible) judgment in the Circuit Court at McMinnville at its February Term 1867 in favor of David Ramsey and Samuel L. Colville, administrators of William Ramsey, deceased. This 5 February 1867.
Wit: J.C. Ross   Signed: Joseph Ramsey
     W.S. White   A. Hodge
Reg: February 20, 1867   G.W. Ramsey

Page 143 - Samuel L. Colville and David Ramsey, admrs. Of Wm. Ramsey, deceased, VS Joseph Ramsey, A. Hodge and G.W. Ramsey. Whereupon came into court C.J. Spurlock and confessed judgment in favor of the plaintiff and against said defendants. This 5 February 1867.
Reg: February 20, 1867   Signed: John S. Ramsey, Clerk

Page 143 - Daniel Boone Deed to Francis E. Lacy. Washington County, Arkansas. This 18 June 1866. Daniel Boone of County of Madison, State of Arkansas of one part and Francis E. Lacy of Washington County, Arkansas of second part. Said Daniel Boone sold unto Francis E. Lacy land which was laid off and set apart after the death of William Boone, deceased, out of the lands of said deceased of which he died seized and possessed for his widow Margaret Boone dower. Said land being in two parcels lying in Bedford County and in civil District No. 22 on the waters of Flat Creek and adjoining lands of John Stone, Jordan Hale, Joseph Parker, P.S. Dean, Richard Mullins, W.G. Harris and others. Containing in all 321 acres and a fraction, said undivided interest of said Daniel Boone of the first part being one ninth of said dower and to take effect at the death of Margaret Boone.
Wit: Joseph Watson   Signed: Daniel Boone
     Jos. D. Porter
Reg: February 20, 1867

Page 145 - S.M. Brown Deed to James P. Taylor, 39 acres. I, S.M. Brown, have sold unto James P. Taylor a tract of land in Bedford County and District No. 10 and containing 39 acres and 1 pole and bounded by a tract that John Jackson purchased of

William Allison, and to the center of Weakley Creek. This
December 25, 1865.
Reg: February 21, 1867   Signed: S.M. Brown

Page 145 - B.F. Sikes Deed to J.M. Black. I, B.F. Sikes, have
sold unto James M. Black a tract of land in Bedford County and
Civil District No. 2 and on the south side of the road leading
from Wartrace Depot to Manchester, and on the head waters of
Knob Creek waters of the Garrison Fork of Duck River, and
bounded by John Anderson's old south boundary line now John
Cauthron's. Containing 3 acres. This 3 March 1866.
Wit: E. Keeling   Signed: Benj. F. Sikes
     R. Morgan
Reg: February 21, 1867

Page 146 - William Baldin Deed to J.M. Black. I have sold unto
J.M. Black a tract of land in Bedford County and Civil District
No. 2 on the head waters of Dotis Creek and bounded by James
Finch's line, and to a tract of land known and owned by Buckner
and W.R. and A. Smith's line. Containing 55 acres. This
January 1859.
Wit: Thos. Barnett   Signed: Wm. Baldin
     G.W.W. Anderson
Reg: February 21, 1867

Page 147 - G.W. Gregory and James Gregory, Extrs. Deed to John
Wallace. We, the executors of Thos. Gregory, Sr., deceased,
having with the will annexed advertised the lands of said
Gregory for sale which lands in Bedford County and Civil
District No. 8 being the same that said Thomas Gregory lived on
at his death. John W. Wallace being the last and highest bidder
for lot No. 2 in the division of said land. Said land adjoins
W.G. Cowan's corner, by Robert Cowan's corner, and by Wm. G.
Cowan's line. Containing 34 acres and 120 poles. Lot No. 3 now
owned by Robt. Cowan. This 12 January 1867.
Reg: February 22, 1867   Signed: G.W. Gregory
                                     James Gregory

Page 147 - T.C. Whiteside and G.F. Blakemore Deed to William
Gosling, House and Lot. We, Thos. C. Whiteside and Geo.F.
Blakemore, have sold unto William Gosling a tract of land with
the improvement in Bedford County and in the corporate limits of
the Town of Shelbyville and bounded by the junction of Union
(now called Walworth) Street with the Nashville, Murfreesboro
and Shelbyville Turnpike Road, by a line between said lot and
the lot now owned by D.J. Christopher on which he resides, and
to the dividing line to its west side of Brittain Street. It
being the lot on which Geo. T. Blakemore now resides and which
was conveyed by Young and Martha Wilhoite to said Thos. C.
Whiteside by deed dated October 2, 1863. This 20 February 1867.
Reg: February 21, 1867   Signed: Thos. C. Whiteside
                                     Geo. F. Blakemore

Page 148 - Lucy Ann Kimmons Deed to Thos. Kimmons. I, Lucy Ann Kimmons of Greene County, Missouri, being the daughter of Lewis Whitesell, deceased, and his only child and heir at law and in his right the owner of an undivided interest in the dower land of her grandmother Milly Whitesell and B.B. Kimmons the husband of said Lucy Ann Kimmons, have this day sold to Thomas Kimmons of Bedford County all our right title claim and interest in said dower tract containing about 63 acres in the 20th Civil District of Bedford County on the waters of Sinking Creek. This 25 January 1867.
Reg: February 22, 1867   Signed: B.B. Kimmons
                                        Lucy Ann Kimmons

Page 149 - Peter Burrow Deed to James A. Knott. I, Peter Burrow, have sold unto James A. Knott a tract of land in Civil District No. 11 of Bedford County and in the Village of Unionville and bounded by W.C. Blanton, to Purity and Peter, M.W. McConnell's corner, by the smoke house, and by J. Moore's line, being established lines between the lots and each of said Burrow and McConnell lives, ourselves and keep up half of the line of fence between us. This __ day of __ 1867.
Reg: February 23, 1867   Signed: Peter Burrow

Page 150 - J.P. Hoover Deed to E.C. Moorland. This 28 October 1862. J.P. Hoover of Bedford County sold unto E.C. Moorland of Rutherford County, Tennessee a tract of land in Bedford County and bounded by Hoover's north boundary line, and by J.P. Hoover's north boundary line. Containing 17 acres.
Wit: J.H. Woodfin   Signed: J.P. Hoover
     Wm. Hoover
Reg: February 23, 1867

Page 151 - William Hord Deed to J.L. Black. I, William Hord, have sold unto James L. Black a tract of land in Bedford County and Civil District No. 2 on Knob Creek of the Garrison Fork of Duck River and on the road from Wartrace Depot to Manchester and adjoining at the sycamore spring the south west corner of a small lot that fell to Mrs. Finch in the division of the E. Hord land, and by Pepper's line. Containing 3 acres and 115 poles. Also another tract of about 2 acres. This __ day of February 1867.
Reg: February 26, 1867   Signed: W.M. Hord

Page 152 - Jas. T. Williams Deed to Jno. T. Fisher. 64 or 65 acres. I, James T. Williams, have sold unto Jno. T. Fisher a tract of land in Bedford County and District No. 8 and 11 and bounded by a 25 acre tract granted to James Williams, and by the east side of the Franklin Road, by a 1500 acre tract granted to Lan(illegible). This 28 January 1867.
Wit: Jos. Anderson   Signed: J.T. Williams
     T.F. Simmons
Reg: February 26, 1867

Page 152 - Presley Prince Deed to William Bomar. This 21 May 1863. Presley Prince sold unto William Brown, both of Bedford County, a tract of land in Bedford County and Civil District No. 24 on the head waters of Thompson Creek and bounded by R.C. Daniel's line. Containing 91 acres including the buildings and improvements.
Wit: Chas. Pearson   Signed: Presley Prince
     Manuel Ray
Reg: February 27, 1867

Page 153 - John H. Oneal Deed to book agents of the Methodist Episcopal C. S. I, John H. Oneal, have sold unto the book agents of the Methodist Episcopal Church, South, a tract of land in Bedford County and District No. 7, containing ¾ of an acre and bounded on the north east by the Unionville Turnpike, and the north west corner of a lot belonging to Thomas S. Sharp, and by a stable. It being the house and lot now occupied by Thomas Trollinger as a residence and a part of the vacant lot north and west of said enclosed lot. This 3 December 1860.
Reg: February 27, 1867   Signed: John H. Oneal

Page 154 - A.H. Redford, agt. &c Deed to Martha J. Haynie, House and Lot. I, A.H. Redford, agent of the Publishing House of the Methodist Episcopal Church (South), have sold unto Martha J. Haynie a piece of land in Bedford County and Civil District No. 7 and within the corporate limits of the Town of Shelbyville and bounded by the Unionville Turnpike, and by Thomas S. Sharp. Containing ¾ of an acre. It being the house and lot now occupied by Gilbert Wynn and part of a vacant lot. This 21 February 1867.
Reg: February 28, 1867   Signed: A.H. Redford

Page 155 - Sterling C. Brown Deed to James Wadley, 17 ½ acres. I, Sterling C. Brown, have sold unto James Wadley a tract of land in 7th Civil District of Bedford County and bounded a dry branch. Containing 17 ½ acres. It being a portion of the lands of which George W. Brown, my father, died the owner and which subsequent to his death was sold by Joseph H. Thompson and by me purchased. This 26 February 1867.
Reg: February 28, 1867   Signed: Sterling C. Brown

Page 155 - Thos. M. Winsett and others Trust Deed to John E. Haskins. Thos. M. Winsett, David H. Winsett and Mary D. Winsett, have sold to John E. Haskins a tract of land in Bedford County and Civil District No. 8 and 9 and bounded by lands of Len Clark and the Widow Hoover, by the lands of Quina E. Morton, and the Widow Mary Dozier, by the lands of John PArsons and Peyton S. Vincent, and by the lands of the Widow Hoover and N.O. Burton. Containing in all about 198 acres. It being the tract of land originally owned by Jason Winsett and is the same land sold by Lewis Tillman, C&M. This 1 January 1867.
Reg: February 28, 1867   Signed: T.M. Winsett
                         D.H. Winsett
                         Mary D. Winsett

Page 156 - W.A. Neely, Declaration. It is my intention to claim the benefit of a home stead. According to Section 2115, I hereby as a housekeeper and head of a family do execute this declaration of intention to claim as such Homestead the following described tract of land in Bedford County and Civil District No. 8 and bounded by Martha Smith's corner. This 27 February 1867.
Reg: February 28, 1867   Signed: W.A. Neely

Page 157 - Wm. M. G. Cowan et als, Contract. Wm. S. Cowan has sold to W.T. Myers and John T. Blackwood the following property, one lot of ground in Bedford County and District No. 7 known as Cowan's tan yard and bounded by an alley, by ___ Street, by a spring branch, and by lands formerly owned by Gen. Robert Cannon. Containing 1 ½ acres. This 27 February 1867.
Reg: March 1, 1867   Signed: Wm. G. Cowan
                                   W.T. Myers
                                   John T. Blackwood

Page 158 - John Trice, Lien of stock to Jas. L. Adams. I, John Trice of Bedford County, give to James L. Adams of same place a lien of one bay mule called Mike, one other bay mule called Tom, and one bay mare. I, John Trice, purchased of said J.L. Adams a lot of bacon on 27 March 1866 which remains unpaid. This February 18, 1867
Wit: Joseph Trice   Signed: John Trice
     W.A. Trice
Reg: March 1, 1867

Page 158 - William H. Mathews Deed to Rebecca Mathews. I, William H. Mathews of Bedford County, have sold to Rebecca Mathews all my undivided title and interest in and to a tract of land in Bedford County and within the corporate limits of Shelbyville on which is situated the frame dwelling house in which said Rebecca Mathews now resides and bounded on the Scull Camp Road Wm. Gosling's corner, by a fence erected by R.P.S. Kimbro in 1857, and by the lot now owned by Peyton Evans or on which he resides. It being the lot or land sold by R.P.S. Kimbro to Andrew Mathews, deceased, by deed dated 29 July 1858 and registered in Book AAA, pages 191 and 192. Containing ¾ of an acre, also in interest in any other lien or land owned and conveyed by said Kimbro's (illegible). My undivided title or interest in said lot or tracts of land being one undivided 1/3 part thereof as a child of said Andrew Mathews, deceased, subject to the dower of said Rebecca Mathews. This 26 February 1867.
Reg: March 2, 1867   Signed: William H. Mathews

Page 159 - Henry Dean Deed to Richard Mullins, 5 acres. This 3 July 1849. Henry Dean sold unto Richard Mullins, both of Bedford County, land in Bedford County on the head waters of Big Flat Creek in District No. 22 and bounded by McLain's line, by the big road leading from New Herman to Isaac Williams, passing McLain's old corner, to said Mullins' line, to a fork of the

road where one goes to Isaac Williams and the other to the
tanyard belonging to Wm. Woodward. Containing 5 acres. This
July 3, 1849.
Wit: Jordan Mullins   Signed: Henry Dean
Reg: March 5, 1867

Page 160 - J.A.S. Shannon, Bill of Sale to B.F. Duggan. I,
J.A.S. Shannon, have sold to B.F. Duggan, Sr. one Jack named Red
Rover and two black mules, one horse and one mare mule. B.F.
Duggan, Sr. has stayed a debt before R.H. Stem, Esq.,
(illegible) to J.W. Clary on a note given by F.M. Ray and by him
trustee to said Clary. This 25, February 1867.
Wit: R.H. Stem   Signed: J.A.S. Shannon
Reg: March 5, 1867

Page 160 - Lemuel Broadway Deed to Samuel Bobo. This 15
December 1866. Lemuel Broadway of Bedford County sold unto
Samuel Bobo of Lincoln County, Tennessee, a tract of land in
Bedford County on the waters of Big Flat Creek, containing 18
acres and bounded by the road leading from Shelbyville to
Lynchburg near the mouth of a lane leading to the meeting house
near Mathew Cunningham's smith shop, and near the graveyard.
Reg: March 5, 1867   Signed: Lemuel Broadway

Page 161 - John W. and Wm. C. Crunk Deed to Floyd Lodge No. 106.
This 7 March 1860. John W. Crunk and Wm. C. Crunk sold unto
John C. Ray, M.W. Watson, E.H. Reager and G.M. Ray present
election officers of Floyd Lodge No. 106 I.O.O.F. all the right
title claim and interest it being one half what we have in and
to a certain house and lot of ground lying in Bedford County and
in the Village of Flat Creek and known as the Coldwell Store
House and lot bounded by the center of the road the north east
corner of Thos. Hutson's lot, and by the old school land.
Containing in all 83 ½ poles including the store house &c.
Wit: S.T. Farrar   Signed: J.W. Crunk
     C.A. Crunk   Wm. C. Crunk
Reg: March 6, 1867

Page 162 - Joseph Fox Deed to W.E. Moorland. This 12 September
1864. Joseph Fox of Rutherford County, Tennessee sold unto W.E.
Moorland of same place a tract of land in Bedford County and
bounded near a little gate in the east boundary line of a 6 acre
tract that said W.E. Moorland bought of J.P. Hoover, by Jno. P.
Hoover's line, and to the top of a ridge. Containing 15 acres.
Wit: W.F. Gibson   Signed: Joseph Fox
     Henry Gibson
     Abram McMahan
     W.J. Davis
Reg: March 6, 1867

Page 163 - J.L. Cooper et als Deed to John A. Mclean. On 2
January 1865, James L. Pucket executed a Deed of Conveyance to
John L. Cooper for the benefit of Mary G. Pucket wife of James

308

R. Pucket a tract of land registered in Book FFF, pages 90 and
91. This 5 March 1867.
Reg: March 7, 1867   Signed: J.L. Cooper
                                  M.G. Pucket
                                  Jos. R. Pucket

Page 164 - Robert Mathews Deed to Robert J. Mathews, Lot. I,
Robert Mathews of Bedford County, have conveyed unto Robert J.
Mathews, my son, for the love and affection I bear for him a
parcel of ground in the Town of Shelbyville and bounded by the
lot formerly owned by me (purchased from Clement Cannon) part
conveyed to Martha A. Mathews by deed, the lot hereby conveyed
is 100 feet long and 50 feet wide on the north side of Bridge
Street and on the south side of the Bank Lot and bounded by a
street or alley. This 6 March 1867.
Reg: March 7, 1867   Signed: Robt. Mathews

Page 164 - J.S. Roberts Deed to G.R. Raney, undivided interest.
I, J.S. Roberts of Bedford County, have this day 5 March 1867
sold unto George R. Raney of Bedford County my undivided
interest in a tract of land in District No. 20 of Bedford County
on the waters of Sinking Creek and bounded by a 640 acre entry
of Phillips & Campbell, by Rezin Smith's tract, by Peter
Robert's widow, by John Roberts' line now owned by T.W. Buchanan
and by Roberts' line and Artemuse (?) Robert's corner, to the
Lincoln County line being the south west corner of a 50 acre
entry in the name of Littleton Meeks, and by Gant's line.
Containing 166 7/8/ acres.
Wit: J.S. Davidson   Signed: James S. Roberts
     W.R. Carigan
Reg: March 8, 1867

Page 165 - R.C. White Deed to G.W. Buchanan. Land being ¼ of a
acre formerly owned by Buchanan & Scudder and located in the
Town of Shelbyville and bounded by a corner or lot D.S. Evans
purchased of R.D. and James H. Deery at the south west corner of
said lot on the north side of the Public Square, by Lot No. 2,
and by Lot No. 1 and 2. This February 11, 1867.
Reg: March 8, 1867   Signed: R.S. White

Page 166 - T.W. Buchanan Deed to R.D. McCullough. I do hereby
convey to R.D. McCullough all the right title claim and interest
that was vested in me by a decree of the Chancery Court of
Shelbyville entered at September Term 1866 and whereon Wm. D.
McClure was complainant and Elizabeth Nance and others were
defendants in one case R.D. McCullough was complainant and
Milton McClure and others were defendants in the other case to a
certain house and lot in the Town of Shelbyville bounded by
Brittain Street, by a lot then owned by C.P. Houston, Jr., now
by R.C. White, by an alley on the south by the Roman Catholic
Church property being the same lot whereon I now reside. This
March 7, 1867.
Reg: March 8, 1867   Signed: Thos. W. Buchanan

Page 167 - Henry Stephens Bond to Rachel Culbertson. November 9, 1860. I am indebted to Rachel Culbertson. I have this day sold unto Rachel Culbertson a tract of land in Bedford County and Civil District No. 11 and bounded by J.J. Long's line, and by A.C. Potts' line. Containing 55 acres and 42 poles.
Wit: M.P.L. Parks   Signed: Henry Stephens
      William Smith
Reg: March 9, 1867

Page 167 - William Collier Deed to Levi Madison. I, William Collier, have sold unto Levi Madison a tract of land in the 21st Civil District of Bedford County and bounded by M. Thompson, 2nd corner in William Morton's line. Containing in all 54 acres and 40 poles, it being the land purchased by me some years ago of one O.W. Knight. Said deed is registered in Book KK, page 409. This 8 March 1867.
Wit: Jos. H. Thompson   Signed: William Collier
Reg: March 9, 1867

Page 168 - Thomas Holland Deed to Joseph H. Thompson, Trustee. I, Thomas Holland of Bedford County, have sold to Joseph H. Thompson land in 7th Civil District of Bedford County and bounded in the McMinnville Road, by Mrs. Eliza McFarland's line, and by Mrs. V(illegible). Containing 6 acres and 53 poles. This conveyance is made for the purpose for and in consideration of my affection for my daughter in law Mrs. Angeline D. Hollamd wife of my son Thomas G. Holland. I desire to secure to her a home and to descend to her children and if she died without children or grandchildren descended from my son Thomas C. Holland. This 21 February 1867.
Reg: March 11, 1867   Signed: Thomas Holland

Page 169 - W.H. Gambill Trust Deed to W.W. Oneal. I, W.H. Gambill of Bedford County do agree with N.C. Gambill, Jr. and W.W. Oneal both of Marshall County, Tennessee that they have and hold all the right title claim and interest that I now have or may obtain in the estate of Newton C. Gambill, deceased, both real and personal for the purpose they are my securities on a note made payable to John W. Greer, admr. &C of said N.C. Gambill, deceased. This February 7, 1867.
Wit: Joseph Trice   Signed: W.H. Gambill
      B.F. Woodward
Reg: March 11, 1867

Page 170 - Thompson, Sheriff, and Deason Deed to G.W. Buchanan & Co. Whereas one R.F. Evans and others recovered a judgment against one D.G. Deason on 23 day of February 1861 and there not being personal property sufficient to satisfy said execution, I lieved on the same on __ day of __ 186_ on a tract of land as the property of said D.G. Deason containing 2 acres lying within the corporation of the Town of Shelbyville and bounded by the Unionville Pike, and by George W. Buchanan. This February 5, 1867.
Wit: R.B. Davidson   Signed: Jo. Thompson, Sheriff

Page 171 - Newcomb Thompson Power of Attorney. I, Fannie M. Owens of the City of New York, have appointed Newcomb Thompson, 2nd of Shelbyville my true and lawful attorney for me and in my name place and stead to collect and receive such money or moneys as maybe now or hereafter due me as one of the heirs of the estate of my father B.C. Owens, deceased, This 4 March 1867.
Wit: Charles Nettleton   Signed: Fannie M. Owens
     Nathaniel Gill
New York City, New York
Reg: March 12, 1867

Page 171 - W.M. Tatum Deed to G.T. Tucker. I, William Tatum of Bedford County, have sold to G.T. Tucker of same place a tract of land in Bedford County and containing 52 acres and bounded by M.F. Williams, and by Hartwell Freeman. This March 13, 1867.
Reg: March 13, 1867   Signed: W.M. Tatum

Page 172 - G.W. and James Gregory &c Deed to James Story. The said executors of Thos. Gregory, deceased, having sold to James Story a tract of land in District No. 8 of Bedford County, containing 120 acres and 87 poles, it being the homestead of Thos. Gregory and Lot No. 1 of the division of said land. Said land bounded by a 10 acre tract belonging to G.T. Tucker and by Wilson Turrentine's line by the south east line of the graveyard. Containing 120 acres and 87 poles.
Reg: March 13, 1867   Signed: G.W. Gregory
                                      James Gregory, Extrs.

Page 173 - Edmund Cooper Deed to Mary J. Thompson. I, Edmund Cooper of Bedford County , have sold unto Mary J. Thompson wife of John W. Thompson a lot of ground in the Town of Shelbyville and bounded by Holland Street, by a lot of ground owned by Thomas C. Whiteside, by the lands owned by Argyle P. Eakin and others, by the lands of Matilda Pannell it being the town lot formerly owned by L.D. Pannell and on which his widow is residing. This 16 November 1863.
Reg: March 15, 1867   Signed: Edmund Cooper

Page 173 - R.P. Shapard Deed to Evander Shapard, House and Lot. I, Robert P. Shapard, have sold unto Evander Shapard a certain house and lot in North Shelbyville in Bedford County and bounded by Silas W. Clay's lot, by Martin Street, and by a new street opened by Thos. Lipscomb. It being the same house and lot I purchased of John T. Stephens in year 1865. This 15 March 1867.
Wit: M. Cannon   Signed: R.P. Shapard
     D.G. Shapard
Reg: March 16, 1867

Page 174 - William G. Smiley, Discharge. William G. Smiley a Private of Lieut. William G. Davis Company (A) 5th Regiment of Tennessee Cavalry Volunteers who was enrolled on the 4th day of September 1862 to serve three years or during the war is hereby discharged from the service of the United States this 25 day of June 1865 at Fayetteville, Tennessee by reason of General Order No. 83 War Dept. May 8, 1865. No objection to his being re-enlisted is known to exist. Said William G. Smiley was born in Jackson County, Alabama is twenty nine years of age, five feet nine inches high, fair complexion, gray eyes, dark hair and by occupation when enrolled a farmer. Given at Fayetteville, Tenn. this 25th day of June 1865.
Francis Jackson, Captain   William G. Davis, Captain
Oath of Identity - William G. Smiley of the Town of ___ of Bedford County, Tennessee on this 16th day of March 1867 personally appeared before me the undersigned a Justice of the Peace for the County and State above mentioned. Wm. G. Smiley who being duly sworn according to law declares that he is the identical Wm. G. Smiley who was a Private in the Company commanded by Captain Lieutenant Davis in the Regiment commanded by Joseph Clift that he enlisted on the 4th day of September 1862 for the term of two years and was discharged at Fayetteville, Tenn. on 24th day of June 1865 by reason of General Order No. 83 War Department.
Reg: March 16, 1867   Signed: William G. Smily

Page 175 - R.B. Rucker Deed to F.J. Harris. I, R.B. Rucker sold unto F.J. Harris a tract of land in Bedford County and Civil District No. 5 and bounded by Anderson Rucker tract, to the Rutherford and Bedford County dividing line, by Wheeler's old corner, by my entire tract, and by Ben Ransom's line. Containing 167 acres. This 16 March 1867.
Wit: J.L. Scudder   Signed: R.B. Rucker
     J.M. Phillips
Reg: March 18, 1867

Page 176 - John L. Harmon Deed to Thomas F. Harmon. I, John L. Harmon conveyed to Thomas F. Harmon one sorrel colt, twenty five barrels corn, one yoke of steers, one red cow, and one sorrel mare. This March 11, 1867.
Wit: N.F. Thompson   Signed: John L. Harmon
Reg: March 18, 1867

Page 176 - W.R. Tinsley to M.T. Griswald. I have this day sold unto M.T. Griswald a town lot in the Village of Wartrace and bounded a street of Nobb Creek Turnpike, and by the corner of the livery stable. This 9 March 1867.
Wit: Thos. H. Watterson   Signed: W.R. Tinsley
     Thos. Hart
     Samuel Tilford
Reg: March 19, 1867

Page 177 - W.Y. Elliott Deed to R.C. White, House and Lot. Rutherford County, Tennessee. I, W.Y. Elliott of Bedford County

have sold unto Robert C. White two town lots lying and being in the Town of Shelbyville, Bedford County and being the same purchased by me on 22 October 1866 and which is registered in Book EEE and containing about 1 ½ acres and known as Lots No. 26 and 27 and bounded by Dawdy Street which divides it feom the Cowan property and the Presbyterian Church, by Jefferson Street which divides it from the Frierson property, by Brittain Street which divides it from the property of William J. Whitthorne and the new Methodist Church. This 4 March 1867.
Reg: March 17, 1867   Signed: W.Y. Elliott

Page 178 - J.A. Taylor Deed to W.S. Taylor. I, J.A. Taylor, have sold unto W.S. Taylor a tract of land in Bedford County and District No. 10 and bounded by J.B. Cooper's corner, by a small tract sold to Alfred Ransom by Wm. S. Taylor, by A. Ransom's corner, by W. Knott's corner, by a stable in Byler's line, and by J.B. Cooper's corner. This January 26, 1867.
Wit: T.J. Taylor   Signed: J.A. Taylor
     J.C. Taylor
Reg: March 20, 1867

Page 179 - Chesley Williams and W.P. Cannon, Extrs. Deed to J.W. McAnally. Whereas Robert Cannon late of Bedford County made and published his Last Will and Testament and afterwards departed this life which will was at the April Term 1864 was duly proved in County Court and therein named his executors Chesley Williams and William P. Cannon. Said Cannon authorized his executors to sell certain real estate. To be sold was all the land or lots that said Cannon had purchased at the sale of the Wilson Coat's estate near the Rail Road east of the Town of Shelbyville. Two lots known as Lot No. 14 and No. 15. Lot No. 14 is bounded by G.W. Gunter, by Blessings, by Lot No. 15, and by Robert Dennis. Containing 8 acres and 28 poles. Lot No. 15 bounded by Lot No. 14, by Blessing, by J.F. Cummings, and by Robert Dennis. Containing 8 acres and 128 poles. This 14 September 1865.
Reg: March 21, 1867   Signed: Chesley Williams, Extr
                                     W.P. Cannon, Extr of
                                     Robert Cannon

Page 180 - R.C. White and Frank Hodgkins Transfer to T.W. Warner, We, Robt. C. White as Trustee of Frank Hodgkins and Frank Hodgkins do sell unto T.W. Warner all the right and interest which R.C. White received from Frank Hodgkins by a Trust Deed made 3 November 1866. Said White and Hodgkins to convey by deed to said Warner all the (illegible) fixtures furniture including the Bake Shop and all the tools, also two billiard tables. This March 22, 1867.
Reg: March 22, 1867   Signed: R.C. White, Trustee
                                     Frank Hodgkins

Page 180 - W.M. Rippey et als Deed to James H. Stephens. We, W.M. Rippey and wife E.A. Rippey and G.A. Cortner, have sold to James H. Stephens 2/6 of a tract of land in Bedford County and District No. 2, containing 250 acres and known as the Francis H.

Keller tract and the place whereon said Stephens now resides and bounded by lands of Joseph Couch's estate, by the lands of Matthias Cortner's estate and John R. Eakin, by the lands of William Pepper's heirs, and by lands of John A. Couch. This March 19, 1867.

Reg: March 25, 1867   Signed: W.M. Rippey
                                     E.A. Rippey
                                     G.A. Cortner

Page 181 - James M. Stephens Deed to James Bramblett. I, James M. Stephens of Bedford County, have sold unto James Bramblett of same place a tract of land being the north part of the land formerly owned by Frank Keller, deceased, lying in Bedford County and District No. 2 and bounded by Myers' line, by Couch's line and Cortner's corner, and by John A. Couch's corner. Containing 126 acres and 83 poles. This 19 March 1867.

Reg: March 25, 1867   Signed: J.M. Stephens

Page 182 - Joel Stallings Deed to H.C. Pickle and wife, 60+ acres. I, Joel Stallings, have sold unto Henry C. Pickle and Margaret E. Pickle a tract of land in District No. 18 of Bedford County and bounded by Thomas Darnell's corner by Hoskins' line, and by Sallie Sykes' corner. Containing 60 acres and 76 poles. This February 2, 1867.

Wit: R.S. Montgomery   Signed: Joel Stallings
     J.B. Montgomery
Reg: March 26, 1867

Page 183 - J.T. Williams Deed to W.F. Clary, House and Lot. I, James T. Williams of Bedford County, have sold unto W.F. Clary a tract of land &c belonging, situated in the Village of Unionville, District No. 11 of Bedford County and bounded by Meredith Blanton's lane, by the Protestant Methodist Church Camp Ground, by Benjamin Blanton's line, and by B. Blanton's and Lucy Smith's line. Containing 2 ¾ acres. This March 21, 1867.

Wit: W.C. Blanton   Signed: J.T. Williams
     Robt. Allison
Reg: March 26, 1867

Page 183 - Minos C. Jordan's Certified Copy 200 acres land. Bedford County on 1st Monday in August 1866 being 5 September 1866. Wm. N. Haily, administrator of Thomas R. Morton, deceased, VS R.S. Dwiggins, Nancy J. Morton and Lula L. Morton. Report that in pursuance of an (illegible) decree in the case on 29 May 1866 - that he advertised the land mentioned in the Shelbyville "Expositor" that on 15 August 1866 (day for the sale) Minos C. Jordan bid and became purchaser. This August 20, 1866. NOTE: Long document.

Reg: March 26, 1867   Signed: Lewis Tillman, C&M

Page 185 - John W. Wells and wife Deed to Charles H. Blake. We, John W. Wells and Sarah Elizabeth Wells, have sold unto Charles H. Blake lands in District No. 3 of Bedford County and bounded

by the center of the Nashville and Chattanooga Rail Road in the
north boundary line of the Depot Grounds at Wartrace, by J.
Cleveland's line, and by H.B. Coffey's corner. Containing 29
acres and 17 poles, the same being a portion of lands allotted
to said Sarah E. Wells in the partition of the lands of our
deceased grandfather John McQuiddy. This March 16, 1867.
Reg: March 27, 1867   Signed: John W.wells
                                   S.E. Wells

Page 186 - William Little Deed to James Waddy. I, William
Little, have sold unto James Waddy a tract of land in Bedford
County and District No. 18, containing 30 acres and 50 poles and
bounded by Benjamin Earnhart's line. This March 26, 1867.
Reg: March 27, 1867   Signed: Wm. Little

Page 186 - W.M. Cully, Jr. Deed to R.M. Smith. I have sold unto
R.M. Smith as agent, a tract of land in Bedford County and Town
of Rowesville and bounded by G.W. Heard's line. Containing 2
acres. This November 18, 1863.
Wit: C.P. Houston. Jr.   Signed: W.M. Cully
     J.N. Dunaway
Reg: March 28, 1867

Page 187 - James S. Newton Deed to Wm. A. Allen. Land purchased
of the west end of school land Lot No. 4, containing 19 acres
and 27 poles and bounded at the corner between J.M.H. Coleman
and said Wm. A. Allen, by R.H. Sims' line, by the Section line,
and by the school land tract. This 25 March 1867.
Wit: C.S. Dudley   Signed: Jas. S. Newton
     J.M.H. Coleman
Reg: March 30, 1867

Page 188 - J.S. Newton Deed to J.M.H. Coleman. J.M.H. Coleman
purchased part of school land Lot No. 4, containing 19 acres and
37 poles and bounded at a corner between Wm. A. Allen and J.M.H.
Coleman, and by Richard H. Sims' line. This 25 March 1867.
Wit: Wm. A. Allen   Signed: Jas. S. Newton
     C.S. Dudley
Reg: March 30, 1867

Page 188 - H.H. Huddleston Note and Lien to J.J. Reese. I
promise to pay J.J. Reeves for one gray horse and one mule.
This 23 March 1867.
Wit: J.C. Snell   Signed: H.H. Huddleston
     W.J. Brown
Reg: April 3, 1867

Page 189 - Susan and J.G. King Trust Deed to W.W. Oneal. We,
Susan King and Joseph King of Lincoln County, Tennessee sold
unto N.C. Gambill and W.P. Oneal of Marshall County, Tennessee
in the estate of N.C. Gambill, deceased, both real and personal.
It being our undivided interest. Said N.C. Gambill and W.W.

Oneal are our securities and note made payable to John W. Greer, admr. (with the Will annexed) of Newton C. Gambill, deceased. This February 27, 1867.

Wit: Joseph Trice   Signed: Susan King
     S.H. Price   J.G. King
Reg: April 2, 1867

Page 189 - N.C. Thompson Deed to B.F. Duggan, Sr. ½ acre lot. I, N.C. Thompson of Bedford County, have conveyed unto B.F. Duggan, Sr. of same place a certain lot or piece of land in Bedford County and Civil District No. 11 in the Village of Unionville and bounded by the edge of the road from Unionville to Enon Church being the M. Blanton's corner, by Wm. Collins' line, by Wm. H. Moon's corner, by J.T. Williams & Co., and by J.W. Clary's line, and by B.F. Duggan's lot purchased from W.C. Blanton. Containing ½ acres. This 17 March 1867.

Wit: A.G. Vincent   Signed: N.C. Thompson
     Jesse Covington
Reg: April 3, 1867

Page 190 - Jane Gill Deed to Elisha Conwell. I, Jane Gill of Lincoln County, Tennessee, have sold unto Elisha Conwell all my right and interest in the estate of my father Thomas Conwell who is yet living but owing to mental incapable of transacting business consisting of one tract of land in District No. 22 of Bedford County and adjoining the lands of William Campbell, by the lands of Joseph Parker, by the lands of Samuel Morris and the heirs of Henry Dean, and by the lands of Katy Leathers. Containing 410 acres. My interest therein being the one seventh part thereof.

Page 190 - Thomas Hatchett Power of Attorney to S.W. Hatchett. I hereby appoint my son S.W. Hatchett my attorney in fact to demand and receive from Bennett Fields, admr. Or executor of Harriet Chaffin, deceased, and who resides in Bedford County, my share to the estate willed me by said Harriet Chaffin, deceased. I hereby authorized S.W. Hatchett to give all necessary receipt. This 18 July 1865.

Reg: April 3, 1867   Signed: Thomas Hatchett

Page 191 - Willliam Thomas et als Deed to Wm. Murphy. We, William Thomas, John Thomas and Smith Bowlin, have sold to William Murphree a tract of land in Bedford County and Civil District No. 5, containing 67 acres and 83 poles. Bounded by William Murphree, also (illegible) tract of 100 acres, by William Tatum, by the Fifer line, and Wm. F. Cooper. This 27 July 1860.

Wit: R.D. Blair   Signed: Wm. Thomas
    W.B. Norville   John Thomas
Reg: April 3, 1867   Smith Bowlin

Page 192 - W.R. Tinsley Deed to John A. Mackey, 20 acres. I, W.R. Tinsley, have sold unto John A. Mackey a tract of land in Bedford County and District No. 3, containing about 20 acres and bounded by the old bridge where the McMinnville Road crosses the Wartrace Creek running west in the creek to where the road leaves the creek, by Coble's branch, by the lands of Henry Coffey, and by Nathan Evans. This 2 April 1867.
Reg: April 4, 1867   Signed: W.R. Tinsley

Page 193 - J.T. Wheelhouse Deed to T.N.B. Turner. I, J.T. Wheelhouse, have sold unto T.N.B. Turner a tract of land in Bedford County and District No. 9 (except ¼ of an acre which has been heretofore sold to M.W. Turner and J.L. Turner and the same deeded to them by Elijah Williams). Containing 45 acres. Said land bounded by W.S. Brame, by T.N.B. Turner, by Mrs. M.F. Hoover and L.M. Rankin, by J.T. Wheelhouse, it being the land of the heirs of Elizabeth Williams. This 2 April 1867.
Reg: April 2, 1867   Signed: J.T. Wheelhouse

Page 193 - J.N. McCullough Trust Deed to F.M. Johnson. I sold unto F.M. Johnson a certain yellow mare. This April 2, 1867.
Reg: April 3, 1867   Signed: J.N. McCullough

Page 194 - Thomas H. Bledsoe Deed to Mary E. Hamilton. I, Thomas H. Bledsoe of Lincoln County, Tennessee, have sold unto Mary E. Hamilton a tract of land in Bedford County and district No. 21 and bounded by or near James L. Hix's house, to the center of the road, to the center of a branch, and by Matilda Hall's dower line. Containing 100 acres. This September 21, 1865.
Wit: J.K.P. Holt   Signed: Thomas H. Bledsoe
     Square Pickle
Reg: April 5, 1867

Page 195 - Joel Stallings Deed to Nancy E. Darnell. I, Joel Stallings, have sold unto Nancy E. Darnell a tract of land in Bedford County and District No. 18 and bounded by E.A. Adkinson's corner, and by Churnell Glasscock's line. Containing about 60 acres and 125 poles. This 28 January 1862.
Reg: April 25, 1867   Signed: Joel Stallings

Page 195 - R.T. Cannon Trustee &c Deed to B.K. Coble. Whereas James Wortham by Trust Deed dated 9 March 1861 and registered in Bedford County on 11 March 1861 in Book CCC, pages 491 and 492. Conveyed to me in trust amongst other property the town lot and also power conferred on me to sell the property and by me paid over to B.K. Coble one of the beneficiaries in said trust deed paid to me by B.K. Coble. I have this day sold unto B.K. Coble all the right title claim and interest which I have in and to one house and lot in the Town of Shelbyville and bounded by lands of Thomas Eakin, by lands of W.H. Wisener and S.F. Crutcher, by an alley, and by lands of Mrs. Eliza Harrison's

land at present occupied by Mrs. A.B. Knott. This 27 February 1865.
Reg: April 5, 1867   Signed: R.T. Cannon

Page James McCrutchen Deed to William Swinny, 175 acres. I, James McCrutchen of Dyer County, Tennessee, have sold unto William Swinny two certain tracts of land adjoining and now constituting one tract containing 175 acres in Bedford County and District No. 19 and bounded by a 50 acre corner bought by me of John Putman and wife, it being a corner of John Larue, by a corner of a 125 acres bought by J.N. Porter of Isaac B. Larue it being H.M. Oneal's corner on J.R. Jones' line, by M.B. Hamilton's corner, and by Sophia Chapman's corner. This 31 December 1858.
Reg: April 6, 1867   Signed: James McCutchen

Page 197 - Hodge & Ramsey Deed to W.E. Coleman. We, Alexander Hodge and Joseph Ramsey, Jr., have sold unto Wilford E. Coleman a tract of land in 3rd District of Bedford County and bounded in the center of Butlers Creek in James J. Miller's, by the Overton tract, by Mullins' corner lettered (M), to the center of the lane leading from Mullins' line to beginning corner except 2 acres and 18 poles heretofore conveyed by Wm. Young to James Mullins near said Mullins Mill except 3 ½ acres heretofore conveyed by said Young to his father James Young. Containing in all 160 acres. This 3 April 1867.
Reg: April 6, 1867   Signed: Alexander Hodge
                                    Joseph Ramsey

Page 198 - A.A. Cooper Trustee &c Trust Deed to Mary B. Murphrey. By a Deed of Trust to me executed by Mrs. Jane R. Murphy on 2 December 1865. I, A.A. Cooper, have sold to Mary B. Murphy the dower interest of Mrs. Jane R. Murphy in a tract of land in Civil District No. 2 and bounded by lands of Erwin & Eakin, by lands of Erwin, by lands belonging to the heirs of Archibald Murphy. Containing about 145 acres, it being her dower interest in the estate of her deceased husband Archibald Murphy. This 25 February 1867.
Wit: John H. Alderman   Signed: A.A. Cooper, Trustee of
     Alonzo Murphy   Mrs. Jane R. Murphy

Page 198 - C.W. Holden, Agt. Deed to J.G. and Joseph Arnold. I have this day sold unto J.G. and Joseph Arnold a tract of land in Bedford County and Civil District No. 9 and bounded by P.J. Curle's corner in Frazier's line, by S.G. Thompson's line to Mrs. Vaughn's corner, by Mrs. Vaughn's and Elben's corner, and by J.R. Puckett's line to P.J. Curle's line. Containing 80 acres. This March 21, 1867.
Wit: S.G. Thompson   Signed: G.W. Holden
     J.F. Key
Reg: April 8, 1867

Page 199 - J.R. Christy Trust Deed to N. Thompson, 2nd. I, J.R. Christy, have sold unto N. Thompson, 2nd one gray stallion now in my possession. This April 4, 1867.
Reg: April 8, 1867   Signed: J.R. Christy

Page 200 - R.A. Shapard and Frank Hodgkins, Articles of Partnership. We, R.A. Shapard and Frank Hodgkins of Bedford County, do bind ourselves under the style of Shapard & Hodgkins to carry on the business of Bakery & Confectioners in the Town of Shelbyville sharing equally the profits. This 22 March 1867.
Reg: April 8, 1867   Signed: R.A. Shapard
                                   Frank Hodgkins

Page 200 - J.S. Newton Procession Deed. Bedford County, February 28, 1867. I went on the premises of Jas. S. Newton this day and proceeded to survey &c the tract of land on which Jas. S. Newton now lives in District No. 21 and bounded at the center of the Shelbyville and Fayetteville Pike Road in R. Dixon's north boundary line, and by Rich'd Phillips' corner. Containing 398 acres and 46 poles. NOTE: Plat on page 201.
J.B. Dixon, CC   C.S. Dudley, SBC
M.E. Campbell,CC
Reg: April 9, 1867

Page 201 - Thos. C. Whiteside Trustee &c Deed to Samuella Winchester. Whereas John R. Eakin by deed dated 18 November 1857 and registered in Book EEE, pages 185, 186 and 187 conveyed in trust to William S. Eakin a tract of land and known as the Willolock(?) place containing 80 acres. Thos. C. Whiteside was then appointed by said trust deed in the room of Wm. S. Eakin resigned &c. Thos. C. Whiteside as trustee did on 6 April 1867 sold to said Samuella Winchester being the highest bidder. Said land being in Bedford County upon the waters of the Garrison Fork of Duck River (illegible) the former residence of the said John R. Eakin buildings, vineyards &c. One tract of about 20 acres purchased by said Eakin and conveyed to him by William J. Webster, trustee for Mrs. A. Erwin. Another small tract conveyed to said Eakin by Whiteside, Lipscomb & Armstrong of about 8 acres by deed dated 13 September 1853. Also another small tract conveyed to said Jno. R. Eakin by Archibald Murphy about the same time of about 2 acres. Also another small tratc on which the vineyard is situated conveyed to said Eakin by Jno. Q. Davidson. Containing about 3 acres. This 6 April 1867.
Reg: April 11, 1867   Signed: Thos. C. Whiteside

Page 203 - Jane Gill Deed to Elisha Conwell. I, Jane Gill of Lincoln County, Tennessee, have sold unto Elisha Conwell all my right title claim and interest in the estate of my father Thomas Conwell who is yet living and owning to mental (illegible) incapable to transacting business, consisting of one tract of land in District No. 22 of Bedford County and adjoining the lands of William Campbell, by lands of Joseph Parker, by the lands of Samuel Morris and the heirs of Henry Dean, and by lands

of Katey Leathers.   Containing about 410 acres.   This 21 March
1867.
Wit: W.N. Bryant   Signed: Jane Gill
     Zacheus Conwell
Reg: April 11, 1867

Page 204 - F.S. Brown Deed to J.P. Taylor and Jno. W. Clary. By
Trust Deed dated 24 April 1865 and conveyed the trust to John W.
Clary for the purpose of securing sundry debts and registered 25
April 1865. I, F.S. Brown, have sold unto James P. Taylor and
John W. Clary one tract of land in Bedford County and District
No. 10, containing 151 acres and bounded by Jordan Rucker, by
the lands of Alford Poplin and A.F. Knott, by the lands of
Keziah Strout(?), and by lands of F(illegible) Thompson and
Lemuel Call. I am also indebted to Sawyer Scales, with James P.
Taylor, William Taylor and Chesly Williams as my securities.
Part of the purchase money going to Robert Pate for the land. I
am also indebted to H.C. McC(illegible), also to Thomas Johnson.
Other names in document are Robert Reid, William Taylor, James
P. Taylor, William Brown, R.H. Stem, H.V. Taylor, J.P. & C.P.
Taylor, Vincent Taylor, deceased, Alford Poplin, William
Collins, James Lawrance, James Williams, T.D. Tarpley, and B.F.
Puckett. This 11 April 1867.
Reg: April 13, 1867'   Signed: F.S. Brown

Page 206 - Thomas Warren and Jno. Nichols Deed to W.L. Shaddy.
We, John Nichols and Thomas Warren, have sold unto W.L. Shaddy
my interest in a tract of land in Bedford County and District
No. 20 and bounded by the north east corner of the tract this
day conveyed to H. Bledsoe, and to the center of the pike near
the 11 mile post. Containing 30 acres and 136 poles. This 27
February 1860.
Wit: Edm'd Copoer   Signed: Thomas Warren
     Hillsman Bledsoe   John Nichols
Reg: April 12, 1867

Page 207 - Jo. Thompson, Sheriff, Deed to W.E. Galbreath. Wm.E.
Galbreath recovered a judgment against Robt. S. Dwiggins before
Jno. C. Martin a Justice of the Peace for Bedford County on 12
September 1863. I levied on 11 March 1865 on a fraction of Lot
No. 76 on the plan of the Town of Shelbyville, adjoining Pascal
Rowzee, on Spring Street running to the corporation line in Duck
River below the factory, said lot was sold as part of the late
estate of Gen. Robt. Cannon and purchased by James S.Newton and
by him sold to Robt. S. Dwiggins. Sale 15 July 1865 to Wm. E.
Galbreath being the highest bidder. This 1 September 1865.
Wit: W.J. Brown   Signed: Jo. Thompson, Sheriff
     Thos. H. Coldwell
Reg: April 13, 1867.

Page 208 - W.W. Gill Deed to Charles A. Warren. Whereas Robt.
S. Dwiggins by three trust deeds dated 1st on July 10, 1856,
second dated 25 June 1858, and also other dated November 21,
1860, conveyed his real estate to me in trust for the purpose of

securing creditors. Winston W. Gill as trustee have a tract of land and being in the Town of Shelbyville on which the steam mill is situated and Charles A. Warren being the highest bidder and which he did on 7 August 1865 executed his two notes. This 7 August 1865.
Reg: April 15, 1867   Signed: W.W. Gill

Page 208 -
M.L. Dismukes Deed to I.P. and G.R. Dismukes. On 8 April 1867 the undersigned Marcus L. Dismukes made a conveyance to John P. Steele a tract of land. At sale Asa L. Stamps became purchaser. Whereas my sons Isham P. Dismukes and George R. Dismukes have agreed to pay debt of mine. Money received by Peterson Smith, admr. Of Goodrich, to Goodlow Wood, Extr. Of James H. Cobb, to Sarah Miller guardian of her children, to Wm. M. Dismukes, and also three debts in favor of parties not now remembered stay by C.C. Grizzard. Land in Bedford County and District No. 21 and bounded by the west bank of Big Flat Creek, by James Dixon, by Robert Dixon lans, by Jacob Greer's line, by Grant's line, by Matilda Holt's line, and by John Koonce's line in Jacob Kizer's line. This 13 April 1867.
Reg: April 15, 1867   Signed: M.L. Dismukes

Page 209 - A.H. McLean Deed to John D. Webb. I, A.h. McLean, have sold unto John D. Webb a tract of land in the 9th Civil District of Bedford County adjoining the lands of said Webb and others. Containing about 65 acres it being the same tract now held as dower by Mrs. Clark widow of James K. Clark, deceased, and title to which has been vested in her for and during her natural life my interest in the same being an undivided eleventh part thereof. This 11 May 1865.
Wit: Robt. Taylor   Signed: A.H. McLean
     L.N.B. Turner
Reg: April 15, 1867

Page 210 - Ro. B. Davidson Deed to Michael Green. Whereas on 2 March 1861 by deed recorded in Book CCC, page 483 Phillip Hodge conveyed to me a tract of land in Bedford County besides other property, in trust, to secure the payment of certain debts therein to sell said land for cash or credit and whereas I have sold to Michael Green 59 acres part of aforesaid tract. Land bounded by Nowlin's north west corner. This 2 April 1867.
Reg: April 15, 1867   Signed: Ro. B. Davidson

Page 211 - Lewis Tillman C&M Deed to B.G. Green, 192 acres. Lewis Tillman, C&M, to B.G. Green. On 13 November 1865 in the case of Mary Cheatham against Benjamin F. Duggan and others, and Benjamin F. Duggan, extr. and others against Mary Cheatham and others, did sell to B.G. Green on 23 December 1865 a tract of land in District No. 6 of Bedford County, containing 192 acres and bounded by a 640 acre tract of land granted to Ephraim Payton, by Tillman's line, by Benjamin McCuistian's corner, by a tract granted to Joshua Hadley and the line of the school land,

and by a 200 acre tract sold to Freeman Burrow. This 13 March 1867.
Reg: April 15, 1867   Signed: Lewis Tillman, C&M

Page 212 - Thomas Thompson Deed to Alexander Sanders. I, Thomas Thompson, have sold to Alexander Sanders a tract of land in 7th District of Bedford County and bounded by the east boundary line of James Story's land, and by Claiborn McCuistian tract. Containing 111 acres and 54 poles. To have and to hold with the exception of the graveyard on said land, containing about 1/8 of an acre. This April 13, 1867.
Reg: April 17, 1867   Signed: Thos. Thompson

Page 212 - Alexr. Sanders Deed to Thomas Thompson. I, Alexander Sanders, have sold to Thomas Thompson a tract of land in 7th Civil District of Bedford County and bounded by the center of the Shelbyville Road. Containing 111 acres and 10 poles. This 13 April 1867.
Reg: April 17, 1867   Signed: Alexander Sanders

Page 213 - J.H. McGill Note to Thos. A. Woosley. I promise to pay Thomas A. Woosley $90 for one sorrel mare. This 1 June next.
Reg: April 17, 1867   Signed: J.H. McGill

Page 213 - S.N. Stephenson Deed to James H. Neely. This 13 April 1867. I have sold to said Neely a certain lot or parcel of land in District No. 18 being Lot No. 5 which I inherited as an heir of my father D.G. Stephenson, deceased, and bounded by James Thorn's corner, by Lot No. 7, and Lot No. 6, by a tract in the name of Dromgoole & Ransom, by D>G. Stephenson's tract, and by Lot No. 5 and Lot No. 4.
Wit: W.J. Brown   Signed: S.N. Stephenson
     J.H. Moore
Reg: April 18, 1867

Page 214 - G.W. Heard Deed to R.M. Smith. This 15 February 1866. G.W. Heard of Gibson County, Tennessee and R.M. Smith of Bedford County sold a tract of land in Bedford County on the waters of Shipmans Creek and bounded by J.H. Scott's lot in the Village of Rowesville, by the Hillsboro Road, west by the bridge on the mill race, to the mouth of the race and opposite the Cave Spring, and then crossing the creek near a fish trap.
Wit: S.K. Whitson   Signed: G.W. Heard
     W.L. Smith
Reg: April 18, 1867

Page 215 - Jo. Thompson, Sheriff, Deed to N. Thompson, 2nd. Whereas an order of sale No. 4662 issued against L.S. Myers and others came to my hand on 28 May 1866, to sell as the property of W.T. Myers and L.S. Myers one tract of land containing __ acres in the 2nd Civil District of Bedford County known as the

Erwin and Myers factory lot and also as their property. One other tract of land in said District, containing about 50 acres it being the land bought by W.T. Myers & Co. of one Jno. B. Eakin and which said order directed me to sell as the property of Jonas Myers a tract of land in 2nd Civil District on which said Jonas Myers then as now resides. Containing upwards of 400 acres, and which said tract adjoins the lands of J. Cleveland and others. This 12 April 1867.
Reg: April 19, 1867   Signed: Jo. Thompson, Sheriff

Page 216 - Jo. Thompson, Sheriff, Deed to N. Thompson, 2nd. An execution No. 7465 in favor of W.H. Christopher against W.S. Jett and N. Thompson, 2nd came to my hands the 17 January 1867 and whereas another execution No. 7464 in favor of N. Thompson, 2nd against W.S. Jett came to my hands 24 January 1867 and there being no personal property of the defendant W.S. Jett to be found in my county I levied both of said executions on a tract of land in 4th Civil District of Bedford County as the property of said Jett which said land is known The Clark Land, contains about 500 acres and bounded by lands of N. Sugg and others, by lands of Bingham and others, by lands of R.D. Blair and others. This March 2, 1867,
Reg: April 19, 1867   Signed: Jo. Thompson, Sheriff

Page 217 - Mary E. Stanfield and W.W. Stanfield to Isiah Parker. William W. Stanfield and Mary E. his wife sold unto Isiah Parker a tract of land being the same allotted to said Mary E. in the division of the lands of her father Alford Campbell, deceased, being in 22nd District of said county on Goose Creek of Flat Creek and bounded by Lot No. 4 assigned to Caroline Landers, by T.S. Word's corner, by Isiah Parker's corner, and by S. Dean's corner. Containing 91 acres. This 15 April 1867.
Reg: April 20, 1867   Signed: Mary E. Stanfield
                                      W.W. Stanfield

Page 218 - Lewis Tillman, C&M, Deed to Martin Glenn. I, Lewis Tillman in the case of "Chesly Williams and William P. Cannon, executors of Robert Cannon, deceased, against Minos T. Cannon, Eliza J. Nelson, Ann S. Fay," did sell (among other lots and lands at the same time sold) a town lot on 15 September 1865 to Martin Glenn Lot No. 8 being 44 feet and 6 feet front on "street bounded by Lot No. 7" purchased by J.H. McGrew by Lot No. 3 purchased by Moses Marshall and the "Brick Block", by Lots No. 9, 10, 11, 12, and 13". Registered in Minute Book pages 117, 125, 127, and 129. This 13 April 1867.
Reg: April 20, 1867   Signed: Lewis Tillman, C&M

Page 219 - David Thornesberry Deed to Joel N. Thornesberry. I have sold unto Joel N. Thornesberry a lot of land in Bedford County and Civil District No. 2, containing 1 acre and adjoining James M. Chilton. This April 4, 1867.
Reg: April 23, 1867

Page 219 - Joseph Anderson Deed to Jonathan Claxton, 61 acres and 130 poles. I have sold unto Jonathan Claxton a lot of land in Bedford County and Civil District No. 11 and bounded by the plantation where said Claxton now lives, by Bellifant's line, and by the lot fence. Containing 61 acres and 130 poles. This 29 March 1867.
Wit: C.C. Covington   Signed: Jos. Anderson
     J.H. Ogilvie
Reg: April 23, 1867

Page 220 - Jo. Thompson, Sheriff, Deed to B.K. Coble. An execution was issued in favor of Joseph H. Thompson, commissioner, against M.J. and P.P. Gilchrist as principals and P. Fay and George W. Buchanan as securities came to my hands as Sheriff on 14 April 1864 and by which I was commanded that of the goods and chattels lands and tenements of said defendant to make the sums of $958 and costs &c. and whereas there being no personal property of said M.J. and P.P. Gilchrist to be found in my county, I levied said execution on a tract of land in 3rd Civil District of Bedford County and contains 600 acres and bounded by lands of James J. Miller and William Young, by lands of Isham Reeves and others, by lands of John A. Moore, and by lands of Jno. W. Norville. B.K. Coble being the last best and highest bidder became the purchaser. This 12 July 1864.
Reg: April 24, 1867   Signed: Jo. Thompson, Sheriff

Page 221 - Charlotte and Garrett Phillips Deed to John H. White. We, Charlotte Phillips and her husband Garrett Phillips, have sold unto John H. White a tract of land as one of the children and heirs at law of Joshua White her father (now deceased) and is bounded by lands of Madison Neal and Robert Marshall, by B.F. White, by Duck River, by lands of Robt. Wallace, and by lands of heirs of Thos. Townsen. Containing 248 acres. This 3 November 1866.
Reg: April 25, 1867   Signed: Charlotte Phillips
                                      Garrett Phillips

Page 222 - Charlotte and Garrett Phillips Deed to John H. White. We, Charlotte Phillips and Garrett Phillips, have sold unto John H. White a tract of land in Bedford County and Civil District No. 11 and bounded by lands of Alex. Cooper, by lands of B.F. White, by lands of Fletcher Osteen, and by B.F. White and Daniel Collins.   Containing 32 acres it being part of the land belonging to Mrs. Phillips' father Joshua White that is in Bedford County that was assigned to Mrs. Phillips in the division of the same. This 3 November 1866.
Reg: April 26, 1867   Signed: Charlotte Phillips
                                      Garrett Phillips

Page 222 - Wm. J. Whitthorne Deed to Wm. S. Eakin. I have sold to William S. Eakin of Davidson County, Tennessee all my right title claim and interest in and to two cotton factories and mills known as the Shelbyville Cotton Factory situated on Duck River in the Town of Shelbyville and the factory and miles two

324

miles below Shelbyville on Duck River with all lands improvements water power and machinery. This 25 April 1867.
Reg: April 26, 1867   Signed: W.J. Whitthorne

Page 223 - Lewis Tillman Deed to Gray Lynch. Whereas I, Lewis Tillman, became the purchaser at Sheriff's sale on 30 June 1866 of a tract of land bounded by lands of E.A. Mosley, deceased, by John and William Thomas, by R.D. Rankin and which had been levied on as the lands of Gray Lynch and on which he then lived and now lives and which tract of land Joseph Thompson executed to me as well as other tracts purchased at same time and is registered in Book EEE, page 421 and 422. This April 25, 1867.
Reg: April 26, 1867   Signed: Lewis Tillman

Page 224 - George W. Fisher Mortgage to Wm. B.M. Brame. This 26 April 1867. George W. Fisher of Bedford County conveyed unto Wm. B.M. Brame of same place, a tract of land in District No. 11 of Bedford County and bounded at George Fisher's corner and J.F. Thompson's line. Containing 40 acres.
Reg: April 27, 1867   Signed: George W. Fisher

Page 225 - M. Cannon Trust Deed to Jas. M. Elliott. I, M. Cannon, have sold unto James M. Elliott, as trustees, all my stock of goods, wares and merchandise now in my business house in which I am doing business and selling goods until 25 December 1867 consisting of books, shoes, hats, ready made cloths, trunks and other articles. I am also indebted to W.J. Whitthorne in a due bill. I owe my sister Mrs. Wortham, also owe James M. Elliott. Other names in document were English, Coble and J.L. Scudder. This 26 April 1867.
Reg: April 29, 1867   Signed: M. Cannon

Page 226 - Thos. Lipscomb Deed to J.W. Jackson. I, Thomas Lipscomb, have sold unto J.W. Jackson a lot of land in Bedford County and District No. 7 north of the Town of Shelbyville and adjoining a lot of land sold by me to Joseph Anderson, and by the old Nashville Road. Containing 3 acres. This 27 April 1867.
Reg: April 29, 1867   Signed: Thos. Lipscomb

Page 226 - W.J. Blackwell Trust Deed to George W. Greer. I, William J. Blackwell, have sold unto George W. Greer one bay small mule it being the same bought by me of Dean. I also sold to said Greer one black filly. This 27 March 1867.
Reg: April 29, 1867   Signed: Wm. J. Blackwell

Page 227 - Mary A. Brittain Deed to Margaret C. Claxton. I, Mary A. Brittain, have sold to Margaret C. Claxton a tract of land in Bedford County and Civil District No. 8 and bounded a tract of land sold by Newcomb Thompson, Sr. to George W., Jacob F. and N. Thompson, 3rd, and by the bank of Fall Creek. Containing 9 acres and 103 poles. This 4 January 1867.

Wit: Thomas H. Coldwell   Signed: M.A. Brittain
Reg: April 30, 1867

Page 228 - F. Batte Deed to Wm. Brown. I, Frederick Batte, have
sold unto William Brown a tract of land in Civil District No. 9
in Bedford County and bounded by A. Lytle's corner, by
I(illegible) Morris' line, and by Finney's line to Micky
Atkinson's corner. Containing 84 acres and 80 poles. This 18
October 1861.
Wit: Robert Allison   Signed: Frederick Batte
     F.S. Brown
Reg: April 30, 1867

Page 228 - Catharine M.E. Garth Deed to J.W. Rainwater. I,
Catharine M.E. Garth, have sold to J.W. Rainwater a tract of
land in Bedford County and District No. 5, containing 6 acres,
adjoining the Dugan's line. This January 25, 1867.
Wit: H.W. Adcock   Signed: Catharine M.E. Garth
     J.W. Johnson
Reg: April 30, 1867

Page 229 - W.C. Gordon Deed to Allen Coble, re-registered. We,
W.C. Gordon and Sarah Gordon, have sold unto Allen Coble of
Bedford County, the dower tract in Civil District No. 25 of
Bedford County upon which R.J. Williams now resides and which
was assigned as dower to his wife Polly Williams as the widow of
Jacob Coble, deceased. Said land contains about 133 acres and
our interest in same being an undivided one eleventh. This 4
March 1858.
Reg: May 1, 1867   Signed: W.C. Gordon
                                  Sarah Gordon

Page 230 - D.W. Barnes and wife Deed to S.D. C(illegible). This
2 July 1866. D.W. Barnes and Virginia W. Barnes wife of said
D.W. Barnes. The former of Bedford County and the latter of
Rutherford County, Tennessee, a tract of land in District No. 9
on Alexanders Creek in Bedford County and bounded by G.W.
Holden's corner. Containing 20 acres.
Wit: C.L. Cooper   Signed: Virginia W. Barnes
     J.B. Gordon   D.W. Barnes

Page 231 - Martin Hancock Deed to C.F. Lowe and Jos. W. Lowe.
Land in Bedford County and Civil District No. 4 on the Wartrace
Creek and bounded by E.A. Mosley's line, to the center of
Wartrace Creek, to the water gate, to the center of the Rail
Road, by Muse's line, and by Ben Merritt's line. Containing 311
acres and 44 poles. This 8 November 1866.
Wit: John T. Hancock   Signed: Martin Hancock
     Thos. F. Hall
Reg: May 3, 1867

Page 231 - M.H. Card Contract with S.H. Card. I, M.H. Card of
Bedford County, have rented from S.H. Card about 21 acres of
land. S.H. Card my security to a note to Wm. H. Stephenson.
Also on a note to Martin Sims. I also owe Jas. H. Neil. This
February 15, 1867.
Reg: May 4, 1867   Signed: M.H. Card

Page 232 - Robt. H. Thomas Deed of Gift to Sarah M. Thomas. For
the love and affection I have for my beloved wife Sarah M.
Thomas formerly Sarah M. Miller. I, Robert H. Thomas of Bedford
County do give and convey unto my said wife all the right title
claim and interest that I now have as may hereafter have in and
to a lot of land in Bedford County and Civil District No. 23 and
bounded by lands of Thomas C. Ryall, by lands of Benjamin
McFarland, and by lands of John W. Brewer's heirs. Containing 2
acres. This being the same land deeded to Sarah M. Miller by
Benjamin McFarland my right to the same being only (illegible).
This 3 May 1867.
Wit: M.E.W. Dunaway   Signed: Robert H. Thomas
Reg: May 4, 1867

Page 232 - John W. McAnally Deed to Wiley Richards. Land a part
of the tract known as county land designated as Lots No. 14 and
15 in plat of said Coat's land being in Civil District No. 7 of
Bedford County and bounded by Ramsey's line, by Cunnins' line
and by the Mill Road and Robert Dennis' line. Containing 17
acres. This April 25, 1867.
Reg: May 4, 1867   Signed: J.W. McAnally

Page 233 - Perkins M. Sims Power of Attorney to J.C. Wilson.
Whereas Thomas Allison, deceased, late of Bedford County by his
Last Will and Testament did give and bequeath unto the heirs of
Briggs G. Sims and Matilda S. Sims, his wife, a legacy of __
dollars. Lemuel Call of Bedford County was duly appointed
administrator of Thomas Allison, deceased, and on __ day of
September 1866 John W. Clary of Bedford County was duly
appointed trustee of the heirs of Briggs G. and Matilda S. Sims
to receive, keep and preserve the above mentioned Legacy in
trustfor said heirs. I, Perkins M. Sims, son of Briggs G. and
Matilda S. Sims and of Greene County, Missouri, having arrived
at the age of 21 years, have appointed John C. Wilson of Bedford
County my true and lawful attorney for me and in my name to ask
demand and receive of and from John W. Clary, trustee, the
Legacy. This 20 April 1867.
Reg: May 7, 1867   Signed: P.M. Sims

Page 234 - Elizabeth J. Stockard Power of Attorney to Bryant
Landis. We do appoint Bryant Landis of Bedford County our
attorney in fact to demand and receive for us and in our names
from one Burrell Ward, Jr., administrator of Burrell Ward,
deceased, late of Bedford County for our distributive shares
which descended to us from said Burrell Ward, now deceased.
This 24 May 1867.
Izard County, Arkansas   Signed: Elizabeth J. Stockard

Reg: May 6, 1967   Signed: Pleasant F.Thompson
                                  John C. Stockard

Page 235 - T.N.B. Turner Deed to Silas Williams, 45 acres. I,
T.N.B. Turner, have sold unto Silas Williams all my interest in
a tract of land in Bedford County and District No. 9 except one
fourth of an acre which has been heretofore sold to M.W. Turner
and J.L. Turner and the same deeded to them by Elijah Williams.
Containing 45 acres. My interest being one ninth part of said
land and bounded by W.S. Brame, by T.N.B. Turner, by M.F. Hoover
and T.M. Rankin, and by J.T. Wheelhouse it being the land of the
heirs of Elizabeth Williams. This May 6, 1867.
Reg: May 8, 1867   Signed: T.N.B. Turner

Page 236 - Dennis Hemby Deed to Dulcing Reddin, 52 acres. This
March 5, 1867. Dennis Hemby sold to Dulcy Reddin, both of
Bedford County, a tract of land on the head waters of Gages
Creek. Containing 52 acres.
Wit: Isaac Glasgow   Signed: Dennis Hemby
     Burrell Blackman
Reg: May 8, 1867

Page 236 - Thomas J. Gambill Deed to Joseph Darnell, 54 acres.
Land in Bedford County and Civil District No. 18 it being the
land I bought of W.F. Barnett and bounded by Caroline Barnett
and by my own land, by Mrs. Bryant, and by Mrs. Durham and
Alexander Dysart. Containing 54 acres. This May 18, 1867.
Wit: John Wai(illegible)   Signed: Thomas J. Gambill
     G.W. Hammins(?)
Reg: May 8, 1867

Page 237 - W.L. Riggins and wife Deed to J.C. Lemmings. This __
March 1867. W.L. Riggins and Frances Riggins, his wife, sold
unto J.C. Lemings all the right title claim and interest to
which said Frances Riggins is entitled to as sister and heir at
law of John T. Weaver in a tract of land situated lying and
being in Bedford County and Civil District No. 25 on the waters
of Norman Creek and bounded by Z. Weaver, by Normans Creek, by
g. Huffman, by J.H. Huffman, by Holland's line, and by
Caleghan's line. Containing 70 acres.
Reg: May 9, 1867   Signed: W.L. Riggins
                                  Frances Riggins

Page 238 - W.L. Riggins Deed to J.C. Lemmings. This 25 March
1867. W.L. Riggins sold unto J.C. Lemmings, both of Bedford
County, all right title and interest the same being three shares
in a tract of land in Bedford County and bounded by Zephaniah
Weaver's corner, by Normans Creek, by George Huffman's line, by
G.H. Huffman's corner, and by Holland's line. Containing 70
acres.
Wit: A.E. Disham   Signed: W.K. Riggins
     George Huffman
Reg: May 10, 1867

Page 239 - Nimrod Burrow Copy of Judgment VS W.G. Smiley et als. Nimrod Burrow VS W.G. Smiley, C.C. Word and J.M. Hix - Action, No. 172. Henry Yancy, James Pratt, Richard Foreman, Robert Mosly, N. Thompson, 2nd., W.W. Payne, Wm. Mc(illegible), Thos. J. Muse, D.B. Shriver, Wm. G. Word, Thomas freeman, and G.W.C. Morton and being elected to speak upon the issue say they find in favor of the plaintiff &c. This May 9, 1867.
Reg: May 11, 1867   Signed: James H. Neil, Clerk

Page 240 - J.F. Thompson Deed to W.B.M. Brame. I have sold unto Wm. B.M. Brame a tract of land in Bedford County and Civil District No. 11 bounded by A.B. Parsons' corner, and by the south side of the Columbia Road. Containing 49 acres and 67 poles. This 17 April 1867.
Reg: May 13, 1867   Signed: J.F. Thompson

Page 240 - W.T. Davis Deed to James Evans, FMC. I, William T. Davis have sold to James Evans (a free man of color) a tract of land in 19th Civil District of Bedford County and bounded by a tract of land known as the Yancy land. Containing 10 acres. This 11 May 1867.
Reg: May 14, 1867   Signed: W.T. Davis

Page 241 - George W. Foster and wife Deed to Phillip D. Meroney. We, George W. Foster and Margaret A. Foster, of Lincoln County, Tennessee, have sold unto Phillip D. Meroney a tract of land in Bedford County and District No. 22 and bounded by lands of R.S. Dwiggins and Lewis Hix, by lands of Robt. Or Harrel Evans, by lands of H.F. Holt, and by lands of W.W. Gill and R.S. Dwiggins. Containing 222 ½ acres. Our interest being only (1/9) one ninth of said land and is the same land that was descended by the Last Will and Testament of Joshua Holt, Sr., deceased, and by Jane L. Phillips. This 13 May 1867.
Reg: May 14, 1867   Signed: George W. Foster
                                   Margaret A. Foster

Page 242 - A.L. Adams Deed to Henry Buford, FMC. I, A.L. Adams of Bedford County, have sold unto Henry Buford, a free man of color, a tract of land in 7th Civil District of Bedford County near the Town of Shelbyville and near the Shelbyville Branch Rail Road and bounded by a lot known as the McAnally's lot, by lands of Philip Brooks, by a lot known as the Cummings' lot, and by a lot owned by George W. Thompson. Containing about 1 ¾ acres. The same being a portion of the land known as the "Coat's Dower" and which several years ago sold under decree of County Court the lot conveyed being the lot purchased by me of George Edmundson. This 10 May 1867.
Reg: May 15, 1867   Signed: A.L. Adams

Page 242 - Martha A. Thompson Deed to N.C. Thompson. I, Martha A. Thomas, have sold to N.C. Thompson a lower tract of land of Elizabeth Thompson, said land is on the north side of Duck River, District No. 11 and bounded by land set apart to Geo. A.

Thompson in the division of the entire tract of land of Joseph Thompson, deceased, of which the dower was a part and allotted to Elizabeth Thompson the widow of the deceased, by Philis (Felix) Turrentine, by M.S. Jones, and by lands of Martha A. Wade and Richard Turner. Containing about 100 acres and said tract being one twentieth of the same. Also my entire interest in and to the twenty five acre tract above mentioned to Geo. A. Thompson, deceased, and which is bounded by Isabella Lock, by Richard Turner, by Felix Turrentine, by my dower. Also being one twentieth part of said land of 25 acres. This 14 May 1867.
Reg: May 16, 1867   Signed: M.A. Thompson

Page 243 - R.C. Russ Deed to Jo. D. Wilhoite, House and Lot. I have sold unto Jo. D. Wilhoite a house and lot in Camp White near Shelbyville in Civil District No. 7 of Bedford County and adjoining a corner of a lot sold by James M. Elliott to M.E.W. Dunaway, by Camp Street, by a corner Lot No. 8 as known in the plan of the lots sold by Clement Cannon in Camp White, by M.E.W. Dunaway's ot, by the west side of Poplar Street, and by Locust Street. Containing 113 1/3 sq. poles. This 14 May 1867.
Reg: May 17, 1867   Signed: R.C. Russ

Page 244 - R.C. Russ Deed to Jo. D. Wilhoite. I have sold unto Joseph D. Wilhoite my Printing Press, type, material &c. This 14 May 1867.
Reg: May 17, 1867   Signed: R.C. Russ

Page 244 - John F. Swan Deed to Silas Dice. I, John F. Swan of Bedford County sold unto Silas Dice of Smith County, Tennessee my interest in a tract of land in Bedford County it being the tract on which I now reside and borders E.S. Wortham's line. Containing 106 acres. This 8 May 1867.
Wit: M.B. Fisher   Signed: John F. Swan
     T.B. Allison
Reg: May 20, 1867

Page 245 - Berry & Dunoville et als Deed to Elizabeth O. Sandridge. This 7 May 1867. Berry & Dunoville of Davidson County, Tennessee. Edmund Cooper as trustee of Mrs. Mary J. Erwin wife of Andrew Erwin. Andrew Erwin and Mrs. Elizabeth O. Sandridge wife of James S. Dandridge. By said Cooper as trustee by deed dated November 5, 1863 and recorded in Book DDD, pages 336 and 337 and said Edmund Cooper as trustee of said Mary J. Erwin in deed of November 5, 1863 to Berry and Dunoville all of her right title and interest to said Mrs. Elizabeth O. Sandridge property in Bedford County and District No. 2 of Bedford County adjoining lands of John R. Eakin, by lands owned by the heirs of Archibald Murphy, by lands owned by the heirs of Wm. Pepper, by south side of the Garrison Fork of Duck River, and by the east side of the Rail Road known as "Beechwood". Containing 250 acres.
Reg: May 21, 1867   Signed: Berry & Dunoville
                                   J.F. Dunoville
                                   Edm'd Cooper, Trustee

A. Erwin
Mary J. Erwin

Page 246 - Mary J. Erwin Power of Attorney to Edmund Cooper. Whereas by marriage contract entered into between Andrew Erwin my husband and my self before our marriage the property then owned by me was to remain my sole and separate property to sell or dispose of the same as I might desire was vested in Edmund Cooper of Bedford County the trustee. Therefore being desirous of selling the "Beechwood" and place in District No. 2 of Bedford County. Containing 250 acres. This 7 May 1867.
Reg: May 21, 1867   Signed: Mary J. Erwin

Page 247 - Robt. H. Tucker Bond to J.A. Pucket.   I have sold unto J.A. Pucket.   By the satisfaction of the said J.A. Pucket of a judgment which (illegible) Edwards obtained against me in Bedford County a tract of land in Bedford County and Civil District No. 5 and bounded by lands of R.W. Couch, by lands of Morlan(?), and by lands of C.W. Harris and M.C. Miller. Containing 132 acres, being the lands owned by my father Lewis Tucker and my mother Harriet Tucker and is vested by me. This 1 January 1867.
Reg: May 22, 1867   Signed: R.H. Tucker

Page 248 - W.J. Whitthorne Deed to S.A. Cunningham. I have sold unto S.A. Cunningham all the right title claim and interest which I have in a lot of ground.   One lot of ground in the corporate limits of the Town of Shelbyville fronting on the west side of the Public Square, by an alley running from Dwiggins Mills north to Bridge Street, bounded on the south by property of the estate of Erwin J. Frierson, deceased, known as "Council Row," and north by Bridge Street. This 18 May 1867.
Wit: Edm'd Cooper   Signed: W.J. Whitthorne
     William Frierson
Reg: May 22, 1867

Page 248 - A.L. Stamps Deed to Harry Ray, FMC. I, A.L. Stamps, have sold unto Harry Ray a tract of land in Bedford County near the Town of Shelbyville and Civil District No. 7 and bounded by a street running east and west which connects Lots No. 17, 15 and 18, to the center of the street which runs north and south, to corner of Wade's Lot No. 12.   Containing about 1 acre.   It being the same lot purchased by me of W.J. L(illegible) on 14 January 1860. This 18 May 1867.
Reg: May 22, 1867   Signed: A.L. Stamps

Page 249 - Edmund Cooper et als Deed to Hardy Prince. Edmund Cooper many years ago conveyed all his right title claim and interest in the tract of land to Wm. B. and James B. Phillips. Said Wm. B. Phillips and James B. Phillips by date November 4, 1857 conveyed said land to Wiley Riggins and wife Margaret Riggins.   Deed contains about 23 acres of the original tract situated on the east side of the Rail Road and one house and lot conveyed to Hardy Prince by William Word by deed dated 30 December 1865. This 18 May 1867.

Reg: May 23, 1867   Signed: Edmund Cooper
                                   Wiley Riggins
                                   Margaret Riggins

Page 250 - W.N. Gwinn Deed to J.M. Neely. I have sold unto J.M. Neely a tract of land in the 18th District of Bedford County and bounded in a glade, by Neely's line, and Earnhart's line. Containing 112 acres, it being the place known as the G.T. Neely's place. This 21 May 1867.

Reg: May 23, 1867   Signed: W.N. Gwinn

Page 251 - Copy of Court Decree to Jas. L. Woods. It appearing to the satisfactory of the Court from the statement of James H. Neil, Clerk of Circuit Court of Bedford County and executor of John T. Neil former clerk of this court that this court at its December Term 1849 did decree the sale of a tract of land of Orville Muse and others heirs at law of Isaac Muse, deceased, as the property of said Isaac Muse, to wit, a tract of land in Civil District No. 2 of Bedford County and bounded by the lands of Scruggs, by lands of G.G. Osborne, Finch, and Scruggs, by lands of Osborne, and by the dower tract of Mrs. Isaac Muse. Containing 221 acres and 141 poles. It also appeared from the affidavit of said James H. Neil and William T. Tune that on the __ day of February 1850 said land was sold, that all the parties interested, to wit, Orville Muse, Permelia Wood the heirs of M(illegible) Rayburn, deceased, and Martha J. Muse were present on day of sale and were satisfied that the said James L. Woods became the purchaser of the land. NOTE: A very long document.

Reg: May 24, 1867   Signed: James H. Neil, Clerk

Page 252 - James C. Dryden Deed to N.L. Dryden. Whereas by descent from Thomas Dryden, deceased, Joseph W. Dryden, John D.L. Dryden, Nathaniel L. Dryden, Thomas E. Dryden, Daniel M. Dryden, Eleanor H. Dryden, Thomas A. White and wife Hannah M. White and James C. Dryden have derived title to and now hold equal and undivided interest in a tract of land in Bedford County and Lincoln County, Tennessee, said land being situated on the line between said counties and partly in both and in District No. __ of Lincoln County, Tennessee and bounded by the lands of William H. Dyer, by lands of Thomas A. White, by lands of Jackson King and others, by lands of Margaret Bradshaw. Now I, James C. Dryden, have sold said land to Nathaniel L. Dryden. This May 22, 1867.

Reg: May 28, 1867   Signed: James C. Dryden

Page 253 - W.B. Neely et als Deed to Price C. Steele. This 27 May 1867. Mary W. Neely, Iva J. Neely, William B. Neely, Elizabeth C. Crawford, and Newton D. Crawford sold to Price C. Steele, all of Bedford County, all our undivided interest in and to a tract of land in Bedford County and Civil District No. 5 on Fall Creek and bounded by a 5000 acre tract granted by the State

of North Carolina to Caleb Phifer, deceased, and Levi Johnson's corner, and to center of Fall Creek. Containing 40 acres.
Reg: May 30, 1867   Signed: W.B. Neely
                                   Iva J. Neely
                                   M.W. Neely
                                   E.D. Crawford
                                   N.D. Crawford

Page 254 - John Noblett and wife Deed to R.S. Montgomery. We, John Noblett and Lucy Noblett his wife, have sold unto R.S. Montgomery all the right title claim and interest of one sixth part that we have in and to a tract of land formerly owned by Joseph N. and William H. Card in District No. 18 and bounded by lands of Samuel H. Card, Drumgoole & Ransom, and the heirs of John H. Lewell and the heirs of Thomas Shearin and others. This 2 May 1867.
Reg: May 31, 1867   Signed: John Noblett
                                   Lucy M. Noblett

Page 254 - Allen Cotton Receipt to C.L. Pyrom. Received of C.L. Pyrom $2200 with interest and cost in full which is in satisfaction of the within Deed of Trust consequently the Deed of Trust is void. This 25 May 1867.
Reg: June 3, 1867   Signed: Allen Cotton

Page 255 - Alexander Sanders Deed to James R. Sanders. Land sold to James R. Sanders a tract of land bounded by Thomas Thompson's tract of land, and by James Story's corner. Containing 17 acres and 5 poles. Also one other tract bounded by Thompson's corner in the Wilhoite's line, by Frazier's line on Tillman's line, and by Lewis Tillman's corner. Containing in all about 48 acres, except about one fourth of an acre which is reserved as a grave yard. This 1 June 1867.
Reg: June 4, 1867   Signed: Alex. Sanders

Page 255 - George Cortner Deed to Mathew Cortner. I, George Cortner, have sold unto Mathew Cortner a lot of land lying in Bedford County and District No. 25. This April 27, 1867.
Wit: J.W. Cowan, Sr.   Signed: George Cortner
     Wm. H. Wilson
Reg: June 4, 1867

Page 256 - A.H. Coffey Deed of Gift to H.C. Haggard. This 10 May 1860, between Alexander H. Coffee and Hamilton C. Haggard. A.H. Coffee, for the love and affection and friendship which he has and bears toward said Hamilton C. Haggard, have given unto him a tract of land in Bedford County near the Nashville & Chattanooga Rail Road and in the Village of Wartrace lying on the south side of a street running from Robert Buchanan's Tavern on the house formerly occupied by him as such to Jeremiah Cleveland's west line, and on the west side of another street running near the spring in said A.H. Coffey's field, and by an alley. Containing about one half acre.

Wit: Thos. C. Whiteside   Signed: A.H. Coffey
    A.J. Greer
Reg: June 6, 1867

Page 257 - D.A. Ozment Deed to S. and T. Lamb. I, D.A. Ozment
of Bedford County, have sold to Sally and Tabitha Lamb of the
same place, a tract of land in Bedford County and Civil District
No. 11 and bounded by the big road the south west corner of the
Male Academy lot in Unionville, Tennessee, by Thomas Allison's
corner, by D.A. Ozment's line, and by J.W. Clary's line.
Containing 7 ¼ acres. This January 26, 1867.
Wit: S.?. Moon   Signed: D.A. Ozment
    W.C. Blanton
Reg: June 6, 1867

Page 258 - W.P. Green Deed to S.R. Haily and H.W. Holt. I,
William P. Green of Bedford County, have sold unto S.R. Haily
and H.W. Holt Lots No. 2 and 3. Containing 66 feet in front and
128 feet in the rear together with the building situated thereon
&c. Bounded by Lot No. 4 at present by A.E. Mullins the same
situated in Wartrace, Bedford County. This January __ 1862.
Wit: J.W. Tilford   Signed: W.P. Green
    B.D. Holt
Reg: June 6, 1867

Page 258 - J.J. Long Deed to Michael Fisher. I, J.J. Long, have
sold unto Michael Fisher a tract of land in Bedford County and
District No. 11, containing 100 acres and bounded by a corner of
the original tract, by a 1500 acre tract of land granted to Wm.
Lanor, by C.L. Burns' corner, by a 300 acre tract granted to
John Thompson, and by the school land tract. This 16 November
1866.
Wit: G.W. Parsons   Signed: J.J. Long
    John F. Thompson
Reg: June 7, 1867

Page 259 - A.M. Webb Deed to Benjamin Webb, Re-registered. I,
A.M. Webb of Bedford County, have sold unto Benjamin Webb of
same place a tract of land in Bedford County, containing 128
acres and 83 poles and bounded by Benjamin Webb's tract of land
which he now lives, by a corner of Parsons' tract of land, and
by S.G. Miller's line. This 28 July 1857.
Wit: B.F. Webb   Signed: A.M. Webb
    M.H. Webb
Reg: June 10, 1867

Page 260 - Martin Thompson Deed to John Thompson, Re-registered.
I, Martin Thompson, have sold unto John Thompson a lot or parcel
of land purchased by P.J. Thompson and myself from Michael Marsh
which land is now undivided one half is mine being in District
No. 18 of Bedford County and containing 1 acre and 47 ¼ poles,
bounded by Ransom Stephen's line, and by the pike. This 14 July
1860.

Page 261 - William Campbell, adm. &c Deed to E.A. Reagor. On 21
October 1862 Alford Campbell sold to C.A. Crunk a tract of land
on the waters of Big Flat Creek and gave his bond, and whereas
C.A. Crunk and J.W. Crunk and Jordan Hale on 3 April 1866
appointed that part of said land should be conveyed unto E.A.
Reagor, which part is bounded by Lot No. 1. Containing 17 acres
and 39 poles. Part No. 2 bounded by a road. Containing 11
acres and 45 poles. This 11 July 1866.
Reg: June 10, 1867   Signed: Wm. Campbell, Admr. Of
                                    A. Campbell

Page 262 - D.F. Jett Deed to George W. Thompson. I, Duncan F.
Jett, have sold to George W. Thompson all the right title claim
and interest which I have in the southern part of the house and
lot on Martin Street in the Town of Shelbyville purchased by me
at a public sale in the case of Mathew Shearin and wife and
others James K.P. Carlisle and others and the title of which was
vested in me by decree of the 20 October 1860 and bounded by a
margin of Martin Street the south west corner of this lot
conveyed by me to William Gosling, by an alley, and by a corner
of George W. Thompson's lot purchased at the sale sale. This 27
May 1867.
New York City, N.Y.
Wit: Thos. Sadler   Signed: D.F. Jett
     John E. P(illegible)
Reg: June 10, 1867

Page 263 - William H. Wisener Deed to George W. Thompson. Land
in Bedford County and Civil District No. 7 and a short distance
west of the Town of Shelbyville being a part of the John T. Neil
tract and conveyed by A.L. Stamps to said Wisener by deed dated
July 12, 1862. Land adjoining a forks of the road and street
laid off in the fall of 1856, by Wisener's plank fence at the
commencement of the war, by a tract of land formerly owned if
not now by Patrick Fay by one A.H. Berry, and by Sims Bridge on
Duck River. Containing something over 3 acres and is subject to
an easement of fifteen feet within said boundaries on the north
side. This 24 April 1867.
Reg: June 11, 1867   Signed: Wm. H. Wisener

Page 264 - W.S. Jett Deed to George W. Thompson. This 1 January
1867. I, William S. Jett, have sold to George W. Thompson a
tract of land in 7t^h Civil District of Bedford County and
bounded by the east side of the Shelbyville and Fayetteville
Turnpike, near the dwelling house, by a lane to Andrew Reed's
boundary, and by the center of Flat Creek. Containing 132 acres
and 69 poles. This 6 June 1867.
Reg: June 11, 1867   Signed: Wm. S. Jett

Page 265 - Edmund Cooper Deed to Winsler(Winston?) Rowzee. I,
Edmund Cooper, have sold unto Winsler(Winston?) Rowzee a town

lot, being one half of the same conveyed to me by deed executed by William S. Jett and the entire lot being the livery stable lot conveyed by A.L. Adams to William S. Jett by deed dated 13 June 1867 and bounded by a corner of Holland and Jones lot on which the livery stable is situated, and by corner to Jones lot, beginning at a corner of lot owned by A.L. Adams and owned by R.N. Jones, and by Brittain Street to an alley. It being the lot upon which the livery stable stands. This 29 May 1867.
Reg: June 11, 1867   Signed: Edmund Cooper

Page 266 - Samuel L. Reagor Trust Deed to George Castleman, Trustee. I, Samuel L. Reagor, have sold unto G.H. Castleman the following property in 22nd District commonly called the Burrow District of Bedford County, to wit, all my undivided interest in the real estate which descended to me and my co-heirs from the estate of my father Abraham Reagor which real estate is occupied by the widow and heirs of said Abraham Reagor. And also a house and lot in Flat Creek Village in Ray's District and occupied by me and formerly by Dr. James J. Crunk. And also all my books of accounts for medical services, and a gray mare and buggy. I am indebted to William Campbell, to Jacob Kizer, to Wm. J. Cochran in the office of Wm. Galbreath to Jesse Coleman, to one Graham of Jackson County, Alabama, to Samuel Lacy, to Jordan Hale, and to Davidson & Buchanan. This 7 June 1867.
Reg: June 11, 1867   Signed: Sam'l L. Reagor

Page 267 - Phebe A. Oneal et als Power to John H. Larue. Henderson County, Texas. We, Phebe A. Oneal wife of Wiley J. Oneal, Wiley J. Oneal, Elizabeth M. Larue wife of Isaac Larue, Isaac Larue and Joseph M. Larue, all residents of Henderson County, Texas, except Wiley J. Oneal and Isaac Larue husband of above heir, of the estate of John Larue, deceased, being administrated upon in Bedford County, do appoint John H. Larue our attorney in fact to demand and receive from all persons from whom any money effects or interests may be coming to us through the estate of said John Larue, deceased, in Bedford County. This 13 May 1867.
Wit: P.T. Tennehill   Signed: Phebe A. Oneal
Reg: June 10, 1867   Wiley J. Oneal
                                               Elizabeth M. Larue
                                               Isaac Larue
                                               Joseph M. Larue

Page 268 - R.B. Wilhoite Deed to Thomas W. Warner. This 1 February 1867. Richard B. Wilhoite of Bedford County sold unto Thomas W. Warner of same place a tract of land in the 21st District in Bedford County situated on the south side of Duck River and bounded by lands of J.L. Stephens and R.H. Temple, by Thos. Lipscomb, and by L.T. Williams and others. Containing 10 acres.
Reg: June 17, 1867   Signed: R.B. Wilhoite

Page 269 - Ebenezer Wilson VS Copy of Decree Robert Terry and others. At September Term 1865 of Chancery Court on the 8

September the decree was pronounced by said court the Hon. Jno.
P. Steele, Chancellor, presiding in the case of Ebenezer Wilson
VS Robert Terry and others - Decree. This came to proceed and
sell the land in the pleadings that he sell for cash and that he
pay over the proceeds when collected. Report. I advertised the
tract of land in the "True Union" a newspaper published in the
Town of Shelbyville, to be sold at the Court House for cash 24th
October 1859. Said land containing 10 acres and sold off to
Jno. P. Steele, and before complying to the term of the sale
relinquished his bid to Robert Terry, he (Terry) proposing to
take the land and pay E. Wilson debts and costs of the cause.
This 24 October 1857.

William J. Whitthorne, C&M

It is further decreed that all right claim and interest of James
Sanders and John P. Steele in said tract of land in District No.
8 of Bedford County adjoining the lands of Ebenezer Wilson,
Samuel Bomar and Isreal Harris. Containing about 10 acres and
on which James Sanders is living be de-vested of them and vested
in Robert Terry.
Reg: June 19, 1867   Signed: Lewis Tillman, C&M
                       By Deputy L. Tillman, Jr.

Page 270 - James J. Smith Deed to Phillip D. Maroney. I, James
J. Smith, have sold unto Phillip D. Maroney a tract of land in
22nd District of Bedford County. One tract bounded by lands of
J.L. Hicks and Robert S. Dwiggins, by lands of Herod F. Holt, by
lands of A.H. Evans and Harrel Evans, and by the lands of Robt.
S. Dwiggins and A.H. Evans. Containing in all 220 acres which
tract is known as the Jarrel Smith farm out of which dower has
been heretofore assigned to his widow my interest being one
eleventh undivided one eleventh. I being one of the children of
said Jarrel Smith. I also convey to said Maroney all my
interest being an undivided one eleventh in the whole in the
following tract in the 22nd District and bounded by the lands of
James Reese, and by lands of Petty's heirs. Containing 18
acres. This 8 June 1867.
Reg: June 19, 1867.   Signed: James J. Smith

Page 271 - Minos T. Cannon Deed to Jo. D. Wilhoite and C.A.
Warren. I have sold unto Jo. D. Wilhoite and C.A. Warren a
house and lot in the Town of Shelbyville on the south side of
the Public Square in Civil District No. 7 Bedford County and
bounded by M.T. Cannon's Hotel lot, and by Jo. D. Wilhoite's
lot. This June 15, 1867.
Wit: J.C. Stamps   Signed: Minos T. Cannon
Reg: June 19, 1867

Page 272 - M.S. Dean Trust Deed to E.W. Dean. I, Martin S.
Dean, do convey unto E.W. Dean a tract of land containing about
59 acres in 24th Civil District of Bedford County being the
tract on which said E.W. Dean now lives, and also one sorrel
mule and all my household furniture. I am indebted to the
estate of David Wise, to Thos. Anderton, and Watson & Pearson.
This 17 June 1867.
Reg: June 19, 1867   Signed: M.S. Dean

Page 272 - Joseph Thompson, Sheriff, Deed to Wm. H. Ransom. On 20 October 1863, T.W. Jordan sued out of the office of the Clerk of Circuit Court of Bedford County a writ of attachment against Daniel L. Reeves and which attachment came into the hands of T.R(B?). Laird, coroner of Bedford County, and there being no personal property of said D.L. Reeves, he levied on a tract of land in District No. 1 of Bedford County and bounded by lands of L.P. Fields and James Johnson, by lands of McMichael, by lands of A. Jacobs, and by lands of W.F. Robinson and Kendle. Containing from 500 to 700 acres as the property of defendant Reeves. NOTE: A long document. This 18 June 1867.
Reg: June 19, 1867   Signed: Jo. Thompson, Sheriff

Page 273 - W'mson Haggard Deed to R.B. Parks. I, Williamson Haggard of Franklin County, Tennessee, have sold unto Rufus B. Parks a tract of land of 114 ½ acres in District No. 2 of Bedford County and bounded by lands of G.G. Osborne, by lands of Robert Waite, by lands of Jeremiah Cleveland, being the same tract of land owned and occupied by Samuel Haggard at his death. This 17 June 1867.
Reg: June 20, 1867   Signed: W'mson Haggard

Page 274 - Isham Martin, Col., Mortgage to T.B. Ivie. I have sold unto T.B. Ivie my entire crop of corn growing on his farm my interest herein conveyed being one half of all I may make on said farm, but this conveyance is made upon the express condition that is I pay a note this day executed by me and signed by said Ivie as my security payable to ___ Stegall due 1 December 1867. This 18 June 1867.
Wit: H.H. Holt   Signed: Isham Martin
Reg: June 21, 1867

Page 275 - P.H. Thompson Deed to J.T. Williams. I have sold unto J.T. Williams all my right title claim and interest I have in a tract of land in Bedford County and District No. 11 and bounded by lands of T.B. Jeffress, E. Batte, H. Clark, J. Green, the Thompson's heirs &c. This June 24, 1867.
Wit: C.C. Covington   Signed: P.H. Thompson
     W.L. Thompson
Reg: June 25, 1867

Page 275 - Robert B. Maupin Deed to Wm. C. Germany. I, Robert B. Maupin, have sold unto William C. Germany a tract of land in Bedford County and District No. 25, containing 10 acres and bounded by the (illegible) dam on the Barren Fork of Duck River, and by Reed's line to the head of the island. This October 19, 1866.
Wit: J.S. Maupin   Signed: Robert B. Maupin
     C.L. Pyrom
Reg: June 25, 1867

Page 276 - W.S. Smith Deed to P.D. Maroney. I, William S. Smith, have sold unto Phillip D. Maroney a tract of land in 22nd

District of Bedford County. One tract is bounded by lands of J.L. Hix and Robert S. Dwiggins, by lands of Herod F. Holt, by lands of A.H. Evans and Harrel Evans, and by lands of Robt. S. Dwiggins and A.H. Evans. Containing in all 220 acres. Said land is known as the Jarrel Smith farm out of which dower has been heretofore assigned to his widow. My interest being one unduvuded one eleventh not encumbered by dower. I being one of the children of said Jarrel Smith. I also convey to said Maroney a tract of land bounded by James Reese, by lands of said Reese, and by lands of Petty's heirs. Containing 18 acres. This 24 June 1867.
Reg: June 25, 1867   Signed: William S. Smith

Page 277 - Robert B. Maupin Deed to Marion Stone. I have sold unto Marion Stone a tract of land in Bedford County and District No. 2, containing 54 acres and 49 poles and bounded by Mary Franklin, deceased, south boundary line and Wm. And Samuel Yates' corner, to the center of the Nashville and Chattanooga Rail Road, by James Chilton's corner, by R.B. Maupin's line, and by Elias Holt's line. This February 16, 1867.
Wit: J.S. Maupin   Signed: Robert B. Maupin
     J.H. Maupin
Reg: June 25, 1867

Page 278 - Robert Clark, Trustee &c et als Deed to William B. Wallace. This 22 June 1867. Robert Clark, Trustee &c James Finch and L.P. Fields and William B. Wallace. Said James Finch by deed dated 16 November 1864 and registered 13 March 1865 in Book DDD conveyed in trust to said Robt. S. Clark for a tract of land in Bedford County on the waters of Straight Creek and said James Finch sold a portion of said tract of land to said L.P. Fields has this day sold said portion of said tract of land purchased by him to said William B. Wallace. Said land in Bedford County in Civil District No. 2 on Straight Creek adjoining Mrs. Couch's east line, to top of the ridge, to Scott's line, and by John S. Davis' corner. Containing 250 acres.
Reg: June 26, 1867   Signed: R.S. Clark
                                      James Finch
                                      L.P. Fields

Page 279 - Mary Foreman, Extrx &c Deed to Adolphus Strassman. I, Mary Foreman, executrix of Richard Foreman, deceased, by virtue of the power conferred on me by the Will and Testament of said Richard Foreman, deceased, do sell to Adolphus Strassman a tract of land in the Town of Shelbyville, Bedford County and bounded by a lot belonging to John H. Oneal, by the street leading by the Female Academy to the Unionville Turnpike, by the old Nashville Road and a lot of the property of Richard Foreman, deceased, by the south by the Unionville Turnpike Road, and by lot hereby conveyed containing one half acre. This May 30, 1867.
Wit: Walter S. Bearden   Signed: Mary Foreman
Reg: June 25, 1867

Page 280 - Jo. A. Blakemore and Jno. H. Oneal Deed to Jerry Cowan and others, Church. This 25 June 1867 between J.A. Blakemore and John H. Oneal of the Town of Shelbyville of one part and Jerry Cowan, Nathan Cowan, Buford Green, Robert Pepper, and Jesse Davidson, Trustees in Trust. That said J.A. Blakemore and John H. Oneal sold unto the successors for the use and purpose all the estate right title claim and interest &c to a certain lot of land in Bedford County and in the Town of Shelbyville and fronts on what is known as Martin Street near a piece of ground occupied by L.B. Knott as a machine shop and fronts on Martin Street, it being a part of a lot owned by Julius Terry and which was sold by adm. of said Terry, and upon which an African Methodist Episcopal Church now stands. NOTE: A long document.
Wit: J.H. Thompson   Signed: J.A. Blakemore
Reg: June 27, 1867   John H. Oneal

Page 282 - Wm. Stewart Trust Deed to Wm. H. Wisener, Sr. Conveyed to William H. Wisener, Sr. one ox wagon and two oxen yoke ring and steeple. I am indebted to said Wisener. This 27 June 1867.
Reg: June 28, 1867   Signed: William M. Stewart

Page 282 - Winn Rowzee Deed to W.M. Dalton and Brother. I, Winfred Rowzee for cash in hand paid by plastering &c of house of Parkel Rowzee and the other executed 27 March 1867 payable to Winn Rowzee and signed by W.T. Dalton and Brothers for land in Bedford County in the Town of Shelbyville on the north side of the Female Academy Pike near its entrance with the Unionville Pike, have this day sold unto W.M. Dalton, L.A. Dalton and T.A. Dalton and S.P. Dalton, partners under the name and style of Wm. Dalton and Brothers, a tract of land in Bedford County and Civil District No. 7 in the Town of Shelbyville on the north side of the Female Academy Pike near its entrance with the Unionville Pike and bounded at Joseph Cox's corner on the north side of the Female Academy Pike, and by E. Daniel's corner, Containing 1 acre and 26 poles. This 27 March 1867.
Reg: July 2, 1867   Signed: W. Rowzee

Page 283 - C.N. Blake Deed to R.S. Clark et als. I, Chas. N. Blake, have to promote the cause of education and to exert useful influence in Society &c, I hereby grant and convey to R.S. Clark, O.P. Arnold, J.J. Phillips, M.T. Griswell and L.E. Rawlings as a board and trustees a certain piece or parcel of land lying in Bedford County and near the village of Wartrace Depot it being a portion of the 26 acres bought by me of Mrs. Jno. W. Wells formerly Miss Betty Shoffner and designated on W.J. Osborn's survey and plat of land as Lots No. 16 and 17. This Deed of Gift is made for the purpose the said board of Trustees is to build a house on said lot of land to be used as a school house and place of religious worship. This 1 July 1867.
Wit: Daniel Stephens   Signed: Charles N. Blake
     A.A. Cooper
Reg: July 3, 1867

Page 284 - A copy - W.W. Lacy by his guardian Jno. Wilhoite VS
R.S. Dwiggins and John C. Hix. Final Decree. Robert S.
Dwiggins and John C. Hix, Robert S. Dwiggins was the guardian
of defendant and J.C. Hix his security. This June 27, 1867.
Reg: July 3, 1867   Signed: Lewis Tillman, C&M
                                 By L.T. Tillman, Jr. DC

Page 285 - George E. Calhoun, Trust Deed to Jason T. Cannon. I,
George E. Calhoun, have sold unto Jason T. Cannon, as trustee,
the whole and entire interest of property which I have in the
firm of Calhoun & Goodwin in the livery stable business
consisting of seven horses, some six buggys and harness, two
hacks and harness, one wagon and harness, and corn and hay and
other feed on hand in said livery stable. Also three saddles
and bridles and all other property which I have. I am also
indebted to Wm. Shearin's estate who died with cholera in
September last. N.F. Calhoun and J.J. Mankin are my securities.
I am also indebted to John Wilhoite as security of one Rozier or
to said Rozier in a judgment before Moses Marshall, Justice of
the Piece for Bedford County. Also indebted to J.D. Wilhoite
and other names in original document were: P.S. English, W.S.
Jett, B.M. Brown and Budd Gaither. This 21 July 1867.
Reg: July 5, 1867   Signed: G.E. Calhoun

Page 286 - W.H. Moon &c others Power of Attorney to G.B. Moon.
We, Wm. H. Moon, John A. Moon, Susan C. Wallis and R.F. Wallis
her husband, M.A.R. Landis and A. Landis her husband and N.C.
Moon guardian for Elizabeth J. Moon, all of Bedford County, do
appoint G.B. Moon of same place out true and lawful attorney,
for us and in out name to have the Rail Road stock in the N.& C.
Rail Road formerly owned by A.B. Moon now deceased regularly
transferred to us by an equal division. This March 25, 1867.
Reg: July 9, 1867   Signed: J.A. Moon
                                        S.C. Wallis
                                        R.F. Wallis
                                        M.A.R. Landis
                                        J.A. Landis
                                        Sallie L. Moon
                                        N.C. Moon, guardian for
                                        Elizabeth J. Moon
NOTE: This name MOON could be MOORE.

Page 287 - Jas. S. Maupin Deed to Jas. L. Black. I, James S.
Maupin, have sold unto James L. Black for the sole use and
purpose of Nancy A. Cason, a tract of land in Bedford County and
District No. 2, containing 47 ½ acres and bounded by James S.
Maupin's line, by the Nashville and Chattanooga Rail Road, by
James Chilton's corner, by David Thornberry's line, and by
Buchanan's line. This 20 February 1867.
Reg: July 9, 1867   Signed: James S. Maupin

Page 288 - John W. McAdams, Discharge - John W. McAdams a
Private of Captain Cutbert B. Word Company (E) 10th Regiment of
Infantry Tennessee Colunteers who was enrolled on the 20th day

of May 1862 to serve three years or during the war is hereby discharged from the service of the United States this 23rd day of June 1865 at Knoxville, Tennessee by reason of Rodgers from War Dept. No objection to his being re-enlisted is known to exist. Said John W. McAdams was born in Bedford County, Tennessee is twenty two years of age, five feet six inches high, fair complexion, blue eyes, dark hair and by occupation when enrolled a cooper. Given at Knoxville, Tennessee, this 23rd day of June 1865.

Otto Jacobs, Captain

Oath of Identity – John W. McAdams of the Town of Shelbyville, Bedford County, Tennessee on this 1st day of July 1867 personally appeared before me the undersigned a Justice of the Peace for said County and State and the above mentioned Jno. W. McAdams who being duly sworn according to law declares that he is the identical Jno. W. McAdams who was a Private in the Company commanded by Captain C.B. Word in the Regiment 10th Tenn Int. commanded by Col. A.C. Gilliam that he enlisted on the 20th day of May 1862 for the term of three years or during the war and was discharged at Nashville, Tennessee on the 3rd July 1865 by reason of Order from War Department.

Reg: July 9, 1867   Signed: John W. McAdams

Page 288 – D.F. Jett Deed to William Gosling. I, Duncan F. Jett, have sold unto William Gosling all right claim and interest I have and to the north part of the brick house and lot on Martin Street in the Town of Shelbyville south of the lot purchased by Robert Cannon and west of the lot bought by G.W. Thompson & Co. sold under decree of the Chancery Court at Shelbyville and in the case of Mathew Shearin and wife and others VS James K.P. Carlisle and others, and bounded by Martin Street, by the partition wall between said house and the one conveyed to George W. Thompson. This 27 May 1867.

Wit: E. Sadler   Signed: D.F. Jett
     John E. Post
New York, N.Y.
Thos. Sadler, Commissioner for State of New York
E Sadler, Commissioner for State of Tennessee
Reg: July 9, 1867

Page 289 – Milton S. Jones, Declaration &c. I, Milton S. Jones, do hereby declare my intention to claim the benefit of the exemption expressed and contained in Section 211 and page 430 of the Code of Tennessee, to wit, my household to the value of five hundred dollars consisting of dwelling house, out buildings and land (illegible) &c. And I, Milton S. Jones, do hereby give notice to all that I shall from this day claim the benefit of said exemption above referred to and provided by law the homestead on which I now live lying and being in Bedford County, District No. 11 and bounded by lands of D.C. Jones, by Martha Wade, by Elizabeth Thompson, by Duck River and by lands of Felix Turrentine. This 8 July 1867.

Wit: James A. Moore   Signed: Milton S. Jones
     J.E. Wade
Reg: July 11, 1867

Page 290 - John Wortham Deed to George Sparrow, FMC. George
Sparrow, a person of color. I, John Wortham, have sold unto
George Sparrow a certain lot of land in Civil District No. 11 of
Bedford County and bounded by Jonas Sikes' line, and by the edge
of the Thompson's Ford Road. Containing 2 acres, being the same
I purchased of M.D.L. Parks by deed dated October 4, 1865. This
6 July 1867.
Wit: M.E.W. Dunaway   Signed: John Wortham
Reg: July 11, 1867

Page 291 - James F. Cummings Deed to W.S. Jett. Re-registered.
James F. Cummings sold unto William S. Jett a tract of land in
Bedford County and District No. 7 and bounded a tract of land
being the north east corner of a tract of land owned by the
heirs of Erwin J. Frierson, deceased, by the line of Chamberlain
& Galbraith's 1000 acre grant, by corner of Thomas B. Cannon,
and by Thomas B. Cannon's line to Andrew Reed, by the line of
Flat Creek. Containing 220 acres. This 3 February 1860.
Reg: July 15, 1867   Signed: J.F. Cummings

Page 291 - Jno. L. Burt Trust Deed to Hugh Thompson. Whereas
myself and Theo. Thompson, have purchased of Wheeler & Millock A
"No. 1 Wheeler & Millock and a six horse lever power" for which
we have executed to them our note. We are joint and equal
owners in the same, but of the said Theo. Thompson is bound on
the note. I convey to him all my right title claim and interest
in said "Thrasher & Power." This 15 July 1867.
Reg: July 16, 1867   Signed: J.L. Burt

Page 292 - Robert S. Dwiggins Trust Deed to Jno. Wilhoite and
Wm. Campbell. Robert S. Dwiggins has sold to John Wilhoite and
William Campbell the following property, to wit, one hundred
head of stock hogs and three bay mare mules. I am indebted to
W.W. Arnold. This July 9, 1867.
Reg: July 18, 1867   Signed: Robt. Dwiggins

Page 293 - C.L. Pyron Deed to W.C. Germany. I have sold unto
W.C. Germany a tract of land and mills known as the "3 Forks
Tract", bounded by Rufus Smith, by Robert Maupin, by Elisha
Read, and by the heirs of Daniel Hooser and Rufus Smith.
Containing 47 acres. This May 31, 1867.
Reg: July 20, 1867   Signed: C.L. Pyron

293 - George W. Greer Deed to Mrs. M.A. Couch. Note executed to
me by M.A. Couch and Wm. Word. I, George W. Greer, have sold
unto Mrs. M.A. Couch a tract of land in 20th District of Bedford
County and bounded by lands of Josephus A. Cunningham, by lands
of said Cunningham, by lands known as the Richard Anderson
tract, and vy lands of Charles A. Warren and Bradly Gambill.
Containing 126 acres being the same land purchased by me of
James Carlisle on 2nd March 1866 and said deeded to me is
registered in Book EEE. This 17 July 1867.
Reg: July 20, 1867   Signed: G.W. Greer

Page 294 - L.W. Barrett Deed to John A. Barrett. I have sold to John A. Barrett a tract of land in Bedford County and Civil District No. 20 on the waters of Sugar Creek and bounded by R.S. Dwiggins' corner. Containing 200 acres. This 19 July 1867.
Reg: July 24, 1867   Signed: L.W. Barett

Page 295 - Henry Stephens Deed to Hiram G. Culbertson. I have sold unto Hiram G. Culbertson a tract of land in Bedford County and District No. 11 and bounded by Emily Neill's corner. This 20 July 1867.
Reg: July 25, 1867   Signed: Henry Stephens

Page 295 - I, Claracy R. Hardin widow of William C. Hardin, deceased, and daughter of John Larue, deceased, and being a resident of Bedford County hereby nominate and appoint Miles Pardee my attorney in fact to demand and receive money effects and interest may be coming to me through the estate of said John Larue, deceased, in Bedford County and all businesses to execute in my name &c. This 18 July 1867.
Wit: Thomas R. Myers   Signed: Claracy R. Hardin
Reg: July 25, 1867

Page 296 - J.P. Hoover and S.A. Batton Deed to J.M. Hoover. This 9 July 1867. John P. Hoover of Bedford County and S.A. Batton of Rutherford County, Tennessee sold unto James M. Hoover of Bedford County a tract of land in Bedford County and District No. 4 adjoining John P. Hoover's tract, and corner by the 640 acre tract of Martin Hoover, deceased, and to a gate post. Containing 12 acres.
Wit: Daniel D. Hoover   Signed: J.P. Hoover
     R.T. Cooper   S.A. Batton
Reg: July 27, 1867

Page 297 - A.J. Bingham Deed to E.G. Davis. I, Andrew J. Bingham, have sold unto E.G. Davis a tract of land in Bedford County and Civil District No. 4 on the west side of the Wartrace Fork of Duck River and contains 139 acres and 39 poles, adjoining Nathan Chaffin's, deceased, corner, to the center of the Wartrace Creek, by a rock fence south end of W.F. Pearson's water gate which is also a corner of R.B. Bingham's 23 acre tract, and to the center of the Liberty Gap Road. This October 24, 1865.
Wit: D.D.. Hoover   Signed: A.J. Bingham
     N. Sugg
Reg: July 27, 1867

Page 298 - Joel H. Burditt and others Deed to E.W. Carney. Whereas on 27 February 1865 E.W. Carney purchased a lot of ground on one B.K. Coble within the corporate limits of the Town of Shelbyville and bounded by lands of Thomas Eakin, by lands of W.H. Wisener and the lot known as the Crutcher lot, by the lot known as the Ledbetter lot, and by lands hereto by Mrs. Eliza W. Harrison and a stone. Containing something under 2 acres.

Record of deed was destroyed. We, Joel H. Burditt, James
Wortham, George W. Buchanan, W.H. Wisener and S.D. Coble do
relinquish any and all claims which we have in said lot to said
E.W. Carney. This __ June 1867.
Reg: July 27, 1867   Signed: Joel H. Burditt
                                    Geo. W. Buchanan
                                    Wm. H. Wisener
                                    James Wortham
                                    S.D. Coble

Page 299 - B.K. Coble Deed to E.W. Carney. I, B.K. Coble, have
sold unto E.W. Carney all the right title and interest which I
have in and to one house and lot in the corporation of the Town
of Shelbyville and bounded by lands of Thomas Eakin, by lands of
W.H. Wisener and S.F. Crutcher, by an street, and by the lands
of Mrs. Eliza W. Harrison and at present occupied by Mr. A.B.
Knott. This 27 February 1865.
Wit: J.D. Coble, Admr.   Signed: B.K. Coble
Reg: July 27, 1867

Page 299 - Martin Glenn Deed to C.L. Randolph. C.L. Randolph
furnish boarding, washing and tuition to Martin Glenn for the
space of eighteen months commenting 1st Monday in August 1867.
I, Martin Glenn, a citizen of Shelbyville, Bedford County, do
hereby sell to C.L. Randolph, a citizen of Lincoln County,
Tennessee, all my right title claim and interest in and to a
certain lot in the Town of Shelbyville, Bedford County and known
as Lot No. 8, adjoining __ Street, by Lot No. 7 purchased by
J.H. McGrew, by Lot No. 3 purchased by Moses Marshall and the
brick block, by Lots No. 9, 10, 11, 12, and 13. This July 27,
1867.
Wit: H.H. Holt   Signed: Martin Glenn
Reg: August 1, 1867

Page 300 - A.G. Moore Deed to Henry Cooper. I, Arch Moore, sold
unto Henry Cooper a tract of land in Bedford County and District
No. 23 and bounded by the old road leading from Shelbyville to
Winchester, and by Johnson's line. This August 2, 1867.
Reg: August 2, 1867   Signed: A.G. Moore

Page 300 - Lewis Tillman, C&M, Title to Henry Stevens. I, Lewis
Tillman, C&M of the Chancery Court at Shelbyville, Bedford
County did sell on 27 October 1865 in the case of John and
William Crowell, administrators &c and others against Joseph
McKinly Crowell and others at public sale to Henry Stephens a
tract of land in Bedford County adjoining the lands of Felix
Turrentine, by lands of Michael Crowell, and by lands of Jacob
M. Parsons' heirs. Containing 320 acres. John D. Clark and
wife Sarah Clark, Phillip Parsons and wife Catharine, B.F.
Parsons and wife Jennie, E.H. McGowen and wife Nancy, J.H. Potts
and wife Isabella W., Mary Capley, Mary Ann Crowell, Jacob B.
Delk and wife Annie, Samuel Crowell, Rosena Goor (complainants)
Joseph McKinley Crowell, Mary Crowell, John Crowell (minors),
Zilphia Cartwright wife of Phillip Cartwright and Jimmie Parsons

(defendants). John Crowell and William Crowell as administrators
of Samuel Crowell, deceased, as heirs at law of Samuel Crowell.
Joshua Crowell, Michael Crowell and others listed. This 27
April 1865.
Reg: August 3, 1867   Signed: Lewis Tillman
NOTE: A very long document.

Page 301 - Rowland Newsom Deed to Robert Reeves. I, Rowland
Newsom, have sold unto Robert Reeves all the right claim and
interest which I have in the land devised to the heirs at law of
Chaney G. Newsom, deceased, who was a daughter of Isham Reeves,
deceased, by the said Isham Reeves in his Last Will and
Testament and duly recorded consisting of two small parcels.
One tract containing 30 acres and bounded by Duck River. One
other tract containing 5 acres and 50 poles adjoining a corner
of F.F. Arnold and wife's tract, and by a corner of Robert
Reeves' tract. My interest being the one fifth part of the two
tracts of land. This 5 August 1867.
Reg: August 5, 1867   Signed: Rowland Newsom

Page 302 - Quinn E. Morton Deed to Stephen Sanders. I, A.E.
Morton, have sold to Stephen Sanders a tract of land in Bedford
County and District No. 9 and bounded by E. Wallace'' corner.
Containing 25 acres and 155 1/2 poles.
Wit: H.C. Turner   Signed: Quinn E. Morton
     W.D. Burge
Reg: August 6, 1867

Page 303 - W.B. Neely Mortgage to T.B. Marks. I, Wm. B. Neely
of Bedford County, do hereby transfer to T.B. Marks of same
place my interest in a tract of land owned by my deceased
father, J.G. Neely, in Civil District No. 5. The place where my
mother Mary W. Neely now lives. I was indebted to T.B. Marks.
This April 12, 1867.
Reg: August 6, 1867   Signed: W.B. Neely

Page 303 - Henry H. Fouch and wife Deed to Robert Reeves. We,
Henry H. Fouch and Mary E. Couch, have sold our interest to
Robert Reeves the land devised to the heirs of Chaney G. Newsom,
deceased, who was a daughter of Isham Reeves and by said Isham
Reeves consisting of two small parcels. One tract containing 30
acres bounded by the Duck River. The other tract containing 4
acres and 50 poles and bounded by a corner of F.F. Arnold and
wife, and by corner of Robert Reeves' tract. Our interest being
one fifth of the two tracts. This 5 August 1867.
Reg: August 8, 1867   Signed: H.H. Fouch
                                     M.E. Fouch

Page 403 - F.P. McElrath Deed to Daniel Earnhart. This 29 July
1867. F.P. McElrath sold unto Daniel Earnhart a tract of land
in Bedford County and Civil District No. 18 and adjoining lands
of H.H. and D.E. and by A.C. (illegible) original south boundary
line. Containing 14 acres and 98 poles.

Reg: August 9, 1867   Signed: F.P. McElrath
                               R.S. Dwiggins

Page 305 - David Altman & Co. Trust Deed to A. Alder, Trustee.
We, D(illegible)Blanberger and David Altman and Bernard Schwartz
as partners and under the firm name of D. Altman, Blanberger &
Co. have sold unto A. Allen as trustee two steam boilers and
engine, five tubs, two copper plates, one copper cooler, one
mash tub, five large tubs, one pump with pipe shafts and which
one grinding malt mill and every articles &c. of machinery of
every kind in conducting the business of distilling. The
distilling on the north west corner of the Public Square of
Shelbyville as well as all stock and material on hand one horse
and wagon and harness consisting of all corn about 200 bushels
of corn or all on hand in said distillery, all the meal on hand
50 bushels of rye, all barley on hand about 25 bushels and all
the malt on hand. NOTE: A very long document. This 5 August
1867.
Reg: August 13, 1867   Signed: David Altman
                               David Altman

Page 307 - Wiley Thompson et als Deed to Samuel Gosling et als,
Trustee. We, Wiley Thompson and Joseph Robinson, have granted
to Samuel Gosling, Sampson Thompson and Thomas Streeter as
trustees of Colored Baptist Church a certain tract of land in
Bedford County and Civil District No. 7 and bounded by the old
Flower Swift line. Containing one half acre. This 3 August
1867.
Reg: August 13, 1867   Signed: Wiley Thompson
                               Joseph Robinson

Page 308 - Sally Lamb and Talitha Lamb Deed to John W. Clary.
We, Sally Lamb and Talitha Lamb of Bedford County, have sold to
John W. Clary of same place, a certain parcel or lot of land in
Bedford County and Civil District No. 11 and bounded by the big
road the south west corner of the Male Academy lot in
Unionville, Tennessee, by Thos. Allison's corner, by Ozment's
line now G.W. Harrison's line, and by J.W. Clary's line.
Containing 7 ¼ acres. This April 15, 1867.
Wit: John A. Ganaway   Signed: Sally Lamb
    T.B. Allison   Talitha Lamb
Reg: August 13, 1867

Page 308 - George F. Allen Contract with John Mathews. I, Geo.
F. Allen of the Town of Wartrace, Bedford County, to me in hand
paid at on or before the delivery by John Mathews my store goods
and groceries taken July 29, 1867. This 29 July 1867.
Wit: Edward J. L(illegible)   Signed: Geo. F. Allen
    D.C. Norvill
Reg: August 13, 1867

Page 310 - James T. Turpin Deed to Margaret J. Trolinger.   I
have sold unto Margaret J. Trolinger a lot or parcel of ground

in Bedford County and within the corporation of said town in the north west part of the Town of Shelbyville and bounded by Ary Kincaid's lot at the edge of a street. This August 8, 1867.
Reg: August 13, 1867   Signed: James T. Turpin

Page 310 - F.B. Woods Deed to J.W. Coffey. F.B. Woods sold unto J.W. Coffey a tract of land in Bedford County and Marshall County, Tennessee on the waters of Rock Creek and bounded by the dividing line between said Coffey and James L. Adams it being said Adams' north west corner, by German Woodward land, and by L.B. Blackwell land.   Containing 21 ½ acres.   This 11 March 1867.
Wit: W. Woods   Signed: Francis B. Woods
Reg: August 14, 1867

Page 311 - W.H. Stephenson Deed to Edward B. Stephenson. I have sold to Edward B. Stephenson a tract of land in Bedford County and District No. 18 on Little Sinking Creek and bounded by the west bank of Sinking Creek in the south boundary line of the old Clift tract.   Containing 83 acres and 149 poles.
Wit: C.S. Dudley   Signed: William H. Stephenson
     James A. Stephenson
Reg: August 14, 1867

Page 312 - M.E. and M. Payne Deed to Robert W. Couch. Whereas by descent from the late Joseph Couch, Catharine Couch widow of said Joseph Couch, deceased, Elijah Couch since deceased, leaving seven children Reuben C. Couch, John A. Couch, Robert W. Couch, Mary Hickerson wife of Washington Hickerson, Emily Maupin wife of Robert Maupin, Jr., and Joseph Cunningham son of his deceased daughter Sarah E. Couch who had intermarried with Washington Cunningham, and John P., Joseph E., William J., James M., Henry M., Nancy C. Stephens, but since the death of intestate intermarried with Willis M. Keller, and Martin D. Stephens his grandchildren being children of his deceased daughter Nancy W. who had previously intermarried with Daniel Stephens, and my self (Margaret Payne wife of Micajah Payne) have title to and now hold equal and undivided interest in two tracts of land in Bedford County and District No. 2 and 23 and bounded by said Joseph Couch, deceased, lived at the time of his death, by lands of the Singleton's heirs, by lands formerly owned by James Finch, by lands of John A. Couch and the Keller heirs, by lands of Cortner's heirs, and by lands of G.G. Osborne.   Containing in former deed 266 acres.   Also a tract of land on Flat Creek in Bedford County and containing 160 acres jointly owned by the heirs of the said Joseph Couch, deceased, and the heirs of his son Elijah Couch, deceased, and bounded by the lands of Wm. McGill, by lands of the heirs of Elijah Couch and Warren Bridges, and by lands of John Bearden's heirs and S.B. Gordon.   This 3 July 1867.
NOTE: A very long document.
Wit: Daniel Stephens   Signed: M.E. Payne
     William Thomas   Micajah Payne
Reg: August 14, 1867

Page 313 - F.B. Woods and Abasolum Mosley Deed to James L. Adams. All the right title claim and interest which I have in and to a tract of land partly in Marshall County and Bedford County and bounded by T.W. Brents' corner, to a lane James Price's line, and by Coffey's line. Containing 111 ½ acres. This 17 September 1866.
Wit: W. Woods   Signed: Francis B. Woods
Reg: August 14, 1867   Absamum Mosley

Page 314 - John W. Wells and wife Deed to R.S. Clark. We, Jno. W. Wells and Sarah E. his wife (formerly Miss Shofner), have conveyed a tract of land in Bedford Conty and within the limits of the corporation of Wartrace it being a portion of the 26 acres sold by us to C.N. Blake and known in W.J. Osborn survey and plat as No. 16 and 17 to R.S. Clark, O.P. Arnold, J.J. Phillips, M.T. Griswell, L.E. Rawlings VS a board of Trustees. This August 5, 1867.
Reg: August 14, 1867   Signed: Jno. W. Wells
                                      S.E. Wells

Page 315 - C.J. Burrow Deed to Stanford Sutton. I, Calvin J. Burroe, have sold unto Stanford Sutton a tract of land in Bedford County and Civil District No, 23 and bounded by a corner of Miss Kiser's line, by Miss Kiser's and Miss Muse's line to John Woodward's line, and by William Smiley. Containing 6 acres. This 10 October 1864.
Reg: August 14, 1867   Signed: C.J. Burrow

Page 315 - James J. Smith Deed to Mrs. E.P. Kingree. I, James J. Smith, have sold unto Mrs. E.P. Kingree a tract of land in Bedford County and District No, 20 and bounded by lands of W.W. Gill, by lands of Nathan Evans, deceased, by lands of John R. Wright, and by lands of Jesse Ortner. Containing 78 acres. This 10 August 1867.
Reg: August 15, 1867   Signed: James J. Smith

Page 316 - B.A. Smith Deed to Phil D. Meroney. I, B.A. Smith, have sold to Phillip D. Meroney a tract of land in 22nd District of Bedford County. One tract in said District bounded by lands of J.L. Hix and Robert S. Dwiggins, by lands of Herod F. Holt, by lands of A.H. Evans and Harrel Evans, and by lands of R.S. Dwiggins and A.H. Evans. Containing 250 acres. This 7 August 1867.
Reg: August 15, 1867   Signed: B.A. Smith

Page 317 - William A. Allen Deed to A.M. Webb. I have sold unto A.M. Webb a tract of land in Bedford County and Civil District No. 18 and containing 10 acres and 40 poles and bounded by R.H. Sims' line and Edw'd Stephenson's corner. This 13 August 1867.
Reg: August 15, 1867   Signed: William A. Allen

349

Page 317 - W.K. Ransom Deed to Sarah S. White. I, William K. Ransom of Bedford County, convey unto my daughter Sarah S. White wife of Barkley White for the love and affection I bear to and for my said daughter the following described land in Bedford County and Civil District No. 5, bounded by Wm. K. Ransom's land. Containing 150 acres. It being the tract I purchased from William Hughs and conveyed to me by deed dated 16 August 1856 and recorded. This 13 August 1867.
Reg: August 16, 1867   Signed: W.K. Ransom

Page 318 - W.K. Ransom Deed to William Ransom. I. William K. Ransom of Bedford County, convey unto my son William Ransom land. One tract containing 128 ½ acres and bounded by McKindley's corner, and by J.W. Spence's corner. It being all the tract of land purchased by me from Jno. G. Russell by deed dated 5 September 1850. Also all that tract of land purchased by me on the west of the above described land from the heirs of Jno. W. Spence and conveyed to me by decree of court and recorded in Book HH on 22 July 1856. Said land in Civil District No. 5 of Bedford County and bounded by Isiah Webb's corner. In all 62 acres. In all conveyed as one tract 191 poles. To him said William Ransom my said son for the love and affection I bear for him. This 13 August 1867.
Reg: August 20, 1867   Signed: W.K. Ransom

Page 319 - William S. Jett and R.S. Dwiggins Deed to Edmund Cooper. R.S. Dwiggins in trust deed dated 5 January 1863 and registered in Bedford County in Book DDD, pages 251 and 252 conveyed the trust of land to William S. Jett in trust to secure the payment of debt. William S. Jett is authorized to sell said land at public sale and on 24 May 1864 registered in Book DDD, page 395 conveyed same tract of land to William S. Jett to secure payment of debts. And whereas John C. Hix as a judgment creditor of Robert S. Dwiggins, which judgment has been registered on 22 October 1866. Land sold unto Edmund Cooper. Said land purchased by Randolph Newsom being in Bedford County and District No. 20 on the waters of Sugar Creek and adjoining lands of A.M. Webb and H.H. Nease, by lands of L.W. Barrett and J.S. Newton, and by lands of James F. Arnold. Containing 500 acres. This 14 August 1867.
Wit: William Frierson   Signed: Wm.S. Jett
     R.P. Frierson   R.S. Dwiggins
Reg: August 21, 1867   J.C. Hix

Page 320 - R.S. Dwiggins Trust Deed to John H. Wells. Robert S. Dwiggins sold unto John H. Wells the lots of land and mills in the Town of Shelbyville being my steam grist mills and lots on which my mill and other houses stand bounded by Water Street and including that part of the street purchased from the corporation of the Town of Shelbyville, by the lot belonging to Rowzee's estate, by the corporation line not including the lot I purchased from Gen. Cannon and executors. This 14 August 1867.
Reg: August 21, 1867   Signed: R.S. Dwiggins

Page 321 - Jas. D. Jeffrees Deed to Thos. B. Jeffrees. We, James D. Jeffrees, Robert W. Hoover and Mary J. Hoover his wife do relinquish all right title claim and interest unto Thomas B. Jeffrees a tract of land whereon the said Thos. B. Jeffrees now lives. Containing 193 acres in Bedford County and Civil District No. 11 on the waters of North Fork of Duck River and adjoining the lands of E. Batte, Henry Clark and others. This 11 February 1867.
Wit: E.D. Wortham   Signed: J.D. Jeffrees
Reg: August 21, 1867   M.J. Jeffrees
                               R.W. Hoover

Page 322 - C.T. Philpot Deed to Lucinda Green. I have sold unto Lucinda Green a tract of land in Bedford County which I purchased of Thomas H. Coldwell as executor of the Last Will and Testament of Rolin Reed, deceased, and bounded by James Reed's corner, by Dunaway's line, and by Mrs. Rogers' corner. Containing about 23 acres. This 16 August 1867.
Reg: August 22, 1867   Signed: C.T. Philot

Page 323 - William H. Wisener, Sr., securing executor of F. Swift Deed to T(illegible) Hall. Whereas many years ago Flower Swift executed his Last Will and Testament and after which he died and said will was duly proved in Bedford County Court of which Swift was at and before his death a citizen. He directed his property (illegible) of which he gave to his wife during the natural life of his widow both real and personal to be sold by his executors and when he appointed William H. Wisener executor and Catharine Swift. Return of said will and when in year 1863 Catharine Swift departed her this life leaving said William H. Wisener the surviving executor. Said will was destroyed in the Shelbyville Court House by fire in March 1863. Said land was sold to one Thomas W. Warner and John V. Hall. Land survived by C.S. Dudley and bounded by James Story's line, and by bank of Duck River. Containing 159 acres and 12 poles. This 5 August 1867.
Reg: August 22, 1867   Signed: Wm. H. Wisener

Page 324 - James H. Neil Deed to Elijah Floyd. Whereas John C. Ray administrator of Watson Floyd, deceased, filed against Pauline Floyd and others heirs of Watson Floyd, deceased, for the sale of the lands of said Watson Floyd which lands were ordered to be sold. The tract of land known as the mill tract and containing 29 acres on which there is a lien for purchase money to Elijah Floyd. This 17 August 1867.
Reg: August 22, 1867   Signed: James H. Neil, C &c

Page 325 - Minos T. Cannon Deed to James L. Scudder. I, Minos T. Cannon, have sold to James L. Scudder a portion of a town lot and buildings thereon in the Town of Shelbyville and on the south side of the Public Square being on the square. Bounded by a corner of a lot of ground sold by me to Warren & Wilhoite being the corner of the north west corner of the Brick Tavern,

the brick wall of the tavern, by south through said brick house and tavern to the street, and to the alley &c. Being a strip of land 18 ½ front and that wide all the way to the street. This 17 August 1867.
Reg: August 23, 1867   Signed: Minos T. Cannon

Page 326 - Catharine Wise Deed of Gift to Sarah E. Sharp and Margaret C. Arnold. Whereas on 20 January 1858, I, Catharine Wise at that time known by the name of Catharine Arnold by deed of that date is registered in Book ZZ, page 367 which is here referred to, give to my two children Sarah E. Arnold and Margaret C. Arnold a tract of land reserving to myself a life estate in said land and also for the purpose of aiding my said children in the use and occupation of said tract of land for love and affection I have for my two chilldren. Land on the east of the road, by Mc. E. and G.G. Arnold's spring, by John Powell's line, by school land, by W.B. Blanton's line, and by Presley Prince's line. Land in Bedford County and Civil District No. 24. This August 1867.
Wit: Alex. Philpot   Signed: Catharine Wise
     Isaac Williams
Reg: August 23, 1867

Page 327 - W.P. Bridges Deed to W.C. Snell. Warren P. Bridges sold unto Willis C. Small tracts of land in Bedford County and Civil District No. 24 and bounded by the center of a spring, by Nancy E. Bearden's corner, by the dower line, by Barnett Stephen's line, and by W.P. Bridges. Containing 25 acres and 63 poles being the tract conveyed by Joseph S. Cates to myself and the said Snell dated 7 March 1859. The other tract also adjoining at the center of said spring, by Stephen's tract, and by the dividing line between J.W. and Eli Bearden. Containing 50 acres which said tract of land was conveyed to myself and said Snell by Eli Bearden by deed dated 11 September 1865. This 17 August 1867.
Reg: August 24, 1867   Signed: Warren P. Bridges

Page 328 - James Russ, Sr., Deed to James P. Taylor. I have sold unto James P. Taylor a tract of land which W.M. Boyce now resides upon in District No. 10 of Bedford County and bounded by lands of A. Boyce, by John King, by William Jackson being the tract of land conveyed to me by Sheriff's deed dated 24 May 1864 and registered in Book DDD, pages 398 and 399 and 400. This 15 August 1867.
Reg: August 24, 1867   Signed: James Russ

Page 328 - N. Thompson, 2nd Deed of Gift to Eliza Owens. For the love and affection which I have for my daughter Eliza Owens and wife of Thomas B. Owens. I have sold unto her land in 21st Civil District of Bedford County and bounded by a 2000 acre survey of Thomas Tolbert, to center of the Shelbyville and Lewisburg Turnpike, by the line of Berry Owens' land, to the center of a fence between me and the heirs of B.C. Owens, and by

Mrs. Susan Burt's line. Containing 125 acres. This 20 August 1867.
Reg: August 26, 1867   Signed: N. Thompson, 2nd.

Page 329 - N. Thompson, 2nd Deed to Thomas B. Owens. I, Newcome Thompson, 2nd have sold to Thomas B. Owens a tract of land in 21st Civil District of Bedford County and bounded by the center of Shelbyville and Lewisburg Turnpike, by the east side of a fence known as a line fence between myself and A.J. Greer, to A.J. Greer's line, and by McPhail's line. Containing 150 acres. The same being known as the Rev. John T. Muse land and by me purchased at a sale made by W.J. Whitthorne, C&M. This 20 August 1867.
Reg: August 27, 1867   Signed: N. Thompson, 2nd

Page 330 - J.B. Morris Deed to E.W. Stone. J.B. Morris sold to E.W. Stone a tract of land in Bedford County and District No. 22 on the head waters of Big Flat Creek and bounded by a lane between Wm. Casteel and said Stone, Casteel's corner, by Martha Woodward's field, to top of the ridge, and by L. Logan's line. Containing 24 acres and 18 ¾ poles. This 25 December 1866.
Wit: F.M. Morris   Signed: J.B. Morris
     Thomas Wise
Reg: August 27, 1867

Page 331 - Bedford County, Tennessee - July 27, 1866. I do hereby certify that I went on the premises of J.F. Ray. I proceeded to survey the lands of said J.F. Ray which I find to his title papers to be as one tract adjoining the south bank of Duck River Jasper Dicken's corner. Containing 98 acres and 120 poles. Also one other tract adjoining the center of the old Amy Jackson spring on the north bank of Duck River, and by the east end of Tuckers Bluff the beginning corner of the Newsom tract. Containing 73 acres and 46 poles.
NOTE: Plat on page 331.
Wit: B.S. Parsons, CC   Signed: C.S. Dudley, Surveyor
     John R. Click, CC
Reg: August 27, 1867

Page 332 - W.P. Gowan Deed to Catharine Morrow. I have sold unto Catharine Morrow a tract of land in Bedford County and Civil District No. 24 on the head waters of Mulberry Creek. Containing 55 acres. This 9 November 1866.
Wit: Thos. H. Coldwell   Signed: W.P. Gowan
Reg: August 27, 1867

Page 332 - Aaron D. Hart and wife Mary J. Hart Power of Attorney to B.F. Wiggins. Wilcox County, Alabama. We, Aaron D. Hart and Mary Jane Hart his wife of said county and state do hereby appoint B.F. Wiggins of Bedford County our true and lawful attorney in fact for us and in out name to demand and receive for any and all moneys that may be due said Aaron D. Hart in right of his wife said Mary Jane Hart from the estate of Jackson

M. Greer, deceased, late of Bedford County and where estate is now being administered in the County Court. This 19 March 1867.
Reg: August 27, 1867   Signed: A.H. Hart
                                       Mary J. Hart

Page 333 - J.R. Shepperson Power of Attorney to Gabriel Cohn. I have this day appointed Gabriel Cohn my attorney in fact to collect and receive all money or monies which may be due me from the Government of the United States for additional county as a soldier serving in the 5 Regiment Cav. Volunteers on a claim lately forwarded by Robert Galbraith to the Department at Washington for collection. This 27 August 1867.
Wit: H.H. Holt   Signed: J.R. Shepperson
Reg: August 28, 1867

Page 334 - J.W. McGill Deed to Wm. McGill. Whereas Jas. McGill departed this life vested in Bedford County, leaving a tract of land and bounded by R.H. Terry, by lands formerly belonging to Jas. McGill, by lands that formerly belonged to Jas. McGill, by lands of A.W. Elkins and Newton Templeton and by which will the widow had an estate for life and whereon said Jas. McGill left seven heirs surviving him of which number I am one. I do hereby hereto sold unto William McGill a tract of land. This August 27, 1867.
Reg: August 28, 1867   Signed: J.W. McGill

Page 334 - Young Wilhoite Deed to Sidney M. Wilhoite. I, Young Wilhoite, sold unto Sidney M. Wilhoite tracts of lands in Bedford County and Civil District No. 7 and 8. In District No. 7 bounded on the north of Duck River. Containing 146 acres and 68 poles. The second tract in District No. 8 on the south bank of Duck river and bounded by the south end of Warners Bridge, by the west of Fishing Ford Road, by Ben. Earnhart's land, by land owned now by Benjamin Earnhart, by lands of Geo. Earnhart, Mrs. Nancy Streeter and Thos. Lipscomb, and by lands of said Thos. Lipscomb. Containing 86 acres. This 20 June 1867.
Reg: August 29, 1867   Signed: Young Wilhoite

Page 335 - W.W. Hopkins Deed to William R. Adams. I, William W. Hopkins of Bedford County, did on 25 September 1865, sold unto William R. Adams a tract of land in Bedford County and Civil District No. 11 and bounded by A.M. Cooper's corner, by William Wilson's line, and by a line of the tract bought of Lucinda Dilliard. Containing 100 acres. This 26 August 1867.
Wit: W.G. Lynch   Signed: William W. Hopkins
     M.E. Hopkins
Reg: August 30, 1867

Page 336 - D.G. Norville Deed to W.R. Norville. I have sold to William R. Norville all the interest to the estate of John W. Norville, deceased, as one of the heirs &c of said estate both in real and personal estate. Said property being one seventh and the interest in the real estate being the one sixth of 344

acres and __ poles in Civil District No. 3 of Bedford County
being the place on which the said John W. Norville, deceased,
resided at the time of his death. This 30 August 1867.
Wit: S.H. Whitthorne   Signed: D.G. Norville
      Evander Shapard
Reg: August 30, 1867

Page 337 - Minos T. Cannon Deed to J.R. Stegall. I, Minos T.
Cannon, have sold to J.R. Stegall a tract of land on the south
west of Shelbyville, Bedford County, a part of the tract willed
to me by my father Robert Cannon on the south side of Duck
River, adjoining Word's corner, south from the forks of the
Turnpike Road being the Shelbyville and Fayetteville Turnpike
Road, and by R.S. Dwiggins' corner. It being the same land
surveyed for me to be sold to said Stegall by William Galbreath
on 27 August 1867. This 30 August 1867.
Reg: August 31, 1867   Signed: Minos T. Cannon

Page 337 - George E. Calhoun Deed to Wm. S. Jett. I, George E.
Calhoun, have sold unto William S. Jett personal property, five
head of horses, two black mules, one top buggy, two open top
buggies, one wagon and harness, one hack and harness, one lot of
bridles and saddles, one lot of spades and shovels, one lot of
sundries of chairs &c., it being in the livery stable of Goodwin
& Calhoun but which I have this day purchased and now own. I am
indebted to E.J. Jett and W.S. Jett and W.B.M. Brame. This 30
August 1867.
Reg: September 2, 1867   Signed: G.E. Calhoun

Page 338 - J.M. Neeley Deed to Trustees of Methodist E. Church.
James M. Neeley, sold unto E.B. Stephenson, Jas. N. Dryden,
James M. Baxter, James M. Neeley, G.T. Neeley, E.D. Jones and
J.C.J. Paschal, Trustees of the Mount Lebanon Methodist
Episcopal Church of the United States of America, all of the
18th District of Bedford County. For the love and affection
that I the said James M. Neeley have for the neighborhood and
the M.E. Church, I hereby give grant and convey to the named
Trustees and their successors in trust that said promises shall
be (illegible) kept maintained and disposed of as a place of
Divine Worship for the use of the ministries and membership of
the Methodist Episcopal Church of the U.S. of America subject to
the disciplin usage and ministry appointments of said church as
from time to time authorized and declares by the General
Conference of said church &c. The church house is now erected
and adjoins a lane it being the south east corner of a tract of
land formerly owned by A.J. Greer in M.F. Earnhart's line.
Containing 3 acres and 13 poles. This 29 August 1867.
Wit: M.F. Earnhart   Signed: James M. Neeley
      James H. Neeley
Reg: September 3, 1867

Page 339 - J.M. Neeley Deed to Michael Earnhart. This 2 May
1859. James M. Neeley of Bedford County have sold unto Michael
Earnhart of same place a tract of land in Bedford County on

355

Sinking Creek and bounded by said Earnhart's corner of a tract of land formerly belonging to Aaron Bledsoe. Containing 20 acres and 53 poles.
Wit: Samuel ?. Harrison   Signed: James M. Neeley
     Henry Lawwell
Reg: September 3, 1867

Page 340 - Hillsman Bledsoe et als Deed to J.W. Bledsoe. We, Hillsman Bledsoe and Jas. W. Bledsoe, Icy H. Neeley, have sold a tract of land in Bedford County and Civil District No. 20 which descended to us by Aaron Bledsoe and bounded by a ridge, and by Bledsoe's line. Containing 109 acres. This September 2. 1867.
Reg: September 3, 1867   Signed: Hillsman Bledsoe
                                        James M. Neeley
                                        Icy H. Neeley

Page 341 - John F. Ray Deed to Trustees of M.E.C.S. I, John F. Ray of Bedford County, have donated unto the following Trustees, to wit, John Landers, John Anderson, W.W. Hopkins, John F. Ray, Asa S. Stem, D.F. Osteen, William R. Adams, M.B. Fisher and G.W. Beavers, a tract of land in Bedford County and Civil District No. 11 and containing 2 ½ acres. The above tract of land for to erect a church and school house on and do give and desire that the Methodist Episcopal Church and the Methodist Protestant Church each have the right to organize a class at said house and same be used as a school house to be managed by the named Trustees. This 11 September 1866.
Wit: Alex D. Hopkins   Signed: John F. Ray
     D.D. Dickens
     Thomas J. Davis
Reg: September 3, 1867

Page 342 - J.F. Cummings Deed to Thos. M. Coldwell. I, James F. Cummings, have sold unto Thomas M. Coldwell a certain lot of ground in the Town of Corinth, Mississippi and bounded by Lot No. 1 in Block No. 5 as known in Town of Corinth, it being a lot of ground in which a small frame building now stands, and also the same lot sold by H.C. (illegible) to Coldwell and Cunnings on the 30 August 1859. My interest in the same being an undivided one half of the whole. This 26 May 1860.
Reg: September 4, 1867   Signed: J.F. Cummings

Page 342 - Andrew Vannoy Deed to Jeremiah B. Boothe. I, Andrew Vannoy, have sold unto Jeremiah B. Boothe a tract of land in Bedford County and District No. 6, containing 57 ¼ acres and bounded by B.G. Green's corner, and E. Payton's 640 acre tract. It being the tract of land conveyed to me by John C. McCuistian by deed on 28 March 1846. This 4 September 1867.
Reg: September 5, 1867   Signed: Andrew Vannoy

Page 343 - Jasper N. Dickens, Discharge - Jasper N. Dickens a Private of Captain Cuthbert B. Word Company (E) 10th Regiment of Infantry Tennessee Volunteers who was enrolled on the 1st day of

March 1863 to serve three years or during the war is hereby discharged from the service of the Unites States this 23rd day of June 1865 at Knoxville, Tennessee by reason of Orders from War Department. No objection to his being re-enlisted is known to exist. Said Jasper N. Dickens was born in Bedford County, Tennessee is twenty eight years of age, five feet ten inches high, fair complexion, gray eyes, dark hair and by occupation when enrolled a farmer. Given at Knoxville, Tenn. This 23 June 1865.

A(illegible) Jacobs, Captain

Oath of Indentity - Jasper N. Dickens of the Town of Shelbyville, Bedford County, Tennessee on this 5th day of September 1867 personally appeared before me the undersigned a Justice of the Peace for County and State above mentioned - which was duly sworn according to law declares that he is the identical Jasper N. Dickens who was a Private in the Company commanded by Captain Cuthbert B. Word in the Regiment commanded by J.W. Scully, that he enlisted on the 1st day of March 1863 for the term of three years and was discharged at Knoxville, Tennessee on the 23rd day of June by reason of Order from War Department.

Reg: September 5, 1867   Signed: Jasper N. Dickens

Page 344 - James Frizzell Deed to William Smith. I, James Frizzell of Bedford County, have sold unto William Smith a tract of land in Bedford County and Civil District No. 1 and bounded by the top of a ridge James Scrugg's corner and Lucy Zollicoffer's corner, and by Emily Hatchett's corner in Jo. P. Kelly's line. Containing 60 acres and 113 poles. This 24 August 1867.

Wit: Jo. P. Kelly   Signed: James Frizzell
     Wm. J. Osborn
Reg: September 7, 1867

Page 345 - G.W. Buchanan Deed to R.P. Teeter. Re-registered. I hereby convey to R.P. Teeter a lot of land being one half of Lot No. 3 and which Lot No. 3 is one of them that I purchased of N. Thompson, 3rd, and which is bounded in the middle of the branch at the corner of Neil's lot No. 2, and by the corner of Lot No. 4. Reserving out of said tract a street or part of a street of five feet along the east and west boundary line. This December 29, 1859.

Reg: (no date)   Signed: Geo. W. Buchanan

Page 345 - R.P. Teeter Deed to G.W. Buchanan. I, R.P. Teeter, have sold unto George W. Buchanan all that certain one half or parcel of lands which I heretofore purchased from G.W> Buchanan and who executed his deed to me on 29 December 1859 and the deed from him being registered in Book BBB, page 421. I hereby convey to him one half of the lot so purchased of him, it being the west half adjoining at Trollinger's line, and by corner of Lot No. 4 now owned by James Golithan. This August 7, 1867.

Reg: September 9, 1867   Signed: R.P. Teeter

Page 346 - Ro. B. Davidson Deed to Mariah E. Phillips. I, Ro. B. Davidson of the Town of Shelbyville, sold unto Mariah E. Phillips of Bedford County a tract of land adjoining the Town of Shelbyville, being the same land conveyed to me by T.W. Jordan on 6 July 1860 and recorded in Bedford County in Book EEE, page 414 on the 5 July 1866. Said land bounded by or near two large gate posts on the north side of the Rowesville Road, and by the line of the late Gen. Robert Cannon the same being what has for many years been known as the Wilson Coat's line. Containing 5 acres. This 31 August 1867.
Reg: September 10, 1867   Signed: Ro. B. Davidson

Page 347 - George W. Thompson Deed to William H. Wisener, Sr. George W. Thompson sold to William H. Wisener, Sr. a small piece of land near Shelbyville and this day conveyed to me by said Wisener. Two notes were made. Land being in Bedford County and Civil District No. 3 and being a part of the old Thomas Holland tract and bounded by a one acre purchased by James G. Barksdale of Thomas Holland, by the north side of Air Creek and the Holland spring. It inclusion of the dower tract, by a tract sold by Nathan Ivey to said Wisener, by the McCuistian Grant and also the Gilchrist line, by the Dougherty Entry and Holland tract, by a land owned now by William Gosling, formerly one John McGuire and before him by one __ Holt, also what one James G. Barksdale corner of his purchase of Robert Moffat tract of land and also land sold by Thomas Holland to said Barksdale. This 24 April 1867.
Reg: September 10, 1867   Signed: G.W. Thompson

Page 348 - L. Tillman, Trustee and B.m. Tillman Deed to E.F. Scruggs. Whereas Barclay M. Tillman on 9 November 1860 executed to Lewis Tillman a Deed of Conveyance with certain terms and condition to secure the payment of a note covering his tract of land in Civil District No. 1 of Bedford County and on 1 December 1866 said Barclay M. Tillman by further Deed of Trust conveyed to Lewis Tillman and Blount G. Green as trustees certain real and personal property, among the other real property the aforesaid of land in Civil District No. 1 and a certain other tract of land bought of J.C. Word also land described, The first tract of land bounded by lands of T.B. Mosely and Benj. Beechboard, by lands of Jas. L. Armstrong, by lands of John E. Scruggs, by lands Scruggs & Wynn Thomas. Containing 330 acres. Other boundaries were: by Thos. B. Mosely, John Tillman, the Murfreesboro Road, and John E. Scruggs. Other names in document were: James C. Word, Stephen Gallaghy, J.G. Patton, S. Gallaghy, and G(illegible) tract, Edward F. Scruggs, L.P. Fields, Jo. P. Kelly, and B.G. Fields.
NOTE: Long document.
Reg: September 11, 1867   Signed: Lewis Tillman
                                       Barclay M. Tillman

Page 350 - Epps Parker and T.L. Roberts Deed to Joseph Reagor. We, Epps Parker and T.L. Roberts, have sold unto Joseph Reagor a tract of land in 24th District of Bedford County and bounded by lands of H.C. Ferguson, by lands of T.L. Roberts, by lands of

Loton Anthony, and by lands of Jno. Martin. Containing 170 acres. This __ of __ 1867.
Wit: M.L. Roberts   Signed: Thomas L. Roberts
     T.A. Roberts
Reg: September 11, 1867

Page 351 - James C. Davison and J.A.R. Davison Power of Attorney to R. Whitehead. Tallahatchie County, Mississippi. I, James C. Davison and Jo. A.R. Davison his wife of same place do appoint R. Whitehead of Fayette County, Tennessee our true and lawful attorney for us and in our name to receive all monies that may be coming to us as heirs at law of the estate of Thomas Mason, late of Bedford County, deceased. This 29 August 1857.
Reg: September 12, 1867   Signed: Jas. C. Davison
                                  J.A.R. Davison

Page 352 - J.H. Whitehead Power of Attorney to R. Whitehead. I, Joseph H. Whitehead of Pippah County, Mississippi, have appointed Redding Whitehead of the County of Fayette County, Tennessee my true and lawful attorney in fact for me and in my name and behalf any sum or sums of money due to me and to which I am entitled from any person or persons in the counties of Coffee and Bedford County, Tennessee. I am or may become entitled as one of the heirs at law of the estate of Thomas Mason, deceased, late of Coffee County, Tennessee. This 11 October 1858.
Reg: September 12, 1867   Signed: J.H. Whitehead

Page 353 - John Whitehead Power of Attorney to R. Whitehead of Colorado County, Texas, have appointed Redding Whitehead of Fayette County, Tennessee my true and lawful attorney for me and in my name to ask, demand, sue for and receive from the clerk of the Chancery Court of Bedford County and also of the clerk of the County Court of Coffee County, Tennessee, all the legacy given and bequeathed unto me by my uncle Thomas Mason, late of Bedford County, all otherwise coming to me by the death of my said uncle. This 13 August 1861.
Reg: September 12, 1867   Signed: John Whitehead

Page 353 - Tempey Teague and Wm. Teague Power of Attorney to R. Whitehead. We, Wm. Teague and wife Tempy Teague formerly of Fayetteville County, Tennessee, do hereby appoint Redding Whitehead of same place, our true and lawful attorney in fact for us and in our name to demand and receive from the clerks of the County and Chancery Court of Coffee County, Tennessee and also of Bedford County, as heirs of Thos. W. Mason, deceased. This 2 September 1867.
Reg: September 12, 1867   Signed: Wm. Teague
                              Tempy Teague

Page 354 - William Brown Deed to A.W. Manier. I, William Brown, have sold unto A.W. Manier for the consideration of trust of land in Rutherford County, Tennessee, District No. 10, a tract

of land in Bedford County and District No. 9, bounded by A. Lytle's corner, by Ira Moore's line, by Finney's line, and by Mickey Atkinson's corner. Containing 840 acres and 80 poles. This 29 March 1867.
Wit: Wm. T. Johnson   Signed: William Brown
     N.R. Taylor
Reg: September 13, 1867

Page 355 - George W. Thompson Deed to Jo. D. Wilhoite. I have sold unto Joseph D. Wilhoite a certain house and lot on the west side of Martin Street in the Town of Shelbyville and bounded by said Martin Street, by an alley, by the corner of a lot now owned by said Joseph D. Wilhoite, and by the center of the partition wall of a lot recently purchased by said Joseph D. Wilhoite from Wm. Gosling. This 12 September 1867.
Reg: September 13, 1867   Signed: G.W. Thompson

Page 355 - William Gosling Deed to Jo. D. Wilhoite. I, Wm. Gosling, have sold unto Jos. D. Wilhoite all the right title claim and interest which I have in and to the north part of the brick house and lot on Martin Street in the Town of Shelbyville south of the lot purchased by Wm. C. Fletcher and east of the lot bought by G.W. Thompson. It being the house and lot I bought of O.F. Jett. It being bounded by Martin Street, and along the partition wall between said house and the one belonging to G.W. Thompson. This 28 August 1867.
Reg: September 14, 1867   Signed: Wm. Gosling

Page 356 - Joseph Ramsey Deed to Ann Frierson, Col. I, Joseph Ramsey of Bedford County do sell to Ann Frierson (col) a tract of land adjoining Robert Dennison, by McNally's line, and by Cowan's line. Containing 2 acres in the 7th District of Bedford County about one mile east of Shelbyville. It being part of a 50 acre tract of land sold by the executors of Robert Cannon, deceased, and bought by William W. Gunter and by him conveyed to me. This 12 September 1867.
NOTE: Plat on page 356.
Wit: W.W. Gunter   Signed: Joseph Ramsey
     R.A. Shapard
Reg: September 14, 1867

Page 356 - Barnett Stephens Deed to E.B. and F.H. Williams. This September 1867. Barnett Stephens of Bedford County, sold unto Elijah B. Williams and Francis H. Williams of same place, a tract of land in Bedford County on the east waters of Big Flat Creek south branch of Duck River and in the 24th Civil District and bounded by a spring branch.
Reg: September 16, 1867   Signed: Barnett Stephens

Page 357 - Louis Mankel Deed to Nimrod Burrow and Wiley T. Snell. James H. Neil as Commissioner and Clerk of the Circuit Court for the benefit of the estate of Wiley F. Daniel, where executor Edmund Cooper holds the claim. I, Louis Mankel, have

sold unto Nimrod C. Burrow and Wiley T. Snell all the right claim and interest which I have in and to a tract of land in Bedford County and District No. 23 and bounded by a tract of land running north to a stone and poplar stump and by a road, by Mrs. Edmondson's tract at the south of the lane, and to the fence. Containing 115 acres and 149 poles. This 14 September 1867.
Wit: Edm'd Cooper   Signed: Louis Mankel
    William Frierson
Reg: September 16, 1867

Page 358 - William gosling Deed to Mrs. S.C.A. Enochs. I, William Gosling, for and in consideration of the fact of Mrs. S.C.A. Enochs and G.A.J. Enochs having released all interest that they had in a mill and the land lying around to George W. Thompson by deed executed 14 September 1867, do release transfer unto Mrs. Sarah C.A. Enochs all the right interest and benefit that I may have under and by virtue of t Trust Deed executed by G.A.J. Enochs and C.A. Enochs, his wife on the __ October 1865 to me by which Trust Deed the interest of Mrs. C.A. Enochs had in the estate of Stephen N. Dance, deceased, in Lincoln County, Tennessee was conveyed. This 24 September 1867.
Reg: September 16, 1867   Signed: Wm. Gosling

Page 359 - James T. Terpin Deed to Sarah Trollinger. Re-registration. I, James T. Terpin, have sold unto Sarah Trollinger a tract of land in Bedford County and Town of Shelbyville being part of the Lot No. 133 and a tract of land adjoining said lot, by Newcomb Thompson's line, by Clement Wright's line, by Hugh Jones' line, by Arthur Brooks' line, and by John T. Neil's line in the Columbia Road. Containing ¾ of an acre. This 12 January 1853.
Reg: September 16, 1867   Signed: James T. Terpin

Page 359 - James N. Trollinger Deed by his Attorney W.W. Bobo to J.M. Trollinger. James N. Trollinger by his attorney in fact W.W. Bobo, have sold to John M. Trollinger his undivided interest the same being one eleventh in a certain lot or parcel of land in the Town of Shelbyville and bounded by former Newcomb Thompson now the heirs of M.F. Thompson, by Clement Wright, by James Stallings and Pauline Carpenter, and by the Shelbyville and Unionville Turnpike. Containing 120 poles. This 12 July 1867.
Reg: September 17, 1867   Signed: James N. Trollinger, by
                             W.W. Bobo

Page 360 - R.P. Teeter and S.A. Teeter Deed to Jno. M. Trollinger. This 16 September 1867. R.P. Teeter and his wife Sarah A. Teeter sold unto John M. Trollinger their undivided interest (the same being one eleventh) to a tract of land lying in the Town of Shelbyville and bounded by formerly Newcomb Thompson now the heirs of M.F. Thompson' line, by Clement Wright, and by James Stallings and Pauline Carpenter, by the

Shelbyville and Unionville Turnpike. Containing 120 poles.
This 16, September 1867.
Reg: September 17, 1867   Signed: R.P. Teeter
                                     S.A. Teeter

Page 361 - Wm. Gosling Deed to G.W. Thompson. I, William
Gosling, have sold unto George W. Thompson a tract of land with
the mills thereon being in Civil District No. 21 of Bedford
County and bounded by Flat Creek, by the old Dixon tract of
land, by the Cummings's land, by the lands formerly owned by
Joseph Thompson purchased by him from Josiah Stephenson and the
lands now owned by George W. Thompson and purchased by him from
William S. Jett and known as the old John B. Cummings' land.
Containing 23 acres. The property conveyed known as the Holt
Mills. This 14 September 1867.
Reg: September 17, 1867   Signed: Wm. Gosling
                                     G.A.J. Enochs
                                     Sarah C.A. Enochs

Page 362 - M.W. Turner and Henry Clark Attorney Dawson and
others to John D. Webb. We, James W. Clark, Thomas J. Clark,
Daniel Clark, Levi A. Clark, W.S. Dawson and wife Frances J.
Dawson, Joseph Harrison and wife Rebecca Harrison, N.J. Winston
the purchasers of John W. Clark's interest, M.W. Turner the
purchaser of Moses B. Clark's interest by our attorney in fact,
M.W. Turner and Henry Clark and we, M.W. Turner and wife Mary A.
Turner and Henry Clark for our individual part as the heirs of
the estate of James K. Clark, deceased. We the above named
heirs by our attorney in fact M.W. Turner and Henry Clark hereto
constituted by power of attorney dated 5 January 1860 and
January 25, 1861 be recorded, have this day bargained and sold
to John D. Webb a tract of land in Bedford County and District
No. 9 and bounded by W.S. Brame's land, by the heirs of J.T.
Wheelhouse and L.M. Rankin, by the dower of Mrs. Frances Clark,
and by Preston Frazier's line. Excepting one half an acre which
was formerly given to the Meeting House (Friendship) by James K.
Clark, also one half an acre to the graveyard. Containing 64
acres and 95 poles. This 24 January 1867.
Wit: H.C. Turner   Signed: Thos. J. Clark
     W.D. Cates   James W. Clark
Reg: September 18, 1867   Levi A. Clark
                                      Daniel Clark
                                      W.S. Dawson
                                      Frances J. Dawson
                                      Joseph Harrison
                                      Rebecca Harrison
                                      N.J. Winston
                                      M.W. Turner, by
                                      Atty M.W. Turner
                                      Henry Clark
                                      Mary A. Clark

Page 363 - Jack Norville Deed to Wm. R. Norville. I have sold
unto William R. Norville all my right title claim and interest
as a distributee in the estate of my father John W. Norville,

deceased, both real and personal to William R. Norville.   This 17 September 1867.
Wit: S.H. Whitthorn   Signed: Jack Norville
     Evander Shepard
Reg: September 18, 1867

Page 364 - Mary Byrum and others Copy of Decree - Elisha Leech et als.   Mary Byrum, administratrix of John Byrum, deceased, E.S. Byrum, J.W. Byrum, John M. Byrum, M.C. Byrum, Geo. W. Byrum, W.H. Anderton and wife Mary E. VS Elisha Leech and wife J.F. Leech, B.J. Byrum and Mary Ann Dean - Final Decree. This cause came for final hearing 12 January 1866 being the December Term of Circuit Court of Bedford County.   Clerk's Report - In this cause the undersigned who was appointed begs leave to report that advertising the time and place and term of sale by notices at three or more public places in Bedford County &c, he attended on the premises on the 2nd January 1866 and offered all right title claim and interest of the heirs of John Byrum, deceased, in and to said lands subject to the widow's dower on a credit.   Land was struck off to Geo. W. Byrum.   Had notes on W.H. Anderton and S.K. Farris. This 17 September 1867.
Reg: September 18, 1867   Signed: James H. Neil

Page 365 - Jasper N. Smith and others Deed to T.N. Stokes. We, Jasper N. Smith, James Caruthers, Nancy A. Caruthers, William T. Sugg and Mary E. Sugg and Kinchen Younger have this day sold unto Thomas N. Stokes all our right title claim and interest in a tract of land in 3rd Civil District of Bedford County and bounded by lands of Gilchrist and Shriver, by lands of T.N. Stokes and Abram Shriver, and by lands of N.T. Stokes and James Ault.   Containing 100 acres.   It being a part of the lands of which Kinchen Stokes (illegible) the owner and is the portion assigned to the children and grand children of Mary Smith in the partition of the lands of said Kinchen Stokes.   The said Mary Smith having been a daughter of said Kinchen Stokes.   This 3 January 1867.
Reg: September 19, 1867   Signed: Jasper N. Smith
                                         Kinchen Stokes
                                         James Caruthers
                                         W.T. Sugg
                                         Nancy A. Caruthers
                                         M.E. Sugg

Page 366 - Simpson Gunn and wife Deed to J.Y. West. We have sold unto J.Y. West a tract of land of Isaac West, deceased, that Sarah D. West lived on at her death lying in Bedford County and Civil District No. 3.   This April 11, 1867.
Wit: J.H.C. Scales   Signed: Simpson Gunn
Reg: September 23, 1867   Frances Gunn

Page 367 - C.W. Phillips Power of Attorney to Jo. H. Smith. I, Caledonia Phillips of Craighead County, Arkansas, do appoint Joseph H. Smith of Bedford County my true and lawful attorney for me and in my name to collect all money due me from Alexander

Dizard my guardian from my mother Jane Phillips' estate and all others money due me in Bedford County. This 20 May 1867.
Wit: H.M. Cole   Signed: C.W. Phillips
     J.W. Willingham
Reg: September 23, 1867

Page 368 - Robert Allison Deed to Robt. S. Brown. I, Robert Allison, Trustee of David T. Chambers, have sold to R.S. Brown he being the highest and best bidder the tract of land in Bedford County and Civil District No. 10 and bounded by Robert Hall's corner, by W. Perry's corner, and by Wynn's line. Containing 98 acres and 144 poles. This 31 August 1867.
Wit: A. Wilson   Signed: Robert Allison
     Robert C. Maupin
Reg: September 23, 1867

Page 369 - Edward N. Stephenson Deed to E.B. Stephenson. Edward N. Stephenson conveyed to E.B. Stephenson, both of Bedford County and Civil District No. 18, a tract of land adjoining E.B> Stephenson's line the same being Edward N. Stephenson's corner. Containing one half acre. This __ day of __ 1867.
Reg: September 24, 1867   Signed: E.N. Stephens

Page 370 - R.H. Calaway and wife Deed to S.D. Coble. We, R.H. Calaway and wife Catharine Calaway formerly Catharine Coble, do sell and convey unto S.D. Coble all our right claim and interest we have or may heretofore acquire in one undivided tract of land containing 134 acres and being the place on which Mary Williams now lives and bounded by lands of Daniel Hoosier's estate and B.K. Coble, deceased, by lands of Mary Kimbro and Mrs. Webster, by lands of Wm. Jenkins and Martin Euliss, by Duck river. The same being in Bedford County and Civil District No. 25. It being on which said Mary Williams now lives and holds as dower. She being the wife of Jacob Coble, deceased, and to which we are entitled at the death of said Mary Williams. This 21 September 1867.
Reg: September 24, 1867   Signed: R.H. Calaway
                                         Catharine Calaway

Page 371 - Jos. Anderson Deed to Thos. F. Simmons. I, Jos. Anderson, have sold to Thomas F. Simmons a tract of land he now lives on in Bedford County and Civil District No. 11 and containing 119 ½ acres and bounded by said Anderson's line, by one old lot clover lot in side the woods lot, by Mary Sugg's old corner now E.S. Wortham's, by a cross fence, by or near a field on Sam'l Crowell's old line, and by said Anderson's old line. This __ day of September 1867.
Wit: B.S. Parsons   Signed: Jos. Anderson
     William Crowell
Reg: September 26, 1867

Page 372 - Jos. Anderson Deed to Wm. Crowel. I, Jos. Anderson, have sold unto Wm. Crowel a tract of land No. 1 of the division

of land between David Anderson's heirs in Bedford County and District No. 11. Said land is the north west lot of said Anderson's land. Bounded by Wortham's heirs' land and said Jos. Anderson's corner, by Lot No. 2, and by David Anderson's old tract of land. Lot No. 1 making 12 acres and 80 poles. This 21 August 1867.
Wit: B.S. Parsons   Signed: Jos. Anderson
     J.C. Claxton
Reg: September 25, 1867

Page 372 - John Murry and wife Mortgage to E. Wilder & Co. Louisville, Ky. We, John Murry and wife Charlotte Murry of Bedford County securing E. Wilder & Co. of Louisville, Jefferson County, Kentucky in a note, one house and lot in the Town of Wartrace, Civil District No. 3 of Bedford County and registered in Book FFF, page 131 February 7, 1867. This 25 September 1867.
Reg: September 27, 1867   Signed: John Murry
                                   Charlotte Murry

Page 373 - A.L. Stamps Deed to William H. Wisener, Sr. Asa L. Stamps on 22 November 1856 sold to William H. Wisener, Sr. a tract of land in Bedford County and Civil District No. 7 and on the west of the Town of Shelbyville being a portion of the JohnT. Neil tract and bounded by the center of Lane Street, and by Kimmons' tract. Containing 30 acres and 20 poles. This 22 September 1867.
Reg: September 28, 1867   Signed: A.L. Stamps

Page 374 - J.A. Jarrett Deed to Elizabeth Woods. I have sold to Elizabeth Woods a tract of land in Bedford County and District No. 8 on the south bank of Fall Creek and bounded by the center of Fall Creek opposite Head's old corner, and by Claxton's corner. Containing 60 acres. This 26 January 1867.
Wit: G.C. Douglass   Signed: James A. Jarrett
     C.S. Dudley
Reg: September 28, 1867

Page 375 - W.P. Bridges Deed to Benjamin F. Read. I. W.P. Bridges of Bedford County, have sold to Benjamin F. Read a tract of land in Bedford County and Civil District No, 23 and bounded by a ridge, by the old section line, and to near the branch. Containing 40 acres and 74 poles. The same being part of the tract on which I now live. This 28 September 1867.
Wit: Thos. C. Whiteside   Signeds: W.P. Bridges
     S.B. Gordon
Reg: September 30, 1867

Page 375 - James L. Wood Deed to John Wood. For the love and affection I entertain for my son John Wood, I hereby give to him two tracts of land in Bedford County and Civil District No. 2. The first whereon he now lives and contains 8 acres and 199 poles and is bounded by the dower of Nancy Muse commencing on her east boundary line, and by Nancy Muse's line. The other

tract containing 30 acres and 20 poles and bounded by G.G.
Osborne's corner, by the Richard Muse's tract, and by William
Finch line. This September 30, 1867.
Reg: September 30, 1867   Signed: James L. Wood

Page 376 - J.C. Leming Deed to L.F. Sherrill. I, J.C. Leming,
have sold to L.F. Sherrill a tract of land in Bedford County and
District No. 25, containing 33 64/100 acres and bounded by the
mouth of a lane. This April 23, 1867.
Reg: October 1, 1867   Signed: J.C. Leming

Page 377 - J.C. Leming Deed to Nathan Leming. I, J.C. Leming,
have sold to Nathan Leming a tract of land in Bedford County and
District No. 25, containing 60 ½ acres.   This September 16,
1867.
Reg: October 1, 1867   Signed: J.C. Leming

Page 377 - Hardy Prince Deed to J.C. Leming. This May 10, 1867.
I, Hardy Prince, have sold to J.C. Leming a tract of land it
being three shares lying on the waters of Normans Creek, Civil
District No. 25 and bounded by Z, Weavers' corner, by G.
Huffman's line marked G.H. Huffman's corner, by Holland's line,
and by Caleghan's line.
Reg: October 2, 1867   Signed: Hardy Prince

Page 378 - Louis Mankel Deed to Jo. D. Wilhoite. I, Louis
Mankel of Bedford County, have this 2nd day of October 1867,
have sold to Joseph D. Wilhoite of same place, a house and lot
in the 7th Civil District of Bedford County and bounded by
JohnC. Coldwell, by lot of Mary Thompson, by ___ Street, and
being the place on which said Louis Mankel now resides. This 2
October 1867.
Reg: October 2, 1867   Signed: Louis Mankel

Page 379 - Thomas Holland Deed to L.B. Knott. This 12 August
1867. I, Thomas Holland, Sr. of the town have sold to L.B.
Knott my half of a lot of land in the Town of Shelbyville known
by Lot No. 44, Henry Yancy owing the other half, lying on Pike
and Adams Streets and adjoining at the corner of PIke Street,
and by Adams Street.
Reg: October 4, 1867   Signed: Thomas Holland

Page 379 - T.M. Winsett and others Deed to J.W. Parson. We,
T.M. Winsett, D.H. Winsett and John E. Haskins, have sold unto
John W. Parson a tract of land in Bedford County and District
No. 9, containing 18 acres and 67 poles and bounded by the
center of North Fork Creek Stephen Sander's corner, and by a
watering gap. This 4, October 1867.
Reg: October 4, 1867   Signed: T.M. Winsett
                                    D.H. Winsett
                                    J.E. Haskins

Page 380 - C.P. Houston Bond to C.P. Houston, Jr. I bind myself to pay C.P. Houston, Jr. Whereas I have sold to said C.P. Houston, Jr. a tract of land in Bedford County on the east side of the turnpike road between my home tract and said road being the part of the John Knott land lying east of said road and for which I hold the bond of John P. Steele for title. Containing 52 acres for the consideration in part of one third interest in the land and mills on Duck River above the Town of Shelbyville and including stock of hogs and all other things pertaining to said mill as sold by the firm of Steele, Hammonds & Co. and which I this day __ the bond for title of John P. Steele. This July 31, 1863.
Reg: October 5, 1867   Signed: C.P. Houston

Page 381 - C.P. Houston Bond to Wm. Houston. I bind myself to pay William Houston. I have sold to said William Houston my tract of land in District No. 6 of Bedford County and bounded by the lands of John Overcast, by the Murfreesboro Turnpike Road, by lands of Wiley Ellis, by lands of C.P. Houston, Sr. and containing 100 acres. This 5 September 1867.
Wit: J.J. Houston   Signed: C.P. Houston, Jr.
     Ann Pinson
Reg: October 7, 1867

Page 381 - T.M. Winsett et als to S.D. Green. We, T.M. and D.H. Winsett and A.B. Green and wife Sarah A. Green and John E. Hoskins, have sold to Stephen D. Green a tract of land in Bedford County and District No. 8, containing 13 acres and bounded by a corner of Jason Winsett's old tract, by a corner between the Jason Winsett and the Peyton Vincent tracts, and by the line between Thomas Landers and the Winsett land. This September 17, 1867.
Reg: October 8, 1867   Signed: T.M. Winsett
                                      D.H. Winsett
                                      A.B. Green
                                      S.A. Green
                                      A.E. Hoskins

Page 382 - Minos T. Cannon Deed to J.R. Stegall. I have sold a tract of land in Bedford County beginning in the middle of Duck River, on the east side of Shelbyville and Fayetteville Turnpike Road about 100 yards south of the forks of Shelbyville and Lewisburg Road, and on the east side of said Fayetteville Road. Said land lying about half mile south of Shelbyville. Plat made by William Galbreath 7 August 1867. Containing 5 acres. This 7 October 1867.
Reg: October 9, 1867   Signed: Minos T. Cannon

Page 383 - Robert Terry Deed to N.B. Parsons. I, Robert Terry, have sold to N.B. Parsons a tract of land in Bedford County and District No. 8, containing 6 acres and 137 poles, adjoining N.B. Parsons' line, by a tract belonging to said Parsons, and by the Shelbyville Road. This 3 February 1866.
Wit: C.S. Dudley   Signed: Robert Terry

G.W. Parson
Reg: October 9, 1867

Page 383 - Giles P. Hastings Deed to John S. Cates. I, Giles P. Hastings, have sold to John S. Cates all of my right title claim and interest in a tract of land in the 23rd Civil District of Bedford County and bounded by the lands of John S. Cates, by lands of Joshua Woosley and others, by lands known as the dower of the widow of John Hastings, and by lands known as the Spencer Brown land. Containing __ acres. It being a portion of the lands of which my father John Hastings died seized and possessed in Bedford County except the portion now known as the dower. My interest being an undivided one eighth in the whole except the dower. This 8 October 1867.
Reg: October 9, 1867   Signed: G.P. Hastings

Page 384 - Jno. C. Anderson Deed to Wm. Crowell. I, Jno. C. Anderson, have sold unto Wm. Crowell a small tract of land in Bedford County and District No. 11, beginning in the lane south of said Wm. Crowell's dwelling house, Thomas H. Wortham's corner, containing 54 acres and being a part of said land I lately bought of George Smith. This 28 January 1867.
Wit: Jos. Anderson   Signed: John C. Anderson
     B.S. Parsons
Reg: October 9, 1867

Page 385 - George Smith Deed to John C. Anderson. I have sold unto John C. Anderson a tract of land in Bedford County and District No. 11 and bounded by William Crowel's corner, by the north bank of Duck River, and by Newsom old corner. Containing 108 acres and 130 poles. This January 19, 1867.
Wit: William Crowel   Signed: George Smith
     B.S. Parsons
Reg: October 10, 1867

Page 385 - John T. Martin Extr. Bond to F.E. Lacy. I bind myself to F.E> Lacy. Whereas F.E. Lacy has purchased of me at public sale a tract of land in Civil District No. 25 and 23 of Bedford County sold by me as executor of James Rippy, deceased, on the 5 October 1867 and bounded by Jno. W. Gardner and Mrs. Kimbro, by David Low, by the lands formerly owned by Wiley Daniel, and by Taylor Haily. Containing 210 acres and 11 poles. This October 8, 1867.
Wit: W. Bearden   Signed: John T. Martin, extr of
Reg: October 10, 1867   James Rippy, deceased

Page 386 - Jo. Thompson, Sheriff, Deed to S.D. Coble. I, Joseph Thompson as Deputy Sheriff of Bedford County on 31 October 1860 sold a tract of land in Civil District No. 7 of Bedford County and east of Shelbyville Depot of the Nashville and Chattanooga Rai Road adjoining the lands of Robert B. Davidson, Robert Cannon, deceased, and ___ Cowan. Containing 2 ½ acres. Sale of land issued from the Circuit Court of Bedford County in favor of

368

W.B.M. Brame against James F. Calhoun and others to Thomas C.Whiteside he being the highest bidder for the same of ten dollars. This September 18, 1867.
Reg: October 11, 1867   Signed: Jo. Thompson, Sheriff
                                James H. Calhoun

Page 387 - S.D. Coble Deed to Mariah E. Phillips. I, S.D. Coble, have sold unto Mariah E. Phillips a tract of land in 7th District of Bedford County near the Town of Shelbyville and the Depot of the Nashville and Chattanooga Rail Road of the town and bounded by the lands of Mariah E. Phillips, by the Rowesville Road, by the lands of the heirs of Gen. Cannon, deceased. It being same land sold and deeded to me by Joseph Thompson as Sheriff and James F. Calhoun. This 8 October 1867.
Reg: October 11, 1867   Signed: S.D. Coble

Page 388 - James Thorne Copy of Decree VS James Pickle and others - Final Decree. This cause came for final hearing 11 September 1867 - And the answer of James F. Stephenson and Wm. H. Stephens and (illegible) order to the adult defendants and answer of guardian for the minor and proof and exhibits. It appearing to the court that the complainants purchased of J.J. Neely as the agent of defendants on the 25 November 1854 the tract of land mentioned in the bill for which he executed his notes and took possession of said land and has been in possession ever since and that he has paid the purchase money for said land long since except a small amount going to James F. Stephenson and Wm. H. Stephenson which he has since the filing of this bill. The land is bounded by lands of D.G. Stephenson, deceased, by lands of Theophilus Williams and Thomas L. Gaunt, and by D.G. Stephens, deceased, and __ Shearin. Containing 126 acres. Which land in Bedford County and Civil District No. 18. (illegible) all the right title claim and interest that James Pickle, John Pickle, Thomas Pickle, Jonathan Legitt and wife Nelly Legitt, Nancy Stephenson, James F. Stephenson, Wm. H. Stephenson, Edward Stephenson, P.M. Pickle, Geo. W. Cook and wife Elizabeth Cook, Charnell Pickle, Thomas Pickle, Jr., Margaret Pickle, George Pickle, Rosannah Pickle and Henry Pickle and Square Pickle have in and to the above tract of land and every part thereof be divested out of them forever and vested in James Thorn forever. This September 30, 1867.
Reg: October 11, 1867   Signed: Lewis Tillman, by C&M

Page 389 - G.K. Hemphill and E.B. Kelly Bond to M. Owen and others. George K. Hemphill sold to Matilda Owen, Martha Ann Owen and Mary Jane Owen a tract of land containing 55 acres which land formerly belonging to the ___ Nelson family and conveyed by the heirs to David Perseller and Perceller to Wm. Little. Now we, George K. Hemphill, Enoch B. Kelly and Langston Lamb bind ourselves unto the said Owens for said land. This 13 February 1867.
Wit: W.G. Osborne   Signed: Geo. K. Hemphill
     Chesly Williams   L. Lamb
Reg: October 11, 1867   E.B. Kelly

Page 389 – G.K. Hemphill Deed to M. Owen and daughters. I, George K. Hemphill of Williamson County, Tennessee, have sold to Matilda Owen, Martha Ann Owen and Mary Jane Owen of the same place, a tract of land in Bedford County and District No. 10 and bounded by a tract of land purchased by Stephen Wood from David Peebles, and by Haley's corner. Containing 55 acres, it being the tract of land conveyed to me by Wm. Little on 1 April 1861. This 13 February 1867.
Wit: Chesly Williams   Signed: Geo. W. Hemphill
     W.G. Osborne
Reg: October 12, 1867

Page 390 – N. Thompson, 3rd and wife Deed to W.H. Shepperson. We, N. Thompson, 3rd and Francis J. Thompson, have sold to William H. Shepperson a tract of land in the 7th Civil District of Bedford County and bounded on the Rowesville Road south east of the lands of Mrs. Moody, and by a "wood" lot. Containing 25 acres, it being a part of the lands belonging to the estate of Gen. Robert Cannon and by Francis J. Thompson bought of George W. Thompson. This October 12, 1867.
Reg: October 12, 1867   Signed: N. Thompson, 3rd
     Fannie Thompson

Page 391 – C.T. Philpott et als Deed to N. Pope. We have sold unto N. Pope a tract of land in Bedford County and District No. 8 and bounded by the center of Fall Creek Wm. Phillip's corner. Containing 37 acres and 59 poles. This 24 September 1866.
Reg: October 14, 1867   Signed: R.R. Philpott
     J.H. Philpott
     C.T. Philpott

Page 392 – T.M. Winsett and others Deed to N.O. Burton. We, T.M. Winsett and D.H. Winsett and A.B. Green and wife Sarah A. Green and John E. Haskins, have sold to N.O. Burton a tract of land in Bedford County and District No. 8. Containing 13 acres and bounded by a line between Winsett and Peyton Vincent, and to the mouth of Burton's lane. This April 17, 1867.
Reg: October 14, 1867   Signed: T.M. Winsett
     D.H. Winsett
     A.B. Green
     S.A. Green
     J.E. Haskins

Page 393 – Jo. Thompson, Sheriff, Deed to Thos. H. Coldwell. Whereas John Wilson did institute suit in Bedford County on the _ - day of December 1858 against John Bennett and came to the hands of James Wortham then Sheriff of Bedford County and there being no personal property of said John Bennett to levy said attachment upon the same was levied on 8 December 1860 on all the right claim and interest which said John Bennett had in a tract of land in Bedford County and bounded by lands of W.W. Gill and Mrs. Chandler, by lands of Mrs. Chandler and a tract formerly owned by Isaac Shook, by lands of W.W. Gill. Sale of land 10 October 1860 which came to the hands of Garret Phillips,

then Sheriff of Bedford County. John Wilson did transfer judgment to Thos. H. Coldwell and said Coldwell did bid became the purchaser. This __ October 1867.
Reg: October 14, 1867   Signed: Jo. Thompson, Sheriff

Page 394 - James L. Woods and wife Deed to James E. Chilcoat. This 14 October 1867. Amelia Woods of Bedford County sold to James E. Chilcoat of same place all the right title claim and interest as one of the heirs of Isaac Muse, deceased, in and to all that tract of land on which Nancy Muse, widow and relict of said Muse, now lives, it being 90 acres as laid off to said widow as her dower. Said land is one fourth of said 90 acres at the death of her mother said Nancy Muse and the Amelia Woods doth defend the right and title of the above, said land. This 14 October 1867.
Reg: October 16, 1867   Signed: Amelia Woods
                                     James L. Woods

Page 394 - W.P. Turner Trust Deed to H.K. and J.M. Stokes. I have sold to H.K. Stokes one bay mare. This conveyance is made to secure him and John M. Stokes as my security on a note payable to James Mullins due and payable in November 1868 which is given for the rent of the Bowles land for 1868. This 17 October 1867.
Reg: October 18, 1867   Signed: W.P. Turner

Page 395 - G.H. Castleman Trust Deed to Martin Euliss and W.J. Shofner. I, G.H. Castleman, have sold to Martin Euliss and William J. Shofner my plantation on which I now reside in Bedford County and adjoining the lands of John C. Hix, Hampton Evans and others. Containing 270 acres. Also all of my interest in the estate of Jacob Castleman on Goose Creek in Bedford County and in Davidson County, Tennessee. Also all my interest in the tannery of Castleman & Goggin in Bedford County including all leather hides, stock and fixtures therein. Also two gray mares, one sorrel mule, two mules, twenty head of pork hogs and all of my stock &c. Other names in document were John Cash, Jacob Wilhoite, James and Wm. McGill, Samuel Bobo, Jesse Tucker, Baston Castleman, John Enochs, Silas Bivins, B.F. Pannel for notes. Other names Wm.J. Shoffner, F(illegible) Lyon, H.P. Reeves, John Tune, Joseph Parker, Frank Lacy, Wm. P. Hicks, Felix Davis, Thomas Williams, Mrs. Morton, Jesse Coleman, E.A. Reagor, Elisha Womack, Joseph D. Wilhoite, Wm. Russell, John W. Cowan, Dr. J.H. McGrew, B.A. Burrow, Geo. W. Floyd, Wm. P. Wells, and Daniel Jenkins, all accounts and notes.
NOTE: Long document. This 18 October 1867.
Reg: October 19, 1867   Signed: G.H. Castleman

Page 396 - John Jakes Deed to G.W. Jakes. I, John Jakes, have sold unto George W. Jakes a tract of land in Bedford County and District No. 1 on Scots Branch of the Garrison Fork of Duck River and bounded by the top of a ridge George Jakes' corner, and by John Jakes' corner. Containing 96 acres. This January 10, 1860.

Wit: Wm. Eoff   Signed: John Jakes
Reg: October 19, 1867

Page 397 - George Jakes Deed to George W. Jakes.   I, George
Jakes of Bedford County, have sold unto George W. Jakes also of
Bedford County, a tract of land in Bedford County on the head
waters of Murrows Branch in District No 1 and being a part of
the tract whereon I now live, containing 40 acres. Land bounded
by John Jakes' line. Also said land is a part of the tract of
land whereon I now live and which I conveyed in a deed in trust
to G.G. Osborne, executor of Mary Shaw, deceased, and John Jakes
as trustee on 7 August 1865. This 4 October 1867.
Wit: G.W. Cherry   Signed: George Jakes
     H.W. Eaton
Reg: October 19, 1867

Page 398 - James M. Stephens Deed to Reuben W. Couch.   This 6
December 1860.   James M. Stephens sold unto Reuben W. Couch,
both of Bedford County, a tract of land in Bedford County and
bounded by the south west corner of said tract and corner of the
land of William Cully and D.W. Hall, and on Cully Branch.
Containing 131 acres and 99 poles.
Wit: G.A. Cortner   Signed: J.M. Stephens
     Jno. R. Muse
Reg: October 21, 1867

Page 399 - R.W. Couch Deed to James W. Stephens.   Reuben W.
Couch to James W. Stephens. Deed to 92 ¾ acres This December
1860.   Both of Bedford County.   Land containing 92 ¾ acres and
26 poles in Bedford County and on the ridge between the waters
of the Garrison and the Barren Fork of Duck River and bounded by
a running spring in the head of Bear Wallow which is the corner
of a tract of land belonging to the heirs of Edmond Hord,
deceased, by Mrs. Eliza Davidson's tract of land, and by Fergus
Hall's line.
Wit: O.P. Arnold   Signed: R.W. Couch
     R.C. Couch
Reg: October 21, 1867

Page 400 - William Gosling Deed to J.M. Brown.   I, William
Gosling, have sold unto J.M. Brown a tract of land in Bedford
County and Civil District No. 3 and bounded by a corner of the
Corbitt's tract of land.   Containing 22 acres and bounded by
lands of Wisener, Patterson and Davis' land, by lands of Wm.
Lane's heirs and Davis land, by William H. Wisener, and by J.M.
Brown. This 20 October 1867.
Reg: October 21, 1867   Signed: Wm. Gosling

Page 400 - James M. Baker and wife Deed to Martin Friddle. We,
James M. and C.F. Baker of Bedford County, have sold unto Martin
Friddle of same place a tract of land in Bedford County and
Civil District No. 22 on Big Flat Creek and bounded by the
Columbia Road it being one of said Friddle's corners, and by a

tract of land belonging to the heirs of A.R. Reagor, deceased. Containing 6 acres and 52 ½ poles. This 21 October 1867.
Reg: October 22, 1867   Signed: James M. Baker

Page 401 - R.C. Ogilvie Deed to Jasper Ogilvie. I, Robert C. Ogilvie, have sold unto Jasper Ogilvie a tract of land in District No. 5 of Bedford County, containing 16 acres, it being a part of Lot No. 7. The lot originally allotted to me by decree in the partition of the estate of James Ogilvie, deceased, and bounded by the north west corner of Lot No. 7 sold to B.F. Whitworth by me, by corner of lot No. 6 belonging to Jasper Ogilvie, by a line of G.W. Bell, by one half of Lot No. 8 which we R.C. and Jasper Ogilvie have this day deeded to B.F. Whitworth. This 21 October 1867.
Reg: October 22, 1867   Signed: R.C. Ogilvie

Page 401 - R.C. and Jasper Ogilvie Deed to B.F. Whitworth. We, Robert C. Ogilvie, have sold unto B.F. Whitworth a tract of land in Bedford County and bounded by the original tract of land belonging to the late James Ogilvie, deceased, known as Lot No. 8 in the division, by B.F. Whitworth's line, and by George Bell's line. Containing 41 acres and 30 poles. This 21 October 1867.
Reg: October 22, 1867   Signed: R.C. Ogilvie
                                     Jasper Ogilvie

Page 402 - S.P. Fuller and G. Carter Transfer to Jno. W. Cowan, Sr. We do transfer to him all that is coming to us from the Commissioners of said jail, for work on the County Jail. This 23 October 1867.
Wit: J.M. Elliott   Signed: S.P. Fuller
     W.H. Wilson   G. Carter
Reg: October 24, 1867

Page 403 - Wm. Hoover Deed to Ursula Jane Hoover. I, William Hoover husband of Ursula Jane Hoover heretofore since my marriage with her have received of her money about the sum of $785 and whereas said Ursula Jane has this day joined with me in a Deed of Conveyance to William C. Orr of 38 acres and 15 poles of land in Bedford County. Land in 4th Civil District of Bedford County and bounded by the center of Wartrace Creek, by the Chaffin land, near spout spring, by A.J. Bingham's water gate, and to the center of the road. Containing 23 acres and 63 poles. This 24 October 1867.
Reg: October 24, 1867   Signed: William Hoover

Page 404 - Wm. Hoover and wife Deed to Wm. C. Orr. We, William Hoover and his wife Ursula Jane Hoover formerly Ursula Jane Orr, have sold a tract of land in 8th Civil District of Bedford County, containing 38 acres and 15 poles and bounded by a corner of Lot No. 3 in the division of lands under decree in the case of William C. Orr and others VS David A. Hall and others. This 27 October 1867.

Reg: October 25, 1867   Signed: William Hoover
                                       U.J. Hoover

Page 405 - Thomas C. Martin Trust Deed to James Martin.   I,
Thomas C. Martin, have sold unto James Martin two tracts of land
on the head waters of Flat Creek in Bedford County. One of the
tracts was conveyed to me by William Pearce by deed dated 31
January 1857.   The other was conveyed to me by C.R.P. King by
deed dated 18 September 1854.   And also personal property, to
wit, one mule, one old mare, three colts, one yellow pony, one
cow and calf, one large yoke of oxen, and other items listed in
original document. This 25 October 1867.
Reg: October 25, 1867   Signed: Thomas C. Martin

Page 406 - Joseph Ramsey Deed to Mary Davidson.   I, Joseph
Ramsey of Bedford County, have sold unto Sarah Davidson (col'd)
and her mother Mary Davidson (col'd) a tract of land in Bedford
County and Civil District No. 3 and adjoining in the center of
the Rowesville Road about one mile east of Shelbyville.   It
being the south east corner of a 10 acre tract belonging to
Lewis Erwin (col'd), and by Henry Cooper's line.   Containing 1
acre.   This October 26, 1867.
Wit: J.B. Dixon   Signed: Joseph Ramsey
     Thos. B. Cannon
Reg: October 26, 1867

Page 406 - Robert Mosley and wife Deed to John Brown.   We,
Robert Mosley and his wife Cynthia Mosley formerly Cynthia
Brown, have sold unto John Brown a tract of land in Bedford
County and Civil District No. 19 and containing 50 acres and
bounded by the land of Wm. Woods and James Russell, by lands of
William Woods, by lands occupied by said Robert Mosely, by lands
of Henry Hazlett it being the same tract conveyed to said
Cynthia for life remainder to her heirs by John A. Blakemore.
This 29 October 1867.
Reg: October 30, 1867   Signed: Robert Mosley
                                     Cynthia Mosley

Page 407 - P.H. Reaves and James P. Newsom Deed to J.J. Burrow.
We, P.H. Reaves and James P. Newsom, have sold to J.J. Burrow a
tract of land, viz, the seven eighths of the following tract of
land in Bedford County in Civil District No. 22 and bounded by
lands of George H. Castleman, by Wm. Campbell, by John Wilhoite
and Wm. Campbell, by J.J. Burrow and known as the old Archibald
Reaves farm upon which P.H. Reaves now lives and which is said
ReAves and Newsom own property. This 19 September 1867.
Wit: John Wiloite   Signed: P.H. Reaves
     Wm. C. Wilhoite
Reg: October 31, 1867

Page 408 - John Woods Deed to Jasper McMillan. John Woods sold
to Jasper McMillan all the right title claim and interest I have
in two tracts of land in Bedford County and Civil District No.

2. The first whereon I now live and containing 8 acres and 139 poles and bounded by the dower of Nancy Muse. The other containing 35 acres and 20 poles and bounded by G.G. Osborne's corner, by Richard Muse tract, and by William Finch. This October 8, 1867.
Reg: October 31, 1867   Signed: John Woods

Page 409 - Edmund Cooper Deed to H.H. Nease. I, Edmund Cooper, have sold unto H.H. Nease a part of a tract of land in District No. 20 of Bedford County and bounded by H.H. Nease's corner. Containing 10 acres and 2 rods and 20 poles. This 31 October 1867.
Reg: October 31, 1867   Signed: Edm'd Cooper

Page 409 - J.L. Gibson Deed to Artimice(?) Roberts a tract of land adjoining the center of a road, and by Gibson's original line. Containing 6 ¼ acres.
Wit: W.C. Wagster   Signed: J.L. Gibson
     William Morton
Reg: October 31, 1867

Page 410 - John Bailey Power of Attorney to Gabriel Cohn. I have this day appointed Gabriel Cohn my attorney in fact to collect and receive all money which may be due me from the Government of the United States for additional county as a soldier serving in the 5th Regiment of Tennessee Cavalry Volunteers or application lately forwarded by W.B. Overcast to the department at Washington for collection. I appoint Gabriel Cohn my attorney in fact to take any step which may be necessary to aid in the collection of the claim. This 31 October 1867.
Reg: November 1, 1867   Signed: John Bailey

Page 410 - Mary Foreman Deed to William Brown. I, Mary Foreman, executrix of Richard Foreman, deceased, have sold unto William Brown a tract of land containing about 1 acre lying in the Town of Shelbyville on the north side of the Unionville Turnpike Road and east of the entrance of the old Nashville Road and bounded by Thomas Foreman and James Story. This 1 November 1867.
Wit: H.H. Holt   Signed: Mary Foreman
Reg: November 1, 1867

Page 411 - W.J. Whitthorne, C&M, Deed to Bryant Landers. Whereas on 19 August 1857 Nancy Ogilvie, Eliza Jane Ogilvie and Barclay M. Tillman as administrator. Heirs of R.C. Ogilvie filed their bill in the Chancery Court at Shelbyville for the sale of a tract of land in Bedford County against Sarah E. Ogilvie and Talitha Ogilvie and said proceedings were held at August Term 1867. Said land was sold at public sale and purchased by Bryant Landers and bounded by A. Wilson's land, a creek, Bryant Landers' corner, by Larisa Covington, by the corner of the lot of the Unionville Female Academy, and by Jennings Moore's line. Containing 184 acres and 18 poles. This 4 November 1858.
Reg: November 1, 1867   Signed: W.J. Whitthorne

Page 412 - John Murray Trust Deed to J.J. Phillips. I have sold to J.J. Phillips my entire stock of goods in the Village of Wartrace consisting of drugs, medicine and notions. Said stock is now in the house in which I have been doing business for the last three years and belongs to S.R. Haley. I owe J.J. Phillips a balance on a note. I also owe G.W. Morris of Louisville, Kentucky, D.P. Searcy, W.W. Tollen of Nashville, Tennessee, E.G. Blatherwick of Nashville, Tennessee, and H.S. Buckner of Louisville, Kentucky. This November 1, 1867.
Reg: November 2, 1867   Signed: John Murray

Page 413 - Josiah S. Webb Mortgage to James S. Webb. This 10 October 1867. Josiah S. Webb of Williamson County, Tennessee is indebted to said James S. Webb and as executor of William S. Webb and as administrator of Samuel Webb, deceased, and is liable and has assumed to pay said Josiah S. debts. Executed a tract of land sold by James S. to Josiah and the title to which said tract of land herein after conveyed is vested in said Josiah by title bond and to make a deed when purchase money on two notes. Also one George M. Neal of Huntsville, Alabama has obtained judgment against said Josiah in the Circuit Court of Lincoln County, Tennessee at its November Term 1866 at which judgment was issued and is now in the hands of the Sheriff of Williamson County, Tennessee and cost to be paid by James S. Webb. James S. Webb as executor of William S. Webb, deceased.
NOTE: Long document
Also a note due owing by Josiah S. to Miss Mollie L. Jackson. Others named in document were W.W. Crockett and Adelaid C. Webb.
Reg: November 4, 1867   Signed: J.S. Webb

Page 415 - M. Holland and Elizabeth Moss, Contract. I, M. Holland agree to take Elizabeth Moss' land dower as it is and manage it as I choose during her life time and I further agree to pay her five barrels of corn per year annually as long as she may and after the first year five dollars in cash. I bind myself to pay every year during the lifetime of said Elizabeth Moss. She, Elizabeth Moss, on her part agrees to let said Holland have said land to cultivate and manage as above stated. This 6 October 1865.
Wit: N.M. Spear   Signed: Middleton Holland
     Nathan Spear   Elizabeth Moss

Page 416 - John Roberts and wife Deed to W.R. Norville. We, John Richards and wife Rosetta Emaline formerly Rosetta Emaline Norville, have sold to William R. Norville all the right title claim and interest said Rosetta Emaline Richards has in the estate of her father John W. Norville, deceased, both real and personal as heir of said estate. This interest including interest in the widow's dower. This November 5, 1867.
Wit: Walter L. Bearden   Signed: John Richards
Reg: November 6, 1867   Rosetta Emaline Richards

Page 417 - Elizabeth Kimbro Deed to Narcissa Ann Coffey. I, Elizabeth Kimbro, have sold unto Narcissa Ann Coffey a tract of

land in Bedford County and District No. 2 on the waters of Knobb
Creek and bounded near the right hand hollow not far from its
head, by B.M. McClure's spring and by his land, and by David
Vance and James Finch's line. Containing 55 ¾ acres. This
October 6, 1866.
Wit: J.W. Cully   Signed: Elizabeth Kimbro
      Robert Morgan
Reg: November 6, 1867

Page 418 - Thomas Holland, Sr. Deed to Mary Ann Huffman. For
the natural love and affection that I have for my daughter Mary
Ann Huffman and her children, I give to her said Mary Ann
Huffman wife of Jarrett B. Huffman, and her children who may be
living at her death, a tract of land and all of the improvements
thereon in Bedford County and Civil District No. 7 near the
Village of Shelbyville, containing 6 acres and 106 poles and
adjoining a corner of Elizabeth Jones' lot, by the widow
McFarland's line, and by Thomas Holland's Sr. land. This 9
August 1867.
Reg: November 8, 1867   Signed: Thomas Holland, Sr.

Page 418 - Robert F. Evans Deed to William H. Wisener, Sr. On
28 October 1865 the C&M at Shelbyville sold a lot of land in
Bedford County on the west being a part of the Fair Grounds and
north east part of the same bounded by lands formerly belonging
to William Little now owned by Mrs. Margaret Cummings, by the
middle of the road or street on the west side of the lot of land
sold by William H. Wisener, Sr. by the Cultural and Mechanical
Society. Containing 1 acre and 105 ½ poles and Robert F. Evans
bid off the same. This 9 November 1867.
Reg: November 9, 1867   Signed: R.F. Evans

Page 419 - William H. Ladd Deed to Mary E. Trice. I, W.H. Ladd
of Williamson County, Tennessee for the love and affection that
I have for Mary E. Trice wife of Joseph trice and my sister have
this day November 9, 1867 given to her two mules, one called
Hiram (brown), and one sorrel horse mule.
Reg: November 16, 1867   Signed: William H. Ladd

Page 420 - J.C. Claxton Deed to J.S. and J.B. Dwyer. I, James
C. Claxton, have sold unto John S. Dwyer and Joseph B. Dwyer a
tract of land in Bedford County and Civil District No. 5 and
bounded by John Sutton's, deceased, corner. Containing 26 acres
and 54 poles. This November 28, 1863.
Wit: Moses Marshall   Signed: James C. Claxton
      J.M. Elliott
      C.T. Philpot
Reg: November 16, 1867

Page 421 - J.S. and J.B. Dwyer Deed to Rosetta Emaline Richards.
J.S. and J.B. Dwyer, have sold unto Rosetta Emaline Richards
during her life time and then to Sallie George Norville and
assignees from John S. Dwyer, a tract of land in Bedford County

and Civil District No. 5 and bounded by John Sutton's, deceased, corner. Containing 26 acres and 54 poles. This November 16, 1867.
Reg: November 18, 1867   Signed: J.S. & J.B. Dwyer

Page 421 - John Nixon, Jr. Power of Attorney to Jennie C. Nixon. City of New Orleans, Louisiana. I, John Nixon, Jr. of the City of New Orleans, Louisiana, have appointed my wife Mrs. Jennie C. Nixon at present residing in Bedford County my true and lawful attorney for me and in my name to grant bargain sell and convey all lands owned by me in the State of Tennessee and sell and convey any other property owned by me in the State of Tennessee. This 11 October 1867.
Wit: Garrett S. Lowe   Signed: John Nixon, Jr.
     Wm. Shannon
Reg: November 18, 1867

Page 422 - John Nixon and wife Deed to Thos. H. Coldwell. I, John Nixon, have conveyed unto Thomas H. Coldwell a tract of land in Bedford County and Civil District No. 6 and bounded by lands of Mrs. Jane C. Nixon and Mary C. Fite, by lands of Mary C. Fite, by lands of Morgan Smith and John McAdams, and by lands of Thomas C. Whiteside. Containing 120 acres. The same being the lands conveyed to me by John C. Coldwell, J.C. Fite and others. This 2 November 1867.
Reg: November 18, 1867   Signed: John Nixon, Jr. by
                                        Jennie C. Nixon, his atty.

Page 423 - Jane C. Nixon and John Nixon, Jr. Deed to Thomas H. Coldwell. We, Jane C. Nixon in her own right and John Nixon, Jr. in right of his wife Jane C. Nixon, have sold to Thomas H. Coldwell a tract of land in Bedford County and Civil District No. 6 and bounded by lands of C.P. Houston, by lands of Mary C. Fite, by lands of John Nixon, Jr., and by lands of Thomas C. Whiteside. Containing 180 acres the land being the same conveyed to us by John C. Coldwell. This 2 November 1867.
Reg: November 18, 1867   Signed: Jennie C. Nixon
                                        John Nixon, Jr. by
                                        Jennie C. Nixon, atty.

Page 424 - John G. Shine Deed to G.W. Thompson. I have granted and sold unto George W. Thompson of Bedford County a tract of land in Bedford County and District No. 21 and bounded in the center of Flat Creek east of a spring which spring is on the west side of said creek, by Jo. Thompson's place, and by the turnpike road. Containing 55 acres and 20 poles. I have and do hereto here and now set my hand and seal in the State of Alabama this 18 May 1867.
Colbert County, Alabama.
Reg: November 19, 1867   Signed: Jno. G. Shine

Page 425 - Thomas B. Hastings Deed to Joseph H. Cates. I, Thomas B. Hastings, have sold unto Joseph H. Cates a tract of

land in Bedford County and Civil District No. 23 and bounded by the lands of John S. Cates, by lands of Joshua Woosley and others, and by lands known as the Spencer Brown land. Containing in all about __ acres. It being the portion of the lands of which my father John Hastings died seized and possessed of and in all of the land of which my father died seized and possessed of in Bedford County except the portion now known as the dower. My interest being an undivided one eighth in the whole except the dower. This 16 November 1867.
Reg: November 19, 1867   Signed: Thomas B. Hastings

Page 425 - Henry Cooper Bond to C.P. Houston, Jr. I am firmly bound unto C.P. Houston, Jr. I have heretofore sold to C.P. Houston, Jr. a tract of land in the Town of Shelbyville, Bedford County and bounded by a corner of W.B.M. Brame's lot, and by a lane leading to Mrs. R.D. Deery's gates. The same being the lot upon which I lately resided. This November 5, 1867.
Reg: November 19, 1867   Signed: Henry Cooper

Page 426 - John Presgrove and wife Deed to N.B. Parsons. We, John and Harriet Presgrove, have sold unto Newton B. Parsons a tract of land in Bedford County and District No. 8 containing 10 acres and 80 poles and bounded by corner No. 3, and by G.H. Wheeler's line. This 23 September 1867.
Wit: John W. Parsons   Signed: John Presgrove
     James M. Presgrove
Reg: November 20, 1867

Page 427 - C.A. Crunk Deed to Thomas H. Hutson. I, C.A. Crunk of Bedford County, have sold to Thomas H. Hutson of same place, a tract of land in Bedford County on Big Flat Creek in Civil District No. 24 and bounded by where the Shelbyville and Lynchburg Road and the Winchester and Columbia Road crosses. Containing 2 acres.
Reg: November 20, 1867   Signed: C.A. Crunk

Page 428 - H.H. Smith Mortgage to James L. Adams. I, Harbert H. Smith of Bedford County, give unto James L. Adams of same place a lien on two bay mules called Molly and Jake, one two horse wagon and about fifty barrels of corn. James L. Adams to go my security. This 21 November 1867.
Reg: November 21, 1867   Signed: H.H. Smith

Page 428 - Nicey Sharp and W.G.P. Sharp, Agreement. Whereas Anderson Sharp, late of Bedford County, departed this life intestate being at the time of his death owner of 205 ½ acres of land in Bedford County on which he resided at the time of his death in year 1863 being in Civil District No. 3 and bounded by J.N. Smith and H.C. Kinniard and Eliza George, by lands of Widow Isabella George, by lands of Daniel Gilchrist heirs and Archibald Prewett, in which said tract of land the undersigned Nicey Sharp was entitled to dower of one third for life which was assigned to her with any intervention dated __ 1863 signed

by the heirs of said Anderson Sharp, to wit, W.G.P. Sharp, W.J. Sharp, Isabella R. Golithan and Mary Ann Sharp. This 22 November 1867.
Reg: November 22, 1867   Signed: Nicey Sharp
                                        W.G.P. Sharp

Page 429 - Mary J. Shriver Deed to Jo. D. Wilhoite. I have sold unto Joseph D. Wilhoite all the right claim and interest I have in a lot, whereon I now live, in Bedford County and Civil District No. 7 and bounded on the north side of the street, by the street lying between said lot and Mrs. Mary Cannon, by John Woosley, and by Joel Burditt. This November 18, 1867.
Reg: November 22, 1867   Signed: Mary J. Shriver

Page 430 - J.D. Wilhoite and Mary J. Shriver. I hereby bind myself to (illegible) to M.J. Shriver the property described in the deed if the sum of $1100 is paid to me by her within twelve months from the date of conveyance. November 21, 1867.
Reg: November 22, 1867.   Signed: Jo. D. Wilhoite

Page 430 - W.J. Sharp Deed to W.G.P. Sharp. Whereas I, William J. Sharp of Bedford County did on 24 November 1866 convey to my brother W.G.P. Sharp in a Trust Deed, all my undivided interest in and to a tract of land in Bedford County and District No. 3 and bounded by James Caruthers, by the heirs of Samuel Phillips, by H.C. Kinnaird, Jasper N. Smith &c., and by lands of the Gilchrist. Containing 205 acres. Also my undivided interest in the dower of the widow of A. Sharp. This 22 November 1867.
Wit: William Frierson   Signed: W.J. Sharp
     T.S. Steele
Reg: November 23, 1867

Page 431 - John M. Hastings Deed to John S. Cates. I, John Hastings, have sold unto John S. Cates a tract of land in 25th District of Bedford County and bounded by the lands of John S. Cates, by lands of Joshua Woosley and others, by lands known as the dower of the widow of John Hastings, and by lands known as the Spencer Brown land. Containing about __ acres. It being a portion of the land of which my father John Hastings, deceased, seized and possessed, and is all of the land of which my father died seized and possessed in Bedford County except the portion now known as the dower. My interest being one eighth. This 21 November 1867.
Wit: J.H. Cates   Signed: John M. Hastings
     Thomas Hastings
Reg: November 23, 1867

Page 432 - N. Thompson, Sr. Deed to S.E. Yancy. For the love and affection I have for my grand daughter Sarah E. Yancy wife of Wm. Yancy and daughter of Michael F. Thompson, deceased. I have granted unto said Sarah E. Yancy a town lot lying in the corporation of the Town of Shelbyville, it being the west half of the lot bounded by the Shelbyville and Unionville Turnpike

Road, by the Shelbyville, Unionville and Eagleville Turnpike Road, by a street leading from said pike north to Mrs. Kincaid's residence, by a lot of John Trollinger's heirs, and by a lot of Joseph Anderson. This 14 September 1867.
Reg: November 23, 1867   Signed: N. Thompson, Sr.

Page 432 - D.W. Terry and wife Deed to G.W. Gregory. I have sold to G.W. Gregory a tract of land it being Lot No. 5 of division of the Edward Whitman land and bounded by T.H. Coldwell, by Susan Gregory's dower, by Sophrona Williams, and by Coldwell's line. Containing 15 acres. This January 1, 1867.
Wit: C.S. Dudley   Signed: D.W. Terry
     W.M. Tatum   S.P. Terry
Reg: November 25, 1867

Page 433 - T.B. Kaar and wife Deed to James Lemmings. This November 23, 1867. T.B. and Mary Kaar his wife sold unto James Lemmings all the right title claim to which T.B. and Mary Karr his wife is entitled to as a sister and heir at law of John T. Weaver, deceased, a tract of land in Bedford County and District No. 25 on the waters of Normans Creek and bounded by Z. Weavers' corner, by G. Huffman's line, and by Holland's line. Containing 70 acres and 69 poles.
Reg: November 26, 1867   Signed: Thomas B. Karr
                                        Mary Kaar

Page 434 - R.H. Sims, Exr. &c Deed to Fannie M. Reed. This 7 October 1867. I, Richard H. Sims of Bedford County was appointed executor of the Last Will and Testament of Berry C. Owen late of Bedford County. Whereas the said will directs that the real and personal estate of said Berry C. Owen shall be sold. I exposed at public sale the real estate in Bedford County on 7 October 1867 and Fannie M. Reed of the City of New York purchased the hereafter described portion of said estate. Said land is in the 21st District of Bedford County is part of the lands known as the lands of Berry C, Owen and is bound by the center of the road leading from Sugar Creek from the turnpike to Mrs. Burt's said stake being in the south boundary line of Mrs. Burt, and to the center of a lane to sugar Creek, by A.J. Greer's line then crossing the Lewisburg Pike. Containing 224 acres and 85 poles.
Reg: November 25, 1867   Signed: Richard H. Sims

Page 435 - W.B. Armstrong Deed to Arch. Prewitt. I, William B. Armstrong of Bedford County, have sold unto Archibald Prewitt of same place, a tract of land bounded by the lands of John Gilchrist and H.C. Kinnaird, by lands of Archibald Prewitt, by the lands of John A. Gilchrist, by lands of Nicey Sharp being in District No. 3 of Bedford County. Containing 83 acres. This 14 November 1867.
Reg: November 25, 1867   Signed: Wm. B. Armstrong

Page 435 - F.C. Holden Deed to Mrs. L.P. Vaughn. I, F.C. Holden, have sold unto Mrs. L.P. Vaughn a tract of land in Bedford County and District No. 9, containing 40 acres and bounded by the north and east by the lands of J.W. Key, and by Samuel G. Thompson, by G.W. Holden, it being a part of 50 acre tract which G.W. Holden purchased of Moses Faulkner. This 25 July 1864.
Wit: Jos. R. Puckett   Signed: F.C. Holden
     J. I. Shed(?)
Reg: November 27, 1867

Page 436 - William H. Jackson Deed to D.C. Jackson. I, William H. Jackson, have sold unto D.C. Jackson a tract of land in Bedford County and District No. 10, containing 26 acres. It being Lot No. 3 and the land that I drew from the estate of John Jackson, deceased, as one of his heirs and bounded by Lot No. 2 of the dower, to the center of the creek, and to the water gate. This Quin E. Morton   Signed: William H. Jackson
     Stephen Sanders
Reg: November 28, 1867

Page 437 - John Hart Bond to L.R. Coy. I, John Hart as Trustee of my heirs bind myself to pay to L.R. Coy as Trustee of Mrs. S.W. Coy $5000. The condition is such that whereas said L.R. Coy has purchased of me a tract of land in Bedford County and District No. 6 and bounded and known as the J. Lain tract and as the 5Lot of the A. McAdams tract being at T.C. Whiteside's corner in margin of the Shelbyville and Murfreesboro Turnpike, and by J.H. and J.W.H. Hart's corner. This 9 October 1867.
Wit: R.F. Evans   Signed: John Hart
     J.M. Elliott
Reg: November 29, 1867

Page 437 - Lewis Tillman, C&M &c Title to Town Lot. Castleman & Goggin. Title to Town Lot in Shelbyville. At a sale of the real estate made by me in the case of Chesly Williams and Wm. P. Cannon, executors of Robert Cannon, deceased, against Minis T. Cannon, Eliza J. Nelson and Ann S. Fay on 15 September 1865 on the Public Square in Shelbyville the lots in said town were purchased by Castleman & Goggins Co.
NOTE: Plat on page 438.
This 27 Novewmber 1867.
Reg: November 29, 1867   Signed: Lewis Tillman, C&M

Page 438 - Temperance McMahan Power of attorney to T.M. Mason. I, Temperance McMahan of Webster County, Missouri, do appoint Thomas M. Mason of Rutherford County, Tennessee my true and lawful attorney for me and in my name to demand and receive of and from any person or persons having or holding the same money coming to me from Thomas Mason, deceased, late of Coffee County, Tennessee, I being an heir of said Thomas Mason and entitled to a share in the estate of said Thomas Mason. I also empower said Thomas M. Mason to use all legal means to collect my said share. This 11 September 1867.

Wit: W.J. Thompson   Signed: Temperance McMahan
Reg: November 30, 1867

Page 439 - Samuel J. Adams Deed to Epps Parker. I have sold to
Epps Parker a tract of land it being in Bedford County and
District No. 19 and bounded at what is called Cook's Spring, by
Thomas Allison, by Martin Smith, and by David Patrick.
Containing 164 acres. This November 29, 1867.
Reg: November 30, 1867.   Signed: Samuel J. Adams

Page 440 - Samuel L. Davidson Mortgage to Mike Shoffner, Agt. I
purchased a mouring machine for which I gave my note to W.A.
Woods & Co. for the machine, one Mike Shoffner. This 23
November 1867.
Reg: December 2, 1867   Signed: Sam'l L. Davidson

Page 440 - Henry E. McGowan Deed to Edwin H. McGowan. I, Henry
E. McGowan, have sold unto Edwin H. McGowan a tract of land in
Bedford County and District No. 11, containing about 90 acres
and called McGowan & Reads place on which Rebecca J. McGowan has
a dower. This 20 December 1867.
Reg: December 3, 1867   Signed: H.E. McGowan

Page 441 - I, A. Wilson, special deputy surveyor, do hereby
certify that I went upon the lands of Tennessee G. Wilhoite wife
of R.B. Wilhoite which was willed to her by her father Trayson
N. Stewart on 15 November 1867. I proceeded to survey &c her
land and it adjoining Mrs. Martin's corner, by the old Phifer's
line, by the Widow Robinson's line, by James Phillips' corner,
by Jarret Phillips' corner, by R.G. Green's corner, and by Widow
Nowlin's corner Andrew Vannoy's corner. Containing 283 acres.
NOTE: Plat on page 441.
Reg: December 3, 1867   Signed: A. Wilson, Surveyor

Page 442 - I, A. Wilson, special deputy surveyor of Bedford
County. I went upon the land of Henry Brown on the 14 November
1867 and proceeded to survey his land. Land adjoining west bank
of Duck River it being the place designated in the notices to be
the proper corner adjoining Hiram Harris' line, and by the bluff
of the river. Containing 89 acres and 60 poles. This 14
November 1867. J.B. Phillips
Reg: December 3, 1867   Signed: A. Wilson, S.D. Surveyor

Page 442 - Mary C. Hight et als Deed to Benjamin Holder et als.
This 30 October 1867. Mary C. Hight, Mathew Roberts and wife,
J.S. Roberts, Mary C. Hight, Susan C. Bradberry, James G. Hill,
R.S. Hill of first part and Benjamin Holder of second part. The
said M.C. Hught, Mathew Roberts and wife, J.S. Roberts, Mary E.
Hight, Susan Bradberry, James G. Hill, R.S. Hill has sold to
said Benjamin Holder five sixths of a tract of land in Bedford
County and District No. 25 on the south side of Duck River and
bounded by Andrew Emerson's line, to the top of the ridge, by

John E. Wells' corner, to near Mathew Moss' fence, by Jacob
Hyles' line, to near where Simmons got some nails and shingles,
and by John Ewell's line. Containing 47 acres.
Rutherford County, Tennessee.
Wit: William A. Hill   Signed: Mary C. Hight
     J.G. Putman   M. Roberts
Reg: December 4, 1867   J.S.A. Roberts
                                      Mary E. Hight
                                      Susan J.C. Bradberry
                                      James G. Hill
                                      Rosanna T. Hill

Page 444 - J.M. Wheeler Deed to J.R. Stem. I, Jesse Wheeler,
have sold unto J.R. Stem a tract of land in Bedford County and
Civil District No. 11 and bounded by the center of a road Mrs.
Winsett's corner. Containing 16 acres. This 23 November 1867.
Wit: A. Wilson Brown   Signed: J.M. Wheeler
Reg: December 4, 1867

Page 444 - S.W. Jones Deed to G.W. McLain. I, S.W. Jones, have
sold unto G.W. McLain a tract of land in Bedford County and
District No. 9, containing 32 acres 1 rod and 16 poles and
bounded by K. Tucker, deceased, tract of land, by Jo. A.
McLain's line, and by John A. Webb's line. This November 13,
1867.
Wit: J.A. McLain   Signed: S.W. Jones
     H.C. Turner
Reg: December 4, 1867

Page 445 - Nicholas Hanaway Deed to Salina A.L. Griffith. I
have sold unto Salina A.J. Griffith a tract of land in Bedford
County and Civil District No. 18 and containing 49 acres and 4
poles and bounded by the side of a sink hole, by Leroy T.
Williams, and by William A. Allen's land. This 3 December 1867.
Wit: Wm. A. Allen   Signed: Nicholas Hanaway
     M.J. Allen
Reg: December 5, 1867

Page 445 - James W. Lowe and Martin Hancock Deed to D.A. Vaughn.
We have sold unto D.A. Vaughn a tract of land in Bedford County
and Civil District No. 4 it being a portion of the Orville Muse
tract and also a portion of Martin Hancock land. Bounded by a
corner of Martin Hancock's land, by said Muse's land, by the
edge of the Fairfield and Shelbyville Road, by the Casey
McGrew's tract, by line of Charles and James Lowe, and by the
bank of Wartrace Creek. This March 19, 1867.
Wit: John T. Hawkins   Signed: James W. Lowe
     Jas. W. Lowe   Martin Hancock
Reg: December 6, 1867

Page 446 - A.W. Manier Deed to Frederick Batte. I, A.W. Manier,
have sold to Frederick Batte a tract of land in Bedford County
and District No. 9 and bounded at a sink hole in A. Lytle's

corner, by Iza Wood's line, and by Micky Atkison's corner.
Containing 84 acres and 80 poles. This 15 April 1867.
Wit: William Brown   Signed: A.W. Manier
    W.M. Brown
Reg: December 9, 1867

Page 447 - Moses Rollins Power of attorney to Newton B.
Cunnings. We, Moses Rollins and Sarah Rollins his wife, Thomas
Terry and Elizabeth Terry his wife, and Lucy Cummings wife of
Newton B. Cummings of Washington County, Arkansas, do appoint
Newton B. Cummings of said County and State our true and lawful
attorney for us and each of us and in our names to demand
receive &c for all money that may be due and coming to us from
the administrators of the estate of James McGill, deceased, late
of Bedford County. This October 22, 1867.
Reg: December 11, 1867   Signed: Moses Rollins
                                      Sarah Rollins
                                      Thomas M. Terry
                                      Elizabeth Terry
                                      Lucy Cummings

Page 448 - Q.E. Morton and wife Deed to D.C. Jackson. We, Nancy
M. Morton and Q.E. Morton her husband, have sold to D.C. Jackson
a tract of land in Bedford County in Bedford County and District
No. 10(?). Containing 32 acres, it being Lot No. 5 and the land
that we drew from the estate of John Jackson, deceased, as one
of the heirs and bounded by Lot No. 4, by J.P. Taylor's line.
November 25, 1867.
Wit: William H. Jackson   Signed: Nancy M. Morton
     Stephen Landers   Quin E. Morton
Reg: December 14, 1867

Page 449 - James Hastings Deed to Lucy A.T. Edde. I, James
Hastings, have sold to Lucy A.T. Edde a tract of land in Bedford
County on the south waters of Big Flat Creek and part of the old
Hiram Edde's tract and bounded by center of the road, containing
7 acres and 64 poles. This 14 December 1867.
Reg: December 16, 1867   Signed: James Hastings

Page 449 - Lewis A. Ray Deed to W.R. Adams. I, Lewis A. Ray of
Bedford County, have sold unto William R. Adams of same place a
tract of land in Bedford County and Civil District No. 11 and
bounded by William R. Adams' corner, and by Bellefant's line.
Containing 2 ½ acres. This 26 August 1867.
Wit: W.W. Hopkins   Signed: Lewis A. Ray
     M.R. Fisher
Reg: December 16, 1867

Page 450 - E.H. Conwell Deed to Jane Gill. I, Elisha H. Conwell
of Bedford County, have sold unto Mrs. Jane Gill all the
interest she sold to me by deed dated 31 March 1867 and
registered in Bedford County her interest to me being the one
eleventh part thereof and the interest said Jane Gill sold to me

385

was her interest in her father Thomas Conwell lands lying in Bedford County and District No. 22 adjoining the lands of William Campbell, by lands of Joseph Parker, by lands of Samuel Morris and the heirs of Henry Dean, and by the lands of Caty Leathers. Containing 410 acres.
Reg: December 18, 1867   Signed: E.H. Conwell

Page 451 - D.M. Holden Deed to T.N. McLain. I have sold unto R.N. McLain a tract of land in Bedford County and Civil District No. 7 and bounded by J.E. Hawkins' corner, and by D. Wheelhouse's line. It being the same tract that I purchased from G.W. Holden and he from J.A. McLain and W.S. Puckett. Containing 102 acres and 100 poles. This December 11, 1867.
Wit: J.B. Holden   Signed: D.M. Holden
     F.C. Holden
     T.J.B. Holden
Reg: December 20, 1867

Page 452 - George D. Hastings Deed to Martha A. and Eliza T. Cates. I, George D. Hastings, have sold to Martha Ann Cates and her infant daughter Eliza Tennessee Cates all of my right title claim and interest in a tract of land in the 22nd Civil District of Bedford County and bounded by lands of John S. Cates, by lands of Joshua Woosley and others, by lands known as the dower of the widow of John Hastings, and by lands known as the Spencer Brown's land. Containing about __ acres. It being a portion of the lands of which my father John Hastings died seized and at the time of his death in Bedford County except the portion now known as the dower and included one eighth in the whole except the dower. This 20 December 1867.
Reg: December 21, 1867   Signed: G.D. Hastings

Page 452 - W.R. Muse Deed to J.C. Chilcoat. This 20 December 1867. William R. Muse of Bedford County, sold to James C. Chilcoat of same place all the right title claim and interest as one of the heirs at law of Isaac Muse, deceased, in and to a tract of land on which Nancy Muse widow and relict of said Isaac Muse now lives it being 90 acres as laid off to said widow as her dower during life.
Reg: December 21, 1867   Signed: W.R. Muse

Page 453 - Margaret E. Castleman and others Deed to Castleman Goggin & Co. We, Margaret E. Castleman, John R. Wright and wife Nancy H. formerly Nancy H. Castleman, Cynthia Castleman and Mary L. Castleman, Emily V. Castleman, sold to George H. Castleman, James H. Castleman, Robert W. Castleman and William M. Goggins by the firm name of Castleman Goggins and being in Civil District No. 22, being a part of Jacob Castleman tract of land adjoining Wm. Chandler's line. Containing 4 acres and 19 poles. This 19 June 1865.
Wit: N.B. Rees   Signed: M.E. Castleman
     J.A. White   Emily Castleman
     J.M. White   Cynthia Castleman
     O.W. Wise   L.M. Castleman

Reg: December 23, 1867   Nancy H. Wright
                                          John R. Wright

Page 454 - L.B. Knott Deed to J.A. Reagor. I have conveyed to
Joseph A. Reagor a tract of land lying on Thompson Creek and
Civil District No. 24 of Bedford County and bounded by a corner
of the house, crossing Thompson Creek, to a rock hillside,
crossing Hornaday Branch where it enters the Mill Pond, and to
the Anderton Branch. Containing 8 acres and 102 poles. This 23
December 1867.
Reg: December 23, 1867   Signed: L.B. Knott

Page 455 - Mariah E. Phillips and R.S. Dwiggins Deed to S.M.
Thompson. This 10 October 1867. Mariah E. Phillips and Robert
S. Dwiggins sold unto Samuel M. Thompson. Whereas on __ day
November 1860 said Robert S. Dwiggins conveyed in trust to the
said Mariah E. Phillips a tract of land in Bedford County and
within the corporation limits of the Town of Shelbyville on the
south side of the Scull Camp Ford Road and bounded by said road,
by the lot of land of M.E.W. Dunaway, and by the Shelbyville
College lot, by the lot of land now owned by Charles A. Warren
and on which he resides. Containing 1 acre being the lot of
land sold and conveyed by Wm. S. Jett to said Dwiggins. This
Thos. C. Whiteside   Signed: Mariah E. Phillips
     Joseph H. Thompson   R.S. Dwiggins
Reg: December 24, 1867

Page 456 - J.M. Floyd Deed to W.T. Vernon. I, John M. Floyd,
have sold to William T. Vernon a tract of land in Bedford County
and District No. 10, containing 63 acres. Adjoining James H.
Floyd's tract of land tract he purchased from A. Baulch (Balch).
This 24 August 1867.
Wit: Thomas M. Corbell   Signed: John M. Floyd

Page 457 - John M. Floyd Deed to W.H. Floyd. I, John M. Floyd,
have sold unto William H. Floyd my undivided interest in a tract
of land containing 104 acres that our father purchased of A.
Baulch (Balch) lying in District No. 10 of Bedford County which
makes my interest in said tract of land 34 ½ acres. This
November 6, 1867.
Wit: Thos. M. Corbell   Signed: John M. Floyd
Reg: December 25, 1867

Page 457 - C.T. Philpot Deed to Thos. Lipscomb. I, Charles T.
Philpot, have sold unto Thos. Lipscomb a certain house and lot
in the Town of Shelbyville, Bedford County, on which the widow
of Leonard Marbury at present lives and which is bounded by the
street or road called the Unionville Pike, by U.E. Peacock's
lot, by G.W. Buchanan's lot, by James H. Neil's lot supposed to
contain 2 ½ acres. This 25 December 1867.
Wit: A. Frierson   Signed: C.T. Philpott
     H.L.W. Little
Reg: December 26, 1867

Page 458 - John N. Lawrence et als Power of Attorney to Jas. L. Turner. Whereas Joel Lawrence late of Bedford County, deceased, died intestate on or about the _- day of __ 185_ and whereas we, John N. Lawrence and Alexander J. Lawrence both of Laclede County, Missouri are children and heirs at law of said Joel Lawrence and are entitled to a share of the estate of said Joel Lawrence, deceased. We have appointed James L. Turner of Shelbyville, Bedford County our true and lawful attorney for us and in our name to demand and receive from the administrators of said Joel Lawrence, from any person or persons who may have in charge or custody the estate of Joel Lawrence. This 7 September 1867.
Reg: December 26, 1867   Signed: John N. Lawrence
                                        Alexander J. Lawrence

Page 458 - Mankin & Crick Mortgage to W. Rowzee. We have sold unto Winn Rowzee nine horses and six buggies. This 26 December 1867.
Reg: December 27, 1867   Signed: Mankin & Crick

Page 459 - J.W. Cochran Deed to W.C. Whitthorne. I, J.W. Cochran of Davidson County, Tennessee, have sold unto W.C. Whitthorne, several listed notes, a certain tract of land or ground in District No. 7 of Bedford County and bounded by lands of J.W. Cowan, by lands of Robert Mathews, and by Union Street. Containing 6 acres and 3 poles. This November 1, 1867.
Wit: C. Robinson   Signed: W.J. Cochran
     S. Watson
Reg: December 27, 1867

Page 460 - A.W. Manier Deed to D.C. Manier, July 2, 1866. I, A.W. Manier, have sold to David C. Manier a tract of land in Bedford County and District No. 10, containing 66 acres and 2 rods and 20 poles and bounded in the center of the pike in Isaac Phillips' line, and by the dividing line of A.N. McCord and Manier.
Wit: J.C. Blanton   Signed: A.W. Manier
     W.C. Dunn
Reg: December 28, 1867

Page 450 - W.T. Thompson and wife Deed to Mary E. Maddox. We, William T. Thompson and wife Huldah Thompson, have sold unto Mary E. Maddox a tract of land in Bedford County and District No. 7, containing 3 acres and 85 poles and bounded by the road leading from Shelbyville to Columbia crossing Duck River at the Warner Bridge or Ford in W.B. Offitt's line, also said Thompson's line, and to the edge of a field. This 27 December 1867.
Reg: December 29, 1867   Signed: William T. Thompson
                                        Huldah B. Thompson

Page 461 - W. Rowzee Trustee &c Deed to Jo. D. Wilhoite. By the powers vested in me in a Trust Deed made by Frankfort T. Fowler

on 1 December 1866 and registered in Book FFF, pages 13 and 14.
I have sold at public sale to Joseph D. Wilhoite a house and lot
in the Town of Shelbyville, Bedford County known as the foreman
House on Washington Street, being the house and lot whereon said
Frankfort T. Fowler were doing business at the making of said
Trust Deed, and bounded by the lot of Mrs. Braden, by the lot of
Hodgkins and Shires, by the vacant lot and by the west by
Washington Street, being __ acres. This 28 December 1867.
Reg: December 30, 1867   Signed: W. Rowzee

**Page 462 - W.H. Christopher Deed to Alexr. F. Rankin. I,
William H. Christopher, have sold to Alexander F. Rankin a tract
of land in Marshall County, Tennessee near Farmington in Civil
District No. 6. Said tract sold in exchange for land in Bedford
County and Civil District No. 18 and bounded by James Stallings.
Containing 197 acres. It being the same tract of land deeded to
me by G.W. Thompson and C.A. Warren on 27 April 1866 and
recorded. This 30 December 1867.**
Reg: December 31, 1867   Signed: W.H. Christopher

******
***
*

INDEX

Index by Timothy J. Edwards

www.ingramcontent.com/pod-product-compliance
Lightning Source LLC
Chambersburg PA
CBHW021843020426
42334CB00013B/161